A HISTORY OF CHRISTIANITY
IN THE UNITED STATES AND CANADA

A History
in the

of Christianity
United States and Canada

Mark A. Noll

WILLIAM B. EERDMANS PUBLISHING COMPANY
GRAND RAPIDS, MICHIGAN

Library of Congress Cataloging-in-Publication Data

A History of Christianity in the United States and Canada /
by Mark A. Noll.
    p.   cm.
Includes bibliographical references and index.
ISBN 0-8028-0651-1 (pbk)
ISBN 0-8028-3703-4 (cloth)
1. United States — Church history. 2. Canada — Church history.
I. Noll, Mark A., 1946-
BR515.H57   1992
277.3 — dc20   92-3651
                              CIP

This book incorporates in rewritten form a much briefer account of
Christianity in North America that appears in *Christianity: A Social and
Cultural History* (New York: Macmillan, 1991).

To
George Rawlyk and Grant Wacker

Contents

CONTENTS

Contents

CONTENTS

Contents

CONTENTS

Contents

CONTENTS

xiv

Acknowledgments

THIS BOOK WOULD NOT HAVE BEEN POSSIBLE WITHOUT THE MANY scholars who have contributed so magnificently to the wealth of outstanding writing on North American religious history of recent decades. It is invidious to single out any in that number for special mention, but I cannot forebear a word of thanks to David Wills for holding up the ideal of making African-American Christian history an integral part of general Christian history and to Robert Handy for pioneering efforts at writing the story of the churches in Canada and the United States as one story.

For specific help in the preparation of this volume, it is a privilege to thank David Malone and Maggie Noll for reducing the quantity of mistakes, infelicities, and inanities; John Clark, Roger Finke, Beatrice Horne, Nathan Hatch, George Marsden, Charles Middlebrook, Sara Miles, Todd Nichol, Alvaro Nieves, Bob Patterson, Jon Pott, Tim Straayer, and Ina Vondiziano for much-appreciated assistance along the way; and Hans-Peter Caulien, Paul Heidebrecht, Michael de Ridder, Ann Coleman, Don Lewis, Neil MacLean, John Stackhouse, Marguerite Van Die, and especially George Rawlyk for being such patient mentors concerning things Canadian.

The book is dedicated to two historians whose expertise has illuminated subjects that were unfamiliar to me, but who are valued even more as friends than as experts.

Tables

Introduction

THIS IS A HISTORY OF CHRISTIANITY IN THE UNITED STATES AND CANADA. As a history, it is intended to provide certain basic information about some of the most important themes, events, leaders, and changes in the Christian churches that have populated the upper two-thirds of the North American continent over the last four centuries.

Historical studies, however, are always more than just sources of information. Authors must select what to include and not to include, they must decide how to slant what is written, and they must highlight certain themes at the expense of others. Even textbooks constitute arguments, embody prejudices, and sometimes even preach sermons. These implicit arguments, prejudices, and sermons usually communicate what the author considers to be some kind of current consensus about the subject of the text, but they also express the author's personal point of view. This book is no different.

Its presentation is self-consciously influenced by important recent currents in the study of American religious history. In particular, the fresh attention being paid to the experiences of women, nonwhites, and "ordinary" people who did not leave extensive written records has left its mark on the pages that follow. It may still not be entirely clear how to integrate such groups fully into the written story of Christianity in America, which until recently has been dominated by leaders of elite groups who did leave extensive published records. But this text is written under the conviction that it is important, nevertheless, to strive toward that goal. In addition, although the book deals extensively with what might be called "high culture" — public ecclesiastical, political, or intellectual aspects of religious history — it also attempts to recover the experiences of common people. It benefits especially from recent studies of the hymns ordinary people sing, what it has meant for them to go to church, and how private individuals have

1

pursued personal or family nurture in the faith. At the start of almost every chapter, a hymn is presented in order to suggest something about how people were worshiping during the period under consideration.

A wealth of recent scholarship has also shown persuasively that there has been a great variety of Christian experience throughout all of North American history. While New England Puritans may have left the best records from the seventeenth century, the Christian story of that century also included significant developments among Catholics in New France, Quakers in Pennsylvania, and Episcopalians in Virginia. And these were developments that anticipated later patterns of American church history more directly than those of the Puritans. In the same way, the white Protestant churches of British heritage dominated the public perception of Christian life in the nineteenth century, but it is increasingly clear that the experiences of black Protestants, German and Scandinavian Lutherans, Roman Catholics of several ethnic varieties, and even Orthodox from Eastern Europe were adding diversity, complexity, and unexpected dynamism to the Christian story of the period. History does require a narrative thread, and the place of Protestants of British background supplies that thread in this text. But its overall pattern also reflects other important threads and a more complicated, more varied fabric that contemporary interests and recent scholarship make it easier to see.

Another helpful emphasis of recent historical study is the value of comparison. Increasingly in the late twentieth century, historians are discovering what students of language have known for a long time. "Who really knows English," they ask, "who knows only English?" For the historian of Christianity, the question becomes "Who really knows the experience of believers in the United States who does not take seriously regional differences within the country, and — even more — the history of Christianity in parallel societies?" In this text, the chief sustained comparison is between the churches of the United States and the churches of Canada. Much is similar between these two countries that trace their political histories from a common British source and whose border has always been wide open to the exchange of cultural influences, including religion. But much is also different.

An examination of these similarities and differences over several centuries has several advantages. It allows us, first, to outline the main developments in Canadian church history. These developments constitute by themselves a most interesting story that is all too often neglected by citizens of the United States. But they also present a fascinating counterpoint to major developments in the churches on the "American" side of the border. A sociologist, Seymour Martin Lipset, recently made the case for social comparison that I hope to carry out for the history of Christianity when he said, "knowledge of Canada or the United States is the best way to gain insight into the other North American country. . . . The more similar the units being compared, the more possible it should be to isolate the factors responsible for differences between them. Looking intensively at Canada and the United States sheds light on both of them."

In one way, however, this volume swims deliberately against the tide of recent scholarship. It is a history of Christianity, not a history of religion. Recent advances in theoretical study of "religion" — considered as a general human phenomenon — have greatly enriched the study of particular faiths, whether Christianity, Judaism, Islam, or others. A number of path-breaking books on American subjects (several of them mentioned in the bibliographies below) have shown how useful it can be to study Christianity from the perspective of universal religious experience. The result has been a flourishing over the past two decades of outstanding books devoted to "religion in America." A history of Christianity, however, is not the same as a history of religion. It is no disrespect to common religious experience to say that the Christian churches have nurtured a distinct set of convictions, practices, and institutions. While it is a noble enterprise to blend the history of distinctions into a common religious story, it is also a valuable enterprise to study the history of Christianity on its own particular terms.

There are several advantages in maintaining a specifically Christian focus in what follows. First, by concentrating on Christian experience, we are able to avoid the assumption that the story of Christianity in America is primarily a story about America. We are, in other words, provided with a focus that makes it possible to include citizens of the United States and Canada in the worldwide story that had its origins in the era of the New Testament. It also makes it easier to pay serious attention to a whole range of believers who, at least when they were alive, were not considered particularly central to "mainstream American" experience. In other words, I hope that this can be a text more concerned with how the Christian religion has fared in America than with how Christians have added their bit to the story of America.

Second, concentrating on Christian experience permits a more natural interpretation of events from standards of Christian faith than would an objective account of generically religious life. Since the interpretations I care about most depend on specifically Christian resources, and since the "lessons" with which I am most concerned are lessons pertinent to the churches, a concentration on the story of Christians makes it possible to express those interpretations and lessons openly. My readings may all be wrong, but at least it should be clear where they are coming from: they are coming from the perspective of a Christian who happens to live in the United States.

One of the convictions that shapes the material in this book might be called a charitable benefit of the doubt. It is the assumption that if historical figures and groups call themselves "Christian" and if they are recognized by others as "Christians," they should be treated that way in a textbook history of Christianity. This judgment, too, reflects sentiments that are stronger in the late twentieth century than they were in earlier centuries. During former ages, Catholics and Protestants regularly read each other out of the kingdom, as did mutually antagonistic Protestants and even sometimes factions within the Catholic Church. In a book of this sort, to write sympathetically about those who called themselves "Christian" is not to endorse every belief, institution, practice, or opinion reported. It does, however, reflect a theological conviction — namely, that the church consists of all who name the name of Jesus Christ. Christians, whether theologians and historians or laypeople and ministers, should be concerned about quality control, about the application of ideal Christian norms to their own lives. Those who are not Christians also have every right to challenge the churches on their understanding of the truth, their integrity of action, and their insight into the human condition. But on the question of who counts as a "real Christian," a historian may be excused for exercising a judgment of charity.

The "plot" of this text centers on the rise and decline of Protestant dominance in the United States. Along the way, full consideration is paid to Canadian contrasts, both Catholic and Protestant. I have also tried to be as sensitive as possible to the many polarities that inform the history of Christianity in North America — especially the polarity between blacks and whites but also that between Catholics and Protestants and between North and South. In addition, I have sketched the histories of major denominations. Yet in order to provide coherence and an orderly sequence, I have organized the book to show how an "evangelical America" arose out of colonial pluralism and the tumults of the Revolutionary era, how the hegemony of evangelical Protestantism began to erode with the Civil War, and how it came to an obvious end by the 1920s. A stress on the Christian, as opposed to the North American, elements in the story will, I hope, make this plot an occasion for edification rather than nostalgia.

Finally, at several points along the way we pause to hear what foreign visitors have to say about the churches in North America. Claude-Jean Bertrand of the University of Paris offers a good recent example of such commentary. Bertrand sees, first, much to condemn: "it seems undeniable that, collectively, the American churches have encouraged puritanism, philistinism, manicheanism, and racism. They have encouraged the cult of

4

individual material success growing out of raw capitalism and the imperialism of a good conscience (the two fundamental ingredients of Americanism in the eyes of its internal and external adversaries)." But he also sees much to praise: "at the same time, the inculcation of individualism, nonconformity, and Protestant freedom have combined to preserve the country in its whole history from the worst horrors of totalitarianism. Religion has nourished the dynamism, egalitarianism, tolerance, generosity, humanity, and idealism of this great people — the only one in history which has mixed all the major ethnic groups and built a great world power without ever falling under the heel of a tyrant or a military oligarchy. Religion has helped this immense continent, filled with all sorts of people, to acquire a soul, to forge itself into a nation, and to anchor itself in its diverse past without ceasing to look toward the future."

To grasp the whys and wherefores of such apparent contradictions is one of the central goals of this book. If it fulfills that purpose, we may find that we can learn not just about Christianity in America but also about Christianity itself, as it has come to expression in the United States and Canada.

Further Reading

At the end of each chapter, a few works are cited that speak directly to the concerns of that chapter. A bibliography at the end of the book includes more general studies and collections of documents, many of which contain material covering the whole sweep of the story.

Albanese, Catherine L. *America: Religion and Religions.* 2d ed. Belmont, CA: Wadsworth, 1991.

Bertrand, Claude-Jean. *Les Eglises aux Etats-Unis.* Paris: Presses Universitaires de France, 1975.

The Encyclopedia of Religion. Edited by Mircea Eliade. New York: Macmillan, 1987.

Handy, Robert T. "Dominant Patterns of Christian Life in Canada and the United States: Similarities and Differences." In *Religion/Culture: Comparative Canadian Studies.* Toronto: Association for Canadian Studies, 1985.

Lipset, Seymour Martin. *Continental Divide: The Values and Institutions of the United States and Canada.* New York: Routledge, 1990.

Marty, Martin. "The American Religious History Canon." *Social Research* 53 (Autumn 1956): 513-28.

Sweet, Leonard I. " 'Ringmasters,' 'Blind Elephant Feelers,' and 'Moles': The

Textbook Literature of American Religious History." In *Critical Review of Books in Religion 1988*, pp. 89-118. Atlanta: Journal of the American Academy of Religion and Journal of Biblical Literature, 1989.

Wills, David W. "The Central Themes of American Religious History: Pluralism, Puritanism and the Encounter of Black and White." *Religion and Intellectual Life* 5 (Fall 1987): 30-41.

Zikmund, Barbara Brown. "The Contributions of Women to North American Church Life." *Mid-Stream* 22 (July-Oct. 1983): 373-77.

PART I

BEGINNINGS

ALMOST AS SOON AS THERE WERE EUROPEAN SETTLERS IN NORTH AMERICA, there were also several varieties of Christianity. Despite popular impressions, the English Puritans did not arrive first. Even in the territory that would become the United States, the Puritans were preceded by their near, but not very dear, fellow Englishmen, the state-church Episcopalians. Representatives of Holland's Reformed Church were also fairly well established in New Amsterdam (later New York) before the main body of Puritans first glimpsed Boston in 1630. Soon German-speaking believers of many types joined English Quakers in William Penn's Pennsylvania, Swedish Lutherans were in Delaware, and Presbyterians from Scotland and the north of Ireland had established a foothold on Long Island, in New Jersey, and in Pennsylvania.

Even before any British Protestants had appeared on the scene, however, there was already a substantial Catholic presence in the New World. From Spain, Catholic priests had come to convert the Native Americans of the great Southwest. In what is now Canada and along the Mississippi River, Catholic missionaries from France were pursuing their work among Indians before missions by English Protestants had even made a start.

The early pluralism was also cultural. Before there were English Puritans in Massachusetts and almost as soon as there were Catholic missionaries in the Southwest, black-skinned immigrants from Africa had arrived in Virginia. Although the twenty Africans off-loaded in Virginia by a Dutch trader in 1619 were not slaves in a strict sense, slavery had already become an essential building block of European expansion in the New World. From the first Portuguese explorations in West Africa to the later and more numerous colonies planted in the Western hemisphere by the Spanish, the French, the Dutch, and the English, human bondage was a central reality — socially,

7

politically, and economically. It was also a religious reality. Africans, who made up virtually all of the slaves, were largely deprived of their native religions when they lost their freedom. At first in small bits and pieces, but then in a more systematic fashion (and often in surprising ways), many of the slaves in North America began to accept the native religion of the Europeans. From the start, Euro-American Christians, even as they proclaimed the freedom of the gospel, held slaves or benefited from the slave trade. The interplay between colonization, slavery, and faith existed from the first.

Diversity and cultural conflict were, thus, the rule from the beginning of Christianity in North America. The diversity and the conflict had not begun in the Western hemisphere but grew naturally from the European circumstances that prevailed at the time of the first efforts to colonize the Western hemisphere. When Columbus sailed in 1492, he was simply a loyal son of *the* church. When the gleam of New World evangelization first shone in the eyes of European Christians, there was only one recognized form of European Christianity. But within two generations the Protestant Reformation and a countervailing surge of reform within the Roman Catholic Church left Europe religiously divided. These divisions, in turn, set the stage for the Christian pluralism of North America.

In more recent centuries, American ties to Third World Christians have grown stronger as missionaries from Canada and the United States have circled the globe and as Christian immigrants from many regions have come to North America. For the first centuries of Christian settlement, however, North America was a "receiving," not a "sending," region. It was a place where Christian heroism, Christian exploitation, and the quiet realities of day-to-day Christian life were all defined by the experiences, the assumptions, and the values of the European churches.

CHAPTER 1

European Expansion
and Catholic Settlement

Within a lodge of broken bark
　　The tender Babe was found,
A ragged robe of rabbit skin
　　Enwrapp'd His beauty round;
But as the hunter braves drew nigh,
　　The angel song rang loud and high —
Jesus your King is born, Jesus is born,
　　In excelsis gloria.

*　　　*　　　*　　　*　　　*

O children of the forest free,
　　O sons of Manitou,
The Holy Child of earth and Heav'n
　　Is born today for you.
Come kneel before the radiant Boy,
　　Who brings you beauty, peace and joy —
Jesus your King is born, Jesus is born,
　　In excelsis gloria.

*This carol was written in the language of the Huron Indians by Jean Brébeuf,
pioneer Jesuit missionary, in 1642.*

🏵　　　　　🏵

God and the Colonies

THE EUROPEAN DISCOVERY OF AMERICA BEGAN IN THE LATE FIFTEENTH century, only a generation before the start of the Protestant Reformation. The European exploration of America was intensified during the second half of the sixteenth century, in the same era as the reform of the Roman Catholic Church sometimes called the Counter-Reformation. And the European settlement of America took place largely in the seventeenth century, when the divisions and subdivisions of the European Reformation assumed institutional and intellectual permanence. For better and for worse, these events in the Old World dictated the shape of Christianity's early history in the New.

The age of Reformation was a time of social, intellectual, national, and economic expansion as well as religious change. Western Europe entered the sixteenth century stronger and more aggressive than it had been at any time in its history. French political power was growing steadily, and its citizens' achievements in finance, art, and literature were often spectacular. After 1485, the English throne was held by the energetic Tudors. Especially under Henry VII (ruled 1485-1509), Henry VIII (1509-1547), and Elizabeth I (1558-1603), monarchs as filled with love for their country as they were with ambition for themselves, England emerged as a major European power. In Spain during the last years of the fifteenth century, the kingdom was united under Ferdinand and Isabella, the last strongholds of the Muslim Moors were overcome, and the nation took the lead in exploring the New World. One result of growing strength among these great nations, and also lesser ones such as Portugal and Holland, was competition in Europe. Another was competition for empire overseas.

The European nations wanted profit from their American explorations, but only Spain found it, and only for a brief period. Yet the drive for raw materials from the colonies, and then a more general pursuit of trade, became a permanent feature of European life. It was this drive that inserted the trade in human beings so deeply into the cultures of North and South America. The spirit of the Renaissance also stimulated exploration across the Atlantic, for the virgin territory of America held out the promise of new knowledge, personal glory, and a liberation from stifling European traditions. Expansion to America, in other words, shared fully in the energies that drove Europe as a whole during the early modern period.

Also from the start, however, European believers took a religious interest in America. As the career of Christopher Columbus illustrates, it was an interest with both the fidelity and the tragedy that would characterize the whole history of Christianity in North America. Columbus's very first entry in the diary that recorded his journey to America in 1492 expressed the hope that he could make contact with the native peoples in order to

The cruel impieties acted out upon the Native Americans by the sailors who accompanied Columbus were matched, if not necessarily excused, by the sincere piety of Columbus himself. *Library of Congress*

find out "the manner in which may be undertaken their conversion to our Holy Faith." On his second journey in 1493 Columbus took with him Catholic friars whom he hoped could convert the Indians that he had seen on the first voyage. To the Spanish monarchs, Columbus insisted that profits from his voyages be used to restore Christian control over Jerusalem. And he had a very high sense of divine calling. In a lengthy manuscript penned after his third voyage, *A Book of Prophecies,* Columbus recorded the many passages from Scripture that he felt related to his mission to the East Indies: "neither reason nor mathematics," he wrote in this manuscript, "nor world maps were profitable to me; rather the prophecy of Isaiah was completely fulfilled" (i.e., Isa. 46:11 — "the man that executeth my counsel from a far country").

The other side of the picture, however, concerns Columbus's conception of himself and the effects his activities had on the inhabitants of the New World. Columbus's zealous belief in his own messianic mission seems at least partly the result of delusions of grandeur. Moreover, the way Columbus's subordinates treated Native Americans was often anything but Christian. The forty sailors he left behind on the Island of Hispaniola to construct a fortress in 1492 so wantonly raped and pillaged that the Indians rose up and slaughtered them. For such resistance, however, the Europeans got an almost total revenge: in 1492 Hispaniola had an Indian population in the millions, but within sixty years that population was virtually wiped out because of contact with the newcomers.

Modern reactions to Columbus's "Christian mission" are, not surprisingly, very mixed. For some Catholic ethnic groups he is a hero, the first of a host of self-sacrificing, faithful missionaries. To others, as suggested by a resolution from the National Council of Churches of the United States in 1990, he bears significant responsibility for "genocide, slavery, 'ecocide,' and the exploitation of the wealth of the land."

Catholic concern for the Americas was by no means unique to Columbus. A year after Columbus's first voyage, for instance, Pope Alexander VI issued a bull aimed at settling the competing territorial aspirations of Spain and Portugal, the eventual effect of which was that Brazil came to speak Portuguese and the rest of Latin America Spanish. The pope held that the major reason to "seek out and discover certain islands and mainlands remote and unknown and not hitherto discovered by others" was that the explorers "might bring to the worship of our Redeemer and the profession of the Catholic faith their residents and inhabitants." In 1529 Charles V, king of Spain and Holy Roman Emperor, justified his sponsorship of an expedition to the New World by describing his "chief motive" as the conversion of Florida's Indians. The Dominican priest Bartolomé de Las Casas (1474-1566), who had served as a colonial official in Hispaniola, eventually became an ardent defender of the Indians. One of his proposals to help the Native Americans, a proposal with tragic consequences, was to substitute slaves from Africa for the Indian slaves the Spanish had taken. (Las Casas later repudiated this suggestion.) He also formulated a missionary strategy of "evangelical conquest" that focused on the presentation of the gospel while at the same time preserving the lives and dignity of the Indians. Las Casas's fellow Dominican, Francisco de Vitoria (1483-1546), a leading theologian at Spain's Salamanca University, also defended Indian rights. Because he felt that Christian truth should affect every area of life, he offered moral guidelines for Spanish treatment of American inhabitants that helped establish modern international relations. Vitoria thought he could justify an enlightened rule of Native Americans by Europeans, but only if the rulers protected the property, the lives, and the souls of the Indians.

The first well-established Christian institutions in the New World came from the work of Catholics. Before the English settled permanently at Jamestown in 1607, thousands of Indians had become at least nominal believers under Catholic missionaries in the New Mexico territories. The first printed hymnbook in America was not the Puritans' *Bay Psalm Book* of 1640 but the *Ordinary of the Mass* in Mexico City in 1556. It had music set beside the words, a feature the British-American hymnals would not incorporate until the eighteenth century. The Protestant impact on Canada and the United States has been great in nearly every way, but such names as St. Augustine, San Antonio, and Los Angeles; Vincennes, Dubuque, and Louisville; and (in Quebec) St. Paul-du-Nord, Notre-Dame-de-Rimouski, and St. Jean testify to the fact that Catholics were here first.

Roman Catholicism in New Spain

Spanish settlement with Spanish varieties of Christianity lasted in North America from the early sixteenth century to the mid-nineteenth. Unfortunately for the Native Americans conquered by the Spanish, Old World Christian ideals were difficult to translate into practical realities in the New. Conquistadors such as Cortez in Mexico and Pizarro in Peru were accompanied by priests, and although these priests sometimes protested when military rulers treated the Indians like animals, they could not prevent brutal exploitation of the native population. One such protest by Dominican colleagues of Las Casas in New Spain, Bernardio de Minaya and Julian Garces, led Pope Paul III to issue in 1537 a formal declaration *(Sublimis Deus)* affirming that Indians were, in fact, people and could indeed become Christians.

Colonial administration was heavy-handed and often displayed anything but the ideals of Jesus. Yet Spanish Catholicism had a notable history in the early days of European settlement. In 1542 the Franciscan priest Juan de Padilla became the first American missionary martyr when, having left the company of Vasquez Coronado to make a preaching tour, he was slain by Native Americans in what is now Kansas. In New Mexico, as many as thirty-five thousand Christian Indians had gathered around twenty-five missionary stations by the year 1630.

In 1634 a Franciscan, Alonso de Benavides, described to the pope what life in a pueblo was like for the overworked brothers. Since it was very expensive to bring religious workers from the old country, a single friar might be responsible for the spiritual instruction of four or more villages. The friar had to say mass, perform baptisms, and carry out other religious duties. At his residence, he would establish a school "for the teaching of praying, singing, playing musical instruments and other interesting things." He would also instruct the Indians in raising crops and cattle because, as

Carmel Mission, founded 1770, Monterey County, California. Spanish church architecture in California and the Southwest is an enduring reminder of the early Catholic
presence in America. *Courtesy of the Billy Graham Center Museum*

Benavides put it with an attitude typical for his time, "if he left it to their
discretion, they would not do anything." Benavides reported that ten Franciscans had been killed in pursuing this work but that they had become "a
lighted torch to guide" the Indians "in spiritual as well as temporal affairs."

Over the next two centuries dedicated missionary activity continued
in the American Southwest and in California. Franciscans such as Junípero
Serra (1713-1784) took the lead in establishing a Christian presence in
California. Serra had been born in Mallorca and had been named a professor
in his native island when at the age of thirty-five he came to New Spain to
administer the Franciscan College of San Fernando in Mexico City. Twenty
years later he led the Franciscans into California. From 1769 to 1845, 146
Franciscans helped found twenty-one missions stations in that future state.
Together they baptized nearly one hundred thousand Indians. Serra was
patient in teaching habits of settled agriculture to his converts, fervent in
promoting spiritual discipline among his fellow workers, and sharp with
Spanish officials who impeded his work.

At the same time, modern Christian sensitivity about the dignity of
all peoples has led to questions about Serra's relationship with the Indians.
Reflecting the common attitudes of his day, Serra held that missionaries
could and should treat their converts like small children. He instructed that

15

This heroic statue of Junípero Serra stands in the U.S. Capitol. But the corridors of power he cared about most were heavenly rather than earthly. *Library of Congress*

baptized Indians who attempted to leave the missions should be forcibly returned, and he believed that corporal punishment — including the whip and the stocks — also had a place. In a reversal of ordinary roles, a California governor once complained that this time *the friars* were punishing the natives too severely. When in the twentieth century the Roman Catholic Church began to investigate Serra as a candidate for sainthood, it was faced with a dilemma. Proponents pointed correctly to his self-sacrificing commitment; opponents, also correctly, accused him of short-changing the dignity of the Indians as image-bearers of God.

Limitations in Serra's work arising from the cultural distance between the Spanish friars and their Indian converts were not untypical. Even more damaging was the callousness of Spain's grip on the colonies. Priests and friars were not immune to European ethnocentricism, but in general they tried to preserve the spiritual priorities of their faith. On the other hand, viceroys and generals, who were sometimes sincere in personal faith, regarded the Indians much more as submissive workers than as potential converts. The situation in the Spanish settlements was complicated by the fact that the popes had granted complete authority over the church in New Spain to the Spanish government. This meant that civil officials controlled church finances and church appointments. The general result was to impede seriously the long-range effectiveness of missionary work.

In addition, conversions among the Indians tended to be shallow. With a few exceptions, Native Americans remained Christian only so long as Spanish colonial rule was secure. One of the problems was simple difficulty in receiving the Spanish imperial culture with which Christianity was bound up. Another was that the friars made little progress at translating Christian material into native languages or enlisting Indian converts for leadership in the church. Yet a third was the fact that missionaries seemed to hold out the promise that a better way of life would follow conversion, yet disease, intertribal conflict, and onerous subjection to the Spanish seemed to belie that promise.

The result was native resentment and, on occasion, even revolt. When the Pueblos near Santa Fe arose in 1680 under a native religious teacher named Popé, for example, they singled out the missionaries for special retribution. Most of the Spanish were simply driven away, but twenty-one of the region's thirty-three missionaries were killed. The insurgent Pueblos also went out of their way to burn churches, destroy baptismal records, and eradicate evidence of the friars' work. Within fifteen years, missionaries had returned to the Pueblos under the protection of a restored Spanish rule. But never did they succeed in adding more than a thin overlay of Catholicism to the indigenous religion of the region.

In other words, despite valiant efforts by Spanish missionaries, the message of a universal saving faith was rarely able to bridge the cultural divide separating Europeans and Native Americans. With variations, the history was mostly the same in territories settled by the English. In New France it was, at least briefly, a different story.

Catholic Missions in New France

The government of France held sway in Canada and what would later be the midwestern United States from the founding of Quebec by Samuel de Champlain in 1608 until 1759, when a British army defeated the French forces on the Plains of Abraham outside that city. Thereafter, the province of Quebec, though now under British control, remained a center of French-Catholic culture. As such, its presence in Canada would be one of the most significant features differentiating that society from the emerging nation to the south. Whereas Roman Catholics in significant numbers came relatively

While the explorer Louis Jolliet sought a waterway to the sea, Fr. Jacques Marquette (shown here sailing down the Mississippi River in 1673) was looking for lost souls.
Library of Congress

late to what would be the United States, they were present as the first permanent settlers of Canada and so provided a foundational contribution to later Canadian civilization.

Like their counterparts in New Spain, the traders, trappers, and settlers of New France were accompanied by Catholic priests, nuns, and brothers. Missionary work among the Native Americans in Canada had been going on for two generations before the most famous French explorations of the United States took place. But the way they combined secular and religious purposes was much the same throughout the course of French exploration. Around 1630, the explorer Jacques Cartier left this record of how contact with Native Americans affected him: finding them "living without God and without religion like brute beasts, I thereupon concluded in my private judgment that I should be committing a great sin if I did not make it my business to devise some means of bringing them to the knowledge of God."

When Louis Jolliet explored the upper Mississippi River valley in 1673, a Jesuit, Fr. Jacques Marquette (1637-1675), was his companion. Jolliet was seeking trade and establishing French claim to the region. Marquette was seeking souls. He had long heard of the Illinois Indians, rumored to be a vast multitude inhabiting the midlands of the continent, and Jolliet's expedition gave him the chance to find them. As Marquette put it, he wanted "to seek toward the south sea [the Gulf of Mexico] nations new and unknown to us, in order to make them know our great God of whom they have been up to now ignorant." His initial contacts with these and other Native American groups were promising, but, worn out by his years of arduous travel in the New World, Marquette died in 1675, still short of his thirty-eighth birthday.

Franciscan missionaries made a significant contribution to the colonization of New France. One of them, Louis Hennepin (1626–ca. 1705), explored modern Minnesota with René-Robert de La Salle. The county in which Minneapolis is now found was named in his memory. But most of the Canadian missionary work was carried on by the Jesuits. Jesuits, whose missionary service in the Far East had been marked by an effort to adapt the faith to Asian cultures, showed some of the same cultural sensitivity in North America.

The best example of that sensitive spirit was probably Jean de Brébeuf, who came to Canada when he was thirty-two, in 1625. Brébeuf helped found mission stations near Georgian Bay, where he enjoyed considerable success at winning the friendly Huron Indians to the new Western religion. In his capacity as senior missionary, he regularly counseled his fellows to adapt, as far as possible, to the ways of the potential converts. Louis Hennepin would later write that "the way to succeed in converting the Barbarians, is to endeavour to make them men before we go about to make them Christians." Brébeuf's attitude was different: "You must have sincere affection for the Savages," he wrote in 1637, "looking upon them as ransomed by the blood of the son of God, and as our Brethren with whom we are to pass the rest of our lives. . . . You should try to eat their sagamite or salmagundi in the way they prepare it, although it may be dirty, half-cooked, and very tasteless. As to the other numerous things which may be unpleasant, they must be endured for the love of God, without saying anything or appearing to notice them."

Jesuit success among the Hurons owed something to the fact that Brébeuf and his colleagues arrived at a time of increasing pressure on the Hurons from neighboring Iroquoian Indians. Expanding Native American societies were harder to evangelize than those, like the Hurons, that had become increasingly dependent on the French and who, as a result, were suffering from acute self-doubt brought on by the ravages of contagious disease that swept through their people. Still, the spirit of Brébeuf also

In this graphic painting depicting the martyrdom of Jesuit missionaries in what is
now Canada, Fr. Jean de Brébeuf is the priest chained to the stake in the right front.
If anything, this is a muted depiction of the torture administered, the agonies endured, and the admiration won through these gruesome trials.
Picture Collection, The Branch Libraries, New York Public Library

contributed to conversions. Among his most notable efforts was the preparation of Christian literature for the Hurons, not only in their own language
but also (to at least some extent) in the idiom of their culture. One of the
examples of that literature is the Christmas carol "Jesous Ahatonhia" ("Jesus
Is Born"), which is quoted at the start of this chapter.

Brébeuf and his fellows carried on their work among the Hurons for
more than a decade. But then warfare forced the Hurons to move, and many
of the leading missionaries, including Brébeuf, were killed by the Hurons'
enemies, the Five Nations Iroquois. Brébeuf's martyrdom came in 1649
when he was captured by a band of Iroquois. It says something of the stature
he had gained among the Native Americans that when he was finally killed,
after excruciating torture, the Iroquois cut out his heart and ate it so that
they might receive a share of his courage.

French Canada also offered considerable opportunities for women missionaries. Marie Guyart (1599-1672), who came to be known as Marie of the Incarnation, was a French widow from Tours in France who joined the Ursuline order and eventually came to Canada as the first woman missionary in the New World. From her new residence in Quebec, Marie took an active interest in the various Indian groups of the region and played a major part in writing grammars, liturgies, and catechisms in Huron and Algonquian for the native converts. She also wrote back thousands of letters to France in which she poured out her concern for her family in the old country and gave expression to a deep, mystical faith. By the time of her death she had been joined by several younger women in religious orders who continued her work.

Some of the missionaries' most notable converts were also women. Catherine Tegahkouita from upper New York was converted in 1676 through the work of the Jesuit Jacques de Lamberville. Despite opposition from her family, Catherine became an example of piety before her early death in 1680. Thereafter her tomb was the object of pilgrimages, and miracles were said to occur there. Such notable conversions remained rare, however. In New France, as historian Jay Dolan has written, "the exploits of the missionaries, not the conversion of the Indians, was the real success story."

The Emergence of a French-Catholic Society

French colonial officials were considerably more enlightened than their Spanish counterparts. They encouraged mission work but also tried to make active religious life a part of the developing French colonies. The first permanent French settlements were noteworthy for their unusually persistent leaders and the unusual form of Catholicism they promoted.

French Canada has always been regarded, and properly so, as a Roman Catholic region. In the very early days of settlement, however, a degree of religious toleration unusual for the age also marked the new colonies. This development can be attributed to events taking place in France. When King Henry IV promulgated the Edict of Nantes in 1598, French Huguenots gained a measure of liberty for which they had been struggling since the early days of the Reformation. These Huguenots were Reformed or Calvinistic Protestants who largely came from the rising class of traders and merchants. One of the Huguenots, Pierre du Gua de Monts, helped finance early voyages of exploration to New France and early attempts at permanent settlement. Other Huguenots invested in these ventures, which involved colonies in what would later be called Quebec as well as in Acadia (the Maritimes). De Monts, for example, helped outfit an Acadian expedition in

1604 that sought to establish a colony in Port-Royal (near modern Annapolis Royal). With a body of 120 workers he also sent out a Huguenot minister and two Roman Catholic priests. Although the clergymen argued with each other constantly, the colonists seemed to have taken a more modern, or at least a more charitable, attitude. When the minister and one of the priests died from scurvy at almost the same time, the colonists — at least so the story goes — buried them together in a single grave with the expressed hope that they would now at last rest peacefully together.

The Huguenot presence in New France was pronounced only until the mid-1620s. Despite quarrels with Catholic officials, Huguenots worshiped openly in Quebec, and several Huguenots obtained high positions in the colonial government. Open Huguenot activity was brought to an end by Cardinal Richelieu when he became the head of France's royal council. In 1627 Richelieu reorganized the company in charge of Quebec in such a way as to underscore the dominance of the Catholics, and he revoked the application of the Edict of Nantes in the French colonies (fifty-eight years before it would be revoked in France itself). Thereafter, Huguenots retained a residual influence, but the movement toward Roman Catholic hegemony in French Canada had definitely begun.

The French settled first on the Atlantic coast, but their interest in Acadia remained mostly mercantile. While the settlement of Quebec soon established its own economic, political, and religious traditions, settlements in the Atlantic region remained more closely tied to the mother country. The Jesuits, who would play a major role in the history of Quebec, first arrived in Acadia in 1611. But they did not stay for long. In 1755 the British forcibly removed many of the Acadians from their ancestral land on the grounds that they constituted a threat to Britain's security. By that time 115 Roman Catholic priests had ministered to the people there over a period of nearly 150 years. The ratio of priests to laymen was always low. As a result, the Catholicism that developed among the Acadians was more pragmatic and less authoritarian than that which which was established along the St. Lawrence River. A pragmatic, informal variety of Roman Catholicism also appeared in Newfoundland, which developed as a fishing colony under British control. By the 1730s Irish Roman Catholics made up a large part of the seasonal work force imported to ply the important fishing trade.

In Quebec, the work of settlement sometimes took a back seat to the exploitation of such natural resources as furs. But religious concerns were always part and parcel of colonization when it took place. Samuel de Champlain (ca. 1570-1635), a sincerely religious person with Huguenot influences in his background and many Huguenot associates, was always eager to see Quebec serve as a center for Indian missions. He was almost as eager to promote the faith among the French colonists who soon after the founding of Quebec City in 1608 began to settle in the lands along the St. Lawrence. Champlain had brought Franciscan Récollets with him to the New World. But soon after the first Jesuits arrived in 1625, they took the lead in organizing the church of New France. In this task they demonstrated the same kind of enterprise, skill, and determination that won them respect (and, from other quarters, condemnation) as missionaries to the Indians.

Administrative blunders and intramural battles were every bit as prominent in Quebec as in France during that period. Early efforts by Jesuits to establish high standards of religious practice were compromised by the travel required by the fur trade and by a lack of coordination between colonial and church leaders. When another French order, the Sulpicians, arrived in the 1650s and took charge of religious life in the recently founded city of Montreal, the Jesuits from Quebec City were more offended than pleased. Eventually, however, a series of strong leaders set Quebec firmly on the religious path that it would not leave until the mid-twentieth century.

The most important of these early leaders was François-Xavier de Montmorency Laval, who was the chief religious authority in New France from 1659 to 1684. Laval was a Jesuit who did not look kindly on efforts by the Sulpicians to exert their influence in Canada. Yet he was always more pious than partisan, more an ecclesiastical builder than a church politician. Under his direction, the church won secure backing from the colonial government and gained the right to tithe the settlers ($\frac{1}{26}$ of their annual crops). Laval secured large land grants for the church in general and the Jesuits in particular. He was concerned about the integrity of France's presence in the New World and so struggled to protect the native population from unscrupulous trappers and rum traders. Eventually he succeeded in restricting the liquor traffic with the Indians. He took steps to ensure the church's control over all education in the colony and in 1663 established a seminary in Quebec (later called Laval University) to train clergy, encourage the colony's intellectual development, and centralize the organization of the church. Laval also promoted the work of several women's orders that had been started before his time. These included the educational work of the Ursulines (for whom Marie of the Incarnation had worked), the Hôtel Dieu Hospital in Quebec which had been founded by three female Augustinians, and the schools staffed by the Congregation of Notre Dame of Montreal, which had been established by Marguerite Bourgeoys in 1658. When in 1674 Laval was named the first bishop of Quebec, it was more a recognition of service already rendered than a summons to wider authority.

Laval was also important for his influence in transforming the inner character of Catholicism in Quebec. In the sixteenth and seventeenth centu-

François-Xavier de Montmorency Laval became the first Bishop of Quebec in 1658, more than 130 years before there was a Catholic bishop in the territory of the United States. As bishop, Laval was distinguished by piety, by his concern for education, and by his efforts to protect Native Americans from the liquor trade. *Archives nationales du Québec à Québec*

ries France was a strongly "Gallican" country, which is to say that the king was the chief player in the church and Catholicism was as much an instrument of French nationalism as a servant of the papacy. But Laval turned Roman Catholicism in the New World away from Gallicanism toward "ultramontanism," the Catholic tradition in which authority in the church is conceived as coming from "over the mountains" — that is, from Rome rather than from local authorities such as the king of France. This influence from Laval made a great difference in the later history of Quebec. While the Roman Catholic Church in France was caught up in the Enlightenment and in the French Revolution, Catholicism in Quebec remained spiritually and intellectually conservative. It continued to take its orders from the pope, it aspired to a nearly medieval control over the lives of French Canadians, and it promoted a piety based on traditional rather than modern Catholic practices.

Although bishops and church administrators after Laval often fell short of his high standards, Quebec faithfully maintained its ultramontane Catholicism. At the time of Anglo-French tension that led to the eventual defeat of the French, for example, the leader of the Quebec church was Bishop

Henri-Marie Dubreil de Pontbriand. While Pontbriand expended considerable energy in promoting France in its dynastic struggle with Britain, he exerted even more effort at encouraging the internal life of the church. Thus it was that, even as Quebec "fell" into the hands of the British in 1759, Pontbriand was strengthening traditional bonds between church and state as well as traditional forms of Catholic life by founding new orders for sisters to work in Quebec's hospitals and schools.

Quebec's ultramontanist Catholicism was a target of endless hostility from the British and their largely Protestant colonies. Britain took control of Nova Scotia in 1713 and treated the Acadians there with caution for nearly forty years. But then in 1755 the British governor, Charles Lawrence, expelled most of them, fearing that they would support the French during the Seven Years' War.

The mutual suspicion between the French and the British extended far beyond politics to almost every aspect of religious life. The life of Sébastian Rale (1657-1724) illustrates this tension. Rale was a French-born Jesuit who became a missionary to Native Americans in both Quebec and Acadia. He was an energetic preacher as well as a gifted linguist. Rale was tireless in his efforts to organize churches among the Native Americans and he also helped to develop written forms for a couple of their languages. In the eyes of Britain and its colonists, however, Rale was perceived mostly as an agitator among the Native Americans. For some twenty years before his death, Rale was regarded as a political threat by the British because of his influence among some Native-American bands that opposed Indian groups allied with the British. In 1724, at a time of heightened French-British tension, Rale was killed in a battle initiated by troops recruited in Massachusetts. The rumor, then and since, is that a bounty had been placed on his head. The unquestioned fact is that triumphant New Englanders paraded through the streets of Boston with his scalp.

Such incidents remind us that during the seventeenth and eighteenth centuries religious differences extended deep into culture and that they could be, literally, matters of life and death. They also remind us that by the 1720s a Christian society had been founded in French Canada that looked very different from the forms of Protestant culture being established in the British colonies. Through the succeeding centuries Quebec's French-Catholic culture remained an important counterpoint to the Protestant societies of North America and even to the more pluralistic Catholicism that eventually came to play such a large role in the United States and elsewhere in Canada. The "founding fathers" of Christianity in America included Brébeuf, Champlain, and Laval as well as those Protestant leaders whose names might be more familiar.

The Death of Father Sébastian Rale. *National Archives of Canada*

Roman Catholics in Maryland

In contrast to Quebec, where steady support from church and state led eventually to a deeply rooted Catholic culture, the beginnings of Catholic settlement in what would become the United States was more haphazard. George Calvert (1580?-1632) and his son Cecil (1606-1675), the First and Second Lords Baltimore, were the founders of Maryland, the only one of the original thirteen American colonies with a significant Roman Catholic population. George Calvert, who converted to Catholicism in 1625, was a secretary of state under James I of England, but he was forced to resign this post when he refused to swear allegiance to the Church of England on James's death and the succession of his son, Charles I. The new king was nevertheless eager to repay the Calverts for loyal service rendered to his father and to himself, and so he gave the family a large proprietary grant in the New World. The colony that resulted was named Maryland in honor of Charles I's Catholic queen, Maria Henrietta of France.

The Calverts hoped to do two things with this grant of land: provide a haven for English Catholics and increase the family fortune through rents. On both accounts they had only a modest success. Despite the Catholicism of the Calverts, the number of Protestants among the original settlers in their colony was high. English Catholics were reluctant to leave England at a time when Charles I was looking more favorably on their religion. And Cecil Calvert felt it necessary to reassure Protestants in England that Maryland would not become a hostile Catholic enclave, so he gave strict instruc-

Many Europeans talked about communicating the Christian faith to Native Americans; the Jesuit Fr. Andrew White was one of the few who did it. *The Archives of the University of Notre Dame*

P. Andreas Vitus, S.J. Angl, in Anglia et Marilandia Americæ Provincia, Apostolicis laboribus clarus. Obijt in Anglia prope octogenarius. A° 1655.

BAPTISM OF KING CHILOMACON, BY FATHER ANDREW WHITE.
FROM TANNER, "SOCIETAS JESU," 1694

tions to his brother Leonard, the lieutenant governor on site, not to antagonize the Protestant settlers.

Soon after the arrival of the first settlers in 1634, Catholic missionaries began work among the Native Americans in the colony, while most of the other settlers turned to the raising of tobacco. The mainstay of the missionary enterprise was the Jesuit Andrew White (1579-1656). White was a determined proponent of Thomas Aquinas's theology and had labored as both a priest in England and a teacher in France before coming to aid the Calverts. In the New World, White preached energetically to the European colonists. For these efforts, ironically, he was reprimanded by the Calverts for endangering their colony (by stirring up the Protestants). But White's most important work was among the Piscataway Indians. Through very difficult conditions, which led to the death of several coworkers, White persisted in his efforts to record Piscataway in a grammar and dictionary and to prepare Christian literature in that language. He also witnessed what seemed to him miraculous signs in his work among the Native Americans. Once White reported that a warrior, speared through the chest, was healed by the application of a sacred relic of the Most Holy Cross that White always carried about his neck. When colonists from Virginia briefly overthrew the Calverts' rule in 1645, White and the other Jesuits were forced to leave. At the age of seventy, White made efforts to return to his Indian work in Maryland from exile on the Continent, but it was not to be. While much of England was embroiled in civil war, White died peacefully in his native land.

The changing circumstances in England associated with the Puritan Revolution established an important milestone in the New World, however. In 1649 Cecil Calvert issued the justly famous "Act concerning Religion." Born more out of a desire to protect Catholic interests against the Puritan parliament in England than out of a theoretical commitment to freedom of religion, Calvert's declaration was nonetheless a notable step in a direction that the other colonists took more than a century to follow. The act stipulated penalties for those who blasphemed the Trinity, cast aspersions on the Virgin Mary, or employed such terms as "heretic, schismatic, idolator, puritan, Independent, presbyterian, popish priest, Jesuit, Jesuit papist, Lutheran, Calvinist, Anabaptist . . . or any other name or term in a reproachful manner relating to matter of Religion." But for the rest, "no person or persons whatsoever within this Province, or the islands, ports, harbors, creeks, or havens thereunto belonging professing to believe in Jesus Christ, shall from henceforth be any wise troubled, molested or discountenanced for or in respect of his or her religion nor in the free exercise thereof." This movement toward toleration did not have a wide influence, but it was a straw in the wind indicating what would one day transpire much more widely in the United States.

In 1691 the original Maryland charter was stripped from the Calvert family, only to be returned in 1715, when the Fourth Lord Baltimore entered the Church of England. Maryland remained a proprietary possession of the Calverts until the American Revolution. It was later the home of the first Catholic bishop in the United States, and it was the center of American Roman Catholicism for an even longer time thereafter.

❀   ❀   ❀

The history of Roman Catholicism in the early years of European colonization is important for at least two reasons. First, the firm presence that the Roman Catholic Church established among the families and other permanent settlers who eventually came to Canada offered a prominent — and sometimes deeply disquieting — contrast to the Protestants busy subduing the areas that would become the rest of Canada and the United States. Second, the fact that Roman Catholic missions, settlements, and institutions were established in the sixteenth and seventeenth centuries, *before* their more visible Protestant counterparts, sets a useful standard for historical comparison. In the late twentieth century, *after* Protestant hegemony has faded in both the United States and Canada, it may for the first time be possible to evaluate the early history of Catholicism in America for generally Christian, as opposed to narrowly sectarian, purposes. That early history may turn out to offer modern Roman Catholics warnings about the dangers of mechanistic views of conversion as well as inspiration in missionary zeal. And if it still provides modern Protestants with reservations about church-state entanglements, it also offers useful guidelines for cross-cultural evangelism and the support of Christian education. In other words, it may have taken the more secular modern period to show both Catholics and Protestants how the early church history of Sante Fe, Quebec, and Maryland belongs to all the Christians who have followed.

Further Reading

American Jesuit Spirituality: The Maryland Tradition, 1634-1900. Edited by Robert Emmett Curran. New York: Paulist Press, 1988.

Bowden, Henry Warner. *American Indians and Christian Missions: Studies in Cultural Conflict.* Chicago: University of Chicago Press, 1981.

Brigham, Kay. *Christopher Columbus: His Life and Discovery in the Light of His Prophecies.* Barcelona: Library CLIE, 1990. A positive assessment of the morality of Columbus's work. For a radically contrasting view, see Kirkpatrick Sale's *Conquest of Paradise,* listed below.

Canada's Huguenot Heritage. Toronto: Huguenot Society of Canada, 1987. Includes John S. Moir's essay "Canada and the Huguenot Connection, 1577-1627" and Marc-André Bedard's essay "La Presence Protestante en Nouvelle-France."

Dolan, Jay P. *The American Catholic Experience.* Garden City, NY: Doubleday, 1985.

Sale, Kirkpatrick. *The Conquest of Paradise: Christopher Columbus and the Columbian Legacy.* New York: Knopf, 1990.

Sandos, James A. "Junípero Serra's Canonization and the Historical Record." *American Historical Review* 93 (Dec. 1988): 1253-69.

Walsh, H. H. *The Church in the French Era: From Colonization to the British Conquest.* Toronto: Ryerson, 1966.

CHAPTER 2

The English Reformation and the Puritans

Psalm 121

I to the hills lift up mine eyes,
    from whence shall come mine aid.
Mine help doth from Jehovah come,
    which heav'n & earth hath made.
Hee will not let thy foot be mov'd,
    nor slumber; that thee keeps.
Loe hee that keepeth Israell,
    hee slumbreth not, nor sleeps.
The Lord thy keeper is, the Lord
    on thy right hand the shade.
The Sun by day, nor Moone by night,
    shall thee by stroke invade.
The Lord will keep thee from all ill:
    thy soule hee keeps alway,
Thy going out, & thy income,
    the Lord keeps now & aye.

This metrical psalm is from the Bay Psalm Book, *printed by the Puritans of Massachusetts Bay at Cambridge in 1640, the first English-language book printed in America and — through twenty editions and seventy printings — one of the most popular.*

THE VITALITY OF ENGLAND AND ITS CULTURE GREW EVER STRONGER throughout the sixteenth century and on into the seventeenth. It was a time of literary splendor, climaxed by the incomparable works of William Shakespeare. It was a time of swashbuckling derring-do, exemplified by the exploits of sea captains such as Sir Francis Drake and John Hawkins, who (with the aid of a great storm) defeated the Spanish Armada in 1588. It was a time of population growth and economic activity, with new wealth flowing to several levels of society. It was a day of political triumphs and political uncertainty. And it was a time of religious tumult and renewal.

Henry VIII initiated the reformation of the English church in the 1530s largely for personal political reasons. When his first wife, Catherine of Aragon, failed to bear him a male heir, he sought to divorce her in order to marry Anne Boleyn. When the Roman Catholic Church refused to accommodate him in this matter, he undertook a series of steps aimed at dissolving the ties between the papacy and the English church. It was not really Henry's intent to introduce ecclesiastical reform for its own sake, much less to introduce Protestant doctrine into the English church, but once it was set in motion, the English Reformation did in fact proceed to affect doctrine, personal devotion, public worship, and ecclesiastical organization. And the broader effects of this Reformation eventually played a large role in the Christian history of America.

The English who played the major part in settling British North America were Protestants of a distinct type. When the youthful Edward VI succeeded Henry VIII in 1547, his Protestant advisors greatly accelerated the pace of religious change in England. They enhanced the authority of such leaders as the Archbishop of Canterbury Thomas Cranmer, whose liturgical theology was a subtle blend of Lutheran and Reformed emphases seasoned by the wisdom of the early church. And they encouraged the removal of Roman Catholic practices and customs that had survived under Henry VIII. In this reforming context the most advanced group of Protestants seized the opportunity to push reform in England to what they thought was its logical conclusion.

The pace of Protestant reform came to a rapid halt, however, when Edward, never a healthy youth, died in 1553 and was succeeded by his ardently Catholic half-sister Mary Tudor. Under her rule, 288 Protestants, common people as well as leaders such as Cranmer, went to the flames for their convictions. But others, including some of the most important voices of English and Scottish reform, managed to lie low in England or escape to the Continent. The experience of the exiles proved especially decisive not only for later events in Britain but also for long-term developments in America.

Until the mid-1550s, the English Reformation was a fairly thorough mixture that combined some impulses from Luther, some borrowings from other Protestant leaders in Europe, and a number of native English tendencies. When Protestants fled England during the reign of Mary, however, they were not able to go to Lutheran lands. Defeats in warfare and intramural disputes in the wake of Luther's death (1546) made it difficult for Lutheran regions in Germany and Scandinavia to accept the English refugees. The situation was much different in Reformed and Calvinist regions. Calvin had secured a thoroughly Protestant settlement in Geneva early in the 1550s, and he welcomed the English refugees eagerly. Similar hospitality was extended by Reformed leaders in other Swiss cities and in southwestern Germany. In these Reformed regions, many of the English refugees caught a vision of how they would like to see their native land renewed if ever the opportunity presented itself again. What Calvin and other Reformed leaders were attempting was a systematic restructuring of society on the basis of the Bible and their understanding of its message. Under such influence, some of the English refugees began to wonder if the eclecticism of England's previous reform had been enough.

When Mary Tudor died in 1558 after a short reign, the English refugees were able to return home. Under the new monarch, Queen Elizabeth I, they joined the many who had remained in England to push for a further, more systematic reform of England's religion. That drive for greater purity in the Church of England led to the rise of Puritanism in England. It also provided a major impetus for the settlement of English colonists in North America.

Puritanism in England

The Puritans thus arose as the "advanced" or "precise" party among English Protestants. Defined negatively, the Puritans wanted to wipe out the vestiges of Roman Catholic worship and doctrine that survived within the Church of England as governed by Queen Elizabeth I (1558-1603), James I (1603-1625), and their clerical advisors. Defined positively, the Puritans wanted to finish the Reformation and finish it now. One of their most extreme representatives, the congregationalist Robert Browne, published a stirring tract entitled *Reformation without Tarrying for Any* in 1582. The sentiment expressed in the title was common to many others whose views were not quite as radical.

The main convictions of the English Puritans were eventually carried to America by their descendants in the 1630s. For that reason, they are worth summarizing briefly. First, Puritans believed that humankind must depend entirely upon God for salvation. Like Martin Luther and John Calvin, Puritans were Augustinians in theology. They held that humans are sinners who will not choose to be reconciled with God unless God initiates the process of their salvation. The Puritans went beyond the Continental Reformers in their emphasis on conversion, however. Early leaders in England, as well as emigrants to New England such as the Reverend Thomas Shepard (1605-1649) of Cambridge, took great pains to trace the progress of the soul from rebellion to obedience.

Second, the Puritans emphasized the authority of the Bible. Specifically, they believed that the Bible exerts a "regulative" authority, which means that Christians, so far as possible, should do only what the Scriptures explicitly direct. In this belief, they went considerably beyond Martin Luther and their Anglican fellows, who held that the Bible was supreme in the sense that believers should do nothing *prohibited* by Scripture. Among themselves, however, Puritans could not always agree on what exactly the Bible demanded. The issue of church organization proved to be a controversial sticking point. Some Puritans (mostly in England) defended a presbyterian church-state organization (churches ruled by elders, whom the members at large elect, with elders meeting together to guide the church as a whole, and with the state actively supporting the church). Most of the Puritans who came to New England, on the other hand, held that the Bible teaches a congregational organization, albeit an organization in league with the state (i.e., that churches are organized individually but cooperate with godly magistrates to promote the total reformation of society). A few Puritans, of whom Roger Williams was the most famous in New England, held that the Bible mandated a congregational organization separate from the state.

Third, Puritans believed that God created society as a unified whole. Church and state, the individual and the public, are not unrelated spheres of life but are complementary, intimately connected by God's acts of creation and his continuing providence. This conviction lay behind the Puritan effort to reform all of English society. It also provided the stimulus for the Puritan effort to fashion colonies in the New World in which all parts of colonial life would reflect the glory of God. The results of this Puritan conviction were decidedly mixed. On the one hand, it led to the high-handedness and intolerance that Puritans sometimes displayed in both Britain and America when they were in control. Since they presumed to know the will of God so clearly, they felt it was only right that they could force others to comply, even if those others did not understand God the same way they did. On the other hand, this belief allowed the Puritan faith to break free from narrow religiosity and to shape substantial spheres of life: Puritan activity had

For the Puritans, the congregation of believers dispersed in the world was the real church of Christ; this belief, nonetheless, made them eager and faithful to attend the "meeting house" for worship and instruction on Sundays.
Courtesy of the Billy Graham Center Museum

something to do with the promotion of democracy, it liberated great energy in literary creativity, it provided a foundation for the first great political revolution of modern times (orchestrated by Oliver Cromwell in England), it offered a supportive environment for the rise of modern science in Britain, it gave several thousand immigrants the courage to brave the howling wilderness in the New World, and it gave those colonists a social vision the comprehensive character of which has rarely been matched in America.

Finally, Puritans believed that God always works with people through covenants, or solemn agreements. They believed that the Bible explains the terms and conditions of the covenants through which God approaches the world. Salvation for individuals comes about through a "covenant of grace" whereby God bestows the merit of Christ's saving work upon those who exercise faith in Christ (it is a covenant of *grace* because God is also the giver of faith). Congregationalist Puritans insisted that local churches arise when individual believers covenant together to serve God as a unit and to follow his will. Almost all varieties of Puritans also held that God enters into covenants with nations, especially those that are granted special insight into the truths of the Bible. Guidelines from the Bible indicate to nations what they must do to enjoy divine blessing, while scriptural examples concerning ancient Israel provide harrowing warnings about what will happen to nations that violate their covenant with God. The Puritans were much inclined to view England and, by extension, her American colonies in this light.

Puritanism derived much of its strength from the subtle interweaving of these covenants. John Cotton, who would become early Boston's foremost minister, claimed that God had appointed humans to "live in Societies, first, of Family, Secondly Church, Thirdly, Common-Wealth." Another early leader drew the bonds even tighter: "The Covenant of Grace is cloathed with Church-Covenant in a Political visible Church-way." The secret of understanding the Puritans lies in realizing not only that energies from private religious life flowed readily into church and society but also that they flowed in the other direction as well.

The great Puritan migration to the New World took place when it appeared as if opportunities for reform were closed off in England. It was bad enough that Charles I, who succeeded James I in 1625, had Roman Catholic sympathies. But Charles also was determined to rule England with a view of divine right that deeply offended the Puritans and their allies in Parliament. Charles quarreled with several Parliaments, and then from 1629 he tried to rule England without calling Parliament into session. He also commissioned his Archbishop of Canterbury, William Laud, to root out his opponents from the Anglican Church. In 1628 a group of Puritans leaning toward congregational church organization purchased a controlling interest in a trading company that had been set up earlier as a profit-seeking venture. After this New England Company was reorganized to emphasize colonization instead of commerce, and after it obtained a new charter from the king that provided for more self-government, the first migration brought over a thousand settlers to Massachusetts Bay in 1630. During the next decade, while leading Puritans in England continued to resist the programs of Charles and Laud, and while some future leaders of Puritan England including Oliver Cromwell wondered if they should go to Massachusetts, over twenty thousand more settlers actually made the hazardous trip to America. By no means all of the these early settlers were heartfelt Puritans in a religious sense. But their leaders were, and few came to Massachusetts and its sister colonies who were not content with a society ordered by Puritan beliefs.

New World Settlements

By the time the Puritans established Massachusetts, however, there were already two other English colonial ventures that had secured a foothold in the New World. In different ways the Puritan surge had also figured in their establishment.

John White's map illustrating "The Arrival of the Englishmen in Virginia" is not especially accurate in its details, but it does capture the strangeness felt by the Europeans who approached this coast in the early seventeenth century. *Library of Congress*

Virginia

England's first permanent settlement was the Virginia colony, established at Jamestown in 1607. Historians have customarily contrasted the secular character of the founding of Virginia with the more overtly religious settlements of Puritans to the north in Plymouth and Massachusetts Bay. It is true that the Virginia Company of London was more interested in turning a profit than the Massachusetts Bay Company that later settled Boston and its environs. It is also true that the dispersed pattern of settlement in Virginia was not conducive to the close spiritual fellowship that was possible in the northern English colonies. Still, if the Virginians were never entirely Puritan, some of the same religious impulses that inspired the settlers to the north were also at work in Virginia.

As soon as the first settlers arrived in May 1607, for example, they joined the Rev. Robert Hunt ("an honest, religious, and courageous Divine" according to Captain John Smith) in holding a service of communion. When Lord De La Warr, a new governor, arrived in 1610 as the colony teetered on

36

This filiopietistic depiction of the baptism of Pocahontas presents a sentimentalized version of Virginia's early history. *Library of Congress*

the brink of collapse, his first action was to organize a worship service in order to issue a biblical call for sacrifice and industry. Virginia's earliest legal code made attendance at Sunday services compulsory and contained harsh laws prohibiting violations of the Sabbath, adultery, and excessive dress. All of these were also concerns of the Puritans. Even the missionary motive was not absent. John Rolfe married the legendary Pocahontas in part to share the Christian faith: "I will never cease," he wrote of his desire to have Pocahontas become a Christian, "untill I have accomplished, & brought to perfection so holy a worke, in which I will daily pray God to blesse me, to mine, and her eternall happiness." Alexander Whitaker, the leading minister in Virginia's early history, never lost his desire to convert the Native Americans, even as he maintained a regular ministry among the English settlers.

As part of Virginia's incorporation, the Church of England was made the colony's established church. This establishment would eventually lend a very different flavor to religion in the Chesapeake region than it had in New England. Other circumstances of Virginia's early history also contributed to its differences from New England, especially an early turn to growing tobacco for export and an early introduction of black chattel slavery. Still, it is possible to glimpse in the early years of the colony some of the same devotion and the same Puritan fervor that played such a large part in the settlement of New England.

Plymouth

England's next permanent colony bore the stamp of Puritanism much more definitely. The settlers who arrived in 1620 at Plymouth in southeastern Massachusetts were in some senses even more consistent than those who came later to Boston. While other Puritans were still contending in England for the thorough reform of the church and the religious life of the nation, the Plymouth settlers had largely abandoned that effort in order to carve out a separate society for themselves. Among the more extreme Protestants who were deeply disappointed when the Scottish James I, successor in 1603 to Queen Elizabeth, did not embrace the Puritan cause, were local congregations that had begun to meet together beyond the jurisdiction of the national church. One of these in Scrooby, Nottinghamshire, grew so uneasy with the course of religious events in England that it resolved to migrate to a more friendly environment. Under its pastor John Robinson, this congregation chose first to go to Holland. But in that land they were disappointed. The Dutch allowed them to worship as they pleased, but the English immigrants found the Dutch culture unappealing. They were also worried that their children were being led astray by alternative faiths and by opportunities for economic gain. So after a dozen years they resolved to move much further afield to find the space they needed to worship and live as they thought best. As their chronicler, William Bradford (1589-1657), wrote of that move, "so they left the godly and pleasant city which had been their resting place . . . ; but they knew they were pilgrims and looked not much on those things but lifted their eyes to the heavens, their dearest country, and quieted their spirits."

These "pilgrims" secured the sponsorship of English merchants in the Virginia Company and eventually surmounted an unremitting series of difficulties to board the *Mayflower* on September 6, 1620, for the New World. They sailed for Virginia but were blown off course to Cape Cod, where they arrived in early November. They decided to stay. But before leaving the ship, the male passengers (not all of whom were members of the congregation) signed an agreement, or compact, in which the mingled motives of their venture were reflected: "having undertaken for the Glory of God, and Advancement of the Christian Faith, and the Honour of our King and Country, a Voyage to plant the first colony in the northern Parts of Virginia; [we] Do by these Presents, solemnly and mutually in the Presence of God and one

This realistic picture, which comes from the reconstructed "Plimouth Plantation" in Plymouth, Massachusetts, captures the simple dignity of the Pilgrim mothers and fathers. *Photo courtesy of Plimoth Plantation, Inc., Plymouth, Massachusetts*

another, covenant and combine ourselves together into a civil Body Politick, for our better Ordering and Preservation, and Furtherance of the Ends aforesaid."

William Bradford, who would soon become the governor of the colony, left a deeply moving record of the ravages of the first winter. Half of the Pilgrims died. Heroic toil by Captain Miles Standish, Elder William Brewster, Bradford, and a few others pulled them through to the spring. Despite that bleak beginning, these humble settlers soon had established a secure dwelling. The colony remained small, with only three hundred residents by 1630, but it prospered. It enjoyed the liberty to plant a congregational form of worship and instill a deeply pious sense of community. William Bradford lived long enough to wonder if the colony's very success had not distracted it from early spiritual commitments. But at least he and a few others among the aging original settlers never lost the wonder of their experience. "Thus out of small beginnings," he wrote in his justly famous narrative of Plymouth Plantation, "greater things have been produced by His hand that made all things of nothing, and gives being to all things that are; and as one small candle may light a thousand, so the light here kindled hath shone to many, yea in some sort to our whole nation; let the glorious name of Jehovah have all the praise."

Puritan Life and Faith in America

As significant as early Christian experience was in New Spain, New France, and Virginia, it is the record of the Puritans in New England that has dominated modern perceptions of America's religious past. There are a number of reasons why this is so. The early American Puritans were blessed — or cursed, some would say — with dominant personalities. From the leaders of the first settlements, such as Gov. John Winthrop (1588-1649) and the Reverend John Cotton (1584-1652), to the last defenders of "The New England Way," such as the Reverend Cotton Mather (1663-1728), himself a descendant of John Cotton and Richard Mather, another famous minister of the first generation, Puritans enjoyed a long stream of vigorous spokesmen. These leaders, moreover, were often involved in obviously important (and sometimes sensational) events. The religious influence, for example, was very strong in the governments of early New England, where, without necessarily intending to, Massachusetts and its fellow Puritan colonies advanced the cause of democracy. It was equally strong in the Salem witch scare of 1692, an event that ever after has been a source of shame to friends of the Puritans and a proof of hysterical instability to their enemies. The Puritans were also a highly verbal people who left a full written record of their thoughts and actions. Long after the founding of the United States, Boston continued to be the publishing capital of North America. Until after the Civil War, most educational programs in the United States, from grade schools through universities, were modeled on patterns established during the first generations of Puritan settlement.

Most important, the Puritan moral vision was so strenuous that almost all Americans since have been forced to react to it in some way. Throughout the mid-nineteenth century, Puritan morality was widely thought to provide the foundation for the great success of the United States. Then for the next century or so it was thought that Puritan morality was the great nemesis to be exorcised from the American past. Not all have agreed with the judgment of Perry Miller, one of the twentieth century's greatest historians, that "many amenities of social life have increased in New England and in America, in direct proportion as Puritanism has receded. But while we congratulate ourselves upon these ameliorations, we cannot resist a slight fear that much of what has taken the place of Puritanism in our philosophies is just so much failure of nerve." Yet almost all who have investigated the Puritans agree with Miller that their moral energy was indeed unusual.

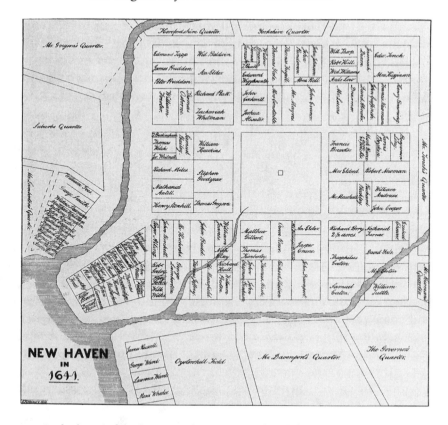

At the heart of Puritan sacred space, as in this early plat of New Haven,
Connecticut, was the town square (symbolizing the unity of the community).
And at the heart of the town square stood the church.
Picture Collection, The Branch Libraries, New York Public Library

The Puritan Way

Puritanism was the dominant religion in four American colonies: Plymouth,
settled as we have seen by separatistic congregationalists; Massachusetts, the
main Puritan colony, which absorbed Plymouth in 1691; New Haven,
founded in 1638 under the leadership of the Reverend John Davenport and
Gov. Theophilus Eaton and probably the strictest experiment in New World
Puritanism; and Connecticut, which came into existence in 1636 when
several ministers under the direction of the Reverend Thomas Hooker led
settlers from Massachusetts to a new home on the Connecticut River near
modern Hartford. In 1662 a new charter from England added New Haven
to Connecticut.

41

For the first generation of settlement, it seemed as if the New England Puritans could achieve the total reform of life that had eluded them in old England. The three other colonies did not follow the Massachusetts system in every particular, but its "New England Way" set a standard for them all. Almost as soon as they arrived, the Massachusetts ministers and magistrates agreed on a more visible measure of conversion than they had practiced in England. Now a new stress was placed on relating an experience of conversion as a prerequisite for full church membership. In the Old World, merely choosing to associate with the Puritans had set people apart; in the New World it seemed necessary to encourage a higher standard. Prospective members were expected to accept Puritan doctrines and live moral lives, but they were also expected to confess before their fellows that they had experienced God's saving grace. Those who could testify credibly to their redemption in this way joined together to form churches by covenanting with each other. The stroke of genius, which transformed ecclesiastical purity into social purity, was to open the franchise only to those males who had become full members of covenanted churches. (Women in New England had somewhat more rights before the law and, in general, more church privileges than in England, but nowhere in the world in the seventeenth century did women as a class take a direct part in political life.)

To put it in the Puritans' own terms, the covenant of grace qualified a person for church membership and a voting role in the colony's public life. This public life fulfilled the social covenant with God, since the leaders selected by the church members promoted laws that honored the Scriptures. Moreover, the church covenant linked converted individuals to the social project without requiring the burden of a church-state machinery such as the one that had persecuted them in England. New England was, thus, no theocracy, where ministers exercised direct control of public life. It was, however, a place where magistrates frequently called upon the reverend fathers for advice, including how best they might promote the religious life of the colonies. The churches were also nonseparating. Local congregations had responsibilities for the good of the whole, not just for themselves.

For a while the system worked. John Winthrop (1588-1649), a man of unusual self-restraint and public-spirited faith, served as Massachusetts's governor for most of its first two decades. Under his direction, Massachusetts saw up to half of the colony's male citizens join the churches and participate in government. An even higher percentage of women citizens became members. The churches by and large flourished. The colony's laws provided for all healthy-bodied individuals to attend church, a stipulation against which almost no one protested. Tumults in England during the 1640s, when Puritans in league with Parliamentarians made war on the king,

John Winthrop, first governor of Massachusetts Bay, was every bit as serious as this picture portrays him, but quite a bit more humane. *American Antiquarian Society*

provided an occasion for the New Englanders to compose a formal statement of their distinctive "way."

This Cambridge Platform of 1648 was the clearest declaration by the Massachusetts settlers of their convictions. The synod of ministers that drew up the Platform had been called together by the colony's legislative assembly, which was alarmed that a few residents, leaning to Presbyterianism, threatened to take their case against New England's congregational practices back to England. By the time the synod met, however, circumstances had changed in England, and Presbyterianism was out of favor there. The synod was therefore at liberty to make a positive statement about its own congregationalism. The Platform accepted as "very holy, orthodox & judicious in all matters of faith" the Westminster Confession, a statement of Calvinist orthodoxy that had just been prepared in England at the request of Parliament. But the Platform differed with the Westminster Confession's presbyterian views of church government. The New Englanders agreed that the "Catholick [universal] Church" consisted of all Christians, but it stated that local churches were to be made up only of professed Christians and their children. The Platform dissociated itself from extreme separatism but did proclaim the substantial independence of each local congregation. Synods (or meetings) of ministers were to play an advisory role — but no more — in the local churches. The Platform also allowed for the influence of godly magistrates in church matters. It authorized pastors, teachers, ruling elders, and deacons as church officers. It is, in sum, the best place to look for an authoritative statement of what early Massachusetts Congregationalists thought their churches should be.

Early on as well, the Puritans worked hard to construct an educational system that could preserve their experiment. In 1636 the Massachusetts legislature authorized a college, which got under way two years later when a young minister, John Harvard, left a library of four hundred volumes to the new institution. (By contrast, the first college in Virginia, William and Mary, was not founded until 1693.) The purposes of Harvard College from the beginning were broader than just the training of ministers, although Harvard remained the prime source of New England's Congregational clergy well into the eighteenth century. Nor did lower levels of education escape the attention of the Puritan leaders. In 1642 the legislature threatened town leaders with fines if they did not see that all children were trained to "read & understand the principles of religion & the capitall lawes of this country." Five years later it passed the famous "ould deluder, Satan," bill, which ordered each town of at least fifty households to appoint a teacher. This attention to learning made New England one of the world's most literate places by the end of the century.

Puritan spirituality also proved a fertile medium for poetry. A scrupulous respect for the Ten Commandments made the Puritans nervous about the use of pictures, drama, and decorations in church, but they were wide open to uses of the word. A number of New England Puritans wrote verse, among whom the most notable were Anne Bradstreet (1612-1672), the wife of a prominent Boston citizen, and Edward Taylor (1645-1729), the quiet minister of the church in Westfield, Massachusetts. Bradstreet, who enjoyed a loving relationship with her husband, Simon, and their numerous children, considered the events of her daily life occasions for seeing more of God. One of her most famous poems describes the terror and the ache she experienced when her home burned to the ground. But at the end she was able to affirm,

> Thou hast an house on high erect
> Fram'd by that mighty Architect,
> With glory richly furnished,
> Stands permanent tho' this bee fled.
> It's purchased, and paid for too
> By him who hath enough to doe.

Taylor's poems, which were not published until the twentieth century, were written as an aid to meditation. Deeply affected by the deaths of two of his children, he began the practice of writing a meditative poem as a way of preparing for the celebration of communion. Taylor's verse was intricate, even to the point of convolution, but like the work of England's metaphysical poets John Donne and George Herbert, it could rise to sublime heights. The following stanza suggests some of his metaphorical power (and also shows that the Puritans maintained a more "realistic" view of the Lord's Supper than they are sometimes thought to have held). It is a stanza that rises from the bread of communion to Jesus the Bread of Life, as Taylor reflects on how God,

> The Purest Wheate in Heaven, his deare-dear Son
>> Grinds, and kneads up into this Bread of Life.
>> Which Bread of Life from Heaven down came and stands
>> Disht on thy Table up by Angells Hands.

At the heart of the Puritan experiment in New England was the weekly gathering in church for worship, fellowship, and instruction. The "meeting houses" where Puritans worshiped were invariably the largest and most centrally located buildings in their communities. At these gatherings they sang the psalms as paraphrased in the example from the *Bay Psalm Book* at the head of this chapter. Puritans at first sang only the psalms, and usually without accompaniment, because they considered other hymns and the use of musical instruments forms of Roman Catholic perversion. But by the start of the eighteenth century, attitudes began to soften toward music. The practice of an elder or deacon "lining out" hymns — the leader singing or speaking a phrase or two which the congregation then bawled out together — gave way to more refined singing in parts, to the printing of music with words, and to other refinements that the first generation of New Englanders would have considered a scandal. By the end of the eighteenth century the Puritan tradition had even produced a few composers of genuine merit. William Billings (1746-1800), whose *New England Psalm-Singer* of 1770 was the first book of American-composed music published in the New World, stands at the head of these composers.

But at the heart of Puritan worship was always the sermon, the means by which the people expected to receive instruction from the very word of God. Sermons were of two kinds: "regular" (preached twice a Sunday in almost all of New England's towns) and "occasional" (preached at the first meeting each year of the legislatures, on special days of fasting or thanks-giving, before local militia companies, and at other signal moments in a

Frontispiece of William Billings's *New England Psalm Singer*. Billings, the first of New England's own memorable composers, lived in the second half of the eighteenth century. Even that late, however, the singing of the psalms remained the staple of Puritan music in church. *The William Clements Library, University of Michigan*

community's life). Most of the sermons that New England ministers published were "occasional"; most that they preached were "regular." "Regular" preaching remained remarkably constant in New England from the first generation of preachers in 1630 to the fifth generation at the time of the American Revolution. The Bible was the only acceptable source for sermon themes. The content was constant for over 150 years: individuals are sinners who need divine salvation; God has provided that salvation by grace, from his mercy alone; saved sinners now have the right and privilege to serve God by following his law.

From the start, New England's ministers preached a covenant of grace in regular sermons and a national covenant in occasional sermons. In the former it was affirmed that sinners are totally dependent upon the divine mercy. In the latter, redeemed sinners were exhorted to do good works in

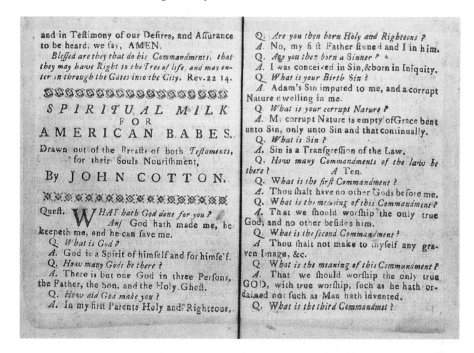

and in Testimony of our Desires, and Assurance to be heard, we say, AMEN.

Blessed are they that do his Commandments, that they may have Right to the Tree of life, and may enter in through the Gates into the City. Rev. 22 14.

SPIRITUAL MILK
FOR
AMERICAN BABES.

Drawn out of the Breasts of both *Testaments*, for their Souls Nourishment,

By JOHN COTTON.

Quest. *WHAT hath God done for you?* Ans. God hath made me, he keepeth me, and he can save me.

Q. *What is God?*
A. God is a Spirit of himself and for himself.

Q. *How many Gods be there?*
A. There is but one God in three Persons, the Father, the Son, and the Holy Ghost.

Q. *How did God make you?*
A. In my first Parents Holy and Righteous.

Q. *Are you then born Holy and Righteous?*
A. No, my first Father sinned and I in him.

Q. *Are you then born a Sinner?*
A. I was conceived in Sin, & born in Iniquity.

Q. *What is your Birth Sin?*
A. Adam's Sin imputed to me, and a corrupt Nature dwelling in me.

Q. *What is your corrupt Nature?*
A. My corrupt Nature is empty of Grace bent unto Sin, only unto Sin and that continually.

Q. *What is Sin?*
A. Sin is a Transgression of the Law.

Q. *How many Commandments of the law be there?*
A. Ten.

Q. *What is the first Commandment?*
A. Thou shalt have no other Gods before me.

Q. *What is the meaning of this Commandment?*
A. That we should worship the only true God, and no other besides him.

Q. *What is the second Commandment?*
A. Thou shalt not make to thyself any graven Image, &c.

Q. *What is the meaning of this Commandment?*
A. That we should worship the only true GOD, with true worship, such as he hath ordained not such as Man hath invented.

Q. *What is the third Commandment?*

John Cotton was the most powerful (and most beloved) of the early Puritan ministers in Massachusetts Bay. His catechism for young children bespoke the love of Puritan parents for their children and their belief that the youngsters were included in the covenant of God's grace. *Library of Congress*

order that their society might flourish and that they might avoid God's judgments. The way in which New Englanders linked the covenant of grace and the national covenant defined the way in which New England's sense of mission evolved over time. At first, that mission was both to restore the primitive purity of early Christianity and to be a "city on the hill" for those who remained in Europe. By the late eighteenth century the New England mission was often described in more general terms as a search for liberty, a search that could have both religious and political connotations.

Because the sermon was the dominant form of communication in colonial New England, its history is in many ways *the* history of New England. Most New Englanders who lived a full life would have heard seven thousand sermons (averaging nearly two hours each) while at the same time reading very few books and having little recourse to newspapers and other forms of communication that are taken for granted today. Once the importance of the sermon for all New England is established, it is easier to see why shifts in the form of the sermon had such a broad impact. One such shift was introduced in the 1740s by George Whitefield, whose spontaneous preaching affected virtually every aspect of Christian worship and practice in the region.

Troubles

Apart from notable dissenters in its early days, to whom we turn in Chapter 3, the major opponent of the Puritan system was time itself. As the 1640s gave way to the 1650s, more and more children of the earliest settlers failed to experience God's grace in the same fashion as their parents, and hence they did not seek full membership in the churches. The problem became acute when these children began to marry and have children of their own. Under the Puritans' Reformed theology, converted people had the privilege of bringing their infant children to be baptized as a seal of God's covenant grace. Now, however, many of those who had been baptized as infants were not stepping forth on their own to confess Christ. Yet they wanted to have their children baptized. The Puritan dilemma was delicate: leaders wished to preserve the church for genuine believers, but they also wanted to keep as many people as possible under the influence of the church. Their solution was to propose a "halfway" covenant whereby second-generation New Englanders could bring their third-generation children for baptism and a halfway membership. Participation in the Lord's Supper remained a privilege for those who could testify to a specific work of God's grace in their lives. This plan was formalized by a special synod of ministers in 1662. Its implementation, though opposed by some as a dilution of Puritan spirituality, did preserve the interlocking covenants of person, church, and society. And so with this adjustment the Puritans pushed on through the middle decades of the seventeenth century.

Even more severe crises arose toward the end of the century, however. Warfare with Indians in 1675 and 1676 wrought great havoc on outlying towns and left several thousand colonists dead. In 1685 the New England colonies were deprived of their representative assemblies and placed with New York and New Jersey into an administrative Dominion of New England. This action was taken by the Roman Catholic James II, who had become England's king in 1685, in order to rein in the extreme Protestants of the New World. The Dominion did not last long: a measure of self-rule was returned to the colonies after Parliament replaced James II with his daughter and her husband, William and Mary, in 1688. But Massachusetts's new charter of 1691 provided a much more secular basis for government than the colony had had before. It stipulated that the governor be appointed by

The proceedings against witchcraft at Salem were rarely as dramatic as this image of George Jacobs's trial. But even without artistic exaggeration, they dealt a blow from which the Puritans' reputation has never recovered. *Library of Congress*

the king. Even more momentously, it established the right to vote for the colonial legislature on the basis of property ownership rather than church membership. The New England Way was beginning to dissolve, and there were many signs of strain.

A "Reforming Synod" in 1679 had allowed Massachusetts ministers to contend "that God hath a controversy with his New-England People." The ministers thought they saw an increase in Sabbath-breaking and other forms of ungodliness. Although the ministers called upon their fellow New Englanders to repent and seek again the spiritual fervor that drove their predecessors into the wilderness, they were preparing for the worst.

But no one was prepared for the devastation that broke out in Salem Village north of Boston in 1692. Prosecution and execution for witchcraft was by no means unknown in New England, but the alarm at Salem went much further than previous incidents. A number of factors fueled the alarm: political strife between Salem Village and the larger town of Salem, voodoo practices associated with a West Indian slave, the recent republication of an ancient book presenting ways to combat witchcraft, recent tension with

DEPOSITIONS OF MRS. ANN PUTNAM AND ANN PUTNAM, JR. BEFORE
MAGISTRATES HATHORNE AND CORWIN, SALEM VILLAGE,
MAY 31, 1692.—

INDICTMENT AGAINST ABIGAIL HOBBS OF TOPSFIELD,
"FOR COVENANTING WITH THE DEVIL" 1692.

Original Salem witchcraft documents.
Courtesy Essex Institute, Salem, Massachusetts

marauding native Americans and their French allies, judges and ministers
nervous about the colony's spiritual decline and eager to find ways of check-
ing it, simmering community hostility against a few lonely old women and
a few new families, a wide range of occult practices, and adolescent hysteria
in a few teenage girls along with judicial hysteria in a few old men. The

result was several months of anguished excitement and the execution of twenty souls (nineteen hanged, one pressed to death for refusing to testify). Finally, when accusations arose against men and women of spotless character and when such leading citizens as the Boston minister Increase Mather spoke out against the proceedings, the incident came quickly to an end.

Even given the number of supposed witches killed at Salem, the number of executions for witchcraft in New England was proportionately less than in most of the countries of western Europe. New England nonetheless suffered considerably from this wild outburst. Its own citizens came to the conclusion that the devil had been extraordinarily active at Salem Village, not so much in those accused of being witches as in those who had accused them and those that had harkened to the accusations. In 1697, several years after the trials, one of the judges, Samuel Sewall, publicly confessed his guilt for "the Blame and shame of it" in a moving statement read aloud in his church. But such repentance has not removed the blot of the Salem witch trials from the history of the Puritans.

Historians have long argued whether, or in what ways, Puritan New England "declined" in the late seventeenth and early eighteenth centuries. A judgment from the twentieth century might be mixed. It would note, as some ministers and laypeople of that time also did, that the pursuit of prosperity was becoming more important than the pursuit of godliness for at least some merchants in Boston and some common people on the land. At the same time, however, the church still exercised the central role in defining the grand questions of society and orienting life in the daily round. And the church's basic message was still the same, that God saves individuals by his grace and calls them together for worship and service into the nurturing fellowship of the church. From the standpoint of the late twentieth century, what the Puritans saw as decline we may be pardoned for regarding as a relatively undiminished version of the white-hot faith that had led to the founding of New England.

Massachusetts and Virginia: A Comparison

One of the ways to put religious developments in the English colonies in perspective is to compare Massachusetts and Virginia. Such a comparison not only tells us something about the seventeenth century but also begins to clarify the history that came later. Some of the differences that affected Christian faith were more generally social than specifically religious. Immigrants to Massachusetts, for example, tended to be older than those to Virginia, and Massachusetts settlers more often arrived with their families.

More important, the Massachusetts colonists were determined "localists," offended by Charles I's efforts to control the churches, economies, and militia of their English communities. Immigration offered an opportunity to preserve the values — religious, political, and social — of those local communities. Those who came to Virginia, on the other hand, were much more likely to be "adventurers," men looking to make their fortunes. Immigration offered them a chance to succeed after past failures or to fulfill personal aspirations. The contrast in value systems shows up strikingly in attitudes toward space: New Englanders clustered around meetinghouses, whereas Virginians dispersed along rivers in the effort to preserve their individual privacy.

Circumstances in the New World made it possible for the values that the two societies imported to flourish in their respective colonies. New England's climate and soil were similar to what the colonists had known in England (and thus settlers could rapidly re-create English agricultural patterns), New England offered no obvious product for profitable export, and European diseases had significantly reduced the Indian population in the region. The result was an environment nourishing the communal self-sufficiency that the New Englanders had brought with them from the old country. It was an environment that made Congregationalism in the Puritan pattern possible. On the other hand, the combination of values and settlement patterns in Virginia encouraged independent estates and a cult of manhood that fostered extravagant gambling. It also nurtured black slavery, a system in which all whites stood in authority over a population of subservient workers.

These different contexts did much to shape religious life in the two regions. For example, while New Englanders believed that the Bible taught congregationalism, they also defended it as part of a much larger struggle for control of local institutions that had marked Puritan experience in England as well as America. The "Bible Commonwealth" in Massachusetts succeeded for as long as it did not only because its settlers were pious but also because New England provided a favorable environment for virtually all the values that the settlers — who were jealous of their local political and military rights as well as of their Puritanism — wished to preserve. Cracks began to appear in the Puritan Way during the early years of the eighteenth century not primarily because of flagging spirituality but because the outside world — in the shape of Indian wars, military taxes, and centralized political authority — finally disrupted the stability of local life. It is striking to observe that the English Puritans, who never enjoyed the localism that flourished in Massachusetts and Connecticut, never succeeded in implementing an encompassing Puritanism and that New England Puritanism succeeded as a social system only so long as it preserved its localism. In Virginia, again by contrast, the Church of England always had difficulty creating cohesive ecclesiastical institutions. Later in Virginia's history, wealthy planters, even if only nominally Anglican, took great offense when upstart Presbyterians and Baptists dared to challenge their control of a social structure that included the church.

Ecclesiastical developments in the future can be explained, at least in part, by the circumstances in which the churches first put down roots in the New World.

Further Reading

Boyer, Paul, and Stephen Nissenbaum. *Salem Possessed: The Social Origins of Witchcraft.* Cambridge: Harvard University Press, 1974.

Bradford, William. *History of Plymouth Plantation* (many editions).

Breen, T. H. *Puritans and Adventurers: Change and Persistence in Early America.* New York: Oxford University Press, 1980.

Collinson, Patrick. *The Elizabethan Puritan Movement.* Berkeley and Los Angeles: University of California Press, 1967.

Haller, William. *The Rise of Puritanism.* New York: Columbia University Press, 1938.

Hambrick-Stowe, Charles, ed. *Early New England Meditative Poetry: Anne Bradstreet and Edward Taylor.* New York: Paulist, 1988.

McGiffert, Michael. "Grace and Works: The Rise and Division of Covenant Divinity in Elizabethan Puritanism." *Harvard Theological Review* 75 (Oct. 1982): 463-502.

Miller, Perry. *The New England Mind.* Vol. 1, *The Seventeenth Century.* New York: Macmillan, 1939. Vol. 2, *From Colony to Province.* Cambridge: Harvard University Press, 1953.

Miller, Perry, and Thomas H. Johnson, eds. *The Puritans: A Sourcebook of Their Writings.* Rev. ed. 2 vols. New York: Harper & Row, 1963.

Morgan, Edmund S. *The Puritan Dilemma: The Story of John Winthrop.* Boston: Little, Brown, 1958.

————. *Visible Saints: The History of a Puritan Idea.* Ithaca: Cornell University Press, 1963.

Stout, Harry S. *The New England Soul: Preaching and Religious Culture in Colonial New England.* New York: Oxford University Press, 1986.

Winslow, Ola. *Meetinghouse Hill, 1630-1783.* New York: Macmillan, 1952.

CHAPTER 3

Other Beginnings

When sun doth rise the stars do set,
    Yet there's no need of light;
God shines, a sun most glorious,
    When creatures all are night.

The very Indian boys can give
    To many stars their name,
And know their course and therein do
    Excel the English tame.

English and Indians, none enquire
    Whose hand these candles hold,
Who gives these stars their names
    More bright ten thousand fold.

Roger Williams may not have intended this short poem to be sung, but its insertion in his Key into the Language of America *in 1643 showed how American experiences were beginning to affect hymnody. The hymn also shows Williams's capacity for drawing unexpected contrasts between the self-confidently "civilized" English and the supposedly "savage" Native Americans.*

ROMAN CATHOLIC QUEBEC AND PURITAN MASSACHUSETTS WERE THE most visible regions on the Christian map of North America during the seventeenth and eighteenth centuries. But Christianity was also appearing in many other forms during this period. By the time of the American Revolution, these other forms had spread along the American coastline and beyond to the interior. Some of these were self-conscious protests against the Puritan way of life that had been established in the New World, some were imported from Britain, and some came from the Continent. Important as the growth of dominant forms of Catholicism and Puritanism were in Quebec and Massachusetts, respectively, the appearance of a wide variety of Christian expressions anticipated more clearly the shape that the faith would take in the later development of the United States and Canada.

Alternatives to the Puritans

Early New England dissent was often more Puritan than the colonial establishments themselves. By the mid-seventeenth century, a number of individuals and groups had challenged the "New England Way." Some of these were shunted off to the neighboring colony of Rhode Island, which soon became a byword for eccentricity and extremism to the leaders of Puritan New England. Others eventually gained an uneasy acceptance in Massachusetts and Connecticut. Their persistence contributed to a rising Christian pluralism that, despite Puritan opposition, came close to setting the norm for colonial America.

Baptists in Early America

Baptists, who shared many convictions with the Puritans, appeared in Massachusetts shortly after the first migrations and soon arrived elsewhere in the colonies as well. In light of their subsequent importance in America, it is appropriate to sketch briefly the background of these lively and ardent Protestants.

The earliest Baptists arose among English separates who, influenced by the Puritan criticism of the religious establishment, felt it was necessary to pull out of the Church of England entirely in order to preserve true Christian life. The lot of separatists in England was difficult; many were put in prison or forced to seek exile abroad. One of the groups that sought refuge in exile went to Holland under the leadership of John Smyth (1565-1612). Here these dissenters came into contact with Dutch Mennonites —

Anabaptists (i.e., rebaptizers) who practiced the baptism of adults on the basis of their confession of faith. Under this influence Smyth too came to feel that adult, believer baptism was the norm established in the New Testament. So in 1609 he baptized himself and several others who together formed the first English Baptist church. When Smyth wanted to enter into a deeper fellowship with the Mennonites, most of his early followers broke with him. Returning to England under the leadership of Thomas Helwys (1550-1616) and John Murton (1583-1630), they established in 1612 the first Baptist church on English soil, near London in Spitalfields. Before leaving Holland, these early Baptists also issued a declaration proclaiming what at that time were radical beliefs: local churches should control their own business, magistrates should not be given power over church affairs, and "baptism or washing with water is the outward manifestation of dying to sin . . . and therefore in no wise appertaineth to infants."

Those in this first group were called "General" Baptists since they believed that Christ's death was equally effective for all people. Another prominent strain of Baptists arose in the 1630s as an offshoot of English Congregational churches established earlier in the century by Henry Jacob (1563-1624). These called themselves "Particular" Baptists because they believed that Christ's death had a saving significance only for those particular souls regenerated by the Holy Spirit. (Thus, General Baptists were more in line with continental Arminianism, and Particular Baptists were more in line with the Calvinistic tradition.)

In the late 1630s the Particular Baptists began to immerse candidates for baptism. Baptists had adopted the practice of pouring, or affusion, from the Mennonites, but immersion rapidly became a trademark of all Baptists. The 1644 London Confession of the Particular Baptists spelled out why they baptized like this: "the way and manner of dispensing this ordinance the Scripture holds out to be dipping or plunging the whole body under water."

Both General and Particular Baptists grew rapidly during the Cromwellian period (1640-1660). They were among the stalwarts of Cromwell's New Model Army, the military marvel of the seventeenth century. Cromwell in turn gave them an unprecedented degree of freedom. By 1660 there were nearly three hundred Baptist churches in England.

The first Baptist congregation in America was formed in 1639 with the help of Roger Williams (1603?-1683) in Rhode Island. The English and Welsh individuals who made up this body agreed with Williams that the life of the church should not be governed by the state. Although Rhode Island continued to be a center for colonial Baptists, Williams himself remained a Baptist for only a few months. (Thereafter he held that no one church in the modern period properly represented true Christianity.) Baptist churches

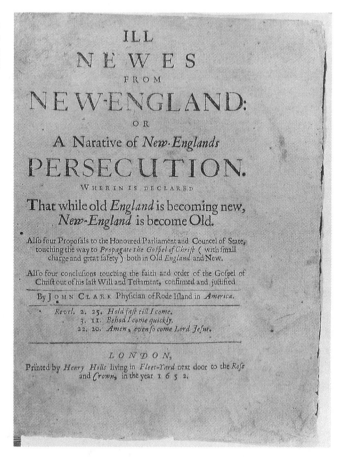

Title page from
John Clarke's
*Ill News from
New England*

in colonial Rhode Island tended to be "General." But in Pennsylvania, the other stronghold of religious liberty in early America, "Particular" Baptists (principally from Wales) predominated. The Philadelphia Association, founded in 1707 by these Particular Baptists, was the first organized fellowship of Baptist churches in America.

The leading Baptist in colonial New England, John Clarke (1609-1676), arrived in Rhode Island in 1639 to found the town of Newport. During the next several decades he and his followers irritated their neighbors by making frequent forays into Plymouth and Massachusetts, where they persuaded some to accept their beliefs.

Clarke also exasperated the Puritan colonies by publishing in London his *Ill News from New England* (1652). This work condemned the Massachusetts Congregationalists for persecuting Baptists in the same manner the Anglicans in old England had attacked the Puritans. Colonial Baptists were also encouraged when Henry Dunster (1609-1659), the president of Harvard College, became convinced that the baptism of infants was unscriptural and in 1654 left his post to join with the Baptists, who at the time were all but illegal in Massachusetts. Persecution by the Puritans was not just a figment of Baptist imagination, as the example of the Rhode Island layman Obadiah Holmes (1607?-1682) showed. In 1651 Holmes was apprehended in Massachusetts as he was paying a visit to an elderly fellow Baptist. The Boston court imprisoned him, convicted him of promoting "Anabaptism," and had him whipped in public.

Partially because of such opposition and partially because of more general conditions in the colonies, Baptist growth was slow. General Baptists from England did establish a few congregations in the South, and Rhode Island remained a haven for General Baptists in New England, but until the Great Awakening of the 1740s, Baptists achieved only a slight presence in the New World.

Despite the relatively small numbers of Baptists, Puritans perceived them as something of a threat, especially because of their insistence that the state had no role to play in the churches. They also feared that Baptist baptismal practices sundered the bond between personal faith, church guidance, and participation in the larger society. And they almost certainly distrusted the Baptists because they had received aid from one of Massachusetts's great nemeses, Roger Williams.

Roger Williams

Williams was born in England around 1603 and came to Massachusetts in 1631 after establishing a reputation as a faithful Puritan preacher. Yet Williams's Puritanism was always so excruciatingly thorough that he had great difficulty fitting into the closely regulated Massachusetts system. Although called to serve churches in both Boston and Salem, Williams refused, choosing rather to settle in Plymouth, where he felt largely free from what he viewed as the compromises of the Puritans. All who knew Williams testified to his gentle spirit and Christian demeanor, but many who came to disagree with him wished he could have kept his opinions to himself, since they were disquieting in the extreme. He held that the Puritans had no right to the Indian lands in the New World and hence that colonial charters were invalid. Moreover, he asserted that individuals who had not confessed Christ could not be held accountable to a social covenant. He also felt it was wrong in principle for magistrates to enforce attendance at church and other spiritual duties, since true Christian action proceeds from the heart. "Christening

As suggested by this portrait, Roger Williams was constantly looking for the genuine church of the apostles. If he never found it, he nonetheless discovered principles of "soul liberty" that one day would become the American norm. *Illustration by Rosemary Ellis*

makes not Christians," he stated, and then went on to argue that attempts to force nonbelievers to act like believers were simply self-defeating. Williams was a separatist of exquisite purity who saw no future in a Christian faith compromised by attempts to rule in the world.

Such views could perhaps have been ignored when whispered in a Plymouth corner. But when in 1633 Williams finally accepted the repeated call from the Salem church to serve as its minister, these views drew the immediate wrath of the Massachusetts authorities. His opinions were perceived as imperiling nearly every aspect of the colony's life. And so in relatively short order Williams was expelled from the colony as a dangerous threat to its continued existence. John Winthrop arranged to have Williams's banishment postponed to the spring, when conditions for the move would be better, but Williams chose to leave Massachusetts in October 1635. After a brutal winter, he finally arrived at the head of Narragansett Bay in April 1636, where he founded the city of Providence in honor of the power that had carried him through the winter.

In his later career Williams remained consistent with his early beliefs, though he did change in some other ways. As the poem at the start of the chapter suggests, he enjoyed excellent relations with Native Americans; he was one of the few English settlers to take time to learn their languages. Yet during a 1637 war with the Pequots, Williams made his knowledge of their ways available to the Puritan soldiers attacking them. As we have seen, he helped

Baptists settle in Rhode Island, but he himself remained a Baptist for a few months, thereafter becoming (as he put it) a "seeker" after the true church of the apostles. He later published important tracts criticizing John Cotton and the Massachusetts Puritans, most notably *The Bloody Tenent of Persecution for Cause of Conscience in a Conference between Truth and Peace* (1644), in which he argued against the use of force to coerce Christian faith or practice. But later, when Quakers descended on Rhode Island, he drafted arguments opposing their distinctive beliefs. He did not want Rhode Island to constrain people in religion as Massachusetts had, yet he spent several years as an old man in England trying to secure a stable charter that would provide some regulation for the sizable handful of lawless settlers who took advantage of the free air of Rhode Island. Before his death in 1683, he also came to oppose the pacifism of the Quakers on the grounds that all responsible citizens should be required to defend the common good in times of military peril.

Roger Williams is known as America's greatest early "democrat," and that reputation is not entirely unjustified. Under his direction, Rhode Island became the first place in the North American colonies where freedom of religious worship was defined as a human right for all groups (or almost all — open atheists were still excluded). It was also the first American colony to attempt a separation between the institutions of religion and the institutions of the state. Even more than he was a democrat, however, Williams was a thoroughgoing Puritan. His reasons for favoring soul liberty and the separation of church and state were themselves religious. Only God knew the heart, he insisted, and only God could promote a truly spiritual life. That being the case, ministers and magistrates must protect with greatest respect the relationship between God and his servants on the earth.

Anne Hutchinson

Just as unsettling to the Puritan authorities, but also just as Puritan, was the challenge of Anne Hutchinson (1591-1643). Mrs. Hutchinson and her family emigrated to Massachusetts in order to remain under the ministry of their English pastor, John Cotton, who had come to Boston in 1633. In particular, she hung on Cotton's message of God's free grace. Once in New England, Hutchinson began a midweek meeting to discuss Cotton's sermon of the previous Sunday and also to take up other spiritual concerns.

This type of meeting, made up at first of women only, was to become a common feature of New World Christianity. Women would not play a public, visible role in the churches for centuries to come, but their labors in organizing communities, building support fellowships, and faithfully at-

Anne Hutchinson was not as dramatic in her preaching as this painting suggests, but even her low-key activities as a quasi-independent woman exhorter proved too much for the Massachusetts Bay authorities. *Picture Collection, The Branch Libraries, The New York Public Library*

tending midweek gatherings for prayer established a foundation for Christian life in America as it had been in Europe before. Men too were involved in this nurturing side of the faith, but here, as in many other spheres out of the public eye, women were the pioneers.

All went well with Anne Hutchinson's private meetings until some magistrates and ministers came to fear that her views were edging toward Antinomianism (the assertion that Christians do not need the law). In her home she argued that a believer possessed the Holy Spirit and thus was not bound by the requirements of law. She also held that the mere fact that a person obeyed the laws of the land (of Massachusetts, for example) did not signify that that person was really a Christian. As John Cotton taught so clearly, salvation was by grace and not by works of the law.

Hutchinson's views were in fact a legitimate, if unusual, extension of basic Puritan theology. The difficulty came in the clash of such notions with the Puritan Way in New England. If individuals were left on their own, even as Christians, where would the godly society be for which the Puritans longed so dearly? The Massachusetts authorities were displeased and demanded an accounting. Through many days of a formal judicial proceeding in 1638, Mrs. Hutchinson held her own against the colony's leaders, including John Winthrop, who, when he ran out of arguments, complained that Mrs. Hutchinson's theologizing was somehow unnatural for a woman. Her case rested on a thorough knowledge of Scripture and careful reasoning.

Just when it seemed as though she had finally silenced her opponents, however, Anne Hutchinson made a fatal mistake. She claimed that the Holy Spirit communicated directly to her, apart from Scripture, and this the Massachusetts authorities could not tolerate. As a result of her rash assertion, she and those who followed her were banished. After stopping briefly in Rhode Island and Long Island, she settled in the colony of New York, where she and most of her family were soon killed in an Indian attack. Massachusetts Puritans nodded grimly upon hearing the news, as they had earlier upon receiving the report that Mrs. Hutchinson had given birth to a severely deformed child. God, they reasoned, was punishing the wicked.

Less involved observers can regret that this woman of unusual spiritual intelligence did not live longer to promote her distinctive interpretation of the Puritan faith, for it was a reading that would be echoed time and again in North America. Throughout its entire history, liberation by God's grace, apprehended through faith, has been the heart of the Christian message. But an enduring problem, especially for the most ardent Christian communities, has also been the construction of religious institutions and religious regulations that seem to quench the faith they are put in place to embody. As elsewhere, so too in America, the delicate balance between law and gospel defined by the apostle Paul proved difficult to maintain.

The Mosaic Takes Shape: Protestants outside of New England

Almost as soon as Roger Williams and Anne Hutchinson were making their protests against the hegemony of Puritan rule in New England, other expressions of Christian faith were gaining a foothold elsewhere in the New World. The variety of these expressions and their different approaches to the church's day-to-day life began, already in the seventeenth century, to constitute a mosaic of Christian faiths. This mosaic only became more diverse as the decades rolled by.

The Church of England

Outside of New England, the Church of England was the major religious presence in the early British colonies. It was the established church in Virginia, the Carolinas, Georgia, Maryland after 1691, and parts of New York City after 1693. Yet in the American environment, that establishment was often very thin. English experience provided no precedent for the vast New World parishes (the size of the average Virginia parish was 550 square miles in 1724). And it offered precious few resources for dealing with the rough, individualistic, honor-driven, slave-holding society of the southern colonies.

Difficulties of communication with the mother country were also a persistent problem. Anglicans in the colonies never enjoyed the services of their own bishop. At first the failure to name a bishop for America seemed merely an oversight, a simple failure of creativity in the face of new opportunities, rather than anything deliberate. After 1700, however, talk of a colonial bishop began to raise fears that Parliament might use this means to limit the political freedom of its colonies. The absence of a bishop created severe strain. In the polity of the Church of England, it took a bishop to confirm (that is, to make a baptized person into a full member of the church) and to ordain new candidates for the ministry. Furthermore, in England bishops provided a cohesion and sense of overall purpose that was conspicuous by its absence in the colonies. A final problem for colonial Anglicans involved their ministers. At least a few Church of England clerics who came to the New World were individuals who had failed at home and were pinning their hopes on service in America as a desperate last chance. Though never a majority among the Anglican clerics, a few wastrels gave the entire ministerial corps a bad name that has taken the Anglican community literally centuries to overcome.

This is not to say that the Church of England was an insignificant or insubstantial body in the colonies. It did enjoy the services of many faithful leaders. James Blair (1655-1743), for example, served with considerable effect as the commissary (or administrator) of the Virginia church for over half a century. Blair's achievements included the founding of a college (William and Mary), determined advocacy of the church's position before the Virginia legislature, and faithful support of the colony's clergy. Similarly effective was Thomas Bray (1656-1730), the commissary for the Church of England in Maryland from 1696 to 1700. During his short stay in the colonies, he founded two agencies that continued to have an effect long after he left America: the Society for Promoting Christian Knowledge (SPCK) provided books in theology and related subjects for ministers and interested

Eighteenth-century SPG bookplate. The Church of England was not particularly effective in reestablishing its institutions in the American colonies, but the Anglican Society for the Propagation of the Gospel in Foreign Parts did more in providing Christian literature than any other organization from the Old World. *Courtesy of the Billy Graham Center Museum*

laypeople, and the Society for the Propagation of the Gospel in Foreign Parts (SPG) sponsored missionary work on behalf of the Church of England, first among the Native Americans and later (to the great consternation of the Puritans) in settled areas such as New England.

Other Anglican ministers who made a sincere effort to carry out their tasks were simply overwhelmed by American ways. Such a one was John Wesley, the founder of Methodism, who during the mid-1730s spent a frustrating eighteen months in Georgia as a young missionary. Wesley was earnest, perhaps to a fault; he diligently preached to Native Americans and the local settlers. But his mission — complicated by a miscarried love affair, by strident controversy with local leaders, and by the indifference of both Native Americans and colonists — was an abject failure. Indirectly, however, it may have been important for Wesley's own spiritual development, for his conspicuous lack of success seems to have driven him to a new reliance on divine grace. At the end of his time in America Wesley wrote in his journal, "it is now two years and almost four months since I left my native country, in order to teach the Georgian Indians the nature of Christianity. But what have I learned myself in the meantime? Why, what I the least of all suspect, that I, who went to America to convert others, was never myself converted to God." Not for the first time, nor for the last, an experience of failure drove the defeated individual to God.

Ironically, the Church of England eventually had its greatest successes in regions where it was not the established church. During the revivals that came in the mid-eighteenth century, New Englanders seeking a church of more repose and less enthusiasm turned in considerable numbers to Anglicanism. And without the protection of an establishment, Anglican missionaries eventually established a limited number of strong churches in Pennsylvania, New Jersey, and Long Island.

In the last analysis, the Church of England's great importance in early America derived not primarily from its intrinsic strength or weakness but from the fact that it was still England's established church. So long as the colonies remained English, the Church of England played a major role in its religious life — for some an example of Old World corruption, for others a point of stability in the hurly-burly of the wilderness.

The Quakers and Pennsylvania

Given the significance of English settlement in the New World, it could only be expected that other varieties of British Christianity would also soon find their way there. Quakers, or Friends as they called themselves under their first leader, George Fox (1624-1691), appeared in New England within a generation of the founding of Massachusetts. In July 1656, two Quaker women, Ann Austin and Mary Fisher, came to Boston with their message of the Inner Light of Christ and their criticism of formal, external religion. The Puritan authorities immediately sent these Quaker witnesses packing. But the Friends kept coming back despite the fines and whippings they endured at the hand of the authorities. Eventually the patience of Massachusetts's leaders ran out, and in the period from 1659 to 1661 (at a time of unusual political unrest in England when little attention was being paid to the colonies), four Quakers were hanged in Massachusetts for sedition, blasphemy, and persistent disturbance of the peace.

Rhode Island offered much more freedom for beliefs that the Puritans judged to be deviant, so it soon became the site of a considerable Quaker settlement. Roger Williams had no love for Quaker doctrines, and he said so in unmistakable terms to George Fox himself when the latter visited Rhode Island in 1672. But grudgingly he still gave them room.

The colonial settlement that put the Quakers permanently on the

William Penn, the leading Quaker in England by the end of the seventeenth century, was instrumental in founding four colonies that eventually became the three states of New Jersey, Delaware, and Pennsylvania. *Picture Collection, The Branch Libraries, The New York Public Library*

American map was Pennsylvania, and the man who accomplished the deed was William Penn (1644-1718). Penn was born in London, raised there and in Ireland, and given all the privileges befitting his station as the eldest son of Admiral Sir William Penn, who captured Jamaica from the Dutch in 1655. By 1661, however, a very worldly William Penn had begun to fall under the influence of Friends, and by 1666 he had joined their number. A prolific writer throughout his life, Penn ran afoul of the law in 1668 for writing a tract attacking the doctrines of the Church of England. While in prison in 1669 he wrote the devotional classic *No Cross, No Crown,* an exposition concerning Christian suffering that has rarely been out of print since. After his release from prison, Penn grew steadily more disillusioned about the prospects for Quakers in England.

He took his first step toward finding a refuge by backing a Quaker expedition to New Jersey in 1677 and 1678. In 1681 Penn acquired a huge tract of land from King Charles II in settlement of a debt owed to his father. Pennsylvania ("Penn's Woods") thereafter became the most secure home for religious toleration in the world. In 1682 the city of Philadelphia was laid out and, certainly of equal importance, Pennsylvania's "Frame of Government" was published. This constitution set out the terms of Penn's

This well-known painting, "Penn's Treaty with the Indians," by Benjamin West, is a testimony to the painter's skill, but also to William Penn's unusually even-handed dealings with Native Americans. *Pennsylvania Academy of the Fine Arts*

"Holy Experiment" in the New World. It allowed unprecedented freedom of religion to all who believed in one God; it was also, for its time, a liberal document politically. Although Penn realized very little profit from the colony, Pennsylvania flourished from the start. One of the reasons was Penn's vigorous promotion on the European continent; another was Pennsylvania's spreading reputation for toleration. The source of many of the early immigrants was memorialized in the name chosen for a town founded in 1683, Germantown, as a grant from Penn to a group of German Mennonites and Dutch Quakers. One of the most appealing features of the Penn administration was its fair and just treatment of Native Americans.

Penn was able to remain in his colony for only two brief periods (1682-1684 and 1699-1701), and his later life was filled with constant troubles, but a modern historian has correctly described him as a "compassionate humanitarian, mystic, theologian, and profound political theorist" — or more simply "the Renaissance Quaker."

The faith of the Friends remained an important counterweight to the dominant religions of colonial America. In the eighteenth century, the Quaker John Woolman (1720-1772) became one of the era's most effective advocates for peace and the abolition of slavery. Woolman's family helped settle Quaker West Jersey, where Woolman earned his living as a tailor. After 1746 he embarked on a series of colonial tours to argue against slaveholding and war. His diplomacy was mild but firm. He showed compassion for the slaveholder as well as for the slave. But he would brook no compromise with the evils of the system, insisting, for example, on paying slaves when they performed personal services and eventually rejecting food which they grew or cloth which they dyed. His antislavery efforts had an impact in Rhode Island, where wealthy Quaker shipowners had long taken part in the slave traffic, but even more in Pennsylvania. In his tract *Considerations on the Keeping of Negroes* (1754, 1762) he contended that slavery affronts common humanity as well as the "inner light of Christ" that has been placed in all people. Woolman also played a role in the withdrawal of Pennsylvania Quakers from the government of their colony during the French and Indian War (1756-1763) in an effort to follow the Quaker "peace testimony" rather than promote the conflict.

Woolman's mystical piety represented an important development in Quaker thought as well as in Quaker social action. His *Journal* reveals an individual who viewed physical life as an intimate reflection of the spiritual world, an individual who devoutly reverenced the work of God in both nature and other humans. He was a man of rare spiritual sensitivity who exerted more of an influence on public moral values, at least among the Quakers, than many of the would-be reformers who have filled America throughout its history.

Presbyterians

With emigration to America growing from Scotland and the north of Ireland, the colonies were soon home also to increasing numbers of Presbyterians. Francis Makemie (1658-1708), born in Ireland, educated in Scotland, and commissioned in Northern Ireland to serve as a missionary to America, was the individual most responsible for their early organization. Makemie evangelized throughout the English-speaking New World — in New England, New York, Maryland, Virginia, and North Carolina, as well as Barbados. He established the first Presbyterian congregation in America at Snow Hill, Maryland, in 1684. The Mathers of New England spoke highly of his work, and Congregationalists in general wished him well. In 1706 he succeeded in bringing together Presbyterians of different backgrounds (English, Welsh, Scottish, Scotch-Irish, and some from New England) as the Presbytery of Philadelphia. Its purpose was "to meet yearly and oftener, if necessary, to consult the most proper measure for advancing religion and propagating Christianity in our various stations." Despite differences in emphasis and custom, these Presbyterians did agree to take their stand on the Westminster Confession's statement of Calvinist theology. In 1707 Makemie was arrested by New York's governor, Lord Cornbury, for preaching without a license in a private home on Long Island. Makemie defended himself by appealing to the English Toleration Act of 1689, which granted religious freedom to Quakers, whose views were much further from the Establishment's than those of the Presbyterians. He was acquitted, but he did have to pay the high costs of his trial. This event solidified the image of Presbyterians as defenders of freedom in the public mind and won new respect for the denomination in America.

A notable Presbyterian contribution to America's general religious life also occurred at this time. In Scotland and then Northern Ireland, the Presbyterians developed a singular way of celebrating the Lord's Supper. They would gather once or twice a year for a series of sermons stretching over several days. The sermons stressed repentance and the need for forgiveness of sins in Christ. Then, after careful preparation and the presentation of a special token, the gathered multitude would advance to large tables where a communal sharing of the bread and wine took place. When Presbyterians brought these "communion seasons" with them to the New World, they provided an outlet for religious expression that would be especially important on the frontier. The "camp meeting" that developed as the mainstay of American revivalism in the 1790s and following years was in many cases a direct descendant of these early communion seasons.

The Reformed and Continental Pietists

The New World also made room very early on for religious groups from other places in Europe. The Dutch, who controlled New York until 1664, brought their hereditary Calvinistic, or Reformed, faith with them to that colony. As an established church, the Dutch Reformed in New Amsterdam, as it was then called, labored under many of the same difficulties besetting the established Church of England elsewhere in the Americas. Only after the colony was taken over by the British did vigorous Dutch churches emerge in New York and New Jersey. These more vital beginnings were fueled by both fresh waves of immigration and a more vigorous clergy.

Hard on the heels of the Dutch came immigrants with similar Re-

This Dutch Reformed church, erected in Albany, New York, in 1715, combines notions of what churches looked like in the Old Country with the purposes they had to serve in the New World. Regrettably, the structure no longer survives.
Library of Congress

formed views from the south of Germany. Civil war, strife with France, and intolerant rule by Lutherans and Roman Catholics drove considerable numbers of the German Reformed to the New World, where by 1740 they were gathered into fifty congregations, mostly in Pennsylvania.

The Dutch and German Reformed were part of a little-noticed trend. Especially in Pennsylvania, but soon in other colonies as well, it was apparent that the New World offered space for religious life that settled European circumstances did not afford. To other European bodies North America was a ripened mission field, ready to be harvested. So it was that before the middle of the eighteenth century a number of Continental Christian groups, drawn especially by a desire for religious liberty, began to wend their way to America.

Many of these groups were influenced by the European pietist movement, which had received its earliest expression in the work of the German Lutheran pastor Philipp Jacob Spener. Spener's *Pia Desideria* ("The Piety We Desire") of 1675 appealed for a general reform of the church and a special renewal of individual spirituality. Realized in small groups devoted to prayer and fellowship, increased missionary concern, and a wide range of social outreach, pietism affected many strands of European life. Included among the pietists who exerted an influence in America were the Dutch Reformed awakening preacher Theodore Frelinghuysen (1691-1747), the great organizer of colonial Lutheranism Henry Melchior Muhlenberg (1711-1787), and two promoters of renewal among the German Reformed, Michael Schlatter (1718-1790) and Philip William Otterbein (1726-1813). Pietist influences were also felt among the Mennonites, German Baptists, Schwenckfelders, French Huguenots, and the German immigrants who founded the Ephrata community in Pennsylvania.

The most notable European pietist to visit America was Count Nikolaus Ludwig von Zinzendorf (1700-1760). Zinzendorf is remembered as the leader of the Moravians, but he looked upon his ministry as an effort to unite all believers in love to Christ and service to the world. During his time in America (1741-1743), he helped found the Moravian community in Bethlehem, Pennsylvania, but also served a Lutheran church as pastor and promoted interdenominational synods until he was rebuffed by others who wanted to preserve their distinctive traditions. The many hymns that Zinzendorf wrote illustrate the importance of music among the pietists. With John and Charles Wesley, both of whom had extensive contacts with the Moravians, Zinzendorf employed music as a way of expressing the personal faith that he and like-minded awakeners sought to promote. So it was with a well-known hymn that he expanded from an earlier German source and which was used widely in English-speaking circles after being translated by John Wesley:

> Jesus, thy Blood and righteousness
> > My beauty are, my glorious dress;
> Midst flaming worlds, in these arrayed,
> > With joy shall I lift up my head. . . .
> Lord I believe thy precious Blood
> > Which at the mercy-seat of God
> Forever doth for sinners plead,
> > For me, e'en for my soul, was shed.

This kind of European pietism contributed greatly to the renewed Calvinism stimulated among Congregationalists, Baptists, and Anglicans by the Great Awakening of the 1740s. And it became an important general source for emphases that would predominate among all Protestants, and even some Catholics, in later decades.

John Wesley *(left)* and Count Nicholaus von Zinzendorf *(right)* did not meet during the visits each paid to America. But with doctrines of graces learned in substantial part from Zinzendorf's Moravians, Wesley's Methodists became the largest denomination of Christians in the New World by 1840. *The Bettman Archive*

Early Protestants in Canada

Although the main non-Catholic settlements in what is now Canada arose following the American Revolution, a few Protestants were already moving into Nova Scotia by the second decade of the eighteenth century in the wake of British and French imperial struggle. In 1710 the British took control of Acadia on the Atlantic coast, but with the Treaty of Utrecht in 1713 they guaranteed the French-speaking Acadians the right "to enjoy the free exercise of their religion according to the usage of the Church of Rome so far as the laws of Great Britain do allow." An era of toleration prevailed until further French-British conflict in the 1740s dramatically altered the pattern of settlement.

New Englanders had joined the British to capture the French fort of Louisbourg on Cape Breton Island in 1745. But then Britain gave the fort back to the French. To placate New England anger at this move and to set up a counterforce to Louisbourg, the British erected a fortified colony at Halifax in Nova Scotia. Several thousand settlers soon arrived, some from England, but many also from Scotland, Ireland, and the Continent, as well as a large contingent of New Englanders. The result was instant religious pluralism. The Anglican Society for the Propagation of the Gospel in Foreign Parts had supplied school teachers to the region from the 1720s, and the first official Nova Scotia Assembly of 1758 virtually made the Church of England the established church. But toleration was extended to all Protestants — New Englanders (who were trying to establish a Puritan kind of Congregationalism), German Lutherans, Swiss and French Huguenots, Presbyterians from Scotland as well as from Northern Ireland and Pennsylvania, and a sprinkling of Baptists and Quakers. It also extended to a small number of Jews who had joined the Halifax settlers. Most amazingly, the toleration even extended to the hereditary Roman Catholics in the region.

The establishment of Halifax led to immediate conflict between the augmented British colony and the Acadians. Finally, in 1755 the British administrators ordered the evacuation of the Acadians (numbering then about 9,000) from Nova Scotia. Despite this terrible event, surprisingly good Catholic-Protestant relations ensued. Abbé Maillard, the spiritual leader of the Acadians and the largely Catholic Micmac Indians, had a more irenic disposition than his predecessor. For their part, the British responded by giving an annual grant to the Catholics through Abbé Maillard. Thomas Wood, a Church of England minister in Halifax, became a friend of the Abbé and eventually conducted his funeral according to Anglican rites before a friendly audience made up of Halifax gentlemen, Catholic Acadians, and Micmac Indians.

Church life in the eighteenth-century Atlantic provinces, therefore, witnessed some of the Roman Catholic–Protestant admixture that would later make religious life in Canada different from that in the United States. It also saw a tighter relationship between governmental authority and religious life, a feature of Canadian church experience that also foreshadowed later differences from the United States.

Native Americans and Slaves

Before the first century of British colonization was over, the diversity that would later flower into American religious pluralism had gained a secure foothold in North America. What had not yet been established in the British colonies, however, was a Christian presence among Native Americans or black slaves. Compared to French efforts among the Native Americans of Canada, English missions were largely ineffectual. The seal on the charter of the Massachusetts Bay Company was emblazoned with the image of an Indian and words the apostle Paul had heard from Macedonia in a dream:

"Come Over and Help Us." But, with some exceptions, British contact with the Indians did much more to harm than to help the spread of the faith. Until at least the mid-eighteenth century a similar situation prevailed among African-Americans in the colonies. They were everywhere in direct contact with European settlers (usually against their will), but the religion from Europe remained the religion of the Europeans.

Native Americans

Two early Massachusetts pastors, John Eliot (1604-1690) of Roxborough and Thomas Mayhew, Jr. (1621-1657), of Martha's Vineyard, did make a significant effort to evangelize Native Americans. Eliot succeeded in gathering a number of converts into "praying towns," which he organized after models he found in the Pentateuch. With the help of several Native Americans, Eliot also translated the Bible into Algonquian. On Martha's Vineyard and the nearby islands of Nantucket and Chappaquiddick, Mayhew, his father, and other members of the family had even more success than Eliot, perhaps because they allowed a little more Native-American culture to remain in the Christian civilization they established.

King Philip's War (1675-1676) proved the undoing of the Native American mission on the mainland. Conversions had been tenuous before then, especially because of the rigidness with which the English missionaries imposed their conceptions of settled order on potential converts. Eliot, for example, held that the Native Americans must "have visible civility before they can rightly enjoy visible sanctities in ecclesiastical communion." The problem was not racism as such, for Eliot could be every bit as unbending in rebuking sins among his white congregation as in attacking what he saw as barbarism among the Indians. The problem lay rather in an inability to realize that "Indian Christianity" might not turn out to look exactly like "English Christianity." This prospect would not be explored until centuries later, especially among the Cherokee in the Southeast during the early nineteenth century and in several twentieth-century groups. The result was that when warfare broke out in 1675, all Native Americans, including Eliot's converts (and Eliot too), fell under suspicion. The Christianized Native Americans were quarantined on Deer Island in Boston Harbor, and bad blood colored future attempts at bringing the Christian message to any that had previously not been reached. Only on Martha's Vineyard, relatively secure because of its physical distance from the conflict, did considerable numbers of Native Americans retain their allegiance to Christianity.

John Eliot's translation of the New Testament into Algonquian was the first Bible printed by Protestants in the New World. *Picture Collection, The Branch Libraries, The New York Public Library*

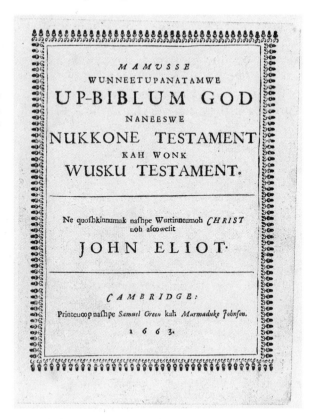

MAMUSSE
WUNNEETUPANATAMWE
UP-BIBLUM GOD
NANEESWE
NUKKONE TESTAMENT
KAH WONK
WUSKU TESTAMENT.

Ne quofhkinnumuk nafhpe Wuttinneumoh *CHRIST* noh afcowefit

JOHN ELIOT.

CAMBRIDGE:
Printeuoop nafhpe *Samuel Green* kah *Marmaduke Johnfon.*
1 6 6 3.

The most effective mission in what would become the United States was conducted by the Moravians, who had been established in their modern form by the assistance of Count Zinzendorf. Soon they became pioneers of Protestant missionary efforts throughout the world. In the British colonies, evangelization among the Native Americans was spearheaded by David Zeisberger (1721-1808), who pursued his work in extraordinarily difficult circumstances for over sixty years. Perhaps because the Moravians themselves were people on the margin of colonial America, without wealth or influence of their own, they seemed much readier to adapt to Native American ways. With the Jesuits of New France, they were the most effective witnesses to Christ among the native peoples.

Zeisberger began his work in 1748 among the Iroquois of Pennsylvania's Wyoming Valley, but the disruptions of the French and Indian War ended that work, and he shifted his attention to the Delawares. Soon his message bore fruit, and he organized the converted groups into peaceful, productive villages. But warfare again intervened. Whites accused the con-

"Baptism of Indians in America."
Perhaps because they were themselves strangers and wanderers in the world,
Moravians proved to be the most effective Protestant missionaries in America.
(A = a Moravian preacher; B = Native Americans being baptized;
C = Native American lay workers; D = the Native American congregation)
Picture Collection, The Branch Libraries, The New York Public Library

verts, who had in fact accepted the pacifism of the Moravian missionaries, of aiding the armed Native-American struggle against the settlers. Under mounting pressure, Zeisberger led his converts to Philadelphia, where they lived for over a year in straitened circumstances. Zeisberger wanted to settle the Native Americans near Bethlehem, but hostility against non-Moravians was too strong, and so he moved further west to establish a new town, Friedenshütten ("Sheltered by Peace"), on the Susquehanna River. The Delawares flourished, peaceful among themselves and fruitful in their farming, but again the thrust of white settlement disrupted their community. In 1772 Zeisberger moved the community into the Ohio territory, where other Native Americans converts came to join the Delawares. Again, however, success in constructing useful, peaceful lives lasted only so long as the region remained a wilderness. When conflict during the late stages of the American Revolution intruded into the Ohio region, the Indian settlement was forced to move again, this time to upper New York state and Ontario. In 1782, ninety of their number, divided about equally among men, women, and children, returned to Ohio to collect the last of their possessions. There they were apprehended by American patriots and brutally slain — "clubbed, scalped, and burned" in the words of a recent historian. Zeisberger arranged for a new location in Gnadenhütten ("Shielded by Grace"), Ontario, where the Indians at last found a refuge and where Moravian Native-American churches survived for generations.

Slaves

Contacts between European Christians and African slaves were, if anything, even more skewed than those between Europeans and Native Americans. Indentured servants from Africa were brought to Virginia in 1619, but indenture soon became slavery for most of the forced immigrants from Africa. Slavery rapidly became a major element in Southern ways of life as well as a common feature in the northern colonies. Throughout the New World, slavery was a major economic force: the selling of human beings enriched many merchants in New York, Newport, Boston, and other trading centers in the North as well as providing chattel labor for the South. Virtually no individuals or denominations questioned the propriety of slavery in the seventeenth century. In a tract from 1706, *The Negro Christianized,* Cotton Mather defended vigorously the essential humanity of blacks, but he was not prepared to attack their systematic enslavement.

To be sure, a few years earlier a faint protest had been made against slavery. Quakers and a small band of German Mennonite immigrants in Germantown, Pennsylvania, questioned in 1688 what they considered a violation of God's intentions for humanity. After referring to the biblical principle — "there is a saying that we should do to all men like as we will be done ourselves" — they asked pointedly, "Have these poor negers not as much right to fight for their freedom, as you have to keep them slaves?" But such voices were very few and far between in the first century of British colonization.

From their side, slaves and free blacks were slow to accept Christianity, and understandably so. Into the eighteenth century, differences of language and culture, not to mention the immense barriers erected by the slave system itself, effectively prevented the transmission of Christianity to slaves. In the minds of many English settlers, the offer of Christianity seemed to contradict the purpose for which blacks had been brought to America. An observer in 1682, John Barbot, noted that "Christians in America . . . take very little care to have their slaves instructed. . . . There,

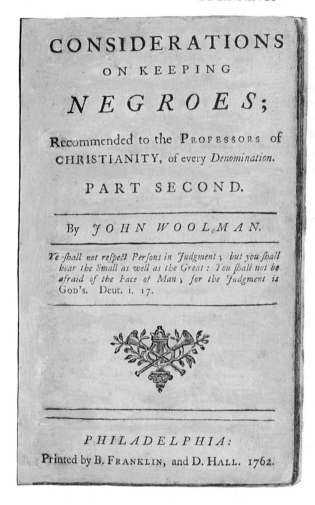

CONSIDERATIONS
ON KEEPING

NEGROES;

Recommended to the PROFESSORS of
CHRISTIANITY, of every *Denomination.*

PART SECOND.

By *JOHN WOOLMAN.*

*Ye shall not respect Persons in Judgment ; but you shall
hear the Small as well as the Great : You shall not be
afraid of the Face of Man ; for the Judgment is*
GOD's. Deut. i. 17.

PHILADELPHIA:
Printed by B. FRANKLIN, and D. HALL. 1762.

The Society of Friends
(Quakers) pioneered in
Christian protest against
the institution of slavery.
Of all colonial Quakers,
John Woolman produced
the most pointed and
effective antislavery
polemics.
*Picture Collection, The
Branch Libraries, The New
York Public Library*

provided that the slaves can multiply, and work hard for the benefit of
their masters, most men are well satisfied without the least thought of
using their authority and endeavors to promote the good of the souls of
those poor wretches." Barbot in 1682 and Bishop George Berkeley in 1731
both contrasted the somewhat greater concern for the spiritual life of
blacks that was found in Catholic regions, New Spain and New France,
with the widespread indifference among English settlers. One of the strategies used by those who were concerned about offering Christianity to the
slaves was the argument that Christian instruction made slaves better
workers than they otherwise would have been. Some slave owners heeded
this message, but others were not convinced, especially when Christianity
among slaves came to be associated with revolt. Such was the case in South

Carolina in 1725, when a group of slaves, inspired it seems by apocalyptic passages in the Bible, rose up against their masters.

Still, there were a few early signs of what would become, despite the offense of slavery, a large-scale turn to Christianity by African Americans. In 1641 a female slave of the Puritan minister in Dorchester, Massachusetts, was baptized and received into full communion in the local church. Several of the ministers supported by the Anglican Society for the Propagation of the Gospel in Foreign Parts took a special interest in working with slaves. One of these was the Reverend Francis Le Jau, who during the early eighteenth century established a parish in South Carolina when blacks in that colony outnumbered whites roughly ten thousand to six thousand. Le Jau wrote in October 1709 of his efforts at introducing blacks to the faith:

> On Sunday next I design God willing to baptise two very sensible and honest Negro Men whom I have kept upon tryal these two Years. Several others have spoken to me also; I do nothing too hastily in that respect. I instruct them and must have the consent of their Masters with a good Testimony and proof of their honest life and sober Conversation: Some Masters in my parish are very well satisfyed with my Proceedings in that respect: others do not seem to be so; yet they have given over opposing my design openly; it is to be hoped the good Example of the one will have an influence over the others.

Before he would baptize black converts, Le Jau required them to affirm they were not planning to use baptism as an excuse for seeking their freedom.

In the earliest decades of colonization, the spiritual life of blacks was often entirely neglected by European settlers. If they took an interest, it was in preventing the practice of religions carried with the slaves from Africa. Eventually, animated by the sorts of motives that the apostle Paul in another context referred to as "pretense and truth," whites began to communicate the Christian message to blacks. From the start, however, the message the whites thought they were conveying was not what the blacks were hearing. As historian Albert Raboteau has put it, "the meaning which the missionary wished the slaves to receive and the meaning which the slaves actually found (or, better, made) were not the same. The 'inaccuracy' of the slaves' translation of Christianity would be a cause of concern for missionaries for a long time to come." For the slaves themselves, that "inaccuracy" became a source of unanticipated hope. When they found, for example, that the Bible had more to say about Jesus lifting burdens than slaves obeying masters, blacks discovered a secret their masters did not want them to know.

What then can we conclude about Christianity in North America after a century or so of colonization? First, European patterns continued to dominate Christian religious life. Whether Puritan in New England, Anglican in Virginia or Nova Scotia, Quaker and Mennonite in Pennsylvania, or Roman Catholic in Quebec and Maryland, most Christians in North America sought in their religious lives what they had earlier found in Europe. But, second, from the outset, the new environment worked changes in that European deposit. The goal of religious domination, even in restricted areas, was harder and harder to achieve. The open environment of the New World encouraged a larger role for lay participation in religious leadership. Early efforts to combine the civilizing and converting of non-Europeans (Native Americans, blacks) were not particularly successful, but some significant inroads were made nonetheless. What Christians from Europe told slaves from Africa in the fields, barns, and houses of America soon yielded some surprising results.

Third, although evidence is fragmentary, it does seem that many colonists remained in contact with nontraditional forms of religion. A terrific jumble of religious practices could be found in early America — occult rituals, palm reading, consultation of "wise" men and "wise" women, witchcraft (black and white), astrology, and the interpretation of portents in, on, and under the earth. The line between some of these practices and more conventional expressions of Christianity was often quite thin. But despite difficulties of crossover and competition from informal religion, Christian observance continued. Full church membership in the colonies was relatively low — rarely higher than a third of adult New Englanders, and by some estimates as low as five percent of adults in the South — but "adherence," or relatively regular participation in religious activities and church-going, seems to have been quite high. Detailed study of diaries, missionary reports sent back to England, and other fragmentary evidence suggests that in 1700 as many as one half to three-fourths of the colonists attended some kind of religious service with some regularity. The situation, then, was the reverse of that in the modern United States, where formal church membership (around sixty percent in the 1980s) has been considerably higher than actual church attendance.

Finally, the distribution of churches reflected the ethnic and denominational heritage of the early settlements. In 1740, the population of the thirteen colonies that later became the United States was about 900,000. Three of the largest four denominations among that population were English and Protestant — Congregationalists (423 churches), Anglicans (246), and Baptists (96). The fourth was Scottish (or Scotch-Irish) and Protestant, the Presbyterians with 160 churches. Then came three largely Continental groups: Lutherans, mostly from Germany (95 churches), the Dutch Reformed (78), and the German Reformed (51). At the time there were twenty-seven Roman Catholic churches, mostly in Maryland. A wide scattering of smaller Continental bodies could be found in Pennsylvania and adjoining territories. When Britain formally assumed control of Canada in 1763, church organization had only just begun among a Maritime population of roughly 3,000 to 4,000 Acadians (who had escaped expulsion or returned) and slightly more than 10,000 newer settlers, among whom New England Congregationalists were the largest contingent. In Lower Canada, with slightly more than 60,000 people, the Bishop of Quebec oversaw three ecclesiastical "governments" — Quebec itself with fifty parishes, Trois-Rivières with twenty, and Montreal with forty-one.

In 1742 New York City contained nine churches representing eight denominations. Alone among the New World's urban centers, it reflected in one place the Christian pluralism that would increasingly become the norm throughout most of North America.

Further Reading

Bonomi, Patricia U., and Peter R. Eisenstadt. "Church Adherence in the Eighteenth-Century British Colonies." *William and Mary Quarterly* 39 (April 1982): 245-86.

Bowden, Henry Warner. *American Indians and Christian Missions: Studies in Cultural Conflict.* Chicago: University of Chicago Press, 1981.

Butler, Jon. *Awash in a Sea of Faith: Christianizing the American People.* Cambridge: Harvard University Press, 1990.

Gaustad, Edwin S., ed. *Baptist Piety: The Last Will and Testimony of Obadiah Holmes.* Grand Rapids: William B. Eerdmans, 1978.

———. *Liberty of Conscience: Roger Williams in America.* Grand Rapids: William B. Eerdmans, 1991.

Hall, David D., ed. *The Antinomian Controversy, 1636-1638: A Documentary History* (Anne Hutchinson). Middletown, CT: Wesleyan University Press, 1968.

Raboteau, Albert J. *Slave Religion: The "Invisible Institution" in the Antebellum South.* New York: Oxford University Press, 1978.

Scherer, Lester B. *Slavery and the Churches in Early America, 1619-1819.* Grand Rapids: William B. Eerdmans, 1975.

Schmidt, Leigh Eric. *Holy Fairs: Scottish Communions and American Revivals in the Early Modern Period.* Princeton: Princeton University Press, 1989.

Stoeffler, F. Ernest, ed. *Continental Pietism and Early American Christianity.* Grand Rapids: William B. Eerdmans, 1976.

Walsh, H. H. *The Church in the French Era.* Vol. 1, *A History of the Christian Church in Canada.* Toronto: Ryerson, 1966.

Woolverton, John F. *Colonial Anglicanism in North America.* Detroit: Wayne State University Press, 1984.

PART II

AMERICANIZATION

D URING THE SECOND CENTURY OF COLONIZATION, EVENTS IN AMERICA began to shape the character of Christian life and faith more decisively. From the early eighteenth century to the early nineteenth, three such events were especially important. First, the loosely connected revivals of the 1730s and 1740s, known as the Great Awakening, gave colonial piety a distinctive American cast. These revivals also altered the way that churches related to their surrounding societies. Second, the War for Independence from Great Britain drove a wedge between loyalist and patriotic churches, bequeathed a spirit of freedom to religion in the United States, and created a new Protestant world in Canada. Third, the Christian churches were also chief players in applying the cultural meaning of the American Revolution — what *did* the newly won freedoms, couched in the language of republicanism, actually mean for day-to-day life? In and through these events the churches in the United States helped define what it meant to be "American," while at the same time what it meant to be "American" had much to do with the development of the churches.

Nowhere is it easier to see this interplay between inherited faith and the new national environment than in a comparison of the United States with Canada. Where the States marched onto a path of self-government, and so defined themselves over against Europe, Canada chose instead to remain with Britain. As a result, its religious development, though not unaffected by life in the New World, remained much closer to European patterns and so offers a sharp contrast to the development of Christianity in the United States.

To be sure, the influence of Europe on North America did not slacken in the eighteenth century. Immigration continued from many parts of Western Europe. England continued to exert a powerful cultural sway (in fact,

83

intellectual elites in the colonies were becoming more English in their tastes and habits even as they broke from the rule of king and Parliament). And Americans still spoke of religious life in terms largely defined by British and Continental debates in the areas of formal theology, general conceptions of the church, and practical Christian experience. Yet the situation that Alexis de Tocqueville discerningly described in the 1830s — that Christianity was unusually prominent in American character, and the principles of America's political self-definition unusually prominent in Christianity — had begun to emerge more than two generations before.

CHAPTER 4

A Renewal of Piety, 1700-1750

Samuel Davies

Eternal Spirit, source of light,
    Enlivening, consecrating fire,
Descend, and with celestial heat
    Our dull, our frozen hearts inspire.
Our souls refine, our dross consume!
    Come, condescending Spirit, come!
Come vivifying Spirit, come,
    And make our hearts thy constant home!

Henry Alline

Ye sons of Adam lift your eyes,
Behold how free the Saviour dies,
    To save your souls from hell!
There's your Creator, and your friend;
Believe and soon your fears shall end,
    And you in glory dwell.

During and after the Great Awakening a new style of hymnody appeared in America. It featured songs that appealed just as directly for conversion and just as forcefully for individual piety as Charles Wesley's more famous hymns from Britain's contemporary Methodist movement. Two of the most prolific writers of these hymns were a Presbyterian minister in Virginia, Samuel Davies, author of the first stanza above from a hymn published in 1769, and Henry Alline, an

85

independent-minded revivalist from Nova Scotia, author of the second stanza above from a hymn published in 1781.

D URING THE FIRST HALF OF THE EIGHTEENTH CENTURY, THE CHURCHES in the thirteen colonies that would become the United States were transformed. In all regions population boomed — quadrupling for New England (from 90,000 to 360,000) and increasing fivefold in both the mid-Atlantic and the southern colonies (from 50,000 to 270,000 in New York, Pennsylvania, and New Jersey; from slightly over 100,000 to well over 500,000 in the South). The result for the churches was both strain and opportunity. The strain involved especially the need to establish stable yet energetic churches for a population that expanded into the hinterlands almost as fast as it was expanding in size. The opportunity was to spread the gospel to wider circles of colonists as well as to make it come alive for those in the coastal settlements. In the face of these challenges, leaders of the churches strove to shore up ecclesiastical organization, largely along lines inherited from Europe. But they also tried to exploit the effects of a wide-spread colonial revival. So it was that as the churches became more Americanized, they pursued both the security of structures and liberation in the Holy Spirit. This combination of countervailing forces became quintessentially American.

The Early Eighteenth Century

Although the generations between the founding of American colonies and the outbreak of the Great Awakening are often passed over in relative silence, they did enjoy the work of several outstanding Christian leaders. Two of these, the New Englanders Solomon Stoddard (1643-1729) and Cotton Mather (1662-1728), would have been extraordinary figures in any era.

Solomon Stoddard and Cotton Mather

"Pope" Stoddard, as his opponents called him, was the minister in Northampton, Massachusetts, from 1672 until his death fifty-seven years later. He was known in his day especially for innovations in church discipline. Stoddard sought to go beyond the "halfway" system of church membership by proposing that all people who lived outwardly decent lives should be allowed to take communion. At the same time he also urged the churches of Massachusetts to develop a "connectional" or "presbyterian" plan of oversight to guide local churches and their ministers. These proposals have led some historians to praise Stoddard for his democratic tendencies (in opening up the Lord's Supper) and others to condemn him for being antidemocratic (in proposing tighter outside controls for local churches). But in fact Stoddard was most concerned about the conversion of the lost. Because he believed that communion offered a way for people to "learn the necessity and sufficiency of the Death of Christ in order to [find] Pardon," he thought it could be a "converting ordinance," and hence as many people as possible should take part. Likewise, Stoddard thought that tighter control over the churches would preserve the purity of the gospel.

For his labors, Stoddard experienced five "harvests" of souls in Northampton. In general, however, those who followed his lead on church discipline showed less interest in the unconverted. But Stoddard's concern for revival was shared by his grandson, Jonathan Edwards, who became his colleague minister in 1724 and his successor when he died. Edwards eventually repudiated his grandfather's ideas on the Lord's Supper, but his efforts in the 1730s and 1740s to promote renewal marked him as his grandfather's heir in spirit as well as in fact.

One of the clergymen who organized opposition to Stoddard's "open communion" was Cotton Mather, colleague-pastor to his father, Increase, at Boston's Old North Church for his entire ministerial career. Cotton Mather has been an inviting target for successive generations of Puritan-bashers in America. He was ostentatiously pious, shamelessly self-promoting, overbearingly moralistic, and his 469 separate books and pamphlets suggest that he never had a thought he felt was unworthy of publication. (In fact, however, his largest work, a massive reference work and commentary on the Bible, has never been published.) Yet superficial treatments do not take the measure of this extraordinarily learned and preternaturally active clergyman.

Mather did champion the Congregationalist's New England Way as if it were the closest thing imaginable to heaven, but he also was remarkably tolerant of other expressions of Christianity. He even had an open-eyed curiosity about non-Christian religions. Toward the end of his life he participated in the ordination of a Baptist minister when such a step was still quite radical. He did defend a painstaking kind of supernaturalism (Mather recorded several conversations with angels in his private study and defended the use of spectral, or invisible, evidence at the Salem witch trials). Yet he was also a wholehearted promoter of science. He corresponded with mem-

The artist had to work fast to complete this portrait of Cotton Mather, for Mather was on the go most of his life — publishing more than four hundred books, writing several more mammoth manuscripts that were never published, pastoring a busy church in Boston (with his father, Increase), and carrying on a correspondence throughout the whole Western world. *Courtesy of the Billy Graham Center Museum*

bers of Britain's Royal Society about natural phenomena in New England, and he wrote an impressive treatise, *The Christian Philosopher*, on the harmony of theology and science. He also introduced inoculation for smallpox in Boston at a time when that too was a radical step. Mather was a man between the times, pulled back out of love and nostalgia for the virtues of New England's pioneering generations but also energetic in his efforts to provide for the religious, social, and intellectual needs of his contemporaries. Mather's efforts at evangelism and the moral reform of society anticipated prominent features of the evangelicalism that would become so prominent in later American history.

Regional Developments

In New England more generally, clergymen besides Stoddard and Mather were making an effort to solidify the place of the churches in their society. Concerned about what they saw as the growth of indifference, a loss of respect for churches (and their ministers), or, especially in coastal towns, a heightened competition from economic interests, some clergymen responded with efforts to make the churches more formal and better established. For some, the Church of England became an attractive model, with its liturgies and latitudinarian doctrine. A tendency to equate the spirituality of the minister with the spirituality of society was occasionally evident. The same tendency lay behind efforts at tightening up procedures for ordination and proposing new forms of church order.

In Connecticut, ministers met in the spring of 1708 at the behest of the colonial legislature in order to correct what it called "defects of the discipline of the churches." Members of the legislature were troubled by forces that seemed to be fragmenting Connecticut society. Later that year, twelve ministers and four laymen met at Saybrook to draft fifteen "Articles for the Administration of Church Discipline." This "platform" committed Connecticut Congregationalists to the doctrine of the Savoy Confession (a Congregationalist variation of the Calvinistic Westminster Confession) and it instituted presbyterian features in the Connecticut churches. Henceforth, county "consociations" of ministers and laymen were empowered to judge disputes arising in local churches. County "associations" and a colony-wide "General Association" of ministers were also formed, though their duties were not precisely defined. The acceptance of the Saybrook Platform solidified the corporate influence of Congregationalism in Connecticut, but it may also have indicated a decline in the internal vigor that had earlier driven the Congregationalists into the wilderness. In Massachusetts a similar proposal for a tighter church organization had been made in 1705, but despite fairly wide support it was never accepted by that colony's churches.

In the middle colonies, the most important structural developments were centered in Philadelphia and the neighboring Delaware River valley. In that region a pattern that would later become the norm in the United States was developing: representatives of a number of denominations (in this case, Quakers, Baptists, Presbyterians, and soon Lutherans and other bodies of Continental origin) managed to live and work together in relative harmony. Whether these groups were in principle inclined toward such cooperation or not, their overlapping settlement forced them to live together without any one of them exercising proprietary rights as an established church. Each may have thought it possessed the one true interpretation of biblical faith, but none was strong enough to impose that interpretation on the others. The result was a degree of interdenominational tolerance probably unknown anywhere else in the world at that time.

But the pattern also led to some heightened denominational consciousness. Quakers, who had begun as a sectarian protest movement in England, had by 1690 achieved a degree of formal organization unanticipated in the Old World. In that year George Keith, a Scottish Friend, complained about the haughtiness of "Public Friends" (i.e., ministers). The result was a schism that led to even greater authority for the Philadelphia Yearly Meeting among those Quakers who did not depart with Keith.

Middle-colony Baptists and Presbyterians also worked to solidify their positions. The Philadelphia Baptist Association was formed in 1707 and gradually became a leading guide to the English and Welsh Baptists who migrated into the region. The Presbyterian Synod that Francis Makemie helped organize in 1707 drew together immigrants from Scotland, Northern Ireland, England, and New England. Their alliance was later weakened by internal differences, but it nonetheless exerted an increasingly regulatory effect on Presbyterians. It too was centered in Philadelphia. Among these groups a quintessentially American pattern was taking shape — religious pluralism in society as a whole combined with growing respect for church structure within the various denominations.

In the South the major Christian development around the start of the eighteenth century was a tragedy. This was the time when the slave system was finalized and the churches were enlisted as agents enforcing that system. After 1680 ambiguities associated with both the legality of slavery and the restriction of slavery to blacks were resolved. At about the same time, the Church of England brought a measure of order into the formal life of the southern colonies. The two developments bore an unfortunate relationship. The establishment of the Church of England kept Protestant dissenters (and the threat of "gospel liberty") from gaining a foothold until the mid-eighteenth century. The same establishment also made clear that its efforts to convert slaves and incorporate them into the churches would be undertaken without questioning the slave system. The almost inevitable result was that the religion of Anglicanism became a prop for unusual social deference and the legitimization of the slave system.

By the 1730s, it was possible to discern three distinct religious patterns in the thirteen colonies: New England, with its heritage of Puritanism as a vital people's religion, was the scene of some uneasiness about the decline of ecclesiastical influence. In the middle colonies a Protestant pluralism was in place, though it was neither celebrated nor always even noticed. In the South the Anglican Church had become part of a deferential culture in which slavery was a key feature, both economically and ideologically. Under these conditions, the mid-century religious quickenings proved explosive, both in simple Christian terms and with respect to the churches' relationship to the social order. New England ministers may have sought revival to shore up their status, mid-colony preachers may have thought revival would expand the outreach and deepen the spiritual life of their denominations, and southern Anglicans may have hoped that a deeper piety could be assimilated within a stable establishment. When it arrived, however, the colonial Great Awakening was a surprise. Its currents of renewal outran the expectations of the clergy and from Nova Scotia to Georgia changed the rules of the game for the American churches.

The Great Awakening

The colonial revival was called a *great* awakening because it touched so many regions and so many aspects of colonial life. Although the Great Awakening represented more a general upsurge of revivalistic piety than a distinct event, it was vastly important for both the churches and American society. In New England the revival brought new life to many Congregational churches and greatly stimulated the growth of the Baptists. In the middle colonies the Presbyterians and the Dutch Reformed, after initial divisions over revival practices, ended by growing rapidly because of its emphases. In the southern colonies, which were affected in the last phases of the Awakening, the revival led to new growth for Baptists and began to prepare the way for the great Methodist movement of the post-Revolutionary period. It also bridged the yawning cultural divide between blacks and whites. The Awakening was made up of local revivals, but it did have two "national" leaders, an English preacher, George Whitefield, and a New England theologian, Jonathan Edwards.

George Whitefield

George Whitefield (1714-1770) may have been the best-known Protestant in the whole world during the eighteenth century. Certainly he was the single best-known religious leader in America of that century, and the most widely recognized figure of any sort in North America before George Washington. Whitefield was an ordained minister of the Church of England, who had cooperated with John and Charles Wesley in a "Holy Club" at Oxford during the 1720s and 1730s. Whitefield later introduced the Wesleys to some of the practices that would characterize their Methodist movement, including preaching out of doors and directing the message of salvation to common people neglected by the established churches. Whitefield visited Georgia briefly in 1738 to aid in the founding of an orphanage. When he returned to the colonies in 1739, his reputation as a dramatic preacher preceded him. His visit became a sensation. When he preached in New England during the fall of 1740, Whitefield addressed crowds of up to 8,000 people nearly every day for over a month. This tour, one of the most remarkable episodes in the whole history of American Christianity, was the key event in New England's Great Awakening. Whitefield returned often to the American colonies, where in 1770 he died as he had hoped he might, in the midst of yet another preaching tour.

Unlike later American revivalists, Whitefield was a Calvinist. He broke with John Wesley over theological matters in 1741, Wesley holding to a

George Whitefield did not inspire unusual confidence with his good looks. (This realistic contemporary engraving shows why his detractors called him "Dr. Squintum.") But when Whitefield started to preach, no one had ever heard anything like it before. He was probably the most compelling religious "presence" in all of American history.
Courtesy of Susan Lundin

moderate Arminianism. (Later Wesley and Whitefield were reconciled as friends, though not in theological opinion, and Wesley preached a sermon of warm commendation after Whitefield's death.) But Whitefield was much more interested in preaching than in theology. Although he affirmed the doctrines of predestination, election, and the definite atonement — all themes of traditional Calvinism — he confessed in a letter to John Wesley early in his career that "I never read anything Calvin wrote; my doctrines I had from Christ and His apostles: I was taught them of God." It was this sense of divine purpose that made Whitefield an effective preacher and a model to other aspiring revivalists in America.

Whitefield's greater cultural significance was his innovative approach to preaching. He was not a good organizer, as the Wesleys were, so those quickened by his preaching had to find their own ways to Anglican or Methodist congregations in England or to Congregational, Presbyterian, and Baptist churches in America. Whitefield did know how to address plain people in plain language, however, and he did so with a new appreciation for the dynamics of the marketplace. As a youth Whitefield had been drawn to the stage, an aspiration he renounced after his conversion. But he remained an actor nonetheless, with an unusual sensitivity to what it takes to secure an audience. He appealed to the heart, he knew how to play on emotions, and he was casual in the extreme about denominational differences. He also knew how to exploit the rising tide of newsprint and he even engaged in what would today be called "publicity stunts." Besides these innovations, Whitefield also preached his sermons *ex tempore,* speaking directly without notes on the strength of his own charisma and the force of his message.

In all these ways Whitefield contributed to the more democratic and popular style of Christianity in America. And these qualities made him a much-respected figure in his own day. Benjamin Franklin, for example, was an admirer of Whitefield, if not necessarily of his message. Skeptical about reports of great crowds coming out to hear the traveling preacher, Franklin once conducted an experiment during one of Whitefield's sermons out of doors in Philadelphia. He came away convinced that Whitefield could in fact be heard by up to 30,000 people at one time. Many others in America and Britain also had a chance to hear Whitefield, for it is estimated that he preached 15,000 times during his thirty-three-year career.

For all his innovations and for all the excitement he created with his dramatic "media events," Whitefield remained most fundamentally an agent of his message. God's grace for guilty sinners was the heart of his concern. Having attended one of his sermons in 1740, at Middletown, Connecticut, an ordinary farmer from nearby Kensington left a record of that message and the power with which Whitefield could drive it home. To Nathan Cole, it was one of the great days of his life:

> When I saw Mr Whitfield come upon the Scaffold [that had been erected for the sermon] he Lookt almost angelical; a young, Slim, slender, youth before some thousands of people with a bold undaunted Countenance, and my hearing how God was with him every where as he came along it Solemnized my mind; and put me into a trembling fear before he began to preach; for he looked as if he was Clothed with authority from the Great God; *and a sweet sollome solemnity sat upon his brow* And my hearing him preach, gave me a heart wound; By Gods blessing: my old Foundation was broken up, and I saw that my righteousness would not save me; then I was convinced of the doctrine of Election: and went right to quarrelling with God about it; because that all I could do would not save me; and he had decreed from Eternity who should be saved and who not.

It was several months before Nathan Cole found the doctrine of God's electing power a consolation instead of a conundrum. As he did, however, he was ushered into a new mode of existence. Touched to the core of his

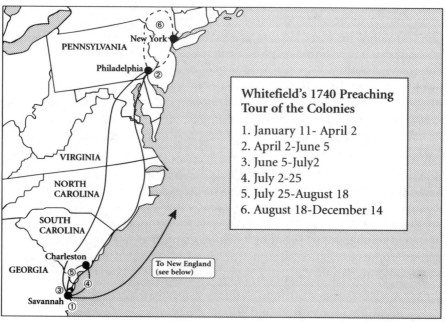

Whitefield's 1740 Preaching
Tour of the Colonies

1. January 11- April 2
2. April 2-June 5
3. June 5-July2
4. July 2-25
5. July 25-August 18
6. August 18-December 14

To New England
(see below)

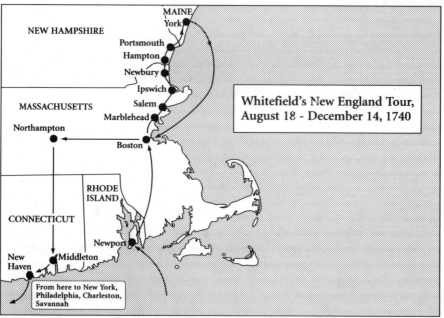

Whitefield's New England Tour,
August 18 - December 14, 1740

From here to New York,
Philadelphia, Charleston,
Savannah

George Whitefield's travels, including his momentous preaching tours of 1740,
sketched above, may have taken him through more of the American colonies than
any of his contemporaries. Beyond doubt, he was the most widely known
"American" before George Washington.

being by the message Whitefield had conveyed, he experienced an altogether transforming sense of God's presence. As his diary goes on to explain, Cole also experienced a new level of love and concern for others who had been touched by a similar message. His revived religious life did, to be sure, lead him to withdraw from the parish Congregational church and to develop a somewhat censorious attitude toward those who had not been affected as he had. But what Cole found in rushing off to hear Whitefield was what countless others in his generation and succeeding generations discovered. It was the reality of such religious experience that Whitefield's preaching sought. It was the power of that reality that nay-sayers in Whitefield's age of Enlightenment as well as in subsequent ages of self-confident economic, social, and psychological "explanations" have never been able to fathom. The realities of heartfelt conversion Whitefield facilitated, even more than the extensive changes he brought to the practices of religion, are why he was such an important figure in his age and why his legacy has remained at the heart of the history of Christianity in America.

Jonathan Edwards

If Whitefield was the most important preacher of the Great Awakening, Jonathan Edwards (1703-1758) was its most important apologist. Questions of revival became the occasion for a string of works that made Edwards America's greatest early theologian and a figure whose work is still the subject of serious academic study and the source of popular theological stimulation. Some of Edwards's works grew out of his efforts to defend the colonial revivals, while others were attempts at discriminating between true and imitation godliness. His *Faithful Narrative of the Surprising Work of God in the Conversion of Many Hundred Souls in Northampton, and the Neighbouring Towns and Villages of the County of Hampshire, in the Province of the Massachusetts-Bay in New-England* (1737) was Edwards's first widely distributed work. It described a time of renewal that had descended upon Northampton after Edwards preached a lengthy series of sermons on justification by faith. This book not only set out a model for reporting on extraordinary spiritual works but also established evangelical connections with such leaders as John Wesley in England and James Robe in Scotland who longed for similar results from their work.

A revival sermon, "Sinners in the Hands of an Angry God," preached at Enfield, Connecticut, in 1741, is Edwards's best-known work. Yet on balance he spent much less time and energy depicting the wrath of God than he did preparing sermons about the beauties of Christ's perfections

This nearly expression-less portrait of Jonathan Edwards fails altogether to suggest his passion for God and only hints at the surpassing range of his intellect.
Library of Congress

and writing formal theological treatises. In a major examination of revival phenomena, published in 1746 as *A Treatise concerning Religious Affections*, he argued that true Christianity is not revealed by the quantity or intensity of religious emotions but is rather present where a heart had been changed to love God and seek his pleasure. After he died, Edwards's friends published a work of his entitled *The Nature of True Virtue* (1765), in which he suggests that an experience of God's grace is the only basis for ultimate and enduring morality (ordinary human experience can account for ordinary human goodness but not for "true virtue").

One of Edwards's earlier books, *Freedom of the Will* (1754), presents traditional Calvinistic ideas on the nature of man and salvation in a powerful new shape. Its basic argument is that the "will" does not constitute a real entity but is an expression of the strongest motive in a person's character. A sinful human nature, in other words, cannot desire to please God unless God, by a miraculous infusion of his grace, changes the sinner's character. Edwards supported the thrust of this work with another, entitled *Original Sin* (1758), in which he argues that all of humanity was present in Adam when he sinned and so all people share the sinful character and the guilt that Adam brought upon himself.

Jonathan Edwards was a theologian overwhelmed by the majesty and the splendor of the divine. The major themes of his theology are the greatness and glory of God, the utter dependence of sinful humanity on God for salvation, and the ethereal beauty of the life of holiness. Edwards was not only a fervent Christian person; he was also a theological genius. He spent part of his time studying the best philosophy and science of his day, especially from his near-contemporaries Isaac Newton and John Locke, in order to explore the workings of the world that Edwards believed God had made for his own glory. In later generations, American revivalists were more likely to follow Edwards in appealing for the new birth than were American theologians in defending the broadly Calvinistic themes so central to his concern.

In the Wake of Revivals

The revivals that Whitefield and Edwards encouraged led, at least for a time, to a rapid increase in the number of people making personal profession of their faith and joining a church. In Connecticut, for which good records remain, an average of eight people had joined each of the colony's congregations each year from 1730 to 1740. (This formal step usually required a testimony to God's work of grace in one's life.) But in 1741 and 1742, at the height of the Awakening, the average reached thirty-three a year. Similar rates of growth were experienced elsewhere, as in the Carolinas following renewed Baptist preaching in the 1750s.

One must be careful not to claim too much for these statistics, however, for the same church records in Connecticut show that the number of new members declined rapidly in the late 1740s to levels below those of the 1730s. For the whole period 1730 to 1750 in Connecticut, about the same proportion of the population joined the churches through a profession of saving faith as had joined during the preceding thirty years. And throughout the colonies, responses to revival preaching represented surges in formal church membership rather than long-lasting proportionate gains. Accurate information on church membership and attendance is very hard to come by for the colonial period, but it does seem as if both church membership and church "adherence" (or reasonably regular attendance) declined gradually from 1700 to the time of the American Revolution. At the same time, periods of revival, inspired by preaching that imitated Whitefield, and interpreted along theological lines suggested by Edwards, measurably strengthened many churches throughout the colonies.

Regional Effects

Clearly the Great Awakening had different effects in different regions. Whitefield preached everywhere in the colonies and hence constituted a common force, but otherwise the revival's effects were various. In New England the bonds among the Puritan churches were strained before the 1730s, but after the revival such unity as there had been was broken irreparably. In its wake, the revival left four distinct ecclesiastical parties, each of which looked upon itself as the proper heir or worthy successor of the English dissenting tradition. Those who followed the libertarian themes of revival eventually separated from the state-church establishment or became Baptists, to whom we will turn at greater length in due course. Congregationalists such as Edwards were often called "New Lights" because they promoted a view of conversion that looked for God to shine afresh into the sinner's soul. Congregationalists of this sort hoped to maintain the traditional ties between church and state, but they were willing to sacrifice the church's authority over the population at large in order to purify the church of nominal members. (This issue led to a break between Edwards and his Northampton congregation.) Third, a party of traditionalists, sometimes called Old Calvinists, was torn between delight at the renewal of religion and fear for the disruption of church and society. The Old Calvinists remained traditional not only in belief but also in holding to the Puritan notion of a unified, hierarchically structured social order. Finally, a more rationalistic party of Congregationalists, joined in spirit by latitudinarian Anglicans, found in Enlightenment trends from Europe an antidote to what they considered the overheated supernaturalism of the revivals. Led by Boston ministers including Jonathan Mayhew and Charles Chauncy, these rationalists were "liberal" in their notions of Christianity but "conservative" in their disdain for the intemperate enthusiasms of the common people. The course they chose led eventually to Unitarianism.

If New England witnessed the fragmentation of its hereditary church as a consequence of the revival, the middle colonies experienced something different. There the revivals provided a common set of experiences in a number of denominations. Some of those denominations, including the Presbyterians and the Dutch Reformed, cracked under the strain. Formal schisms took place between parties eager to participate in the revivals and parties fearful of losing Old World forms in the hurly-burly of America. Among both the Presbyterians and Dutch Reformed, the future belonged to the American revivalists. Divisions occurred in the 1740s, but things were patched back together over the next two decades. Having surmounted the schisms, both denominations retained a strong sense of their European

Charles Chauncy,
the most active opponent
of the colonial Great
Awakening, was known
as "Old Brick." This
portrait shows why.
*Courtesy of the Billy
Graham Center Museum*

traditions, but both had also come far along the path to more egalitarian, more pietistic, less formal conceptions of the church. These sorts of broadening changes were even more profoundly effected in less conservative denominations with weaker ties to their European past. A spirit of evangelical pragmatism grew rapidly in the middle colonies in a wide range of British, German, Dutch, and other bodies. Unlike New England, where strife over revivals fragmented an inherited unity, the middle colonies, where extraordinary religious diversity had existed from the first, saw their churches emerge from the revivals moving toward a common pattern of evangelical faith and practice.

In the South, where the Baptists were the first great beneficiary of the evangelical Calvinism promoted by the Great Awakening, the most important effect of the revivals was to create an alternative to the Church of England. This alternative involved the popularization of emotional personal faith as opposed to formal ceremonial worship. It involved the popularization of new models of intimate Christian fellowship as opposed to external religious observances. And it involved challenges to the standing order. Methodist missionaries would not appear until the 1770s, and Methodist organization would not follow for another decade after that, but the currents of revival that had entered the South by the 1750s were the harbingers of a great Methodist movement. Even more than the rise of the Baptists, that Methodist movement would soon transform not just the Christian faith of the South but the whole of North American Protestantism.

The Great Awakening and the Baptists

In New England, many of the awakened believers came to doubt the wisdom of the church-state establishment. Their heavy stress on the conversion experience also led many to conclude that it would be appropriate to administer baptism after conversion. Not surprisingly, then, many believers who moved from the established Congregational churches to Separate (or independent) Congregational churches eventually became Baptists. In such churches enthusiasm for evangelism and reform lasted long after the revival fires had cooled in the Congregational churches.

The ongoing work of the Baptists in New England was led by Isaac Backus (1724-1806). After being converted during a revival, Backus pastored a Separate Congregational church for a few years. He then served for five years as the minister of an "open" church that did not make convictions about baptism a test for membership. When this arrangement proved unsuccessful, Backus formed a Baptist church in Middleborough, Massachusetts. He then played a major role in the influential Warren Association of Baptist Churches (founded in 1767) and became a diligent historian of the Baptist movement. The manuscripts that Backus collected and his own historical writings are still valuable sources for the early history of the Baptists in America. Later Backus also led the fight in Massachusetts during the American Revolution for the separation of church and state.

The Baptists in New England remained largely Calvinistic in theology. Backus even spoke of "our Edwards" in approving Jonathan Edwards's Calvinistic defense of the revival. Baptists differed with Edwards and Whitefield principally in their assertion that adult baptism upon profession of faith should be the only form of baptism and that New England's traditional governmental support for the churches was unwise. Having once embraced the tide of revival, the Baptists in New England grew rapidly — from 25 individual churches in 1740 to 312 by 1804. An added sign of maturity was the founding of a Baptist college in Rhode Island (1764), which later became Brown University. The Baptist commitment to religious freedom is evident in the college's charter, which specifies an intent to uphold "Absolute and uninterrupted Liberty of Conscience" and "freely" admit "youths of all Religious Denominations." (The Awakening also figured, directly or indirectly, in the founding of several other colleges — Princeton by Presby-

As historian, organizer, pastor, and campaigner for religious liberty, Isaac Backus led New England's Baptists to new commitment and respectability in the age of the American revolution.
Library of Congress

terians in 1746, Queens [later Rutgers] by the Dutch Reformed in 1764, and Dartmouth in 1769 by Congregationalists with a special interest in providing higher education for Native-American converts.)

In the southern colonies the tide of revival and the spread of the Baptists both came later — and had an even greater effect. A Bostonian, Shubal Stearns (1706-1771), and his brother-in-law Daniel Marshall (1706-1784), moved into the Carolinas in the 1750s with expressly evangelistic purposes. Together they formed a Baptist congregation in 1755 at Sandy Creek, North Carolina. Three years later enough new churches had been started to establish the Sandy Creek Association of Baptist churches. By the early 1770s Baptists numbered in the thousands in Virginia and the Carolinas. This phase of Baptist growth also witnessed the emergence of the farmer-preacher as a mainstay of Baptist ministry. The sturdy yeoman who worked his farm during the week and proclaimed the gospel on Sunday built a foundation for the later spread of the Baptists in regions where formally trained ministers were conspicuous by their absence.

Baptist growth in the South was often not appreciated by the wealthy planter classes on the seaboard. In their view, the Baptists and other dissenters undermined order by refusing to defer to their social betters and

University Hall, Brown University, was built in 1770, less than twenty years after Rhode Island Baptists founded the college to perpetuate the gains of the colonial Great Awakening. *Brown Univerity Archives*

by insisting on the rights of absolutely everyone to act on the gospel message. A report of what happened in 1771 when a small Baptist congregation tried to organize in Tidewater Virginia suggests something of this antagonism:

> Brother Waller informed us . . . [that] about two weeks ago on the Sabbath Day down in Caroline County he introduced the worship of God by singing. . . . The Parson of the Parish [who had ridden up with his clerk, the sheriff, and some others] would keep running the end of his horsewhip in [Waller's] mouth, laying his whip across the hymn book, etc. When done singing [Waller] proceeded to prayer. In it he was violently jerked off the stage; they caught him by the back part of his neck, beat his head against the ground, sometimes up, sometimes down, they carried him through a gate that stood some considerable distance, where a gentleman [the sheriff] gave him . . . twenty lashes with his horsewhip. . . . Then Bro. Waller was released, went back singing praise to God, mounted the stage and preached with a great deal of liberty.

Public baptisms, as depicted in this Pennsylvania scene from the second half of the eighteenth century, worried Anglicans, Congregationalists, and Presbyterians but also suggested the fervor that was making Baptists one of the fastest growing denominations in North America. *Courtesy of the Billy Graham Center Museum*

Despite such violence, the Baptists' ability to communicate a living faith to all classes, especially those of little account, swiftly made them a powerful new force throughout the region.

For some time, churches belonging to the older Philadelphia Association of Particular Baptists looked on Marshall and Stearns with suspicion. Members of the Association, styling themselves "Regular" Baptists, considered these "Separates" too emotional and too undisciplined. But in 1787 Separates and Regulars set aside their differences. Both groups committed themselves to the Calvinistic standards of the Philadelphia Association while reaffirming the primary authority of the Bible. The Separates also agreed with the Regulars that interchurch cooperation was a worthy goal for all to pursue.

From English Puritanism to American Evangelicalism

The revivals were also a major stimulus for promoting a more active, more individualistic form of Protestantism. In communities visited by revival, it became customary for laypeople to take the initiative for gathering to pray, read the Scriptures together, and exhort one another to godliness. In Jonathan Edwards's Northampton, Massachusetts, renewal rolled through the community in waves from 1735 through 1742. The result was a population that, at least temporarily, set aside personal quarrels, practiced its business more diligently and more honestly, and took greater delight in the exercise of religion. But this sort of religion did not spread without opposition. Before the 1740s were over, Edwards lost favor with his own congregation when he altered the long-standing Northampton practice of allowing all members of the community to participate in the Lord's Supper even if they had not yet joined the church by a profession of faith. Edwards's new proposal, that only the "professedly regenerate" be allowed to take communion, upset many of the town's leading citizens, who had come to look upon church membership as an important glue preserving the traditional order of the community. After bitter debate, Edwards was dismissed from his pulpit. The dismissal was a blessing in disguise for theology in America, since Edwards spent most of his last years as a pastor to small Native-American and white congregations in Stockbridge, Massachusetts, where he was able to give nearly all his time to study and writing. It also showed that a faith empowering the laity would not always win its way easily in the face of inherited European traditions.

The clash in Northampton is indicative of the sorts of changes in religious practice that were produced by the Great Awakening. Similar changes were also taking place in the most visible Protestant movements on the Continent. It can be called a shift in sensibilities from Puritanism to evangelicalism. The transition was subtle, and it occurred in different areas in different ways. The revivalists' appeal to the individual and their implied challenges to the traditional authority of settled ministers and of established bonds between church and state contributed significantly to this transition. The practice of Whitefield was central to the change. Historian Harry Stout has recently summarized Whitefield's reversal of the reigning assumptions: "instead of invoking authority as a means of popular control and influence, Whitefield would make himself popular and, on the basis of that popularity, claim authority and status."

Puritans had opposed the formal and external aspects of Roman Catholicism and Anglicanism, but they had also assumed that such inherited institutions as the family, the church, and even the covenanted English nation as a whole mediated salvation. In the rising tide of evangelicalism, it was a key tenet that salvation is unmediated by anything other than the spoken and written word. Puritans had protested against religious nominalism, but they nonetheless acted as if inherited institutions of church and society were simply given. The evangelicals who emerged from the Great Awakening took it upon themselves to create their own communities; at first they sought to remake the churches, but then (in the United States) they set their sights on creating a Christian nation. Puritans, who challenged the authority of corrupted authorities, nonetheless sought ministers whose training and orthodoxy set them apart as responsible authorities. After the Great Awakening, the evangelical tendency increasingly was to seek leaders distinguished by charismatic power. Puritans sought vital individual spirituality, but they fenced in enthusiasm with the formal learning of their ministers, a respect for formal confessions, and deference to traditional Protestant interpretations of Scripture. The new evangelicals, however, were much more kindly disposed to the power of religious emotion (what the eighteenth century called "enthusiasm"), and they sought to determine its boundaries only by drawing on the wisdom imparted by leaders they themselves had selected, by individual Bible reading, and by the intuitive persuasion of personal religious experience. The Great Awakening by itself did not bring about the change from a Puritan style of religious life to an evangelical style, but it had much to do with facilitating that shift, and thus it contributed forcefully to the shape of later religious life.

Preaching to the Under Classes

Also as a result of the revivals, the Christian message came more directly to the downtrodden and despised of society. Some readers still find inspiration in the spiritual diary of David Brainerd (1718-1747), which Jonathan Edwards edited for publication. Brainerd was just one of a number of ardent souls who were led by the revival spirit to become missionaries among the Native Americans. Brainerd's own work was with the Mahicans of Massachusetts and the Delawares of New Jersey and Pennsylvania. But other sons of the revivals such as Brainerd's brother, John (1720-1781), had much more success in bringing religious and humanitarian aid to Native Americans. John Brainerd's work among the Delawares was sponsored by the Scottish Society for the Propagation of Christian Knowledge, which suggests something about the many connections in the era between the Church of Scotland and American Presbyterians and Congregationalists. Compared to other missionaries, Brainerd was less hostile to the particular cultural habits of Native Americans, though he did feel, with almost all of his white contemporaries, that converted Native Americans would naturally rise to higher levels of civilization. He put it this way: "we do not despite them for their color, but for their heathenish temper and practices. . . . When they become Christians, and behave as such, they shall have the same treatment as white people." Unfortunately for Brainerd and the generous handful of his Native-American converts, corrupt local treaties and the English settlers' lust

David Brainerd, a missionary to Native Americans throughout New England, is perhaps best known for his diary, edited and published by Jonathan Edwards. Brainerd's career was brief: he died of tuberculosis on October 4, 1747, at the age of twenty-nine. *Courtesy of the Billy Graham Center Museum*

for land repeatedly disrupted his Christian settlements. Despite good intentions and a genuine boost of concern for Native Americans from the Great Awakening, the result was another failed opportunity to communicate the universal promise of the gospel.

The Awakening also stimulated evangelism among slaves. Gilbert Tennent (1703-1764), a Presbyterian from New Jersey, was delighted during a preaching tour in Massachusetts that "multitudes were awakened, and several had received great consolation, especially among the young people, children and Negroes." Tennent's Presbyterian colleague Samuel Davies (1723-1761) took an especially earnest interest in blacks during his itinerations in Virginia. As a pioneering preacher to several Presbyterian congregations in Hanover County, Virginia, in the late 1740s, he took time to preach specifically to slaves. Many of his hymns, like the one quoted at the start of the chapter, were written expressly for his work among African Americans. And Davies was always eager to invite converted blacks to share in regular church observances, including those that featured the celebration of the Lord's Supper. He wrote in 1757, "what little success I have lately had, has

Samuel Davies was the first great non-Anglican church leader in Virginia. A notable hymn-writer and diligent evangelist among slaves as well as a faithful Presbyterian itinerant, Davies died while serving as president of the College of New Jersey, which later became Princeton University. *Courtesy of the Billy Graham Center Museum*

been chiefly among the extremes of Gentlemen and Negroes. Indeed, God has been remarkably working among the latter. I have baptized about 150 adults; and at the last sacramental solemnity, I had the pleasure of seeing the table *graced* with about 60 black faces." Whitefield also made an effort to preach to black slaves, but among the first generation of leading revivalists, little attention was paid to the institution of slavery itself.

The period of the Awakening had great significance with respect to the status of African Americans, because it was under the impulse of the revival that the chasm between white and black cultures was breached. The revival message of personal experience with God was a message that not only resonated with the American experiences of blacks but also echoed aspects of African religions. Especially in the Calvinist overtones of the major revivalists of the period, slaves heard the message that only God's grace mattered. Social standing, the possession or absence of wealth, the ability to exercise power over others, or abject dependence upon a master — these issues were all irrelevant to the promise of forgiven sins. In the absence of their own testimony, it is not always clear exactly what the first black converts heard from the revivalists. Samuel Davies's advice to blacks inquiring about the gospel indicates, however, that experiential elements predominated over the social or the institutional: "you will say perhaps 'other negroes are baptized; and why not I?' But, consider some other negroes have been in

The revival message of a personal experience with God resonated with blacks in both the North and South, as can be seen in this free blacks' prayer meeting in the pre–Civil War North. *Courtesy of the Billy Graham Center Museum*

great trouble for their souls; their hearts have been broken for sin; they have accepted Christ as their only Saviour; and are Christians indeed; and when you are such, it will be time enough for you to be baptized."

In this era of intensified revivalism, churches organized by and for blacks gradually made their appearance. The formation of black churches was beset with every kind of social prejudice and legal disadvantage, but emerge they did. Perhaps as early as 1758, white followers of Shubal Stearns helped slaves on the plantation of William Byrd III on the Blackstone River in Virginia establish a more formal fellowship for their own worship. The honor for the first continuing black church is usually given to the Silver Bluff Church in Aiken County, South Carolina, where around 1773 or 1774 an African-American preacher, David George, established a congregation. This body was ministered to by other black leaders until 1791, when Jesse Peter led the congregation to nearby Augusta, Georgia, and it was incorporated as the Springfield Baptist Church. The significance of such preliminary moves was profound. From the religion of the slaveholders itself, slaves were discovering a faith that, in the midst of involuntary servitude, gave a measure of purpose to their lives.

Longer ranging currents from the revivals eventually did make an impact, if only for a brief period, on white toleration of slavery. When some of the younger followers of Jonathan Edwards became pastors, they began to apply insights of their teacher more broadly. In particular, they expanded ideas from the revival about the essential dignity of all created beings stemming from the fact that they shared the "Being" of their Creator. This theme was developed from the ideas in Edwards's *Nature of True Virtue,* even though Edwards himself had never thought to apply them to human bondage and had himself actually kept a household slave. With such notions, a distinct movement of social reform grew from the Awakening.

Samuel Hopkins (1721-1803), who had studied personally with Edwards, eventually became troubled about the existence of slavery in America. By the time of the Revolution, Hopkins was a minister in Newport, Rhode Island, where he had a chance to view the slave trade firsthand. Increasingly, he came to feel that slavery violated the essential "being" of the kidnaped Africans and that the practice of slave trading made a mockery of Christian efforts to spread the gospel among Africans. In 1776 he published a pamphlet which he sent to all members of the Continental Congress. How could the Congress complain about "enslavement" to Parliament when it so casually overlooked the real slavery imposed upon hundreds of thousands of blacks in the colonies? Hopkins further asked his readers to "behold the *sons of liberty,* oppressing and tyrannizing over many thousands of poor blacks, who have as good a claim to liberty as themselves." In this attack on slavery Hopkins was joined by other followers of Edwards, including Levi Hart in Connecticut, Jacob Green in New Jersey, and Edwards's own son, Jonathan, Jr., who was also a minister in Connecticut.

At least some blacks also sensed a connection between the liberation from sin proclaimed by the awakeners and a human dignity to be found even in the yoke of bondage. When George Whitefield died, one of many published memorials came from the pen of Phillis Wheatley (1753?-1784), who had been born a slave but had been emancipated by the Boston family that had originally purchased her. She eventually became America's first published black poet, and her first published poem was the memorial to Whitefield. It was in many ways a conventional effort, but it also went out of its way to note the hope that Whitefield's message had brought to African Americans:

> . . . Thou didst in strains of eloquence refin'd
> Inflame the heart and captivate the mind. . . .
> The greatest gift that ev'n a God can give,
> He freely offer'd to the num'rous throng,
> That on his lips with list'ning pleasure hung. . . .
> "Take him, ye Africans, he longs for you,
> Impartial Saviour is his title due;
> Washed in the fountain of redeeming blood,
> You shall be sons and kings, and Priests to God."

Phillis Wheatley (1753?-1784), a freed slave, was America's most famous black poet of the eighteenth century. *Courtesy of the Billy Graham Center Museum*

Revival did not mean the end of slavery, but it did serve to direct new attention to the spiritual lives of African Americans. And that attention, as so often in the history of Christianity, had far-reaching consequences the revivalists did not foresee.

The Awakening and America

The series of local revivals known collectively as the Great Awakening stimulated considerable renewal in the American churches. To be sure, revivals did not halt the general trend of secularization in colonial society, a trend that accelerated with great loss to the churches during the trying days of the 1770s and 1780s. Yet they provided new energy, new recruits, new concern for preaching to the unconverted, and new impetus for dealing with marginalized members of society.

The revivals, along with the general turn to a more pietistic religion, also had a significant effect on American society more generally. The Awakening, for instance, was America's first truly national event. Whitefield and his exploits were common matters of discussion in every British colony. Ministers throughout North America corresponded with each other to en-

The mature Gilbert Tennent, as shown in this portrait, had become a benevolent champion of evangelical Presbyterianism. Earlier in his career, however, he was as fiery a gospel preacher as the Presbyterians possessed in promoting revival in the middle colonies. *Courtesy of the Billy Graham Center Museum*

courage revival. On the other side, ministers opposed to revivalistic "enthusiasm," such as Charles Chauncy of Boston, also gathered information from a wide network to bring the movement into discredit. The end result was the same: events with a local significance were transformed into events linking larger and larger sections of the continent.

The revivals also served as something of a melting pot, giving immigrant communities more contact with other colonists. The career of Gilbert Tennent, whom we have already met as an awakener from a prominent Presbyterian family, shows how the revival joined different groups together. Tennent was born in northern Ireland of Scottish descent, he was schooled by his own father in upstate New York, his Presbyterian congregation in New Jersey included some settlers from New England, his preaching tours took him as far away as Piscataqua, Maine, and Hanover County, Virginia, and Tennent's own understanding of Christianity was influenced by Theodore Frelinghuysen (a German-born, Dutch-educated minister pastoring a church of immigrants from the Netherlands in New Jersey). The process that would lead to European immigrants identifying themselves as "Americans" had begun.

The other side of the process that led colonists to identify themselves as "Americans" was an increase in general suspicions about Europe. During the Awakening and after, religious leaders among Dutch, Scottish, and German immigrants came into conflict with European leaders who did not grasp the dynamics of North American piety. As might be expected, tensions were strongest with respect to the Church of England, already suspect for its close ties with crown officials. After the Awakening, Anglicans were the object of even more suspicion because of their indifference to revivals. And when it was again suggested that a bishop should be sent to the colonies, many North Americans were distressed at the prospect of losing the religious freedoms that the revivals had won. Such resentment had more than casual implications when political tensions rose between the colonists and Parliament. Suspicion of the Church of England fueled the larger distrust of England.

The Great Awakening also gave more energy to such already powerful terms as *liberty, virtue,* and *tyranny* that were most often applied to spiritual realities during the 1740s and 1750s. In addition, when revivalists spoke of the millennium, they mostly had in mind the spread of personal liberation as a result of the spread of Christianity, but the time was soon to come when, for example, Gilbert Tennent's appeal to seek "everlasting Liberty" from "Bondage and Servitude" would assume a different shading. It was far easier, when the tyrant on the horizon was Parliament rather than sin, to make fruitful use of the capital that these terms had acquired in the revivals.

Perhaps most important for later American history, however, was the new model of leadership that emerged during the mid-century revivals. The Awakening was sustained by traveling evangelists; they encouraged laypeople to perform religious duties for themselves and not to rely on an elite clergy or magistrates. Whitefield did not read his sermons like so many ministers of his century but rather spoke directly to the audience. His style drove home the message that it was not formal education or prestige in society that mattered most but the choice of the individual for or against God. Whitefield seems not to have thought about the political implications of such a style, but his form of public speaking, and the implicit message of his ministry moved in a democratic direction. And as a symbol for a new form of piety, Whitefield also became an agent for new forms of social order. His ministry represented the strongest possible demonstration of a new confidence in the religious powers of the people. Whitefield was a Calvinist who did not believe in a natural human capacity to choose God. But he did believe that God's grace made it possible for even the humblest individual to take a place alongside the greatest of the saints. He always remained an Anglican, and yet he paid very little attention to ecclesiastical structures. This spirit — incorporating both a frank expression of popular democracy and the sharpest attack yet on inherited privilege in colonial America — had much to do with the rise of a similar spirit in politics later on.

In light of such connections, one of the most bizarre incidents of the

Revolutionary period begins to make more sense. In 1775, colonial troops were mustered near Newburyport, Massachusetts, in preparation for an expedition to Canada. The hope was that a show of force to the north would draw Canadians into the struggle for independence from Britain. Before the troops set out, however, they paused for a sermon from a young chaplain, the Reverend Samuel Spring. After the message, Spring and some of the officers visited a nearby crypt. It was the tomb of George Whitefield, who had died in Newburyport only five years earlier. Together the minister and officers pried open the coffin and removed the clerical collar and wrist bands from the revivalist's skeleton. Somehow it was thought that the spirit of America's greatest preacher of spiritual freedom would assist them in this struggle for political freedom. Whatever powers the living Whitefield enjoyed, his relics did not work. The expedition ultimately failed. For reasons discussed in Chapter 5, the Canadians were not impressed.

Further Reading

Bonomi, Patricia U. *Under the Cope of Heaven: Religion, Society, and Politics in Colonial America.* New York: Oxford University Press, 1986.

Bowden, Henry Warner. *American Indians and Christian Missions: Studies in Cultural Conflict.* Chicago: University of Chicago Press, 1981.

Bumsted, J. M., and John E. Van de Wetering. *What Must I Do to Be Saved? The Great Awakening in Colonial America.* Hinsdale, IL: Dryden, 1976.

Butler, Jon. *Awash in a Sea of Faith: Christianizing the American People.* Cambridge: Harvard University Press, 1990.

Crawford, Michael J. "The Spiritual Travels of Nathan Cole." *William and Mary Quarterly* 33 (1976): 89-126.

Gaustad, Edwin S. *The Great Awakening in New England.* New York: Harper, 1957.

Hatch, Nathan O., and Harry S. Stout, eds. *Jonathan Edwards and the American Experience.* New York: Oxford University Press, 1988.

Isaac, Rhys. "Evangelical Revolt: The Nature of the Baptists' Challenge to the Traditional Order in Virginia, 1765 to 1775." *William and Mary Quarterly* 31 (July 1974): 345-68.

Murray, Iain. *Jonathan Edwards: A New Biography.* Edinburgh: Banner of Truth, 1987.

Sobel, Mechal. *Trabelin' On: The Slave Journey to an Afro-Baptist Faith.* Westport, CT: Greenwood, 1979.

Stout, Harry S. *The Divine Dramatist: George Whitefield and the Rise of Modern Evangelicalism.* Grand Rapids: William B. Eerdmans, 1991.

CHAPTER 5

The Churches in the Revolution

Independence

The states, O Lord, with songs of praise
    shall in Thy strength rejoice.
And blest with Thy salvation
    raise to Heav'n their cheerful voice. . . .
No King but God.
To the King they shall sing Hallelujah.
And the continent shall sing:
    God is our rightful King, Hallelujah.
And the continent shall sing:
    God is our gracious King, Hallelujah. . . .
May American wilds be filled with his smiles
and may the native bow to our royal King.
May Rome, France and Spain and all the world proclaim
The glory and the fame of our royal King.
God is the King. Amen.

In times of social excitement, hymn writers often compose music to fit the occasion. So it was during the American Revolution. This text was written by William Billings, New England's first recognized musician, and was published in 1778. Thankfully, such lyrics do not usually survive in the churches.

CHRISTIAN VALUES PLAYED A CENTRAL PART IN THE TUMULTUOUS EVENTS of the Revolutionary period. Many believers promoted the movement for independence from Great Britain in the 1770s, and they also rendered great service to the patriot cause during the Revolutionary War itself. From the other side, Christian reasoning was central for many Loyalists who rejected patriotic arguments and who were often banished from the thirteen new states for their views. Christian principles were also the key to the witness of America's considerable minority of pacifists, who felt that all who fought in the War for Independence, on whatever side, were making a mistake. Between the end of actual fighting in the early 1780s and the reorganization of government under the Constitution at the end of that decade, Christian leaders in the United States commented less directly on public affairs. Yet they did attempt to put the momentous events of the age in moral and religious perspective in this period. The Revolutionary era was a great turning point in American history, and also for the churches. In Canada, where independence was rejected at least in part for religious reasons, the impact of the Revolution was hardly less.

The Christian Patriots

Before and during the Revolutionary War, Christian faith played a political role for patriots on two levels. It contributed to the content of the period's dominant political ideology, and it was also a significant force in the actual outworking of the war. Most significant in this regard was the relationship between the Puritan tradition, which was evolving into a uniquely American form of evangelical Protestantism, and the ideology that would justify a break from Britain.

Republicanism

Two crises dominated the political history of this era. The first was a crisis of the British Empire, which was resolved by the American Revolution. The second was a crisis of government in the new United States, which was resolved by the delegates who convened in Philadelphia during the summer of 1787 to write the Constitution. In simplest terms, both crises involved efforts to preserve the virtues of *republican* government.

Christians and the Christian faith played a substantial, if ambiguous, role in the shaping of republicanism. In eighteenth-century Britain and America, republicanism was an ideal rather than a sharply defined system.

It arose among the political theorists of the Italian Renaissance, of whom Machiavelli is the best known. It took on a special British cast during the English civil wars of the seventeenth century. While the Puritan Oliver Cromwell and the armies of Parliament waged war against King Charles I for corrupting and oppressing the English people, philosophers of public life struggled to define how government should support the well-being of society.

In simple terms, the republicanism of this period can be defined as the conviction that the exercise of power defines the political process and that unchecked power leads to corruption even as corruption fosters unchecked power. Furthermore, the arbitrary exercise of unchecked power must by its very nature result in the demise of liberty, law, and natural rights. Republicans, therefore, tended to favor separation of power in government rather than its concentration. They usually held that a good government must mix elements of popular influence, aristocratic tradition, and executive authority rather than be simply democratic, simply aristocratic, or simply monarchical.

The process of the formation of republicanism involved numerous individuals and groups over a long period of time, but Christians contributed their fair share. The Puritans who supported Cromwell and the Scottish Calvinists who agitated for the independence of their Presbyterian Kirk linked republican values with Scripture. They felt that republicanism represented a political recognition of the Bible's realistic teaching about human sinfulness and the ongoing struggle between Christ (who promoted true liberty) and Satan (who represented the worst possible tyranny). Other influences, however, were deistic or agnostic, including some of Britain's "real whigs" of the early eighteenth century, who had given up traditional Christian faith for a religion of nature that had no place for miracles, the Incarnation, or special revelation.

Republicanism was critical for the relation of religion and politics in the Revolutionary era in the sense that the beliefs of American Christians paralleled republican principles in many particulars. This in turn led to the widespread assumption that republican principles expressed Christian values and hence could be defended with Christian fervor.

Together, the republican and the Puritan traditions shared many formal similarities. In the first place, they both held to a view of human nature that recognized the human capacity for evil as well as for good. Puritans dwelt at length on the natural tendency toward evil that arose as a consequence of Adam's fall. Republicans dwelt at length on the natural tendency to abuse official power as a consequence of the corrupting nature of power itself.

116

This Massachusetts broadside, publicizing the 1798 law prohibiting "profane Cursing and Swearing," shows how much of the old Puritan morality remained in the early years of the new American republic. *Courtesy of the Billy Graham Center Museum*

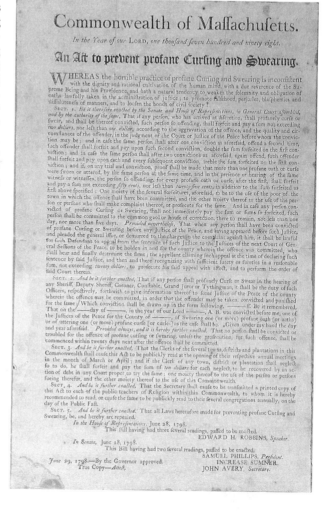

Puritans and republicans also defined virtue, freedom, and social well-being in very similar terms. Both saw virtue primarily as a negative quality: Puritans as the absence of sin, republicans as the absence of corrupt and arbitrary power. Puritans looked on freedom as liberation from sin, republicans as liberation from tyranny. The Puritans defined a good society as one in which sin was vanquished and in which people stood vigilantly on guard against its reappearance. Republicans defined a good society as one in which political freedom from tyranny was preserved and in which citizens resolutely resisted any tendencies toward the corruption of power.

With similar views on virtue, freedom, and social well-being, it is not surprising that republican and Christian points of view began to merge during the Revolution. It was only a small step, for example, to expand concern for the glorious liberty of the children of God into concern for the glorious freedoms imperiled by Parliament.

Republicans and the evangelical heirs of the Puritans also shared a common view of history. Both regarded the record of the past as a cosmic struggle between good and evil. To American Christians good and evil were represented by Christ and anti-Christ; to republicans, by liberty and tyranny. Both republicans and Puritans longed for a new age in which righteousness and freedom would flourish. Both hoped that the Revolution would play a role in bringing such a golden age to pass.

A lively tradition of millennialism also helped to forge a link between political freedom and Christian liberty. Speculation of this sort encouraged the notion that the great conflict between God and Satan was somehow being played out in the struggle with Britain, and that a victory over Parliament might signal the near approach of God's rule on earth, the millennium. During the war, several ministers preached sermons pointing out how closely British oppression resembled the beast described in the thirteenth chapter of Revelation. At least one New Englander thought that America might be the stone from the book of Daniel that strikes "the image of the beast," becomes "a great mountain" filling all the earth, and leads to the time when "discord shall cease, and Tyrants be no more."

This millennial speculation fit comfortably with many shades of theology, from Samuel Hopkins's orthodox Calvinism to the biblical universalism of the Philadelphia minister Elhanan Winchester. It was also embraced by some of those who promoted a more radical restructuring of American society and some who backed a conservative revolution. Throughout the Revolutionary period, millennial speculation usually remained spiritual. Only in the most heated moments did ministers and lay theologians apply their millennial theories directly to political events. Nevertheless, during the Revolution an established tradition of millennialism, hitherto largely apolitical, may have become the most important vehicle for melding evangelical Christianity and republican political theory into the morally charged ideology that fueled the War for Independence. And there is some evidence that later on several varieties of biblical millennialism may have made a more important contribution to the egalitarian ideology of Thomas Jefferson's Democratic-Republican party than is usually thought.

These Christian ideas grew closer toward republican ideals during the French and Indian War (1755-1763) as British colonists rallied against their enemies. To them the French represented the epitome of evil both because they accepted absolute monarchy and because they supported the Roman

Catholic Church. After that conflict, when the British Parliament began to tighten its control of the colonies, a shift in interpretation occurred. Tyranny promoted by Parliament and the Church of England replaced the tyranny represented by France and Roman Catholicism as the great terror in many colonial eyes. Republicanism and this variety of evangelicalism became virtually inextricable as the crisis with the British Parliament grew more intense.

Contributions to the Cause

During the actual conflict with Britain, Christian political action played a leading role in the achievement of independence. On the most general level, a broadly Puritan ethic set the tone for the patriots' political exertions. In the Puritan heritage, patriots found a seriousness about the vocation of "public servants," individuals who sacrificed private gain for the public good. The same source provided an example of perseverance in the face of adversity — just as the earliest American settlers had continued to work hard and trust God when their enterprise was threatened by the forces of nature, so too patriots could labor on and pray when the tide of battle ran against them. Similarly, the Puritan link between personal virtue, the exercise of frugality, and the enjoyment of liberty served as a model for how the same qualities could be joined together in an independent United States. On this level, Christian values shaped political behavior quite generally, but still with telling effect.

Other strands of Christian influence also served to justify the patriot cause. In the middle colonies, ministers of the various Reformed churches (Dutch, German, Presbyterian) drew during the crisis on a theological tradition stretching back to the Reformation and into the Middle Ages. It was a tradition occupied with questions about the application of natural law, the Bible's commentary on equity, and the proper criteria for a just war. In these terms a case could be made that British impositions had created a situation in which it was just to act in self-defense. During the War itself, some of these Reformed voices from the middle colonies also took up the theme of a "chosen nation" more common in New England. But the fact that they were also employing another strand of theological reasoning suggests something about the fluidity of religious patriotism.

Despite these contributions from the middle colonies, the tone of Revolutionary Christian patriotism was set further to the north. New England preachers had long stressed the special relationship between God and that region. As war approached, many of them cast the conflict with Great

Britain in cosmic terms. God had called his people to religious and political freedom in the New World; certainly he would now sustain them as they fought off the tyrannical imposition by Parliament. New England was the scene of the sharpest early tensions with Britain. Boston patriots led in resisting parliamentary efforts to sustain a tax on tea (the Boston Tea Party), and the first actual battles of the War took place in Massachusetts (Lexington and Concord, Bunker Hill). It was thus of great significance for the whole American effort against Great Britain that a long New England tradition had recognized God as the Lord of Battles actively intervening on behalf of his people.

Sermons encouraging a defense of political liberty, however, were by no means restricted to New England. Presbyterians in New Jersey and the South preached a similar message, as did representatives of the Baptists and other smaller denominations. Even some clergymen of the Church of England, contradicting the official allegiance of their denomination, denounced the grasp of Parliament. One of the most notable of these patriotic sermons was the effort by Presbyterian John Witherspoon at Princeton on May 17, 1776. Witherspoon had emigrated from Scotland eight years before to become the president of the College of New Jersey (later Princeton University). Now he was calling on especially his fellow Scottish immigrants to realize that the time to choose had come. The title of the sermon was "The Dominion of Providence over the Passions of Men." Its twin themes were the propriety of resisting unjust tyranny and the necessity of believing that God could bring good out of the evil situation of the day: "the ambition of mistaken princes, the cunning and cruelty of oppressive and corrupt [parliamentary] ministers, and even the inhumanity of brutal soldiers, however dreadful, shall finally promote the glory of God, and in the meantime, while the storm continues, his mercy and kindness shall appear in prescribing bounds to their rage and fury." Less than two months after preaching this sermon, Witherspoon, as a delegate from New Jersey, became the only clergyman to sign the Declaration of Independence.

In general, the services of believers to the patriot cause were great and multiform. Ministers preached rousing sermons to militia bands as they met for training or embarked for the field. Many ministers served as chaplains. Ministers joined Christian laymen on the informal committees of correspondence that preceded the formation of the new state governments. Other ministers served gladly as traveling agents of the new governments who wanted them to win over settlers in outlying areas to the support of the patriot cause. Throughout the conflict, common soldiers were urged to their duty by the repeated assertion that Britain was violating divine standards.

Surprisingly enough, the patriot cause also received support from the

Many Congregational, Presbyterian, and Baptist pulpits became rallying points for patriotism during the American War for Independence. *Courtesy of the Billy Graham Center Museum*

small Catholic community in the English-speaking colonies. Such support was surprising because of the hostility toward Roman Catholicism that was everywhere present in the colonies. One of the leaders of a prominent Catholic family in Maryland, Charles Carroll, was reminded in 1773 of how thoroughly the deck was stacked against Catholics in British America. In a newspaper exchange with the loyalist Daniel Dulany, Jr., Carroll defended the rights of Americans that then seemed threatened by Parliament. For his pains, Carroll was reminded that "he is disabled from giving a vote in the choice of representatives, by the laws and constitution of the country, *on account of his* [religious] *principles,* which are *distrusted* by those laws. . . . He is not a Protestant." Yet Carroll steadfastly stuck to his convictions. He eventually signed the Declaration and during the war served his state and new national government in several important posts. In Carroll's mind, current laws against Catholics were not most important; he invested in the hope of a better day to come. "When I signed the Declaration of Independence," he wrote, "I had in view not only our independence of England but the toleration of all sects, professing the Christian religion, and communicating to them all great rights." In Quebec, Catholic sentiment was different,

121

as Carroll discovered when he accepted an appointment to serve on a committee charged with drawing French Canada to the side of the patriots. But for most Catholics in the colonies, the prospect of independence promised more good than harm.

The direct political activity of Christians had important consequences. Opponents recognized the importance of the Christian element immediately. A Hessian captain in Pennsylvania wrote, "call this war ... by whatever name you may, only call it not an American Rebellion, it is nothing more or less than an Irish-Scotch Presbyterian Rebellion." Joseph Galloway, a moderate opponent of Parliament who eventually chose loyalty to Great Britain over colonial Independence, wrote that the colonial insurrection was led by "Congregationalists, Presbyterians, and Smugglers." From the patriot side the connotations were different, but the message was largely the same.

Loyalists

Not all Christians in America supported the push toward independence so completely, or even supported it at all. A substantial number remained loyal to Great Britain. Because of independent developments in Canada, there was a notable lack of enthusiasm for Independence north of the border as well.

Somewhere between a fifth and a third of the residents in the thirteen colonies either remained loyal to Great Britain during the Revolution or harbored loyalist sentiments of some sort. Among these were many individuals who felt a religious duty to remain faithful to the mother country. The most visible spokesmen for a Christian loyalism were members of the Church of England, but at least a few loyalists could also be found among Congregationalists, Presbyterians, and Baptists (mostly cultural conservatives who thought the Revolution would drift into anarchy) and Roman Catholics (who, unlike Charles Carroll, were grateful for the benign neglect they enjoyed in Britain's American colonies).

Loyalist arguments sometimes stressed a different understanding of the Bible than that found among patriots. Jonathan Boucher, an Anglican minister in Maryland, for example, preached a sermon in 1775 entitled "On Civil Liberty, Passive Obedience, and Nonresistance." His text was Galatians 5:1, which speaks of "the liberty wherewith Christ hath made us free." Boucher denied that this verse justified political self-determination, arguing instead that the New Testament teaches clearly that "obedience to Government is every man's duty. . . . It is enjoined by the positive commands of God." Other Anglican loyalists worried more generally about what would happen to religious life and the orders of society supported by religion if the Revolution should prevail. Miles Cooper, the president of King's College (later Columbia University), expressed such a sentiment after the fighting had begun: "when once [the people] conceive the governed to be superior to the Governors and that they may set up their pretended Natural Rights in Opposition to the positive law of the state, they will naturally proceed to despise dominion and speak evil of dignities and to open a door for Anarchy, confusion, and every evil work to enter." Such loyalists as Boucher and Cooper likely shared certain republican fears about the accumulation of power, but they also valued an organic relationship among all elements in society as well as a respectful attitude toward properly constituted government. In the crucible of the Revolution, the latter values prevailed over the former for the loyalists.

Canadian Loyalism: Quebec

Canadians, who would be greatly influenced by the emigration of loyalists from the United States, had their own reasons for rejecting the patriotic appeal. When the French ceded Quebec to Britain by treaty in 1763, 196 priests were serving the province's 60,000 residents, almost all of whom were Roman Catholic. Because of continuing tensions between France and England, the supply of priests from overseas was greatly restricted. Otherwise, however, Quebec adjusted harmoniously to its new Protestant rulers. Britain's official policy after the Treaty of Paris in 1763 was to anglicize the French Canadians, including their religion. But in practice, successive governors allowed the Catholic Church to go its own way, realizing that anglicization simply was not realistically possible. A series of delicate negotiations involving Quebec's senior clergy, the British governor, and the papacy was required to secure the appointment of the first bishop under British rule. This bishop, Jean-Olivier Briand, whose consecration finally took place in March 1766, turned out to be an effective guide to his Catholic parishioners and an irenic conciliator with the British. Thus, despite its anomalous status as a Roman Catholic enclave in the antipapist British Empire, Quebec maintained its course.

Britain's accommodating spirit toward its new colony became controversial when Parliament passed the Quebec Act in 1774. This legislation gave up the pretense of anglicization and formally bestowed a number of rights and privileges on the Catholic Church. It was given clear title to its hereditary land, it was granted the right to tithe its members, and French civil law was recognized as the legal procedure of the colony (though at the same time English criminal law was instituted). Most remarkably, Catholic citizens re-

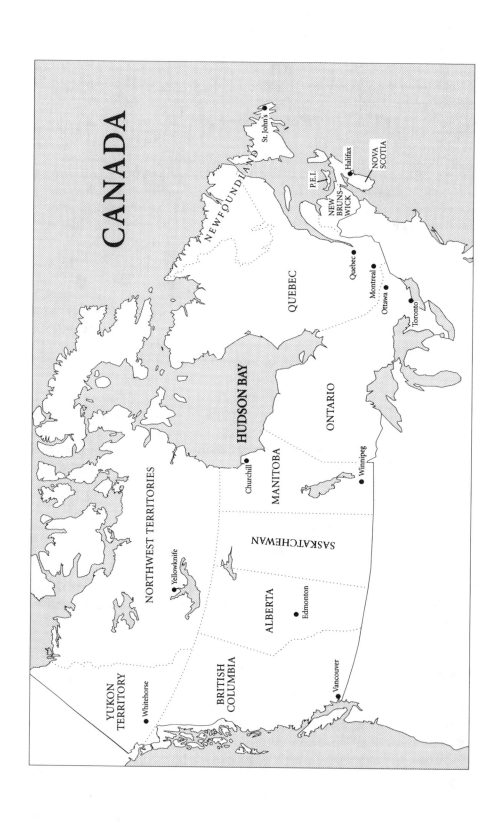

Paul Revere produced this engraving satirizing Britain's Quebec Act for the *Royal American Magazine* in 1774. The implication is that the mother country intended to establish Anglican (or even Catholic) bishops as a way of dominating the colonies.

ceived full civil rights — fifty-five years before their fellow religionists in Britain received a similar dispensation. In the colonies to the south, where ardent anti-Catholicism flourished, these measures seemed to prove that Britain was eager to promote tyranny, since nothing was more obvious to America's strictest Protestants than that the Catholic Church was a foe of liberty. Given these sentiments in the thirteen colonies, it is little wonder that Quebec looked very coolly on the suggestion by the Continental Congress that it join the Revolution against Britain. Nor was it odd, given the tension over the Quebec Act, that the French Canadian colony would open its doors to American loyalists who felt compelled to leave the new United States.

During 1775 the rebellious American colonies launched a two-pronged attack on Quebec. In response to these invasions, a few British merchants from Montreal who had been offended by the liberal provisions of the Quebec Act went over to support the invaders. A handful of French *habitants* disgruntled with their superiors also joined the American cause, but they were significantly outmatched by the Quebec citizens who took up arms to assist the British garrison. Most *Québecois,* however, remained neutral. But the same could not be said of their religious leaders, who, guided by Bishop Briand, lined up solidly behind the British. George Washington had issued a proclamation to Quebec in 1775 in which he claimed that God was smiling "upon the virtuous efforts" of the rebels, so that "the hand of tyranny has been arrested in its

Bishop Briand rallied support among the clergy in Quebec for the British during the American attack on Quebec in 1775. *National Archives of Canada*

ravages." But Bishop Briand, who insisted that aid to the *bostonnais*, as he called the rebel forces advancing from New England, was heresy. Also in 1775, he reminded Quebec's Catholics about "the remarkable goodness and gentleness with which we have been governed by his very gracious Majesty, King George the Third . . . [and] the recent favours with which he has loaded us, in restoring to us the use of our laws and the free exercise of our religion." The conclusion, to Briand, was obvious: "your oaths, your religion, lay upon you the unavoidable duty of defending your country and your King with all the strength you possess." Later Briand instructed his clergy to refuse the sacraments to Canadians who supported the Americans.

The result was the continuation of British rule over French Canada and the preservation of an increasingly well-entrenched Catholic culture. Quebec's response to the American Revolution was also a harbinger of what would come when France rose in revolution short years later. As Quebec had rejected the democratic republicanism of the American Revolution, so too would it reject the free-thinking nationalism of the Revolution in France.

Canadian Loyalism: The Maritimes

Prospects for American patriotism seemed considerably better in the Maritimes than in Quebec. A majority of the residents in the 1760s were immi-

Halifax, Nova Scotia, was still a new city when this drawing was made in the 1760s or 1770s, but already its loyalty to King George III and its government's support for churches had set it upon a "Canadian" pattern of religious life different from what would be pursued in the United States. *The Public Archives of Nova Scotia*

grants from New England, and most of them shared the Puritan or evangelical convictions that were merging so easily with republican patriotism. But like the situation in Quebec, religion proved to be a decisive factor in the rejection of independence. (To be sure, it was not the only factor. The large British fortress in Halifax as well as a history of antagonism against New England privateers helped to keep the Maritime population, which had reached barely 15,000 by 1770, on the side of the British.)

The religious factor in the revolutionary situation was sparked by the conversion of a talented but troubled person, Henry Alline (1748-1784). Alline had been born in Newport, Rhode Island, but at age twelve came to Falmouth, Nova Scotia, with his parents. After several years of religious seeking and near-mystical experiences, he underwent a powerful conversion in March 1775. Soon thereafter he began to preach the new birth wherever he could gather a crowd. In a sense, Alline was extending the revivalism of George Whitefield, since he too stressed the power of Christ's death to reconcile women and men to God (see the hymn quoted at the start of Chap. 4). In another way, however, Alline represented a departure from Whitefield, since he was aggressively anti-Calvinistic. Even more relevant to the 1770s, the revived Christian faith he experienced and preached was strongly apolitical. (From the time of the French and Indian War, Whitefield, by contrast, had regularly added anti-French, anti-Catholic, and antityrannical themes to his sermons.)

To a people torn by doubts about the war and still insecure as recent immigrants in an outpost of empire, Alline's message was a tonic. From 1776 to 1783 he preached to responsive audiences in most of Nova Scotia's communities. (In 1784 Alline died of tuberculosis shortly after beginning a preaching tour in New Hampshire.) Alline's message seems to have been one of the factors that predisposed Nova Scotians to political neutrality. In the first instance the War was a distraction. When Alline was offered a militia commission in 1775, he replied that he had "a Commission from Heaven to go forth and enlist my fellow mortals to fight under the banner of King Jesus." The thought of warfare may also have violated the mystical ethics that flowed from Alline's work. Though not a systematic thinker, Alline nonetheless called for highest expressions of concern for the downtrodden and neglected, and these are attitudes that might have disposed him against war in general. The Nova Scotia revival also provided an outlet for more democratic self-assertion from the insecure settlers in the Maritimes. They may have viewed the pursuit of "New Light" Christian faith as their own Declaration of Independence. For whatever combination of spiritual, psychological, and cultural reasons, the revival promoted by Henry Alline helped make citizens of the Atlantic region unwilling to join the side of the American patriots.

The War did, however, eventually bring dramatic changes to the churches of the Maritimes. As a result of antagonism in the newly independent states, about 35,000 loyalists moved to Halifax and the surrounding regions, tripling the population in one fell swoop and cementing a loyalty toward the mother country. Shortly after the War, churches that had been gathered around Alline's type of New Light Baptist faith moved into more conventional Baptist circles or were absorbed by the surge of Methodist preaching in the colony. Methodist itinerants such as William Black, from Yorkshire in England, and Freeborn Garrettson, from what had become the United States, effectively planted the seeds for what would become become a powerful Methodist movement. The community of Presbyterians also increased in size and confidence.

Finally, with the coming of the loyalists, it could only be expected that the Church of England would also be strengthened. After the great loyalist immigration, the British Parliament divided the region into three separate colonies. Most of the loyalists were situated in New Brunswick, to the east toward Quebec. Cape Breton Island became a separate colony. In Nova

Henry Alline was called "the Whitefield of Nova Scotia." Like Whitefield's ministry, Alline's preaching affected the whole tenor of society, as well as the individuals who heeded his message. Shown here is the title page of a posthumously published collection of his hymns. *Courtesy of the Billy Graham Center Museum*

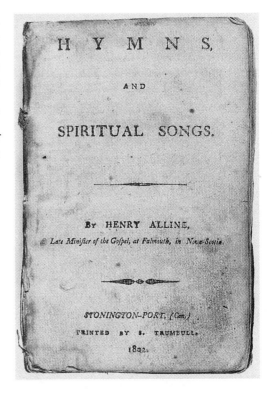

HYMNS,

AND

SPIRITUAL SONGS.

By HENRY ALLINE,
Late Minister of the Gospel, at Falmouth, in Nova-Scotia.

STONINGTON-PORT, *(Con.)*
PRINTED BY S. TRUMBULL.
1802.

Scotia, official sentiment for Anglicanism ran high. The first meeting of the Nova Scotia legislature formally established the Church of England, even though the plurality of Protestant bodies already present prevented a re-creation of the English situation. Irish-born Charles Inglis had been rector of Trinity Church in New York City and a feisty opponent of American independence. After patriots burned his church in 1777, Inglis moved to London, where he spoke before the government on behalf of the American loyalists. In 1786 Inglis was named Anglican bishop in British North America, the first colonial bishop in the Church of England. Inglis's rhetoric continued to be sharp, as when he lamented the damage done to traditional faith by "these times of Democratic rage and delusion." But he proved to be an accommodating negotiator with other Christian leaders as well as a strong leader for the Anglicans.

Protestantism in the Maritimes, in short, had been born within an American context, but the influence of Alline's New Light revival, the rejection of Independence, and the massive influx of loyalists left Canada's Atlantic region with a heritage neither entirely British nor entirely American. The Maritimes resembled the new United States with their plurality of Protestant denominations, but they also resembled the old country with their fidelity to the crown and British traditions. In other words, a "third way" had been established, a path for Canadian churches lying between the traditionalism of the Old World and the innovations of the New.

Canadian Loyalism: Upper Canada

Quebec also received a number of loyalist refugees as the War for Independence drew to a close. Most of these settled in the eastern part of the province along the St. Lawrence River and to the north of the Great Lakes. Religious factors played a smaller role in this migration and the establishment of English-language communities in what had formerly been a largely French-speaking region. But almost as soon as these loyalists arrived, they became dissatisfied with the French and Catholic conventions of Quebec and so petitioned Parliament for the rights, legislatures, and religious freedoms of Englishmen. The result was a Constitutional Act that was implemented in 1791. It divided Quebec into Lower Canada (largely French and Catholic) and Upper Canada (largely English and Protestant), roughly corresponding to modern Ontario. In the establishment of English government in Upper Canada, provision was made for state support of religion and for the designation of tracts of land for that support (later called the Clergy Reserves). Although the terms of these provisions were vague enough to be a source of nearly endless contention among Protestants for half a century, they testified to a determined opposition to patterns taking shape in the new United States. Part of loyalism in Upper Canada, as also in the Maritimes, was the belief that the institutions of the church had an official public role to play in a responsible civilization. For these Canadians, freedom was meant to protect traditional values as well as to provide for individual opportunity. The sharp separation of church and state was an American, but never a Canadian, principle. This circumstance, the ramifications of which expanded through the decades, turned out to be one of the main differences dividing those who held that God ordained the American Revolution from those who felt he had not.

Pacifists

The several groups of Christian pacifists in the colonies joined the loyalists in questioning the American recourse to arms but went beyond them to criticize all use of military force. The most vocal pacifists during the War

Christopher Sauer (or Sower) was the leading German-language printer in colonial America. His press brought out the first European-language Bible printed in the British colonies (it was Martin Luther's German translation, the title page of which is shown here). During the Revolutionary War, Sauer's press was destroyed by patriots because he insisted on printing pamphlets by Loyalists as well as the Patriots. *From the collection of Charles W. Turner, BMH Books*

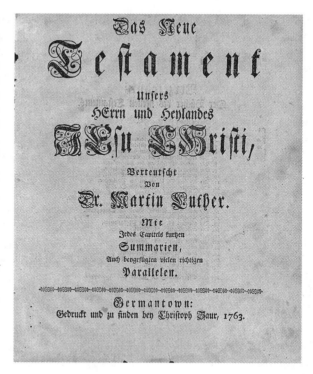

were Quakers, but their sentiments were shared by Mennonites, Moravians, Schwenckfelders, members of the Church of the Brethren, and a few early Methodists. Where pacifists lived in fairly large communities with each other, they were usually able to work out some kind of peaceful agreement with the new patriotic authorities to avoid military service. But where pacifists were isolated and where they refused to submit payment in lieu of military duty, they were sometimes forced to pay large fines or forfeit their property. Despite unfriendly treatment from both loyalists and patriots, pacifists several times offered notable service to prisoners, to soldiers wounded in battle, and to refugees from the fighting. In 1783, for example, three Mennonite farmers near Lancaster, Pennsylvania, gave food and temporary shelter to several escaped British prisoners. For feeding the hungry and giving the thirsty drink, they were fined and sentenced to lengthy terms in prison. It took an appeal to General Washington to effect a suspension of the prison sentence and a reduction of the fines. Earlier, patriots in Pennsylvania had taken other kinds of similarly aggressive actions against that state's large pacifist population. In 1777, the printing press of Christopher Sauer, Jr., a member of the Church of the Brethren who served most of Pennsylvania's German communities, was destroyed by patriots. Sauer had courageously continued to print pacifist tracts even after local authorities expressed their disapproval.

The Philadelphia Quaker Anthony Benezet (1713-1784) was the most outspoken public critic of warfare during the struggle for Independence. In a tract published in 1778, for example, he stated his position with great economy: "[Christ] positively enjoins us, to love our enemies, to bless them that curse us; to do good to those that hate us, and pray for them which despitefully use and persecute us. . . . On the other hand, War requires of its votaries that they kill, destroy, lay waste, and to the utmost of their power distress and annoy, and in every way and manner deprive those they esteem their enemies of support and comfort."

The record of Christian pacifists, like that of the loyalists, is instructive. Large in the mythology of U.S. history is the notion that "God has stood by us." One of the reasons this notion has gained such currency is that little attention has been paid to the voices that opposed the merger of American and Christian values during the Revolutionary period. When they are recovered, these voices offer an instructive Christian alternative to what became the majority opinion. And they remind later listeners that the story of Christianity in America is never just the story of American (or patriotic) Christianity.

The Faith of the Founders

The relationship of Christianity to the founding of the United States goes beyond what the churches did in the Revolution. Also relevant is the question of what Christianity meant to the leading patriots, the men who established the new nation. On this matter, it is important to advance with care. Most of the leading founders were sincerely religious persons. At the same time, the most influential of their number practiced decidedly nontraditional forms of Christianity. In addition, even the more traditional Christians among the founders do not seem to have viewed the crisis with Britain as a cause for special religious reflection. They tended to view it as a political struggle to be adjudicated by natural political axioms, not the special insights of faith.

To be sure, a number of the leading patriots were also well known as Christian leaders. We have noted that the Presbyterian clergyman John Witherspoon and the Catholic layman Charles Carroll signed the Declaration of Independence. Roger Sherman of New Haven, Connecticut, a faithful member of the Congregational church pastored by Jonathan Edwards, Jr.,

This sentimental portrait depicts the first prayer in the U.S. Congress. The year was 1789. *Courtesy of the Billy Graham Center Museum*

was also a signer as well as an influential delegate to the Constitutional Convention. John Jay of New York, the first chief justice of the Supreme Court and an important ambassador of the early United States, and Patrick Henry, famous for his "Liberty or Death" speech before the Virginia House of Burgesses in 1775, were low-church Anglicans whose personal faith could also be characterized as evangelical. And Elias Boudinot of New Jersey, who carried out important civilian tasks for General Washington during the War and who played an important part in the early national legislatures, was a dedicated Presbyterian layman. Boudinot eventually came to devote his entire energy and much of a substantial fortune to the promotion of such Christian causes as the American Bible Society, which he served as its first president. These patriots and a few more like them suggest that faithful believers played no small role in the founding of the new nation.

At the same time, however, the leading founders were much less traditional in their religion. Benjamin Franklin appreciated a good sermon and had an especially warm spot in his heart for George Whitefield, but he viewed Jesus much more as a model from whom we could learn humility than as God's incarnate Son. If humans were to improve, Franklin thought, they would pretty much have to do it on their own. George Washington served faithfully on the vestry of his Anglican parish, but his faith was mostly a social convention. In the words of a recent biographer, Marcus Cunliffe, "he was a Christian as a Virginia planter understood the term. He seems never to have taken communion; he stood to pray, instead of kneeling; and he did not invariably go to church on Sundays."

The religious views of Thomas Jefferson and James Madison are even more unusual, since they combined great respect for faith with extreme distrust of traditional Christianity. As a young man Jefferson (1743-1826) had thrown over his inherited Anglicanism in favor of faith in reason and commitment to liberty. But after the vituperative presidential campaign of 1800, in which his Federalist opponents denounced him as an infidel, Jefferson underwent something of a conversion. This change grew out of his growing conviction that republican government needed a stronger moral fabric than classical ethicists such as Epicurus could provide. And it reflected the influence of a Unitarian friend, Joseph Priestley, who convinced Jefferson that a demythologized Christian morality was superior to the ethics of even the greatest classical philosophers. Thereafter, Jefferson continued to scoff at the notion of a Trinity, to suspect the clergy of being hungry for power, and to stand firm for freedom in religion ("I have sworn upon the altar of God eternal hostility against every form of tyranny over the mind of man"). He still held that the Bible's account of miracles was "a ground work of vulgar ignorance, of things impossible, of superstitions, fanaticisms, and fabrications." Yet he also came to assert "that *I* am a *real Christian,* that is to say, a disciple of the doctrines of Jesus." By this he meant that Jesus' teaching, once shorn of its unreasonable aspects, could light the way to a better humanity. Jefferson praised Jesus as a teacher of monotheism, for his focus on the heart as a wellspring of action, and especially for what he regarded as Jesus' efforts to encourage universal benevolence, "not only to kindred and friends . . . but to all mankind." Jefferson twice prepared private abridgments of the Gospels for his own use, cutting out those stories and sayings he held to be unseemly. His faith was profound, but it was also profoundly heterodox.

James Madison (1751-1836), principal author of the Constitution and Jefferson's successor as president, was always intensely private about his own religion. He was a graduate of John Witherspoon's Princeton College, where he also studied divinity (and other subjects) in an extra postgraduate year with Witherspoon. Madison's first political activity on the eve of the Revolution showed his concern for religious matters: in the face of opposition from Virginia's Anglican planter class, Madison went out of his way to support the granting of civil rights to Baptists. To the end of his days he

James Madison, the fourth president of the United States, joined his colleague and friend Thomas Jefferson in trying to remove the sphere of government from all dealings with churches and formal expressions of Christianity. *Courtesy of the Billy Graham Center Museum*

was an ardent champion of religious liberty. As an old man he offered the opinion that the separation of church and state that took place in Virginia immediately after the War was the best thing that had ever happened to the churches in that state: "We are teaching the world the great truth that Governments do better without Kings and Nobles than with them. The merit will be doubled by the other lesson that Religion flourishes in greater purity, without than with the aid of Government." For himself, Madison seems to have drifted toward the deism that was so prevalent among men of his position in Virginia during the early years of the United States. But his attitude toward faith was always respectful, and he rarely if ever made the kind of disparaging comments about traditional Christianity that pepper the letters of Jefferson. In the words of Madison biographer Ralph Ketcham, "Madison took notes on the meaning of the Scriptures, while Jefferson compiled his own condensation of the New Testament. The difference in method and pretension is significant."

The God of the founding fathers was a kindly deity, more like the God of eighteenth-century deism or nineteenth-century Unitarianism than of the early Puritans or later American revivalists. This God had made the world an orderly and understandable place. He was "nature's God," as the

Declaration of Independence put it, who had created humankind with nearly infinite potential. The men who put the nation together were sincere moralists and great humanitarians. They were entirely convinced that human exertion and goodwill could make America into a nearly ideal place, perhaps even a millennial place. What Daniel Boorstin, a former librarian of Congress, once wrote about Jefferson and his friends applies more generally to most of the founders: they had found in God what they most admired in humanity.

The founders were a noble group. Many of their actions were clearly compatible with traditional Christian values. Others, such as the continuation of racial chattel slavery in a "free" United States, were not.

The Religious Problem of Slavery in the American Revolution

For American blacks, the War for Independence provided scattered moments of opportunity to expand Christian activities and church organization. Events surrounding the first permanent Baptist church for blacks in Silver Bluff, South Carolina, were not typical but did indicate what the upsetting conditions of the War made possible. David George (1742-1810), after having run away from his slave birthplace in Virginia, having served as a servant among Natchez Indians, and having been sold to a plantation on the Savannah River, was converted to Christianity in this new location by another slave, named Cyrus. Soon George began to exhort his fellow slaves and became, in effect, the on-site pastor of the Silver Bluff church. When Britain occupied nearby Savannah in 1778, George's patriot owner abandoned the area. George and most of the congregation moved into Savannah, where he preached for the next three years. When the British abandoned Savannah, George went with them to Nova Scotia, where he helped established a tradition of black Baptist churches that survives to this day. For ten years George labored in Nova Scotia, often against vicious racial antagonism ("they came one night and stood before the pulpit and swore how they would treat me if I preached again"). In 1793 George emigrated with a small company of other blacks to Africa, where he helped found the nation of Sierra Leone and also the first Baptist church to be established in West Africa.

One of George's coworkers at both Silver Bluff and Savannah was George Liele (ca. 1750-1820), the slave of a Baptist deacon named Henry Sharp. After a white minister introduced Liele to Christianity, his master encouraged him to exhort fellow slaves. Before the British occupation of Savannah began, Deacon Sharp, a loyalist, liberated Liele, and Liele joined

David George is shown here leading an open-air meeting in Nova Scotia, thus beginning a tradition of black Baptist churches there like that in South Carolina.
Courtesy of the Black Cultural Center for Nova Scotia

the tide of blacks streaming into Savannah, where they were promised freedom by the British military governor. Like George, Liele left Savannah when the British occupation came to an end, but his destination was Jamaica. In Kingston, Liele established a church that soon flourished, attracting nearly 350 members by 1791. Its members were mostly slaves, but it also included free blacks and a few whites. Liele does not seem to have been an active opponent of slavery as such, but his substantial Jamaica congregation and his wide-ranging connections with Baptists in Nova Scotia and throughout the southern United States made him a formidable leader in the push for African-American religious stability.

Among the last people Liele baptized before leaving Savannah were Hannah and Andrew Bryan (1737-1812). Bryan had been converted while a slave and was then encouraged to exhort by his owner, who thought such

This plantation church was considerably more substantial than many of the sites in which slaves were allowed to worship. *Courtesy of the Billy Graham Center Museum*

preaching would pacify his other slaves. When other black leaders departed with the British, Bryan rapidly became a leader in the Christian African-American community. In 1788, with the cooperation of a white Baptist, Abraham Marshall, and David George's successor in Silver Bluff, Jesse Peters, Bryan was ordained and installed as the organizing minister of the "Ethiopian Church of Jesus Christ" in Savannah (which exists to this day as the First African Baptist Church of Savannah). For slave owners eager to clamp down after the more liberal treatment of the British, exhortation was one thing, but a free-standing church was another. Bryan was continually harassed, and in 1790 he was imprisoned along with about fifty members of his congregation. As their white friend Abraham Marshall reported, "the whites grew more and more inveterate; and taking numbers of them before magistrates — they were imprisoned and whipped . . . particularly *Andrew, who was cut and bled abundantly*. . . . He held up his hand, and told his persecutors that he rejoiced not only to be whipped, but *would freely suffer death for the cause of Jesus Christ.*"

Bryan's master was sympathetic and helped him reestablish the congregation in a barn on his plantation a few miles outside of Savannah. There the work flourished. Bryan was able to purchase his own and his wife's freedom after their master died. By 1800 the congregation numbered seven hundred, and Bryan reported that they enjoyed "the rights of conscience to a valuable extent, worshiping in our families and preaching three times every Lord's-day, baptizing frequently from ten to thirty at a time in the Savannah, and administering the sacred supper, not only without molestation, but in the presence, and with the approbation and encouragement of many of the white people." Soon the Second and Third Baptist churches in Savannah sprang from this work, and when Bryan died the white Baptist association of the city eulogized him as one who had endured "inexpressible persecutions in the cause of his divine Master" to proclaim "a knowledge of the truth as 'it is in Jesus.'"

The Revolution, which white patriots regarded as a struggle for freedom *from* Britain, became for at least a few blacks an occasion for freedom *in* America. The sphere in which that African-American freedom was first and most powerfully exercised was the church.

The Revolution not only created a few new opportunities for blacks but also drew attention to the question of slavery itself. From the very beginning of agitation against Britain, at least a few Christians sensed a great hypocrisy. How was it that so much moral indignation could flow against Britain for the *threat* of "slavery" ostensibly implied by Parliamentary actions (often misguided, even stupid, but rarely malicious), when white Americans calmly continued to enslave hundreds of thousands of black Africans? Founding fathers such as Thomas Jefferson may have been secretly troubled by such a question, but to the extent that a protest existed at this time, it was mounted by religious leaders. The protests against slavery directed by Samuel Hopkins and other followers of Jonathan Edwards at the Continental Congress and then at sessions of the new Congress of the United States were echoed by abolitionist actions from other Christian leaders. Methodists Francis Asbury, James O'Kelly, Freeborn Garrettson, Lorenzo Dow, and William McKendree; Presbyterians Jacob Green and David Rice; Baptist David Barrow; and poet and publicist Thomas Branagan — all these raised their voices against the enslavement of blacks, and all to some degree did so for Christian reasons.

Soon, however, this antislavery agitation began to die down. Economic changes in the South as a result of mechanized processing of cotton, the allure of other pressing projects of reform and evangelism, and the gradual elimination of slavery in the North eventually undercut what had been at least a mildly serious challenge to the slave system arising from the marriage of Revolutionary and Christian values. After Christian abolitionist agitation had begun to die down, two Christian veterans of the Revolutionary struggle paused to regret their part in enshrining slavery in the Constitution. John Jay of New York and Elias Boudinot of New Jersey had both played prominent roles in securing the passage in the Constitution that spoke of the

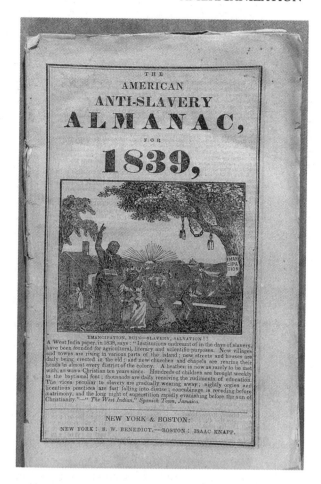

THE AMERICAN ANTI-SLAVERY ALMANAC, FOR 1839,

By 1839 Christian agitation against slavery was growing in the Northern United States, but the Christian defense of slavery was becoming just as vigorous in the South. *Courtesy of the Billy Graham Center Museum*

enslaved as "other persons" to be counted as three-fifths for the sake of congressional representation. In addition both shared an active Christian faith that led them to promote a wide variety of mission and reform activities. In 1819 Boudinot sent Jay a brochure describing the work of a New Jersey antislavery society. Jay responded by ruminating on the troublesome clause in the Constitution, confessing sadly that "the word *slaves* was avoided, probably on account of the existing toleration of slavery, and of its discordancy with the principles of the Revolution; and from a consciousness of its being repugnant to . . . the Declaration of Independence."

What Jay and others could see clearly enough as whites was etched even more sharply in the perception of blacks. The principles of America's founding documents, like the principles of Christianity, could be put to use for human liberation, but they could also be twisted to justify the status quo between masters and slaves. It was an ex-slave, Frederick Douglass, who best captured the hypocrisy, for both national and religious principles, in a memorable address two generations after the Revolution was past. It was given on Independence Day, 1852, to the Ladies' Anti-Slavery Society of Rochester, New York. In it Douglass presented a vision of America's founding and its connection to Christianity that few of the whites in attendance had ever faced before:

> What, to the American slave, is your 4th of July? I answer; a day that reveals to him, more than all other days in the year, the gross injustice and cruelty to which he is the constant victim. . . . You boast of your love of liberty, your superior civilization and your pure Christianity, while the whole political power of the nation . . . is solemnly pledged to support and perpetuate the enslavement of three millions of your countrymen. . . . You can bare your bosom to the storm of British artillery to throw off a three-penny tax on tea; and yet wring the last hard-earned farthing from the grasp of the black laborers of your country. You profess to believe "that, of one blood, God made all nations of men to dwell on the face of all the earth" [Acts 17:26], and hath commanded all men, everywhere, to love one another; yet you notoriously hate (and glory in your hatred) all men whose skins are not colored like your own. . . . The existence of slavery in this country brands your republicanism as a sham, your human-ity as a base pretense, and your Christianity as a lie.

Not for the first time in the history of nations and in the history of the Christian church, the noblest ideals and the most altruistic actions failed to eradicate malignant oppression. The irony of slavery coming out of freedom, and of the churches' complicity in the deed, was an enduring legacy of the Revolutionary era.

Further Reading

Bloch, Ruth H. *Visionary Republic: Millennial Themes in American Thought, 1756-1800.* New York: Cambridge University Press, 1985.

Essig, James D. *The Bonds of Wickedness: American Evangelicals against Slavery, 1770-1808.* Philadelphia: Temple University Press, 1982.

Foner, Philip S., ed. *The Life and Writings of Frederick Douglass.* New York: International, 1950.

Griffin, Keith L. "Reluctant Revolutionaries: The Middle Colony Reformed Idea of a Just Resistance." Ph.D. diss., Fuller Theological Seminary, 1989.

Hatch, Nathan O. *The Sacred Cause of Liberty: Republican Thought and the Millennium in Revolutionary New England.* New Haven: Yale University Press, 1977.

Hennesey, James. *American Catholics: A History of the Roman Catholic Community in the United States.* New York: Oxford University Press, 1981.

Jefferson's Extracts from the Gospels. Edited by Dickinson W. Adams. Princeton: Princeton University Press, 1983.

Kaplan, Sidney. *The Black Presence in the Era of the American Revolution.* Washington: Smithsonian Institute Press, 1973.

MacMaster, Richard K. *Land, Piety, Peoplehood: The Establishment of Mennonite Communities in America, 1683-1790.* Scottdale, PA: Herald, 1985.

Moir, John S. *The Church in the British Era: From the British Conquest to Confederation.* Toronto: McGraw-Hill Ryerson, 1972.

Noll, Mark A. *Christians in the American Revolution.* Grand Rapids: William B. Eerdmans, 1977.

Noll, Mark A., George M. Marsden, and Nathan O. Hatch. *The Search for Christian America.* Rev. ed. Colorado Springs: Helmers & Howard, 1983.

Rawlyk, George A., ed. *Henry Alline: Selected Writings.* New York: Paulist, 1987.

————, ed. *Revolution Rejected, 1775-1776.* Scarborough, ON: Prentice-Hall, 1968.

CHAPTER 6

The Revolution in the Churches

Bigotry Reported

A horrid thing pervades the land,
The priests and prophets in a band,
   (Called by the name of preachers,)
Direct the superstitious mind,
What man shall do his God to find,
   He must obey his teachers. . . .

Is this religion? God forbid,
The light within the cloud is hid,
   My soul be not deceived;
The Great Redeemer never told
The priests to separate his fold,
   And this I've long believed. . . .

Let Christians now unite and say,
We'll throw all human rules away,
   And take God's word to rule us;
King Jesus shall our leader be,
And in his name we will agree,
   The priests no more shall fool us.

This hymn was written early in the nineteenth century by Joseph Thomas, an itinerant preacher in the upper South who called himself simply a "Christian" as a protest against all restrictive hereditary forms of belief.

A FTER THE GREAT AWAKENING AND THE WAR FOR INDEPENDENCE, THE third most important "circumstance" of the eighteenth century that served to fashion a uniquely American Christianity was the effects of the Revolution. Churches were faced with the question of how they would adjust to the new political freedom won in battle against Great Britain. Even more pressing was the issue of how they would adjust to the ideology of democratic republicanism that had driven the war. The answers involved formal institutions of church and state, new aspirations among "the people," and far-reaching changes in religious thought.

The Separation of Church and State

The First Amendment to the United States Constitution, with its provision that "Congress shall make no law respecting an establishment of religion, or prohibiting the free exercise thereof," took effect in 1791. At that time, five of the nation's fourteen states (Vermont joined the Union in 1791) provided for tax support of ministers, and those five plus seven others maintained religious tests for state office. Only Virginia and Rhode Island enjoyed the sort of "separation of church and state" that Americans now take for granted — government providing no tax money for churches and posing no religious conditions for participation in public life. With less than a handful of exceptions, even the defenders of religious liberty in Rhode Island and Virginia did not object when Congress or the president pro-claimed national days of prayer, when the federal government began its meetings with prayer, or when military chaplains were appointed and funded by law.

In light of these conditions in the states, we might well ask how the First Amendment came to coexist with what, from a modern vantage point, looks like a thorough intermingling of church and state. The answer involves matters of both principle and practice. Experiencing fear about the potential for governmental tyranny so common in the Revolutionary period, more and more Americans came to affirm that religion was a matter of conscience between God and the individual and should be exempt from the meddling of government at any level. A growing number also spoke out much more strongly for the spiritual benefit to be derived from separating church and state. One such individual was the leader of New England's Baptists, Isaac Backus. During the Revolution, which he supported, Backus asked Massachusetts and Connecticut why they maintained establishments of religion that forced Baptists and other non-Congregationalists to support forms of Christianity that they conscientiously opposed. If the colonists were fighting Britain for liberty, Backus asked, why did the new states themselves not grant religious liberty to their own residents?

On a practical level, the idea that the national government should simply not address the question of religion seemed more and more necessary if there was to be a national government at all. At both the Constitutional Convention in 1787 and the first Congress in 1789, which was responsible for the First Amendment, such leaders as James Madison realized how explosive and how complicated the question of religion was throughout the nation. Any effort to establish one particular faith would have drawn violent protests from adherents of other faiths. Any effort to deny the importance of religion would have deeply offended the substantial numbers who still believed that the security of a nation depended on the health of its faith. The compromise chosen by the founding fathers was to avoid the issue. If they were going to have a Constitution for all of the people, they somehow were going to have to get the government out of the religion business. By leaving such matters to the states, it was hoped, they could establish a government for the nation without being forced to decide what the nation's religion should be.

At the same time, however, the colonial background of the new states was so overwhelmingly Protestant that it was simply assumed that such things as Sunday legislation, laws prohibiting atheism and promoting public morals, and the regular use of Christian language by governmental officials were appropriate. The distance between the new United States and our modern period is suggested by the fact that during the Constitutional period Catholics and Jews protested against the form, but not the existence, of religious tests for office-holding in the states. When Pennsylvania's first state constitution required legislators to "acknowledge the Scriptures of the old and new Testaments to be given by divine inspiration," the Philadelphia Synagogue protested by noting that "Jews are as fond of liberty as their religious societies can be." Furthermore, these loyal Philadelphians pointed out that "in the religious books of the Jews, which are or may be in every man's hands, there are no such doctrines or principles established as are inconsistent with the safety and happiness of the people of Pennsylvania, and that the conduct and behaviour of the Jews in this and the neighbouring States, has always tallied with the great design of the Revolution." The Philadelphia Jews were protesting not the religious test as such, but their own exclusion under the specifically Christian stipulations of the Pennsylvania test. From local discussions like this one the conviction steadily grew

After Independence, some Americans became concerned about efforts by other Americans to maintain moral behavior through governmental action. This print from the Philadelphia engraver James Akin satirizes moralists who wanted to keep the government from moving the mail on Sundays. *American Antiquarian Society*

that the federal government should keep as far away from contested religious questions as possible.

Interpreting the First Amendment

On the related question of how religion in general might bear on public life, the founders were divided. What Thomas Jefferson thought the First Amendment meant is well known. As he put it to the Danbury Baptist Association in 1802, there was to be "a wall of separation between Church and State." Jefferson also felt that debate over the famous Virginia Statute for Religious Freedom in 1785 formed the essential background to the First Amendment and that the Virginia Statute was intentionally written to guarantee full participation in public life on equal terms, as he put it, for

146

After Chief Justice John Marshall, Joseph Story of Massachusetts was the most influential Supreme Court Justice in the early United States. While Story did not want to see any one church supported by the state, he did feel that a general promotion of Christianity was necessary to ensure the health of a republican government. *The Bettman Archive*

"the Jew and the Gentile, the Christian and Mahometan, the Hindoo, and Infidel of every denomination."

Other founders interpreted the words differently. In 1812 Joseph Story became the youngest judge ever appointed to the Supreme Court. Over the course of his lengthy tenure on the bench (1812-1845), he was John Marshall's righthand man in defining the role of the court itself and its jurisdiction over state and national laws. While serving as a justice, Story transformed the Harvard Law School into the nation's premier school for lawyers and also wrote the most influential commentaries on the nation's laws published before the Civil War. His 1833 discussion of the First Amendment, thus, grew out of intimate involvement in the new nation's legal system. It showed how he read the founders' intent. Story began by asserting that "the promulgation of the great doctrines of religion . . . [can] never be a matter of indifference to any well ordered community." "A republic" in particular required "the Christian religion, as the great basis, on which it must rest for its support and permanence." The First Amendment therefore allowed "Christianity . . . to receive encouragement from the state, so far as was not incompatible with the private rights of conscience, and the freedom of religious worship." Moreover, "the whole power over the subject of religion is left exclusively to the state governments," but to the end that "the Catholic and the Protestant, the Calvinist and the Arminian, the Jew and the Infidel, may sit down at the common table of the national councils, without any inquisition into their faith, or mode of worship."

James Madison, the individual most influential in the drafting of both the Constitution and the First Amendment, offered an interpretation more like Jefferson's. On the basis of the First Amendment as well as the general principles of the Constitution, he opposed public payment for chaplains in Congress and the military, spoke out against national proclamations of days of prayer (though as president he did "recommend" them), and while president vetoed congressional efforts to incorporate churches in the District of Columbia. At the same time, Madison frequently suggested that it was appropriate for private citizens to support chaplains and other kinds of semiorganized public religion through voluntary contributions.

Whose "intention" among the founders defines the real "meaning" of the First Amendment? On particular questions, it is difficult to say, but on general matters there was agreement. None of the founders interpreted the First Amendment as prohibiting religiously grounded arguments for general public policies. Nor did they seem to worry about incidental benefits accruing to religious institutions from government measures designed for the benefit of all citizens. On the other hand, they also clearly indicated their belief that the federal government could not support "religion in general" without edging toward the legal establishment of something like a "church." Such an establishment they had experienced under Britain. At least for the nation as a whole, they would have none of it in the new United States.

A New Era of Populist Democracy

The American Revolution stimulated social changes every bit as dramatic as the political changes it brought about. As much as the winds of war offered a marvel to the world — an upstart band of provincials defying the greatest power in Western civilization — the libertarian spirit that sparked the Revolution, with its appeals to self-evident truths, inalienable rights, and the equal creation of all, did even more to reap a democratic whirlwind at home. Historian Nathan Hatch has succinctly noted that the two generations after 1776 witnessed a "cultural ferment over the meaning of freedom." What was true for America at large was no less true for its Christian churches.

The new prominence given to the notion of the sovereignty of the people no doubt had something to do with the gradual decline of Calvinism,

If anything, this depiction of a frontier camp meeting suggests less drama than was typically associated with such events. *Courtesy of the Billy Graham Center Museum*

particularly its insistence on the jealous sovereignty of God. The revival spirit that transformed the American landscape in the early decades of the nineteenth century also drew on the spirit of the Revolution. Revivalists called upon individuals to exert themselves for God. They found traditional church structures largely irrelevant. They encouraged the formation of ad hoc voluntary societies to reform the nation. The revival became the dominant religious force in American Protestantism (and an underappreciated influence among American Catholics), in part because it was so effective in winning the lost but also because it so effectively expressed the country's democratic spirit.

The new tide of democracy eventually washed over some very traditional churches. The number of Episcopalians, for example, was significantly reduced during the Revolution: there had been 318 active parishes in 1774, but there were only 259 in 1789. The official establishment that the church had enjoyed in the four lower counties of New York and all the colonies from Maryland to Georgia vanished in the republican wind. The rebuilding of the church was painfully slow. Because it was no longer a political threat to have American bishops, three church leaders were able to be consecrated for this office (Samuel Seabury of Connecticut in 1784, and in 1787 William

White of Pennsylvania and Samuel Provoost of New York). Together these three, with other associates, succeeded in constituting an independent Episcopal Church in the United States in 1789. As they set about reconstituting their church, Episcopalians, though the most self-consciously British of the major Protestant churches, nonetheless put to use such themes from the anti-British Revolution as "natural rights," "participation of the people," and "representation." The result was hierarchical episcopalianism with a democratic flavor. Church leaders professed their entire satisfaction with the separation of church and state. The denomination's local vestries continued to exercise the powers they had gained during the War, when clerical leadership was scarce. The church's bishops forswore the political power that for centuries had been an accepted part of a bishop's service in England. And the American bishops also yielded a great deal of power to the laity and the lower clergy of the church. Imitating the new U.S. Congress, the church's General Convention consisted of two chambers, a House of Bishops and a House of Clerical and Lay Deputies, with the latter enjoying the unprecedented privilege of overturning actions of the former.

Most Christian bodies were even more directly affected by the democratic surge than the Episcopalians. In particular, a universal passion for liberty fueled the social changes of the Revolutionary period. Restraint — whether political restraint from a corrupt Parliament, ecclesiastical restraint from denominational traditions, or professional restraint associated with the special prerogatives of lawyers, ministers, and physicians — was everywhere a cause for resentment. A Presbyterian minister in 1781 put it bluntly: "this is a time in which a spirit of liberty prevails, a time in which the externals of religion may properly be new modeled, if needful, and fixed upon a gospel plan." Even Isaac Backus, the Baptist who pioneered for religious liberty in New England, was beginning in the 1790s to worry that such radical new groups as the Shakers, the Universalists, and the Free Will Baptists were abandoning too much of the traditional Protestant heritage.

But innovative groups like these flourished naturally in the free air of post-Revolutionary America. Shakers, who believed in community living, religious perfection, and sexual celibacy, had arrived from Britain in upstate New York in 1774 under the leadership of Mother Ann Lee (1736-1784). Universalists, who held to the eventual salvation of all people, had also become well established in the New England backcountry by the end of the War. Led by John Murray (1741-1815), who emigrated to New England in 1770, Universalists appealed especially to ordinary people who found traditional notions of eternal punishment unfair. For their part, Free Will Baptists protested against traditional Calvinist beliefs in the divine control of salvation. They were also organized in New England at about this same time, under such leaders as Benjamin Randall (1749-1808). The common element in the histories of these bodies was their resistance to traditional modes of authority. They also insisted on the corresponding right to promote the beliefs and practices *they* held to be true. Many of the people who ended up in these groups had originally been converts of George Whitefield, and quite a few were caught up in the "New Light Stir" associated with Henry Alline of Nova Scotia. All of them added millenarianism, perfectionism, and anti-Calvinism to the Protestantism they had inherited. Others, known as Come-Outers, Merry Dancers, or Nothingarians, went even further in creating their own forms of Christian expression. Ministers in traditional denominations on the seaboard, as well as laity busy with negotiations over the Constitution's proper division of church and state, may not have paid much attention to the sects in rural New England. But their innovations and the radicals' pursuit of what the Universalists called "gospel liberty" marked them as the wave of an American future.

No Creed but the Bible

One of the practices that the American passion for liberty most affected was Bible reading. A principal reason that so many new denominations sprang to life in America between the War for Independence and the Civil War — Disciples and "Christians" of several varieties, Adventists, Mormons, Cumberland Presbyterians, offshoots of the Methodists, and more — was the new opportunity for unfettered interpretation of Scripture. Americans in the early nineteenth century transformed an earlier battle cry of the Reformation, "the Bible alone," into a distinctly American appeal — "no creed but the Bible!" This appeal, in turn, nurtured expressions of the kind of resentments against inherited hierarchies illustrated by the hymn at the start of this chapter. It led also to a much more democratic style of evangelization.

This blend of Christianity and democracy created a Christian message specifically adapted to the shape of American social realities. That message was, in turn, brought to a wide circle of the previously unchurched by vigorous representatives of a liberated Christian faith. Leaders of the Restoration Movement, for example, such as Barton W. Stone (1772-1844), Thomas Campbell (1763-1845), and his son Alexander Campbell (1788-1866), sought to roll back the corruptions of the centuries and restore the purity of primitive Christianity. Their message was thoroughly imbued with an American spirit. As an old man, Barton Stone wrote that "from my earliest recollection I drank deeply into the spirit of liberty, and was so warmed by the soul-inspiring draughts, that I could not hear the name of

This promotion for a "Rally Day" for the Bible comes from the early twentieth century, but the prominence of the Scriptures in its iconography reflects themes (e.g., "no creed but the Bible") that were common in the United States from its very earliest decades. *Courtesy of the Billy Graham Center Museum*

British, or Tories, without feeling a rush of blood through the whole system." When he and his followers broke with the Presbyterians of Kentucky, he called the move their "declaration of independence." For his part, Alexander Campbell, in an effort to encourage the hearts of his "Christian" followers, would later write that July 4, 1776, was "a day to be remembered as with the Jewish Passover. . . . This revolution, taken in all its influences, will make men free indeed." The Disciples, Christian Churches, and Churches of Christ founded by these leaders effectively evangelized the Upper South and opening West because they had translated the Christian message into an effective American idiom. To one degree or another, the sorts of adjustments of the gospel to the themes of the Revolution's ideology that they made were also evidenced in more traditional groups.

The Effect of Populist Democracy

Various social changes that affected the American churches arose from the new populist democracy. Democratic rhetoric about the rights of the people and democratic resentment of the privileges of the elite filled the sails of these new movements. Yet a steady, even autocratic hand on the tiller was often required as well. The leaders of new movements inevitably had a deep populist streak, a firm commitment to the free choices of the people at large, and an unwillingness to accept inherited beliefs or practices simply because they were inherited.

The effects of such populist democratization on the churches can be shown with a simple statistical comparison. (See Table 6.1.) The Protestant churches that flourished most decisively in the first half of the nineteenth century were the Baptists and the Methodists, the two bodies that succeeded in joining most efficiently a democratic appeal with effective leadership. On the other hand, the leading colonial churches, especially the Congregationalists and the Episcopalians, equivocated about becoming religions of the people and so lost their lead among the American churches. The story of these denominations during the first half of the nineteenth century is told in Chapter 7, but their relative standing at the time of the Revolution and then in 1850 illustrates powerfully what was at stake in the democratization of the American churches.

Table 6.1 Denominational Shares of Religious Adherents: The United States, 1776 and 1850

1776		1850	
(1) Congregationalists	20.4%	(1) Methodists	34.2%
(2) Presbyterians	19.0	(2) Baptists	20.5
(3) Baptists	16.9	(3) Roman Catholics	13.9
(4) Episcopalians	15.7	(4) Presbyterians	11.6
(5) Methodists	2.5	(5) Congregationalists	4.0
(6) Roman Catholics	1.8	(6) Episcopalians	3.5

In addition, by 1850 other bodies had also become statistically important — for example, Lutherans (2.9% of church adherents), Unitarians and Universalists combined (1.9%), German and Dutch Reformed combined (1.9%), "Christian" followers of Barton Stone and Alexander Campbell (1.8%), and Quakers (1.6%). (These figures are from Roger Finke and Rodney Stark, "How the Upstart Sects Won America: 1776-1850," *Journal for the Scientific Study of Religion* 28 [1989]: 31, as supplemented by the 1850 Census of the United States.)

Theology in an American Key

The era of the American Revolution also marked a crucial turning point in Christian thought. In the new nation Christian leaders continued to desire a powerful presentation of the gospel. But in the altered cultural circumstances after the War, this desire led to innovations in thought every bit as important as those that the spread of populist democracy brought into the denominations. The strategy that a wide range of church leaders eventually pursued was to exploit a conservative form of the European Enlightenment as a way of preserving the intellectual relevance of the faith. It was a strategy that gained very much but may also have given away a great deal.

The American Christian Enlightenment

Changes associated with the American Revolution led to the establishment of a Christianized form of the Enlightenment as the dominant intellectual force in the country. Almost all Americans, to be sure, repudiated skeptical or radical forms of the European Enlightenment. The philosophical doubts of Scotland's David Hume and the sneers at religion from the French savant Voltaire found little sympathy in the new nation. Yet important principles of the Enlightenment, as these had been refined by other Europeans of the eighteenth century, came to exert a near-universal domination in America.

The form of the Enlightenment that prevailed in the United States was derived from an important school of Scottish thinkers known as "common sense" philosophers. Guided by the moralist Francis Hutcheson (1694-1746) and the general work of Thomas Reid (1710-1796), these Scots shared the general confidence of eighteenth-century Europe that it was now possible to see the truth — moral, physical, social — with greater clarity than in previous generations. They differed from other thinkers such as Hume and Voltaire, however, by showing how their Enlightenment thought could be compatible with at least the broad outline of received Christianity. Proponents of common-sense philosophy held that it was "realistic" because it asserted that humans could genuinely know true things about the world outside their minds. The key to the Scottish point of view was its appeal to universal (or "common") experience (or "sense"). Even if arguments of so talented a skeptic as David Hume were hard to answer, it still was the case that normal humans everywhere presupposed basic realities such as the connection between causes and effects and the existence of the external world. Even if a scoffing Voltaire ridiculed traditional religion, it still was the case that average human beings throughout the world presupposed a God who would one day judge good and evil. Scottish appeals to "common sense" were developed in sophisticated philosophical treatises. Their great impact in America, however, was less on the plane of recondite philosophy than in open fields of intellectual combat.

Americans found the Scottish philosophy useful in three ways: (1) for justifying the Revolution against Britain, (2) for outlining new principles of social order in the absence of the stability of British rule, and (3) for re-establishing the truths of Christianity in the absence of an established church. During the Revolution, the ethics of Scotland's Francis Hutcheson provided a solid moral basis for resisting British tyranny (it was self-evident "common sense" that a distant mother country should not exercise absolute rule over colonies, especially when the colonies had become populous and economically self-sufficient). After the Revolution, principles of moral reasoning from Scottish sources were joined with insights from John Locke to provide a groundwork for the new Constitution. Common-sense reasoning helped to define what governments should and should not do. It was even possible, as the *Federalist Papers* put it, to construct a "science of politics" from careful observations of human conduct. The founders of the American nation used a wide variety of intellectual sources, but among the most prominent were lines of thought from the Scottish Enlightenment. Jefferson, for example, drew on principles from Francis Hutcheson in writing the Declaration of Independence, and Madison used an even broader range of Scottish sources in his arguments for the Constitution.

Scottish thinking also proved a boon for all those, whether explicitly Christian or not, who hoped to establish a sturdy moral foundation for the United States. It had been only natural for the patriots' fear of Old World political traditions to broaden into a fear of European traditions generally. But would social chaos result if everyone simply threw off the traces of inherited morality? Some of those who wrote the Constitution feared that they could see such developments already in the 1780s, in, for example, a willingness to ignore debts, an inclination to follow demagogues, and a propensity to engage in factional political in-fighting. Christian leaders expressed similar fears for morality as they saw growing disregard for Sabbath observance, declining church attendance, and heightened disrespect for the clergy. Christians in the United States shared the fears about Old World corruptions, but they nevertheless wanted to rescue the faith itself, as well as conceptions of social order allied with Christianity, from the Revolutionary assault upon tradition. In the new United States, however, it would not do simply to appeal blindly to traditional authorities or to invoke the customs of the European churches, for the Revolution had shown how easily these traditions led to tyranny. Moral leaders in the new United States had put themselves in a delicate position. They had led the attack on Old World political traditions, but now they wanted to reassert standards of morality that were usually expressed in the intellectual terms of the Old World.

In this context, Scottish thought provided attractive answers, especially when reinforced by the great respect for the new science of the eighteenth century that was often associated with common-sense philosophy. Scottish reasoning offered an ideal way to defend the traditional faith free from reliance on discredited European traditions. With such a system, both Christian apologists and heterodox moralists such as Jefferson could appeal to assumptions that were common to all human minds — that, for example, a First Cause had brought the world into existence or that individuals presuppose a Perfect Morality when they make moral judgments. From these axioms, sound arguments could be developed for a harmonious social order and also for specifically Christian beliefs. The result was that as American Christians called on principles of Common Sense Philosophy to defend their faith and promote social order, they were able to keep in step with more general national feelings about personal liberty, self-determination, and the need for all men (soon women too) to think for themselves.

The role of science at this stage had more to do with intellectual prestige than with actual explorations of the natural world. Americans held in greatest respect Sir Isaac Newton and the age of scientific discoveries he represented. They were convinced that Newton's scientific triumphs could be repeated in epistemology, ethics, jurisprudence, and other spheres, if only practitioners in those fields were as rigorous and dispassionate as Newton had been in his scientific work. When the principles of Newton (or, even more, the principles of scientific induction championed by Sir Francis Bacon, whom Americans believed had paved the way for Newton) were applied to politics, social ethics, or Christian apologetics, then scientific reasoning could be put to use to ensure political peace, social morality, and even Christian orthodoxy.

What made this system of thought so important for the history of Christianity in America was that most of the leading thinkers in America's most visible Protestant churches embraced some variety of common-sense reasoning for their own use. The Scottish Presbyterian John Witherspoon had brought Scottish common sense with him as the new president of Princeton College in 1768. At Princeton such ideas flourished for over a century, among Witherspoon and his successors at the college, and among the first generations of theologians at the Presbyterian seminary founded at Princeton in 1812. But other religious leaders soon adapted it for their own uses as well, including Congregationalists Timothy Dwight at Yale College and Nathaniel W. Taylor at Yale Divinity School, Unitarians Henry Ware, Jr., and Andrews Norton at Harvard, Baptist Francis Wayland at Brown, Alexander Campbell of the Disciples (who helped found Bacon College), and many others. As this very incomplete roster suggests, the new nation's colleges were thoroughly imbued with common-sense principles.

As president of the College of New Jersey (later Princeton University) during and after the American Revolution, John Witherspoon was the most influential Presbyterian clergyman of his generation. Not only did he sign the Declaration of Independence (he was the only minister to do so), but he also taught generations of students the philosophy of common-sense moral reasoning he had brought with him from his native Scotland. *Independence National Historical Park Museum*

With Scottish common sense to assist them, Protestant leaders expressed new optimism about the ability of all human minds to be drawn to the faith by logically compelling arguments. They worked diligently constructing appeals to neutral reason, grounded in universal moral sense and in science, in order to prove the existence of God, the need for public morality, and the divine character of Scripture. They had, they felt, turned back threats from the more radical forms of the Enlightenment by showing that reasonable arguments could support the faith and the public good.

Although earlier theological emphases did not disappear when American theologians began to exploit common-sense reasoning, much from former days was set aside because of its influence. For example, most Americans who thought about such things in the wake of the Revolution no longer held with the Puritans that a revelation from God was the first necessity in understanding life; they stressed instead that a rigorous, "scientific" chain of reason demonstrated the truth of revelation. Again, most had moved beyond Jonathan Edwards's belief that the inclinations of the heart infallibly determined human choices, arguing instead that self-consciousness seemed to indicate that humans are free to choose between competing inclinations. But whatever had been lost, American theologians now had a message that could be communicated in the democratic landscape of the new nation.

From his pulpits in Great Barrington, Massachusetts, and Newport, Rhode Island, the Rev. Samuel Hopkins propounded a form of Calvinism developing and extending the themes of his teacher Jonathan Edwards. In Newport, Hopkins also joined his colleague the Rev. Ezra Stiles in working against the enslavement of Africans. *Library of Congress*

Theological Developments

The changes introduced in theology by accommodations to the reasoning of the Revolution were subtle but far reaching. Developments among the theologians of New England, who enjoyed the most substantial theological tradition in the new nation, illustrate the changes. Jonathan Edwards's students Joseph Bellamy (1719-1790) and Samuel Hopkins, writing during the Revolutionary period with its concerns for fairness in government and personal responsibility in citizens, began to talk of God as "the infinitely wise and good Governor of the world." They also came to the conclusion that God punishes only the sins that humans actually commit, not a sinfulness inherited from Adam. Hopkins and Bellamy did not repudiate the Calvinistic theology they had inherited from Jonathan Edwards, but the influence of contemporary notions about the imperatives of human happiness and individual rights and the need to justify all intellectual principles at the bar of reason are evident in their work.

A generation later, the same general tendencies were influencing the students of Bellamy and Hopkins. Jonathan Edwards, Jr. (1745-1801), who was very young when his father died and who took his theological training with Bellamy, continued to affirm that only God can bring new life to the

Timothy Dwight, president of Yale College and promoter of revivals within the bounds of reason, was one of the most influential leaders of the Second Great Awakening in New England. *Courtesy of the Billy Graham Center Museum*

sinner. Yet his theology also bent along lines demanded by the era's new fascination with the individual and the law. In fact, Edwards the Younger carried further than his teachers the notion that human sinfulness is a product of each individual's actions rather than a burden inherited from Adam. And he pictured the atonement as governmental (Christ putting to right God's sense of justice) rather than propitiatory (Christ putting to rest God's anger at sin). Timothy Dwight (1752-1817), a grandson of Jonathan Edwards who gained eminence as the president of Yale College, showed how preoccupation with unregulated power could move theology in a republican direction. In a powerful series of sermons preached to Yale undergraduates, Dwight argued that God rules "by motives, addressed to the understanding and affections of rational subjects, and operating on their minds, as inducements to voluntary obedience. No other government is worthy of God: there being, indeed, no other, beside that of mere force and coercion."

Theology of a similar sort from Dwight's contemporary Samuel Stanhope Smith (1750-1819) was the staple at Princeton. Smith used principles of common-sense philosophy to defend the unity of humanity against suggestions from Europe that the different races might indicate a plural origin

159

for human beings. To Smith, these notions were repugnant, not primarily because they contradicted the Bible but because he felt that all people would have to learn common moral principles from studying their own moral natures if there was to be any hope of a well-ordered society or of arguing toward the specific truths of Christianity.

In elite theology, therefore, as well as in populist religion, the Christian faith of the early republic took on something of the character of the American Revolution. In neither popular church life nor more academic theology did these changes alter Christian belief radically. But they did soften the hard edges of many Christian doctrines that earlier believers, whether Puritan or not, had considered crucial. A country convinced of innate human capacities would naturally encourage popular preachers and theologians at the colleges to propose at least modest curbs on the all-encompassing power of God.

Countervailing Trends

At the same time that American churches were absorbing principles from the Revolution, church life in North America was also manifesting a variety of countervailing trends. Some of these were intellectual, some regional, and some both.

In the first place, allegiance to historic Christian confessions by no means died away when the Revolution mounted its assault on inherited intellectual traditions. Many Episcopalians, Presbyterians, Dutch and German Reformed, and growing numbers of Lutherans and Roman Catholics continued to embrace the confessions of Christian faith that their communions had developed in the Reformation or (in the case of Roman Catholics) long before. Each of these confessional Christian bodies made some adjustments to the American environment, but each also affirmed that although much had been learned in the New World, much of the wisdom of the Old still applied.

Immigration of believers from Europe supported the continuing power of confessions. Most new Americans in the first decades of the United States came from the British Isles. Among these were at least a few Presbyterians from Scotland and Northern Ireland who lived and died by the Westminster Confession and a few Anglicans for whom the Thirty-Nine Articles remained a treasured guide. Likewise, after the numbers of Lutheran and Roman Catholic immigrants began to grow in the 1830s and beyond, these new Americans bore strong attachments to, respectively, the Augsburg Confession and the Councils and Decrees of the Council of Trent. As we shall see, immigration also disturbed Old World allegiances, but the fresh supply of Europeans who had grown up in traditional churches exerted a conserving theological influence.

Regional reservations about the tide of democracy were probably even more important than the effects of confessionalism and immigration. In the South a far greater respect for hierarchy survived. With that respect came a certain conservativism in Christian expression. Baptist and Methodist churches flourished in the South, but protests against the older English-language denominations did not go too much further. In addition, a society that embraced the practice of slavery with an increasingly firm grip was not prone to socially disruptive beliefs or practices. It was one thing for white, male Americans to claim "no creed but the Bible," but when a black man did it, there was the devil to pay. In 1800, for example, nearly 1,000 slaves near Richmond, Virginia, revolted under their leader, Gabriel Prosser. Several elements went into Gabriel's Rebellion, including recourse to African practices, key use of the general rhetoric of liberty, and the harshness of local conditions — but an active attention to the Scriptures was also a crucial element. Gabriel's brother Martin even used the Bible to convince fellow conspirators that their lot was like that of the Israelites. If God promised that "five of you shall conquer an hundred & a hundred a thousand of our enemies," it was as true for the present as it had been in days gone by. Needless to say, white response to this free use of Scripture was anything but approving. Gabriel, along with other leaders of the rebellion, paid with his life.

Far to the north a different set of circumstances checked the spread of democratic and republican principles. Almost all Canadian churches throughout the nineteenth century remained closer to their European roots than did churches in the United States. Moreover, Christianity in Canada tended to be, in the words of historian Robert Handy, "more cautious, traditional, and church-oriented" than Christianity in the States. Only a few Canadian believers felt that it was necessary to revise inherited ways in order to accommodate the spirit of either the American or the French revolutions. And since a republican fear of governmental tyranny was conspicuous by its absence, very few Canadians campaigned for strict separation of church and state. The general Canadian solution to church-state issues was to guarantee the rights of minorities over against the majority alliances between church and state rather than to do away with governmental support for religious institutions. Finally, though Canada was huge, it simply did not receive the great number of immigrant and indigenous Christian bodies that the States had received by the early nineteenth century. In a word, when we set Canadian religious history beside that of the United States, the chief contrast is between the Revolution that altered the shape of Christianity in the States and the Revolution that did not take place to the north.

Further Reading

Curry, Thomas J. *The First Freedoms: Church and State in America to the Passage of the First Amendment*. New York: Oxford University Press, 1986.

Finke, Roger, and Rodney Stark. "How the Upstart Sects Won America: 1776-1850." *Journal for the Scientific Study of Religion* 28 (1988): 27-44.

Hatch, Nathan O. *The Democratization of American Christianity*. New Haven: Yale University Press, 1989.

Howe, Daniel Walker. *The Unitarian Conscience: Harvard Moral Philosophy, 1805-1861*. Cambridge: Harvard University Press, 1970.

Hughes, Richard T., and C. Leonard Allen, *Illusions of Innocence: Protestant Primitivism in America, 1630-1875*. Chicago: University of Chicago Press, 1988.

McLoughlin, William G. *New England Dissent, 1630-1833: The Baptists and the Separation of Church and State*. 2 vols. Cambridge: Harvard University Press, 1971.

Marini, Stephen A. *Radical Sects of Revolutionary New England*. Cambridge: Harvard University Press, 1982.

May, Henry F. *The Enlightenment in America*. New York: Oxford University Press, 1976.

Mills, Frederick V. *Bishops by Ballot: An Eighteenth-Century Revolution*. New York: Oxford University Press, 1978.

Noll, Mark A. *Princeton and the Republic, 1768-1822: The Search for a Christian Enlightenment in the Era of Samuel Stanhope Smith*. Princeton: Princeton University Press, 1989.

Wilson, John F. "Religion, Government, and Power in the New American Nation." In *Religion and American Politics from the Colonial Period to the 1980s*. Edited by Mark A. Noll. New York: Oxford University Press, 1990.

PART III

THE "PROTESTANT CENTURY"

W HEN IN 1835 ALEXIS DE TOCQUEVILLE PUBLISHED *DEMOCRACY IN AMERICA*, a book growing out of a lengthy tour of the States, he wrote that "there is no country in the world where the Christian religion retains a greater influence over the souls of men than in America." Tocqueville was struck, however, not just by the simple fact of Christianity but by its character. "In France," he wrote, "I had almost always seen the spirit of religion and the spirit of freedom marching in opposite directions. But in America I found they were intimately united and that they reigned in common over the same country." Generations of historians have seconded Tocqueville's conclusions. Antebellum America was a distinctly religious land, but it was religious in a distinctly American way. How that situation came to be is the subject of this section.

From the vantage point of 1789, the year in which government began under the U.S. Constitution, it would have been difficult to anticipate the picture Tocqueville was to draw fifty years later. To be sure, Christians had contributed a great deal to the War for Independence, both practically and ideologically. In addition, the Christian faith enjoyed a considerable reservoir of support among the population. Where religious assumptions, presuppositions, convictions, or conventions of whatever sort existed among the population, they were almost all Christian in some form or another. Still, the churches were definitely disorganized in the wake of the Revolution, and the role of Christianity in the new national culture was anything but secure. While church adherence remained high at least into the 1770s (with perhaps as much as 40 to 50 percent of the population attending church with some regularity), formal church membership was sinking, and in the 1790s reached an all-time low (somewhere between 5 and 10 percent of the adult population).

The causes of this unsettled situation were many. They included new notions about the separation of church and state, new religious convictions arising from the democratic surge spilling over from the Revolution, and new possibilities created in the vast spaces of the frontier. As it happened, the churches rapidly overcame the confusion of the Revolutionary era to mount vigorous campaigns for evangelizing the populace and Christianizing the civilization. Prominent in these campaigns were representatives of the older colonial-era churches, but even more influential were dynamic leaders of new denominations. Together they formed something of an evangelical Protestant phalanx that dominated the public perception of religion in the United States. In Canada, the Protestant surge may have been even more successful, though the dimensions of its effect were obscured by the continuing strength of Roman Catholicism in Quebec.

At the same time that evangelical Protestantism was exerting its greatest sway, however, the early chapters in the next significant stage in American Christian history were being written. This stage was marked by a pluralism of Christian experience broadening well beyond evangelical Protestantism. It witnessed a cultural diversity that contradicted the notion of the United States as a Protestant "Christian America" and of Canada as "His Dominion." But in the century after the American Revolution, it was the evangelical empire that stood out, and that is the subject of the chapters that follow. Having once traced that story, we will turn to the larger tale of religious pluralism that was in fact gathering strength during the heyday of evangelical Protestantism.

CHAPTER 7

Evangelical Mobilization

I thirst, thou wounded Lamb of God,
To wash me in thy cleansing blood;
To dwell within thy wounds; then pain
Is sweet, and life or death is gain.

Take my poor heart, and let it be
For ever clos'd to all but thee!
Seal thou my breast, and let me wear
That pledge of love for ever there.

How blest are they who still abide
Close shelter'd in thy bleeding side!
Who life and strength from thence derive,
And by thee move, and in thee live.

What are our works but sin and death,
Till thou thy quick'ning Spirit breathe?
Thou giv'st the power thy grace to move;
O wond'rous grace! O boundless love!

This hymn reflects some of the ardent longing for God that was so much a part of the revivals during the first half of the nineteenth century. It is taken from The Wesleyan Sacred Harp: A Collection of Choice Tunes and Hymns for Prayer, Class, and Camp Meeting, Choirs, and Congregational Singing, *which was published in Boston, Cleveland, and New York in 1856.*

165

The Second Great Awakening

The Second Great Awakening was the most influential revival of Christianity in the history of the United States. Its very size and its many expressions have led some historians to question whether a *single* Second Great Awakening can be identified as such. Yet from about 1795 to about 1810 there was a broad and general rekindling of interest in Christianity throughout the country. This renewal, in turn, provided a pattern and an impetus for similar waves of revival that continued throughout the nation until after the Civil War.

The state of Christianity in the United States after the American Revolution was not good. The tide of warfare itself had disrupted many local congregations, particularly where fighting had been most intense — in New Jersey, New York City, the Philadelphia area, and the Carolinas. The Revolution had dealt an especially hard blow to the Episcopal Church, whose ties with England made it particularly suspect. The disestablishment of the churches in the Southern states and attacks on the tie between states and the church in New England also led to uncertainty.

Interest in religion more generally also seemed on the decline. Concern for creating a new nation, for populating the open lands west of the Appalachians, for overcoming the ravages of inflation, and for avoiding foreign entanglements left little time for church. In addition, a well-publicized attack on traditional Christianity convinced some that the old faith was not worth preserving. This attack was led by the deists Ethan Allen, who had captured Fort Ticonderoga during the War "in the name of the Great Jehovah and the Continental Congress," and Tom Paine, whose book *The Age of Reason* (1794, 1796), with its questioning of traditional supernaturalism, was almost as widely discussed as his earlier condemnation of British rule, *Common Sense* (1776). As a result of these varied influences, allegiance to the churches wavered. Well under 10 percent of the population belonged formally to local congregations, and many areas on the frontier were entirely devoid of Christian influence.

To be sure, scattered outbursts of Christian renewal had continued to take place during the War and afterward. Immigrant communities continued to nourish a variety of Christian faiths from the Old World. The Congregational heirs of Jonathan Edwards in New England saw occasional local revivals as a result of their labors. Presbyterians in the middle states also witnessed occasional spurts of religious interest. Baptists, active in the

South in the wake of the colonial revivals, had some encouraging successes. The "Revolutionary Revival" in backcountry New England and New York prepared the way for a spiritual harvest among the ordinary people. These local revivals were important for "awakening" a few individuals who later come to the fore as revival leaders, such as Barton W. Stone in Virginia. But they did not yet amount to a major change of religious direction.

The West

Change, however, was the order of the day from the mid-1790s onward. In the opening frontier, a recovery of faith had its genesis in the dedicated missionary work of Presbyterians such as James McGready and itinerants from the Baptist and Methodist churches. McGready's church in Logan County, Kentucky, began in 1797 to pray regularly "for the conversion of sinners in Logan County, and throughout the world." In 1801 the efforts of McGready and like-minded leaders bore spectacular fruit. In August of that year a great "camp meeting" convened at Cane Ridge, Kentucky. Thousands streamed to this gathering, as many preachers — black and white; Presbyterian, Baptist, and Methodist — fervently proclaimed the Good News. The form of the meeting owed something to the Scottish observance of the "communion season" (described in Chap. 3). But if the pattern of intense evangelistic gatherings lasting several days originated in Scotland, it assumed an unusually powerful force in the backcountry where Scottish immigrants were only part of a mobile population drawn from many sources.

The results at Cane Ridge were electrifying. Some of the unusual bodily effects — the jerks, dancing, laughing, running, and "the barking exercise" — can be attributed to powerful psychological release. Isolated families, subject to a hard and perilous life, were responding with their emotions to stirring messages from charismatic leaders. Other effects — such as the rapid establishment of churches that followed the camp meetings — were more clearly religious. The renewed interest in the faith touched off at Cane Ridge and similar camp meetings led to a rapid growth in Presbyterian churches in the South. By comparison, however, Presbyterian efforts paled beside the accomplishments of the Methodists and Baptists. Methodist circuit riders and Baptist farmer-preachers fanned out through the South and the opening West in unprecedented numbers. By the 1830s these groups had replaced the Congregationalists and Presbyterians as the largest denominations, not only in the South but in the whole United States.

This 1867 *Harper's* depiction of a Methodist circuit rider captures well the determined dedication of this hardy breed. *Courtesy of the Billy Graham Center Museum*

The East

In the East, concern for revival gripped several local Congregational ministers in Connecticut during the early 1790s. By the turn of the century a considerable network of these ministers was exchanging information on signs of religious vitality. Together they were praying and preaching for the revival of church attenders and for the conversion of the indifferent. The work of Timothy Dwight (1752-1817), a grandson of Jonathan Edwards who became president of Yale College in 1795, was the most visible expression of this activity. When he arrived in New Haven, Dwight found many of his students at least superficially attached to the deistical fashions of the French Enlightenment. To meet the challenges of "infidelity," Dwight launched a two-pronged effort. He labored by forthright argument to restore confidence in the Bible, and he began a four-year cycle of sermons designed to communicate the essentials of the faith. Progress was slight at first, but in 1802 revival swept the Yale campus. A third of the 225 students were converted, and many of these became agents for revival and reform in New England, upstate New York, and the West. These college graduates did not so much create the local revivals, which had been taking place for decades in out-of-the-way rural villages, as they expanded their influence. Together with the promoters of local revivals, they spread concern for renewal up and down the East Coast. Soon there was hardly a locale in which Christians were not praying for revival or thanking God for having received one.

First and Second Awakenings Compared

One good way to understand the revivals in early national America is to compare them with the colonial revivals. In both, a concern for personal salvation predominated. Preachers in 1800 no less than in 1740 were telling whoever would listen what they had to do to be saved. In both, as well, concern for revival in America was related to a similar concern for world-wide Christian renewal. Revivalists in both awakenings communicated with colleagues in England, Scotland, and on the Continent. And in both, a network of correspondents arose who learned from each other and rejoiced or sorrowed as revivals waxed or waned in the Atlantic community.

But there were also major differences. Where Congregationalists (Jonathan Edwards), Anglicans (George Whitefield), and Presbyterians (Gilbert Tennent) had spearheaded the first Awakening, Methodists, Baptists, and Disciples (Barton Stone and Alexander Campbell) rapidly came to dominate the second. The second Awakening also left a more permanent legacy than did the first. The great profusion of voluntary societies that sprang up in America in the first third of the nineteenth century can be traced directly to the energies of the Second Great Awakening.

One of Timothy Dwight's pupils, Lyman Beecher (1775-1863), was particularly active in organizing the forces of the revival into permanent organizations designed to evangelize and reform America. Through the efforts of Beecher and people with his vision, the country saw the founding of the American Board for Foreign Missions (1810), the American Bible Society (1816), the Colonization Society for liberated slaves (1817), the American Sunday School Union (1824), the American Tract Society (1825), the American Education Society (1826), the American Society for the Promotion of Temperance (1826), the American Home Missionary Society (1826), and many more organizations. Such agencies gave the second Awakening a long-lived institutional influence that the first had not produced.

Lyman Beecher not only stage-managed many of the enterprises making up "the evangelical united front" before the the Civil War but also left a numerous family, including the pulpiteer Henry Ward Beecher and the novelist Harriet Beecher Stowe, that continued to influence American Protestant life for the rest of the century. *National Portrait Gallery, Washington, D.C. / Art Resources, New York*

The theology of the Second Great Awakening also differed from the earlier revival tradition. Stressing God's sovereignty in all things, Edwards and Whitefield had emphasized the inability of sinful people to save themselves. The theology of leading revivalists in the nineteenth century, both North and South, suggested that God had bestowed on all people the ability to come to Christ. This shift in perspective was related to the larger political and intellectual developments we have already noted, but it also arose from a widespread desire for a theology of action that could encourage and justify the expanding revivals of Christianity.

Exemplary Leaders

Two individuals more than any others embodied the major thrusts of the revival impulse. The first was an Englishman who eventually traveled over more of America than probably any other person in his generation, the Methodist Francis Asbury. The second, a Presbyterian-become-Congregationalist who may have had a greater impact on the public life of antebellum America than any of the nation's politicians, was Charles Grandison Finney.

Francis Asbury and the Rise of Methodism

Francis Asbury (1745-1816) was born in Birmingham, England, where his parents were early followers of John Wesley, the founder of Methodism. Their son was converted at the age of thirteen and began lay preaching three years later. When in 1771 Wesley asked for volunteers for America, Asbury responded eagerly. Upon his arrival, Asbury soon assumed leadership of the four Methodist workers already here. While his colleagues favored a "settled" clergy located in populous areas, Asbury was convinced that preachers should go where the gospel was most needed. His example set the style for the itinerant Methodist minister in early America. Later he would exhort his associates to "go into every kitchen and shop; address all, aged and young, on the salvation of their souls." Asbury's desire to spread the gospel kept him on the move the rest of his life. Before he died, he traveled nearly 300,000 miles, mostly on horseback, on trips that also took him on several occasions into Canada. He crossed the Appalachians more than sixty times to reach the previously unreached Americans. He knew more of the American countryside than any other person of his generation. In turn, he may have been known by more North Americans than any of his contemporaries.

Despite Asbury's energetic efforts, the Methodists did not experience immediate growth. One reason was the War for Independence. When violence erupted in 1775, all of the Methodist missionaries except Asbury returned to England. The Methodists were also hurt by their association with the Church of England, an association that American patriots perceived as disloyalty to the United States. Asbury himself had to retire into Delaware when authorities in Maryland banished him for not signing a loyalty oath to the new state government. It took many years for the American followers of Wesley to overcome the stigma of disloyalty.

But overcome it they did, and with a vengeance. After the War, Asbury guided the Methodists in setting up an organization that bound eastern centers to missionary outposts on the frontier. In addition, when Asbury, at John Wesley's appointment, became "general superintendent" of the Methodists in North America, an unusually effective arrangement was in place for promoting Methodist interests. A paradox was that Methodism would be the "religion of the people" par excellence in the early United States, but Asbury as leader exercised extraordinarily tight control of the movement. This combination of democratic and autocratic tendencies was enshrined in the official organization of the American Methodists, which took place in December 1784 under Asbury's guidance at a famous Christmas Conference in Baltimore. From that time on the church grew rapidly, particularly west of the mountains, where the rough life and the near-

The word *indefatigable* was made for Francis Asbury, who probably walked or rode a horse over more American territory than any other person in the first decades of the United States. *Courtesy of the Billy Graham Center Museum*

barbarism of the population discouraged representatives of more traditional denominations.

Asbury's message in city and wilderness alike was traditionally Christian, with the special Wesleyan emphases: God's free grace, humanity's liberty to accept or reject that grace, and the Christian's need to strive for "perfection" (an end to willful sin after conversion). Asbury used the Methodist pattern of organization — local classes, preaching circuits, and general conferences — to further the growth of the church and, in the process, to civilize the frontier.

Asbury also was a particularly effective spokesman for a distinctly Wesleyan spirituality. This piety did not deny doctrine or repudiate the importance of church structures; rather, it subordinated these matters to the higher goals of communing with Christ and the faithful. The original Methodists opposed formality, sought what historian Gregory Schneider has called "the mystery of intimacy," and insisted that outward behavior should match the inward conversion of the heart. Sentiments like those in the hymn appearing at the start of this chapter were the heart of Methodist spirituality. Combining the tenderest expressions of love and the most demanding stan-

By 1869, when this print was made of "The Central Circle" at the National Camp Meeting, Round Lake, New York, camp meetings had become better organized but also somewhat less powerful than in the earlier history of American Methodism.
Courtesy of the Billy Graham Center Museum

dards of righteousness, Methodist piety — even more than Methodist organization — transformed the Christian landscape of early America.

Asbury's normal activities were strenuous. As he put it in one report in his journal, "my present mode of conduct is . . . to read about one hundred pages a day; to preach in the open air every other day; and to lecture in prayer meeting every evening." His journeys were often difficult, but Asbury was undaunted: "The water froze as it ran from the horse's nostrils. . . . I have suffered a little by lodging in open houses this cold weather; but this is a very small thing when compared to what the dear Redeemer suffered for the salvation of precious souls." His vision of Christianity reached beyond the inner life to take in social responsibilities as well. Asbury established educational institutions, he willed his very modest estate to the Methodist "Book Concern," he argued against slavery, and he urged abstinence from hard liquor.

Statistics can never tell a whole story, but when Francis Asbury came to America in 1771 four Methodist ministers were caring for about 300 laypeople. When he died in 1816, there were 2,000 ministers and over 200,000 Methodists in the States and several thousand more in Canada devoted, as he put it, to "the dear Redeemer . . . of precious souls."

As was the case for the early Puritans, the Methodists' greatest problem may have been their own success. Methodism flourished when its energies were dispersed in rural camp meetings and countless local classes of ordinary believers. When it became more like a traditional denomination — with settled pastors competing for urban pulpits and publicists putting out literature imitating the books of established denominations — the growth began to slow. In this regard the Methodists on a large scale resembled such dissenters of the Revolutionary era as the Shakers, Free Will Baptists, and Universalists. These populists had earlier experienced the same stages that later characterized Methodist history — in the 1780s, powerful proclamation alongside confused or absent leadership; in the 1790s, increasing institutional stability along with more careful definition of theology; by 1820, a growing resemblance to older denominations with traditions and bureaucracies of their own. Early Methodist leadership had been more centralized, but otherwise Methodism followed this pattern. Later, other dissident groups such as the Mormons and the Seventh-Day Adventists would pursue a similar course. A general conclusion explaining the common pattern requires a subtle blend of religious and institutional analysis.

The emergence of the Methodists is one of the great stories in American history, but expert work on the inner character of the movement has only just begun. Clearly the ability of Asbury and his colleagues to control a far-flung populist army of circuit riders is part of the story. But for the rise of the Methodists, spiritual realities were just as important as organizational genius.

Charles Finney and Modern Revivalism

In the generation after Asbury, Charles Grandison Finney (1792-1875) emerged as the best-known revivalist in the United States. Finney's range was breath-taking. He created powerful yet controlled revivalistic "methods" for the frontier (upstate New York, Ohio) at the same time that he orchestrated successful evangelism in the nation's major cities (especially Boston and New York) and overseas in Britain. More than any other individual of his day he succeeded in joining evangelical religion to social reform. Although he never allowed other interests to supersede evangelism, Finney was an effective promoter of benevolence, an abolitionist, a pioneer of coeducation at Oberlin College, a reformer in many areas (temperance, peace, sabbatarianism, and care for the retarded), a promoter of such things as phrenology and the Graham diet, and an opponent of Masonry. In addition, he formalized ties between conservative theology and industrial

Even in a domestic portrait, the penetrating gaze of Charles Finney indicates
why he was such a riveting speaker from the pulpit.
Courtesy of the Billy Graham Center Museum

wealth that still characterize evangelical culture. If this were not enough,
Finney's theological emphases on the Moral Government of God, the powers
of the human will, and the state of entire sanctification played a key role in
the evolution of American Protestant theology.

Finney experienced a dramatic conversion in 1821 while a legal ap-
prentice in Adams, New York. He began preaching almost immediately and
soon acquired a local reputation for vigorous, confrontational sermons. In
1827 he met ecclesiastical opponents from New England at a famous meeting in New Lebanon, New York, and successfully defended his "new measures" against charges of innovation and anarchy. A great revival in Rochester over the winter of 1830-31 catapulted him to national renown. He
soon conducted extended preaching campaigns in Philadelphia, Boston, and
New York. During the early 1830s he completed his break from traditional

Presbyterianism, which he viewed as laboring under burdensome organizational handicaps and a theology unappreciative of native human ability. By the mid-1830s Finney had become the mentor to a growing number of ardent young reformers who wanted to see Christianity as they understood it renewing society as well as individuals. Among these reformers were some of the nation's leading abolitionists. A few of their older associates were influential in convincing Finney that he should move to Oberlin College in Ohio, which they planned as a center of both evangelism and social reform. From Oberlin Finney later traveled to Great Britain and mounted other social campaigns, including his offensive against the Masons after 1860. And at Oberlin, Finney fully supported the admission of women as regular students (it was the first college in the country to do so). Major books spread his views even further, especially his *Lectures on Revivals* (1835) and *Systematic Theology* (1846-47).

Finney's impact was especially great in shaping the practices of revival. His use of the "anxious bench," for example, took over a Methodist practice and made it into a norm of later revivalism. The anxious bench was a specially designated area, usually in front of the auditorium to which Finney called people for prayer or to be admonished about the condition of their souls. It was one of the "new measures," along with the "protracted meeting" (or nightly gatherings for several weeks) for which Finney's evangelism was famous. Revivalists before Finney were more willing to leave the timing of conversions to God. Finney, however, felt that if God had commanded individuals to repent, he had also given them the means to do so *at once*. The anxious bench led to the modern evangelistic practice of coming to the front at the end of a religious service to indicate a desire for salvation. Of the anxious seat Finney himself said, "if you say to [the sinner], 'There is the anxious seat, come out and avow your determination to be on the Lord's side,' and if he is not willing to do so small a thing as that, then he is not willing to do *any thing*." The German Reformed minister J. W. Nevin (1803-1886) spoke for many critics of Finney in such works as his *Anxious Bench* (1843), in which he suggested that Finney's "new measures" put too much emphasis on man's action in conversion and too little on God's. According to Finney, however, the best defense of the practice was that it worked.

Because of his dominant role in the revival tradition, and the dominant place that revivalism assumed in the antebellum period, a good case can be made that Finney should be ranked with Andrew Jackson, Abraham Lincoln, and Andrew Carnegie (or some other representative industrialist) as one of the most important public figures in nineteenth-century America. Beyond doubt, he stands by himself as *the* crucial figure in white American evangelicalism after Jonathan Edwards. In fact, a good case can be made that

This early sketch of Oberlin College shows a revival meeting tent on "Tappan Square," named after New York merchants Arthur and Lewis Tappan, who helped fund Oberlin as a center for higher education and Christian holiness.
Courtesy of the Billy Graham Center Museum

Finney exerted a more significant influence on American life, and certainly on American religion, than such other key figures as the essayist Ralph Waldo Emerson, the political statesman Daniel Webster, the educational reformer Horace Mann, and the historian Henry Adams.

In his theology, Finney was yet more Arminian than John Wesley: Wesley maintained that the human will is incapable of choosing God apart from God's preparatory grace, but Finney rejected this requirement. He was a perfectionist who believed that a permanent stage of higher spiritual life was possible for anyone who sought it wholeheartedly. Following the theologians of New England, he held a governmental view of the atonement whereby Christ's death was a public demonstration of God's willingness to forgive sins rather than a payment for sin itself. And he tended toward a belief that emotions are the culprits that keep reason and will from following God's purposes.

Finney's zeal, his penetrating gaze, and his moral rectitude made him a daunting figure. At the same time, Finney offers a refreshing contrast to at least some who have exploited revivalism as a means of self-promotion. Not for him was the blithe pursuit of mammon that has come to characterize our contemporary television evangelists. In 1837, shortly after giving up a large New York church for the duties of a theology professor at Oberlin, Finney was so pressed for funds that he was forced to sell "my travelling trunk, which I had used in my evangelistic labors." His response was simply to pray and to conclude "that, if help did not come, I should assume that it was best that it should not."

Asbury and Finney were representatives of the most visible religious movements between the Revolution and the Civil War. They were both Arminians who succeeded in modifying a hereditary Calvinism to fit more easily into the ethos of the new republic. They were both charismatic figures who relied on their own native abilities instead of inherited status or educational certification to convince others of their message. They were both great communicators, and both gave the American faith a distinctly populist tone. They both had broad visions of Christian society, not extending (it is true) to questions about the structures of economic life but nonetheless defining Christian social responsibilities as clearly as they defined personal spiritual duties. Together with like-minded leaders of only slightly less influence, they established the revival and the voluntary society as the foundations of American Protestant faith.

Mobilization of the Baptists

The Second Great Awakening also stimulated a burst of Baptist growth. Particularly in the southern and new western states, Baptists became leaders in evangelizing the frontier population. By 1812, there were close to 200,000 Baptists in the United States, with half of them in the states of Virginia, North and South Carolina, Georgia, and Kentucky. By 1850, the total exceeded 1,000,000. By that time, nearly three-fourths of them were also cooperating in national missionary ventures.

Throughout the antebellum period, Baptist theology remained predominantly Calvinistic. An important confession drawn up to serve a New Hampshire association in 1833 became a widely used statement of Baptist faith. Except on principles of church organization, the doctrinal parts of this confession closely resembled the kind of theology promoted by conservative Congregationalists and Presbyterians. At the same time, Baptist practice laid a heavy stress on the experience of personal conversion. Baptists also shared the general American confidence in the powers of a free people. The effect was to soften in practice, at least with many Baptists, the Calvinistic doctrines of unconditional election and limited atonement (i.e., the beliefs that God's foreordination was the fundamental reason why a person became a Christian and that Christ's death was effective only for those foreordained by God for eternal salvation). But throughout the nineteenth century, the Baptists who lined up with the Methodists in their evangelistic zeal continued to resemble the older Calvinists in their formal theology.

Baptists were intense localists. Congregational freedom was a principle only slightly less valued than the authority of the Bible. Yet out of the desire to expand evangelization, at first on the frontier and then around the world, Baptists overcame their feisty independence and found ways to work together. Local associations of Baptist churches, such as the Warren Association that Isaac Backus had developed in New England, were cooperating in evangelistic efforts on the frontier before 1800. The revivals of the Second Great Awakening increased interest in missionary outreach even more. Efforts to provide sponsorship for pioneering overseas workers led in 1814 to the organization of the "General Missionary Convention of the Baptist Denomination in the United States for Missions." This institution, known as the Triennial Convention because it met every three years, commissioned nearly one hundred missionaries in its first two decades.

As early as 1802 the Massachusetts Baptist Missionary Society was sending missionaries to plant churches on the frontier of the upper Midwest. Other state and local associations carried on similar efforts until in 1832 the American Baptist Home Mission Society was formed to coordinate these labors. This body was never as successful as the Triennial Convention, in part because state associations continued to organize their own evangelistic efforts and in part because Southerners complained that its efforts went disproportionately to the North.

North-South tensions eventually led to the most significant of Baptist institutional efforts. In the 1840s, the national mission agencies began to raise increasingly strong objections to certifying candidates who owned slaves. In response, Baptist churches in the South withdrew their support. In 1845 many of these banded together to form the Southern Baptist Convention (SBC), an event marking a new era in the history of American Baptists. For the first time a large number of these independent-minded folk had taken on a fully denominational structure like that of other Protestant bodies. Although not as authoritarian as the bishops of Methodism or the General Assemblies of Presbyterians, the SBC nevertheless provided a degree of centralized authority unknown among Baptists prior to that time. (The comparable development that resulted in the formation of the Northern Baptist Convention did not take place until 1905.)

From the first, however, significant numbers of Baptists in the South resisted the centralizing tendencies of the SBC. Some were uncomfortable with the predominant Calvinism of that body. Following the early teaching of Paul Palmer (d. ca. 1750) of North Carolina, groups of Free Will Baptist and General Baptists continued to affirm doctrines of "free grace," "free will," and "free salvation." Other Baptists resisted the denominational structure of the SBC. These groups refused any compromise to strict standards of local congregational autonomy. For their resistance to the idea of outside, denominational control, these Baptists became known as "Primitive," "Old School," "Regular," "Hard Shell," or "Anti-Mission." These groups tended to be determinedly Calvinistic, and they frowned on coordinated missionary or educational activity that took funds or personnel out of the control of individual churches. Later in the century, what came to be known as the "Landmark" emphasis in the SBC reflected the influence of these Baptist dissenters. This movement, following the lead of Tennessee's James R. Graves's influential book *An Old Landmark Re-Set* (1854), advocated the belief that the church is not in any meaningful sense universal but is rather local and visible. From this viewpoint, a "true" Baptist was one who believed that baptism is valid only when administered by a New Testament (i.e., Baptist) church, that membership cannot be transferred from local assembly to local assembly, and that baptisms administered some place other than the local congregation constituted an "alien" ordinance and had no standing.

The Southern Baptist Convention eventually became the largest Protestant denomination in America. But for all its influence, especially in the South, that body has always been outnumbered by Baptists who chose not to affiliate with the SBC.

Baptists had many important leaders in the antebellum period, though none as visible as Francis Asbury and Charles Finney. What they lacked in visible leadership, however, they made up in vigor. Baptist agencies became, after parallel bodies formed by the Methodists, the most active Protestant institutions in the United States. Their aggressive strategies for outreach, their combination of determined congregationalism and institutional association, and their traditional Calvinism adjusted to the American environment made Baptists a powerful force in the South and on the frontier.

A New Visibility for Women

The revivals of the early nineteenth century also brought women to the visible forefront of the churches and even, to some extent, to the forefront of public life in general. Women had always been the mainstay of the churches in North America. In Puritan New England, men and women had joined the churches in roughly equal proportions during the first years of settlement and in the wake of the Great Awakening. But for the rest of New England's Puritan history, women consistently outnumbered men in church: by the end of the seventeenth century, they constituted three-quarters of those joining some of the major churches of the region. Ratios are hard to determine exactly in other colonies, but the predominance of female membership seems to have been mirrored elsewhere as well.

In the early nineteenth century, women remained the majority of those who adhered most closely to the churches. And it was at this point that changing social conditions and new theological emphases began to offer them more opportunities for public ministry. A more fluid social setting on the seaboard as well in the thinly populated regions newly opened to settlement and the rhetoric of democracy from the Revolution both served to advance women in the public practice of religion. In many areas of the country it soon became conventional to look upon women as the prime support for the nation's republican spirit. Mothers, it was thought, were the ones who could most effectively inculcate the virtues of public-spiritedness and self-sacrifice that were essential to the life of the republic. And such notions were increasingly linked to the idea that women had a special capacity for the religious life, as individuals who could understand intuitively the virtues of sacrifice, devotion, and trust that were so important to the Christian faith.

Phoebe Palmer and the Appeal of Holiness

Perhaps the most important factor in the emergence of women as public figures in the antebellum period was a new emphasis from revivalists (especially the Methodists) on holiness of life. John Wesley's doctrine of "Christian perfection," or freedom from all known sin, had been part of Methodist teaching in America from the start. To that emphasis, revivalists such as Charles Finney added exhortations to go on to "perfect love" or "entire sanctification." The result was new expectations about the work of the Holy Spirit in converted individuals. Those who had been brought to Christ should proceed with the Spirit to seek the perfection promised by God to those who sought him with all their hearts. In these exhortations, especially in the teaching of the Methodists, there were no barriers of gender. Women as well as men could find "the second blessing." Once found, it seemed only natural that women as well as men should promote the work of godliness as energetically as possible. With this theological orientation it became increasingly common for women to take part in revivals and soon also in

181

With her message of Holiness
(or complete surrender to God),
Phoebe Palmer was one of the
most influential Protestant
teachers of any kind during the
nineteenth century in both the
United States and Canada.
*Courtesy of the Billy Graham Center
Museum*

the social reform, especially the temperance and abolition movements, that
grew out of the revivals.

The career of one of the leading holiness advocates illustrates the
power of this teaching. Phoebe Worrall Palmer (1807-1874) was raised in
New York in a conventionally Christian home. Her husband, Walter Palmer,
was a physician, with whom she enjoyed close spiritual as well as domestic
accord. During the early years of their marriage, the Palmers experienced
the devastating loss of three young children. But Mrs. Palmer continued her
activity as a private Bible teacher, and she longed for a deeper experience
of the faith. This was given to her on July 26, 1837, which she always called
thereafter "the day of days." After receiving a special sense of the Holy Spirit's
indwelling power, she began to share the experience, and the life of hope
opened by the experience, with others. Her forum was a weekly gathering
in New York City established by her sister Mrs. Sarah Lankford, who had
experienced the indwelling of the Spirit in 1835. This "Tuesday Meeting for
the Promotion of Holiness" became a magnet for a distinguished group of
believers and soon for prominent teachers of holiness from throughout the
English-speaking world.

Mrs. Palmer was at first reluctant to share her experiences with men
present, but after Thomas Upham, a prominent Congregational minister,

received the fullness of the Spirit under her guidance, she set aside social convention and talked to all who would listen. Soon she also began to write for the religious press. In 1843 a number of essays that had originally appeared in the *Christian Advocate and Journal* were reprinted in a collection entitled *The Way of Holiness*, which proved to be an immediate success both at home and abroad. Years later, Phoebe Palmer confessed that when she set to work on this book, she was in poor health and expected soon to die. But her life was spared, and she went on with her husband to conduct a ministry of personal counseling, publishing, and public speaking in the United States, Canada, and Britain.

In an age when women were not forthcoming in public, Mrs. Palmer proclaimed her message winsomely and without attempting to draw attention to herself. She even published several of her books anonymously. At the same time, she insisted that God's grace was poured out on women and men alike and that all who tasted the heavenly gift had the obligation to pass it on. In 1859 she published *The Promise of the Father*, a vigorous defense of women's right to preach, a work that makes much of such biblical passages as Galatians 3:28 ("there is neither . . . male nor female; for you are all one in Christ Jesus") and Joel 2:28 ("your sons and daughters will prophesy"). So it was that although Phoebe Palmer sought primarily the promotion of holiness, she also furthered the public role of women in the religious life of America.

Public Life

The same passages that Phoebe Palmer had employed to justify her work were also put to use by the Reverend Luther Lee when, in 1853, he presided over the ordination of Antoinette Brown to the ministry of the Congregational Church. This was the first formal ordination of a woman in America, although women, black and white, had been active as regular preachers before this time. The Free Will Baptist revivalist Nancy Towle had preached publicly in New England from about 1815 and then throughout the East Coast. She once was even invited to preach to the United States Congress. Formal ordination, however, was rare in the nineteenth century (Antoinette Brown herself later resigned her ministerial position after she left the Congregationalists for the Unitarians). But such events as Brown's ordination nonetheless testified to a growing involvement of women in the public life of America's churches.

The revivals encouraged women to play a more active part not only in narrowly spiritual matters but also in the larger arenas of social reform.

Many reform-minded church women were active in the woman's suffrage movement. *Library of Congress*

Often in the context of revival, women strove mightily against slavery (Sarah and Angelina Grimké), for better treatment of the mentally ill (Dorothea Dix), for educational opportunities for women (Catherine Beecher), and later in the temperance crusade (Frances Willard) and social work in the cities (Jane Addams).

Intense female involvement especially in the areas of temperance (liberation from the bondage of drink) and abolition (liberation from the bondage of slavery) seemed almost naturally to spill over into growing concern for liberation from the social bondage of women themselves. The religious factor in that move was always prominent. The first formal call for fuller women's rights in society, including the right to vote, was issued from Seneca Falls, New York, in July 1848, when active abolitionists, men and women, white and black, issued an appeal for the public rights of women. Conveners of the meeting were Lucretia Coffin Mott (1793-1880) and Elizabeth Cady Stanton (1815-1902), both of whom had long been nurtured in centers of religious reform, Mott having served as an "acknowledged

184

minister" in the Society of Friends and Stanton having taken a more conventional path through evangelical nurturing to social reform. Significantly, the Seneca Falls meeting took place in the town's Wesleyan Methodist Church, the representative of a denomination that only shortly before had broken from the main group of Methodists precisely out of a desire to promote more vigorously both holiness and abolition.

The new spheres opening up for women in America even came to include the leadership of religious movements. Ann Lee (1736-1784), founder of the "Shakers," had immigrated from her native Manchester, England, to the colonies in 1774. While in prison in England for preaching as a Quaker, she received a vision ordaining her the "Second Pillar of the Church of God," the female counterpart to the male principle revealed in Christ. In America, her teaching proved attractive to many whom revivalists had urged to seek a higher form of spirituality. By the Civil War, about 6,000 adherents in nineteen communities were following the way of celibacy, frugality, communalism, millennialism, pacifism, vegetarianism, spiritualism, and industry that she had marked out for her followers. Ann Lee thus pioneered where other religious founders, including Ellen White of the Seventh-Day Adventists and Mary Baker Eddy of the Christian Scientists, would follow.

A Missionary Vision

One feature of the evangelical mobilization that had dramatic long-range consequences for Christianity in America was the new vision for missionary work that emerged. Protestant missions from English-speaking lands had begun only shortly before with the sailing of William Carey from England to India in 1793. Soon thereafter, Americans followed their English coreligionists in commissioning missionaries for evangelism overseas. What followed was growing concern for bringing the Christian message to unreached peoples abroad and on the American continent. As significant as the overseas work became, however, the great achievement of missions in the nineteenth century was the conversion of American and Canadian citizens. The vision of Asbury, Finney, Baptist farmer-preachers, and likeminded individuals inspired North Americans to take the gospel abroad, but the work done by those who stayed at home to evangelize and civilize America was *the* truly great missionary story of the century.

Enthusiasm for missions work began after a period of revival at Williams College. It then spilled over into the student body of Andover Theological Seminary. Andover was the nation's first full-fledged school for theo-

Through his decades of missionary labor in Burma, Adoniram Judson became the first great missionary hero for Protestant Americans. *Courtesy of the Billy Graham Center Museum*

logical education, which was being founded at that very time (1807) by a coalition of New England's Trinitarian Congregationalists in protest against Harvard College's drift toward Unitarianism. The life of Samuel J. Mills, Jr. (1783-1818), who experienced the events at Williams and at early Andover, illustrates the aspirations of the movement.

With several other students from Williams College, Mills had been forced to take refuge in a farmyard from a summer rainstorm in 1806. While sheltered by a haystack, the students held a prayer meeting, committing themselves to take the gospel across the seas. Along with several of his prayer partners, Mills went on to Andover Seminary, where they created a more formal organization to achieve their missionary goals. With friends, Mills helped found the American Board of Commissioners for Foreign Missions (ABCFM) in 1810. By 1812 this organization had dispatched the first American missionaries to India and the Far East. Poor health prevented Mills himself from going overseas, but in the period from 1812 to 1814 he was sent by the Congregational home missions societies of Massachusetts and Connecticut on extensive tours of the western United States to assess the need for missionaries there. Soon thereafter ministers were sent to frontier areas, one of them becoming the first permanent Protestant minister in the Mississippi Valley (1816). Mills's concern for spreading the gospel on the frontier bore fruit after his death in the establishment of the American Home Missionary Society (1826).

Among the first contingent of five that went to India in 1812 under the American Board was Adoniram Judson (1788-1850), who later became a greatly revered figure among American Protestants. Judson's conversion to Baptist convictions while on board ship to the East estranged him from the ABCFM but led in 1814 to the establishment of the Baptist Triennial Convention. Judson worked as a missionary for nearly forty years in Burma, where reports on his efforts were followed up diligently by a host of Americans eager for news of the progress of the gospel. Americans also took a great interest in the women who served with Judson, especially the first of his four successive wives, Ann Hasseltine Judson (1789-1826). Books on the work of the Judsons were best-sellers in antebellum America, indicating that confidence in the spread of the faith in America was broadening to include eager anticipation of its spread elsewhere.

The Ambiguous Mission to the Cherokees

Innovations in missionary work on the North American continent are well illustrated by efforts to bring Christianity to the Cherokees of Georgia and neighboring states. But the tragedy of this story also speaks of the general ambiguity of American missions of the era, when evangelization often involved a fatal and indiscriminate mingling of Christian and national values. After the Revolutionary War, the United States exacted retribution from the old Cherokee Nation (located in northern Georgia, eastern Tennessee, and western North Carolina) for siding with the British and for blocking national expansion to the southwest. A peace treaty of 1794 stimulated a cultural revival among the Cherokees and also opened the way for white missionaries to begin their work. While the Cherokees built roads, organized politically in imitation of whites, rendered their language in writing, and began to print their own books and newspapers, they also welcomed Protestant missionaries. Moravians, with single-minded spiritual purpose, were among the first to arrive. Presbyterians, Congregationalists, and Baptists, who more thoroughly mingled evangelization and Americanization, were soon on the scene in greater numbers.

What followed was a slow but steady acceptance of the Christian faith. Some of the Native Americans resisted and contributed to the periodic revivals of tribal religion that so distressed the missionaries. Some became all-out converts and took their cues entirely from the missionaries. Still others became Christians and took on American ways, albeit exercising

Missionary work among Native Americans was difficult for missionaries and Indians alike. Sometimes, however, there was success that satisfied both, as in the work of the Reverend Abel Bingham, shown here with two women colleagues and a small group of their converts. *Courtesy of the Billy Graham Center Museum*

considerable discretion in the process, retaining selective elements of Native-American religion in their new faith and using the symbols and doctrines of Christianity to resist total assimilation into white culture. The Cherokee leader Elias Boudinot, who took his name from the first president of the American Bible Society, illustrated how far the twin processes of Christianization and cultural conversion could advance in one generation. Boudinot studied at a local Indian academy, then in a missionary school in Connecticut, and finally for a year at Andover Seminary before returning to Georgia to become a translator, writer, and publisher among his people.

During the administration of President Andrew Jackson, however, the evangelism of the missionaries and the work of selective cultural adaptation by the Cherokees both received a fatal blow. After the discovery of gold in northern Georgia about the time of Jackson's election in 1828, the lust of white settlers for Cherokee land grew even stronger than before. Jackson and his agents for Indian affairs were eager to give it to them. The result was a forced removal of the Cherokees from Georgia to the West. Despite the fact that the Cherokees had adapted to American ways with remarkable skill, the removal proceeded with ruthless finality. The missionaries, who had come to the Native Americans as bearers of civilization as well as of Christianity, faced a terrible dilemma. They now were forced to watch their country, supposedly the embodiment of Christian civilization, turn violently against a people that had responded to their message.

Missionary executives away from the field and many of the missionaries working with the Cherokees caved in to the pressure and acceded peacefully to the removal. But others protested vigorously, even to the point of civil disobedience. Samuel Worcester and Elizur Butler went to jail rather than obey a Georgia state law demanding whites to leave Cherokee land (as a prelude to a forcible takeover). The Northern Baptists Evan Jones and his son John B. Jones fought for Cherokee rights in the southeast and then journeyed with the outcasts to Oklahoma, where they continued the work of evangelization and education. The ministers they trained formed the backbone of a sturdy network of Baptist Cherokee churches that eventually developed in the new tribal lands. So effectively did the Joneses champion their cause that the Cherokees adopted them into the tribe. But missionary support for the Cherokees was not enough, and the brutal removal went on. The United States, bearing the gifts of Christian faith and republican politics, destroyed a tribal people that was working to accept those gifts. Some missionary spokesmen, unlike Worcester, Butler, and the Joneses, played a signal part in that destruction. Such spokesmen were good culture Christians. The agents of Andrew Jackson's Indian policy were good democrats. Together they did the devil's work in the name of the Lord and of his "chosen country."

Interpretations

Historians of a previous generation were prone to contend that Asbury, Finney, Baptist organizers, and such Congregationalist spokesmen as Timothy Dwight and Lyman Beecher, along with leaders of the new denominations on the frontier, represented efforts by Christian clergy to control an American society that was escaping their grip. To some extent this interpretation is valid. The revivalists and voluntary organizers did want to see American life ordered by the precepts of their religion. But it was not simply a process of manipulation. The reformers believed Christianity to be true, and as such it deserved their allegiance. It had also been shown to be an effective shaper of society, and as such particularly useful for helping to organize an expanding and fragmenting civilization. The burgeoning fron-

189

tier (population in Tennessee, Kentucky, and Ohio went from barely 100,000 in 1790 to nearly 1,000,000 in 1810) and the restructuring of urban life through the advance of capitalism created immensely unsettling conditions. More than any other group, it was the Protestant revivalists who ensured the cohesion of Americans and who brought order into the near chaos of American life before the Civil War.

Further Reading

Banner, Lois W. "Religious Benevolence as Social Control: A Critique of an Interpretation." *Journal of American History* 60 (1973): 23-41.

Brumberg, Joan Jacobs. *Mission for Life: The Story of the Family of Adoniram Judson.* New York: Free Press, 1980.

Conkin, Paul K. *Cane Ridge: America's Pentecost.* Madison: University of Wisconsin Press, 1990.

Griffin, Clifford S. *Their Brothers' Keepers: Moral Stewardship in the United States, 1800-1865.* New Brunswick, NJ: Rutgers University Press, 1960.

Hardman, Keith J. *Charles Grandison Finney, 1792-1875: Revivalist and Reformer.* Syracuse: Syracuse University Press, 1987.

Hoffmann, Ronald, and Peter J. Albert, eds. *Women in the Age of the American Revolution.* Charlottesville: University Press of Virginia, 1989.

McBeth, Leon. *The Baptist Heritage.* Nashville: Broadman, 1987.

McLoughlin, William G. *Champions of the Cherokees: Evan and John B. Jones.* Princeton: Princeton University Press, 1990.

———. *Cherokees and Missionaries, 1789-1839.* New Haven: Yale University Press, 1984.

Mathews, Donald G. "The Second Great Awakening as an Organizing Process, 1780-1830." *American Quarterly* 21 (1969): 23-43.

Richey, Russell E., and Kenneth E. Rowe, eds. *Rethinking Methodist History: A Bicentennial Historical Consultation.* Nashville: Kingswood, 1985.

Schneider, A. Gregory. "Social Religion, the Christian Home, and Republican Spirituality in Antebellum Methodism." *Journal of the Early Republic* 10 (Summer 1990): 163-89.

Walls, Andrew F. "The American Dimension in the History of the Missionary Movement." In *Earthen Vessels: American Evangelicals and Foreign Missions.* Edited by Joel A. Carpenter and Wilbert R. Shenk, pp. 1-25. Grand Rapids: William B. Eerdmans, 1990.

CHAPTER 8

"Outsiders"

A few more beatings of the wind and rain,
Ere the winter will be over —
    Glory, Hallelujah!
Some friends has gone before me, —
I must try to go and meet them —
    Glory, Hallelujah!
A few more risings and settings of the sun,
Ere the winter will be over —
    Glory, Hallelujah!
There's a better day a coming —
There's a better day a coming —
    Oh, Glory, Hallelujah!

The former slave Charity Bowery, who reported singing this spiritual with other blacks in North Carolina during the 1830s, also reported that whites tried to stop its use because they discerned a rebellious menace in the phrase "there's a better day a coming."

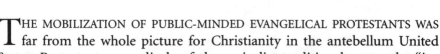

THE MOBILIZATION OF PUBLIC-MINDED EVANGELICAL PROTESTANTS WAS far from the whole picture for Christianity in the antebellum United States. Protestant evangelicals of the revivalist tradition became the "insiders" in American religion, occupying the most visible public space and looking on themselves as proprietors of American life. But a whole host of "outsider" groups, each with its own important story, also inhabited the American landscape. "Insider" and "outsider" are relative terms to be used with care, especially by those who remember the words of Jesus about the last being first and the first being last. Yet they are also useful terms, if only for showing why some Christians of the period took on the role of public guardians while others were more concerned about simply carving out space in which to live. Among the most aggressive outsiders of the period were new Protestant denominations that sprang up in the early years of the republic. The relative freedom of America also offered opportunities for Protestant immigrants from the Continent and for intentional communities that broke away from the traditional churches. Black Americans made up the social group furthest removed from insider control of power or communications. But their communities also experienced dramatic religious developments between the Revolution and the Civil War. To outline the scope of these alternatives to mainstream Protestantism is to show how varied the Christian presence was becoming, even by the midpoint of the supposedly "Protestant century."

Millerites and Mormons

American denominations such the Disciples of Barton Stone and "Christians" of Alexander Campbell, or even the Baptists and Methodists, took pains to distinguish themselves from the older denominations that had dominated the colonial period. But they were not altogether distinct. They did gain ground by presenting themselves as denominations of "the people," opposed to inherited privilege and fiercely democratic in their views of religious life. At the same time, once they had achieved a certain measure of success, they moved easily into the mainstream. Their Protestantism was more an extension of the dominant evangelical trends than a contrast to them. Other groups, however, managed to create substantially different patterns in the open spaces of America, even if many of these patterns drew on themes from the history of Christianity or the history of the United States shared by insider groups.

Two of the most interesting of such bodies were the followers of William Miller and of Joseph Smith — Millerites and Mormons, respectively. The Millerites, who eventually formed several Adventist denominations, were closer to the inside than the Mormons, but both exemplified extraordinary religious creativity in the boisterous climate of the early United States.

"Outsiders"

The Adventism of William Miller

William Miller (1782-1849) was a self-educated farmer from Low Hampton, New York, who was converted as an adult after service in the War of 1812 and a long career of serious reading in religious (and skeptical) writers of his day. From the vigorous study of the Bible that followed his conversion, Miller came to the conclusion that the return of Christ and the end of the world as foretold in Scripture would occur sometime "around 1843." Miller's exegesis paid detailed attention to the minutest parts of the Bible, including its numbers, and so fit well into the American enthusiasm for scientific endeavor that loomed large before the Civil War. This enthusiasm also led to the founding of the Smithsonian Institute, to great advances in machine tooling and manufacturing, to manifold schemes for improving physical health, and to the newfangled sciences of hypnosis and phrenology. Miller's interests were in many ways typical of antebellum American Protestants, including as they did biblicism, revivalism, and millennialism. Miller's followers believed that he was simply following out the logic announced by countless Bible-preaching revivalists in the early United States. His detractors may have been influenced by his intensity to move toward increasingly nationalistic, immanentistic, and liberal forms of religion.

Miller's message was promoted in ways that were also typical of the period. Joseph V. Himes (1805-1895), his main publicist, was a communications genius who popularized Miller's views in something over five million pieces of literature. In response to the media barrage, thousands (perhaps tens of thousands) waited expectantly for the Lord's return on March 21, 1843, and, when nothing happened then, on a second predicted date, October 22, 1844. Many of those who heeded Miller were transplanted Yankee pietists for whom his views were a natural extension of mainstream American themes. That is to say, Miller exhibited optimistic expectation, confidence in the Scriptures, and great belief in the ability of humans to understand the deepest mysteries of the sacred writings. When the End was not manifest, some of those who had accepted Miller's interpretation of the Bible returned to their previous religious commitments, but quite a few persevered. Others continued to maintain Adventist beliefs in a variety of small movements. One of these, under the leadership of Ellen White (1827-1915), concluded that Christ had indeed returned as Miller predicted but that the return was spiritual, into the presence of the Father. Because of their belief in worship on Saturday, followers of White became known as Seventh-Day Adventists. Their steady expansion in the twentieth century has made this an important body worldwide.

This pictorial explanation of William Miller's understanding of biblical prophecy appeared on the front page of Horace Greeley's *New York Tribune* on March 2, 1843, shortly before the day that Miller had designated for the return of Christ.

This portrait of the young Joseph Smith communicates at least a · little of his brooding spirituality as well as his steadiness of purpose. *National Portrait Gallery, Washington, D.C. / Art Resource, New York*

The New Religion of Joseph Smith

If the Millerites lived on the border between evangelical Protestant insiders and sectarian Protestant outsiders, the Mormons under Joseph Smith went even further toward the outside. Joseph Smith (1805-1844) seems an unlikely candidate for the founding of a major religious movement. He was born to New Englanders who never quite succeeded in making a comfortable living in either their native region or upper New York state, to which they moved in 1816. Yet the family was an intensely religious one, and Joseph Smith received powerful religious instruction especially from his mother, Lucy Mack Smith. For her part, Lucy Smith was a spiritual seeker who, despite considerable effort, could not find in traditional denominations the spiritual vitality she sought. Joseph Smith later reported that he began to receive visions from heavenly beings in the early 1820s, a few years before the angel Moroni showed him the unique *Book of Mormon* that detailed God's special dealings with prehistoric settlers in America and long-lost tribes of Israel. When Smith published his translation of the Book of Mormon in 1830, it sparked vitriolic controversy as

Already by 1868, as this early photograph indicates, Salt Lake City had begun to look like a substantial urban oasis in the great Western desert.
Church Archives, The Church of Jesus Christ of Latter-day Saints

well as more friendly interest in what was called the "burned-over district" because of the intense movements of revival and reform that swept over it in this period.

The migration of Smith and his followers to Kirtland, Ohio, in 1831 began the series of moves that eventually led the main body of Mormons on a Great Migration to the basin of Salt Lake (1846-1848). Before he could make that heroic trek, Smith was killed by an angry mob in Carthage, Illinois. Brigham Young, a master organizer, succeeded him and directed the move to Utah. Before they left, however, a segment of Joseph Smith's early followers, apprehensive about the content of Smith's later visions, the autocratic nature of his leadership, and the practice of plural marriage, broke away to form the Reorganized Church of Jesus Christ of Latter-day Saints.

Smith's religion drew on themes prominent in the early national period, including a republican conception of world order and a democratic belief in the ability of common people to grasp religious truth. Even more than this, Mormonism represented a new religious movement, dependent upon the traditions of Jews and Christians but also (in the view of its adherents) transcending these traditions. Thus, the *Book of Mormon* presupposed the Judeo-Christian Scriptures but constituted an addition to the canon. His followers viewed Joseph Smith as a new oracle who reenacted the deeds of prophets in past times. The gathering of the Latter-day Saints amounted to a re-forming of the church of Jesus Christ. The trek to Utah became a kind of exodus, and the new home in the West was a Promised Land for the saints. The result was a religious movement that arose out of specific conditions in the early national period but that also laid the foundation for the worldwide movement that Mormonism has since become.

Alternative Communities

The American landscape made room for many other sorts of outsiders in the early days of the republic. In particular, a number of utopian communities took advantage of the free American setting to attempt to construct a more perfect form of society. The best known of these may have been the Oneida community of John Humphrey Noyes.

Noyes (1811-1886) was a graduate of Dartmouth, where he was converted during a revival in 1831. He then attended Andover Theological Seminary and Yale Divinity School, where his opinions brought him into disfavor. He advocated the concept of sinless perfection, and in 1839 he proclaimed that Jesus had returned to earth in A.D. 70. He asserted that the way to sinlessness now lay through union with Christ. Noyes also came to feel that socialism was the means for perfected Christians to bring the kingdom of heaven to earth. With these views he organized a group of "Bible Communists" who in 1840 settled near Putney, Vermont. In 1846 Noyes's communalism advanced a step when he declared that holding all things in common should extend to wives. This view of "complex marriage" caused a sensation and led to legal charges. In 1848 Noyes moved his group to Oneida in western New York state, where the community was reestablished. Here they prospered, with over two hundred residents by 1851, finding success in farming and light industry. The community attempted to live out Noyes's belief in evangelical perfectionism, Christian communalism, and rational American efficiency. These principles also shaped Noyes's *History of American Socialism* (1870). The group's "free love" was carefully, even eugenically, controlled. Gradually, however, secularization invaded the community; there was less and less concern for sinless perfection and evangelical zeal. And the scandal of Oneida's marriage customs kept pressure on from the outside. Finally in 1879 Noyes fled to Canada in order to escape legal actions. The community became a joint stock company in 1881.

Oneida was far from the only venture of this sort in the century, but

New Harmony, on the Wabash River in northwest Indiana, had been founded by a religious utopian group, the Harmonists, made up of German followers of Johann Georg Rapp. This print shows the town shortly after the Harmonists had moved to Pennsylvania after selling New Harmony to a group of secular utopians following the principles of Robert Owen. *Granger Collection*

many of the others had foreign origins. One of these was the Harmony Society, founded by George Rapp (1757-1847), who had led a group of pietistic believers out of the Lutheran state church in Germany. The community was founded in 1805 at Harmony, Pennsylvania, near Pittsburgh. It moved to New Harmony, Indiana, in 1815 and eventually settled in Economy (now Ambridge), Pennsylvania, in 1825. These earnest German immigrants fervently anticipated the millennium, believed in universal salvation, and confidently set out to perfect their lives through diligent daily discipline. One of the religious features that set them apart from American evangelicals was their practice of regular confession to their leaders. The society sought an economy based on New Testament principles of communalism. Although many such efforts rapidly fell on hard times, the Harmonists prospered as farmers, weavers, brewers, and as innovators in such industrial processes as oil refining. As early as 1807 the society adopted celibacy in an effort to purify its life even further. This was one of the major factors, however, leading to the ultimate demise of the community in 1916.

In general, communal groups were more experiments than long-lived movements of great influence. Still, these nineteenth-century efforts did show how much free space America offered for religious and social experimentation. And these early communes also became an inspiration for further efforts at building separated religious communities in America during the counterculture movement of the 1960s and 1970s.

African Americans Organize Their Own Churches

With respect to other Christians in the new United States, black Christians were the furthest outside. They were set apart by a nearly universal assumption among whites that they were inferior — culturally, educationally, and religiously. Yet in the seriousness with which increasing numbers of African Americans adopted the Christian faith and in the dedication they displayed in organizing churches and denominations for themselves, blacks belied the assumption of inferiority. In the face of great, and sometimes overwhelming, odds, African Americans began to establish churches for themselves. As they did so, they also taught white Americans a lesson about the relation of faith to culture, and, indeed, about the Christian faith itself. Historian Will B. Gravely has described that lesson very well: "because they had participated in the life of biracial congregations and denominations from the outset, black Protestants who removed themselves from white supervision and connections were merely continuing their own experience. That experience, was to affirm, audaciously to many whites, an elemental core within each denominational tradition, and behind that, within Christianity itself, which was not created or controlled by white Christians. That core was as accessible to blacks as to whites, and it was thereby appropriated."

Although the conversion of slaves was often cited as an important purpose for slaveholding by those who supported the institution, in fact white slaveholders did little to promote the evangelization of blacks throughout the whole history of slavery. As we have seen, some slaves and free blacks had begun to accept the Christian faith by the time of the Revolution. The period's rhetoric of freedom created a few more opportunities than before, as did also the relative hospitality of British military officials to black self-organization. After the Revolution, the rapid rise of the Methodists and Baptists also broadened the appeal of Christianity among blacks, since these two groups aimed their message at ordinary people. They taught a Christian faith in which the personal experience of God's grace was much more important than the support provided by the church for the social order. In their early period they were remarkably

When slaves preached to slaves, they typically spoke more directly to the conditions of African-American life than when black preachers spoke to audiences that included whites. *Courtesy of the Billy Graham Center Museum*

egalitarian, and for a few years in the 1780s and 1790s they even made noises against slavery itself.

In the wake of revivals led by itinerant preachers from these denominations and of increased preaching by blacks to blacks, the number of African Americans adhering to churches rose dramatically from the 1770s to the 1830s. During this period, most Christian blacks were formally attached to white congregations and denominations, even though the informal meetings they organized for themselves often provided the deepest sustenance for their religious faith. A few blacks were even ordained for service in largely white congregations. After fighting for the patriots during the War for Independence, Lemuel Haynes (1753-1834) was ordained a Congregationalist minister in 1785, the first black to be ordained in a major white denomination. For over thirty years he served Congregational churches in New England, won a reputation for orthodoxy by defending Calvinism against the spread of universalism, and was given an M.A. by Middlebury College (again the first American black to be so honored). Yet in 1818 he was forced to retire from his Rutland, Vermont, congregation at least in part because of rising racial antagonism. Haynes's life reveals the opportunities for conscientious black leaders during this period, but it also gives an indication of why many of his contemporaries set out to organize churches for themselves.

Richard Allen, founder of the African Methodist Episcopal Church, was as notable for his efforts to assist blacks in bettering their own conditions as he was for a lifelong fidelity to the principles of Methodism.
Courtesy of the Billy Graham Center Museum

Richard Allen and the African Methodist Episcopal Church

One of the earliest and most important of these groups was the African Methodist Episcopal Church. Its story, along with the story of its founder, Richard Allen (1760-1831), tells much about the lengths to which black Christians went to express the faith for themselves. Allen was born a slave and was converted by Methodists at the age of seventeen while working on a Delaware plantation. Immediately he began to preach, first to his family, then to his master, and finally to blacks and whites throughout the region. Allen taught himself to read and write, and after much hard work he managed to purchase his freedom. After pursuing several trades — while regularly preaching as a layman on Methodist circuits — he finally arrived in Philadelphia at the age of twenty-six. Allen reported on that arrival in this way: "I soon saw a large field open in seeking and instructing my African brethren, who had been a long forgotten people and few of them attended public worship. I preached in the commons, in Southwark, Northern Liberties, and wherever I could find an opening. I frequently preached twice a day, at 5 o'clock in the morning and in the evening, and it was not uncommon for me to preach from four to five times a day." Along with other

This early African Methodist Episcopal church building was not an imposing edifice, but it was probably built by black labor, and it belonged to the people who had put it up. *Courtesy of the Billy Graham Center Museum*

blacks, Allen regularly attended St. George's Methodist Church, which was one of the places he was allowed to preach to other blacks early in the morning.

Then a distressing incident at St. George's pushed Allen in another direction. (Traditionally the year is given as 1787, but there is some doubt as to the exact time.) While Allen's friend Absalom Jones was kneeling to pray during a Sunday service, white trustees forced Jones to his feet in an effort to move him out of an area reserved for whites. In response, Jones, Allen, and the other blacks left the church. About the same time, Allen and Jones founded the Free African Society, America's first organization established by blacks for blacks. This nonsectarian society provided aid and spiritual encouragement to Philadelphia's African-American community. It also became a prototype for other black fraternal organizations devoted to religious concerns. In 1793 Jones and Allen led other blacks in providing aid to the entire population of Philadelphia during a dreadful epidemic of yellow fever. In 1794 Jones became the minister of St. Thomas Episcopal Church in Philadelphia, the nation's first black Episcopal congregation.

After years of struggle and much opposition from whites, as well as some doubts by middle-class blacks, Allen succeeded in establishing the Bethel Church for Negro Methodists in 1793. He himself was ordained in 1799 as a Methodist deacon (a "temporary" office preparatory to full ordination in which blacks, unlike whites, were usually allowed to languish). Leading Philadelphia Methodists subsequently tried to prevent Allen and his colleagues from controlling their own property. At one confrontation over this issue, Allen said to a white trustee, "if you deny us your name [as Methodists], you cannot seal up the scriptures from us, and deny us a name in heaven. We believe heaven is free for all who worship in spirit and truth." Finally in 1816 the Pennsylvania Supreme Court ruled that the Bethel Church had the right to control its own affairs and property.

Made uneasy by these efforts of the predominantly white Methodist church, Allen's congregation and other black Methodist churches in 1814 organized their own denomination, the African Methodist Episcopal Church (Bethel). Allen became its first bishop in 1816 and served the growing body as a widely respected leader until his death in 1831. The year before he died, Allen was elected president of the first national black political organization, the National Negro Convention, which grew out of a meeting at Allen's Bethel Church at which forty delegates met to protest systematic discrimination against blacks in America.

Allen considered the Christian message presented by the Methodists to be ideal for black Americans, even if white Methodists often made life difficult for their communion. As he put it, "the plain and simple gospel [of the Methodists] suits best for any people, for the unlearned can understand, and the learned are sure to understand." It was "the plain doctrine and having a good discipline" that made the Methodists successful among blacks. Other denominations "preached so high-flown" that the message went right over the heads of most people. Allen's description of the Methodist message could stand as well for the approach taken by Baptists to preaching and worship: it was direct, it was forceful, it was simple, and it provided a source of hope for blacks and whites alike.

Organization North, Perseverance South

By the time Allen died, other northern blacks had also begun to organize churches for themselves. Local congregations of Methodists, Baptists, and Presbyterians could be found in all of the major urban areas. And some of these congregations led to the formation of denominations or other kinds of religious associations. By 1822 there was a black Episcopal association and three Methodist bodies (the Union American Methodist Episcopal Church, a small group centered in Delaware; Allen's AME Church, centered in Philadelphia; and the African Methodist Episcopal Zion Church head-quartered in New York). Important Baptist congregations with far-flung connections were founded in Boston (the African Baptist Church in 1805), New York (the Abyssinian Baptist Church in 1808), and Philadelphia (the First African Baptist Church in 1809). Black Baptists, like their white coun-terparts, stressed congregational autonomy and so were slower than the Methodists to form national organizations. But after many years of cooper-ating with white Baptist mission agencies, blacks established in 1845 the African Baptist Missionary Society. Earlier, black Baptists to the west had joined together to form several regional associations. These fellowships in Ohio, Illinois, Michigan, and neighboring Ontario pooled efforts to promote home missions. Many of the churches also cooperated with the underground railroad that moved escaped slaves to freedom in Canada.

By the 1820s, black churches and denominations were venturing out-ward in a number of areas. Black churches were also sending their members as missionaries to Liberia, Sierra Leone, and Haiti. Notable among these missionaries was Lott Carey, who in 1821 helped found the First Baptist Church in Monrovia, Liberia. Black ministers also became important leaders of the abolitionist movement. Several of these were pastors of black Pres-byterian and Congregationalist churches that maintained a formal connec-tion with the white parent denominations but that also imitated the style of the black-led Methodists and Baptists. Leaders in all the denominations also lent their energies to other reforming causes such as temperance. Al-though black groups, like white, ordained only men, at least some black women, such as Richard Allen's associate Jarena Lee, did exercise wide-ranging ministries as exhorters and lay preachers. (In 1827 Lee traveled over 2,000 miles and preached on 180 different occasions.)

In the slave South, there were significantly fewer opportunities for organizing churches and voluntary societies. Yet such institutions did come into existence, as in the case of the First African Baptist Church of Savannah, Georgia, whose origins we have already examined. Despite the notorious "slave codes," which prohibited a wide range of meetings and created bar-riers to literacy, Christianity made progress. Some masters encouraged their slaves to attend church with them. Others permitted supervised religious meetings on the plantations. Still others gave grudging approval to the work of white missionaries among the slaves, such as the Methodist William Capers and Presbyterian Charles Colcok Jones, who faced the daunting task of evangelizing blacks while assuring owners that slavery could be Chris-tianized. Even where owners forbade religious meetings, slaves were often able to meet in secret for prayer, exhortation, and preaching with fellow blacks.

At such meetings and on other occasions, songs like the one reproduced at the start of this chapter added immeasurably in expressing a distinct African-American spirituality. Hymns recounting the stories of Abraham, David, Daniel, and Jesus were sung with fervor, both to offer hope for the age to come and to encourage perseverance in the present. Where possible, these songs were also acted out, often in the "shout," a counterclockwise, circular dance that recalled African ritual.

Christianity could be a source of comfort, reconciling slaves to their fate in bondage, but it could also feed rebellion. In some form or other, whether through redemptive images from the Bible or Christian patterns of organization, Christian faith contributed to major slave revolts under Gabriel Prosser in Richmond (1800), Denmark Vesey in Charleston (1822), and Nat Turner in Virginia (1831). Much more commonly, Christianity emboldened slaves to disobey masters in order to meet together for worship and song, to labor diligently with an eye toward freedom at least for coming generations, and even to escape. In this determination to find freedom — in Christ and in this world — the Southern slaves shared the commitments of their Northern peers, where leaders in the church were often leaders in the struggle against slavery as well.

No group stood as far outside America's dominant patterns of religion between the Revolution and the Civil War as the slaves. It is a testimony to their resilience as well as to the transforming power of Christianity that a religion used so often to support the slave system could become a means of counteracting its inhuman influence.

Roman Catholics

An increasingly important outsider in American religion during the nineteenth century was the Roman Catholic Church. Numbers alone cannot tell the whole story, but they are nonetheless of great significance. In 1789 when the election of the first Catholic bishop for the United States was confirmed by the pope, there were about 35,000 Catholics, roughly 60 percent of these in Maryland, and not many more than thirty priests. By 1830, the total number of Catholics had grown to over 300,000. Within the next thirty years, while the nation's population increased two and a half times from 13,000,000 to 31,500,000, the Catholic population leaped nearly tenfold to over 3,100,000. The addition of new territory contributed marginally to Catholic growth, with about 40,000 Catholics added through the purchase of Louisiana and the cessions of the Mexican War. Natural increases through births also contributed substantially to the rise, but the most important reason was immigration, first from Ireland and then from Germany. During the 1840s, when blight ruined successive potato crops in Ireland, nearly 800,000 Irish came to America. In the next decade the total climbed to over 900,000. For a variety of political, economic, and religious causes, nearly 400,000 German immigrants came in the 1840s, and almost 1,000,000 in the 1850s. Although many Irish immigrants to Canada were Protestants, most who came to the United States were Catholic, as were many of the Germans. This infusion transformed the character of Roman Catholicism in the United States and greatly altered the picture of Christianity in America.

John Carroll and an American Catholic Church

As we have seen, the early history of Catholicism in the United States was centered in Maryland and was guided by aristocratic families of English origin. The career of the first Roman Catholic bishop in the United States illustrates that lineage, but it also shows how the events of the Revolution and the democratic tendencies of the new country affected early attempts at organizing the church under the new American regime. John Carroll (1735-1815), the son of a wealthy Maryland merchant, was educated by English Jesuits in France. After entering the Catholic priesthood, he taught in France, traveled, and then in 1774 returned to North America. His cousin Charles was a patriot leader and the only Catholic to sign the Declaration of Independence. With this cousin and Benjamin Franklin, Carroll reluctantly undertook a trip to Quebec in 1776 to try to persuade the Catholic French Canadians to enter the Revolutionary War on the side of the Americans. Although that effort did not succeed, general Catholic support for Independence, along with the help of Catholic France in winning the War, led to greater tolerance for Catholics in the new United States. Some of the state constitutions did discriminate against non-Protestants, but in general Catholics enjoyed as much latitude in the States as in any other Protestant area of the world.

After the War, John Carroll took the lead in strengthening the tiny bands of Catholics in the new country. His *Address to the Catholics of the United States* (1784) was really written for Protestants, defending Catholics against charges of being unpatriotic and less than Christian. As Catholic leaders gained a measure of control over their own affairs, Carroll was the official to whom they looked. In 1784 he was named Vicar Apostolic superior of the mission in the

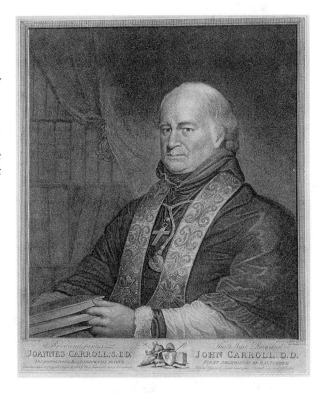

When American Roman Catholics nominated one of their number to become the first bishop in America, John Carroll of Maryland was the overwhelming choice. He was consecrated in 1790. *National Portrait Gallery, Washington, D.C. / Art Resource, New York*

United States. In 1789 Carroll was appointed Bishop of Baltimore, the first American bishop. In 1808, he became the archbishop of Baltimore when four suffragan bishops were appointed to new dioceses in Boston, New York, Philadelphia, and (reflecting active western expansion) Bardstown, Kentucky. Although the Catholic Church in America was largely an immigrant church, most of the bishops throughout the nineteenth century who succeeded Carroll in the metropolitan see of Baltimore were descendants of Maryland's colonial English elite.

Carroll's major accomplishment was his success in bringing European priests and teachers to staff schools, churches, and mission societies in America. Most of these Europeans came from France, where strong anti-Catholicism after that country's Revolution made service in the New World attractive to loyal servants of the Church. Like many of his Protestant counterparts in the early United States, Carroll was deeply committed to education. His interest here led to the founding of Georgetown College for the training of future priests.

Within a generation of Carroll's death, the American bishops met for their First Provincial Council, an occasion that enabled them to solidify much of the work of Carroll's pioneering generation. The Council regularized the authority of bishops over all priests in their dioceses, including those in religious orders. In contradiction of the Protestant stereotype about Catholic suspicion of the Bible, it also declared that the Scriptures, "when used with due care, and an humble and docile spirit," should be read by laypeople "for the edification and instruction of the faithful." (A later archbishop of Baltimore, Francis Patrick Kenrick, published his own English translation of the Bible in the late 1840s as a modern alternative to the older Douay-Rheims English translation.) In addition, in 1829 the Council also declared that all church property was to be held in deed by the bishops.

This last measure spoke to the one area in which Carroll's tenure as bishop had largely failed. In the free American atmosphere, with heady talk of rights and individual liberties, and a context in which Protestant varieties of congregational autonomy abounded, Catholics too tended to think that local communities could and should control the churches, including their property. In the early years of Catholic settlement, when priests were not always present, lay trustees had often had no choice but to organize for themselves and take in hand the construction and maintenance of church buildings. But trusteeism, as it came to be called, clashed with traditional patterns of Catholic authority, which specified that bishops maintain close control over all aspects of the Church's life, including property. Disputes between lay trustees and bishops usually centered on the right to name new priests. Bishops claimed the privilege exclusively for themselves, while trustees claimed a veto power over episcopal appointments. As the Church grew both in numbers and conformity to Rome, trusteeism died away as a movement, but lay protests against seemingly un-American ways of wielding episcopal power could still be heard as late as the 1840s and 1850s.

Protestant Opposition

The presence of ever-larger numbers of Roman Catholics did not always sit well with Protestants who had grown accustomed to thinking of the United States as their special preserve. After he had moved to Cincinnati from his native New England, Lyman Beecher in 1835 published a strongly worded tract entitled *A Plea for the West,* in which he outlined the dangers to freedom and true Christianity if Roman Catholicism should increase its already substantial influence in the opening American frontier. But the greatest clashes between Protestants and Catholics occurred in the cities of the East. There immigrant Catholic labor seemed to threaten Protestant jobs, and able bishops, solicitous for the well-being of their flocks, spoke out against

In the eyes of some American Protestants, the growing number of Roman Catholic immigrants meant only trouble. This cartoon expresses nativist fears that the pope would undermine the schools of the United States. *American Antiquarian Society*

what they saw as favoritism to Protestants. In 1834 a Boston mob burned the Ursuline Convent of Charleston, and Boston Protestants backed the publication of such scandal-mongering books as *Six Months in a Convent* (1835) and Maria Monk's *Awful Disclosures of the Hotel Dieu Nunnery in Montreal* (1836). In 1844 Protestant and Catholic disputes over labor issues led to violent clashes in the Philadelphia suburbs of Kensington and Southwark. Four years before, New York's Bishop John Hughes had petitioned the city's Public School Society to provide money for Catholic schools in a manner similar to its support for Protestant establishments. The result was a bitter, long-lasting quarrel that did not result in subsidies to the Catholics but did lead to the demise of the Society and the emergence of a nonsectarian ideal for New York public education.

The most concerted resistance to the rise of the Catholic Church came when Protestants, worried about the tide of European and specifically Catholic immigration, organized a fraternal-political association to resist the tide. The new body was founded as the Order of the Star-Spangled Banner in 1849 and reorganized in 1852 as the American Party, but its members were popularly called "Know Nothings" because when they were questioned about the group's principles or activities, they would always respond "I don't know." The party had simplistic convictions — immigrants were damaging the Anglo-Saxon stock of "native" Americans, and Roman Catholics were minions of a despotic foreign power, the pope. The American Party enjoyed a brief day in the sun: in 1854 proponents elected seventy-five members of the House of Representatives and in Massachusetts garnered 376 of the 378 seats in the state legislature. It declined very rapidly, however, as a new party (the Republicans) arose to challenge the Democrats and as a new issue (North-South conflict) overshadowed fear of Catholic immigration.

This kind of opposition disconcerted but did not materially affect Catholic efforts to organize, instruct, and mobilize their growing numbers. Traveling Catholic missioners even copied a page or two from evangelical itinerants by adopting strategies to energize nominal Catholics and inspire the committed. First in the upper South and then more generally throughout centers of Catholic population, these Catholic evangelists traveled from parish to parish, held extended meetings during the evenings for a week or more, featured stirring music and affecting oratory, and called on individuals to make spiritual decisions to advance the work of the Church. Prominent in this work of Catholic revivalism were the Vincentians, Franciscans, Passionists, Jesuits, and Redemptorists (who mounted 189 parish missions in the 1850s and another 280 in the 1860s). In this way Catholics put to use styles of outreach that they were learning from the very ones who most resented their presence in America.

Catholic Women

As it did also for Protestants, the American environment opened up a full sphere for the religious work of Catholic women. The long tradition of Catholic religious orders for women was soon extended in America. In 1818 Rose Philipine Duchesne from France established the first convent of the Sacred Heart in America; it was a religious order whose nuns and sisters promoted good works in many forms.

Even earlier an indigenous American Catholic women's order had come into existence through the efforts of Elizabeth Ann Seton (1774-1821). A trip to Italy for the recuperation of her husband's health had unexpected results when Elizabeth Seton was deeply impressed by the personal faith of local Catholics and especially by firsthand experience of the Catholic eucharist. After she returned to her native New York City and engaged in an extended period of discussion with her Episcopalian bishop, Elizabeth Seton finally entered the Catholic Church in March 1805. Friends and family expressed such sharp disapproval that, after consulting with Bishop Carroll

After her husband's early death, Elizabeth Ann Seton entered the Catholic Church in 1805 and shortly thereafter founded the Sisters of Charity, over which she presided with the title of "Mother." She was the first native-born American to be canonized (in 1975) by the Vatican. *Mt. St. Vincent Archives*

and French Sulpician fathers, Mrs. Seton moved to Baltimore. There, with the assistance of the Sulpicians, she opened a school for girls. When several young women came to assist in her work, she was able to secure property near Emmitsburg, west of Baltimore. On this site she established the Sisters of Charity, who carried out a wide variety of tasks in education and care for orphans. (In 1975 Mother Seton became the first person born in the United States to be made a saint by the Roman Catholic Church.) Mother Seton was not alone in her work, however, for by the Civil War fifty-one communities of women religious had been established in the United States. Over the next forty years another fifty-nine would be added. The result was that in 1900 over 40,000 Catholic sisters were active in a great number of services in the Church, especially in education. Almost all of the Catholic Church's nearly 4,000 parochial schools, along with nearly 700 academies for young women, were staffed by the sisters.

Well before 1900, it was clear that the Catholic Church had become a major presence in America. When Prince Napoleon, cousin of the French emperor, visited the United States in 1861, his entourage included a Corsican officer, Camille Ferri-Pisani, who wrote a series of letters on his travels that were eventually published. He was much impressed with the strength of Catholicism in America, but he could not tell if that strength derived from the Church's internal circumstances or its rapid adjustment to America. His conclusion was that "from a theoretical point of view, the application of the *voluntary* system to the Catholic religion offers a system of balanced forces, an intimate alliance of symmetrical principles, and that this conception is very appealing to the mind." The adjustment of Europe's largest and most traditional church to the open spaces and cultural innovations of the New World was by no means complete in 1860. What could be said even then, however, was that the Catholic Church was destined to make an ever-increasing impact on its new environment, just as that new environment was bound in some measure to make an impression upon the Church.

Immigrant Protestants

Yet another important group of "outsiders" in the antebellum period was made up of immigrants from the European continent whose faith, though Protestant, differed at many points from the revivalistic Protestantism already in America. Migrants from Ireland at this time were mostly Catholic, but from Germany came thousands of Lutherans and Protestant Pietists along with many Catholics. Much of the migration from the Netherlands was Reformed, and most of the migrants from Scandinavia were Lutheran. Between 1800 and 1920, the United States received about 40,000,000 immigrants, among whom a substantial minority were Protestant. As was the case with the Catholics, some of the Protestant immigrants never reestablished church ties on this side of the Atlantic, and some maintained only the sort of religion to be found in ethnic fraternal organizations. Others who had practiced nearly sectarian faiths on the margins of the state churches spun off into separate American organizations that retained only general connections with Old World faiths. Examples of such bodies were the Swedish Evangelical Covenant Church of America (later the Evangelical Covenant Church) and the Norwegian-Danish Evangelical Free Church Association (later one of the constituent parts of the Evangelical Free Church of America). Still other immigrants formed American churches that were at first offshoots of European bodies but that later became freestanding denominations. In this category were most of the Reformed and Lutheran bodies.

An early example of how the pietism of immigrant communities could mingle with the religion of English-language Protestants is provided by the life and work of Jacob Albright (1759-1808). Albright's parents were

The middle years of the nineteenth century saw not only the growth of many different Christian denominations in the United States but also an incredible boom in the construction of church buildings. Structures like the one in this early photograph could be found almost everywhere in the settled portions of the country. *Courtesy of the Billy Graham Center Museum*

German-Lutheran immigrants to Pennsylvania. His own faith, however, was only nominal until, at the funeral of one of his own children in 1791, he was movingly converted. Shortly thereafter, Albright made contact with a local class of Methodists who shared his intense attachment to the message of divine forgiveness. A few years later, after overcoming scruples about his lack of education, Albright began to preach to German-speaking residents of Pennsylvania. By 1800 enough had responded to form three small classes on the Methodist model. In 1807 a first conference was held for five itinerants, three settled ministers, and a total membership of about two hundred. The name of this body, which Albright served as bishop, was "The Newly Formed Methodist Conference." Albright worked cooperatively with Francis Asbury and used Asbury's discipline as a model for his own group. Yet when Albright took steps to join the larger body of Methodists, he was rebuffed, because the Methodists were not prepared to accept a German-speaking group into their fellowship. Thereafter the "Albright Brethren" called themselves "The Evangelical Association." (Only in 1968, with the merger of the Evangelical United Brethren and the Methodist Episcopal Church did the descendants of Albright's denomination succeed in joining the Methodists.) Albright himself was a bridge to an American spirituality. With roots in the German community he nevertheless accepted a model for theology and church organization from the Methodists and so hastened the process by which immigrants began to contribute to Christianity in America.

Jacob Albright founded the "Albright Brethren" in the early nineteenth century as a Methodist-style denomination for Americans of German background.
Courtesy of the Billy Graham Center Museum

The Lutherans

The large Lutheran immigrations of the nineteenth century illustrate a different pattern, for in their case a fresh tide of newcomers actually reversed the process of Americanization. During the first decades of the nineteenth century, the Lutheran churches in the United States were largely the product of organizing efforts by Henry Melchior Muhlenberg (1711-1787), who had been sent from the pietist center in Halle to provide guidance for the German Lutheran immigrants who began to settle in Pennsylvania during the eighteenth century.

As these earlier settlers learned English and took on other American characteristics, their religion also assumed an American cast. A leading figure in the creation of this more American Lutheranism was Samuel Simon Schmucker (1799-1873), a graduate of Presbyterian Princeton Seminary, who worked throughout his life for causes that he felt would benefit both Lutherans and other American Protestants. It was Schmucker's conviction that New World Lutherans could profitably conjoin characteristics of American Protestantism to traditional European distinctives. He worked on behalf of the General Synod of Lutheran churches (formed in 1820), became a mainstay of Gettysburg Lutheran Seminary, and pledged himself to fight rationalism and religious indifference with the weapons of the Augsburg

214

Samuel Schmucker, who presided over the Lutheran seminary in Gettysburg, Pennsylvania, was probably the most influential leader in his denomination in the decades before the Civil War. Yet eventually Schmucker's proposals for modifying Lutheranism in an "American" direction lost out to those who wished to perpetuate traditional Lutheran principles in the New World. *Courtesy of the Billy Graham Center Museum*

Confession and Luther's Small Catechism. At the same time, Schmucker's concerns moved beyond Lutheranism. He supported revivalism. He favored the development of interdenominational agencies, such as the Sunday School movement, to spread the gospel and improve national morality. He spoke out on American national issues by expressing fears, for example, concerning immigrants and Roman Catholics. He also was a founder of the American branch of the interdenominational Evangelical Alliance (1846).

But Schmucker's plan to modify the historic Augsburg Confession and reform a few traditional practices proved upsetting to traditional Lutherans. Many were scandalized by the fact that he did not believe in a Real Presence of Christ's body in the Lord's Supper, that he rejected private confession, that he wondered if baptism really brought regeneration, and (in keeping with American, "Puritan" opinions) that he desired a much stricter observation of the Sabbath. On all of these subjects he was adjusting Old World principles to religious standards more common in the New.

Schmucker's point of view did gain momentum among American Lutherans until about mid-century. At that point, however, a reaffirmation of Old World views by a rising tide of immigrants from Germany (and later Scandinavia) combined with a revival of interest in the roots of the Reformation to lessen the influence of "American" views. From 1850 to 1870, the number of Lutheran churches more than doubled from slightly over 1,200 to nearly 2,800, and the value of Lutheran church property multiplied nearly five times. Schmucker's books, including the *Elements of Popular Theology* (1834) and *A Fraternal Appeal to the American Churches* (1838), seemed to the immigrants to be advocating a casual relaxation of essential traditions. The anonymous *Definite Synodical Platform* of 1855, which proposed a revision of the Augsburg Confession along lines favored by Schmucker, precipitated a clash of interests that eventually led to the mobilization of "European" Lutheranism against the trends favored by Schmucker.

In the struggle between "American" and "European" Lutherans, defenders of old ways also enjoyed capable leaders. One of these was the American-born Charles Porterfield Krauth (1823-1883), whose book *The Conservative Reformation and Its Theology* provided a forthright rationale for maintaining strict Old World standards for Lutheran teaching even in the New World. Another was Carl Ferdinand Wilhelm Walther (1811-1887), a native of Saxony who came to the United States in 1838. Walther was every bit as active as an American revivalist, but the goal of his activity was the strengthening of the German Lutheran community. He pastored a church in St. Louis, helped start a training institute for ministerial candidates, founded a publishing house, a newspaper, and a theological journal, and worked to unite the many different bodies of Lutherans in the United States. He was the president of the German Evangelical Lutheran Synod of Missouri, Ohio, and Other States (a forerunner of the modern Lutheran Church–Missouri Synod), and he was a leading figure in the Evangelical Lutheran Synodical Conference of North America that came into existence in 1872. Although Walther leaned toward a congregational form of church government and proclaimed such high views of God's grace that he was called a "crypto-Calvinist," he shared with Krauth the conviction that the main task for Lutherans in the New World was to maintain their Old World distinctives rather than adjusting to the ways of America. Following Krauth, Walther, and like-minded individuals, American Lutherans reemphasized inherited doctrine. As a result, Lutheranism in America remained a largely self-contained, European outsider until the 1930s and the end of large-scale immigration from the European centers of Lutheran strength.

In nineteenth-century America, religious groups had plenty of room to establish their own identity as well as to preserve their distinctive character as new American faiths or old European religions. For all of these groups the evangelical Protestantism that predominated in the public sphere constituted something of a problem. Sometimes that Protestantism actively persecuted the outsiders (especially the Catholics, but occasionally other groups such as the Mormons), sometimes it merely ignored the existence of groups different from itself (as was often the case with the Lutherans),

216

and everywhere it simply took for granted the second-class status of African Americans, whether slave or free. For their part, some of the religious outsiders managed to grow over time, establish more formal norms of organization, and themselves began to look as much like insiders as outsiders. (That process has clearly taken place in the twentieth century for Roman Catholics and Lutherans, and also the Mormons, at least in the Rocky Mountain states.) Others, such as the Seventh-Day Adventists, have remained more unto themselves. Black churches have come closer to the inside over time but still retain much of their original character. That character arose both as black leaders adapted Christianity for themselves and as white society forced blacks to construct alternative Christian institutions. Both the space for new groups to find a haven as outsiders and the tendency to move toward the inside are characteristic of the cultural circumstances of Christianity in America, where fluidity and change are much more the order of the day than stability and tradition.

Further Reading

Allen, Richard. *The Life Experiences and Gospel Labors of the Rt. Rev. Richard Allen*. Philadelphia, 1833. Excerpted in *Afro-American Religious History: A Documentary Witness*. Edited by Milton C. Sernett. Durham, NC: Duke University Press, 1985.

Bushman, Richard L. *Joseph Smith and the Beginnings of Mormonism*. Urbana, IL: University of Illinois Press, 1984.

Carey, Patrick W. *People, Priests, and Prelates: Ecclesiastical Democracy and the Tensions of Trusteeism*. Notre Dame, IN: University of Notre Dame Press, 1987.

Dolan, Jay P. *The Immigrant Church: New York's Irish and German Catholics, 1815-1865*. Baltimore: The Johns Hopkins University Press, 1975.

————. *Catholic Revivalism: The American Experience, 1830-1900*. Notre Dame, IN: University of Notre Dame Press, 1978.

Epstein, Dena J. *Sinful Tunes and Spirituals: Black Folk Music to the Civil War*. Urbana: University of Illinois Press, 1977.

Fogarty, Gerald P. "The Quest for a Catholic Vernacular Bible in America." In *The Bible in America*. Edited by Nathan O. Hatch and Mark A. Noll. New York: Oxford University Press, 1982.

Gravely, Will B. "The Rise of African Churches in America (1786-1822): Reexamining the Context." *Journal of Religious Thought* 41 (1984): 58-73.

Kuenning, Paul P. *The Rise and Fall of American Lutheran Pietism*. Macon, GA: Mercer University Press, 1988.

Lincoln, C. Eric, and Lawrence H. Mamiya. *The Black Church in the African American Experience.* Durham, NC: Duke University Press, 1990.

Moore, R. Laurence. *Religious Outsiders and the Making of Americans.* New York: Oxford University Press, 1986.

Numbers, Ronald L., and Jonathan M. Butler, eds. *The Disappointed: Millerism and Millenarianism in the Nineteenth Century.* Bloomington, IN: Indiana University Press, 1987.

Sernett, Milton C. *Black Religion and American Evangelicalism: White Protestants, Plantation Missions, and the Flowering of Negro Christianity, 1787-1865.* Metuchen, NJ: Scarecrow Press, 1975.

Shipps, Jan. *Mormonism: The Story of a New Religious Tradition.* Urbana, IL: University of Illinois Press, 1985.

CHAPTER 9

"Evangelical America," 1800-1865

Who has our Redeemer heard,
Whose voice was good and kind?
Thus he spoke in holy word:
Seek and ye shall find.

CHORUS:
Ask and it shall be given
Seek and ye shall find,
Every prayer is heard in heaven
That is breathed from a truthful mind.

*   *   *   *   *

Life to all our Lord has shown,
Then be to hope resigned,
When around you doubts are thrown,
"Seek and ye shall find."

CHORUS.

Stephen Foster (1826-1864) is much better known for his ballads than for his church music, but this effort, published shortly before his death, typified much nineteenth-century Protestant hymnody: it echoed the words of the King James Bible, it was sentimental and moralistic, and it inculcated the twin ideals of external and internal spiritual discipline.

THE "PROTESTANT CENTURY"

S HORTLY AFTER THE CIVIL WAR, THE ROMAN CATHOLIC CHURCH SURPASSED the Methodists to become the largest Christian communion in America. At the same time, fresh waves of immigrants (German and Scandinavian Lutherans, Catholics from several countries of Europe, a growing number of Jews, and even a few Orthodox Christians) were further diluting the English-language Protestant character of American religion. Yet for public purposes, with respect to the perceptions that loomed largest in the American media and that first struck foreign visitors, the nation still appeared to be a Protestant country dominated by white denominations of British origin.

Membership figures, though never as accurate as might be wished, tell a revealing story. By 1870, in a total population of nearly 40,000,000 there were about 3,500,000 Catholics and 440,000 Lutherans. The Methodists were the largest of the Protestant denominational families of British heritage, with about as many adherents as the Catholics. Another 2,000,000 were Baptists or Disciples, there were about 1,150,000 in the various Presbyterian bodies, and there were about 480,000 Congregationalists. The last of the major bodies with origins in the colonial period, the Episcopalians, numbered around 440,000. The Universalists were the largest of the denominations that had sprung up after the Revolution, with approximately 140,000 adherents. Other groups with substantial numbers included the German Reformed and the Quakers (each numbering about 90,000-100,000), and the Dutch Reformed (about 55,000). Unitarians, who had divided from the Trinitarian Congregationalists in the first decades of the century, numbered about 30,000. Mennonites, the Church of the Brethren, Winebrennarians, Swedenborgians, and Shakers each claimed about 10,000 adherents.

The diversity of churches was great, and there were also a lot of them. In 1860 the census counted 38,183 church buildings, or an average of one house of worship for every 608 Americans. These churches were served by over 26,000 professional ministers and priests and by well over 10,000 part-time local preachers. The Methodists alone had 19,883 churches in that year. Church-going was most regular along the Atlantic coast and along the northern tier of states in which New England influence was often pronounced. In 1870, between 35 and 40 percent of the population in New England, the Atlantic states, and the eastern belt of Southern states were regular adherents. Further west the rates dropped to about 25 percent, but then climbed to eastern levels in the sparsely populated regions of the far West.

In Foreign Eyes

Visitors from overseas were regularly struck by the vitality of faith in the United States. Andrew Reed, a Congregationalist from England, where he was active in voluntary social service, visited America in the mid-1830s and came away marveling at the Christian energy he saw. Reed took pains to compare the number of churches, ministers, and communicants in British and American cities of similar size (i.e., Liverpool and New York, Edinburgh and Philadelphia, Glasgow and Boston). The Americans, he concluded, were ahead on nearly every count. In comparison to Nottingham, an English city of 50,000 inhabitants with 23 churches and 4,864 communicants, he was flabbergasted to find that Cincinnati, "a city only forty years old, and in the forests" with only 30,000 citizens, had nearly as many churches (21) and almost twice as many communicants (8,555).

To be sure, other foreign visitors interpreted all this American energy differently. Frances Trollope, mother of the novelist Anthony Trollope, lived in Cincinnati from 1827 to 1831 and was definitely not impressed by what she saw of the country's religious life. "The whole people appear to be divided into an almost endless variety of religious factions," she wrote upon returning to England. America's religion seemed to her but a mirror of its wild society. "The vehement expressions of insane or hypocritical zeal, such as were exhibited during 'the Revival,' can but ill atone for the want of village worship, any more than the eternal talk of the admirable and unequalled government can atone for the continual contempt of social order. Church and State hobble along, side by side, notwithstanding their boasted independence." A stranger in the western United States who was looking for regular worship, prayer, or preaching would find, according to Mrs. Trollope, only "that most terrific saturnalia, 'the camp meeting.'"

Other newcomers tended to view the lack of general supervision and the absence of governmental connection with the churches much more as strengths than as weaknesses. Philip Schaff, a native of Switzerland, came from schooling in Germany to teach at the German Reformed seminary at Mercersburg, Pennsylvania, in 1843. When he returned to Germany for the first time in 1853, he was called upon to explain the religious life of the United States. He reported that he had initially doubted the wisdom of America's voluntary organization of religion but that he now took a much more favorable view:

> The nation . . . is still Christian, though it refuses to be governed in this deepest concern of the mind and heart by the temporal power. In fact, under such circumstances, Christianity, as the free expression of personal

221

Philip Schaff, shown here in a portrait from 1891, was one of the many immigrants who helped to shape church life in the United States and Canada during the nineteenth century. As church historian, Bible translator, editor, and organizer of countless conferences and publishing projects, Schaff was also one of the busiest.
The Union Theological Seminary Archives, The Burke Library, New York City

conviction and of the national character, has even greater power over the mind, than when enjoined by civil laws and upheld by police regulations. This appears practically in the strict observance of the Sabbath, the countless churches and religious schools, the zealous support of Bible and Tract societies, of domestic and foreign missions, the numerous revivals, the general attendance on divine worship, and the custom of family devotion — all expressions of the general Christian character of the people, in which the Americans are already in advance of most of the old Christian nations of Europe.

Protestant Life in "Christian America"

Schaff no doubt exaggerated the comprehensive sweep of Christianity in the United States at mid-century, for, in fact, a majority of the population did not then have a regular church attachment, and in some regions of the country organized religion had made only slight headway. At the same time, Schaff did catch the Protestant tone that dominated the nation's public life. During the decades from the post-Revolutionary revivals at least through the Civil War, the country's ethos was predominantly evangelical. In a number of particulars, this was indeed the era of "Christian America" as evangelical Protestants would use the term.

Converting the West and the South

The most striking testimony to the evangelical sway was the conversion of the West and the South. To some extent the history of New England illustrates modern conceptions of so-called secularization theory: its Protestantism remained strong through the mid-nineteenth century, but already it seemed to be thinning out doctrinally and culturally as the cities grew, capitalism took firmer hold, and intellectual innovations from Europe eroded previous dogmatic certainties. In the South and West, however, there was movement in the other direction.

"The West" was not a fixed geographical region but a relatively uninhabited region to the west of those areas that had been settled by white Americans. In the decades before the Civil War, the West comprised regions adjoining and just beyond the Mississippi River and areas along the Pacific coast. In these areas, into which European civilization and Christianity had only recently been introduced, earnest clergymen, Sunday School workers, and organizers of voluntary agencies (many of them women) cooperated with the settlers to impart the institutions and practices of Christian civilization.

Already in the 1830s, a Methodist missionary, Jason Lee (1803-1845), advanced beyond the Rockies toward Oregon, where he established a mission to Flathead Indians in the Willamette Valley. Soon he was followed by the Presbyterians Marcus and Narcissa Whitman and Henry and Eliza Spalding. The Spaldings worked successfully among the Native Americans, but the Whitmans proved to be better publicists about the virtues of life in the far Northwest. After they were killed in an Indian uprising in 1847, their fame grew even more. The result was unprecedented publicity for the possibility of settlement — publicity in which the role of missionary clergymen remained very important.

Experiences in the Iowa Territory, closer to the settled East, were less spectacular but more typical. The seventeenth-century explorations of Father Marquette had given Catholics a beachhead across the Mississippi, and in 1835 the first Catholic church building was constructed in what would later be the state of Iowa. The first bishop, Mathias Loras, arrived four years later. But it was to be Protestant missionary-pastors who exerted the most widespread influence.

Peter Cartwright (1785-1872), an indefatigable Methodist circuit rider best known for his labors in Indiana and Illinois, visited Iowa in 1834 and then dispatched other Methodists to take up the challenge. One of these, Burton Randle, soon was at work in and around Dubuque, where, with an anti-Catholic fervor typical for this age, he hoped to restrict the power of

Peter Cartwright was a vigorous Methodist itinerant with a long and varied career. He preached nearly 15,000 sermons, ran for Congress against Abraham Lincoln, and more than once faced down frontier bullies who attempted to disrupt Methodist services. *Courtesy of the Billy Graham Center Museum*

the Catholic Church while winning converts himself. The story goes that Randle preached first in a tiny town near Dubuque where the only building large enough to host a crowd was the pool hall, to evangelical eyes a den of vice. The owner, showing his respect for the visiting minister, covered his table with a sheet, whereupon Randle, noticing a similarity to a coffin, preached a vigorous sermon that resulted in the conversion of the proprietor and the sale of his hall. By 1838, Baptists, Presbyterians, and Congregationalists had joined the Methodists in establishing churches in the network of farming crossroads and trading centers that were fanning out west from the Mississippi.

Protestant ministers felt like lonely sentinels in their frontier outposts and so importuned eastern missionary agencies for more workers. The first Presbyterian in Iowa, Asa Turner, wrote many such letters to the American Home Missionary Society, but the response, when it came, surprised even him. In 1843 Turner received a letter from twelve young students at Andover Seminary inquiring if it were possible for them to form an "Iowa Band" to help in preaching the gospel and establishing churches there. Turner was very much interested but also slightly skeptical:

> I am happy to hear that a reinforcement from Andover is talked of. I hope it will not end in talk, but I fear. . . . Don't come here expecting a paradise. . . . Come prepared to expect small things, rough things. Lay aside all your dandy whims boys learn in college, and take a few lessons of your

grandmothers before you come. Get clothes firm, durable, something that will go through the hazel brush without tearing. . . . Get wives of the old Puritan stamp . . . those who can pail a cow and churn the butter, and be proud of a jean dress or a checked apron. . . . But it's no use to answer any more questions, for I never expect to see one of you west of the Mississippi river as long as I live.

But eleven of the Andover students did come to the Iowa Territory. Turner let them choose posts where they would. One died during the first five years, but each of the other ten established a church. Together they also perpetuated the ideals of learning they had imbibed at Andover, Yale, and Amherst by establishing Iowa College in Davenport on the Mississippi. It was not an easy life. The settlers were often indifferent. One of the ministers, William Salter, who would serve the same Congregational church for sixty years, reported early in his ministry that "I preached a Thanksgiving sermon this week to a very small congregation. Most of the people were in the fields husking corn." And ministers with New England standards for sermon style and ecclesiastical decorum found the people much readier to assemble for Methodist and Baptist exhorters.

As elsewhere in the open spaces of the United States, the combination of Methodist zeal and organization pushed that denomination to the front in Iowa, which became a state in 1846. The census of 1860 counted 90,000 Methodists, more than twice as many as any other denomination. Presbyterians, Baptists, and Congregationalists, as well as the Catholics, all had 20,000 or more adherents. And by 1860 Iowa was also exhibiting a common American pattern by becoming home to numerous smaller groups of Christians: Reformed from Holland who settled in central Iowa under their leader Hendrik Scholte, Quakers from further east, Swedenborgians moving up from St. Louis, and Mennonites delighted at finding a home in the open prairies. Iowa was also attractive to numerous communal groups. One of these, the Community of True Inspiration, after migrating from Germany and staying briefly in New York State, established Amana in the 1850s, a network of seven villages on 26,000 acres of good farmland in east-central Iowa. The Amana Colony survived as a communal society until social changes introduced by the automobile and the Great Depression led to the establishment of private ownership in 1932. It was, nonetheless, the longest lived and most successful of all communal societies in the history of the United States.

The most impressive statistic of the 1860 census, however, was the number of unchurched — well over 400,000, or nearly two-thirds of Iowa's population. Significant achievements, at the cost of great labor, marked the push of Christianity into new territories like Iowa, but the tasks that remained were daunting. Still, a beginning had been made. The churches, at least to some degree and at least to the time of the Civil War, succeeded in their efforts to keep up with the westward movement of American civilization.

In the South the situation was different, for Christianity had always been present in some form or other in that region. There the problem was not so much establishing a Christian presence as developing a strength to rival other value systems that were also as old as European settlement. Through the early years of the nineteenth century, the dominant Southern culture was confrontational, violent, self-possessed, and driven more by personal honor than by personal religion. The revivals associated with the Second Great Awakening did not change that system of values entirely, but they did exert an enormous influence. Evangelical revivalism gave a new sense of personal dignity to ordinary middle- and lower-class whites especially. It also gave women of all classes means for self-expression and forms for association resting on principles of love instead of the confrontational standards that dominated the lives of aristocratic white men. Except for a few years early in the century, whites did not consciously extend the sense of spiritual purpose and personal self-worth communicated by evangelical religion to black slaves. But despite this unwillingness, blacks, as we have seen, also began to respond to the evangelical message.

The success of revivalistic Protestantism in the South, especially its ability to link ideals of womanhood with the ideals of Christianity, dramatically altered Southern culture. To honor wives and daughters was now much more clearly to respect Christianity. Acting responsibly in the world at large was now much more clearly associated with making a place for the church. No change had a greater effect on the general culture of antebellum America than the progress of evangelical Protestantism in the South. And no change, as historian Donald Mathews has succinctly summarized, involved black Christianity so thoroughly, yet also so ironically, with white:

> As a social, historical process, Evangelical Protestantism in the Old South enabled a rising lower-middle/middle class to achieve identity and solidarity, rewarding its most committed religious devotees with a sense of personal esteem and liberty. From interaction with and participation in this process, blacks created the measure by which southern Evangelicalism itself could be judged, and through their appropriation of Evangelical Christianity expressed a religious-social ethos that could best convey its significance in the Evangelical promise to "preach liberty to the captives."

Because of slavery and because of variations in revivalistic Protestantism, the evangelization of the West and of the South took different forms.

226

Yet in both regions, conversions, the construction of churches, and efforts to build institutions for transmitting Christian civilization succeeded in making the South and the West constituent parts of "Evangelical America."

Mass Communications and Popular Thought

The extent of evangelical influence extended much further, however. It was, for example, evangelical Protestants who drove the great development of popular communication between the Revolution and the Civil War. In that period, evangelicals, whether as individuals or in voluntary societies, literally transformed the ground rules of print. Between 1790 and 1830, nearly 600 religious magazines were founded. Every state in the Union except Mississippi became the publishing home of at least one such effort. By 1830 two of these new journals, a Methodist weekly entitled *The Christian Advocate and Journal and Zion's Herald* and a monthly interdenominational magazine, the *American National Preacher*, each claimed a circulation of 25,000. Nowhere else in the world at the time did any other journal of any kind circulate so widely. Evangelicals such as those who backed the various Bible societies pioneered in print technology (e.g., cheap stereotyping, steam-powered printing, and mechanized papermaking). And they were leaders in conceiving innovative ways of distributing the printed word. In this matter, itinerant Methodist preachers had no peers, for they were always merchants of the written word as well as preachers of the spoken word.

Two organizations were especially important in creating a popular evangelical press — the American Bible Society and the American Tract Society. Along with the entire phalanx of American voluntary societies, these two agencies were driven by missionary motives to convert unreached Americans. They shared a belief in the United States' unique destiny and an optimism about the imminence of the millennium. They were attuned to the democratic ethos that had come to prevail after the Revolution. They became absolute masters of technique — whether the production of books and pamphlets or the organization of contributors and distributors. They were also journalistic pioneers whose writers communicated briskly, understandably, and entertainingly. The result of combining such energy and purpose was a prodigy of print. During the three-year period from 1829 to 1831, the American Bible Society printed and distributed more than 1,000,000 copies of the Scriptures, when the nation's entire population was not yet thirteen million. During the same period, the American Tract Society printed each year an average of five pages for every person in the United States.

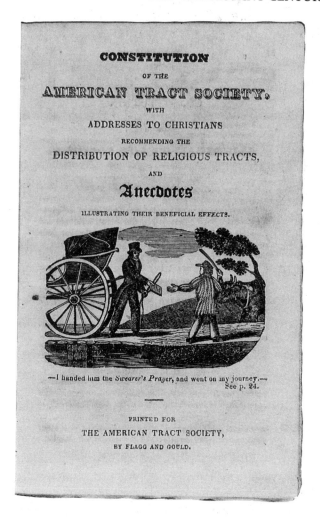

Through innovative use of printing technology, efficient management, skillful fund-raising, and a zeal for the Christian message, the American Tract Society became one of the leading publishers of any kind in the United States before the Civil War. *Courtesy of the Billy Graham Center Museum*

Evangelical Protestants not only provided ordinary Americans with their reading material; they also shaped the patterns of their thought. To the extent that it is possible to discover the popular opinions of Americans who left only letters, an occasional diary, or other fugitive records, it seems as if a deeply religious spirit imbued much of the American population in this period. It was not necessarily a church-going spirit, for more Americans in this period did not attend church regularly than did. In addition, ordinary people do not seem to have given much thought to the messianic character of the United States or to prospects for imminent arrival of the millennium, subjects that did engage the publishing elites. Rather, the mood of common Americans was more at home in the somber universe of Nathaniel

Hawthorne or Herman Melville and much closer to the melancholy of Abraham Lincoln than to the cosmic optimism of Ralph Waldo Emerson or Walt Whitman.

Whatever their formal religious beliefs, ordinary Americans seemed to retain a generally sober, even Calvinistic, view of humanity, concerned much more with human limitations than with human potential. Ordinary people, in a life made difficult by unexpected death, families separated by vast distances, and the unpredictability of weather and crops, tended toward personal resignation. They were earnest, wary of pretension, and above all pessimistic about human nature. They were less concerned with controlling other people for their own ends than with controlling themselves and their immediate environments. Common people had a vital interest in order and a deep-seated fear of disorder. They dealt with these inner needs, it seems, with efforts to control the self, respond to God's particular call for salvation, and accept the more general designs of Providence. Most common people worried about controlling themselves in the face of personal guilt, anxieties due to the vicissitudes of love and marriage, the uncertainties of birth, the unknown possibilities of the West, and the ever-present reality of death. These are generalizations that did not apply to many antebellum Americans, but for many others — perhaps even a majority — this vision of life shaped the daily round.

Education

Evangelical religion was also a major influence in defining the nation's formal education. Again, the voluntary societies led the way. One of the most effective of these agencies was the American Sunday School Union, founded in Philadelphia in 1824. Its first efforts were directed at frontier areas, but the grand design of its promoters was extended much further. A wealthy patron, Arthur Tappan of New York City, put it clearly when he called for "a Sabbath school . . . in every town" of the country. The Union did two important things to advance Sunday School education. As a national organization, it funneled missionaries into unevangelized areas. As a publisher, it provided materials for the weekly lessons. Before the growth of mass public education, Sunday Schools supplied basic education for lower- and middle-class students. The Union helped shift the attention of Sunday Schools to specifically religious concerns: conversion of the lost and spiritual strengthening of Christians. The Union was a major religious force for many decades. Toward the end of the nineteenth century, it was given new life when Dwight L. Moody enlisted his wealthy Chicago friend B. F. Jacobs in

Arthur Tappan, the New York merchant, was a dynamo of activity in support of the publishing, preaching, and social agencies of antebellum Protestant evangelicalism. *Courtesy of the Billy Graham Center Museum*

its ranks. Jacobs put a "uniform lesson plan" into practice whereby Sunday School teachers from various denominations in a locality would gather together at midweek to prepare for the next Sunday's Bible lesson. The influence of the Union can be seen by the fact that its missionaries established well over 70,000 new Sunday Schools during the nineteenth century.

In antebellum America very few young people went to college (no more than 2 percent of the seventeen- to twenty-two-year-old population until the 1880s). But where colleges existed, they were almost always sponsored and staffed by Protestant evangelicals. Exceptions were the colleges founded by Roman Catholics (twenty-seven such institutions before the Civil War) and very occasionally a school such as Harvard, which by mid-century had drifted away from its earlier evangelicalism to a more genteel Unitarianism. Before 1820, almost seventy percent of America's colleges were sponsored by Congregationalists, Presbyterians, and Episcopalians. By the Civil War, Methodists and Baptists staffed a third of the nation's institutions of higher learning, the three large colonial denominations another third, and other religious groups another 10 percent.

The theological seminary was not as well developed before the Civil

By 1868, when this parade of Brooklyn Sunday School Students was featured on the cover of *Harper's Weekly*, Sunday School had become the most widespread form of education for young Americans. The Brooklyn parade remains an annual event. *Photo Collection, The Branch Libraries, The New York Public Library*

THE REISSUE OF

HARPER'S WEEKLY.
A JOURNAL OF CIVILIZATION

VOL. XII.—No. 598.] NEW YORK, SATURDAY, JUNE 13, 1868. [SINGLE COPIES, TEN CENTS. [$4.00 PER YEAR IN ADVANCE.

PARADE OF THE BROOKLYN SUNDAY-SCHOOL CHILDREN, MAY 26, 1868.—SKETCHED BY THEODORE R. DAVIS.—[SEE NEXT PAGE.]

War as it would become in later decades. But the seminaries that did exist enrolled a very high proportion of what are today called "graduate students." (The only serious competition was a few law schools.) Preparation for the ministry had traditionally involved personal study, a call to preach, private instruction from a practicing minister, or (for the older, English-based denominations) training at a liberal arts college. Andover Seminary, founded in 1808 by orthodox Congregationalists to provide an alternative to Harvard Unitarianism, was the first major seminary in what would become a standard American pattern — a school primarily for graduates with previous college training devoted to systematic study of the biblical languages, theology, church history, and preaching. Soon the other colonial denominations founded their own seminaries, and by the time of the Civil War the Baptists, Methodists, Disciples, and other newer groups had also established schools especially for the training of ministers. If these institutions educated only a small minority of the nation's preachers, it was still the case that the seminaries kept alive the ideal of a learned ministry. They also provided a forum for advanced intellectual activity at a time when few educational institutions of any kind were doing so.

What was true for schools was also true for publications. Among the nation's intellectual elite, the periodicals most widely distributed and most generally influential were the theological quarterlies. It was a period when all denominations worthy of the name sponsored at least one such journal and when Methodists, Presbyterians, Episcopalians, Congregationalists, Unitarians, and yet other groups patronized several weighty quarterlies each. Presbyterians, who prided themselves on the care they devoted to religious thought, had the *Southern Presbyterian Review* and the *Cumberland Presbyterian* for readers below the Mason-Dixon Line, the *American Presbyterian* and the *Presbyterian Quarterly Review,* which promoted more activistic, Americanized "New School" views, and the *Biblical Repertory and Princeton Review,* edited for forty-five years by Charles Hodge of Princeton Seminary, to promote more traditional "Old School" opinions. Methodists, Congregationalists, and Episcopalians had a nearly similar spectrum of learned journals. What these journals published also went well beyond normal religious fare. To be sure, they gave full attention to theological issues and questions about the meaning of the Bible, but they also discussed literary and historical subjects, commented at length on current events (especially before and during the Civil War), and provided general discussions of scientific questions that were among the best-informed in the country.

A Flourishing of Protestant Theology

The theologians who staffed the seminaries and produced the quarterlies were the country's most respected intellectuals before the Civil War. The thought of a Ralph Waldo Emerson or a Henry David Thoreau might now seem more interesting than the work of the antebellum theologians, but contemporaries were much more impressed by the theologians. And most of those who exerted the greatest influence either propounded some variety of evangelical Protestantism or advanced their thought in self-conscious dialogue with evangelical traditions.

The work of the major antebellum theologians exhibited several common convictions, which often were also put to use by populist religious leaders in their own anti-institutional and antitraditional ways. Belief in the Scriptures as God's inspired Word was nearly universal. A preoccupation with theological problems as defined by the Puritans' Calvinistic tradition and by such eighteenth-century Reformed thinkers as Jonathan Edwards was also widespread. As an intellectual method, the common-sense philosophy imported from Scotland held wide sway, with its assertion that the physical senses convey reliable information about the external world, and the moral sense (or conscience) about the spiritual world. In addition, most of the major theologians took a proprietary interest in American culture. They affirmed the principles of political liberty, republicanism, and democratic opportunity that had been embraced at the Revolution. In one way or another, they wanted theology and its practical outworkings to guide the nation.

The Heirs of Calvinism

What was called the New Haven Theology represented a last stage in the development of the thought that had originated with Jonathan Edwards and the colonial Great Awakening. Timothy Dwight, grandson of Edwards and president of Yale College at the turn of the century (1795-1817) was a key figure in modifying some doctrines from colonial Calvinism for use in the nineteenth century. But it was Dwight's most outstanding pupil, Nathaniel William Taylor (1786-1858), who developed the New Haven Theology most consistently. In 1822 Taylor became the first professor at the new Yale Divinity School, where he saw himself as the heir of Edwards and a champion against Unitarian innovation in New England. But Taylor differed markedly from Edwards in his convictions about human nature. He once argued, in a famous phrase, that people had a "power to the contrary" when faced with moral choices. By this he meant that sinfulness arises from sinful acts rather than from a sinful nature inherited from Adam. All people do in fact sin, Taylor held, but they are not predetermined to do so by human nature itself. The New Haven Theology was a powerful engine for revival and reform, since it provided a rationale for trusting God while exerting one's own energies to the fullest. This New Haven Theology arose out of the Calvinist tradition, but its emphasis on human capacities carried it in the direction of the Methodism that was then exerting such a dramatic influence on American religion.

The Unitarianism that Taylor and his associates so feared was best represented by William Ellery Channing (1780-1842). Channing had grown up in Rhode Island under the preaching of Jonathan Edwards's most faithful pupil, Samuel Hopkins, and he had undergone an evangelical conversion experience as a Harvard undergraduate. Despite the later de-

Nathaniel W. Taylor *(above left)*, first professor of theology at the Yale Divinity School, joined a concern for revivalism, a modification of New England's historic Calvinism, and Scottish common-sense moral philosophy in promoting his influential teaching on "the moral government of God." William Ellery Channing *(above right)* was the best known of the Unitarians who by 1820 had made a decisive break with New England's Trinitarian Congregationalists. *Taylor portrait courtesy of the Billy Graham Center Museum; Channing portrait courtesy of the National Portrait Gallery, Washington, D.C. / Art Resource, New York*

velopment of Channing's thought, he never regretted his background in the stricter forms of New England Calvinism. In 1803 he became minister of Boston's Federal Street Congregational Church, where he remained the rest of his life. Channing's presence, along with a liberal Harvard College, made Boston the stronghold of Unitarianism. It was not in Boston, however, but in Baltimore that Channing set out most fully the creed of the Unitarians in a sermon preached in 1819. He spoke out against traditional beliefs in the Trinity, the deity of Christ, the total depravity of humans, and substitutionary atonement. In other contexts Channing affirmed the perfectibility of humanity, the fatherhood of God, the moral perfection of Christ, and the reality of the resurrection as well as other New Testament miracles. He believed that the Bible recorded inspiration but was not itself inspired as such. Later in his career, Channing criticized others, such as the Transcendentalists, for moving too far away from traditional Christianity. His own evangelical personality and the strong reforming impulses he shared with his evangelical contemporaries (against slavery and the liquor traffic) may have obscured how far away from traditional conceptions his own faith had traveled.

Another effort to modify traditional Calvinism for use in the dynamic decades of the antebellum period was promoted by Charles Finney (1792-1875), who, as we have already seen, was the period's most prominent revivalist. While still a Presbyterian, Finney read the works of N. W. Taylor and soon concluded that Taylor was correct: humans do have within themselves the power for choosing Christ and living holy lives. After Finney left the Presbyterians, he encountered John Wesley's *Plain Account of Christian Perfection,* and his belief in the possibility of "entire sanctification" was confirmed. When Finney became professor of theology at Oberlin College in 1835, his theology assumed its mature form with these components: (1) a commitment to "new measures" in revivalism, (2) a commitment to moral reform, and (3) a belief in a second, more mature stage of Christian life. The last conviction was developed by various professors at Oberlin who used such terms as "holiness," "Christian perfection," and "the baptism of the Holy Ghost" — terms that would later have a great influence on the development of evangelical, holiness, and Pentecostal theologies. Finney's influence at Oberlin was considerably enlarged by his coworkers, among whom Oberlin's first president, Asa Mahan (1799-1889), was an especially forceful proponent of the Oberlin Theology.

Not all nineteenth-century Calvinists were interested in revising their heritage in response to contemporary circumstances. Among those most insistent on retaining the hereditary faith were the theologians at the Presbyterians' seminary in Princeton, New Jersey. This seminary, founded in 1812, was for more than a century the center of conservative American Calvinism. The convictions of the seminary's first professor, Archibald Alexander (1772-1851), defined the emphases of this theology. Alexander was a man of deep personal piety whose formal theology combined emphases from European Calvinism (Calvin, the Westminster Confession, and François Turretin) and an anti-Catholic defense of Scripture with intellectual procedures defined by the Scottish philosophers of common-sense reasoning.

Alexander's student Charles Hodge (1797-1878) extended this theological viewpoint into a powerful system of thought during his fifty-six years as a Princeton professor. Hodge used the same sources that Alexander had employed to defend the glory of God (instead of the happiness of humanity) as the purpose of life, to affirm the power of the Holy Spirit in salvation (against views of human self-determination), and to champion the Scriptures as the proper fount of theology (against either human religious experience or the dictates of formal reason). Hodge once remarked proudly that there had never been a new idea at Princeton, by which he meant that

This print shows Princeton Theological Seminary flanked by the houses of Archibald Alexander *(left)* and Charles Hodge *(right)*, the two most important theologians at this, the largest Protestant seminary of the nineteenth century.
Courtesy of the Billy Graham Center Museum

Princeton intended to pass on Reformed faith as it had been defined in the sixteenth and seventeenth centuries. Hodge and the Princetonians did adjust in some ways to their time, however, especially by employing current methods of science as a model for their own work. Hodge's formula, "the Bible is to the theologian what nature is to the man of science," was used to preserve traditional Calvinism, but it took for granted concepts and procedures that were very much a part of America's nineteenth-century intellectual life.

In the South, with its more conservative social order, older forms of traditional theology survived with even more vigor than in the North. Thus, although Princeton was the best-known center of conservative Calvinism before the Civil War, such Southern Presbyterians as James Thornwell (1812-1862) and Robert Dabney (1820-1898) were also effective spokesmen for a Calvinism undiluted by modern notions of personal self-determination. Thornwell was associated with South Carolina College and Columbia Theological Seminary, and he was also an active preacher. His Calvinism resembled that of Charles Hodge, with the difference that Thornwell argued more strenuously for the integrity of the church and its higher levels of jurisdiction as a spiritual principle. Dabney became known after the Civil

War for his defense of the Old South against both northern political reform and the spread of industrial materialism. But already before the War he had been developing a moderate form of Westminster Calvinism with special attention to the ways in which divine Providence may be said to operate alongside, rather than in opposition to, the regular course of nature. The conservative Calvinism developed by Thornwell and Dabney was also decisively shaped by their Southern context, for they found it natural to defend both traditional theology and the traditional social order of slavery.

Baptists in the South developed more extensive theological institutions and traditions after the War, but already in the antebellum period distinctive marks of Baptist theologies had begun to appear. A strong "primitivist" streak was prominent in the work of such leaders as J. M. Pendleton (1811-1891) and J. R. Graves (1820-1893), who argued for the strictest form of local church organization and practice. Their "Landmarkism" was derived from a tract of Pendleton referring to Proverbs 22:28 ("remove not the ancient landmark which your fathers have set"). It argued both that Baptist organization and practice was the only Christian form faithful to the New Testament and that churches manifesting such strict Baptist allegiance could be traced back to the New Testament. Closer to Northern convictions and temperament were a generation of Baptist theologians who in the 1850s and 1860s began to construct seminaries on the Northern model. Prominent among these was James Petigru Boyce (1827-1888), who studied at Brown and Princeton Seminary before founding the Southern Baptist Theological Seminary in Greenville, South Carolina (later moved to Louisville). Boyce was an active denominational leader whose own theology presented a moderate Calvinism adjusted to defend adult believer baptism and the particular convictions of Baptist ecclesiology.

Also by the time of the Civil War, the Restorationist movement that had crystallized early in the century led to the establishment of schools, a host of periodicals, and a strong theological tradition. Originating with the work of Barton W. Stone (1772-1844) and Alexander Campbell (1788-1866), restorationists sought to recover the pristine purity of a "Bible only" Christianity. They were avidly antitraditional and anti-Calvinistic, but they did share the conviction of their Protestant contemporaries that a rigorously scientific approach to the Bible would yield the one true Christian theology. They took as their name simply "Christians" or Disciples of Christ in the hopes of uniting all believers in a commonsense, democratic form of the faith. Over time, the inevitable happened, and this antidenominational movement developed a vigorous denominational tradition including such institutions as Alexander Campbell's Bethany College, where the particular tenets of restorationism received an increasingly formal and learned defense.

Southern theology of the antebellum period had more in common with theologies of the North than it had differences. But Southern evangelicalism was distinct in its relative distrust of formal learning, its appeal to absolute forms of ideal New Testament faith, and its powerful insistence that people read the Scriptures for themselves. The last emphasis was not without its ironies, for several well-defined traditions emerged in the South that united considerable numbers of people who were reading the Bible for themselves along lines laid down by influential leaders. But the populist, localist, and restorationist character of Southern theologies enabled them to survive long after many Northern expressions of evangelical Protestantism were drastically changed.

Mediating Theologies

By mid-century a number of other theological traditions, which did not receive much notice or support at the time, appeared as modifications of the dominant evangelical tradition. These varieties of antebellum evangelicalism looked more like deviations than variations from the perspective of the mid-nineteenth century, but from the perspective of the late twentieth century, it is clearer how each represented a strand of evangelical thought that would one day blossom into a major expression of Christian theology.

Horace Bushnell (1802-1876), long-term pastor of a Congregational church in Hartford, Connecticut, was a theologian of Christian experience and so anticipated the sort of Protestant theologies (both liberal and conservative) that would one day make experience a fundamental principle of theology. Bushnell's theological guides were Friedrich Schleiermacher and, even more, Samuel Taylor Coleridge, from whom he learned a more romantic view of God, humanity, and the world. Bushnell's upwardly mobile congregation in Hartford was optimistic about the future of America, skeptical about the vulgarity of the masses, anxious for a more refined sensibility, and yet also serious about maintaining a viable Christian faith. Bushnell's theology spoke to these desires and, by so doing, also anticipated more general changes that came later in theological history. In a treatise entitled *Christian Nurture* (1847) he argued against the crudities of popular revivalism in favor of a Christianity centered in the domestic environment. Bushnell drew fire for his "Dissertation on Language," published in 1849, in which he denied that it is possible to do theology in scientific terms; he argued rather for the metaphorical, aesthetic, or even artistic character of Christian truth. In 1858 he published yet another controversial volume, *Nature and the Supernatural,* in which he hoped to show why it was appropriate to view all things, natural and supernatural, as sharing a spiritual essence. Bushnell's theology was rooted in evangelical experiences, which he hoped to refine out of the polarities of revival to a romantic sensitivity concerning the spiritual potential of all life. His views pointed toward later liberal revisions of Protestant orthodoxy as well as later conservative concentrations on the primacy of Christian experience.

A theological tradition that shared Bushnell's disquiet with revivalistic evangelicalism but which sought theological renewal in a different source was associated with the German Reformed seminary in Mercersburg, Pennsylvania. This theology was primarily the work of John Williamson Nevin (1803-1886) and Philip Schaff (1819-1893), whom we have already encountered as an immigrant from Europe. Nevin studied with Charles Hodge at Princeton Seminary but eventually concluded that Hodge's Calvinism was too "Puritan" and that American evangelicalism in general was too mechanically revivalistic. After he joined the faculty of the tiny Mercersburg Seminary in 1840, Nevin was inspired by his reading in contemporary German theologians who hoped for renewal of Reformation traditions and in the German Reformed Church's doctrinal standard, the Heidelberg Catechism. Responding to these influences, Nevin criticized American revivalism for placing too much emphasis on the self. He also attacked American Calvinistic orthodoxy for deemphasizing the work of Christ and the importance of the Lord's Supper. Schaff, who joined Nevin in 1844, brought with him an appreciation for the new idealistic philosophy of Germany as well as a deep commitment to pietistic church renewal. Schaff contributed to the critique of American ways by arguing for a fuller appropriation of the Christian past, including selective use of the medieval Catholic heritage.

The influence of Nevin and Schaff was slight in the 1840s and 1850s. American Protestants were still wholeheartedly revivalistic, they suspected any form of European thought that did not conform to commonsense categories, and they harbored grave suspicions about any views of the church that seemed to resemble Roman Catholicism, however slightly. The day of influence for the Mercersburg Theology would not arrive until the 1940s, when at least a few Protestants, disillusioned by the appeals of both fundamentalists and modernists, found in these theologians the kind of mediation between traditional Protestantism and modern forms of thought that they felt the church required.

From an altogether different place in the landscape of American Christianity, black thinkers had also begun to construct more formal theologies in the decades before the Civil War. The most important contribution of blacks to Christian theology was intense reflection on the experience of slavery itself. But this theology seldom made it into print. Black ministers

Black pastor Lemuel Haynes *(above left)* broke new ground in the early 1800s by serving a white congregation — a combination that has remained a rarity in American church history. Bishop Daniel Alexander Payne *(above right),* who received his theological training at Lutheran Gettysburg Seminary, was the leading theologian and one of the leading promoters of education in the African Methodist Episcopal churches in the decades after the Civil War. *Haynes etching courtesy of the Billy Graham Center Museum; Payne photo from the collections of the Library of Congress*

who did educate themselves and achieved a formal position in the churches before the Civil War tended to expound varieties of evangelicalism, but even in such standard expositions there were hints of difference. Such a one, as we have seen, was Lemuel Haynes, the first black ordained formally in the United States. Haynes was a conventional New School Calvinistic revivalist who, in his opposition to Tom Paine's deism and Hosea Ballou's universalism, sounded like a typical orthodox Congregationalist. Haynes did not often speak of his race, but on at least a few occasions he did draw attention to the injustice, under God, of perpetuating the slave system. Such comments were not greatly different from antislavery remarks by other heirs of Jonathan Edwards's New Light Calvinism, but they did outline a path for those who, in later years, would move more directly from the general principles of evangelical Protestantism to specifically theological reflection on the conditions of American society.

A later spokesman who moved in that direction was Daniel Alexander Payne (1811-1893), a leading spirit in the African Methodist Episcopal Church from the early 1840s. Payne, who was born a free black in Charleston, South

Carolina, but who was educated for the ministry at the Lutheran Seminary in Gettysburg, became best known as a proponent of education in the A.M.E. church. His own theology reflected the general evangelicalism of the day; he was able to work closely with a more Americanized group of Lutherans and to serve a black Presbyterian congregation before he joined the black Methodists. Payne's ardent advocacy of education, which he felt he had received as a direct commission from God, led him to criticize some traditional worship practices of blacks such as the "ring shout." But he expounded his message of educational improvement as an evangelical shaped by his own experiences. His view of the Deity, for example, differed from that held by many of his white contemporaries, in its emphasis on God's patient working. When the South Carolina legislature passed a law in 1835 that shut down the school he was conducting for other African Americans, he entertained doubts about the goodness of God but then was reassured that, since a thousand years was but a day to the Lord, he should not despair about God's ultimate purpose in bringing an end to this evil system.

Payne's own experience also made him sensitive to the universality of God's love. As might be expected, he complained when white churches or seminaries excluded blacks simply because of their race. But perhaps more surprisingly, he took a strong stand against an A.M.E. church that prohibited a white woman from joining the congregation. His defense of this position angered fellow blacks, but Payne did not equivocate: "I believed that the pastor who would turn away from God's sanctuary any human being on account of color was not fit to have charge of a gang of dogs." Payne's formal theology was ordinary in the antebellum context, but his personal experiences allowed him to make a distinctive contribution to the standard evangelicalism of his day.

Evangelicalism held sway across almost the entire ecclesiastical landscape in the years before mid-century. Quakers, for example, were drawn closer to the evangelical mainstream by the influence of Joseph John Gurney (1788-1847), an English Friend. Gurney visited the states in 1837, shortly after a group of Philadelphia Quakers had left their Yearly Meeting in order to resist evangelical trends in their movement. Gurney, on the other hand, encouraged Friends to combine the distinctives of their tradition, such as reliance on the "Inner Light of Christ," with more general evangelical emphases on the authority of Scripture and the need for a holy life as such holiness was defined by active revivalists.

In a similar manner, even major theological voices in the Catholic Church reflected the influence of dominant evangelical trends. An influential early bishop, John England (1786-1842), defended the propriety of Catholicism with arguments similar to those that evangelical Protestants were using to promote their forms of the faith. And as we will note in more detail below, innovative Catholic thinkers such as Orestes Brownson and Isaac Hecker reflected at least some effects of common evangelical experience in their formulations of Catholic teaching.

The point is not to claim that the theology of Protestant evangelicals created the best of all possible worlds in antebellum America. It was, in fact, a theology that could not solve the issue of slavery and a theology that in emphasizing so heavily the themes of conversion and strenuous holy living certainly underemphasized other essential parts of Christianity. Yet the scope and influence of the theology is unquestioned. For better and for worse, it was America's public theology from the Revolution to the Civil War.

Politics

The influence of evangelical religion extended beyond the intellectual to the political. Here many other influences were also at play. But, at the least, evangelical mobilization for reform also provided a model for action adapted to American circumstances that political reformers increasingly put to use as the century wore on. In addition, styles of revival exerted a long-lasting influence on the organization of political groups that occurred in "the second party system" beginning under Andrew Jackson. Historian Leonard Sweet has written perceptively on one facet of that influence: "the most enduring legacy of the camp meeting was in the realm of politics. The political rally was more than a secular counterpart to camp meetings. It was an actual borrowing of camp-meeting methods by American political party structures, and the nominating convention of today is probably the closest thing to an evangelical nineteenth-century camp meeting that most Americans experience."

Evangelical values also deeply influenced the formal political parties. The Anti-Masonic Party, the Liberty Party (which advocated a more rapid liberation of the slaves), and the Know-Nothing or American Party (which exploited Protestant fears of Roman Catholics) were each important third parties with considerable local (and even national) loyalties for at least an election or two in the forty years before the Civil War. All of them were direct products of evangelical worldviews, apprehensions, and aspirations. The Whig Party, from its rise as the formal opposition to Jackson to its demise in the 1850s, came close to being an embodiment of evangelical public faith. The Whig sense of urgency at promoting righteousness in society, its often confusing alliances with the forces of freedom (religious, social, capitalistic), its ambiguous but persistent uneasiness with slavery — all of these were products of an evangelical worldview. And the Democrats, though opposing the Whigs systematically, also reflected some evangelical influences, especially from the South and especially from Protestants who felt alienated from the larger, more publicly visible evangelical spokesmen.

The importance of evangelical religion for antebellum politics is indicated by the fact that denominational allegiance, in conjunction with ethnic ties, was the best predictor for voting behavior in the period. Thus, in elections through at least the middle third of the century, Whigs or Republicans could count on overwhelming support from Congregationalists, Northern Methodists, Episcopalians, New School Presbyterians, and free black Protestants, as well as substantial support from Disciples, Old School Presbyterians, and most German ethnic groups such as Mennonites and Moravians. Catholics of all ethnic varieties disagreed with Southern Methodists and Baptists on almost all religious questions, but these disparate bodies did unite politically with overwhelming support of the Democrats because of their opposition to the Whig/Republican–Northern evangelical coalition. Some of the newer groups of Lutheran and Dutch Reformed immigrants, likewise uneasy with Whig/Republican evangelicalism, gave consistently reliable support to the Democrats.

The line between religion and politics has always been a thin one in America. In the heyday of "Evangelical America," it was virtually nonexistent.

Antebellum America was "evangelical" not because every feature of life in every region in the United States was thoroughly dominated by evangelical Protestants but because so much of the visible public activity, so great a proportion of the learned culture, and so many dynamic organizations were products of evangelical conviction. Protestant evangelicalism was not as all-encompassing in the antebellum United States as French Catholicism was in Quebec at the same time, and yet in the period before the Civil War, the influence of religion on public life exercised by evangelicals in the United States was so profound and extensive as to be unmatched in the North American context by anything but the situation in overwhelmingly Catholic Quebec.

The achievement of the evangelicals was remarkable: they managed to forge a relatively cohesive religious culture out of disparate elements and make it effective throughout a sprawling, expanding land. If the achievement was flawed by insensitivity to those outside the camp of white evangelicals, and if the intellectual triumphalism of the period grew increasingly hollow as the decades passed, the commitment, zeal, and purpose of these Protestants were nonetheless more impressive religiously than anything that had happened in the United States before, or that was going on in contemporary Europe.

243

As the reference to Quebec suggests, the only comparable sort of culture formation during this period was occurring just over the border to the north. But in nineteenth-century Canada, to which we turn next, the building of a "Christian nation" was complicated by the fact that the task was being pursued by two vigorous, often antagonistic varieties of Christian faith.

Further Reading

Ahlstrom, Sydney E., ed. *Theology in America: The Major Protestant Voices from Puritanism to Neo-Orthodoxy.* Indianapolis: Bobbs-Merrill, 1967.

Finke, Roger, and Rodney Stark. "Turning Pews into People: Estimating Nineteenth Century Church Membership." *Journal for the Scientific Study of Religion* 23 (1986): 180-92.

George, Timothy, and David S. Dockery, eds. *Baptist Theologians.* Nashville: Broadman, 1990.

Holifield, E. Brooks. *The Gentlemen Theologians: American Theology in Southern Culture, 1795-1860.* Durham, NC: Duke University Press, 1978.

Howe, Daniel Walker. *The Political Culture of the American Whigs.* Chicago: University of Chicago Press, 1979.

Mathews, Donald. *Religion in the Old South.* Chicago: University of Chicago Press, 1977.

Miller, Glenn T. *Piety and Intellect: The Aims and Purposes of Ante-Bellum Theological Education.* Atlanta: Scholars Press, 1990.

Nord, David Paul. "The Evangelical Origins of Mass Media in America." *Journalism Monographs* 88 (1984): 1-30.

Powell, Milton B., ed. *The Voluntary Church: American Religious Life, 1740-1860, Seen through the Eyes of European Visitors.* New York: Macmillan, 1967.

Saum, Lewis O. *The Popular Mood of Pre–Civil War America.* Westport, CT: Greenwood, 1980.

Smith, Timothy L. *Revivalism and Social Reform: American Protestantism on the Eve of the Civil War.* Rev. ed. Baltimore: The John Hopkins University Press, 1980.

Sweet, Leonard I. "Nineteenth-Century Evangelicalism." In vol. 2 of *Encyclopedia of the American Religious Experience.* Edited by Charles H. Lippy and Peter W. Williams. New York: Scribner's, 1988.

Swierenga, Robert P. "Ethnoreligious Political Behavior in the Mid-Nineteenth Century: Voting, Values, Cultures." In *Religion and American Politics from the Colonial Period to the 1980s.* Edited by Mark A. Noll. New York: Oxford University Press, 1990.

Wall, Joseph Frazier. *Iowa: A History.* New York: Norton, 1978.

CHAPTER 10

His Dominion: "Christian Canada"

What a Friend we have in Jesus,
All our sins and griefs to bear!
What a privilege to carry
Everything to God in prayer!
O what peace we often forfeit,
O what needless pain we bear,
All because we do not carry
Everything to God in prayer!

$$* \quad * \quad * \quad * \quad *$$

Are we weak and heavy-laden,
Cumbered with a load of care?
Precious Savior, still our refuge —
Take it to the Lord in prayer.
Do thy friends despise, forsake thee?
Take it to the Lord in prayer.
In His arms He'll take and shield thee —
Thou wilt find a solace there.

Joseph Scriven (1819-1886), who emigrated from Ireland to Port Hope, Ontario, as a young man, wrote this hymn to express the comfort he had found during several tragedies in his life. Its message of confidence in Christ was a prominent theme of Canadian religious life in the nineteenth century. When Dwight L. Moody's song leader, Ira Sankey, included it in his first collection of Gospel Hymns *(1875), it became a much-loved hymn in the United States and Great Britain.*

CHRISTIAN DEVELOPMENTS IN NINETEENTH-CENTURY CANADA BEAR STRIK-ing similarities to what was happening at the same time in the United States. Like the faithful in the American republic, Canadian believers mobilized to preach the gospel in new settlements spread over a vast frontier. Canadians also linked the progress of Christianity with the advance of civilization. And they succeeded in bequeathing a Christian tone to the institutions, habits, and morals of public life. After the modern nation of Canada was formed in 1867, Leonard Tilley of Fredericton, New Brunswick, a political leader and a Methodist, applied the words of Psalm 72:8 to the new country: "He shall have dominion also from sea to sea." For several generations thereafter, the vision of "His Dominion" as a nation embodying Christian principles and striving toward Christian goals loomed large. It would shape the aspirations of those who promoted a social gospel, such as J. S. Woodsworth, a Methodist minister turned socialist politician, and those who wanted to preserve traditional formulations of the faith, such as T. T. Shields, a Baptist minister who tried to organize a fundamentalist movement in Canada. Throughout the century, in other words, there was much in Canada to remind observers of what was also transpiring in the United States.

But there was also much that was different. First and foremost, French Quebec and Acadian New Brunswick gave Canada well-established, culturally powerful expressions of Roman Catholicism unlike anything in the United States. Canada was never to know the sort of unified vision of Protestant purpose for the nation that many evangelicals thought had been established in the States. In addition, Canada's ties to the Old World remained much stronger than such ties in the United States. Powerful English, Scottish, Irish, and French influences continued to flow into Canada, where for the most part they were welcomed. The result was that Canada was situated culturally *between* the United States and Europe. Finally, politics shaped the life of the Canadian churches almost to the same extent that it shaped religion in the States, although the nature of the influence was different. Political events that were celebrated in the United States became occasions for Canadians to distance themselves from American principles.

The story of Christianity in nineteenth-century Canada is worth retelling for its own sake. But because of how that history is related to what was happening in the United States, it also provides a telling contrast to American developments. We will begin by examining the political context of nineteenth-century religious history, proceed to consider the fate of Catholicism both in Quebec and elsewhere, and finally look at Protestantism in the Atlantic provinces, Ontario, and the opening Canadian West. In the end, this survey will put us in a position to compare developments in Canada and the United States.

The Canadian Political Context

In Canada, unlike the United States, the most important political events were things that did *not* happen. After the British government in 1791 divided Upper Canada (Ontario) from Lower Canada (Quebec), a modest number of immigrants from the new United States and also from Britain continued to settle in Upper Canada. During the 1790s and the first years of the next century, Britain ruled Canada by benign neglect. Its energies were devoted much more to the great struggle with Napoleon's France than to managing its overseas holdings. Government in Britain's North American colonies was entrusted to aristocrats, would-be aristocrats, or (in Quebec) leaders allied with the Catholic Church. Settlers in Canada's English-speaking regions did not take kindly to aristocratic pretensions, but neither were they particularly concerned about political or international affairs.

The event that focused Canadian Loyalism and also inspired the beginnings of Canadian nationalism was the War of 1812. American textbooks now treat this conflict as a fairly minor skirmish that merely confirmed the independence of the United States. North of the border, by contrast, the psychological impact of the war confirmed Canadians in their differences with the United States. For political and church leaders alike, American invasions across the Great Lakes provided a stimulus for defining Loyalism more exactly. Canadians did, in fact, want to retain continuity with Europe. They did not want the forces of democracy to overwhelm respect for the past, honor to the crown, or traditions inherited from England, Scotland, and pre-Revolutionary France. They did not think that "liberty" was the supreme value; they viewed it simply as one valued commodity to be pursued along with several others. As historian John Webster Grant has put the matter, "the War of 1812 . . . left an indelible mark on the Upper Canadian mentality. Most immediately, it changed colonists' perceptions of the United States and thereby — by a peculiar but well-understood Canadian logic — their perception of themselves." The War of 1812 thus resembled the American Revolution: it was an opportunity for Canadians to join the United States that they chose not to take.

The next important developments of this sort were the rebellions of 1837-38 in Ontario and Quebec. In these situations the Canadians chose not to pursue independence on the American model and not to embrace American political values wholeheartedly. By the 1830s, liberal political voices had arisen in both Upper and Lower Canada calling for more political freedom and heightened autonomy in economic matters. In Quebec, Louis-Joseph Papineau told his followers, *les Patriotes,* that "the democratic flood has poured irresistibly down the slope of time and, growing faster and faster, will topple the unavailing barriers which may be erected against it." Similar words came from William Lyon Mackenzie in present-day Ontario, who told his followers that "if we rise with one consent to overthrow despotism, we will make quick work of it." The problem for Papineau and Mackenzie was that very few Canadians believed them. Following months of increasingly heated rhetoric in 1837, the radical forces blundered into military action against hastily assembled militia loyal to the British government. In the skirmishes that followed, the rebels were decisively defeated. Papineau and MacKenzie fled to the States, and Loyalism received a substantial boost among both elites and most ordinary Canadians. Out of the tumult did come a parliamentary commission to examine Canadian affairs which eventually endorsed several important steps toward more democratic government. But these steps were taken in cooperation with, rather than out of hostility toward, hereditary British rule.

In 1867 the modern nation of Canada was formed by the federation of Quebec, Ontario, Nova Scotia, and New Brunswick. The British North America Act of that year gave Canadians a degree of independence only slightly short of what Americans had achieved in 1776, and it enshrined principles of politics just as democratic as in the States. Yet the spirit of the Act as well as the government it set up were significantly different. Canadian self-government resulted from pragmatic calculations, it did not engender fierce antagonisms, and it did not provide the stuff of legends. "Peace, order, and good government" was the slogan used to sell confederation. This phrase, as many Canadian historians have pointed out, is almost entirely lacking in the appeal to idealism implied by the "life, liberty, and the pursuit of happiness" clause in the American Declaration of Independence.

John A. Macdonald, the architect of confederation and Canada's Tory prime minister for more than twenty years under the new government, won his way by appealing to regional self-interest. The Maritime provinces, fearful of being isolated, were won over with promises of rail connections to central Canada. Most leaders in Quebec favored confederation because of the increased autonomous powers it offered to the province. In Ontario businessmen and politicians saw confederation as a chance to enhance their own influence. The British Parliament was glad to give Canada more autonomy as a way of both reducing its subsidies and protecting British in-

Throughout the nineteenth century, Canadian politics was often expressed in terms of loyalty to Britain versus assimilation by the United States. This early pattern has remained influential in Canada to the present day. *National Archives of Canada*

vestors. To British Columbians and settlers in the Red River Valley (later Manitoba) the British North America Act spelled out procedures for their entrance into the new Dominion as autonomous provinces.

A significant factor in confederation was again the desire to avoid taking the American path. Quebec leaders, who had no great love for the English, feared absorption into the American empire more than they feared the designs of other Canadians. Ontario wanted to be sure that the opening west did not simply fold into the United States. The American Civil War provided an important negative reference point. Political leaders thought the American government had been too weak to prevent disunion but also that the war showed the tyrannical potential of democratic ideology. (The contrast between the handful of casualties in Canada's "rebellions" of 1837 and 1838 and the hundreds of thousands in the American Civil War was for Canadians telling.) At the last moment, negotiators even changed the name of the new country from the "Kingdom of Canada" to the "Dominion of Canada" to avoid antagonizing sensibilities in the United States. Historian Kenneth McNaught has done a good job of summarizing what was at stake in confederation and the system that emerged: "beyond doubt its central meaning was that of survival, and for each of the regions and cultures survival meant maintenance of a protective connexion with Britain. . . . [The result was] a pragmatic politics receptive to change, suspicious of any form of totalitarian democracy, and deeply concerned with the multi-racial and multi-cultural problems that have come to dominate the twentieth century." With confederation, Canada retained the British sovereign and many British traditions, but it also gained virtual autonomy and the freedom to develop its own approach to political-cultural life.

In the wake of confederation, Canada developed steadily. Manitoba became the fifth province in 1870, followed by British Columbia (1871), Prince Edward Island (1873), Alberta and Saskatchewan (both 1905), and finally Newfoundland (1949). By comparison with the United States, economic life stagnated until the mid-1890s but then enjoyed a boom that was sustained through World War I. Again by comparison with the States, Canada's population was very small, only slightly over 3,500,000 at the first Dominion census in 1871 (about the same as the population of the thirteen colonies in 1776). Fifty years later there were nearly 8,800,000 Canadians, but this was considerably less than one-tenth of the American population in 1920 (106,000,000). Nation-building was the dominant theme in Canada's public life over that half century.

It was also in many ways the theme of the churches in the same period. They had helped to shape Canada's emergence as a modern nation even as they were being shaped by it. The persistent fact of French-English multiculturalism, the embrace of Loyalism, the desire for evolutionary as opposed to revolutionary change, the respect for traditions, the knowledge that theirs was a small population in a vast land, a persistent awareness (and wariness) of the United States — these were all aspects of nineteenth-century Canadian history that influenced religion as much as it influenced politics.

The Catholic Story

The center of Catholicism in Canada was and is Quebec. The dominant language of Canadian Catholicism was and is French. But if the heart of the Catholic story in Canada is French-speaking Quebec, it is also true that the Catholic Church has enjoyed a major presence elsewhere in Canada. In fact, Catholicism in Canada has affected almost every aspect of that nation's Christian history, even in regions dominated by Protestants. The history of Catholicism in Quebec, therefore, comes first, even if it is not the whole story.

The Triumph of Ultramontanism in Quebec

By the time of the Canada Act of 1791, more than 100,000 Roman Catholics were being ministered to in 118 parishes under the oversight of the Bishop of Quebec. British acceptance of Quebec's Catholicism was genuine but not particularly secure. Even after French-Canadians confirmed their loyalty to the crown during the American Revolution, influential leaders in the British Parliament repeatedly made noises about "anglicizing" the French in Canada, a process that was automatically assumed to include conversion to Protestantism. These noises continued for a long while, but two developments in the decades immediately after the Canada Act solidified the place of Catholicism in Quebec and also reassured the British that a Catholic colony could be tolerated.

The first of these was the arrival in Quebec of forty-five émigré French priests as a result of the French Revolution. These priests were monarchists who brought profoundly anti-Revolutionary sentiments with them to the New World. In the absence of other significant emigrations from France, and given the relative lack of Canadian-born clergy, the antiliberal influence of this contingent was considerable.

The second development was the eventful tenure of Joseph-Octave Plessis (1763-1825) as Bishop of Quebec. After attaining the bishopric in 1806, Plessis first took pains to fend off attempts by the British government to restrict the free reign of the Church. But the War of 1812 soon presented him with a more significant cause. Despite fears in London that the American invasions would be welcomed by restive *Québecois,* Plessis galvanized his priests and the entire apparatus of the Church to back the British. For this service, the grateful government relaxed its efforts to control Roman Catholicism, increased the subsidy it had been providing under the provisions of the Canada Act, and also added Plessis as an *ex officio* member to the province's legislative council. These actions greatly perturbed the Anglican Bishop of Quebec, Jacob Mountain, who felt that, since Quebec was a British colony, his church should be given the preferences of establishment. Despite Mountain's misgivings, Plessis adroitly exploited his newfound influence by expanding the administration of the Catholic Church in all of Canada. In a series of negotiations that extended over several years and involved delicate dealings with both the British government and the Vatican in Rome, Plessis divided the Canadian Church into separate sees that stretched from Prince Edward Island to the Red River Valley.

Both of these developments confirmed the increasingly ultramontanist character of Quebec Catholicism. As noted in Chapter 5, *ultramontanism* (literally, "over the mountains") was a term originally coined in France to

Joseph-Octave Plessis was the Catholic Bishop of Quebec during the War of 1812. His support for Britain kept French Canadians loyal despite the invitation of Americans to join the United States. *Archives nationales du Québec à Québec*

designate a Catholicism that stressed loyalty to the pope and strict adherence to Church traditions. The opposite tendency, "Gallicanism," emphasized the role of political authorities in guiding the Church and also argued for much greater local autonomy in matters of faith and practice. Quebec had already been leaning in an ultramontanist direction, especially because of its abhorrence for the way the Catholic Church was treated in the French Revolution. The arrival of the refugee priests and Plessis's success at freeing Quebec from tight British constraint moved French-Canadian Catholicism even further in that direction.

Quebec's unalloyed commitment to an ultramontanist faith was not secured, however, until after the troubles of 1837. The liberal political ideas for which Louis-Joseph Papineau contended greatly concerned the hierarchy, not just because of their association with Revolutionary anticlericalism but also because they threatened to displace the Church as the central institution in Quebec society. The artisans, lawyers, doctors, and merchants who paid attention to Papineau seemed, to the critical eye of the bishops, to want the kind of control over their own religious and public destinies that had become commonplace in the United States. When the rebellion of 1837 miscarried and Papineau fled in disgrace to the States, the Church took advantage of the opportunity to solidify its dominance of Quebec society. Led by the first bishop of Montreal, Jean-Jacques Lartigue, who was, ironically, Papineau's cousin, the Church reasserted its centrality in the province's life. Practically, that reassertion involved tighter control over Quebec's educational system, so that for more than a century after 1840 the education of all French-speaking citizens in Quebec was directed by the Church. Ideologically, it meant that Catholics identified themselves with political traditionalism, economic conservatism, social deference, an agrarian society, and resistance to change. The evils that Lartigue and his successors feared were the individualism of American economic life, democratic politics as practiced in the United States (and also to a lesser extent in the rest of Canada), social egalitarianism, urban commotion, and intellectual innovation. In other words, after 1840 the tie between the Catholic Church and French-Canadian culture was tighter than it had been before. Britain, and later the English-speaking Canadians who promoted confederation, tolerated this situation out of gratitude for Quebec's general loyalty to the crown but also because the bonds of Catholic French-Canadian identity had become too strong to dissolve.

Under Bishop Ignace Bourget, who replaced Lartigue in 1840 and whose tenure extended for forty years, Quebec enjoyed a time of spiritual renewal as well as nationalistic and institutional vigor. Bourget was an indefatigable administrator who recruited brothers, nuns, and priests in Europe, oversaw the founding of many hospitals and schools, worked for the establishment of an independent university in Montreal (which was, however, not founded until after his death), started influential periodicals, denounced such fashionable European ideas as positivism, evolution, and revolution, and firmly supported the conservatism of Pope Pius IX. But Bourget was also a man of intense personal piety who not only spent much time in prayer himself but also founded several institutions to encourage prayer among priests, the laity, and the religious orders. He also diligently recruited missionaries for the western Canadian frontier on the assumption that, as he put it, "the best means of preserving the faith is to propagate it far and wide." Bourget was also instrumental in founding an *Institut Canadien* in 1844, which he hoped would provide young intellectuals with an edifying outlet for their interests. Later, when devotees of the *Institut* began to criticize the Church for its tight control in the province, Bourget withdrew his support and campaigned actively against its influence.

An incident involving Bourget in conflict with members of the *Institut* illustrates the extent to which the Church was at the center of Quebec life, but also the way in which resistance to that domination could bubble to the surface. Since ultramontanists were by definition conservative in politics, it

253

Ignace Bourget, Bishop of Montreal for more than thirty-five years in the mid-nineteenth century, founded many new religious communities and colleges, staunchly maintained ultramontane doctrines, and feuded regularly with the liberal *Institut Canadien*. *Archives nationale du Québec à Québec*

was not surprising that Bishop Bourget openly supported John A. Macdonald's Conservative Party against its opposition, the Liberals. Despite the fact that many Conservatives (or Tories) outside of Quebec were ardent anti-Catholics, Bourget was convinced that a politics of preservation was much better than a politics of change. When in 1868 the yearbook of the *Institut Canadien* published articles promoting the virtues of democracy and capitalistic individualism, Bourget responded by placing the yearbook on the Index of Prohibited Books. The next year he issued a pastoral letter forbidding Catholics to belong to the *Institut*. By the end of the year Bourget showed how serious he was in issuing that directive.

In November 1869, Joseph Guibord, a well-known member of the *Institut*, died. Because he had maintained his membership, the Catholic clergy refused to give him the Church's last rites or bury him in a consecrated Catholic cemetery. Much incensed, Guibord's colleagues started legal proceedings that after five years of hotly contested litigation resulted in a decision by the Judicial Committee of the Privy Council in London that Guibord should be interred in a Catholic cemetery. A hostile clash ensued on the streets of Montreal when Guibord's supporters tried to transport his remains from their temporary resting place to a Catholic burial ground. Later they performed the burial in secret, but Bourget ultimately had the last word when he deconsecrated the particular spot where Guibord had been laid to rest.

Bourget resisted political individualism with all the means at his command. After the Guibord incident he instructed priests to pass the word to parishioners that they should vote only for Tories. In the event that the choice lay between an anti-Catholic Conservative and a well-meaning Liberal, Bourget said that no vote should be cast. Voters in doubt should consult with their priests, who, by following the word of the bishop (who in turn followed the pope), would give them instructions from Christ himself. These extreme statements earned Bourget a rebuke from other Canadian Catholics and eventually from the pope. After Bourget was gone, after John A. Macdonald died in 1891, and after Wilfrid Laurier of Quebec became leader of the Liberal Party, Quebec Catholics eventually turned from their massive support of the Conservatives to back the Liberals almost as completely.

The particular style of Bourget's politics had faded away by the end of the century, but Quebec's French-Catholic culture remained. Montreal, as a mercantile center with a substantial English minority, was always more suspect than Quebec City, which remained a bastion of ultramontanism until well after World War II. The Quebec bishops were slow to acknowledge the right of laborers to organize, out of fear that unions upset the hierarchical order given by God. Well past the middle of the twentieth century other characteristics of this singularly Catholic culture remained. The Church ran Quebec's schools and hospitals. Quebec had an extraordinarily large number of priests, nuns, and brothers. (Throughout the century from 1860 to 1960, there was about one priest for every 510 Roman Catholics, and as late as 1941, one man or woman in religious orders for every 87 Quebec Catholics; two-thirds of the nuns and brothers worked in the Quebec schools.) The size of families remained large, with the Quebec population doubling every quarter-century. Pilgrimages to rural and urban shrines were common. And the Church exercised its vigilance in keeping out such subversive ideas as socialism or Freemasonry as well as subversive practices such as attending the cinema on Sunday.

Most Canadian Protestants, and even many non-French Catholics, viewed efforts like those of Bishop Bourget to defend a closed French-Catholic culture as misguided or worse. But for generations of *Québecois*, the successful implementation of an ultramontane Catholicism gave a degree of intellectual, social, and liturgical stability found nowhere else in North America. At the end of the twentieth century, it is appropriate both to marvel at the strength of that French-Catholic synthesis and to wonder if its very thoroughness did not lay the groundwork for the incredibly swift secularization that has befallen Quebec in the last decades of the twentieth century.

Catholicism beyond Quebec and Protestant-Catholic Hostility

The Roman Catholic Church never dominated any other area in Canada as it did Quebec. But it was still a formidable presence almost everywhere. As the various provinces entered the Dominion, Catholics constituted the largest single religious communion in New Brunswick, Prince Edward Island, British Columbia, Saskatchewan, and Alberta. In Nova Scotia, Catholics were almost as numerous as Presbyterians; in Ontario, they were not too far behind the Methodists, Presbyterians, and Anglicans; and in Manitoba, there were only slightly fewer Catholics than Presbyterians or Anglicans. In the mid-nineteenth century most Catholics outside of Quebec were French-speaking, but increasingly as the decades passed, Catholics from the United States, England, Ireland, and the Continent made up a larger proportion of the total.

Canada's history of the relationship between French-speaking Catholics and other Catholics had some similarities to the situation in the United States. Just as tension developed in the States when bishops of English origin were put in charge of Irish, German, Italian, or Polish sees, and later when Irish-American priests were sent to Hispanic parishes, so in Canada considerable friction existed so long as the French remained in charge of the non-French. By the 1880s, for example, French bishops were finding Irish immigrants to Ontario increasingly restive under their care. At the beginning of World War I, all of the Catholic bishops in western Canada were French-speaking, even though most of the faithful were by that time using English or some other European language. The one exception to this pattern was New Brunswick. Over the course of the nineteenth century the French-speaking Acadians, who had been expelled before the American Revolution as a precaution by the British, gradually drifted back. By 1860, there were five predominantly Acadian sees, but all were ruled by Irish or Scottish bishops. Only in the twentieth century have bishops been ethnically matched with their constituencies.

The spread of Catholic settlements beyond Quebec only exacerbated the deep antagonism between Catholics and Protestants that was so much a part of the religious world of the North Atlantic in the nineteenth century. It was not just in Quebec that Catholics feared greatly that the Protestant population would sweep their Church away. From the other side, many Protestants shared the sentiments of Robert Murray of Halifax, Nova Scotia, who told the sixth general conference of the Evangelical Alliance, meeting in New York City in October 1873, that the Catholic Church in Canada was "so strong as to occasion anxiety to the friends of liberty and education." According to Murray, "the most formidable foe of living Christianity among us is not Deism or Atheism, or any form of infidelity, but the nominally Christian Church of Rome." From a foundation of mutual suspicion there arose a series of violent incidents in the 1850s and 1880s as well as ongoing contentions over education that linger to the present.

The violence at mid-century was precipitated by events in the Old World. In 1850, over three centuries after Catholic bishops had been abolished in the reign of Henry VIII, the English Parliament authorized the reestablishment of a Catholic hierarchy. A broad spectrum of Canadian Protestants reacted with hostility to the announcement of this restitution, characterizing it as nothing less than a "papal aggression." Especially aggrieved were members of the Orange Order, Protestant immigrants from Ireland who had carried to the New World organizations and sentiments that had been forged in the Protestant-Catholic strife in their land. At first the violent sentiments were restricted to the printed page, where Orangeman joined other Canadian Protestants in denouncing the tyrannies of Rome, and Irish Catholic immigrants led a more general Catholic defense of Parliament's action and the Catholic Church.

The transition from violent words to violent actions took place in 1853. The galvanizing event was the visit by an Italian ex-priest named Alessandro Gavazzi, who was touring Canada to promote Italian nationalism and expose the errors of the papacy. When Gavazzi tried to lecture in Quebec, rioters stopped the proceedings and injured members of his party. Shortly thereafter, at the end of a lecture in Montreal, troops that had gathered to protect the peace unaccountably fired on the departing crowds. Nearly twenty, mostly Protestants, were killed. Disruptive demonstrations and counter-demonstrations occurred regularly for much of the rest of the decade. In 1855 the murder in Quebec of Robert Cortigan, a convert from Catholicism, increased Protestant ire. For the next several years, marches to commemorate the Catholic St. Patrick's Day and the Protestant Twelfth of July (a celebration of the liberation of Northern Ireland from Catholicism) were marked by hostilities, bloody riots, and fatalities on both sides. Religious antagonisms were heightened still more in the 1860s by the Fenian Brotherhood, a secret organization promoting the liberation of Ireland from England. When members of this American-backed group mounted a comic-opera invasion of Upper Canada in 1866, Protestant outrage again ran high. Only with confederation and provisions in the British North America Act for greater autonomy for Quebec did the violence subside.

Louis Riel, leader of the *métis* in what is now Manitoba, combined an ardent, messianic Catholicism with wounded outrage at the treatment his people had received at the hands of Canada's political leaders. *Archives nationales du Québec à Québec*

Given entrenched Catholic-Protestant hostilities, it is little wonder that Protestant missionary efforts in Quebec bore little fruit or that Catholic attempts to spread their faith among English-speaking residents in Quebec's eastern townships and Montreal's business community had little effect. A redoubtable immigrant from Switzerland, Madame Henrietta Feller, established the Grande Ligne Mission as a pioneering Protestant effort in 1836, and she was later joined by organized efforts of the main Protestant denominations. But the efforts of such groups were usually met with icy hostility and sometimes with violent resistance.

This ongoing antagonism forms the background to the controversial career of Louis Riel (1844-1885). Riel was a *métis* (a person of mixed French-Indian ancestry) from the Red River Valley who had been trained in Catholic schools and who possessed a driven, charismatic personality. When in 1869 the Hudson Bay Company ceded the Red River region to the new Canadian Dominion and the Dominion prepared to admit the area as the province of Manitoba, Riel led the region's *métis*, who had not been consulted on the transfer, in forming a provisional government. Negotiations between Riel and the Canadian authorities came to an abrupt end when Riel allowed his military council to execute Thomas Scott, an Orange-man and agitator. The response in English Canada was outrage, and Riel was soon forced to flee. After living some years in the United States, Riel returned to Manitoba in 1885 to reestablish a government of and for the *métis*. This time the Dominion dispatched an armed force, Riel was captured, and then before the end of the year executed for treason. Riel, who combined a deep spirituality with convictions about his own prophetic powers, became a lightning rod for violent public opinion. To Canadian Protestants, who long remembered the death of Thomas Scott, he was a symbol of Catholic licentiousness; to French-Catholics in Quebec and elsewhere he became a martyr to the imperial pretensions of the English.

Incidents like those associated with Riel became explosive because they grew out of deeply ingrained suspicions between Catholics and Protestants. The ill-feeling that rankled most persistently concerned education. Right from the start of settlement in what became Ontario, and then with increased ardor in the western provinces, French-Catholics and English-Protestants engaged in a never-ending round of recriminations over the funding, control, and maintenance of local schools. Decades of controversy in Ontario matched Protestants, who wanted to see a unified, generically Christian system for all young people, against Catholics, who dug in firmly to support separate schools for the French-speaking population. Finally in 1855 Catholics won the right to set up their own elementary schools with government funding in Canada West (Ontario), but this was by no means the end of controversy. Under the British North America Act of 1867, Canada's provinces were given control over education, so each new addition to the Dominion led to cantankerous debates over schooling. Early legislation in New Brunswick, for example, prohibited the use of taxes for the teaching of French or religion, while in Quebec English-speaking Protestants were allowed to establish their own system. Manitoba came into the Dominion with a dual system, but then legislation in 1890 brought all the schools in that province together into an English-language system. The Manitoba school question was a central issue in the federal political election of 1896, when the leader of the Liberal Party, a Quebec Catholic named Wilfrid Laurier, rode to victory with a delicately balanced platform that promised Manitoba autonomy over its own schools. After the election, Laurier also succeeded in winning some concessions from Manitoba for its French-Catholic students. When Alberta and Saskatchewan joined the Dominion in 1905, arguments flared once again about the educational rights of linguistic and religious minorities.

To this day in Canada, questions linking education and religion remain matters of public debate. More Canadians than Americans have acknowledged that education is never value-neutral and more have been willing to grant provincial funding for the schools desired by children's parents, even if the schools are religious. Regulations differ, but most provinces permit religious or linguistic minorities above a certain size to set up their own primary and secondary schools and to receive funding from the province (for tuition, construction and maintenance, or both). In Newfoundland, all of the schools are based upon denominations. The rights of Catholic and French-speaking individuals are the main concern outside of Quebec, but the debate between French-Catholics and English-Protestants over schooling has meant that smaller religious and ethnic minorities have also been able to provide publicly funded schooling for their own.

The Meaning of Catholic-Protestant Tension

Canada's long history of Catholic-Protestant standoffs is one of the characteristics that most separates its church history from that of the United States. Tension between Catholics and Protestants provided one of the main external props for Quebec's distinct French-Catholic culture. For example, when Protestants reacted angrily in 1850 to the restitution of the Catholic hierarchy in Britain, the backlash in Quebec only solidified the determination of such leaders as Bishop Bourget to defend, fortify, and expand the hold of the Church in that province. After Louis Riel was executed in 1885, reaction in Quebec was so strong that in the next provincial election the *Parti National,* a Quebec nationalist organization alienated from both the national Conservatives and Liberals, swept into power.

The other side of the picture is that a strong French-Catholic presence made Protestants perpetually anxious about their own standing in the Dominion. A telling incident from the 1870s illustrates that anxiety. John William Dawson (1820-1899) was a world-renowned geologist who taught at Montreal's McGill University. Dawson was also an earnest Presbyterian who paid very close attention to the religious as well as the scientific implications of Darwin's new theory of evolution. Because of his eminence as both scientist and lay theologian, Dawson received a very attractive offer from Princeton College in 1878 to take that university's chair of geology. He was tempted, but he eventually turned down Princeton with these words: "I fear that the claims of duty tie me to this place where a handful . . . of protestant people are struggling to redeem this province of Quebec from the incubus of ultramontanism and of mediæval ignorance." A climate of mutual suspicion, exacerbated by political and education-related conflict as well as by the basic differences between the two varieties of Christian faith, colored almost every aspect of Canada's religious life.

J. W. Dawson was for thirty-eight years the principal of McGill University, during a time when it reflected the sturdy Presbyterian faith that Dawson hoped to promote through his work as one of the most widely respected geologists of his day. *Archives nationales du Québec à Québec*

But as with most trying situations, there were also compensations. Because of the divided Christian allegiances of Canadians, they were much less tempted than Protestant Americans to conceive of their nation as standing uniquely in covenant with God. Such notions can stimulate good, but they also lead to a great deal of moral posturing and simple hypocrisy that Canadians have mostly been able to avoid.

Another unintended dividend of the persistent Catholic-Protestant divide was the growth of considerable religious tolerance in public life. In 1896 Wilfrid Laurier, through his shrewd handling of the Manitoba school question as well as through expert attention to his own Quebec constituency, became Canada's first elected Roman Catholic prime minister. This election took place more than thirty years before a Catholic was nominated by a major party in the United States to run for the presidency and more than sixty years before John Kennedy was elected as the first Catholic president. Catholic-Protestant differences have not been absent in Canada's political life, but it has been much easier to take them in stride there than it has been in the States. Since the time of Laurier, Canada has enjoyed the service of several Catholic prime ministers, including the best-known Liberal (Pierre Eliot Trudeau) and Progressive Conservative (Brian Mulroney), in the era after World War II.

As we turn now to Protestant life in nineteenth-century Canada, we will do well to keep in mind the Catholic presence. Just as a grasp of the

Catholic experience in Canada requires constant attention to the reality of Protestantism, the reverse is also the case.

The Protestant Story in the Atlantic Provinces

From the earliest British settlements in the Atlantic region, the Church of England was given special status. But if Anglican preference had had its problems in the thirteen colonies that became the United States, it was even more precarious in Nova Scotia, New Brunswick, and Prince Edward Island. A large Catholic population, especially in French-speaking areas, always had to be accommodated. The resistance of other Protestants, who gained steadily in numbers and influence, also made an effective Anglican establishment impossible. Despite fulminations against democratic leveling by early Anglican bishops Charles Inglis and his son John, who became Nova Scotia's third Anglican bishop in 1825, the tide continued to turn against establishment. For a few decades the Church of England received a stipend from the British parliament, and an Anglican bishop sat on the executive councils of Nova Scotia and New Brunswick into the 1850s, but these were remnants of Old World patterns rather than viable options in the New World.

Of greater long-term influence than efforts at establishing the Anglican Church was the work of lay revivalists and self-educated ministers in other denominations. The "New Light Stir" of Henry Alline from the 1770s and 1780s left an enduring legacy of mystical fervor and lay reliance on Scripture that, though greatly modified over time, could still be glimpsed in the twentieth century. As the New Light movement was co-opted by other groups, it became more formal in practice and more Calvinistic in doctrine. Yet a strong Free Will Baptist movement continued throughout the nineteenth century as a more direct continuation of New Light themes. In Baptist churches especially the hymns of Henry Alline were sung long after the free-form dynamism of his earlier movement had flowed back into more conventional ecclesiastical channels.

Fresh waves of immigration from Britain in the first decades of the nineteenth century decisively shaped Protestantism in the Maritimes. Scottish Presbyterians, in large numbers and of several varieties, made their home in Nova Scotia and Prince Edward Island, where they re-created the forms of worship, emphases in doctrine, and even the willingness to quarrel that they had known in their native land. These Presbyterians also brought with them the hereditary Scottish concern for education and soon were working to establish schools and higher academies in what was still a barely

Thomas McCulloch, Presbyterian
immigrant from Scotland, was the
founder of Pictou Academy in
Nova Scotia and one of the leaders
in creating an "evangelical creed"
for English-speaking Canadians
during the nineteenth century.
*Archives of The United Church
of Canada*

settled frontier. Notable in these efforts was Thomas McCulloch (1776-
1843), a Scottish-born minister who founded Pictou Academy in 1816.
There he became one of the most significant early teachers of what historians
Goldwin French and Michael Gauvreau have called Canada's "evangelical
creed." This depiction of Protestant faith stressed both the supreme authority of Scripture and the necessity for a vital personal experience with Christ.
When taken up by Methodists, Baptists, other Presbyterians, and a significant number of evangelical Anglicans, it became a powerful guide to both
religious and intellectual life in all of Canada. McCulloch, a versatile thinker
who also published some of Canada's notable early humor, became in 1838
the first principal of Dalhousie College.

The direction of Methodism in the Atlantic provinces was altered when
British Wesleyan immigrants began to gain influence at the expense of American Methodism, especially after the War of 1812. The early Methodism of
William Black (who was commissioned by John Wesley to itinerate in Nova
Scotia) and Freeborn Garrettson from the United States was similar in emphases to the New Light faith of Henry Alline. The later Wesleyan Methodists,
by contrast, put greater stress on formal ministerial training, on decorum in
worship, and on a more tightly disciplined approach to the spiritual life.

The Cornwallis Street Baptist Church, built in 1832, was the first church in Nova Scotia owned and controlled by blacks. *Courtesy of the Black Cultural Center for Nova Scotia*

These developments among the Methodists contributed to a general process that saw Maritime Protestantism become more disciplined, more conservative, and more preoccupied with morality (sometimes even moralism). Similar movements in the three major groups of dissenting Protestants — toward Calvinism among the Baptists, toward English decorum among the Methodists, and toward the reconstruction of Scottish forms among the Presbyterians — combined with a general distaste for American patterns occasioned by the War of 1812. The result by the 1820s and 1830s was the creation of a vigorously disciplined Protestant culture that would shape life in the Atlantic provinces well into the twentieth century. Protestants in the Maritimes contributed more than their share to temperance crusades and movements such as the Lord's Day Alliance.

At the same time, however, more general conditions in the provinces curtailed the growth of the churches. As fishing became less important in the North Atlantic economy and as the Maritimes grew increasingly more marginal to the concerns of both the British and central Canadians, the Maritime population leveled off, the economy became stagnant, and a sense of regional alienation grew. Early patterns continued — with strong Catholic minorities, a significant Anglican presence especially in the major cities, and sturdy congregational life among Presbyterians, Baptists, and Methodists. There was even room for significant smaller groups. Of these the most intriguing were the black churches around Halifax, Nova Scotia. By mid-century almost half of Canada's blacks, some descended from the

Loyalists of the 1780s and some more recently escaped from American slavery, lived in the Halifax region. Most worshiped in Baptist churches.

Throughout the twentieth century, levels of church membership, church attendance, belief in traditional Christian teachings, and avoidance of alternative belief systems such as astrology and psychic religions have been consistently higher in the Maritimes than in any other of Canada's other Protestant regions. Since the 1960s and the rapid secularization of Quebec, these levels have been far and away the highest in Canada as a whole.

On the negative side, by the middle of the nineteenth century the sense was also growing that the Atlantic provinces were becoming a backwater of little interest to Britain, the United States, or the rest of Canada. The Atlantic provinces did produce significant Christian leaders, but they tended to make their mark elsewhere — as, for example, William Dawson (Nova Scotia), who, as we have seen, was a distinguished scientist in Montreal, A. B. Simpson (Prince Edward Island), who founded the Christian and Missionary Alliance, and Shirley Jackson Case (New Brunswick), who became an influential proponent of modernist theology at the University of Chicago. In a rough comparison, the Maritimes became to Canada what Scotland was to England — a place of vigorous Christian loyalties that nonetheless remained on the margin of cultural influence, famous as much for sons and daughters who left for other parts as for those who remained behind.

The Protestant Story in Ontario and the West

Important as the Maritime provinces were in providing a beachhead for Protestantism in Canada, it was in Ontario that Protestant expansion exerted its greatest force. The importance of Ontario as a province (known first as Upper Canada, and then from 1841 to 1867 as Canada West) also involves its key role in Canada's Christian history. Although it was virtually unpopulated in the 1780s, by the mid-nineteenth century Ontario had overtaken Quebec as Canada's most heavily populated province. Ontario's current population of about nine million constitutes more than a third of Canada's total. Its economic centrality has been a fact of Canadian life for over a century. And its great metropolis, Toronto, is for Canada's cultural life what New York and Los Angeles are for culture in the United States. To add to its importance for Protestants, Ontario has had a smaller Catholic population, proportionately, than any other province.

To understand the nature of Protestant history in Ontario and the Canadian West, as well as to note important points of contrast with the United States, we will do well to consider several especially important historical developments. First, it is helpful to consider how divergent strands of Protestant experience at the start of the nineteenth century eventually came to assist each other in the creation of an evangelical Protestant civilization. Second, it is also helpful to see how Ontario as the heart of Canadian Protestantism continued to absorb European influences alongside influences from the States and its own indigenous development. Third, an understanding of the strong Protestant culture before Confederation will also allow us to see how that culture was sustained for more than a half century after 1867 by strategic adjustments to changing conditions in thought and society.

A Confluence of Opposites

Ontario's Christian history is instructive in a North American context because the province experienced in barely one century the sequence of pioneering and consolidation that took over 250 years to unfold in the United States. In 1800 Ontario was home to no more than 20,000 widely scattered residents, who were served by about 25 clergymen. A century later the provincial population had grown a hundredfold to about 2,200,000, and there were enough churches to seat every one of its citizens at the same time, with a few spaces left over for visitors. From 1851 to 1871 alone, the number of churches grew from less than 1,500 to nearly 4,100. Anglicans made up the largest denomination at the first reliable census in 1842, but they were soon surpassed by Methodists, and then edged out also by Presbyterians. Catholics were always a significant minority (about 17 percent in 1871). These four groups maintained the allegiance of 80 to 90 percent of Ontario's citizens throughout the century. Baptists were the largest of the smaller bodies, which also included offshoots of many of the period's religious movements from Great Britain and the United States (e.g., Congregationalists, Disciples, Mormons, Adventists, members of the Salvation Army, followers of Edward Irving, Plymouth Brethren, and eventually holiness and Pentecostal bodies), along with a few from the Continent (e.g., Lutherans).

From the very first days of settlement by British subjects fleeing the new United States, the principles of Loyalism exerted an immense impact. While the number of those who migrated northward in order to preserve the bond with king and Parliament soon became a minority, their disposition to social stability and their hostility to unchecked democracy deeply colored the province's history. In the first decades, however, the effects of Loyalism were not foreordained. Early settlers did not want to break from Britain, but neither would they tolerate the heavy-handed administration

266

that had characterized British rule of the thirteen colonies. The earliest effective religious leaders in Ontario were much more likely to be Methodist evangelists in the populist mold of Francis Asbury than socially conservative Anglicans of the sort desired by Canada's British governors. Until the War of 1812, in fact, the embryonic conventicles in Ontario's frontier settlements were more like the Baptist and Methodist churches springing up in the American West than like the settled churches on the Atlantic coast.

The War of 1812 changed this situation dramatically. A few Canadian firebrands did welcome the United States' military invasions of Upper Canada. (It was during one of those invasions that American militiamen burned the city of York [later Toronto], a deed for which the later British destruction of Washington was a reprisal.) But most leaders, social and religious, were deeply offended by the effort to incorporate Canada by force into the United States. The War of 1812, which some Americans thought would be the ideal moment for Canada to enter the Union, was instead for Ontario a stimulus to commit decisively *against* the States.

As a result of the War, church life was changed decisively. The flow of itinerant preachers from the United States, mostly Methodist, was cut off almost entirely. Many Canadian Methodists began to steer their course along lines suggested by the more decorous Wesleyans from England. Anglicanism took on a new respectability as a key link to the mother country. In sum, the chance that Canadian Protestantism might follow the populist, sectarian, fragmenting ways of the United States — certainly a real chance in early decades — came to an end because of the War.

Even after the conflict, however, it was not a simple matter for Loyalism to exert a solidifying influence on the churches of Upper Canada. It was axiomatic to almost all who settled in Ontario after the American Revolution that Christian faith was essential to public well-being. But what kind of Christian faith should it be? There were two prominent but contrasting contenders.

Defenders of Anglicanism, including social leaders of the province and, to a somewhat lesser extent, the Presbyterians, sought a faith featuring order, stability, and social harmony. On the other hand, Methodists, who tended as in the States to draw their most committed support from artisans and farmers, wanted a faith defined by the transforming power of Spirit-inspired revivalism. A clash between representatives of these contrasting viewpoints kept Ontario culture unsettled for the first third of the century. Then, however, Methodists (and to some extent other sectarian groups) began to see more value in harmonious order even as Anglicans (and to some extent Presbyterians) began to recognize the need for emotionally satisfying Christian experience. The result was a confluence of divergent faiths that even-

This Methodist camp meeting in Ontario, sometime around 1840 or 1850, illustrates a process that was also occurring at the same time in the United States. The formal arrangement of tents, the relatively stylish dress, and the general decorum of those in attendance mark a rise in respectability for meetings that in their early days were more emotional, less well organized, and closer to elemental religious feelings.
Archives of The United Church of Canada

tually resulted in a relatively common approach to church, society, and public morality. It was generally agreed that the life-changing experience of conversion was crucial but also that conversion h; d to be joined to public responsibility in the construction of a civilization. So successful was this reconciliation of "enthusiasm" and "establishment" that at least a few Ontario Protestants by late in the century thought their experience might be a harbinger of the millennium.

The way this momentous confluence took place is well illustrated by the lives of the two dominant Protestants of the period, the Anglican John Strachan (1778-1867) and the Methodist Egerton Ryerson (1803-1882). Strachan, who was an immigrant from Scotland, eventually became the Bishop of Toronto and Ontario's most active proponent of an Anglican establishment. He believed that it was the job of the church to promote a godly sense of restraint and balance, since "a love of order is not only essential to the tranquillity but to the very being of any State." Strachan was an especially zealous champion of Anglican rights concerning the Clergy Reserves, a large grant of land designated in the 1791 Canada Act "for the

Egerton Ryerson was Upper Canada's leading Methodist spokesman during the middle third of the nineteenth century. His list of public services was lengthy — from Methodist minister to president of Victoria College and finally director of public education for the whole province of Ontario.
Archives of The United Church of Canada

support and maintenance of a Protestant clergy." (Contention over the income from the Reserves festered until they were at last secularized in 1854.) Strachan also strove to make the Anglican Church the dominant force in English-speaking higher education.

By contrast, Egerton Ryerson's conception of both religion and the public good was shaped irrevocably by the moving conversion he experienced under Methodist guidance as a young man. The essence of Christian faith for Ryerson was the transporting touch of God's grace. In his service as an itinerant minister, editor of an influential Methodist publication, and the founding principal of the Methodists' first college, Ryerson boldly championed the virtues of voluntary church organization and the ongoing need for spiritual rejuvenation. If Strachan held that the establishment of religion was the secret to a Christian society, Ryerson contended that it was the camp meeting.

Strachan expressed his viewpoint with unusual clarity at a public address in July 1825 to commemorate the death of Jacob Mountain, the first Anglican bishop of Quebec. Strachan held that Mountain deserved high praise for trying to construct an orderly, loyal, and well-regulated regime in church and state. As Strachan put it, "a Christian nation without a religious establishment is a contradiction." But as he praised the virtues of an Angli-

John Strachan, eventually Bishop of Toronto, was the leading proponent of a full establishment of the Anglican Church in the early history of English Upper Canada. *Courtesy of Ontario Archives*

can establishment, Strachan also went out of his way to say what was wrong with enthusiasts like the Methodists: they were "uneducated itinerant preachers, who leaving their steady employment, betake themselves to preaching the Gospel from idleness, or a zeal without knowledge, by which they are induced without any preparation, to teach what they do not know, and which from pride, they disdain to learn."

This barb was too much for the young Egerton Ryerson, who provided a full-scale response the next year. First, he pointed out what was wrong with Strachan's idea of religion. "Our savior," wrote Ryerson, "never intimated the union of his church with the civil polity of any country." Anglican ritual, moreover, was "all pompous panegyric." What Canadians needed was what a high and dry Anglicanism could not provide — "preaching the gospel" with passion for repentance and conversion. Ryerson's response catapulted him into public prominence, where he went on to champion without stint the virtues of an experiential, heartfelt Christian faith.

What seemed to be a classic standoff, however, yielded an unexpected degree of reconciliation, and in a relatively short time. As the Methodists grew by leaps and bounds, they took greater and greater interest in the civilizing effects of their mission. As a never-ending series of complications impeded Strachan's push for Anglican establishment, he began to recognize some virtue in a voluntary conception of church order. The loyalty to British

The growing respectability and growing prominence of Protestants in English-speaking Canada are shown by the contrast between these two types of Methodist church buildings — the first in a restrained classical style from about the 1830s, the second in an exuberant Gothic about a half-century later. *Metropolitan Toronto Reference Library*

models that the two groups shared (Ryerson's father had been one of the earliest Loyalist settlers in Ontario) provided a significant point of reconciliation. In any event, the strife gradually cooled, and the former antagonists grew closer together.

The evolution of church architecture provided a graphic example of this confluence. Methodists, who once had built inconspicuous halls that seemed to call people out of the world, now began to construct stately cathedrals that dominated (and, they hoped, inspired) the urban landscape. Anglicans, who once had built churches resembling official government buildings, now began to construct parish churches after models from an idealized rural England. In both cases the move was from trying to protect the distinctives of a particular Christian tradition toward providing churches that both nurtured the faithful and sanctified the world.

When at last Strachan and Ryerson actually met each other face to face during a long coach ride in 1842, they were surprised to find how well they got along. Their meeting was important for education, too. It came after the Methodists had secured provincial legislation to transform their denominational academy into a full-fledged college (Victoria College, which would later join the University of Toronto), and Strachan gave Ryerson advice on how to tap the Clergy Reserves for support of the new institution. Each had begun with the hope of preserving the distinctive Christian emphasis of his tradition, but each found it increasingly easy to integrate that emphasis with the concerns of his former opponent, while together promoting the place of religion in Ontario society.

After long and honorable service to the Methodists, Ryerson became the first director of public education in Ontario. In this post he built the sort of formal structures that Strachan had always favored to provide a vigorous, if general, Protestant education. His attempt was not appreciated by Ontario's Catholic minority, but it did flow naturally from the earlier themes of his career. By the end of his life, Strachan was willing to concede the importance of vital Christian experience, and he gracefully concluded that at least some of the voluntarism once promoted so aggressively by Ryerson was necessary for religion in Ontario. In other words, Ryerson and Strachan came to a rough agreement on how Christianity should be put to use for the benefit of individuals and society.

The faith that resulted from the confluence of Methodist enthusiasm and the Anglican establishment provided both a powerful impetus for personal religion and a vital means for Christianizing Ontario's burgeoning society. Public-spirited church leaders and impressive church buildings dotting the new urban landscapes provided a unifying rather than sectarian impulse to Ontario's religious life.

Protestant energy bore much of the responsibility for transforming Ontario from a frontier outpost into a paragon of advanced (albeit self-conscious) civilization. If some pettiness attended this transformation, and if it was always defined by conventions of Victorian culture, it nonetheless displayed remarkable sacrificial zeal, organizational energy, altruistic dedication, and spiritual power.

The twin concern for evangelical conversion and social construction provided the backdrop for Ontario's characteristic practices in church and state. As the Anglican establishment faded, Ontario did not turn to the ideals of the American First Amendment but rather worked out a distinctly Canadian solution. Churches would be supported by the voluntary activities of their members, but no one in Ontario at mid-century quibbled about disbursing one last round of proceeds from the Clergy Reserves to Anglicans, Presbyterians, Catholics, and even a few sectarian Protestants willing to take the money. The province would fund public education, but it would do so in a broadly Protestant way, while also providing separate schools for Roman Catholics. At the University of Toronto, instruction in the sciences and social sciences would be the responsibility of a religiously neutral, even secular, faculty, but church colleges, supported by public funding, were invited into the structure to teach the arts and train ministers.

Victoria College began as the college of Upper Canadian Methodists in Coburg, Ontario. Later, as shown in this photo, it was incorporated into the University of Toronto, where throughout the nineteenth century confessional colleges like Victoria functioned as integral parts of the larger university. *Archives of The United Church of Canada*

This pattern in higher education has proven very durable in Ontario and throughout the rest of Canada. In 1877, for example, the University of Manitoba was founded as a joint product of three denominational colleges — Presbyterian, Anglican, and Catholic (in 1881 a Methodist institution was added). Later the university itself assumed an increasingly large share of the instruction, but never to the point of entirely excluding the denominational colleges as part of the enterprise. Provision for church-sponsored colleges within public universities continues at the end of the twentieth century.

The structures resulting from the confluence of evangelizing and civilizing motives left Ontario Protestants with a distinct heritage. Compared to the United States, they were more culturally conservative (and hence perhaps slower in responding to change) but also more culturally responsible (and so perhaps less prone to individualistic excesses). They also continued to bear the mark of European circumstances more evidently than was the case in the States.

Between Britain and America

A good example of the way that Old World influences continued to shape Canadian Christian life is provided by the Presbyterians. Presbyterians were, in general, a more important body in Protestant Canada than almost anywhere in the United States, except for some regions of Pennsylvania and the Carolinas, where Scottish and Scotch-Irish immigrants had concentrated. Canadian Presbyterians did not easily forget that the Scottish church from which they came was officially established as the state church, and so they often sided with the Anglicans as champions of a new establishment on this side of the Atlantic. At the same time, however, many Canadian Presbyterians had been affected by evangelical preaching or conversion, and so they had a good deal in common with the Methodists as well.

The best way to see the workings of Old World influence is to follow events among Canadian Presbyterians after the "Disruption" of Scotland's established Presbyterian church in 1843. Presbyterians in Canada were almost all intimately tied to the Scottish Kirk or to the closely related Presbyterian church of Northern Ireland, which meant that they watched Scottish developments closely. When the more evangelical, more activist leaders of Scotland's Kirk found themselves unable to free their church from what they regarded as the excessive control of hereditary aristocrats and the state, about one-third of the clergy and even more of the people broke away to establish the Free Presbyterian Church of Scotland. The fathers of the Scottish Free Church wanted to maintain the establishment of the church, but they walked out of the Kirk in order to defend the principle of the church's control over its own affairs.

The conditions that divided the church in Scotland were next to meaningless in Canada, for by the mid-1840s Ontario was well on its way to ending the vestigial Anglican establishment. Only continuing debates on how to distribute revenues derived from the Clergy Reserves and how to fit the churches into Ontario's emerging universities remained as matters of contention. Canadian Presbyterians, in other words, did not need to divide over what were essentially Scottish issues. But divide they did, with the more evangelical group coming out to form the Presbyterian Church of Canada, which, after the Old World example, was usually called the Free Church. This new denomination grew rapidly, and soon outdistanced the Kirk Synod in Canada that remained in fellowship with the Auld Kirk of Scotland. By 1861 the Free Church had grown to about 150,000 (or roughly 10 percent of Ontario's population), while the Kirk Synod had fallen behind with only 110,000. In that year, the Free Church completed a merger with the United Presbyterian Church in Canada (a New World offshoot of earlier splinters from the Scottish Kirk). These negotiations, in turn, became the vanguard of a more general movement toward Presbyterian union that culminated in the gathering of almost all Canadian Presbyterians into one denomination in 1875.

During its short existence, the Free Church vigorously maintained

Scottish traditions of Sabbath observance, anti-Catholicism, and conservatism in worship and church architecture. But it also took on some habits of North American evangelical Protestantism by vigorously promoting temperance reform and eagerly sponsoring missionary outreach, especially in the opening Canadian west. The most interesting development, however, was the denomination's changing stance on the nature of the church in society. At its beginning, the Free Church was officially establishmentarian — it held, with the Scottish Free Church, that the state should support the church, so long as that support did not undercut ecclesiastical self-rule. Over the course of its existence, however, the voluntary character of the Free Church's experience dissolved the establishment cast of its hereditary thinking. Early on the Free Church disciplined a minister for holding that religion should not seek the help of the state. Within two decades, the denomination's vision had been turned sufficiently from Scotland to Canada — that is, from the remembered ideal to the current reality — to abandon all but the most ephemeral establishment aspirations.

The experience of the Presbyterians was fairly typical for large groups of Canadian Protestants. They were close enough to the Old World to be directly shaped by events in Britain, but they were also sensitive to currents in the States and eager to establish viable traditions of their own in Canada. That combination of influences resulted in churches that in some cases looked more American, in some cases more British, but also, increasingly, more Canadian.

Adjustments after 1867

By the end of the nineteenth century, Ontario Protestants represented a singular blend of North American and British characteristics. They had so successfully employed American techniques of voluntary mobilization that Toronto enjoyed a much more obviously Christian Sunday than did the wide-open cities of the United States. More generally, Ontario's Protestants were evangelical but, because of the Loyalist tradition and the leaven of Anglican influence, not quite as democratically or individualistically evangelical as those in the States. Those same factors also meant that the crises of the late nineteenth century that so profoundly shook America's mainstream evangelical tradition — the immigration of non-Protestants, the growth of industrial giantism, and new ideas about science and the Bible — were received with somewhat greater calm in Canada. Ontario's Protestants could not escape these challenges, and they did not necessarily do better in answering them than did the Americans, but the style of their response tended to be indirect rather than confrontational. The result was an evangelical Protestant tradition that evolved rather than lurched into the twentieth century. The results of that evolutionary development are evident in both theology and social ideals.

Canada's dominant Protestant theology at the end of the nineteenth century was well nourished by the evangelical stream that had begun in eighteenth-century Britain and broadened out in nineteenth-century North America. It was uniquely Canadian in balancing an American openness to innovation, optimism, and personal liberty with a British commitment to order, stability, and tradition. Late nineteenth-century Canadian Protestant theology also owed a great deal to America in its full embrace of Baconian scientific procedure, since the United States was the place where a commitment to empirical induction had the longest and most vigorous life in the Western world. Finally, this Canadian theology also reflected British influence, especially in its endorsement of Christianized versions of evolution and modest views of biblical criticism alongside traditional commitments to evangelical doctrine and piety.

The career of Canada's leading Methodist theologian in the half century before World War I provides an excellent example of how these various strands were woven together. Nathanael Burwash (1839-1910), who was born of Loyalist stock and who experienced a convincing conversion at an early age, served briefly as a Methodist pastor before becoming in 1867 the professor of natural theology at the Methodists' Victoria College. Eventually he was named chancellor of this Methodist institution, and in 1888 he negotiated the incorporation of the college into the University of Toronto. Although he was a lifelong student of John Wesley, Burwash was not a narrow denominationalist. In fact, he became a leader in early negotiations among Methodists, Congregationalists, and Presbyterians that led (after his death) to the creation of the United Church of Canada.

The significance of Burwash in the larger scheme of things was his stance as a "mediating," "moderate," or "progressive" evangelical. The key to his position was that he held to traditional evangelical convictions while adjusting selectively to new intellectual proposals of his day. Thus, Burwash maintained consistently that Christ's atonement was objective and that it really paid the price for sin. He insisted on the reality of original sin and the need for new birth from the Holy Spirit. Throughout his life Burwash consistently preached that the experience of regeneration and the practice of morality were absolutely essential. He resigned as chancellor of Victoria College in 1902, for instance, when he found the rising generation of administrators not as eager to superintend the moral development of female students as he and his wife, Margaret, thought they should be.

Nathanael Burwash, shown here with two infant sons, was the leading Canadian Methodist in the second half of the nineteenth century. By coming to terms with a conservative view of evolution and moderate biblical criticism while maintaining his commitment to the supernatural character of conversion, Burwash exemplified the liberal evangelicalism that was then so common in English Canada. *Archives of The United Church of Canada*

At the same time, Burwash the evangelical was also Burwash the moderate. After the popularization of Darwin's ideas, he adjusted traditional Christian cosmology in an evolutionary direction. When the higher criticism of Scripture became an issue for Canadian Methodists, he publicly defended practitioners of the new views (even as he privately chided one leading proponent of higher criticism for moving too far away from biblical supernaturalism).

Burwash's effort to combine traditional evangelical beliefs with modern intellectual opinions did lead to ironic outcomes. First, he promoted a moral philosophy based on the "facts" of human experience in order to defend traditional evangelicalism, but these "facts" came to be viewed differently by some modern thinkers and were eventually used by others to undercut evangelical convictions. Second, Burwash established the bond between Victoria College and the University of Toronto as a way of securing the church's contribution to modern learning, but over time the university learning he respected came to offer little room for distinctly Christian convictions. Third, Burwash accommodated himself to the new ideas of his own time as a way of preserving traditional Methodist faith, but at least some of his students in the next generation found it easier to promote the new ideas than traditional Methodist beliefs.

These ironies were the price that Burwash and Canada's mediating evangelicals paid to preserve Christianity in the mainstream of Canada's intellectual life. The attempt of the churches to minister to altered social conditions revealed some of the same successes but also some of the same ironies.

As in the United States, Canada's Protestant churches struggled to adjust their ministries to the new conditions created by rapid industrialization, the growth of cities, and the presence of new populations. In Canada, these developments attended the economic boom of the Wilfrid Laurier years (1896-1911), a little bit later than in the States. By that time, growth was also the order of the day for the western provinces, the needs of which became increasingly important for leaders in central Canada.

Canadian Protestants exploited almost as wide a variety of voluntary agencies as were present in the United States to expand the ministry of the churches. Especially important were temperance societies, which carried the hopes of both theological conservatives and theological liberals for the construction of a moral society. A Canadian branch of the Woman's Christian Temperance Union was founded in 1874 under the leadership of Ontario's Letitia Youmans, following by only a few years the organization of the WCTU in the States. In Canada, the WCTU displayed much of the same energy and won much of the same, often grudging respect that the American organization under Frances Willard achieved. Temperance was tied directly to concern for the integrity of homes and the welfare of children, and so it became a cause supported eagerly by promoters of the Social Gospel. It was also high on the agenda of such evangelists as Dwight L. Moody (who visited Toronto in 1885 and Winnipeg in 1897) and such Canadian revivalists as the team of H. T. Crossley and John E. Hunter which during the late nineteenth century visited and revisited most Canadian cities.

Several denominations and large congregations established community centers in cities where traditional churches were giving way before the new industrialism and the spread of urban poverty. Many of these were administered by women. In Winnipeg, a Sunday School class for immigrant children taught by the Methodist Dolly Maguire expanded rapidly to provide a wide variety of assistance to the thousands of new residents streaming into that western city. By 1893, Maguire was overseeing prayer meetings that met several times a week, clinics to care for the sick, an employment bureau, and schooling provided at night. Only a few years later the Walmer Road Baptist church in Toronto sponsored an urban mission of similar scope under the direction of Nellie MacFarland. By the end of 1912 it was ministering to 7,000 people each month. After the turn of the century, several

James S. Woodsworth was a Methodist minister who later passed beyond traditional forms of Christianity in his career as a social reformer. Woodsworth supported the 1919 Winnipeg General Strike and served as a Canadian Member of Parliament for several terms, eventually as parliamentary head of the Co-operative Commonwealth Federation. *Archives of The United Church of Canada*

Protestant bodies created (or re-created) the office of deaconess for women willing to work as urban missionaries. Although arrangements were never entirely satisfactory, since deaconesses occupied an ambiguous position and were rarely paid for the demanding work they attempted, the position did provide a way for women to address the changed needs of the cities. Finally, one of the reasons that the Salvation Army established a more visible presence in Canada than in the United States was its success in mobilizing urban missions in this period. By the start of World War I, the first Pentecostal missions were also opening in Canadian cities.

Changing circumstances at the end of the century stimulated a Social Gospel movement in Canada that was, in its early stages, more closely tied to evangelical Protestant traditions than it was in the United States. A cautious use of modern ideas was not foreign to promoters of the Social Gospel in Canada, but for much of its early history it remained more evangelical than it did in the States. James S. Woodsworth, a Methodist active in Winnipeg, was a shaping force in the practical application of the Social Gospel. Woodsworth later resigned from the ministry when his pacifism was denounced by other Methodists during World War I, and during the Depression he advocated socialism as the remedy to Canada's economic and moral crises. But while he served as superintendent of the Methodist All People's Mission in north

Winnipeg from 1907 to 1913, the mixture of evangelical faith and compassionate social outreach he tried to promote was typical for its day.

Canadian society was profoundly and permanently affected by the great upsurge in immigration that took place after the turn of the century. Proportionate to the United States, Canada had been the destination of relatively small numbers of immigrants before 1900. But thereafter Canadian totals were larger with respect to Canadian population than even the huge number of immigrants coming to the United States in the same period. At a time when Canada's total population had not yet reached 10,000,000, about 3,000,000 immigrants arrived between 1900 and 1914. And whereas most of Canada's earlier immigrants had been from Great Britain, many of these new residents came now from southern or eastern Europe or Asia.

Since most of the immigrants settled in Ontario or the western provinces, these regions quickly become home to a range of new denominations, especially Lutherans and Mennonites, as well as Greek Orthodox and Ukrainian Catholics. The older Canadian churches made some efforts to ease the way for new settlers, but their capacities were hindered by uncertainties about how best to approach immigrant populations. A widespread opinion linked the unity of Canada with the success of the churches. Thus, in one of the works of the popular novelist Ralph Connor a character says that he is working with children in Saskatchewan in order "to make them good Christians and good Canadians, which is the same thing." The Baptist Home Mission Board of Ontario and Quebec issued a pamphlet in 1913 with the same message: the church would "Canadianize the foreigner by Christianizing him." These sentiments did not encourage openness to variant expressions of Christian faith, nor did they reveal much sensitivity to the practical situation of the newcomers. But they did at least encourage the development of settlement houses and community centers such as those managed by Dolly Maguire and Nellie MacFarland.

The tide of immigrants began to swell shortly after the completion of the Canadian-Pacific Railway in 1885. For the country, this event confirmed the possibilities of a genuine nationalism, and for the churches it held out the prospect of expanded missionary efforts. Soon it was obvious, however, that the competition between Protestant denominations that had seemed natural in the Atlantic provinces, Quebec, and Ontario meant less and less on the prairies and in British Columbia. By the time an organized movement to establish a Protestant United Church for all Canada was under way, many small communities in the western provinces had already established union congregations in which older distinctions between Methodists, Presbyterians, Baptists, and sometimes even Anglicans were no longer noticed.

On the whole, efforts by Canadian Protestants to address changing social needs in the decades before World War I were not measurably more successful than similar attempts in the United States. Canadian Protestants had worked wonders in mobilizing British settlers on farms and in small towns. By the end of the century, however, when the social challenges assumed forms alien to both British ancestry and small-town moral economies, they experienced many of the same difficulties that beset the churches in the States. What set the Canadian churches apart in this period, however, was that the response to a changing society was carried out alongside remarkable new efforts to construct a national Protestant consensus.

The Rise and Limits of Protestant Ecclesiastical Nationalism

After Confederation in 1867, Protestants took the lead in seeking to Christianize Canadian civilization, both in existing settlements and in the opening west. The population was small enough and (except for Quebec) Protestant enough to think that a concentrated effort could provide a special Christian bonding for the new nation. As we will see below, during this same period in the United States, fresh waves of immigration and the emergence of African-American denominations were fragmenting the once-dominant Protestant consensus. But in Canada well into the twentieth century there remained more forces working for unification than for disunity. Presbyterians and Methodists had earlier succeeded in consolidating a number of subunits into national denominations in 1875 and 1884, respectively. For their part, Anglicans, who retained the sharpest sense of Old World ties, nonetheless took the lead in exploring cooperation with other Protestants. Baptists never created a national denomination, but they did consolidate into strong regional associations in the Maritime provinces, Ontario and Quebec, and the western provinces.

The movement toward national consensus culminated in a proposal, debated over several decades, to form a united church for all of Canada's Protestants. The idea was brought forward first in the Anglican Church, even though a majority of Anglicans could never be brought around to support the idea. After a number of preliminary discussions, the Methodist General Conference of 1902 formally asked Presbyterians and Congregationalists to move together toward union. Six years later a Basis for Union was completed. It presented a doctrinal platform that skillfully negotiated classical sticking points between Methodist Arminians and Presbyterian Calvinists. But the key matter in the minds of those who prepared the Basis was not so much doctrine as ecclesiastical vision. To them, the goal spelled out in the preamble was the key: "it shall be the policy of the United Church to foster the spirit of unity in the hope that this sentiment of unity may in due time, so far as Canada is concerned, take shape in a Church which may fittingly be described as national." The Congregationalists and Methodists approved the Basis almost immediately. But the intervention of World War I and a prolonged internal debate among the Presbyterians delayed implementation until 1925. Although a substantial number of Presbyterian churches remained out of the Union, approximately 4,800 Methodist congregations, 3,700 Presbyterian congregations, 166 Congregationalist churches, and a number of union churches already existing in the west joined together to make up the United Church.

Aspirations for the new body were extremely high. One Congregationalist, William T. Gunn, hoped to see a day that would bring "other unions still, until we have one great National Church of all that love God, working together to make our Dominion His Dominion from sea to sea and all the kingdoms of this world the kingdoms of our Lord and His Christ." Unfortunately for the architects of the United Church, the timing of its founding was not propitious for the realization of such goals.

In the first instance, World War I undercut utopian visions. More in the pattern of the Old World than the United States, Canadians suffered psychologically from the European devastation in which they had participated for the four full years of the conflict. (Canadian fatalities at 60,000 were only half the Americans' 117,000, but these were from a nation that was still less than one-tenth the size of the United States.) The disillusionment brought by the War also took an institutional form. During the 1914-1918 period, Canadian reformers had at last succeeded in securing prohibition legislation in every province. But even before the War was over, the consensus on this reform began to dissolve. Soon thereafter prohibition was almost completely abandoned as a reforming strategy. The toll, at several levels, was great. Prohibition had united Protestant reformers as the single greatest chance for social reconstruction. Not only was the reform now lost but so too was the coalition that had struggled for its implementation. The historian Robert Wright puts the result in proper focus: "by 1926 all of the provinces except Prince Edward Island had abandoned prohibition. Dead was the most enduring of the social action campaigns in which the churches had been involved and one of the few that had united liberal and conservative evangelicals in common cause."

By the inauguration of the United Church in 1925, there were also considerable signs of theological tension among Protestants. Canadians avoided an all-out fundamentalist-modernist battle such as took place

This photo shows the assembled throng on June 10, 1925, when the United Church of Canada came into existence through the merger of Canada's Methodists, Congregationalists, many of its Presbyterians, and a large number of federated congregations from the Canadian west. *Archives of The United Church of Canada*

among Northern Presbyterians and Baptists in the States, but the once-cohesive evangelical Protestantism was noticeably fraying at both ends. T. T. Shields (1873-1955), pastor of the Jarvis Street Baptist church in Toronto, became active in American fundamentalist circles and also injected a jarring note into Canadian Protestant life. Shields's disillusionment with the Baptists' McMaster University was only one of the issues that caused him to lead an exodus from the Baptist Convention of Ontario and Quebec. From the other end of the spectrum came a criticism of equal intensity, that the churches were proving too conservative in their approach to society. From within the United Church radical critics of capitalism contended that Canadian theology had been captured by nineteenth-century economic conventions. Such criticism propelled leaders including the former Methodist J. S. Woodsworth and the former Baptist T. C. Douglas out of the moderate evangelicalism they once espoused into a search for political solutions to Canada's moral dilemmas.

A more general difficulty affected Canada even as it was also coming to influence the shape of religion in the United States. So successful had Canadian Protestants been in shaping their society that it was almost impossible to discern when, in turn, the expectations of Canadian society began to shape the faith. In the early twentieth century, the problem was particularly acute with the frequent, nonreflective equation of Christian virtues with the values of middle-class culture. When such an unfortunate equation took place, there was little Christian resistance to the instincts of materialist individualism that were becoming increasingly common in all of North America. Canada's Protestants were by no means entirely swept away by the rising tide of affluence and expanding personal choice, but just as these by-products of modern life seriously affected the churches in the States, they also exerted an influence in Canada. They constituted at least one of the reasons why visionary hopes for an expanding, unifying national Protestant church became moribund at almost the same time that the United Church of Canada was born.

The nineteenth-century may properly be regarded as a "Christian century" in Canada. Both in Quebec, where Roman Catholicism provided the dynamism and the institutions for an entire way of life, and in English Canada, where Protestants enjoyed a cultural influence even greater than their counterparts exercised in the United States, the Christian faith provided the foundation for personal and corporate existence. If by the 1920s, the Protestant consensus had begun both to weaken and disintegrate, the achievements of the age were still remarkable. And if, as we shall note below, the twentieth-century history of the Canadian churches offers a sharp secular contrast, it serves only to heighten the sense of what was accomplished as Canadians transformed a wilderness into a significant Christian civilization.

Many of the developments taking place in Canada had their parallels in the United States. But differences were also significant. Compared to Christianity in the States, Christianity in Canada was less fragmented, more culturally conservative, more closely tied to Europe, more respectful of tradition, more ecumenical, and less prone to separate evangelical theology from social outreach. But the greatest difference remains the first difference: Canada was not so much *a* Christian nation as *two* Christian nations, Catholic and Protestant. As we return now to the period of Christian history in the United States when the Catholic Church was growing and the previously dominant Protestant churches were beginning to lose their hold, the contrast offered by Canada's experience should provide not only instructive parallels but also a fresh angle for interpreting the history taking place below the Canadian border.

Further Reading

Desrosiers, Yvon, ed. *Religion et Culture au Québec*. Montreal: Fides, 1986.

Gauvreau, Michael. *The Evangelical Century: College and Creed in English Canada from the Great Revival to the Great Depression*. Montreal: McGill-Queen's University Press, 1991.

Grant, John Webster. *The Church in the Canadian Era*. Rev. ed. Burlington, ON: Welch, 1988.

———. *A Profusion of Spires: Religion in Nineteenth-Century Ontario*. Toronto: University of Toronto Press, 1988.

Handy, Robert T. *A History of the Churches in the United States and Canada*. New York: Oxford University Press, 1976.

———. "Protestant Patterns in Canada and the United States." In *In the Great Tradition*. Edited by J. D. Ban and P. R. Dekar. Valley Forge, PA: Judson Press, 1982.

McNaught, Kenneth. *The Penguin History of Canada*. Rev. ed. New York: Penguin, 1988.

Masters, D. C. *Protestant Church Colleges in Canada*. Toronto: University of Toronto Press, 1966.

Moir, John S. *The Church in the British Era: From the British Conquest to Confederation*. Toronto: McGraw-Hill Ryerson, 1972.

Morton, W. L., ed. *The Shield of Achilles: Aspects of Canada in the Victorian Age*. Toronto: McClelland & Stewart, 1968. Note especially in this volume Goldwin French's essay "The Evangelical Creed in Canada."

Rawlyk, George A. "Politics, Religion, and the Canadian Experience: A Preliminary Probe." In *Religion and American Politics from the Colonial Period to the 1980s*. Edited by Mark A. Noll. New York: Oxford University Press, 1990.

———, ed. *The Canadian Protestant Experience, 1760-1990*. Burlington, ON: Welch, 1991. Note especially in this volume Nancy Christie's essay " 'In These Times of Democratic Rage and Delusion': Popular Religion and the Challenge to the Established Order, 1760-1815"; Michael Gauvreau's "Protestantism Transformed: Personal Piety and the Evangelical Social Vision, 1815-1867"; Phyllis D. Airhart's "Ordering a New Nation and Reordering Protestantism, 1867-1914"; and Robert A. Wright's "The Canadian Protestant Tradition, 1914-1945."

Van Die, Marguerite. *An Evangelical Mind: Nathanael Burwash and the Methodist Tradition in Canada*. Montreal: McGill-Queen's University Press, 1989.

Vaudry, Richard W. *The Free Church in Victorian Canada, 1844-1861*. Waterloo, ON: Wilfrid Laurier University Press, 1989.

Westfall, William. *Two Worlds: The Protestant Culture of Nineteenth-Century Ontario*. Montreal: McGill-Queen's University Press, 1989.

CHAPTER 11

The Last Years of
"Protestant America," 1865-1918

Fanny Crosby

Down in the human heart, Crush'd by the tempter,
Feelings lie buried that grace can restore;
Touched by a loving heart, wakened by kindness,
Chords that were broken will vibrate once more.

CHORUS:
Rescue the perishing,
Care for the dying;
Jesus is merciful,
Jesus will save.

Walter Rauschenbusch

Our Father, we thank thee for the food of our body, and
for the human love which is the food of our hearts. Bless
our family circle, and make this meal a sacrament of love
to all who are gathered at this table. But bless thou too that
great family of humanity of which we are but a little part.
Give to all thy children daily bread, and let our family not
enjoy its comforts in selfish isolation.

*Fanny J. Crosby (1820-1915), though blind, was an incredibly prolific writer
of gospel songs, many of which were collected by Ira D. Sankey in the hymnals
he produced for use by Dwight L. Moody and other revivalists. The verse above
is the third stanza of Crosby's "Rescue the Perishing," from Sankey's* Gospel

286

Hymns, No. 5, *published in 1887. The "grace before meat" that follows is from* Prayers of the Social Awakening, *published in 1910, by Walter Rauschenbusch, America's leading proponent of the Social Gospel.*

🯄🯄   🯄🯄

IT IS APPROPRIATE NOW, AFTER EXAMINING THE CANADIAN EXPERIENCE throughout the nineteenth century, to take up the story in the United States where we left off, at the Civil War. The era of that conflict represents the beginning of a major shift in the public story of Christianity in the United States. Conditions were changing in both society and the churches, and by 1920 the situation was very different. This is not to say that the proprietary Protestants — those groups that saw themselves as the protectors of an American Christian heritage and the builders of a distinctly Protestant society — did not continue to exert a great influence long after the Civil War. But the conditions of American life in which Protestants of British background had flourished were changing rapidly. Non-Protestant and non-English-speaking Christians, as well as non-Christian segments of the population, were growing rapidly in the second half of the nineteenth century. Serious fissures were also emerging among the Protestants themselves. Nevertheless, for a time yet America's public religion continued to be defined by its hereditary Protestants in much the same way that Canadian public life was dominated by French Catholics and British Protestants. The final decades of that dominant "public Protestantism" in the United States is the subject of this chapter.

We will consider the transitions associated with the era of the Civil War, as well as the deep Christian involvement in that conflict, in Part IV of this book. In this chapter, however, we turn to the aspirations of the United States' most visible Protestants, who, especially in the North, thought that the postwar years might provide the opportunity to realize the lofty Christian goals anticipated earlier in the century. Those goals, as it turned out, were ambitious in the extreme: to evangelize the population and the whole world, to reform personal and public life, to redeem the cities, and to effect institutional unification of Protestantism itself.

Evangelists at Home and Abroad

The drive to spread the gospel to those who had not yet embraced it grew even stronger after the war. A revival in 1857-1858, sometimes called "the businessmen's awakening" because of the prominent role urban merchants played in promoting it, had established the form for subsequent urban evangelism in the nation and also raised the expectation for missionary activity overseas. This awakening had featured noontime meetings for prayer in many Northern cities. It had provided spiritual support at a time of increasing political tension and a major financial collapse. It had emphasized themes of inner spiritual peace in the midst of external turmoil. It was at once an unusual occasion of spiritual renewal and an apolitical response to heightened social and political crisis. It promised both personal peace with God and a renewed feeling of community solidarity. The forms and expectations from this earlier lay-led revival played a significant role in both the urban revival crusades and the expanding missionary activity that arose later in the century.

Dwight L. Moody

During the second half of the nineteenth century no evangelist was better known than Dwight Lyman Moody (1837-1899). The achievements of his life fulfilled in many ways the aspirations of a wide spectrum of American believers. After moving from his native New England to Chicago shortly before the Civil War, Moody took an active part in the work of the Young Men's Christian Association, one of the most influential voluntary agencies founded as a result of the antebellum revivals. Moody assisted eagerly with efforts to found Sunday Schools, distribute Christian literature, and bring a general Christian influence to the burgeoning metropolis on Lake Michigan. When in 1873 Moody enlisted a song-leader friend, Ira Sankey (1840-1908), to accompany him on a modestly conceived preaching tour of Great Britain, the results changed their lives. The meetings proved unexpectedly successful, and the Americans remained abroad for two full years. At the same time, in the States there was an increasing appeal by denominational leaders for spiritual renewal and a restoration of Christian sentiment in the entire society. Once again the churches seemed to be flagging. Once again social and political turmoil (this time, the failure of Reconstruction in the South, the perceived threat of Roman Catholic influence, and the uncertainties associated with urban and industrial expansion) imperiled both the sense of local Christian community and the meaning of the United States as a Christian nation. When Moody and Sankey returned to the States, they were everywhere in demand. The results resembled the revivals of 1857-1858, except that this time a single figure (though still a layman) provided a focal point for urban revival.

The YMCA building on Fourth Avenue and Twenty-third Street in Manhattan was typical of the solid structures built by this largely Protestant organization to house and instruct single men in the midst of America's growing cities.
Courtesy of the Billy Graham Center Museum

Moody's manner as a preacher nicely fit the character of his age. He was not as intense as Charles Finney, his famous predecessor, nor did he engage in the theatrical antics of Billy Sunday, his best-known successor. Rather, Moody tried to talk sense to his audiences about God and the need for a Savior. He dressed like a conventional businessman and spoke calmly and plainly. Moody presented a basic Christian message, which he summarized as the "Three R's": Ruin by Sin, Redemption by Christ, and Regeneration by the Holy Ghost. He did not expound learned theology, nor did he promote sophisticated formulas for Christian action in society. Instead, he drew artlessly on powerful themes of Christian sentiment — the same themes that Ira Sankey skillfully evoked with the gospel hymns (like the one quoted at the start of this chapter) that he performed at Moody's meetings. Increasingly Moody's concerns turned away from the reform of society. He saw himself first and foremost as a winner of souls. In his most famous statement about his own work, Moody said, "I look upon this world as a wrecked vessel. God has given me a lifeboat and said to me, 'Moody, save all you can.'"

The many stories Moody used in his sermons illustrated his ability to

289

The duo of Dwight L. Moody (shown here on the left) and song leader Ira Sankey
(on the right) made up the most popular evangelistic team in the last decades of the
nineteenth century. Here they are addressing a rally in Brooklyn.
Courtesy of the Billy Graham Center Musuem

present Protestant conceptions of the gospel in an emotionally powerful
form that spoke especially to American concerns about the loss of traditional
family and community values. He liked to tell the story, for example, of a
father who took a young child into a field on a Sunday afternoon. While
the youngster was gamboling about, the father fell asleep. When he awoke,
he searched with rising panic for the child, only eventually to find that the
child had tumbled over "a precipice" to its death. Moody's moral was characteristic: "I thought as I read that, what a picture of the church of God! How
many fathers and mothers, how many Christian men and women, are sleeping now while their children wander over the terrible precipice right into
the bottomless pit! Father, mother, where is your boy tonight?"

Moody's personal influence was extended through the important institutions he founded. These included a Bible training center for lay workers
in Chicago (later the Moody Bible Institute) and the summer missions
conferences held near his home in Northfield, Massachusetts. From these
meetings came the founding, in 1876, of the Student Volunteer Movement,
a great effort that encouraged thousands of students to seek "the evangelization of the world in this generation."

Missionary Entrepreneurs

Joining Moody as promoters of efforts to take the Christian message around the world were a host of capable and earnest promoters of the missionary enterprise. The Presbyterian A. T. Pierson (1837-1911) organized conferences throughout the 1880s that led to the recruitment of 3,000 young men and women for missionary service. Pierson also was a factor in founding the Africa Inland Mission (1895), one of the largest American faith missions (which asked their recruits to solicit their own support instead of providing it through denominational means). A Boston Baptist, A. J. Gordon (1836-1895), established the Boston Missionary Training Institute in 1889 to prepare laypeople, especially women, for missionary service. In the 1890s A. B. Simpson (1843-1919) set up a missionary network for foreign service and then a North American fellowship to support the missionary endeavor, two bodies that eventually merged to become a new denomination, the Christian and Missionary Alliance. John R. Mott (1865-1955), who had been recruited for missionary service by Pierson, traveled extensively in America and around the world throughout his long life to promote the cause of missions. His widely influential book *The Evangelization of the World in This Generation,* published in 1900, explained what was meant by the Student Volunteer watchword — "giving to all men an adequate opportunity of knowing Jesus Christ as their Saviour and of becoming His real disciples." The book also beseeched Protestants to raise the number of their missionaries from 15,000 to 50,000 as a way of achieving the goal set out in the title.

Perhaps the most visible promoter of missionary service at this time was a Presbyterian layman, Robert Elliott Speer (1867-1947), who was an early administrator of the Student Volunteer Movement and then from 1891 to 1937 the Secretary of the Board of Foreign Missions for the United Presbyterian Church in the U.S.A. Speer was an active promoter of cooperative missionary work and a leader in ecumenical ventures at home. In pursuit of missionary harmony, he was chairman of the Committee on Cooperation in Latin America. Promoting ecumenism at home, he served a term as president of the Federal Council of Churches and, during World War I, as the chairman of the General Wartime Committee of Churches. Speer's exposition of the missionary mandate was the major theme of his nearly seventy books and hundreds of articles. In *Christianity and the Nations* (1910) he admitted that missionaries had often made mistakes in spreading the gospel, but he argued that the task must be carried on whatever the failings of Christians. In one of his last books, *The Finality of Jesus Christ* (1933), he put the case eloquently: Christian missions will be necessary so long as Christ is the only savior of humanity.

291

In an age of rapid missionary expansion, Robert E. Speer served both his own Presbyterian denomination and a wider constituency as a promoter of and apologist for evangelical expansion around the world.
Presbyterian Historical Society, Presbyterian Church USA

Eventually, Speer's effort to promote missionary outreach indiscriminately made him suspect among both theological liberals and theological conservatives. The former did not appreciate his forthright defense of the uniqueness of Christ, and the latter felt he allowed too much latitude for modernism. For his part, Speer tried to steer clear of the theological conflicts that intensified during the first decades of the twentieth century. What was happening, however, was an important sign of things to come. Speer's promotion of missions as the unified effort of an American Protestant phalanx did not survive long in the new century.

American Protestants to the Ends of the Earth

During the last decades of the nineteenth century, however, the rise of Protestant missions from America was very much a part of the expansion of the United States. President William McKinley, who led the nation to war against Spain for control of the Philippines in 1898, felt that he was acting as much from missionary as from national motives. As he told a delegation of Methodists in 1899, he came to a decision to enter the conflict with largely

Missionary interest in the Southern Baptist Convention grew steadily until the Southern Baptists eventually became the largest source of American workers abroad. This photo shows a group of mostly female Southern Baptist missionaries en route to Lagos, Nigeria, circa 1916. *Foreign Mission Board of the Southern Baptist Convention*

religious concerns: "there was nothing left for us to do but to take them all, and to educate the Filipinos, and uplift and civilize and Christianize them, and by God's grace do the very best we could by them, as our fellow-men for whom Christ died." After Senator Albert J. Beveridge of Indiana returned from visiting the Philippines in 1900, he made an even bolder statement: God "marked the American people as His chosen nation to finally lead in the regeneration of the world."

A major factor in the rising missionary interest was the participation of women. When denominational officials expressed ambivalence about giving women full recognition as missionaries, the response was to found mission societies staffed, directed, and funded by women. Abbie Child (d. 1902) led other American women in establishing the World's Missionary Committee of Christian Women, one of the earliest bodies attempting to coordinate the missionary activities of scattered groups in different fields of service. Single women in their own missionary societies and the wives of male missionaries made up 60 percent of the nation's missionary force in the late nineteenth century. By the turn of the century, forty-one women's missionary societies supported over 1,200 missionaries. On the field itself, women often enjoyed opportunities for exercising authority, for public speaking, and for institutional leadership that were not yet available in the States. In many missionary compounds throughout China, for example, women took the lead in providing schooling and medical care for Chinese women and children, they often supervised large staffs of men and women helpers, and they represented both Christianity and Western culture in public gatherings. The disparity between what women did routinely as part of their missionary service and what they were permitted to do in churches at home now appears more significant than it did at that time; nevertheless, the situation pointed to the fact that the Christian message overseas sometimes possessed a flexibility that it lacked in the American home of the missionary volunteers.

At the start of the twentieth century, Americans played central roles in bringing together large groups of missionaries to discuss the state of the world and their common purposes in spreading the Christian faith. In 1900 President McKinley himself addressed the Ecumenical Missionary Conference in New York, which assembled representatives from over 200 missionary agencies. It was the largest such gathering of its kind ever held. Ten years later the World Missionary Conference in Edinburgh, which attracted participants from a wide variety of denominational and theological persuasions, marked the high point of expectant missionary zeal. The conference heard from many Americans, including John R. Mott and Robert Speer. Mott was later appointed chairman of a Continuation Committee that evolved into the International Missionary Conference, which became part of the World Council of Churches in 1961.

To many American Protestants at the end of the nineteenth century and in the early years of the twentieth, it seemed as if the evangelization of the world was within reach. Atlantic civilization was at its peak, and the United States was at the forefront of Christian endeavors in that rising civilization. Clouds of war might be gathering in Europe, economic and political strife might distract the attention of some church members, the relationship of Christianity to modern learning might pose a problem, and a pluralism of religious experience might be advancing rapidly in the country as a whole, and yet it seemed that the rising tide of America also marked the rising tide of Christian expansion, at home and throughout the world.

The ideal of domestic Christianity in the nineteenth century always included a time for family Bible reading and prayers. *Courtesy of the Billy Graham Center Museum*

The Moral Reform of Society

The older Protestant bodies continued also to dominate conceptions of public moral reform at the end of the nineteenth century. The drive to renovate society, which had loomed so large with the antebellum revivalists, continued as a potent force in American life at least through the First World War. Most Protestant reformers maintained that the key to changing society lay in converting individuals, who would then reorder their private lives. The organization of society might now be more complicated — with new industries, new systems of transportation, and new types of immigrants adding to the population — but most public-spirited Protestants still felt that the key to a better life together lay in personal moral reform.

Prohibition

The campaign against drink provides the best example of how such assumptions led to a vast outpouring of energy designed to alter the moral structure of American life. The various temperance and prohibition movements may now appear somewhat quixotic, but they were the direct successors of such antebellum movements as the fight against slavery. Just as Christians had been active to win freedom for the slave, so now after the war they exerted great efforts to free the nation from slavery to alcohol.

Religious reaction to excessive drinking had begun in the early nineteenth century, at a time when Americans really were imbibing a great deal more than in previous generations. Lyman Beecher expressed an influential early aversion to alcohol in a book first published in 1826, *Six Sermons on the Nature, Occasion, Signs, Evils, and Remedy of Intemperance.* As Beecher saw it, drink harmed "the health and physical energies of a nation" as well as the "national conscience or moral principle" and "national industry." Enough concerned New Englanders agreed with Beecher in the 1840s and 1850s to secure passage of various laws in Massachusetts and Maine restricting access to drink. But it was not until after the Civil War that temperance reform became a national cause. Its twin goals were to promote self-discipline by individuals and a Christian communal discipline in society. It was a campaign that carried the ideals of rural and small-town America into the cities, where large populations and the expansion of merchandising had made the trade in drink a major feature of the environment.

Soon after the Civil War, a number of temperance advocates proposed a political party to promote their cause. A convention was held in Chicago in 1869 to decide on further political action. As an indication of how progressive this reform then was, it was the nation's first political convention in which women participated on an equal basis with men. The Prohibitionists, fired with religious ardor, ran a candidate for president in 1872, as they have every four years since. In 1892, at the height of the nation's reforming zeal, the Prohibitionist candidate received over two percent of the presidential vote. Yet even in an America energized by reforming zeal, prohibition was simply too narrow a platform upon which to build a successful political party.

If the Prohibition Party had its difficulties, however, there were triumphs in other areas scored by the denominations and a multitude of voluntary societies. For most of the century before 1919, the Methodist church, with its strong perfectionist theology, spearheaded the drive to outlaw all forms of alcoholic beverages. But most of the other major denominations also sponsored temperance caucuses to promote the cause.

The most dynamic special purpose group was the Women's Christian Temperance Union under the able leadership of Frances Willard (1839-1898). Willard was a Methodist who, after serving as a teacher in Evanston, Illinois, became increasingly active in local and national activities of the WCTU. In the course of a very active public career, she promoted innovative strategies for preserving the values of Victorian America. She urged the

Frances Willard was not only a leader
of the temperance movement but also
a pioneer in carving out a role for
women in American public life.
*Courtesy of the Billy Graham
Center Museum*

Prohibition Party to broaden its concern to take on the general protection of the family, and she succeeded in having the name of the party changed to the Prohibition Home Protection Party (but only for a brief period). She was a colleague of Dwight L. Moody, for whom she helped to organize women's ministries in conjunction with his urban revivals. She also broadened her activities to Europe, where she helped to establish a formidable British counterpart to the WCTU. As she grew older, Willard also grew more interested in the efforts of Christian socialists to repair the defects of industrial society. She was a persistent advocate of women's right to preach, although her denomination, the Methodist Episcopal Church, which did not ordain women, looked coolly on the proposal. More than any leader of her age, she succeeded in mobilizing women for the causes of domestic purification and personal order that the temperance crusade represented. Her public career, as summarized by a recent biography, was determined by principles from her youth, "New England's discipline and intellectual rigor, Methodism's concentration on behavior and spirit."

Willard and the WCTU were joined by several other more directly political organizations toward the end of the century. The American Anti-Saloon League was organized in 1895 by a largely evangelical Protestant constituency. Its leaders called the organization "the Church in Action against the Saloon" and hoped to achieve legislative victories against the liquor traffic by using Protestant congregations as a base for operations.

Temperance reform was one of the first public activities in which women took a
leading role. This print shows an early "pray-in," one of the kinds of direct
action that women took against the retail liquor trade.
Courtesy of the Billy Graham Center Museum

Interest groups like the WCTU and the Anti-Saloon League drew on old
Protestant interests, but they also received considerable assistance from
some members of the Roman Catholic hierarchy. These "dry" Catholics
wished both to prove themselves good Americans and to disabuse their
fellow citizens of the notion that Catholics were anti-American and loose-
living. The drive for prohibition was also successful at crossing theological
lines. Conservatives, who insisted on traditional interpretations of the Christian faith, joined those who were more theologically liberal. Together they
agreed that cooperation for moral reform took precedence over theological
disputes.

As in Canada, the events of World War I heightened fears of social
disorder in America and paved the way for the prohibition amendment to
the Constitution. Growing fears about the evil effects of drink on the un-
savory elements in American society combined with a propensity to link
the crimes of the Kaiser's Germany with the evils of drink. The Eighteenth
Amendment to the Constitution of 1919 was the result. The war had shown
how fragile civilization was and seemed to spotlight the need for more

strenuous measures toward social discipline. In this belief Americans were joined by many from Europe, who also successfully promoted temperance measures of some sort in their countries.

When the Eighteenth Amendment and its prohibition of "the manu-facture, sale, or transportation of intoxicating liquors" took effect in the United States on January 17, 1920, some Christians heralded the dawning of a new era. In Norfolk, Virginia, the revivalist Billy Sunday staged a funeral service for "John Barleycorn." His speech summed up the aspirations that had led to so much Christian political action against the trade in alcohol. "Good-by, John," the revivalist said, "the reign of tears is over. . . . The slums will soon be only a memory. We will turn our prisons into factories and our jails into storehouses and corncribs. Men will walk upright now, women will smile, and the children will laugh. Hell will be forever rent."

Prohibition did bring improvements in the nation's health and welfare, but nothing like the utopia its promoters had foreseen. If the results of national Prohibition did not achieve its lofty goals, however, the movement still illustrated the power of the nation's public Protestants — generally evangelical, almost all white, largely of British background — in translating their moral vision into the law of the land.

The Culmination of Protestant Politics

Christian efforts in politics were not as sharply focused as efforts at moral reform. But the period between the Civil War and World War I saw also in politics a high tide of Protestant influence. Where the nation's earliest politi-cal leaders had, like Jefferson, turned aside from traditional Christianity, or, like Lincoln, practiced a traditional faith in unconventional ways, many of the nation's political leaders of this period saw their public service as a generally Christian enterprise. So it was with the Methodist Rutherford B. Hayes and the Disciples of Christ lay minister James Garfield. (The wives of these Republican presidents lent the temperance crusade their support by refusing to serve alcohol at White House functions.) So it also was with William McKinley, who saw victory in the Philippines as an opportunity for spreading Christian civilization, and to some extent with McKinley's succes-sor, Theodore Roosevelt, whose robust vision of life made room for a mascu-line embrace of the Christian faith.

In general, Protestants in the nation's Progressive Era had few difficul-ties in translating their beliefs in the saving power of Christ and the authority of the Bible into an intuitive but nonetheless powerful political attitude. Most saw reform at home as the natural complement to missionary activity

299

overseas. Protestants might differ with each other on the best way of promoting national reform — traditional leaders continued to stress the altera-
tion of individuals and modernist leaders beginning to think about the
renovation of social structures — but on practical questions, white Protestants from the leading English-language churches took similar positions.
They almost universally supported the temperance crusade, they almost
universally thought of the public schools as means of Christian civilization,
and they almost universally suspected Roman Catholics of undermining
Christian as well as American values. In this last era of a dominant public
Protestantism, the two political leaders who most fully embodied a tradi-
tional public Protestantism (while avoiding some of its worst excesses) were
William Jennings Bryan and Woodrow Wilson, the nation's two leading
Democrats at the end of the nineteenth century and start of the twentieth.

William Jennings Bryan

William Jennings Bryan (1860-1925), a Democratic populist from Nebraska,
carried the standard of his party as its presidential candidate in 1896, 1900,
and 1908. From 1913 to 1915 he served as Secretary of State during Woodrow Wilson's first term in office. Bryan, an active Presbyterian who had
experienced an evangelical conversion as a young man, saw politics as a
forum for promoting principles of a morality both Christian and American.
Bryan took a special interest in the welfare of farmers and workers who were
suffering from the grasp of manipulating financiers and overweening in-
dustrialists. His great speech against the gold standard at the Democratic
convention in 1896 ("You shall not press down upon the brow of labor this
crown of thorns, you shall not crucify mankind upon a cross of gold")
exemplified both his economic policies and the Christian overtones of his
thought. Bryan's reformist campaigns on behalf of ordinary American citizens never entirely succeeded, but he was a valiant political warrior who
left his mark on a whole generation of American politics.

The reasons for Bryan's failures lay partly in the political climate of
the time. Republican policies really did work fairly and beneficially for many
urbanites and the citizens of small northern towns. Bryan's failure also was
partly the result of his own style. He was a crusader who earned his living
between presidential campaigns as an itinerant speaker, and a motivator
whose most famous address was an oft-repeated oration on the example of
"The Prince of Peace." He was not, in other words, the world's best mender
of political fences. Even if he had been, he may still have been defeated, for
he represented the interests of small-town, rural America at a time when

300

William Jennings Bryan, "Boy Orator of the Platte," was a tireless campaigner for his vision of a Christian America oriented to the needs of ordinary people. *Courtesy of the Billy Graham Center Museum*

the nation's politics was moving in the direction of its cities and major manufacturing centers.

Bryan's goals were indubitably worthy. He was a pioneer in promoting better treatment of workers, fairness (as well as the vote) for women, and respect for the values of common citizens. While other Americans hastened toward war, he held out for peaceful means of resolving international conflict. Evidencing a commitment to principle that has been rare in American political history, in 1915 Bryan resigned as Secretary of State when he concluded that President Wilson was needlessly pushing the country toward war with Germany.

After he left Washington, Bryan turned his energies increasingly to the campaign against the teaching of evolution in the nation's schools. In his mind, this effort was simply an extension of earlier efforts to preserve the rights of common citizens against the imperialism of the elite and the values of traditional America against the encroaching naturalism of an alien moral system. He always believed that the social implications of Darwinism constituted a threat that vastly overshadowed any specific difficulties relating to the interpretation of Scripture. Unlike Woodrow Wilson, Bryan never lapsed into disillusionment when his projects were defeated. Yet like Wilson he illustrated the power of public Protestantism as its ideals and its revivalistic style were put to use in the political sphere.

Woodrow Wilson

Woodrow Wilson (1856-1924), the professional academic who went from the presidency of Princeton University to the governorship of New Jersey to the White House in the brief period from 1910 to 1913, was a reforming Democrat who won the nation's highest office in large part because of his record for cleaning up corruption in New Jersey. As president from 1913 to 1921, however, Wilson made his mark most indelibly in foreign policy. First, he tried to preserve American neutrality in the early days of the First World War. When the United States entered that conflict in 1917, he then defined the nation's effort in noble terms as "making the world safe for democracy." After the war, the crowning moment of his career also became his greatest tragedy. At the Treaty of Versailles he tried to establish a new standard for international justice through his Fourteen Points, which included a visionary plan for a League of Nations to solve international disputes peacefully. The tragedy came when he tried to implement the ideal.

Wilson's politics incorporated the general confidence in American democratic ideals that prevailed in the progressive era. Yet they also incorporated his lifelong Christian commitment. He was raised in the home of a Southern Presbyterian minister, experienced a conversion in 1873, read the Bible and prayed faithfully throughout his life, and believed that the American experience witnessed the fullest manifestation of public Christian values in human history. As a statesman, Wilson attempted to flesh out programs of national security and international peace that drew their inspiration from general Christian conceptions of justice and fair play.

Wilson's ideals for both national and international affairs were based on the assumption that general principles of Christian morality could be translated into national policy and that they could also serve as the direct model for international agreement. With this attitude toward political life, Wilson experienced considerably more success in domestic affairs than in international dealings, where his ideals fell foul of the intransigent realities of Europe's conflicting interests. When Wilson traveled to the peace convention in 1919, great crowds in England and France hailed him as the savior of Western democracy. But the leaders of the other European states spoke of him in private as a naive amateur who could not cope with the realities of historic antagonisms and the practicalities of postwar needs.

Wilson's efforts as a crusader for public morality failed most spectacu-

Woodrow Wilson, shown here emerging from the Scottish Presbyterian Church in Paris, brought the same high Christian idealism to his work at the Paris Peace Conference after World War II that had sustained his life as an academic and then in politics. *California Museum of Photography, Keystone-Mast Collection, Univcersity of California, Riverside*

larly when the Senate refused to approve the United States' entry into the League of Nations. When Republican leaders in the Senate balked at approving the treaty, Wilson (political evangelist that he was) took to the stump in response. The exhausting whistle-stop campaign that ensued carried Wilson throughout the country as he gave impassioned addresses in rented halls and from the back of his railway car. In the middle of the trip, Wilson collapsed. Unswayed, the Senate still rejected the Treaty. Wilson had tried to do the political equivalent of what the abolitionist Theodore Dwight Weld and the temperance reformer Frances Willard had also attempted in their efforts to remake the character of America according to a largely religious vision.

No less than these other reformers, Wilson, like William Jennings Bryan, hoped that the country could live up to its highest Christian ideals. If they were trying to solve problems in a twentieth-century pluralistic America with a frame of reference shaped by antebellum Christian values, they were nonetheless public servants of unusual integrity. After Bryan and Wilson, there have been other Christians who made their mark in politics,

303

but none since that time have embodied so thoroughly the aspirations of American Protestantism or fought so ardently for the vision of a Protestant America.

The Cities and the Social Gospel

During this last era of Protestant dominance in America, the reforming impulse extended to the nation's rapidly expanding cities. In an era of rapid business expansion, the cities had become scenes of great wealth but also great squalor. In the period between 1860 and 1920 the nation's population more than tripled, but the number of its businesses increased eightfold, and its net national product became thirty times larger. The cities showed the greatest effects of these changes. They were places of employment for immigrants from Europe as well as vast numbers of people leaving farms and rural villages. They were places to make a fortune. They were also places where social services often broke down, where incredible deprivation lurked just beyond the boundaries of prosperity, and where rootlessness and alienation were becoming ways of life. American Protestants also turned to the cities with an eye toward reform.

The most prevalent Protestant attempts to reform urban life were based on principles of private action and personal responsibility. Many older churches developed programs of social outreach and support to supplement more traditional services. The Salvation Army, which arrived in the States from Britain in 1880, was a pioneer in providing social services from religious motivation. Founded in the 1860s, when William Booth came into firsthand contact with the slums of East London, the Army balanced evangelistic and social outreach in its English work as well as in its work overseas. William's daughter Evangeline (1865-1950) eventually came to head up the work of the Army in the United States, where she promoted the same range of activities that her father had advanced in England — provision of food, shelter, and medical assistance; vocational training, elementary schooling, and internships in manufacturing and farming; and visits to prisons, legal aid for the indigent, and inexpensive coal in the winter. By 1904 the Army had over nine hundred stations, or corps, in the States. It was (and remains) the most comprehensive Christian outreach to the cities.

Better known, however, was the informal, loosely organized Social Gospel movement, which was a force from roughly 1880 to the start of the Great Depression in 1929. Its leaders also attempted a Christian response to the rapid social changes of the period, but one in which an analysis of corporate entities supplemented the appeal to individuals.

304

The Salvation Army's places of worship were often in urban areas, since the Army made a special effort to reach city dwellers whom other churches passed by.
Courtesy of the Billy Graham Center Musuem

The origins of the Social Gospel were both domestic and foreign. The strong link in the American revival tradition between personal holiness and social reform contributed to the genesis of the movement, as did a newer concern for the scientific study of social problems that accompanied the rise of the modern American university after the Civil War. In addition, the example of such Britons as Thomas Chalmers in Scotland and the Christian socialist F. D. Maurice in England, who attempted innovative Christian responses to the problems of industrial society, also influenced Americans desiring a Christian social reform.

Early expressions of the Social Gospel included the work of Washington Gladden (1836-1918), a Congregationalist minister in Springfield, Massachusetts, and Columbus, Ohio. While in Massachusetts he published *Working People and Their Employers* (1876), an appeal for fairness toward labor. Gladden's Ohio congregation included mine owners whose workers struck twice in the mid-1880s for better wages and working conditions. His belief in the justice of their demands led Gladden to appeal more insistently for the rights of labor and the application of the Golden Rule to industrial organization. A different expression of the Social Gospel appeared in the

Washington Gladden, shown here in the study of his Ohio church, was the best-known spokesman for the Social Gospel before Walter Rauschenbusch. *Ohio Historical Society*

work of a clergyman from Topeka, Kansas, Charles Sheldon, whose best-selling novel *In His Steps* (1897) presented a picture of what could happen in a community torn by social dissension if Christians would only ask themselves at every moment, "What would Jesus do?"

The most important exponent of the Social Gospel was Walter Rauschenbusch (1861-1918), a German-American Baptist who ministered for ten years in New York City's "Hell's Kitchen" before becoming a professor of church history at Rochester Seminary in upstate New York. Rauschenbusch's firsthand experiences with industrial exploitation and governmental indifference to workers made him a convinced critic of the established order. His fruitful relationships with such New York City socialists as Henry George offered alternative models for social organization. But Rauschenbusch's main concern was to search the Scriptures for a message to the troubled circumstances of industrial society. The results were published in 1907 as *Christianity and the Social Crisis,* a work that recalled the prophetic denunciations of Old Testament prophets as well as New Testament injunctions about the dangers of Mammon. Rauschenbusch followed this work with other influential volumes, including *Prayers of the Social Awakening* (1910), *Christianizing the Social Order* (1912), and *A Theology for the Social Gospel* (1917). In these works Rauschenbusch combined a prophetic ideal of justice with a commitment to building the kingdom of God through the power of Christ.

The Social Gospel is often associated with more liberal trends in theology. Gladden, for example, was a popularizer of biblical higher criticism, and Rauschenbusch, though more realistic about the intractably fallen character of human nature, nevertheless reinterpreted some traditionally supernatural elements of Christian doctrine. At the same time, however, themes of social service associated with the Social Gospel were also prominent among such more evangelical bodies as the Salvation Army. With the Army, and many local efforts scattered from coast to coast, leaders of the Social Gospel were trying to solve an American dilemma — how to adapt the Protestant tradition of an earlier rural America to the changing demands of a newly industrial society.

The Ecumenical Movement and World War I

As Protestants attempted the reform of their own society, they also seemed poised to make a notable advance in the reconciliation of intramural Christian differences. Interest in cooperation among Christian (especially Protestant) groups had been rising throughout the nineteenth century. Americans formed a branch of the British-inspired Evangelical Alliance in 1867. With much fanfare, the sixth general conference of the Alliance took place in New York, October 2-12, 1873. Before the visitors from overseas and Canada returned to their homes, they were greeted in Washington by leaders of Congress and President Grant. By the end of the century, Americans were playing significant parts in several other notable ecumenical bodies, including the Young Men's and Young Women's Christian Associations, Christian Endeavor, the World Student Christian Federation, a number of missionary agencies, and the worldwide fellowships of the Methodists, Baptists, and Reformed. In addition, inter-Protestant cooperation in the vast panoply of American voluntary societies was a well-established feature of American religious experience. Peter Ainslie, an ecumenical leader from the Disciples of Christ who edited the *Christian Union Quarterly* for many years, proclaimed a goal that many others shared: "henceforth let no man glory in his denomination; that is sectarianism: but let all men glory in Christ and practice brotherhood with men; that is Christianity."

Two events in the first decade of the twentieth century gave further impetus to ecumenical efforts. The first was the formation of the Federal Council of Churches of Christ, established in 1908 by thirty-three Protestant denominations representing 18,000,000 members. The Council's founding documents touched briefly on its theological basis — "to manifest the essential oneness of the Christian churches of America in Jesus Christ as their divine Lord and Savior" — and then expounded more thoroughly on its

John R. Mott, a whirlwind of activity on behalf of foreign missionary work, is shown here presiding over the famous World Missionary Conference held in Edinburgh in 1910. *Yale Divinity School Library, John R. Mott Papers, Record Group 45*

practical purposes — "to secure a larger combined influence for the churches of Christ in all matters affecting the moral and social condition of the people, so as to promote the application of the law of Christ in every relation of human life." The second was the worldwide Edinburgh Missionary Conference of 1910, which, as we have seen, proved to be even more significant by showing Americans how their own efforts at cooperation could fit into the worldwide effort.

World War I also promoted ecumenical cooperation. Although church leaders were divided over whether the United States should enter that conflict, when Congress did declare war in April 1917, virtually all major church bodies — Catholic as well as Protestant — pitched in with enthusiastic support. Only the peace churches, Quakers and Mennonites especially, who were joined by members of a new sectarian denomination, the Jehovah's Witnesses, protested the recourse to arms. But the consensus was overwhelmingly in the other direction. Support for the conflict came from all positions along the political spectrum. The revivalist Billy Sunday, for example, claimed that "Christianity and Patriotism are synonymous terms" and also that "hell and traitors are synonymous." No less direct was a doyen of American religious liberalism,

Shailer Mathews of the University of Chicago Divinity School: "for an American to refuse to share in the present war . . . is not Christian." Exigencies of war led to fresh Protestant cooperation in such agencies as the YMCA, which sent many ministers and young seminarians to Europe to staff canteens and other centers for assisting the soldiers. The war also led Roman Catholics to organize a National Catholic War Council, which later evolved into the National Catholic Welfare Conference, one of the first major cooperative ventures of Catholics on a national scale.

After the war, ambitious Christian leaders, encouraged by religious cooperation during the conflict and backed by seed money from the Rockefellers, established the Interchurch World Movement of North America. Its grand scheme to raise nearly $400 million for the relief of war-torn Europe and to advance social renewal in the States fell far short of reaching its goal. But it did draw further attention to spheres of activity where churches could cooperate rather than compete.

The failure of the Interchurch World Movement did point to deeper trends in American church life. The buoyant spirit that drove reforming efforts in social and political life was passing from the scene. Problems both in the churches and in the churches' relation to society that once seemed manageable began to look more difficult. If the Interchurch World Movement marked a high point of Protestant aspiration to lead and shape American culture, its failure suggested that the day for public Protestantism of this sort was almost past. Why that was so requires us to step back to observe a different range of circumstances that had in fact been undercutting the cohesion and strength of the nation's traditional Protestants since at least the time of the Civil War.

Further Reading

Bordin, Ruth. *Frances Willard: A Biography.* Chapel Hill, NC: University of North Carolina Press, 1986.

Carpenter, Joel A., and Wilbert R. Shenk, eds. *Earthen Vessels: American Evangelicals and Foreign Missions, 1880-1980.* Grand Rapids: William B. Eerdmans, 1990.

Coletta, Paolo E. *William Jennings Bryan.* 3 vols. Lincoln: University of Nebraska Press, 1964-69.

Findlay, James F. *Dwight L. Moody: American Evangelist, 1837-1899.* Chicago: University of Chicago Press, 1969.

Handy, Robert T. *Undermined Establishment: Church-State Relations in America, 1880-1920.* Princeton: Princeton University Press, 1991.

Hunter, Jane. *The Gospel of Gentility: American Women Missionaries in Turn-of-the-Century China.* New Haven: Yale University Press, 1984.

Magnuson, Norris. *Salvation in the Slums: Evangelical Social Work, 1865-1920.* Rev. ed. Grand Rapids: Baker Book House, 1990.

Mulder, John M. *Woodrow Wilson: The Years of Preparation.* Princeton: Princeton University Press, 1978.

Orr, James Edwin. *The Event of the Century: The 1857-1858 Awakening.* Wheaton, IL: International Awakening Press, 1989.

Piper, John F., Jr. *American Churches in World War I.* Athens, OH: Ohio University Press, 1985.

Sizer, Sandra S. *Gospel Hymns and Social Religion: The Rhetoric of Nineteenth-Century Revivalism.* Philadelphia: Temple University Press, 1978.

White, Ronald C., Jr., and C. Howard Hopkins. *The Social Gospel: Religion and Reform in Changing America.* Philadelphia: Temple University Press, 1976.

PART IV

THE EMERGENCE OF
RELIGIOUS PLURALISM

Bᴇᴛᴡᴇᴇɴ ᴛʜᴇ ᴄɪᴠɪʟ ᴡᴀʀ ᴀɴᴅ ᴡᴏʀʟᴅ ᴡᴀʀ ɪ, ᴀɴ ɪᴍᴘᴏʀᴛᴀɴᴛ ᴛʀᴀɴsɪᴛɪᴏɴ occurred in the history of Christianity in America. To be sure, as we have seen, these decades witnessed the high point of American Protestant civilization. Yet at the same time they also witnessed another set of circumstances that undercut the Protestant hegemony that had prevailed from shortly after the Revolution.

In the first instance, an increasingly broad spectrum of Christian expressions either expanded or took root in postbellum America. For example, not only did immigration and natural increase make Roman Catholics the largest Christian communion in America, but the Catholic Church also began cautiously to break from its ghettos in order to participate in the nation's public life. In addition, Protestants of non-British background, especially the Lutherans, established an unmistakable presence in the nation. Black Christians, now liberated from hereditary slavery, organized for themselves. Representatives of various Eastern Orthodox churches made their first appearance. And beyond the Christian orbit, other religious groups, at first Jews but then others as well, began to claim a place in the sun. A majority of Americans still identified themselves as Protestants, and most of these Protestants had some connection to the nation's traditional denominations, but the age of Protestant hegemony was nearly over. The changes that led to this broadened spectrum are discussed in Chapter 13.

But a number of other factors related more directly to the participation of Protestants in the Civil War also undermined the certainties of "evangelical America." These factors — including the way in which the War affected the place of blacks, opened up settlement in the West, promoted contrasting varieties of civil religion, influenced approaches to Scripture, and changed the stakes for education — are taken up in Chapter 12.

311

As a result of changes within the churches and changes affecting the churches' relationship to society, Protestant influence began to decline. As a result of social, political, economic, and intellectual as well as religious circumstances, Protestant control over the nation's organs of communication, its centers of higher learning, and its public morality gradually receded as the nineteenth century gave way to the twentieth. These circumstances did not lead to inactivity among Protestants or other Christians but rather stimulated all sorts to action — theological as well as social, ecclesiastical as well as political. Efforts were made to advance Christian civilization as well as to save it. An inescapable reality had, however, become clear by the mid-1920s: the nation's religious instincts were no longer uniformly Protestant but were instead jumbled and competitive — Protestant versus Protestant, Protestant versus Catholic, and Christian versus non-Christian. That story is the particular subject of Chapter 14 and the general theme of this entire section. As a transition to a fuller examination of the pluralism that developed, we will also take a brief look in Chapter 15 at several legacies from nineteenth-century "Christian America" — involving political activity, literature, and the use of the Bible — that have survived into the twentieth century.

CHAPTER 12

The Civil War

Julia Ward Howe (1862)

In the beauty of the lilies Christ was born across the sea,
With a glory in his bosom that transfigures you and me;
As he died to make men holy, let us die to make men free!
While God is marching on.
Glory! Glory! Hallelujah!
Glory! Glory! Hallelujah!
Glory! Glory! Hallelujah!
While God is marching on.

Henry Timrod (1861)

And what if, mad with wrongs themselves have wrought,
    In their own treachery caught,
    By their own fears made bold,
    And leagued with him of old,
Who long since in the limits of the North
Set up his evil throne, and warred with God —
What if, both mad and blinded in their rage,
Our foes should fling us down their mortal gage,
And with a hostile step profane our sod!
We shall not shrink, my brothers, but go forth
To meet them, marshalled by the Lord of Hosts . . .

*Hymn writers during the Civil War composed contrasting visions of God's
involvement in the conflict. The first stanza above is from the well-known hymn*

313

"The Battle Hymn of the Republic" by Julia Ward Howe (1819-1910), a Unitarian abolitionist from Boston. The second is from the all but forgotten "Ethnogenesis," which Henry Timrod (1826-1867) of South Carolina wrote during the first meeting of the Confederate Congress. Hymns from both North and South shared the conviction that God was on only one side in the conflict.

CHRISTIANITY WAS EVERYWHERE PRESENT IN THE CRISIS LEADING TO THE American Civil War and in the War itself. As during the American Revolution, faith as such was not a cause of the conflict, but it did provide a network of influences which intensified the political, social, and cultural differences that brought on the strife. As intense as the religious commitment to the War was, so wide-reaching were the religious effects it precipitated.

The Civil War as a Religious War

In the long view of history, the Civil War can be seen as the last chapter in the Christian story of the Second Great Awakening. In the North, one of the reforms inspired by the revival was abolition, the drive to abolish slavery. Not all abolitionists were revivalist Protestants by any means, but many of them were. One of the most effective antislavery agents, for example, was Theodore Dwight Weld (1803-1895), a convert under revivalist Charles G. Finney who worked throughout the 1830s and 1840s with equal fervor to convert sinners and end slavery. Harriet Beecher Stowe (1811-1896) was the daughter of revivalist and social reformer Lyman Beecher and the wife of a Congregationalist minister. Her immensely influential novel *Uncle Tom's Cabin* (1852) exerted its great impact at least in part because the book was such a forceful summation of Christian revivalism, Christian domesticity, and Christian abolition. In a similar manner, the 1858 hymn "Stand Up, Stand Up, for Jesus," written by a Presbyterian minister from Philadelphia, George Duffield, nicely combined appeals to eternal religious truths and the temporal challenge (to eradicate slavery).

Even where the antislavery impulse was not the direct result of revivalism, it bore a distinctly religious cast. William Lloyd Garrison (1805-1879), raised in New England under Quaker influence, proclaimed abolition evangelistically in the pages of his influential newspaper, *The Liberator,*

Harriet Beecher Stowe *(above left)*, the daughter of revivalist and social reformer Lyman Beecher, produced one of the most influential documents of the abolition movement, *Uncle Tom's Cabin.* William Lloyd Garrison *(above right)*, who founded the abolitionist newspaper *The Liberator* in 1831, eventually came to doubt the final authority of the Bible, since others of his day were so effective in using Scripture to defend the institution of slavery.
Both photos courtesy of the Billy Graham Center Museum

and in many other ways. The revivalistic tone of Garrison's work is suggested by words he wrote before founding *The Liberator* in an attack on the liquor traffic: "while there remains a tyrant to sway the iron rod of power, or chain about the body or mind to be broken, I cannot surrender my arms. . . . While a soul remains unenlightened, uneducated, and without 'the glorious gospel of the blessed God,' my duty is plain — I will contribute my little influence to the diffusion of universal knowledge." By mid-century, in other words, a growing number of Northerners had come to link the future of the faith as well as the future of the country with an end to slavery.

In the South, where the revival tradition had eventually been merged with social conservatism, it was a very different story. Stung by abolitionist attacks from the North, revivalistic Protestants, who earlier had equivocated on slavery, came to defend the institution. They saw in slavery a means of converting blacks (who would otherwise have languished in heathendom) and preserving the virtues of Christian order. Growing numbers of Protestants in the South believed that Northern attacks on slavery threatened not just a general way of life but specifically religious underpinnings for faith as well.

Denominations that had linked Christians throughout the nation were the first to fall prey to the spiraling cultural antagonism. In 1837 the main body of American Presbyterians divided for reasons that were largely theological and ecclesiastical, but a secondary source of contention did involve sectional politics. The more conservative "Old School" party held that slavery was a secular topic that the church should not address directly. The more revivalistic "New School" group took the opposite view and wanted to see the church act more aggressively to put an end to slavery and other social problems. Not surprisingly, the "New School" was strongest in the North, and the "Old School" derived much of its strength from the South. Sectional conflict was not the major issue at stake for the Presbyterians in 1837, but it soon would become key for even larger Protestant bodies.

In the mid-1840s, the Baptists and the Methodists, which by that time had become the nation's largest Protestant denominations, both divided over slavery. The issue among Methodists concerned the propriety of bishops holding bondsmen. Among the Baptists the specific question was the appointment of slaveholders as missionaries. In both cases, negotiations gave way to recriminations, standoff gave way to schism. For Baptists in the South, the contention over slaveholding missionaries led in 1845 to the formal organization of the Southern Baptist Convention, the denomination that a century later would become the largest of all Protestant bodies in the country. At the time, however, the major consequence of intradenominational strife over slavery was that cultural ties between North and South were weakened, a development that was recognized almost immediately.

In 1844, before the Methodists divided North and South, they were, after the federal government, the nation's largest organization of any kind. In that year, the Methodist Thomas Crowder, himself a Southerner, made predictions that proved chillingly accurate. He contended that if Bishop James Andrew was stripped of his episcopal authority because he held slaves, "the division of our Church may follow — a civil division of this great confederation may follow that, and then hearts will be torn apart, master and slave arrayed against each other, brother in the Church against brother, and the North against the South — and when thus arrayed with the fiercest passions and energies of our nature brought into action against each other, civil war and far-reaching desolation must be the final results."

In 1850, the Southern statesman John C. Calhoun made a similar analysis in his last speech to the United States Senate:

> The cords that bind the States together are not only many, but various in character. Some are spiritual or ecclesiastical; some political; others social. . . . The strongest of these of a spiritual and ecclesiastical nature,

consisted in the unity of the great religious denominations, all of which originally embraced the whole Union. . . . Beginning with smaller meetings, corresponding with the political divisions of the country, their organizations terminated in one great central assemblage, corresponding very much with the character of Congress. . . . All this combined contributed greatly to strengthen the bonds of Union. . . . But, powerful as [these ties] were, they have not been able to resist the explosive effect of slavery agitation.

The result, in sum, was a break at the Mason-Dixon Line between not just large and influential religious bodies but also between significant forces for political cohesion. In the words of historian C. C. Goen, the "broken churches" led to a "broken nation."

A deep longing for the millennium also played its part in heightening the stakes of sectional conflict. Visions of the End of the Age, when Christ would rule the world in a thousand-year kingdom of righteousness and peace, drove revivalists and social reformers to unpredecented personal sacrifices in pursuit of souls and social righteousness. It also lent a sacred aura to the fabric of national civilization that Northerners felt the South was threatening and Southerners felt the North imperiled. The increasing strife between North and South inspired not only loyalty to section but also apocalyptic conceptions of the nation, as in a work published in 1854 under the title *Armageddon; or, The . . . Existence of the United States Foretold in the Bible, Its . . . Expansion into the Millennial Republic, and Its Dominion over the Whole World*.

What was by now the standard American identification of the United States as "God's New Israel" served only to heighten religious conceptions of the conflict. After Abraham Lincoln's assassination at the very end of the War, a great outpouring of sermons mourned his passing. Many of these rehearsed the notion of God's special plan for America. Ministers, for example, affirmed that the meaning of Psalm 147:20 ("He hath not dealt so with any nation") still was "as true of us as of ancient Israel." They expressed their belief that "the Hebrew Commonwealth, 'in which all the families of the earth were to be blest,' was not more of the whole world's concern than is this Republic." Even Isaac Wise, a rabbi, used this language of the Old Testament in calling the American "Israel" to repent of its sins and obey God's law.

Christians elsewhere, including those just over the border in Canada, worried about the results that might come from these notions. But in the States they remained largely unquestioned as the country moved to, through, and beyond the War.

Christian Activity during the Conflict

The War itself was the occasion for a great deal of Christian activity. In the public sphere, Christianity rapidly became a prop for the efforts of both sides. During the conflict, Jefferson Davis called for nine national days of fasting in the Confederacy, and Abraham Lincoln proclaimed four days of thanksgiving for the Union. Special services of worship and prayer were common in all regions, North and South. After one of these, a sermon in November 1864 by the Presbyterian Benjamin Palmer in Columbia, South Carolina, the diarist Mary Boykin Chestnut recorded her response: "What a sermon! The preacher stirred my blood. My very flesh crept and tingled. A red-hot glow of patriotism passed over me. Such a sermon must strengthen the hearts and hands of any people. There was more exhortation to fight and die à la Joshua than meek Christianity, however." On the other side, ex-slaves joined whites in casting the conflict in Christian terms. A black chaplain, William Hunter, preaching after the liberation of Wilmington, North Carolina, described the Union forces as "the armies of the Lord and of Gideon." In April 1865, an observer recorded that black troops with General Sherman marched into Charleston, South Carolina, "singing Methodist hymns."

During the War, Christians and Christian institutions were also active in more strictly spiritual, less overtly ideological areas. Revivals were common in the camps of both the Blue and the Gray. In the field, if not always at the home front, preaching was focused more directly on the spiritual needs of individuals before God and less on a presumed biblical mandate to win the War. The result was a series of deeply moving conversions. In the South, fervor increased along with the tide of Northern advance. Some Southerners, high officers and simple privates alike, apparently expected a supernatural intervention in response to their turn to piety. Others, such as Capt. Daniel Hundley, a prisoner of the Union forces, were coming to different conclusions. "Adversity has its lessons," he wrote at the time, "and those who will take the trouble patiently to master them will in the end be forced to acknowledge that it is oftentimes better to go up to the house of mourning than to the house of rejoicing."

The tradition of volunteering also flourished during the conflict, when thousands enlisted — not to fight the enemy but to assist soldiers and others thrown into difficulty by the War. In the North, the Sanitary Commission looked to the material needs of combatants, and groups such as the Christian Commission and the American Tract Society ministered directly to spiritual concerns. The immense job of assisting released slaves fell largely to the agents of the Freedman's Bureau. In the face of considerable local resistance,

This print, depicting General McClellan participating in a Union worship service, is evidence of the importance of such meetings for both sides during the Civil War. The Southern army demonstrated an even greater interest in religious revivals during the war than did the Northern army. *Courtesy of the Billy Graham Center Museum*

its agents provided shelter, began education, trained for employment, and encouraged spiritually the former slaves. The head of the Freedman's Bureau was Maj. Gen. Oliver Howard. His attitude toward the relation of religion to the War was illustrated by his belief that once Gen. George McClellan had decreed that the Northern Army should, insofar as possible, observe the Sabbath, victory was assured.

In these efforts, as would be the case in other wars, women played especially important parts. The development of more professional standards of nursing owed a special debt to women who worked, at least in many cases, as an expression of Christian compassion. A legendary interchange after the Battle of Shiloh illustrates the spirit in which some of that work was carried out. "Mother" Mary Ann Bickerdyke (1817-1901) was working for the Northwestern Sanitary Commission of Chicago to provide the Union army with medical supplies and other necessities. After Shiloh, an army surgeon encountered "Mother" Bickerdyke as she tended to the wounded soldiers. In the words of the Sanitary Commission's historian, "her kettles had been set up, the fire kindled underneath, and she was dispensing hot soup, tea, crackers, panado, whiskey and water, and other refreshments, to

Practical aid and comfort to soldiers during the Civil War came from many different groups, most of them connected in some way to the churches. This print shows the activities of the Christian Commission, the busiest and most effective of these agencies.
Courtesy of the Billy Graham Center Museum

the shivering, fainting, wounded men." When the surgeon inquired about the authority under which she was working, the reply was instantaneous: "I have received my authority from the Lord God Almighty: have you anything that ranks higher than that?"

In a word, the Civil War was a religious event because it consumed the energies of a religious people. Not surprisingly, however, the character of Civil War religion was dictated by the character of the dominant Protestant faiths in the nation. These faiths were quick to action, eager to discern the mind of God, and deeply convinced of the rightness of their cause. Only occasionally did participants in the War step back from the pressures of the moment and reflect more generally on the mysteries of Providence. The great example of such reflection came from a most unlikely source, the Union's rustic president from Illinois, Abraham Lincoln.

Abraham Lincoln

Abraham Lincoln (1809-1865), sixteenth president of the United States, has become a mythic figure in America's civil religion. Born into relative poverty

Abraham Lincoln,
near the end of his
life. *Library of
Congress*

on the midwestern frontier, he rose from humble origins through self-discipline, honesty, common sense, a considerable measure of ambition, and a ready wit to shepherd the nation through the black days of the Civil War. After his death, Americans found it irresistible to see his achievement in a religious light. It was soon noted, for example, that Lincoln — the "Savior" of the Union — was shot on Good Friday (April 14, 1865), that his efforts to liberate the bondslave and bind up the wounds of war were cut short by "martyrdom," and that his very name — Abraham — spoke of the father of his people. Although Lincoln himself originally saw the Civil War as a political struggle to preserve the Union, he came to regard it as a crusade for truth and right. He spoke of the United States as "the last, best hope of the earth," of its citizens as "the almost chosen people," and of the War as a test to see if a nation "conceived in liberty . . . can long endure."

Considerable uncertainty arises, however, when Lincoln's own religion is examined. On the one hand, it is obvious that Christianity exerted a profound influence on his life. His father was a member of Regular Baptist churches in Kentucky and Indiana. Lincoln himself read the Bible throughout his life, quoted from it extensively, and frequently made use of biblical images (as in the "House Divided" speech of 1858). It was said of him, perhaps with some exaggeration, that he knew by heart much of the Psalms, the book of Isaiah, and the entire New Testament. His life also exhibited many Christian virtues. He was scrupulously honest in repaying debts from ill-fated business ventures of the 1830s. He offered tender sympathy to the widows and orphans created by the Civil War. He pardoned numerous sleeping sentries and other soldiers condemned to death for relatively minor lapses. He kept his head concerning the morality of the contending sides in the War, refusing to picture the North as entirely virtuous or the South as absolutely evil. And during his years as president he did regularly attend the New York Avenue Presbyterian Church in Washington.

On the other hand, Lincoln never joined a church nor ever made a clear profession of standard Christian beliefs. While he read the Bible in the White House, he was not in the habit of saying grace before meals. Lincoln's friend Jesse Fell noted that the president "seldom communicated to anyone his views" on religion, and he went on to suggest that those views were not orthodox: "on the innate depravity of man, the character and office of the great head of the Church, the Atonement, the infallibility of the written revelation, the performance of miracles, the nature and design of . . . future rewards and punishments . . . and many other subjects, he held opinions utterly at variance with what are usually taught in the church." It is probable that Lincoln was turned against organized Christianity by his experiences as a young man in New Salem, Illinois, where excessive emotion and bitter sectarian quarrels marked yearly camp meetings and the ministry of traveling preachers. Yet although Lincoln was not a church member, he did ponder the eternal significance of his own circumstances, a personal life marked by tragedy (the early death of two sons) and difficulty (the occasional mental instability of his wife). And he took to heart the carnage of war over which he presided.

Whether it was from these experiences or from other sources, Lincoln's speeches and conversation revealed a spiritual perception far above the ordinary. It is one of the great ironies of the history of Christianity in America that the most profoundly religious analysis of the nation's deepest trauma came not from a clergyman or a theologian but from a politician who was self-taught in the ways of both God and humanity. The source of Lincoln's Christian perception will probably always remain a mystery, but the unusual depth of that perception none can doubt. Nowhere was that depth more visible than in his Second Inaugural Address of March 1865: "Both [North and South] read the same Bible, and pray to the same God; and each invokes His aid against the other. It may seem strange that any men should dare to ask a just God's assistance in wringing their bread from the sweat of other men's faces; but let us judge not that we be not judged. The prayers of both could not be answered; that of neither has been answered fully. The Almighty has His own purposes." Even more to the point was his reply when a minister from the North told the president he "hoped the Lord is on our side." Responded Lincoln, "I am not at all concerned about that. . . . But it is my constant anxiety and prayer that I and this nation should be on the Lord's side."

The Civil War as Turning Point

The economic and social ramifications of the Civil War certainly stimulated forces that would lead to a more secular America. The War acted as a spur to large-scale industrialization, intensive bureaucratic efficiency, and the mass movement of people from rural America into the cities — all factors working against the settled harmonies of republican Christianity and small-town Christian morality that had prevailed in the antebellum period. At the same time, the most important long-term effects of the War on the churches may have come from its very religiosity. Because of the pivotal nature of the War in American history, the kind of religious commitment made by Christians to the conflict had long-lasting results. Sometimes those results were unexpected, even ironic. As a whole, the curious result was that a war won (and lost) by people who felt that true religion was at stake produced a nation in which the power of religion declined.

Abolition

Revivalistic abolitionism raised the issue of slavery to national attention, but it was the force of arms and political compromise that brought about an end to slavery. Long-time abolitionists added their voices to the Northern crusade for the Union that eventually defeated the Confederacy. With the passage of the Thirteenth Amendment and its prohibition of slavery in December 1865, leading abolitionists felt their job was over. William Lloyd Garrison stopped publishing *The Liberator*. With the passage of the Fifteenth Amendment in 1870 guaranteeing ex-slaves the right to vote, the American Anti-Slavery Society, which had enjoyed extensive support from northern Protestants, disbanded. Most abolitionists traded in their earlier moral fervor for a more pragmatic approach to the times and its needs.

But if slavery was at an end, racism and systemic oppression of black

The Civil War formally secured freedom for American slaves, and so fulfilled the goals of abolitionists, but legal and economic conditions for black families in many areas of the country did not improve for many years. *Library of Congress*

people was not. Jim Crow laws in the South and lynch mobs in the North as well as in the South replaced the formal institutions of slavery to render most of the nation's blacks second-class citizens at best. Warfare, as often in the history of nations, proved to be a powerful opponent of moral reform. Content that the issue of slavery had been formally resolved, Christians turned away from the substantive problems remaining to give attention to other concerns. Some looked eagerly to the fruits of a new wave of evangelism, this time under the inspiration of Dwight L. Moody. Others struggled to make the gospel speak to the changing social conditions of an industrial America. A few began inching toward the contrasting conceptions of the Christian faith that would lead to the fundamentalist-modernist controversy. Political concern for the liberty of America's black citizens would not arise among the white churches for nearly a century.

In short, the crusade against slavery had won — and it had lost. The

The San Xavier del Bac mission near Tucson, Arizona, reminds us of the significant Hispanic Catholic presence that has prevailed throughout the American Southwest from the seventeenth century until today. *Archives of the University of Notre Dame*

proper laws were now in place, but genuine freedom for America's blacks had yet to be realized. After the Civil War, the struggle for that freedom was not of major interest to the nation's white Christians. By 1865 the antislavery revival was over. But human evil turned out to be an intrinsic as well as an extrinsic problem. A perfect state of society, it seemed, required vigilance over the sinfulness of the heart as well as aggressive military action and new laws. For the history of Christianity in America, winning (and losing) the struggle for racial justice marked the high tide of evangelical Protestant reform. Never again would an effort by Christians to reform society be so successful. Never again would a successful reform leave such a long-lasting evil. The ambiguous legacy of abolition may help explain why those who brought it about were losing control of American life.

Opening the West

The Civil War also affected the fate of Christianity in America by the way it helped open the frontier for further settlement. One of the main contentions between North and South had been whether slavery could move west with the spread of the population. The War settled that issue. With slavery prohibited throughout the whole nation, the dominant Protestant churches of the North felt they could now move westward to establish the same sort of settled churches and Protestant civilization that dominated life in many regions of New England and the Middle West. But it was not to be. Despite valiant efforts by Protestant home missionaries in the years after the War, settlement on the prairies, in the mountain states, and on the West Coast

The Indian mission at Fort Yates, North Dakota, was only one of the sites where
Catholics worked to evangelize the country's Native Americans.
Archives of the University of Notre Dame

never evidenced the blend of Protestant and American values that had
dominated public life in the East.

One of the reasons for this situation was that the West was religiously
pluralistic from the start. East of the Mississippi, an awareness of religious
diversity came relatively late in American history. In that region, the weight of
history suggested that white Protestants were "normal" and other groups of
Christians and practitioners of other religions were "exceptions." In the West,
on the other hand, exceptions were the rule. Before Protestants began their
systematic missionary efforts, a large Hispanic Catholic community was securely in place in the Southwest, the Mormon settlements had spread over
Utah and into Idaho, many Indian reservations (with a mixture of indigenous
and Christian faiths) had been set up on the plains, immigrants from Asia with
Asian faiths had arrived on the West Coast, and hardy habits of irreligion were
well rooted among nomadic populations of miners and ranchers.

Some Protestant missionaries to the West did have notable, even heroic,
careers. To mention only a few, the Unitarian Starr King (1824-1864), who
is known for helping keep California in the Union during the Civil War,
regarded himself first and foremost as a minister; his church (First Unitarian
of San Francisco) was a base for far-flung lecturing and preaching. Presbyterian Sheldon Jackson (1834-1909) energetically established churches and

Pierre-Jean de Smet *(above left)*, a Belgian Jesuit missionary, was one of the most active Catholic missionaries in the American West and Upper Midwest during the decades before and after the Civil War. Jean Baptiste Lamy *(above right)* carried out his ministry in the Southwest, serving as the first Catholic archbishop of New Mexico. *Photo of De Smet from the archives of the University of Notre Dame; photo of Lamy courtesy of the Museum of New Mexico*

schools in the Upper Midwest, and then on the plains, before pioneering Protestant missions in Alaska after the late 1870s. Jackson's fellow Presbyterian Sue McBeth was just one of many energetic women who joined in the effort to convert the Indians with her broad-based efforts among the Nez Percé in Idaho. Episcopalians enjoyed the services of several beloved bishops, including Daniel Sylvester Tuttle (1837-1923), who from 1867 to 1886 traveled over 40,000 miles by stagecoach in the Rocky Mountains, and John F. Spalding of Colorado (1828-1902), during whose tenure in the last quarter of the nineteenth century the number of Episcopalian churches rose from seven to one hundred.

Yet such Protestant leaders never succeeded in establishing a Protestant domination like that which Eastern Protestants had enjoyed before the War. They had been preceded in their labors by notable Catholic missionaries, among whom the Jesuit Pierre-Jean de Smet (1801-1873) is most famous. From the early 1850s de Smet served as mediator between Indians and whites, as well as among Indians, even as he energetically planted Catholic churches and catechized whites and Indians. Jean Baptiste Lamy (1814-1888), first Catholic archbishop of New Mexico, had also been working in the Southwest since the early 1850s. Lamy went on to recruit nuns and priests, expand the educational outreach of his diocese, ordain several Native Americans to the priesthood, and perform a whole host of other services. His fictionalized portrait in Willa Cather's *Death Comes for the Archbishop* may be the most fully realized picture of a minister in all of American literature.

Religious pluralism extended far beyond the Catholics. The major Protestant churches arrived in the plains and beyond alongside sectarian Protestants (Mennonites, Hutterites), representatives of the Freethinkers, as well as significant early migrations of Jews. Unlike the situation in colonial Massachusetts, Virginia, or New York, all of these groups stood on equal footing before the law. None had a constitutional advantage. In this context, legal provisions for the separation of church and state probably meant even more than they did in the East, where decades or centuries of tradition allowed the larger Protestant groups to act like establishments, regardless of the law.

No Protestant hegemony was possible on the frontier, however, not just because other faiths were active but because of the very nature of the West itself. California was atypical even in the nineteenth century, but the nature of its rapid settlement created a different society than those in which Protestantism had flourished in the East. After the discovery of gold in 1848, settlement advanced rapidly, but without the regular families, the expectations for education, and the agreed-upon legal procedures that had become commonplace elsewhere in the country. The result was a religious climate in which churches were valued for how they supported the social order and how they maintained the symbols of civilization rather than for how they defined the core values of the community. In the words of historian Sandra Sizer Frankel, California religion possessed "no enthusiasm, no sectarianism, little commitment to religious institutions." These conditions, which were also found elsewhere in the West to one degree or another, ensured that the role of the churches remained auxiliary rather than central to the new societies.

The Civil War, in other words, marked a fresh opportunity for opening the West to settlement and for introducing Christianity. But conditions in the region combined with the instant pluralism of postbellum faiths to shape a context in which religion never meant the same thing, or perhaps as much, as its most earnest adherents had hoped when they contemplated the chance to fill the West with churches as well as settlers.

Republican Virtue

The War may also have signaled an end to the synthesis of republican and Christian values that had dominated American culture since the Revolution.

An important component of that synthesis — as it was realized in colleges, the courts, and the pulpit — was the assumption that Christian virtue was a prime requirement for the support of republican institutions and that republican institutions served as guarantors of the freedom necessary for practicing Christianity. Educators (most of them Protestant ministers) enlisted intellectual methods from the Scottish common-sense philosophers and exploited popularized forms of scientific reasoning to make their case for the interdependence of republican and Christian virtues. The intensity of the debate between the North and the South in the decades before the War derived from the way similar systems of moral reasoning were applied to a common problem but led to radically different conclusions. Southerners felt that Northern busybodies were destroying republican institutions and subverting Christian order. Northern critics of the South countered by pointing out how slavery subverted republican ideals of freedom and so paved the way for the suppression of Christianity. Both used common-sense arguments and an appeal to philosophical (or scientific) evidence to make their case. After the Civil War, the social, political, and cultural circumstances that had made the arguments, the conclusions, and the methods of common-sense moral philosophy so important were unalterably changed. When these conditions changed, so too did the need for common-sense moral philosophy itself.

During the antebellum period, common-sense moral philosophy contributed profoundly to a series of ongoing political arguments about the nature of the Union, the rights of the states, and the imperatives of republicanism. After the War and the securing of the Union, there was little call in national politics for a philosophy of justice concerned with the nature of virtue. Armies, not arguments, had settled the issue of what a republic was and how its parts should fit together. American politics then entered into a long period, from which it has not yet emerged, in which material interests and debates over the role of government — but not arguments over first principles — have determined the horizon of public debate. In such a political situation, common-sense moral philosophy has been all but irrelevant.

With political and social conditions changed, the Christian alliance with common-sense moral philosophy became a problem. Protestants might still rely on common-sense philosophy to articulate public positions, but when they did so, they were speaking a conceptual language whose day had passed. More and more after the Civil War, other forms of reasoning were being exalted as better ways to truth. On one side were advocates of a romantic sensibility who suggested that the innate inner powers of human beings could lead to truth and beauty. On the other side, and much more important in the culture at large, was a new trust in science. Common-sense moral philosophy had once provided a widely accepted method for supporting the link between republican and Christian virtues, but the new arbiters of national intellectual life had little stake in that synthesis. Intellectual method had been the servant of republican religion, but after the Civil War another relationship prevailed. While a few elite Americans turned to a religion of literature and the arts, masses turned to the new religion of science. In such a world the public-spirited constraints that common-sense moral philosophy had once inculcated as a way to preserve both Christianity and republicanism had little meaning.

The Civil War decisively solved many of the public problems about which Americans had quarreled since the time of the Revolution. After the War, it was clear that republican freedom did not include the liberty to leave the Union, and for purposes of preserving the Union, the force of the federal government was more important than details of moral reasoning. The new authoritative notions of public virtue now excluded Southern slavery, but they offered scant morality to the hustling concern for markets that prevailed in the North. In every instance, it was action, not argument, that settled the issues. With the constitutional crisis resolved and the prize of wealth for all becoming ever more important for ever larger portions of the population, there simply was little place for the antebellum system of moral reasoning. To be sure, romantic trust in the self and a deep respect for scientific proof were both present before the Civil War, but these impulses were subservient to a public concern for Christian faith and republican virtue. After the War, that bond between intellectual methods and Christian or republican outcomes was broken. The War, which had been fought on both sides to defend republican Christian virtue, led to a world in which that kind of virtue was not nearly as important as it had been before.

Civil Religion

The War also served to redefine perceptions of the faith itself. In simplest terms, the sectional strife presented a nearly irresistible temptation to express Christianity in terms of a particular region and its principles. The process seemed to move with a kind of inevitability. The divisions among Presbyterians, Baptists, and Methodists from the 1830s and 1840s meant that denominational concerns were increasingly defined in terms of North or South but not both. The intensity of antebellum political debate and then the traumas of the War itself reinforced regional expressions of the faith. At the conclusion of the War and for many decades thereafter, observers on all sides felt that they could see clearly what God had intended to teach them (but not everyone) through victory or defeat. The push, which exerted such force because the issues reached so high, was always in the direction of identifying the interests of a particular region with the concerns of God. "Civil religion" is a term with many possible meanings, but the one that fits this situation best is the sense of a mingling of ultimate allegiance to the universal standards of Christianity with the particular values of a person's nation, region, or way of life.

The course of this civil religion in the War between the States is evident from the way in which Scripture was handled during the conflict. The "nation's book," the Bible, figured large in the era's clash of cultures. Scripture penetrated to such a deep level nationally that it was a major prop for both sides in the conflict leading to open war. Many Southerners viewed the Bible as the sure foundation for their way of life. The Reverend Frederick Ross of Huntsville, Alabama, for one, insisted that Southern slavery was modeled on a biblical pattern: "every Southern planter is not more truly a slave-holder than Abraham. And the Southern master, by divine authority, may today, consider his slaves part of his social and religious family, just as Abraham did." From the North it was a much different story, though based on the same authority. As the Presbyterian Albert Barnes from Philadelphia put it, "the principles laid down by the Saviour and his Apostles are such as are opposed to Slavery, and if carried out would secure its universal abolition."

The sense that the Scriptures supported one side, and one side only, was manifest in the War. Early on in the conflict, for example, a Southern Presbyterian teased 2 Chronicles 6:34-35, King Solomon's prayer for success in battle for Israel, into a biblically worded analysis of Abraham Lincoln's role in the current crisis: "eleven tribes sought to go forth in peace from the house of political bondage, but the heart of our modern Pharaoh is hardened, that he will not let Israel go." In the North, one of the more than four hundred sermons published after the assassination of Lincoln was an exposition of 2 Samuel 18:32, in which David learns about the treacherous slaying of his son Absalom. After an examination of the text, the minister concluded that no one "will be able to separate in thought the murder of the president from Jefferson Davis' persistent effort to murder the Union."

This way of using the Bible was very common. Its persistence only throws into sharper contrast the attitude Abraham Lincoln expressed in his Second Inaugural Address. Lincoln was one of very few in his day who recognized that "both sides read the same Bible and pray to the same God." The president did not proceed from this observation to herald the correctness of his side and the error of the South; rather, he used it as an opportunity to reflect on the mysterious ways of God with humanity. Such reflec-

331

With the Plymouth Congregational Church in Brooklyn as his base, Henry Ward Beecher was probably the best-known preacher and religious author in the United States during the years surrounding the Civil War. *Courtesy of the Billy Graham Center Museum*

tions were notable by their absence in the struggle between two biblical, but also self-righteous, peoples.

Lincoln's effort to view God above the conflict also had few parallels after the War. Many in the North perceived the War as a dramatic vindication of the right. The noted Congregationalist Henry Ward Beecher was asked to speak at Fort Sumter on February 14, 1865, when the Union flag was once again raised over the site where the War began. As Beecher saw it, there was no moral ambiguity whatsoever: "I charge the whole guilt of this war upon the ambitious, educated, plotting political leaders in the South. . . . A day will come when . . . these guiltiest and most remorseless traitors . . . shall be whirled aloft and plunged downward forever and ever in an endless retribution."

In the South, it looked very different. Already in 1866 Jonathan Babcock was writing in the *Southern Presbyterian Review* about the lessons to be learned by the "just" when God chastises his "chosen people." A few years later another Southern Presbyterian, Robert Lewis Dabney, proposed that a book be assembled for the Southern war effort on the model of *Foxe's Book of Martyrs*, the sixteenth-century compendium that had praised the lives and memorialized the deaths of England's Protestant martyrs. It was obvious to Dabney, as well as many other Southerners, that the biblical righteousness of their cause had never been disproved, only defeated.

Effects from the civil religion of the Civil War lingered powerfully. Denominational identities among the Baptists, Methodists, and Presbyterians were long defined by region. The main branches of northern and southern Methodists did not reunite until 1939, and it was not until 1983 that the sectional divisions from the Civil War were overcome among the Presbyterians. Among Baptists, there still has been no reunification of what was divided in 1844. These long-lasting divisions did not mean that all Baptists, Methodists, and Presbyterians thought that only Southerners (or Northerners) were part of God's kingdom. It did mean, however, that the ordinary awareness of a larger "body of Christ" was restrained by the divisions precipitated by the political divisions of a particular place at a particular time.

Similarly, the fact that Northerners and Southerners both exploited the Bible for the conflict did not mean that the Scriptures were wholly prostituted to regional principles, but sectarian use of Scripture was clearly more extensive than it would have been had the Bible not been put to use as a religious weapon during the War. Among Protestants, interpretations of the Bible were subjected to local and regional tests but rarely to broad examination from a range of Christians. The War had taught both sides that the Scriptures could inspire a threatened people. Unfortunately, it had also removed some of the checks and balances that, in other circumstances, kept biblical interpretation responsive to a general Christian framework. America's public culture came to pay less and less attention to the Bible in the decades after the War. One of the reasons was that Christians had paid it the wrong kind of attention before and during the War.

Finally, as the conflict raged, believers in both the North and the South were tempted to make the success of their military efforts the object of their most basic religious concern. To the extent that this took place, a most unfavorable precedent was established. By making such strong commitments to the righteousness of their own side and by regarding the enemy in such deeply religious terms, believers set the stage for other consuming national interests to exert a similar shaping influence on the churches. Once again, the irony was profound. A religious people had devoted great religious energy to "saving the nation." From the side of the North, the effort was successful. From the side of the South, it was not. Success or failure, however, may have been less important than the nature of the effort. To reapply an old saying first used in the early history of Christianity, the believers who married the spirit of the Civil War age found themselves widowed in the age that followed.

Further Reading

Frankel, Sandra Sizer. *California's Spiritual Frontiers: Religious Alternatives in Anglo-Protestantism, 1850-1910.* Berkeley and Los Angeles: Univesity of California Press, 1988.

Goen, C. C. *Broken Churches, Broken Nation: Denominational Schisms and the Coming of the Civil War.* Macon, GA: Mercer University Press, 1985.

Moorhead, James H. *American Apocalypse: Yankee Protestants and the Civil War, 1860-1869.* New Haven: Yale University Press, 1978.

Noll, Mark A. "The Image of the United States as a Biblical Nation, 1776-1865." In *The Bible in American Culture.* Edited by Nathan O. Hatch and Mark A. Noll. New York: Oxford University Press, 1982.

Shattuck, Gardiner H. *A Shield and Hiding Place: The Religious Life of the Civil War Armies.* Macon, GA: Mercer University Press, 1987.

Silver, James W. *Confederate Morale and Church Propaganda.* New York: W. W. Norton, 1957.

Szasz, Ferenc Morton. "The Clergy and the Myth of the American West." *Church History* 59 (Dec. 1990): 497-506.

————. *The Protestant Clergy in the Great Plains and Mountain West, 1865-1915.* Albuquerque: University of New Mexico Press, 1988.

Wolf, William J. *The Almost Chosen People: A Study of the Religion of Abraham Lincoln.* Garden City, NY: Doubleday, 1959.

CHAPTER 13

Non-White, Non-Protestant

O Black and Unknown Bards

O black and unknown bards of long ago,
How came your lips to touch the sacred fire?
How, in your darkness, did you come to know
The power and beauty of the minstrels' lyre?
Who first from midst his bonds lifted his eyes?
Who first from out the still watch, lone and long,
Feeling the ancient faith of prophets rise
Within his dark-kept soul, burst into song?

Heart of what slave poured out such melody
As "Steal away to Jesus"? On its strains
His spirit must have nightly floated free,
Though still about his hands he felt his chains.
Who heard great "Jordan roll"? Whose starward eye
Saw chariot "swing low"? And who was he
That breathed that comforting, melodic sigh,
"Nobody knows de trouble I see"?

      *   *   *   *   *

You sang far better than you knew; the songs
That for your listeners' hungry hearts sufficed
Still live — but more than this to you belongs:
You sang a race from wood and stone to Christ.

It was not until after the Civil War that African-American spirituals were written down. Their power, however, only grew as they passed into print. James Weldon Johnson (1871-1938), a black lawyer, editor, politician, novelist, professor, and organizer for the NAACP, published this poem in the early twentieth century as a memorial to the unknown slaves who created the most distinctly American hymnody.

THE TRIUMPHS AND TURMOILS OF WHITE PROTESTANTS WERE THE MOST visible religious dramas in the United States throughout the nineteenth century. But the history of white Protestantism was by no means the only important Christian story. The Civil War offers a convenient vantage point from which to notice those other stories, for it marked a period of new beginnings for America's black Christians. It also happened to stand just at the start of major new migrations from Europe that introduced large numbers of adherents of an ancient form of Christianity, the Eastern Orthodox, and that transformed the Roman Catholic Church from a large curiosity into a major national force. Increasingly as the nineteenth century gave way to the twentieth, the preeminence of white Protestants faded irreversibly.

African Americans in Control of Their Destinies

The ending of slavery had immediate consequences for church life among people of color. Despite the failure of Reconstruction to secure civil rights for freed slaves in the South, and despite the intensifying racism of the half-century after the Civil War, blacks seized control of their own religious lives. African Americans in previously white denominations abandoned those organizations in great numbers, and new opportunities arose for expanding previously existing black denominations and for forming new bodies.

Denominational Initiatives

Three important developments occurred in the organization of separate black churches. The first was the establishment of new denominations, primarily in the South. Between the end of the War and 1870, for example,

336

This print of the Sunday morning service of an African-American church in the
Virginia Pines probably comes from after the Civil War, since only then were
blacks able to organize their own churches in the South.
Courtesy of the Billy Graham Center Museum

ex-slaves founded the Colored Methodist Episcopal Church and the
Colored Cumberland Presbyterian Church as entities separate from white
denominations. Baptist organization was more fragmented, but of even
greater long-lasting significance. State conventions of blacks in the South
formed slowly, but then looked to even broader venues of fellowship. The
result was the establishment of the National Baptist Convention in 1895.
The two groups that emerged from this body after a split in 1907 (the
National Baptist Convention of the U.S.A., Inc., and the National Baptist
Convention) constitute the largest cluster of black Christians in the United
States.

A second development after the Civil War was the expansion of previously existing Northern denominations into the South. Here the Methodists took the lead, especially the African Methodist Episcopal Church. In
1865 Bishop Daniel Alexander Payne, who thirty years before had been
forced out of South Carolina, returned in triumph to Charleston to establish
his denomination in that area. Soon other Northern bodies followed suit,
which added to the number of national black churches.

The third development was the establishment of numerous independent congregations, at first mostly rural, in which locally supported preach-

337

The National Baptist Convention, U.S.A., represented here by a group photo from one of its early annual meetings, remains one of the largest African-Americn denominations. *Courtesy of the Billy Graham Center Museum*

ers created and maintained their own congregations. These groups, usually Baptist in practice, have continued to be a mainstay of black Christian experience in the South. In later decades, with the vast movement of blacks into cities both North and South, this pattern of independent congregations led to some of the largest and most influential urban congregations as well as to a vast array of smaller churches.

Two other developments in specific denominations are worth noting. First was the heightened self-consciousness among black Roman Catholics. Since African Americans have been predominantly Baptist, Methodist, or independent, it is sometimes forgotten that there is a long tradition of blacks in the Catholic Church. After the Civil War, attachment by blacks to the Catholic Church increased in both the South and the North. Although the attention of the Church during this period was focused most on newcomers from Europe, it also made some efforts at educating an indigenous black leadership. In 1886, Augustus Tolton (1854-1897) of Quincy, Illinois, who had studied with Franciscans in the United States and at the College of the Propaganda of the Faith in Rome, became the first American of pure African descent to be ordained to the priesthood. Three years later the first congress of African American Catholics took place in Washington, D.C. The national census taken the next year counted 100,000 black members of the Catholic Church.

Blacks also played prominent roles in the development of holiness and Pentecostal forms of Christian faith. The Church of God in Christ, for example, was organized in Memphis in 1897 by two ministers, C. H. Mason (1866-1961) and C. P. Jones (1865-1949), who had been urging their Baptist constituencies to seek a postconversion experience of God's grace as a path to holiness. Later, after Mason journeyed to Azusa Street in Los Angeles to explore the Pentecostal vision of special charismatic gifts, he and his followers divided from Jones and others who rejected speaking in tongues. Those who followed Mason kept the name Church of God in Christ, which eventually became the largest of the black Pentecostal

Lane College, Jackson, Tennessee, was one of the numerous colleges that African-Americans founded and staffed, largely through their own efforts, in the wake of the Civil War. It was a college of the Colored Methodist Episcopal Church (later called the Christian Methodist Episcopal Church).
Courtesy of the Billy Graham Center Museum

churches. Jones and his supporters became known as the Church of Christ (Holiness) U.S.A.

Other Institutions

The Constitutional prohibition of slavery also made blacks freer to organize their own institutions of culture and religious outreach. Most of the African-American colleges founded immediately after the War were organized, funded, and directed by white Christian bodies. But after 1880, black Christians were active themselves in establishing colleges for their youth. The Colored Methodist Episcopal Church (Lane College), the African Methodist Episcopal Zion Church (Livingstone College), and the African Methodist Episcopal Church (Morris Brown College) took the lead in this venture, but other groups participated as well, with the result that by 1900 over twenty-five such church-connected colleges had been established in the South.

Church bodies also pioneered in providing books and periodical literature for the black community. The Sunday School Union of the African Methodist Episcopal Church began its own publishing house in 1887. But well before then other local churches and national denominations had brought out books, published magazines, and even begun weekly newspapers. These various forms of publication continued to flow from the black churches well into the twentieth century. They were sources of religious information and spiritual direction but often of more general news and intellectual culture as well.

Once freed from slavery, blacks also made a significant contribution to missionary work. The European partitioning of Africa into spheres of

Amanda Berry Smith was a missionary, social worker, preacher, world traveler, and all-around Christian activist. This print is from her autobiography, published in 1893, under the title *The Story of the Lord's Dealings with Mrs. Amanda Smith.*

influence motivated American blacks to send their own missionaries to Africa, with the hope that the message of the gospel could prevent in their ancestral homelands the exploitation they had known in America. A Baptist Foreign Mission Convention was organized in 1880 and was later absorbed into the work of the National Baptist Convention. The major Methodist denominations also established a large missionary presence in Africa, doing especially strong work in Liberia and Sierra Leone. Like their white counterparts, black women also organized their own missionary societies and sent out energetic (though usually not ordained) workers.

Amanda Berry Smith (1837-1915), who toured India in 1880 and labored for the rest of that decade in Liberia, was a stellar example of such labor. Her life also illustrates the way in which postbellum black Christian experiences intersected with those of white Protestants and yet led in different directions as well. Shortly after the end of the Civil War, Amanda Smith was instructed in holiness teachings at Phoebe Palmer's Tuesday meetings in New York City. Later, through connections with the African Methodist Episcopal Church and as an independent itinerant, she preached holiness at camp meetings in the Atlantic states, in England, and during her time in India and Liberia. After returning to the United States, she moved near Chicago, where she established the Amanda Smith Industrial Orphan Home. Outreach to the disadvantaged was a natural extension of her preaching, as was the case in both the nineteenth-century holiness movement and the more general tradition of black Christianity.

Church and Society

During the last decades of the nineteenth century, black Christianity advanced as much against the wishes of white leaders, including many church leaders, as with their blessing. Blacks who attempted to form freed slaves into effective churches encountered obstructions from both Northern and Southern whites. As just one of many examples, James Lynch (1839-1872), who served as a chaplain to black troops in the War and who eventually worked for the A.M.E. Church in Mississippi during Reconstruction, struggled continually against the unwillingness of both the Southern and Northern white Methodist churches in the effort to secure ordinations, property, or independence for African-American congregations. Lynch was once fired upon during a quarterly Methodist conference, an attack that may also have been linked to his service as Mississippi's Secretary of State during Reconstruction.

When black Catholics met in Washington in 1889, their address to fellow Catholics included a complaint. Given the desperate conditions in which many blacks lived at the time — for the two decades after 1885, there were an average of nearly one hundred well-documented lynchings of blacks each year in the United States — the complaint was gently phrased: "we must admit — only to lament it — the fact that the sacred rights of justice and humanity are still sadly wounded — are still immeasurably obstructed — even in a country where liberty, so long an exile, so long abused, so long a wanderer the world over has found at last a secure refuge, a permanent home, a grand and lasting temple." The appeal spoke to a situation in which the promise of Emancipation had not yet been realized.

Even on the mission fields of Africa, black evangelists often won only suspicion from white colonial officials for their efforts to spread the gospel among native peoples. Persistent shortages of funds also hampered blacks in efforts to strengthen churches and their outreach. Still, if the period between the Revolution and the Civil War was a time in which African Americans turned to Christianity in unprecedented numbers, the period between the Civil War and World War I was a time in which blacks began to control the shape of their own religious lives.

After the Civil War, the black churches rapidly became the center for black culture generally as well as for black religious life. The failure of political Reconstruction — with the end to the protection that had been

This depiction of a worship service in a black church near Yorktown, Virginia, sometime after the Civil War highlights the participation of entire families.
Courtesy of the Billy Graham Center Museum

provided by Union troops, the beginning of violent repression associated with the Ku Klux Klan, and the enactment of Jim Crow laws enforcing a demeaning segregation — meant that freed slaves were stripped of control over every institution except the church. In the North, where the legal situation was better, racial prejudice was nevertheless almost as widespread. And so the political, literary, business, and associational activities that whites carried on in scores of institutions tended among blacks to be concentrated in the churches. The result was dynamic Christian life, but also the suspicion that religion was a compensation for lost possibilities in the "real world." In more recent years, some voices have accused the churches and their leaders of offering a pious expectation of heavenly riches instead of social resistance to the systematic racism of American society. It comes closer to the mark, however, to say that black Christians in the generations after the Civil War found in the churches stability and direction for this life every bit as much as consolation for the life to come.

A contrast between two important leaders illustrates the directions in which African-American Christian faith could travel. Booker T. Washington (1856-1915) is known today as an educational pioneer whose willingness

The Christian faith of Booker T. Washington *(above left)* was one of the elements
that inspired his strategy of training African-Americn young people to work within
the system established by white Americans. Henry McNeal Turner *(above right)*,
shown here as a chaplain in a Civil War regiment, took a different approach and
became one of the most outspoken — and effective — proponents of a Christian
theology that drew directly on the oppressed experience of American blacks.
Both portraits courtesy of the Billy Graham Center Museum

to work within the boundaries set by white society has been regarded both
as a tactical stroke of genius and as an unforgivable accommodation to
injustice. Washington, a lifelong Baptist, was trained at Hampton Normal
and Agricultural Institute in Virginia, the first school established by the
abolitionist American Missionary Association. Throughout his life, and
especially as founder of the Tuskegee Institute in Alabama, Washington
exhibited the Christian moral earnestness that he had learned at Hampton.
In a famous speech at Atlanta in 1895 he urged blacks to win their way in
a white society through self-discipline, moral constancy, and diligence in
farming and the mechanical trades. This speech has been criticized for
conceding too much to the injustices of the time, and yet Washington was
not offering self-restraint or Christian faith as a substitute for justice. Indeed,
three years after the Atlanta speech, Washington attacked what he called
"sentimental Christianity, which banks everything in the future and nothing
in the present." He characterized such faith as "the curse of the race." Yet
Washington's vision of progress was accommodating. He asked blacks to
bear with injustice, to tolerate wrongs, and to proceed patiently along the

path toward freedom. He defined the object of Christian faith as getting "the inner life, the heart right, and we shall then become strong where we have been weak, wise where we have been foolish."

By contrast, Bishop Harry McNeal Turner (1834-1915) of the A.M.E. Church became disillusioned with the focus on inner religion and called for a faith that worked simultaneously for spiritual and social freedom. During Reconstruction, Turner worked in Georgia both to establish the A.M.E. Church and to create a government open to all citizens. When Reconstruction failed and blacks were ousted from Georgia politics, he returned to the church full-time. Yet he did not lose his sense that political conditions reflected ultimate realities. He became the leading black voice against repressive decisions by Congress and the Supreme Court, and he took up again the call for African colonization as an option for African Americans. His bold claim in 1896 that "God is a Negro" was meant to shock the sensibilities of both whites and blacks into pursuing consistency between inner religious peace and justice in society. Unlike Booker T. Washington, who ended his years as a widely respected figure, Bishop Turner died in Canada an embittered observer of black life in his native country.

The contrast between Washington and Turner points to the powerful but diverse roles of Christianity among American blacks. It has offered comfort to those in adversity, but it has also engendered discontent with injustice and inspired many to action. In the decades after the Civil War, each of these functions was well developed and each was pointing toward yet more dramatic developments in the twentieth century.

The Orthodox in America

The problems that the Eastern Orthodox encountered in their efforts to establish a strong presence in America were much different than those that black Christians struggled with, but they proved almost as daunting. They had to grapple not with systematic racial prejudice but with a bewildering array of ethnic divisions complicated by ambiguous ties to European homelands.

Orthodoxy is the hereditary Christian faith of the eastern Mediterranean and much of Eastern Europe. It is a faith distinguished from both Roman Catholicism and Protestantism by its subjection to the authority of the seven ecumenical councils of the early church (through the second Council of Nicea in 787), by fidelity to the liturgies of the first centuries, and by a concept of spirituality in which material forms serve importantly as means by which God communicates aspects of his divine nature to

By the 1930s, Pittsburgh, Pennsylvania, like many American cities, could boast of well-established Orthodox landmarks.
Library of Congress

humans (centrally in the Incarnation of Christ but also through elaborately decorated church structures, liturgical chants, and icons). The Patriarch of Constantinople (later Istanbul) was long the leading primate among the Orthodox, because of Constantinople's central place in the ancient Roman Empire. Later quasi-independent (or *autocephalous*) Orthodox churches developed in Greece, many of the countries of southeastern Europe, the Middle East, and especially Russia. When in the last decades of the nineteenth century immigration on a large scale brought to the United States millions of new residents from these parts of the world, their numbers included many Orthodox Christians.

Continued immigration and natural increase have made the Orthodox family of churches an important part of the story of Christianity in North America. By the 1980s, the various Orthodox groups in the United States and Canada, taken together, numbered about 3,500,000 adherents — more than the Presbyterians, the Episcopalians, or the Congregationalists. Still, the relatively recent arrival of the Orthodox, as well as the bewildering diversity of Orthodox groups, makes it difficult to relate a coherent account of their American experience.

Russian Orthodox monks had been active as early as the 1790s in what is now Alaska, where sporadic missionary efforts continued among the

This iconographic portrait of Saint Herman and Saint Innocent shows that, like the Protestants and Catholics, Eastern Orthodox Christians also had their missionary heroes from the earlier history of the United States.

Eskaleutian tribes through 1867, when Alaska was sold to the United States. These early efforts had some success, in part because of the dedicated work of such leaders as the saintly monk Herman and the energetic Bishop Innocent, both of whom were later canonized by the Russian Church.

The immigration of the late nineteenth century led to the establishment of many Orthodox congregations, first in large port cities and then in other major urban areas. Early in the migration, conflict over Byzantine-rite Christians (known as Uniates), who followed traditional Orthodox practices but who recognized the authority of the Roman Catholic pope, led to some tensions between the Orthodox and Roman Catholics. As a result, some Uniates in America returned to Orthodoxy, and relations with the Catholic Church were strained in the first two decades of the century.

A leader in establishing Russian Orthodoxy in the States was Bishop Tikhon Bellavin (1865-1925), who in 1905 transferred his see from San Francisco to New York in order to minister more effectively to the centers of Russian settlement. Tikhon encouraged greater lay participation in the councils of the Church and also in 1907 convened the first All-American Council, an initial step toward broader cooperation among the Orthodox

Sitka, Alaska, was the site of this Russian Orthodox Cathedral. The print dates from about 1900, after Orthodox monks had been in Alaska for nearly a century. *California Museum of Photography, Keystone-Mast Collection, University of California, Riverside*

in America. Tikhon was later called to Russia, where in 1917 he was elected the Patriarch of Moscow.

The Russian Revolution of that same year brought about a division of loyalties among the Russian Orthodox in the States. One small body, known as the Russian Orthodox Church, became fiercely anticommunist and tenaciously ethnic. Another small group, the Patriarchal Exarchate, remained completely loyal to the Patriarch of Moscow, who was forced to hew to a line drawn by the Kremlin. The third, and largest, Russian body, whose allegiance to the Moscow Patriarchy was always somewhat ambiguous, became known as the Metropolia. In 1970 it was granted an independent status (autocephaly) by the Patriarch of Moscow. Soon thereafter this group, which had proceeded furthest of all Orthodox bodies along the road of cultural adaptation, changed its name to the Orthodox Church in America. Subsequently it has sought to provide a home for Orthodox believers from beyond the Russian immigrant community.

The largest Orthodox body in America is the Greek Orthodox Archdiocese of North and South America, which in the 1980s numbered about 2,000,000 adherents. As with many Orthodox bodies, membership sometimes implies more ethnic identification than active participation. The Archdiocese came into existence as a separate church early in the twentieth century through the efforts of Meletios Metaxakes, a Greek bishop who traveled and worked in the States from 1918 to 1921, and by Athenagoras

Sperou, who served as the head of the Greek Orthodox in the United States from 1930 to 1949. Like the Russian Tikhon, Athenagoras also became head of a world communion when he was elected as the Ecumenical Patriarch of Constantinople in 1949.

Political and religious conflicts in Old World countries and regions — for example, the Ukraine, Byelorussia, Syria, Albania, Bulgaria, Romania, Serbia, Egypt — often disrupted Orthodox immigrant communities in the United States. The upshot was a tangled network of small and sometimes aggressively competitive churches and related institutions. In more recent years, however, a measure of common Orthodox cooperation has been achieved. A Standing Conference of Canonical Bishops in the Americas (founded in 1960) provides for dialogue and a measure of cooperative action (as in the provision of military chaplains). Leading émigré theologians Georges Florovosky (1893-1979) and Alexander Schmemann (1921-1983) also transformed the Russian St. Vladimir's Seminary in New York into an institution serving a broader Orthodox constituency.

For the Orthodox, as for other immigrant groups, the irreversible process of Americanization offers both perils and prospects. The spirit of American culture does threaten to erode the distinctives of Orthodox spirituality and ecclesiology. Thomas Hopko, one of the first American-born professors to teach at St. Vladimir's, has warned that Orthodox susceptibility to either "individualistic relativism" or "crusading sectarianism" could lead to "the deeper weakening (if not the total disappearance) of the Orthodox Christian vision and way of life among many, if not most, of the Orthodox themselves." On the other hand, their presence in America also presents the Orthodox with the opportunity to introduce Protestants and Roman Catholics to what Father Hopko has described as "the essential mystical existence of the one, holy, catholic, Orthodox church — expressed in the integrity of its scriptures, doctrines, sacraments, canons, spirituality and hierarchical structures."

Catholics

Roman Catholics became increasingly important in American life between the Civil War and World War I for two compelling reason. First, their numbers grew dramatically, from about 3,500,000 in 1870 to over 15,000,000 by 1910. Second, an increasing attention to broader American culture also made Catholics more of a force in the nation. Catholics in the nineteenth century underwent a process of assimilation just as Protestants of British background had in earlier centuries and as non-British Protestants, the Orthodox, Jews,

This Italian family, disembarking at Ellis Island, New York, joined the millions of European immigrants who poured into the United States in the half-century between the end of the Civil War and the start of World War I. *George Eastman House Collection*

and members of other immigrant groups had in the nineteenth century. Catholic assimilation, however, had a distinct character because of the way local expressions of that faith still functioned, though not without strain and controversy, as parts of a worldwide Christian Church.

An Immigrant Church

A great surge in immigration over the last third of the nineteenth century brought millions of Catholics to the United States from southern and central Europe. The newly arrived Catholics created both problems and opportunities for the American hierarchy, in which the Irish, followed by Germans, were now most prominent. The problems included simple survival in an alien environment as well as intramural clashes among Catholics about how best to adjust to startlingly new circumstances. The opportunities included a chance to adapt an ancient tradition to a new setting as well as increasing opportunities to shape the larger world of Christianity in the United States.

Between the Civil War and World War I, Catholics predominated in the streams of immigrants from Bohemia, Croatia, Hungary, Italy, Lithuania, Poland, Slovakia, and elsewhere. Upon arriving in the United States, all of these groups formed "national parishes" in which the Catholic faith was offered alongside social, domestic, economic, political, and cultural services. Yet the experiences of immigrant Catholics were not uniform, as the story of Italians and Poles indicates.

During the 1890s, 700,000 Italians arrived in the United States; another 2,000,000 came during the next decade. Of all Catholic immigrants, these were among the least securely tied to the Church. Many arrived with scant religious instruction and little interest in more than nominal attachment to the Church. Looking back on the early twentieth century, Bishop Thomas Becker confided that "it is a very delicate matter to tell the Sovereign Pontiff how utterly faithless the specimens of his country coming here really are. Ignorance of their religion and a depth of vice little known to us yet, are the prominent characteristics." Other immigrants were offended by the coolness of the American hierarchy to the reunification of Italy (and consequent loss by the papacy of its political power). Still others took umbrage when local bishops criticized as superstitious or decadent the exuberant festivals for patron saints that were part of rural Italian culture. Ethnic suspicions of a predominantly Irish hierarchy did not ease the tension. In these unsettled religious conditions, aggressive American Protestants, led by Methodists, Baptists, and Presbyterians, established several hundred churches for Italians and commissioned missionaries in search of converts. Eventually, however, the Catholic Church proved much more successful in winning back Italian-American loyalty than were Protestants in overcoming it. Early in the first decade of the century there were about one hundred Italian priests working in New York City alone, and comparably energetic labors were undertaken in other cities. Italian-Americans became a solidly entrenched part of American Catholicism, but not without a struggle.

Difficulties for the more than 2,000,000 Poles who emigrated to the United States between 1850 and 1924 were of a different sort. Polish newcomers, who were overwhelmingly Catholic, turned instinctively to the church for spiritual support, social stability, and access to the new land. Religious workers, first from Poland but then from America, volunteered in large numbers to staff a burgeoning network of Polish-American institutions. By 1914, for example, 2,200 sisters were teaching more than 128,000 Polish-American children. The Poles resembled the Italians, however, in at least one matter: they too resented what appeared to them to be the unsympathetic attention of the American hierarchy. The first Polish bishop was not appointed until 1908, and this only after the immigrant church had

Ethnic Catholic churches, like this Polish parish church in Chicago, were often the center for social as well as religious life and also the institutions that most effectively bridged the gap from the Old World to the New. *State Historical Society of Wisconsin*

petitioned the the pope. A decade before, misunderstanding between German-American bishops and Polish congregations had resulted in an unusual break from the Roman Catholic Church. Under the leadership of Francis Hodur of Scranton, Pennsylvania, and drawing on strength from Polish settlements in Chicago and Buffalo, a Polish National Catholic Church was formed as an alternative to Roman jurisdiction. This breakaway body, while retaining Catholic theology, did make some adjustments to the American environment (including optional celibacy for priests). It remains a substantial denomination to this day (100,000 members in 1983). Continued loyalty to the homeland and to the Roman Catholic Church has been much more typical among Polish-Americans, however. Upward mobility, movement to the suburbs, and broader educational opportunities have altered, but not replaced, the hereditary Catholic loyalties of most Polish Americans.

With much struggle, immigrant Catholic churches developed their own educational institutions. After trying unsuccessfully to secure rights for Catholic students in public schools, Catholics developed an extensive system of parochial education. Catholic higher education, already well in place before the Civil War, was strengthened even further by a multitude of new colleges and seminaries, as well as by the establishment of the national Catholic University of America in Washington, D.C. When its cornerstone

351

was laid in 1888, Bishop John Spalding of Peoria drew attention to the larger meaning of the event: "the special significance of our American Catholic history . . . lies in the fact that our example proves that the Church can thrive where it is neither protected nor persecuted, but is simply left to manage its own affairs and to do its work." A Catholic university of this kind demonstrated to Catholics that they could make it in America at the same time that it demonstrated to Americans that they had nothing to fear from Catholics.

Despite some uneasiness in the hierarchy, Catholic laity also worked actively to organize workers and promote their rights. Bishops objected to oaths of secrecy standard among some labor organizations, and they worried lest labor organizing drift into violence or promote socialism. But when prominent labor organizations such as the Knights of Labor renounced the use of violence, they continued to attract widespread support from the Catholic laity and eventually won approval from the hierarchy as well.

The diligent activity of thousands of sisters in religious orders was a constant feature in Catholic adjustment to America. Nuns cared for the sick in hospitals, sheltered orphans, provided for the elderly, established settlement houses in cities, and operated many other institutions of social assistance. But above all they were teachers. By 1900, there were over 3,800 Catholic parochial schools in the United States and another 663 academies for girls, almost all of which were staffed by nuns. Though subject to all common human foibles, many of the nuns were heroic figures. Their larger-than-life presence is responsible for the powerful memories — some frankly ambiguous, some painful, others tender beyond words — that linger powerfully among American Catholics even after the decline in vocations witnessed since the 1960s. That the legends were rooted in fact is suggested by examples, such as a historian's recent description of Sister Blandina Segale, a Cincinnati Sister of Charity, who in 1878, at the age of twenty-two, moved to the West to serve as a teacher and much else. During her eighteen years in Colorado and New Mexico, "she put up a school and a hospital without prior resources, ended the lynch law in New Mexico, tamed Billy the Kid, built the tallest building in the territory, and proved herself more than the equal of the forces of greed and violence that surrounded her." Archbishop Jean Baptiste Lamy is the Southwest's best-known Catholic leader of the period, but had he not had the help of Sister Blandina and her associates, the Catholic presence would have been much reduced.

Catholic laity were also active in establishing their own American organizations. In the last decades of the nineteenth century, ethnic Catholics founded almost as many fraternal organizations, with almost as many purposes, as had the Protestant voluntarists before the Civil War. The laity also

Sister Blandina Segale was a pioneering member of the Cincinnati Sisters of Charity, who, for nearly twenty years toward the end of the nineteenth century, carried on a wide-ranging ministry in Colorado and New Mexico. *Courtesy of the Museum of New Mexico*

patronized a wide range of spiritual activities associated directly with the churches, including sodalities devoted to Our Lady or the Holy Spirit and societies of the Rosary or the Sacred Heart of Mary. Lay congresses were held in Baltimore in 1889 and Chicago in 1893 to encourage broader participation in the Church. Reading circles, magazines of every description, and special courses during summer vacations added to the variety of Catholic lay experience. In a word, Catholics were not just present in increasing numbers but were establishing the social and religious infrastructure that would sustain a vital church life once the crises of immigration had become only a family memory.

Journey to Rome: Isaac Hecker

One of the signals that the Catholic faith was adjusting to the New World environment was its ability to attract the interest of Americans raised in Protestant traditions. The most notable of many hereditary Protestants to make the spiritual journey to Rome was Isaac Hecker, whose life itself serves as an important gauge of Catholic influence in America. Even more, the uses to which "lessons" from Hecker's life were put after his death precip-

Isaac T. Hecker, founder of the Paulist Fathers, was a leader in providing an effective message to those outside the Catholic Church as well as in offering support to Catholics newly arrived in American cities. *Library of Congress*

itated a major debate between the Vatican and Roman Catholics in America, in which the question of Catholic adjustment to the Americas was probed even more intensively.

Hecker (1819-1888) was born in New York City into a home that was nominally Dutch Reformed. But the shaping religious influence of Isaac Hecker's early life was his mother's Methodism, to which she turned with great fervor when Isaac was a child. Although Hecker came to appreciate Methodist zeal, the Methodist rejection of Calvinism, and Methodist optimism concerning natural human capacities, he did not find his mother's faith satisfying. It took him some time to find one that was. As a young adult he explored Unitarianism, he poured himself into the reformist activities of New York's Equal Rights Party (the "Loco-Focos" whom one historian has styled "Methodists of Democracy"), he felt the tug of Mormonism and its vision of radical social reorganization, and eventually he fell under the spell of the New England romantic Orestes Brownson (1803-1876). Through Brownson, Hecker came into the orbit of the Transcendentalists, with whom he spent nearly two years.

Hecker's search for a satisfying form of spirituality finally ended when he became a Roman Catholic in 1844. He devoted the rest of his life to accommodating an expansive vision of God to the structures of Catholicism and to ardent labors on behalf of his new faith. In 1845 he became a member of the Redemptorists, an order that had recently arrived in the United States to work with German immigrants and — of special attraction to Hecker — to evangelize in Catholic churches and in the American population at large. When Hecker sensed a slackening of missionary zeal among the Redemptorists in the late 1850s, he founded the Paulist order and directed it especially toward the conversion of Americans. The Paulists also reflected Hecker's emphasis on the immediate work of the Holy Spirit and were thus less rigid in structure than traditional Catholic orders. Until his health broke in 1871, Hecker performed prodigious amounts of work for the Paulists — traveling extensively to lecture before Catholics and Protestants, organizing evangelistic forays, publishing books, launching periodicals (e.g., *The Catholic World* in 1865), and overseeing a large parish in New York City.

Hecker was the most influential church leader among the substantial number of Transcendentalists who turned to Catholicism, a group that included also Brownson and Mrs. George Ripley. These Americans had grown up in the democratic Protestantism of the early national period, a Protestantism that had largely set aside Calvinistic convictions on original sin and sovereign grace and was full of enthusiasm for the spiritual potential of individuals and the religious significance of America. Hecker never lost the perfectionist bent, the reformist utopianism, the American messianism, the belief in the extraordinary activity of the Spirit, or the reliance on infused grace that characterized the egalitarian evangelicalism of the antebellum period. Yet he was not content with ecclesiastical anarchy, excessive individualism, and rampant anti-intellectualism, which he thought this Protestantism also nurtured. And so he turned to Rome, because Catholic spirituality, especially in its mystical expressions, offered a resting place for his own romanticism. It is, thus, no surprise that after Hecker's death his approach to Catholicism — or at least what was perceived to be his approach in its extreme form — became the center of controversy between the papacy and Roman Catholics in the United States.

"Americanism"

The affair came to be known as the "Americanist Controversy" because it raised the question of how far the traditions of the Catholic Church could be accommodated to New World notions of freedom, evangelism, and spiritual illumination. After Hecker's death in 1888, a Paulist father, Walter Elliott, published a biography, *The Life of Father Hecker,* which praised his goals and methods highly. When it was translated into French in 1898, some European Catholics were upset. They found in the work evidence that the liberal soil of the New World was nourishing a break from Catholic traditions. The upshot was a clash, or at least the appearance of a clash, between Pope Leo XIII and leaders of the American hierarchy.

That hierarchy had come to include capable spokesmen arguing that the Church was compatible with American patterns of life. Among its leading representatives were bishops John Ireland and James Gibbons, whose careers illustrate the way in which leading Catholics were attempting to retain a balance between fidelity to their inherited faith and sensitivity to the American situation. John Ireland (1838-1918) was the influential archbishop of St. Paul, Minnesota, who spent his active life campaigning for full Catholic participation in American education, politics, and society. Born in Ireland, the archbishop maintained a lifelong commitment to aiding the immigrants and laborers whose experiences in the New World matched those of his own family. Ireland aligned himself with other "Americanizing" leaders against German, Polish, and conservative Irish Catholics who wanted to see a European-style Catholicism established in the United States. With the other "Americanists," Ireland argued for strong Catholic education in both public schools and a separate parochial system. He supported the Catholic University of America but also took an active interest in public higher education. He urged American Catholics to be active in politics. Unlike many of his fellow religionists, he leaned toward the Republican party, in large measure so that the Democrats would not take the immigrant Catholic vote for granted. His enthusiasm for America led him to work with the railroads in bringing immigrants to the upper Midwest. He summed up his feelings on the place of Catholics in the United States with these words in 1894: "there is no conflict between the Catholic Church and America. . . . The principles of the Church are in thorough harmony with the interests of the Republic."

James Gibbons (1834-1921), Archbishop of Baltimore, was an even more influential figure. The great burden of Gibbons's career was to bring Catholic practice into the mainstream of American life without at the same time forsaking traditional Catholic teaching. Gibbons, as archbishop of the leading archdiocese in America and after 1886 a cardinal, was known as a liberal because of his views on the church-state issue. Unlike traditionalists, he thought Catholics could flourish in a society without the official support of the government. Gibbons was the son of immigrants from Ireland; he spent much of his active life exploring ways to assimilate Catholic immigrants into American society as well as into the Church. Much of his effort was spent in rebutting the virulent anti-Catholic opposition to the new waves of immigration. His willingness to support "American" reforms such as prohibition and to cooperate on a limited basis with Protestants earned

James Cardinal Gibbons was the best-known and most influential prelate of the Roman Catholic Church in the United States during the last decades of the nineteenth century. His shrewd handling of the "Americanist" controversy satisfied both Europeans nervous about American innovations and Americans eager to establish their own style in the New World. *Library of Congress*

him the scorn of conservatives. Yet his own works, such as *The Faith of Our Fathers* (1877), presented traditional Catholic doctrine in a winsome, attractive way.

European responses to Elliott's biography of Hecker precipitated a widely publicized exchange between Rome and leading bishops including Gibbons and Ireland. In 1895, Pope Leo XIII addressed American Catholics in an encyclical, *Longinqua Oceani*, which praised them for what they had accomplished in the New World but also cautioned against making American church-state relations the norm for all places. Four years later he issued another encyclical, *Testem Benevolentiae*, in which he attacked notions alleged to have been spread abroad in America, such as the idea that church teaching may be altered in order to accommodate to special local conditions. Leo said that if American Catholics did indeed teach certain doctrines — such as that the Church should "show some indulgence to modern popular theories" or that more freedom should be given to individual interpretations — they must stop.

Conservative Catholics in America and in Europe were satisfied that the pope had put an end to dangerous experimentation. For his part, Cardinal Gibbons responded in a famous letter of March 17, 1899, saying that American Catholics were in fact loyal children of the Roman Church and that no such heresies as the pope described were tolerated in America.

Confusion reigned for a brief period. No American Roman Catholics left the Church specifically over this controversy, although it did lead to extra caution on the part of such leaders as Gibbons and Ireland in their efforts to promote Roman Catholic traditions in America.

Growing Maturity

The maturation of Catholicism in America can be measured in two seemingly contrasting areas: the development of spirituality and expertise in politics. In different ways, their growth in both these areas testified to the way in which Catholics were becoming at home in America.

The development of New World spirituality naturally drew on Old World models. Yet by the 1870s and 1880s, American Catholics were making distinctive contributions of their own in promoting the specifically Christian sensibility of their adherents. A leader in this effort was John Joseph Keane (1839-1918), who became the first rector of the Catholic University of America. Before being named to that post, he had served as Bishop of Richmond, in which position he had designed special exercises of devotion to the Holy Spirit. The "Confraternity of the Servants of the Holy Ghost" that he organized, along with the book he wrote to assist the worshipers, eventually encouraged more than a thousand Richmond parishioners to join regularly throughout the year to celebrate the Third Person of the Trinity. The materials Keane prepared included hymns, readings from Scripture, and prayers centered on the seven gifts of the Holy Spirit — wisdom, understanding, counsel, fortitude, knowledge, piety, and the fear of the Lord. Protestants would not mistake these Catholic liturgical materials for their own. But for those with eyes to see — even at a time when Catholic-Protestant strife remained high — it was evident that American Catholics were making signal contributions to the internal stability of faith as well as its external struggle to survive.

The political sphere was another arena in which Catholics negotiated to bring Old World habits into line with New World circumstances. Protestant fear that Catholics would ignore the separation of church and state now seems adventitious, for Protestants had themselves worked out innumerable informal arrangements to exert their will on the body politic. Yet with Catholics largely aligned on the side of the Democratic party and with the manifest authority given to bishops in classical Roman teaching, Protestants continued to worry that the influx of Catholic immigrants would poison the political system. Catholics had their most persistent difficulties when they asked for equal time in the public schools, where Protestant

Bishop John Joseph Keane was equally adept as an administrator and a promoter of Roman Catholic spiritual life. *Archives of the University of Notre Dame*

prayers, Protestant moral sensibilities, and the use of Protestant biblical translations were usually taken for granted. Parochial schools were part of the Catholic answer, but so was a never-ending series of delicate negotiations between bishops and political leaders. Protestant zealots were ever at hand to pounce on situations, especially in the cities of the East and Midwest, in which Catholic leaders exerted a public influence. But as the years passed, the exercise of that influence was honed to an art.

At the same time, important Catholic leaders took care to warn off the faithful from indiscriminately mixing religion and politics and to reassure Americans at large of the Catholic eagerness to adjust to American ways. That overarching purpose helps explain the wounded outcry of Bishop Bernard McQuaid of Rochester, New York, in 1894 after Archbishop John Ireland invaded his state to campaign on behalf of the Republican party. The campaign at issue was a curious one, for it concerned the legislature's election of regents to the board of the state university. Through understated, behind-the-scenes negotiations, McQuaid had positioned himself for one of these appointments. The line between exerting legitimate influence and shameless politicking was a fine one, but McQuaid thought Ireland had crossed it, and so he delivered a stinging rebuke: "I want it understood that it is the policy of the Catholic Church in this country that her bishops and priests should take no active part in political campaigns and contests; . . . that neither have any right to become tools or agents of any political party."

Stated principles were not the only thing that moderated the fears of those who worried about Catholic political power. The self-determination of Catholic politicians also played a role. During World War I, for instance, Boston's Cardinal William O'Connell was distressed about a proposed amendment to the state's constitution that prohibited public aid to religious institutions. To fellow Catholics in the state legislature, including John W. McCormack (later Speaker of the United States House of Representatives) and Martin Lomasney (the political boss of Boston's West End), O'Connell proclaimed that the proposal was a "gratuitous insult." In reply, Lomasney simply said, "tell His Eminence to mind his own business."

Catholic political engagement reached an institutional high point during the First World War, when a National Catholic Welfare Conference was established to coordinate the public services of the Church. This body subsequently evolved into the National Catholic Welfare Conference, which in 1966 became the National Conference of Catholic Bishops. It is one of the ironies of American religious history that in the nineteenth century Protestants feared Catholic political corruption, but in the twentieth century Catholics, through these national conferences, have sponsored some of the most responsible and most Christian commentary on the political, social, and economic life of the nation.

The maturation of Catholics in the United States has depended upon two changes. One was a change in Americans at large to accept, however grudgingly in some quarters, the Catholic Church as a rightful participant in American public life. This change has been substantially completed in the second half of the twentieth century. The second change, however, was internal. It involved the transformation of insular immigrant communities into a self-confident actor on the American stage. That was a change well under way by the early twentieth century.

A Changing Landscape

Numbers hide as much as they reveal, but the following census figures do reinforce the theme of this chapter. If during the two generations after the Civil War many Americans and foreign observers still thought of the United States as a white Protestant country of British heritage, they were not altogether wrong, even on demographic terms. But in the practical week-by-week participation of adherents in religious activities, the reality was changing steadily. Remembering that all figures for adherence to church and

Table 13.1 Proportions of Church Adherents in the United States, 1860-1926

	1860	1890	1906	1926
White Protestants of British Background	69.4%	52.7%	44.5%	42.7%
Roman Catholics	21.4	25.8	32.4	29.5
Black Methodists and Baptists	1.7	13.3	11.4	10.4
Lutherans	2.6	4.3	4.8	6.2
Jews	1.3	1.1	1.6	6.0
Eastern Orthodox	—	—	0.3	0.4

Sources:
Roger Finke and Rodney Stark, "Turning Pews into People: Estimating Nineteenth Century Church Membership," *Journal for the Scientific Study of Religion* 25 (1986): 180-92; Roger Finke, letter dated 19 April 1991; Edwin Scott Gaustad, *Historical Atlas of Religion in America*, rev. ed. (San Francisco: Harper & Row, 1976); Arthur A. Goren, "Jews," in *Harvard Encyclopedia of American Ethnic Groups*, ed. Stephan Thernstrom (Cambridge: Harvard University Press); United States Census reports for 1890, 1906, 1916, and 1926.

synagogue are at best rough estimates, Table 13.1 shows how the growing strength of non-British Protestants (e.g., Lutherans), nonwhite Protestants (especially black Methodists and Baptists), non-Protestant Christians (Roman Catholic as well as the Eastern Orthodox), and non-Christians (e.g., Jews) undermined the hereditary dominance of white Protestants of British background. For black Protestants, the three decades after the Civil War were critical for getting large-scale organization under way. For Lutherans, immigration from Germany and Scandinavia combined with natural increase to ensure steady growth throughout the period. For groups drawing strength from immigration, the breakthroughs came late in the nineteenth century and early in the twentieth century. From 1890 to 1906, for example, the number of Roman Catholics that were counted leaped from 6,241,000 to 12,079,000 (and these figures were probably low by 15 percent). The number of Eastern Orthodox found by the census takers in the same period went from 600 to 129,600. The number of Jews in the United States went from an estimated 700,000 in 1906 to over 4,100,000 in 1926.

Table 13.1 reports the percentage of church adherents in America belonging to major groupings. During the period from 1860 to 1926 (the year of the last satisfactory census of religious groups conducted by the federal government), the nation's population grew from 31,500,000 to over 117,000,000. In the earlier year about 37 percent of Americans were members of churches; by the latter year that figure stood at 58 percent. This rising rate of church affiliation indicates that the body of religious adherents other than white Protestants of British background was growing not just in absolute numbers but also at a faster pace than either the population at large or the total population of those who identified themselves as church adherents. Thus, although the estimated number of white Protestants of British background — Methodists, Baptists, Presbyterians, Episcopalians, Congregationalists, Disciples, and the like — grew over threefold from 1860 to 1926, from over 8,000,000 to nearly 30,000,000, their proportion in the churchgoing population declined from nearly 70 percent to considerably under 50 percent during this period.

Further Reading

Ewens, Mary. "The Leadership of Nuns in Immigrant Catholicism." In *Women and Religion in America*, Vol. 1, *The Nineteenth Century*. Edited by Rosemary Radford Ruether and Rosemary Skinner Keller. San Francisco: Harper & Row, 1981.

Farina, John. *An American Experience of God: The Spirituality of Isaac Hecker.* New York: Paulist, 1981.

Garrett, Paul D. "Eastern Christianity." In *Encyclopedia of the American Religious Experience*, vol. 1, ed. Charles H. Lippy and Peter W. Williams. New York: Scribner's, 1988.

Hennesey, James. "Roman Catholics and American Politics, 1900-1960." In *Religion and American Politics from the Colonial Period to the 1980s*. Edited by Mark A. Noll. New York: Oxford University Press, 1990.

Hopko, Thomas. *All the Fulness of God: Essays on Orthodoxy, Ecumenism and Modern Society.* Crestwood, NY: St. Vladimir's Seminary Press, 1982.

[Keane, John Joseph.] *Devotion to the Holy Spirit in American Catholicism.* Edited by Joseph P. Chinnici. New York: Paulist, 1985.

Lincoln, C. Eric, and Lawrence H. Mamiya. *The Black Church in the African American Experience.* Durham, NC: Duke University Press, 1990.

Mays, Benjamin E. *The Negro's God as Reflected in His Literature.* 1938; reprint, New York: Atheneum, 1973.

O'Connell, Marvin R. *John Ireland and the American Catholic Church.* St. Paul: Minnesota Historical Society, 1988.

Walker, Clarence E. *A Rock in a Weary Land: The African Methodist Episcopal Church during the Civil War and Reconstruction.* Baton Rouge: Louisiana State University Press, 1982.

Wills, David W. "Beyond Commonality and Plurality: Persistent Racial Polarity in American Religion and Politics." In *Religion and American Politics from the Colonial Period to the 1980s*. Edited by Mark A. Noll. New York: Oxford University Press, 1990.

CHAPTER 14

Protestantism Shaken

The Fullness of Pentecost

What is the fullness of true Pentecost —
    What does the Latter Rain bring?
Heart-thrilling moments of worship and praise
    Unto our glorious King!
Blessed revealings that God doth prepare
    Thus to unfold to His own;
Glimpses of Christ in His beauty most rare
    Unto our hearts clearly shown.
    Fullness of joy,
    Blessings untold —
    Jesus thy Lord
    Thus to behold.

      *   *   *   *   *

What of the fullness the Comforter brings
    To witness for God each day?
Emboldened like Peter, Christ's name to declare
    The Life, the Truth, and the Way.
The power Christ promised we thus may receive
    Anointed to sound His name;
To men of all nations and tribes and tongues
    His marvelous grace to proclaim.
    Spirit of God,
    This very hour
    Breathe upon us
    Fullness of pow'r!

As earlier in the history of Christianity, the emergence of powerful new move-ments was marked by an outburst of hymns. This one, by Alice Reynolds Flower from 1938, is representative of the many new songs that were written as part of the Pentecostal movement at the start of the twentieth century.

T HE CHANGE THAT WAS PERHAPS MOST TELLING FOR THE SORT OF WHITE Protestants that had dominated nineteenth-century religious life in the United States was a simple statistic. In 1870, 9,900,000 Americans (or 26 percent) lived in towns and cities with 2,500 people or more. By 1930, the absolute number had risen to 69,000,000 Americans and the national pro-portion to 56 percent. The shift in population to the cities did not mean that revivalistic, evangelical, voluntaristic Protestantism passed away. But it did mean that the small towns and rural settlements where Protestantism had dominated culture as well as provided the stuff of religious life were no longer as important in the nation as a whole. The urban environment provided more intense commercial pressure, greater access to higher edu-cation, and more opportunities for contact with representatives of diverse religious and ethnic groups — all of which worked in some degree to un-dermine the evangelical character of the national religion. Space in the cities for other forms of Christianity and for simple inattention to the faith stimu-lated the religious pluralism that had always been part of the American scene. It may have been that these sorts of social changes were the primary reasons for the shaking of white Protestantism in the period between the Civil War and World War I. But changes of this kind were also matched by intellectual dislocations that testified to the fragmentation of the Protestant Christianity that for a century or more had dominated public religion in the United States.

Intellectual Challenges

Intellectual challenges to the old Protestantism occurred in both form and content. Formal developments included the reshaping of American univer-sities in response to changing intellectual conventions abroad and changing demands for higher education at home. Shifts in content included the gathering momentum of new ideas that eventually made unbelief as respect-able as belief among the country's intellectual elite.

364

The New University

The modern American university was created in the decades after the Civil War. When the innovative Charles Eliot became president of Harvard in 1869, and when in 1876 the Johns Hopkins University was founded in Baltimore for the express purpose of providing specialized, graduate instruction on the model of the German seminar, the change had begun. In the generation that followed, important new universities (e.g., Stanford and the University of Chicago), the most substantial older colleges (e.g., Yale, Princeton, and Columbia), and many of the newer state universities (e.g., Michigan and Wisconsin) joined Harvard and Johns Hopkins in developing a new form of higher education.

Funding for the new universities was coming from new sources of influence in American society. The federal government made its first efforts to support higher education primarily in the form of land grants. But much more money, with many more strings attached, came from the nation's new class of fabulously wealthy entrepreneurs. Ezra Cornell (telegraph, banking), Johns Hopkins (banking, railroads), Cornelius Vanderbilt (steamships, railroads), Leland Stanford (railroads), James Duke (tobacco), and John D. Rockefeller (oil) were only a few of the prominent businessmen who poured vast sums into the creation of modern universities. These entrepreneurs were not paying for moral uplift but for the means to advance a vision of the good life that increasingly stressed the powers of free choice and the pleasures of personal consumption.

As more money came to the universities, so also did more students. Where less than 2 percent of the nation's eighteen- to twenty-one-year-olds attended college in 1870, the number had risen to over 12 percent by 1930.

Nearly unnoticed amid the great influx of dollars and students was the steady weakening of traditional Christian habits. At Harvard, for example, compulsory chapel came to an end in 1886. As money from businessmen increased, so also did the concern that boards of trustees and college administrators function in a businesslike way. So it was that businessmen replaced clergymen as trustees, and professional educators replaced ministers as presidents. In 1839, fifty-one of the fifty-four presidents of America's largest colleges were clergymen (forty either Presbyterian or Congregational). By 1900 that proportion was greatly reduced.

Another part of the academic revolution was the growing appeal of the German model of academic life. Education in America, as also in Britain, had traditionally stressed character formation. In the last half of the century, however, the German emphasis on specialized, advanced scholarship became increasingly attractive. Under the influence of the German model, the new

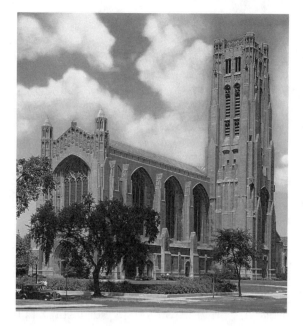

The Rockefeller Chapel at the University of Chicago is a monument to the generosity of the Rockefeller family to this one-time Baptist institution as well as evidence of the grip of an imagined gothic European past over the minds of America's rising wealthy classes.
University of Chicago Archives

university placed increasing stress on its freedom from petty sectarian control. Andrew Dickinson White, the founding president of Cornell University, promised that his institution would "afford an asylum for Science — where truth shall be sought for truth's sake, where it shall not be the main purpose of the Faculty to stretch or cut sciences exactly to fit 'Revealed Religion.'" White also wrote an influential book, *A History of the Warfare of Science with Theology in Christendom* (1895), in which he argued that organized Western religion had stymied the advance of science.

White's confidence in science was nearly unbounded. And it was widely shared. Many of America's new university leaders felt that by following its guidance they could escape the intellectual sterility of the traditional sects. And the champion of the new science, who seemed to embody everything positive in the disinterested pursuit of truth, was Charles Darwin. Darwin's *Origin of Species,* published in 1859, seemed to offer a model for rigorous, critical pursuits of all sorts. But Darwin's science, summarized recently as "a scientifically credible theory of random and purposeless change," sharply contradicted traditional intellectual habits in American intellectual life. In particular it seemed to call into question a treasured proof for God's existence, the Argument from Design. Protestant and Roman Catholic theologians alike had long argued that the world itself, with all its splendor and complexity, could not be explained except by the kind of creating and sustaining God of which the Bible spoke. Protestant educators in America

Early in the era of the fundamentalist-modernist controversy, evolution became an emotional symbol of all that the more conservative side felt was wrong with modern education as well as much else in American society. *Courtesy of the Billy Graham Center Museum*

ANOTHER PIED PIPER

for decades had grounded their religious instruction on the proposition that the Argument from Design showed that belief in God is intellectually as well as spiritually respectable. Especially as backed by the commonsense reasoning taught in the colleges, the Argument from Design had become a mainstay of American higher education.

When applied generally, the evolutionary perspective seemed even more devastating to traditional Christian beliefs. Darwin's British popularizers, including Herbert Spencer and Thomas Huxley, were suggesting that evolutionary theories could provide a whole philosophy of life. Humanity, in this view, was advancing from simpler to more complex tasks, from a primitive to a sophisticated state of existence. Christianity, in this reading, may have been helpful in aiding primitives to cope, but it was a primitive religion, and as such needed to be carefully reconsidered. In the American university, leaders such as the educationist and public philosopher John Dewey turned aside from the traditional effort to promote Christianity and a better society in tandem. They embraced instead the vision of a future ennobled by science. Historian Bruce Kuklick has well summarized that vision: "loyalty to science would enable human beings to achieve existential integration most adequately. Mankind would make its greatest advance when the scientific method was applied to questions of ethics. Control would grow ever more rich and complex. The quality of human experience would change for the better and, consequently, human selves also."

Such proposals were changing the intellectual environment for Christianity in America. As the dominant Protestant cultural consensus weakened, the universities were being reformed. The enthusiasm of their most visible leaders for the life of science was nearly religious. As the sociologist Edward Shils has suggested, "at a time of faltering theological conviction . . . the universities were able to become, in a sense, the heirs of the churches." That kind of transition took place only for selected audiences, and it was never a complete transition. But by altering the context in which Christian intellectual life took place, it decisively influenced the general climate for Christian faith.

Historical Criticism of Scripture

If general notions about science and evolution affected America's traditional higher education, specific proposals concerning the Bible seemed even more revolutionary. Much of the advanced scholarship from the Continent toward the end of the century seemed to undermine the hereditary confidence most American Christians had placed in the truthfulness of Scripture. (American Protestants had long been notorious for their inability to interpret the Bible in anything like a harmonious fashion, but before the 1870s only a very few believers of any sort had doubted the fact that, however interpreted, the Bible was true in largely commonsensical ways.) A rapid increase in knowledge about the ancient world was one of the factors that led some scholars to consider Christianity as merely one of the many similar religions of the ancient Near East. If other cultures had their stories about great floods or the appearance of gods on earth, why should Christianity be considered unique? An increased willingness to regard historical writing as a product of the historians' worldviews and habits of mind as well as of the actual events reported led other academics to question some or all of the miracle stories in the Bible. And advances in the study of ancient texts and their transmission convinced still other scholars that many writings in the Bible were actually composed, or at least collected, centuries later than Christians had traditionally thought was the case.

These new academic conclusions were, however, probably not the critical factor in promoting new approaches to Scripture. It was rather that the more general religious climate had changed in such a way as to provide an eager reception for such notions. As John Dillenberger and Claude Welch once put it, "the new conception of the Bible which came to characterize Protestant liberalism [did not originate] simply as a reaction to the discoveries of historical criticism. In fact, the situation was more nearly the reverse.

368

Leaders of Protestant fundamentalism worried about
the influence of new views
of Scripture that they sometimes associated with the
decadence of modern
German civilization.
*Courtesy of the Billy Graham
Center Museum*

The Critics: "Calm yourself, friend; we are only putting in a few new planks to make
her float better."

It was new conceptions of religious authority and the meaning of revelation
which made possible the development of biblical criticism." These new
conceptions transformed the Bible from an unquestioned foundation of
religious authority to a problem demanding increasing attention and gener-
ating increasing controversy.

Moderates, Mediators, and the Unexpected

Since the 1920s, strife among Protestants over how best to adjust to modern
life has been a permanent feature of the religious landscape. That fact,
however, has obscured the differences between the earliest responses to the
modernist challenge and the later responses. In fact, the first Protestant
adjustments to modern social conditions and modern critical ideas were
relatively trauma-free. The Protestant sea was not placid in the last third of
the nineteenth century, but neither was it roaring with wild storms, and
such squalls as did arise in the earlier period did not divide the waters in
ways that fit the stereotypes of the late twentieth century.

Attitudes to evolution provide an example. In the first decade and a
half after the publication of Darwin's *Origin of Species* in 1859, religious
leaders followed scientists in showing great skepticism toward the theory of

evolution by means of natural selection. Advanced thinkers such as Horace Bushnell joined conservatives such as Charles Hodge and moderates such as Phillips Brooks, a Boston Episcopalian with a nationwide reputation as preacher, author, and hymn-writer ("O Little Town of Bethlehem"), in rejecting the theory as an affront to moral sensibilities and theistic assumptions. On the other hand, the most notable early proponent of Darwin in America was Asa Gray, a Harvard botanist who insisted that evolutionary theory was in fact compatible with God's purposeful design of the universe as well as with orthodox, trinitarian Christianity. Gray once wrote that he was "scientifically, and in his own fashion, a Darwinian, philosophically a convinced theist, and religiously an acceptor of the 'creed commonly called the Nicene,' as the exponent of the Christian faith."

Later, as the scientific establishment gradually came around to accepting general evolutionary principles, Protestants began to divide among themselves. Charles Hodge considered the evolution that Darwin proposed to be "atheism" because, as Hodge read the *Origin* and Darwin's later *Descent of Man*, he found no allowance for divine purpose to control the physical world. Hodge spoke for a considerable body of those who rejected evolution for theological reasons of this sort, or simply because they could not square evolutionary notions with their reading of the book of Genesis. Far on the other side were thinkers who radically altered traditional Christian conceptions to fit an evolutionary model, but there were not too many of these until the twentieth century.

Much more common than either outright rejection of or outright capitulation to Darwinism were efforts to make minor adjustments to both received Christian thinking and popular conceptions of the cosmos. At Yale, for example, most of the leading academics during the the presidencies of Theodore Dwight Woolsey (1846-1871) and Noah Porter (1871-1886) saw themselves as evangelicals who were working to support both the advancement of religion and the morality of society. They did differ from earlier Yale generations in the extent to which they viewed themselves as practitioners of specific academic disciplines instead of clerical generalists concerned primarily about moral instruction. They also absorbed a great deal from the more conservative idealists in German universities and from contemporary English sentiments as represented by Thomas Arnold, famed headmaster at Rugby. But the major Yale scholars of the period — geologist J. D. Dana and historian G. P. Fisher, along with Woolsey and Porter — saw themselves as enlisting modern learning in support of Christian truth and social progress. At Princeton College in the same period, a similar influence was being exerted by James McCosh, a Scottish-born Presbyterian who served as president of the New Jersey college from 1868 to 1888. The source of McCosh's intellectual inspiration lay in Scottish developments in technical philosophy and practical Christian outreach. McCosh thought his primary purpose was to develop the Christian lives of his students in a context responsive to his own time. Thus, while he tried to make Princeton more professional by hiring well-trained academics, he also promoted campus revivals and even invited Moody and Sankey to campus in 1876. For our purposes, the most interesting aspect of the Yale and Princeton Protestants, however, was that both felt that a traditional Christian faith and a traditional belief in God's divine ordering of the world could be integrated with belief in some form of evolution.

The range of leaders who agreed was, again by late twentieth-century expectations, surprisingly wide. Benjamin B. Warfield (1851-1921) of Princeton Theological Seminary was the nation's most forceful defender of the Bible's "inerrancy" at the end of the nineteenth century. By inerrancy, Warfield meant that all of Scripture's statements were truthful if interpreted according to the sense in which the biblical authors had intended them. In 1881 Warfield wrote with his colleague A. A. Hodge that "the Scriptures not only contain, but ARE THE WORD OF GOD, and hence . . . all their elements and all their affirmations are absolutely errorless, and binding the faith and obedience of men." At the same time, however, Warfield also felt it was possible to show how such a view of the Bible could accommodate theories of evolution accounting for the development of all life, including humans. In 1888 he wrote, "I am free to say, for myself, that I do not think that there is any general statement in the Bible or any part of the account of creation, either as given in Gen. I & II or elsewhere alluded to, that need be opposed to evolution."

The themes advanced by McCosh, the Yale moderates, and Warfield were capable of endless variation. Individuals who tried, as these scholars had, to retain the hereditary faith with some admixture of modern elements did not necessarily agree among themselves, but they were the dominant theological voices at the turn of the century. For example, William G. T. Shedd (1820-1894), a Presbyterian who taught at Union Seminary in New York, defended the Calvinism of the Westminster Confession but also borrowed from Germany the idea that history develops organically rather than remaining static. Shedd also edited the complete works of England's Samuel Taylor Coleridge, an influence more often associated with liberal strands of nineteenth-century theology. The northern Baptist A. H. Strong (1836-1921) propounded an influential theology that combined traditional Reformed emphases, distinctive Baptist convictions about the organization of churches, and a relative openness to evolution and the higher criticism of Scripture. Charles A. Briggs (1841-1913), Shedd's successor at Union, accepted the findings of biblical higher criticism (and

371

B. B. Warfield, who taught theology at Princeton Theological
Seminary for thirty-five years, is
shown here shortly before his
death in 1921. Warfield was the
last of a long line of academic
Calvinist theologians who, with
varying shades of opinion, had
dominated formal theology in
America since the time of the
Puritans. *Courtesy of the Billy
Graham Center Museum*

so won the wrath of B. B. Warfield) and also proposed other modifications
to the Presbyterians' traditional Calvinism (and so was forced out of that
denomination). Yet after the passage of a few years, Briggs's defense of the
supernatural in Christianity as well as of the Bible's general authority, even
when understood with the new criticism, made him look more, rather than
less, like the conservative foes of his early public life. The Southern Baptist
Edgar Youngs Mullins (1860-1928) guided his denomination in drafting a
conservative confession in 1925 and steered it away from evolution. But
Mullins also defined Christian life in terms of experience rather than
doctrine, a move associated since the beginning of the nineteenth century
with Friedrich Schleiermacher, who is often called the father of modern
Protestant liberalism.

The differences among such theologians were considerable. But what
they displayed in common, even when expounding their differences, was a
Protestantism still bearing the marks of the nineteenth century — conserving as much or more than innovating, concerned to accommodate (or at
least consider fully) the latest advances in general learning, willing to employ
combinations of theological resources that by the next century became
incompatible, and writing their theologies to guide general culture as well
as simply the church.

At least into the early twentieth century, therefore, leading Protestant theologians largely took the new learning in stride. Their responses were not necessarily predictable by the canons that have come to dominate American religion in the twentieth century. At the same time, the new learning did disrupt the settled relationship between evangelical Protestantism and the nation's intellectual life, and that for several reasons. It ended Protestant control of American higher education. It opened the doorway to secular interpretations of life especially by creating a possibility that had not existed before — a willingness by some intellectuals to question the very existence of God. And it did act in different ways upon Protestants. The effect on the latter was to produce diverging forms of theology which, if they were not as prominent as the mediating varieties that developed during the late nineteenth century, created the backdrop for disruptive differences in the twentieth century.

The Disruption of Protestant Theology

In the unfolding of the twentieth century, two poles of Protestant theology did emerge as striking opposites. These divergent extremes have been called "modernist" and "fundamentalist." The two names speak for a great divide, but they also mask significant similarities between the two. Both parties grew out of American Protestant experience. Both, after the fashion of the nineteenth century, hoped to arbitrate for American society as a whole. Both made a very great deal of how the best forms of science supported their positions. And each felt that the other was damaging the defense of the faith in the modern world.

Yet if modernists and fundamentalists drew on common habits of mind, their division was still very real on its own terms. Public contentions over the nature of the faith represented a divide in the stream of nineteenth-century Protestantism that has not yet been repaired. It was also one of the key factors that ended the Protestant hegemony that representatives of both parties were struggling to preserve.

Modernism

Modernists were Protestants who felt that it was necessary for the Christian faith to adjust self-consciously to the norms defining modern culture. They believed that God is best understood as working *within* human societies, and so they were convinced that the evolving shape of modern life as well as the developments in learning conveyed the realization of God's work in the world. Thinkers of this sort drew some inspiration from the theology of Horace Bushnell, who, as we have seen, had held that the traditional language of Scripture and the Christian creeds was closer to poetry than to precisely descriptive language. Bushnell had wished to revise traditional doctrines into language that emphasized intuition, human potential, social progress, and the redemptive potential of the world. In his own times these ideas had attracted more opposition than support, but by the end of the century there were many who followed in his train.

Theodore Munger (1830-1910), for example, was a Congregationalist pastor who served churches in New England and, for a brief period, California. Munger championed the idea that modern views amounted to revisions rather than rejections of older truths. He felt that it should be possible to see Christian faith and the laws of nature coming together into one form of truth. On this basis, old Christian doctrines such as "reconciliation" and "atonement" began to take on new meanings, involved much more with the divine development of the human spirit than with supernatural or juridical views of God's activity over against humanity. This "New Theology," as it was called, gave modern reason a more central role in religion, since, as Munger put it, it was reason that would "replace the excessive individuality of the old theology by a truer view of the solidarity of the race."

Modernism won its most important victories in centers of higher learning rather than in the churches, where a moderate conservatism tended to prevail throughout the early twentieth century. Arthur Cushman McGiffert (1861-1933), professor of church history and then president of Union Seminary in New York, exemplified the academic trajectory of much modernist thought. He had studied with the famed Adolph Harnack in Germany before returning to a teaching career in the United States. Out of his German training and his own theological predilections, he stressed three matters in his teaching: the centrality of the life of Christ, a commitment to "scientific history," and an allegiance to social ethics. According to McGiffert, Jesus possessed "a vivid realization of God as his father and the father of his brethren." On the other hand, he stated that the apostle Paul had propounded ideals "totally at variance with Christ's." It was Paul who founded historic Christianity, a movement distorted by its overemphasis on the divinity of Christ and the institutional prerogatives of the church. Now, however, with a scientific form of academic inquiry that concentrated on natural means of historical explanation, McGiffert thought it was possible to recover the essence of Christian faith as service to humanity in imitation of Christ's own virtues. Such teachings marked McGiffert as a leader of

Shailer Mathews was dean of the Divinity School at the University of Chicago for twenty-five years in the early part of the twentieth century. As a teacher and writer, he was one of the most popular voices calling for Christianity to be adjusted to "modern" views of science, society, and human learning. *University of Chicago Archives*

liberal Protestantism but also led to his being forced out of the Presbyterian Church.

The University of Chicago was an even more influential center of modernist thought than Union Seminary. At Chicago, Shailer Mathews (1863-1941) was the key figure for several decades. Mathews's book *The Faith of Modernism* (1924) was the most widely distributed statement of this new reading of Christian faith. Mathews made clear in this volume and elsewhere that he valued classical Christian faith with its proclamation of Jesus as Savior, the human need for salvation, the continuation of life after death, and the Bible as a complete record of revelation. Yet given the great changes that had come over the Western world in the preceding century, Mathews felt that these hereditary Christian doctrines needed to be reinterpreted and reapplied if Christianity were to survive. In short, his work was an effort to recover the power of Christianity in a changing intellectual world. Mathews heaped scorn on fundamentalists because, as he saw it, they simply parroted old slogans in the face of compelling new conditions. "The world needs new control of nature and society and is told that the Bible is verbally inerrant," he wrote. "It needs a means of composing class strife, and is told to believe in the substitutionary atonement. . . . It needs faith in the divine presence in human affairs and is told it must accept the virgin birth of Jesus Christ." Mathews insisted that the untapped potential of Christianity lay in providing a moral basis for reconciling modern strife, both social and intellectual.

Modernism has had a long-lasting influence on the academic study of religion. Especially its desire to translate the dogmatic and sectarian elements of classical Christian faith into more generic religious terms has set an important precedent for study of religion in colleges and universities. Modernism had less impact among the church-going population, although its promotion of the Social Gospel helped keep alive a concern for social reconciliation in the large Protestant denominations of the North. Ironically, modernists may have had the greatest impact on their polar opposites, the fundamentalists, who were intensely preoccupied with the effort to refute modernist reinterpretations of the faith.

Fundamentalism and the Rise of Dispensational Theology

Fundamentalist responses to altered American conditions, and specifically to modernism, ranged across a broad spectrum. A few of the fundamentalist leaders, such as J. Gresham Machen (1881-1937), argued their case in the academy. Machen was a New Testament scholar who taught at Princeton Seminary before establishing Westminster Theological Seminary in Philadelphia in 1929 to provide an alternative to the increasingly inclusive stance at Princeton. In his major polemical work, *Christianity and Liberalism* (1923), he made the case that the theological changes proposed by such modernists as A. C. McGiffert and Shailer Mathews changed the inherited faith so radically as to make up a new religion. With this and other works, Machen won the respect of secular intellectuals such as H. L. Mencken and Walter Lippmann, but he did not win over the modernists.

A much broader range of conservative Protestants, though respecting efforts like Machen's to defend classical orthodoxy, turned to a newer theological expression with which to absorb the shocks of the times. This new theology was premillennial dispensationalism, which, figuratively speaking, dug in its heels at every point against the new ideas of the academy. Dispensationalism arose in modern form from the work of John Nelson Darby (1800-1882), an Anglican minister who left the Church of Ireland to help found the movement that eventually came to be known as the Plymouth Brethren. The theology that he promoted divided the teaching of the Bible into separate dispensations, in each of which God is said to act from common principles but with varying mandates. Prophecy also features large in

John Nelson Darby *(above left)*, who had been a minister in the Church of Ireland before helping to found the Plymouth Brethren movement in Great Britain, was a world traveler who promoted a dispensationalist understanding of Scripture. Cyrus I. Scofield *(above right)* became the most influential promoter of dispensational theology in the early twentieth century with the publication of the Scofield Reference Bible. *Both portraits courtesy of the Billy Graham Center Museum*

dispensationalism, especially the effort to perceive the divine plan for the End of the Age. Dispensationalists feel that promises made to the Hebrews of the Old Testament were not realized in the history of the church as had been commonly held but have yet to be fulfilled. The period between the age of the apostles and the End is "the church age," a historical parenthesis in which believers are to evangelize, separate from ungodliness, and prepare for the return of Christ.

Partially as a result of the influence of Darby, who traveled considerably in the United States and Canada, but also as a result of a widespread desire to understand the subject better, major conferences examining the Bible's teachings on end times took place in the late 1880s. The emphasis on eschatology may be seen as a natural culmination of concern for the return of Christ that had been prominent in various ways throughout Protestant history. It may also have been a defensive reaction to an implicit realization that American culture was slipping away from evangelical Protestant control. Those who attended these conferences generally held a premillennial view of Christ's second coming, or the belief that Christ would return before establishing a literal thousand-year reign of righteousness on the earth. Not all the premillennialists at these conferences or among later Protestants were dispensationalists, for dispensationalists stressed more literal interpretations of the Bible and sharper divisions between periods of history than did other Protestants who shared a conservative attitude toward the Bible.

The most influential formulation of dispensational teaching appeared in 1909 when the Oxford University Press published a Bible annotated by C. I. Scofield (1843-1921). Scofield, a lawyer before becoming a Congregational minister, had undertaken a long period of private study in preparing this edition of the Scriptures, which he intended as a portable guide for missionaries more than as a polished theological system. The impact of the Scofield Reference Bible (published in a revised edition in 1967) has extended well beyond the early centers of dispensationalism to influence a wide spectrum of American Protestants. Dispensationalism, with its great stress on biblical prophecy that has not yet been fulfilled, has remained a potent force in American religious life. In fact, the best-selling book of any sort published in the United States in the decade of the 1970s was a popular dispensational description of the end of the world, *The Late Great Planet Earth* by Hal Lindsey. For the purposes of understanding the late nineteenth century, however, dispensationalism was most important as a theological system that provided some beleaguered Protestants with intellectual ballast in the turbulent seas of modern thought.

Holiness

A counterpart in spirituality to the theology of dispensationalism was provided by a group of related movements among more conservative Protestants known as Victorious Living, the Keswick Higher Life movement, and a variety of other names. The renewed emphasis on holiness of life took many forms. Among Methodists, ecclesiastical separations had occurred throughout the nineteenth century when dissident groups such as the Free and Wesleyan Methodists felt that John Wesley's teaching on Christian perfection was being neglected. The National Campmeeting Association for the Promotion of Christian Holiness, which was formed in 1867 by John S. Inskip and several associates after a successful gathering in Vineland, New Jersey, nurtured holiness expectations among a large but mostly Methodist constituency.

Toward the end of the nineteenth century a resurgence of concern for the doctrines and practices of holiness led to significant breakaway movements from the main Methodist bodies. Methodists who continued to pro-

Like many other new Christian movements before its day (and like the early
Methodist movement after which it was patterned), the Church of the
Nazarene began in humble settings and among ordinary folk.
Courtesy of the Billy Graham Center Museum

mote the possibility of entire sanctification and who looked for a distinct
second work of grace after conversion sponsored a wide variety of camp
meetings, mission initiatives, orphanages, and independent churches. Under
the leadership of Daniel Sidney Warner, the denomination now known as
the Church of God, Anderson, Indiana, broke from the main denomination
in 1881. Phineas F. Bresee (1838-1916), who had been a Methodist minister,
was the first of the holiness advocates to use the name Church of the
Nazarene when in 1895 he organized an independent congregation in Los
Angeles. Soon others from mostly Methodist backgrounds who, like Bresee,
emphasized the direct work of the Holy Spirit moved to create a national
organization. The result was the Pentecostal Church of the Nazarene, organized in 1907. After absorbing other groups with similar aims and after
dropping the name "Pentecostal" in 1919 (Nazarenes do not practice
tongues-speaking), the Church of the Nazarene became a leading institutional proponent of distinctively holiness teachings.

The desire "to lay all on the altar," to be "clay in the potter's hands,"
to experience a "deeper work of grace," a "closer walk" with Christ, the

Among the numerous regional painters who in the early twentieth century drew religious scenes, John Stewart Curry was one of the best. This cartoon-like drawing is of an early holiness or Pentecostal service. *Courtesy of the Billy Graham Center Museum*

"baptism of the Holy Ghost," a "higher life," "victorious living," or "overcoming power" extended far beyond the Nazarenes. Among those of Baptist or Presbyterian background, the holiness impulse did not usually entail belief in a conclusive postconversion experience. But the concern for inner peace and a tangible experience of God drew a wide circle of American Protestants to such teachings. Summer conferences, networks of holiness periodicals, and classic books such as Hannah Whitall Smith's *The Christian's Secret of a Happy Life* (1875) were potent substitutes for more formal ties. In individual denominations as more generally throughout American Protestantism, holiness teachings exerted a wide sway.

As with dispensationalism, the holiness surge at the end of the nineteenth century may be regarded from two perspectives. In one sense, it simply represented another stage in the development of a spirituality that can be traced back through the efforts of Mrs. Phoebe Palmer and the revivalist Charles Finney, the rigorous spirituality of David Brainerd, and the arduous piety of the Puritans to more general founts of mysticism in the medieval and early church. But in another sense, the new emphasis on holiness may have been a way of adjusting to the shifting character of

American religious life — or as historian Douglas Frank has recently put it, "a certain partial letting go of temporal history and a disillusionment with American history in particular" in order to seek "perfect victory centered in a subjective inner kingdom."

Whatever the correct interpretation, proponents of holiness as well as proponents of dispensationalism were making their own adjustments to the tide of American religious life as Protestant modernists had in their way. Although the two movements had different origins, their themes, promoters, and expressions soon overlapped considerably. More than the modernists, the dispensationalists and those in the holiness movements retained the nineteenth century's populist orientation, its commonsense biblicism, and its revivalistic fervor even as they worked out their innovations in Christian life and thought.

Fundamentalist-Modernist Controversy

Discontent among white Protestants with the course of American civilization came to a head early in the twentieth century in a movement known as fundamentalism. The phrase itself came into prominence first when a widely circulated set of booklets called *The Fundamentals: A Testimony to the Truth* were published between 1910 and 1915. They contained nearly one hundred articles by leading evangelicals. Together they defended the "fundamentals," or basics, of the faith that newer forms of thought had recently called into question, among them assertions that the Bible is the inspired Word of God; that Jesus Christ was God in human flesh, was born of a virgin, lived a sinless life, died on the cross for the salvation of men and women, rose from the dead, ascended into heaven, and would return at the end of the age in great glory; that sin is real and not the product of fevered imaginations; that God's grace and not human effort is the source of salvation; and that the church is God's institution designed to build up Christians and to spread the gospel.

Authors of the articles included some of the leading theological conservatives from the start of the twentieth century: Scottish theologian James Orr, Princeton Presbyterian B. B. Warfield, Anglican bishop H. C. G. Moule, American dispensationalist C. I. Scofield, evangelist R. A. Torrey, and Southern Baptist scholar E. Y. Mullins. There were considerable differences among these figures on how to interpret the Bible and define the Christian life, but on the whole they set aside these differences in order to publish *The Fundamentals*. Dispensationalists and confessional Calvinists, ecclesiastical separatists and loyal denominationalists, advocates of holiness and those wary

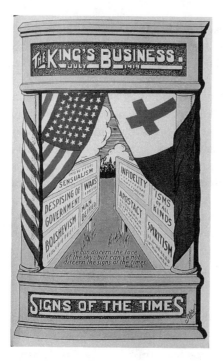

One of the things marking the outbreak of the religious conflict that later came to be known as the fundamentalist-modernist controversy was a growing uneasiness about larger trends in national and religious life. Here a proto-fundamentalist periodical, *The King's Business*, provides a succinct statement of what it felt was wrong with religion in America.
Biola University Archives

of holiness themes all cooperated in this venture as a conserving response to the day's theological challenges. Although hundreds of thousands of the booklets were distributed, their greatest effect may have been to give later historians a useful signpost for what would come. The *Fundamentals* do not seem to have generated a great deal of discussion in academic circles. Some of their authors, such as Scotland's Orr and Princeton's Warfield, tolerated an openness to evolution that would later become anathema among self-designated "fundamentalists." And although some of the essays were vigorously combative, others were much more moderate in tone.

A more sharply defined movement arose shortly after the publication of *The Fundamentals*, especially among northern Baptists and Presbyterians. This fundamentalism, defined by its premier historian, George Marsden, as "militantly anti-modernist Protestant evangelicalism," was a selective continuation of nineteenth-century themes. Revivalist elements were most obvious, but important too were beliefs in the inerrancy of Scripture, a premillennial eschatology, conventions of Victorian morality, and the epistemology of common-sense philosophy. World War I, with its attendant sense of crisis about the fate of Western civilization, mobilized the movement and gave it its initial energy. The term *fundamentalist* itself was coined by Baptist editor Curtis Lee Laws in 1920 as a designation for those who were ready "to do battle royal for the Fundamentals." Laws later called fundamentalism "a protest against that rationalistic interpretation of Christianity which seeks to discredit supernaturalism." Fundamentalists were in fact distinguished at the time from other theological conservatives, often espousing European confessional traditions, who did not sense the same crisis of civilization and who were protected within ethnic or sectarian borders from the troubling changes of modern conditions.

Those who spearheaded the fundamentalist movement, however, felt that the time for action had come. Presbyterian spokesmen such as J. Gresham Machen and the populist William Jennings Bryan (who in the 1920s took a growing interest in the politics of his denomination) along with Baptist leaders such as Laws, William Bell Riley of Minneapolis, and John Roach Straton of New York City agreed that theological indifferentism or outright modernism had gone too far. In particular they were deeply offended by the efforts of moderate or liberal Protestants to promote wholesale accommodation to the newer shapes of modern learning.

The fundamentalists who battled liberals and moderates in the 1920s had an ambiguous attitude toward the United States. Sometimes they spoke of it as "Babylon," far gone in its sins. Sometimes it was "God's New Israel," still at least potentially a light to the nations. Often in the 1920s fundamentalists affirmed both. In this regard, William Jennings Bryan's emergence as a fundamentalist spokesman in the 1920s makes a great deal of sense. In his person Bryan embodied a link with nineteenth-century efforts to establish a Christian America. Bryan's campaign against evolution, which in 1925 culminated in his celebrated clash with Clarence Darrow at the Scopes Trial in Dayton, Tennessee, was not so much a fight against new ideas itself as it was a fight against what he and other fundamentalists felt the new ideas were doing to destroy the nation's Christian heritage.

For their part, leaders in the churches who opposed the fundamentalist movement often minced no words in expressing that opposition. The best example of such speaking out was provided by the Baptist minister Harry Emerson Fosdick (1878-1969). Fosdick was probably the nation's best-known preacher between Dwight L. Moody and Billy Graham. He had been educated at Colgate University and Union Seminary, where he came under the influence of liberal theologians W. Newton Clark and A. C. McGiffert. Fosdick enhanced an already broad fame when on May 22, 1922, as supply preacher for New York City's First Presbyterian Church, he delivered a sermonic challenge entitled "Shall the Fundamentalists Win?"

When this sermon was quickly distributed throughout the country to 130,000 ordained Protestants by Ivy Lee, an associate of John D. Rockefeller,

In his later years as a New York City pastor and professor at Union Theological Seminary, Harry Emerson Fosdick was the best-known preacher in America. Much beloved by his parishioners and many who read his books or heard him on the radio, he was also feared and despised by fundamentalists and other doctrinal Protestant conservatives. *Courtesy of the Billy Graham Center Museum*

Jr., it created a sensation. The sermon's message was, by that date, not unusual from moderate or liberal voices: Christianity did not need the intolerance of the fundamentalists but rather the tolerance of diverse belief practiced by enlightened modernists. Fosdick had experienced some of the theological tensions of his era firsthand in New York, he was kept abreast of strains among both Baptists and Presbyterians through a far-flung correspondence, and he had traveled to the Far East in an effort (vain, as it turned out) to mediate disputes between contending theological parties among the American missionaries. His sermon, coming as it did from a person of his stature, ignited an extended controversy.

In the wake of controversy, Fosdick left the Presbyterians for good but went on to even greater eminence as a national radio preacher and as minister of the Riverside Church in New York City, which was established through the munificence of the Rockefellers. Among the Presbyterians, as among the northern Baptists at just about the same time, inclusivists, who wanted a range of opinions in their denominations, triumphed over the stricter conservatives. The inclusivists can best be regarded as moderates who preferred peaceful coexistence to theological battle. Their victories did establish a measure of harmony, but they also rendered theology considerably less important than it had traditionally been in these northern denominations.

The more militant conservatives considered a willingness to coexist with modernists as tantamount to promoting modernism, and so could not remain. In 1932 the General Association of Regular Baptists was formed as a separate denomination at the last gathering of the Baptist Bible Union, a fundamentalist advocacy group set up within the Northern Baptist Convention only ten years before. In 1936, Presbyterian dissidents under J. Gresham Machen formed an alternative church. The next year these Presbyterian militants, who would not compromise with modernism, found it impossible to compromise with themselves and so divided into two groups that came to be known as the Orthodox Presbyterian Church and the Bible Presbyterian Church. The former represented efforts to preserve a confessional Calvinism, the latter a desire to season modern Calvinism with premillennialism, the prohibition of alcohol, and other more American emphases.

Theological debates among Baptists and Presbyterians in the 1920s had larger and more lasting consequences than might at first appear possible. In practical terms they were an occasion for weakening the position of these denominations in national religious life. Although the cause-and-effect connections are not exact, debates within these groups also had something to do with the increasing propensity of fundamentalists and other nay-sayers to form independent churches. After the 1920s, the number of such churches grew rapidly in the North and, after a few decades, in the South as well.

Outside the churches, the fundamentalist-modernist debates eroded the general influence of Protestantism in American life. The white Protestant phalanx, which had exerted a shaping national influence for much of American history, was no more. Historian Martin Marty has perceptively summarized the situation with these words: "what had come of the conflict of the twenties was a deeply, permanently divided Protestantism. . . . Original-stock Protestantism — from which both sides derived — no longer presented a single front. . . . They were splitting up what was left of a Protestant establishment, leaving it ever less prepared to hold its place of dominance in American culture in the decades to come." It may in fact have been a blessing for Christianity itself that such influence waned, but at the time it was a blessing very much in disguise.

Inside the churches, fundamentalist-modernist strife had a more unambiguously evil effect. The debate left a distortion in Christian self-understanding that has not yet gone away. After the mid-twenties, theological discussion between Protestants in the marketplace of American religion has regularly had a self-defeating character. Those who protest the errors of modernism and attack the intellectual environment in which inclusivism was at home have been pushed toward sectarian and anti-intellectual affirmations of faith for fear of being labeled modernists. On the other hand, inclusivists, moderates, and liberals who scorn sectarianism and the populist environment in which Protestant anti-intellectualism flourishes have been pushed toward expansive and barely Christian definitions of the faith for fear of being labeled fundamentalists. Of the many disquieting legacies of fundamentalist-modernist strife, this is the worst.

Pentecostalism: A New Departure

Meanwhile, events that in hindsight loom as important as the theological pugilism among northern Baptists and Presbyterians were taking place out of the glare of national publicity. These events included the traumas of assimilation among immigrant groups and the portentous beginnings of modern Pentecostalism.

In 1906 an abandoned Methodist church at 312 Azusa Street in the industrial section of Los Angeles became the cradle for this new movement. William J. Seymour (1870-1922), a mild-mannered black holiness preacher, founded the Apostolic Faith Gospel Mission on Azusa Street, where a new emphasis on the work of the Holy Spirit rapidly became a local sensation that eventually gave birth to a worldwide phenomenon. Before coming to Los Angeles, Seymour had been guided by the ministry of Charles Fox Parham (1873-1929), who in his Methodist and holiness upbringing had been influenced by teaching that stressed the work of the Holy Spirit. In his schools in Kansas and Texas, Parham taught that a baptism of "the Holy Ghost and fire" should be expected among those who had been converted and who had gone onward to the perfect sanctification that holiness advocates proclaimed. Parham also pioneered the teaching that a special sign of the Holy Spirit baptism would be "speaking with other tongues." With many in the Methodist and holiness traditions at the end of the nineteenth century, he also placed a stronger emphasis generally on the gifts of the Spirit, including the gift of healing.

The revival that began on Azusa Street in 1906 rapidly attracted attention from the secular media, including the *Los Angeles Times*. It was marked by fervent prayer, speaking in tongues, earnest new hymns such as the one quoted at the start of this chapter, and healing of the sick. One of its most prominent features was the full participation of women in public activities. In an America that still took racial barriers for granted, Azusa Street was also remarkable for the striking way in which blacks and whites joined to participate in its nightly meetings. Soon the Azusa Street chapel became a mecca for thousands of visitors from around the world, who often went back to their homelands proclaiming the need for a special postconversion baptism of the Holy Spirit. These included Florence Crawford, founder of

In this humble structure, the Azusa Street Mission (shown here circa 1906) began the Pentecostal movement that has since spread throughout the whole world. *Assemblies of God Archives*

the "Apostolic Faith" movement in the northwestern United States; missionary T. B. Barratt, who is credited with the establishment of Pentecostalism in Scandinavia and northwestern Europe; William H. Durham of Chicago, early spokesman for Pentecostalism in the Midwest; and Eudorus N. Bell of Fort Worth, first chairman of the Assemblies of God. From a welter of new alliances, networks of periodicals, and circuits of preachers and faith-healers, the Assemblies of God, established in 1914, emerged as the largest Pentecostal denomination.

Denominational concerns were not priorities in the early years of the Pentecostal movement, however. Later observers have noted that Pentecostalism spread most rapidly among self-disciplined, often mobile folk of the middle and lower-middle classes. But an ardent desire for the unmediated experience of the Holy Spirit was a still more universal characteristic of those who became Pentecostals. The testimony of teenager Alice Reynolds concerning what happened in Indianapolis on Easter Sunday 1907 pointed to the kind of experience that made the movement:

> The warmth of God's presence in that service deeply moved me, until there was a complete melting of the reserve that had held me back from a full surrender to God. . . . Spontaneously I rose to my feet, lifting my hands with a glad note of praise, "Thank God for the baptism of the Holy Spirit; praise, O praise the Lord!" . . . As this praise came from my lips, for the first time in my life I felt the physical manifestation of God's power all through my being, and I sank to the floor. God's day of Pentecost had come to a hungry teenager. . . . In a few moments my jaws began to tremble, and the praise that was literally flooding my soul came forth in languages I had never known.

Observers at the time linked Azusa Street with the great Welsh Revival of 1904 and 1905 and the "Latter Rain" movement that had pockets of influence throughout the United States. Today it symbolizes the inaugural dynamism of the fastest growing movement in the Christian world.

In the first decade of the century, however, events at Azusa Street and in the midwestern church where Alice Reynolds testified to the baptism of the Holy Spirit seemed much less important than the well-publicized doings of the major white denominations. Yet over the course of time, the impact of those denominations, weakened by internal strife and uncertain about how best to find their way in the larger culture, declined, while the influence of sectarian movements such as Pentecostalism increased. Shifting currents in the early twentieth century left white Protestantism no less vital a part of the history of Christianity in America. But now it was a divided Protestantism, less capable of shaping the national destiny on its own terms and more aware of internal divisions. Clearly, the day of white Protestant hegemony was over. The significance of that fact in the broader history of Christianity, for better and for worse, became more evident in the decades that followed.

Further Reading

Anderson, Robert Mapes. *Vision of the Disinherited: The Making of American Protestantism*. New York: Oxford University Press, 1979.

Blumhofer, Edith L., ed. *"Pentecost in My Soul": Explorations in the Meaning of Pentecostal Experience in the Early Assemblies of God*. Springfield, MO: Gospel Publishing House, 1989.

Frank, Douglas. *Less than Conquerors: How Evangelicals Entered the Twentieth Century*. Grand Rapids: William B. Eerdmans, 1986.

Hoeveler, J. David, Jr. *James McCosh and the Scottish Intellectual Tradition: From Glasgow to Princeton*. Princeton: Princeton University Press, 1981.

Hutchison, William R. *The Modernist Impulse in American Protestantism*. Cambridge: Harvard University Press, 1976.

Kuklick, Bruce, *Churchmen and Philosophers from Jonathan Edwards to John Dewey*. New Haven: Yale University Press, 1985.

Livingstone, David N. *Darwin's Forgotten Defenders: The Encounter between Evangelical Theology and Evolutionary Thought*. Grand Rapids: William B. Eerdmans, 1987.

Longfield, Bradley J. *The Presbyterian Controversy: Fundamentalists, Modernists, and Moderates*. New York: Oxford University Press, 1991.

Marsden, George M. *Fundamentalism and American Culture: The Shaping of*

Twentieth-Century Evangelicalism, 1870-1925. New York: Oxford University Press, 1980.

Marty, Martin E. *Modern American Religion.* 2 vols. Chicago: University of Chicago Press, 1986-91.

Moore, James R. *The Post-Darwinian Controversies: A Study of the Protestant Struggle to Come to Terms with Darwin in Great Britain and America, 1870-1900.* Cambridge: Cambridge University Press, 1979.

Roberts, Jon H. *Darwinism and the Divine in America: Protestant Intellectuals and Organic Evolution, 1859-1900.* Madison: University of Wisconsin Press, 1988.

Sandeen, Ernest R. *The Roots of Fundamentalism: British and American Millenarianism, 1800-1930.* Chicago: University of Chicago Press, 1970.

Stevenson, Louise L. *Scholarly Means to Evangelical Ends: The New Haven Scholars and the Transformation of Higher Learning in America, 1830-1890.* Baltimore: The Johns Hopkins University Press, 1986.

Szasz, Ferenc Morton. *The Divided Mind of Protestant America, 1880-1930.* Tuscaloosa: University of Alabama Press, 1982.

Turner, James. *Without God, without Creed: The Origins of Unbelief in America.* Baltimore: The Johns Hopkins University Press, 1985.

Wacker, Grant. "The Holy Spirit and the Spirit of the Age in American Protestantism, 1880-1910." *Journal of American History* 72 (June 1858): 45-62.

Weber, Timothy P. *Living in the Shadow of the Second Coming: American Premillennialism, 1875-1982.* Rev. ed. Chicago: University of Chicago Press, 1987.

CHAPTER 15

Legacies of "Christian America"

Like Every Newborn

The Lord is King, and hath put on glorious apparel; the
Lord hath put on his apparel, and girded himself with
strength. (Psalm 93:1)

> Like every newborn, he has come from very far.
> His eyes are closed against the brilliance of the star.
> So glorious is he, he goes to this immoderate length
> To show his love for us, discarding power and strength.
> Girded for war, humility his mighty dress,
> He moves into the battle wholly weaponless.

*Poetry with a Christian focus began in North America with Jean de Brébeuf,
Anne Bradstreet, and Michael Wigglesworth in the seventeenth century. It has
continued to the present, as in these verses for Nativity by Madeleine L'Engle,
which were published in the 1970s.*

AFTER THE 1920S, PROTESTANTS CONTINUED TO EXERT A CONSIDERABLE
influence on the public life of the United States. They had only slightly
less impact on the culture of English Canada. But, as we shall observe in
Chapter 16, dramatic public events of the 1930s and 1940s further weakened
the hold of Protestantism on public life. Developments inside the churches

were also contributing to the loss of Protestant hegemony, including deep divisions among the heirs of nineteenth-century evangelicalism, the rise of the Roman Catholic Church, the increasing strength of other Christian bodies and non-Christian faiths, and the broadening influence of nonreligious sectarianism. The result was to make more obvious the religious pluralism in North America that had been only latent before.

As a new era dawned in which Protestants were more obviously fragmented competitors within a multireligious environment instead of rulers of the religious roost, the earlier emphases of American public religion did not entirely fade away. In fact, much that was forged in the nineteenth-century Protestant furnace remained to shape the course of later religious life. At this point in the story, where the plurality of Christian expressions becomes ever more evident, it is appropriate to discuss some of the habits, customs, forms, assumptions, and practices of the nineteenth-century Christian world that have continued their influence. In the twentieth century, these legacies remain powerful impulses, at least in part because they have entered the lives of Catholics as well as Protestants, whites as well as blacks, residents of the North as well as of the South. Some of those influences may have assumed a civic or even secular form, but their connection to the Protestant culture of earlier centuries reminds us of the power (and also the ambiguity) that these earlier religious experiences enjoyed.

Of many such legacies, three are treated below: first, the shape that revivalism bequeathed to American political life; second, the impact that the preoccupation with Scripture exerted on the general culture; and third, the more specific ways in which Christian themes have shaped main currents in American literature.

A Puritan-Evangelical Politics, with Alternatives

Every time the television networks broadcast a Democratic or Republican political convention, we see in our living rooms a shadow of revivalistic Protestantism. Every time the rhetoric of a political campaign heats up — promising to "save" the world or the United States, offering something "new" to change our lives decisively for the better, announcing a strategy to "reform" the evils of the incumbent administration, or pleading for "commitment" to causes of justice and fairness — we hear echoes of that same revivalism. To be sure, much has changed in modern American politics from the time that conventions, mass campaigns, and fervent stump speaking began in the 1830s and 1840s. In particular, political campaigns almost never directly address questions of specific spiritual concern. But when we

Urban revivals, like this one conducted by J. Wilbur Chapman, provided politicians
with models for their own conventions, publicity, and campaigns.
Courtesy of the Billy Graham Center Museum

examine matters of style and organization, it is clear that a progenitor of
modern American politics was the revival, and, behind the revival, a distinctly reformist approach to Christian life in the world.

The historian Daniel Walker Howe has nicely summarized the debt
that the egalitarian politics of the antebellum era owed to the revival style:
"the hullabaloo of political campaigns in the second party era — the
torchlight parades, the tents pitched outside town, the urgent calls for commitment — was borrowed by political campaigners from the revival preachers. Far from being irrelevant distractions or mere recreation, the evangelical
techniques of mass persuasion that we associate with the campaigns of 1840
and after provide a clue to the moral meaning of antebellum politics."

Long after the Second Party System that began in the era of Andrew
Jackson, the characteristic approach of the revivalist continued to influence
political style. Revivalists were "immediatists" who wanted to see people's
lives change, and the sooner the better. So too has American politics characteristically sought immediate solutions to the problems of society. Revivalists
were "ultraists" who pushed for the reorientation of all of life under God.

So too have American political leaders characteristically talked as if political actions could restructure the entirety of life. Revivalists were "perfectionists" who preached that individuals acting responsibly could, with God's help, reach the goal of total consecration; they have always proclaimed that moral citizens banding together in voluntary agencies could Christianize American society and drive out evil (maybe even ushering in the millennium). So too have politicians characteristically held out the hope of an idyllic society if only votes were cast in the right way.

The approach of revivalists in the early nineteenth century itself reflected a modification of Puritan impulses from the English Reformation. With other Reformed or Calvinist branches of Protestantism, the Puritans, as we have seen, thought it was possible to reform the church and all of society with the same principles that they drew from Scripture for the reform of the self. In the course of American history, Puritanism as a distinct religious movement evolved into a broader evangelical Protestantism adjusted to the democratic themes of the Revolution and the experiential Arminianism of the Methodists. In the course of the nineteenth century, the Roman Catholic Church grew in importance, and at the end of the century a variety of factors that we have examined ended for good the previous supremacy of evangelical Protestant denominations.

While these important religious changes were taking place, however, attitudes toward public life — and especially politics — have remained largely the same. The dominant pattern of American political involvement has always been one of direct, aggressive action. Like the early Puritans, American Christians have moved in a straight line from personal belief to social reform, from private experience to political activity. For the colonial Puritans and the nineteenth-century evangelicals this meant the mounting of religious crusades. Puritans and evangelicals assumed the necessity of moving directly from passion for God and the Bible to passion for the reformation of society. The past century, which has been a more secular period in America, has been no less characterized by crusading zeal. Now, however, it is not so much zeal for God and the Bible as infatuation with science and technique, solicitude for American influence among the nations, or a passion for private rights that has fueled the efforts to renovate society. Still, in the past three American centuries, there has been a common strategy in pursuing political goals that were defined on the basis of private religious belief (or, in the secular period, on the basis of other private beliefs that function as religious beliefs once functioned).

The rise of a more pluralistic society in which secular values have become prominent has changed the substance but not necessarily the form of public activity. In twentieth-century America the language of political reform is more likely to base hope on scientific expertise than on a morality derived from the Bible, and it appeals more naturally to education than to conversion as the basis for social transformation. Modern political leaders also assume that the state will play a more important role in bringing about the good life than would have been the case in the Puritan or evangelical eras. Yet public leaders still act as if the task of politics is to work out their own salvation (however defined) and the salvation of everyone else through the restructuring of public life.

Foreign visitors have remarked upon the "Protestant style" of American politics for a long time. In his classic account from the 1830s, Alexis de Tocqueville noted how the British settlers "brought with them into the New World a form of Christianity which I cannot better describe than by styling it a democratic and republican religion." Under these combined influences, "the Anglo-Americans acknowledge the moral authority of the reason of the community as they acknowledge the political authority of the mass of citizens." As Tocqueville observed the antebellum United States, he thought that Americans considered "society as a body in a state of improvement." And the means of improving the body politic were the same means employed in conversion and the life of Christian faith. He concluded that, in America, "from the beginning, politics and religion contracted an alliance which has never been dissolved."

Almost a century after Tocqueville, another visiting Frenchman, André Siegfried, described in even more explicit terms the connections between Puritan-evangelical Protestantism and the public life of the country. In Siegfried's analysis, the United States was dominated by a "Calvinist" approach to public life, by which he meant not a narrow theological Calvinism but the broadly Puritan-evangelical-Methodist-voluntary pattern characteristic of nineteenth-century white Protestantism as a whole. So defined, "the Calvinist has a mission to carry out," wrote Siegfried — "namely, to purify the life of the community and to uplift the state." Furthermore, in carrying out this work, such a one "cannot admit two separate spheres of action, for he believes that the influence of Christ should dominate every aspect of life." From this tendency, Siegfried concluded, "arises the feeling of social obligation that is so typically Anglo-Saxon."

Writing in the mid-1920s, Siegfried thought it was this heritage that explained why Americans were so energetic as reformers. "Not only do they believe that they have been called to uplift the outside world — a duty toward savages, negroes, and Frenchmen — but they also feel the need of home missions to evangelize their own community" by means of "crusades against cigarettes, alcohol, and the slums, and such movements as feminism, pacifism, anti-vivisection, Americanization of immigrants, and even the gospel of eugenics and birth control." Siegfried also saw clearly that this tendency could take a general political cast. He thought the Puritan-evangelical heritage was the secret behind the American political style that so often perplexed Europeans. "Every American is at heart an evangelist, be he a Wilson, a Bryan, or a Rockefeller. He cannot leave people alone, and he constantly feels the urge to preach."

Siegfried, like Tocqueville before, certainly underestimated the plural forms of Christianity in America. But both of them did see accurately that the dominant style of political life in America was heavily influenced by generations of Puritan and evangelical efforts at public moral reform. The crusading passion, to be sure, can lead in contradictory directions. In recent decades, for example, we have witnessed anti-war activists trading shouts with pro-war supporters, and passionate standoffs between opponents and proponents of abortion. Historically considered, however, the form (if not the substance) of both sides in such confrontations comes from the same Puritan-evangelical root.

Alternatives: Separation, Natural Law, Canada

Puritan-evangelical reformism has dominated American public life, but it has not been the only religious approach to politics in North American history. Other historic approaches have also been present. And in Canada, for a number of reasons, the relationship between religion and politics has never been quite the same as in the United states.

A direct counterpoint to Puritan-evangelical reform is offered by the separatist style that, in European church history, was revitalized by Anabaptist movements of the sixteenth century. The Anabaptist approach to culture is the mirror image of the reformist. At the time of the Reformation, Anabaptists were radical Protestants who felt that the corruption of both church and world required the formation of separated and purified communities. The Anabaptists rejected the baptism of infants for a variety of reasons, including the fact that using baptism both as a basis for citizenship and as an expression of faith struck them as a corrupting mixture of allegiance to church and world. Anabaptists also rejected military service because they felt that the coercion necessary to govern (or reform) an entire society was, in principle, contradictory to the ways of the Prince of Peace. Like the Calvinists, Anabaptists sought a total renovation of life, but they believed that this renovation should take place in alternative communities separated from the sinful world, not by subduing society as a whole for Christ.

From early in the history of European settlement, North America has

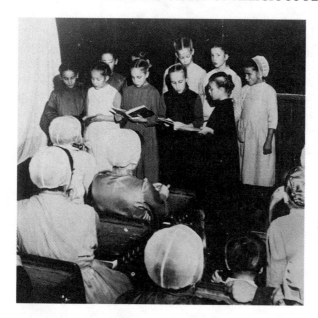

Though sometimes troubled by demands for conformity to more common American patterns, the Amish have been only one of several religious communities to preserve their unconventional religious traditions in the sprawling regions of the North American continent. *Religious News Service*

been home to several varieties of Anabaptists, most notably the Mennonites and their extreme wing, the Amish. Until comparatively recently, these "Stille im Lande" (quiet ones in the countryside) have sought salvation in separation. They have concluded that since efforts to reform all of life and all of society are pretentious folly, true godliness must be cultivated in isolation from the sinful world. Anabaptist communities in both Canada and the United States have gradually assimilated over the decades, so that many Mennonites now promote their beliefs publicly in ways that their religious ancestors — immigrants from Switzerland, Holland, Germany, and Russia — did not. Yet even in recent decades, Anabaptist efforts have not adopted the immediatism, ultraism, and perfectionism that are more common among larger groups of Protestants and citizens at large.

Mennonites have practiced a politics of separation more consistently than other Christian groups, but other varieties of separatism have also appeared from time to time. There was an Anabaptist leaven at Plymouth among the Pilgrims, at least with Governor William Bradford, who wondered late in life if success at subduing the New World had not compromised the spirituality of the Pilgrims. During the nineteenth century, a parade of gifted, charismatic leaders abandoned efforts to reform all of society and instead went off into the wilderness to construct alternative communities in which righteousness and truth could flourish at last. Transcendentalists at Brook Farm, the followers of John Humphrey Noyes at

Oneida, and the Mormons under Joseph Smith and Brigham Young were among the best known who took this path. In the twentieth century a number of groups have followed this Anabaptist strategy — some (e.g., the Bruderhof movement) self-consciously Christian in their communal aspirations, others more secular in their desire to "tune in, turn on, and drop out." Such groups buck a powerful tradition of reformist political instincts, but their persistence is also a reminder that the dominant political-religious connection in America is not the only Christian option.

A similar reminder is provided by the history of Roman Catholics. In the Catholic Middle Ages, the institutions of religion and government mixed elements that Protestants later divided. With the Lutherans who came later, Catholics believed that God exercises his sovereignty through different instrumentalities in the church and in the public sphere. With the Calvinists, on the other hand, Catholics held that the spheres of church and society are parts of one whole. The church and the state are different but nonetheless joined under a common divine sovereignty. Furthermore, Catholics sustained a belief that Protestants set aside — namely, that God has established a hierarchy of ruling in the church that culminates with the pope. This hierarchy not only directs the church but also provides a template for social ordering of whatever kind. Ecclesiastical hierarchy thus becomes a model for political hierarchy. In addition, where institutions of public order and institutions of ecclesiastical order overlap, it is only right for the public to defer to the church. The theologian H. Richard Niebuhr once labeled this standpoint "Christ over culture." In his description, it is a vision of life in which the church offers all other institutions a model of order to which they can aspire. In the centuries since the Reformation, European countries in which Catholicism has remained strong have adopted variations of this standpoint. Official recognition of the church, as well as governmental support for its particular offices, was once the norm.

In North America, this kind of connection between Christianity and politics developed only in Quebec, where it continued until after World War II. Organization of society was modeled on the hierarchical structure of the Catholic Church, which provided oversight for the province's public as well as religious life. Political arrangements were worked out between powerful members of the elite. The result, in comparison with the rest of North America, was a traditionalist politics of deference. But the system, despite occasional vigorous protests from within, also offered a degree of social cohesion not found elsewhere on the continent.

Although the Roman Catholic Church has been the largest Christian communion in the United States for over a century, American Catholics have rarely attempted to reproduce the attitudes toward politics found

397

among their fellow believers in Europe, in South America, or (before 1960) in Quebec. In contrast to the situation in Canada, by the time large numbers of Catholics arrived in the United States, Protestants were too well established to permit experimentation with the "Christ over culture" position. Throughout much of the nineteenth century, Roman Catholics in the United States looked a little bit like Anabaptists, building self-contained enclaves and a comprehensive network of institutions (schools, youth organizations, fraternal orders, insurance societies) as alternatives to the "public" (i.e., Protestant) institutions of mainstream American culture.

When in the twentieth century Catholics did emerge from their immigrant cocoons, they often assumed the reformist attitudes characteristic of their American neighbors. From the first major appearance of Catholics in the public life of America — the participation of several well-known bishops in temperance crusades during the late nineteenth century — Catholics in public have tended to act more like their Protestant fellow Americans than their European fellow Catholics. Catholic efforts to professionalize higher education in the 1930s, to protect the nation from communists in the 1950s, and (through the Bishops' letters on nuclear arms and the economy) to influence the direction of public policy in the 1980s have all resembled the dominant reformist spirit of Protestant politics.

As we will note in a later chapter, one of the reasons for this Catholic experience in the United States was the effort by theologians such as the Jesuit John Courtney Murray (1904-1967) to mediate between a Vatican suspicious about what was going in America and Protestant Americans suspicious of the Vatican. Murray did not want to deny the value of specifically Catholic contributions to public life. He and others sharing his opinions have stressed, for example, that historic Catholic reliance on "natural law" provides a political strategy that avoids the coercion often found in Protestant moral crusades. At the same time, Murray was eager to affirm that some aspects of Protestant concern for freedom and voluntary organization can instruct the traditional Catholic pursuit of political equity and social justice. Catholic influences on public life in the United States have not simply imitated Protestant influences. But unlike the situation in Quebec, the political styles of American Catholics have been more variations on prominent Protestant themes than a re-creation of European patterns.

Among Canadian Protestants there has been yet another variation on the link between politics and Christianity. In its colonial phase and then for its first half century as a Dominion after 1867, English Canada witnessed many Protestant crusades for moral improvement and social reform like those in the States. But most Canadian Protestants — whether Methodist, Anglican, Presbyterian, or Baptist — were also committed to the Loyalist

When the Anglican bishop John Strachan died in November 1867, the dignity of his funeral procession down Yonge Street in Toronto bore testimony to the tight bond that then prevailed in Canada between the churches and the state.
Metropolitan Toronto Reference Library

tradition with its long-standing distrust of unmediated democracy or un-restrained republicanism. Because of that tradition, it was harder to regard the activities of democratic voluntary agencies with the millennial enthusiasm they engendered in the States.

In addition, Canadian Protestants, especially after the War of 1812, were just as likely to follow British models for public life as they were the American models. In Britain, the division between Anglicans of the establishment and dissenting Protestants outside the establishment affected the religious tone of political activity. Anglicans continued to assume a certain hereditary right to influence public life. Dissenters might drift toward political separation or engage in strenuous activity to gain more social rights, but they were always conscious of their status as cultural outsiders. In neither case, however, did the same parallel exist between the ultimate religious concern and practical political activity that prevailed in the States.

The recurrence of separatism, the presence of Catholic alternatives to Protestant dispositions, and the different experiences of Canadians testify to the fact that Christian-political connections have varied in North American history. At the same time, however, these variations have not led to the same kind of general pluralism that prevails in North American Christianity. The dominance of a Protestant political style has continued even after the decline of Protestantism. In sum, the most common religious outlook toward public life throughout American history has been reformist and Puritan-evangelical. Whether early or late, whether in Christian or secular variations, whether from hereditary Protestants or from others, Americans in the political sphere have, in general, first committed themselves to ideals of The Good. Then they have moved as if by second nature to formulate plans for letting all of society share that Good. Finally, they have mobilized followers for the effort of setting America, if not the whole world, to rights. Even in the late twentieth century, a legacy of "Christian America" continues, for better and for worse, to determine the course of North American public life.

America's Book, America's Icon: The Bible

During the nineteenth century, the most pervasive symbol of "Christian America" was the Bible. This fascination with Scripture had roots in the Protestant Reformation, but it was developed in distinctly American ways by the surge of democracy that recast the United States between the Revolution and the Civil War. Since the decline of public Protestantism in the twentieth century, the involvement with Scripture has become very diffuse, but it still makes up a significant aspect of Christian experience in North America. Abraham Lincoln noted in his Second Inaugural Address that "both [sides] read the same Bible," as indeed they did, along with many others before and since. How did the use of the Bible develop? How did it broaden out from its originally Protestant forms? And why does it continue to influence the direction of Christian life even in a twentieth century greatly different from the world in which the Bible was first read and preached in North America?

Printing, Translating, and Distributing

Throughout their entire history, Americans have sustained an incredible rate of Bible publication and an even more stupendous appetite for literature about the Bible. Publication of the Bible has been a lucrative business in America, but not without peril. Before the Revolutionary War, the publication of English-language Bibles was prohibited in America, since the king's printers in England enjoyed an exclusive copyright for printing the Authorized or King James Version (KJV). This meant that the first Bibles printed in America were in languages other than English. In 1743, Christopher Sauer of Pennsylvania brought out an edition of Martin Luther's Bible on type carried from Frankfurt and in so doing established his family as America's leading publisher for readers of German. Even earlier, the Bible had made its appearance in native tongues. Spanish Franciscans were translating biblical liturgies and other Catholic literature for the Rimucuan Indians of Florida in the sixteenth and very early seventeenth centuries, before permanent English colonies existed in New England. Decades later the Massachusetts Puritan minister John Eliot translated the Bible into Algonquian (New Testament 1661, entire Bible 1663). Other laborers since Eliot have translated at least parts of the Bible into a whole series of Native American languages, including Apache, Cherokee, Cheyenne, Choctaw, Dakota, Hopi, Inupiat, Iroquoian, Kuskokwim, Mohawk, Muskogee, Navajo, and Ojibwa.

Once American printers began producing their own editions of the KJV, business boomed. Over 2,500 different English-language editions of the Bible were published in the United States between 1777 and 1957. Mason Weems, who fabricated the story of Washington and the cherry tree, made his living in the early years of the new nation selling Bibles in Virginia. Shortly after 1800, he wrote to his publisher, "I tell you this is the very season and age of the Bible. Bible Dictionaries, Bible tales, Bible stories — Bibles plain or paraphrased, Carey's Bibles, Collin's Bibles, Clarke's Bibles, Kimptor's Bibles, no matter what or whose, all, all, will go down — so wide is the crater of public appetite at this time."

As successful as Bible publishing was in general, however, that success did not extend to marketing new translations. Until well into the twentieth century, the King James Version for Protestants and the Douay-Rheims version for Catholics reigned supreme as the Bibles of choice for Americans. Nineteenth-century publishers who underwrote efforts to produce a Bible specifically for their countrymen found great resistance to any version that departed from the King James. Noah Webster, father of the American dictionary, in 1833 finished a translation of a Bible shorn of British spellings and archaic usages. His contemporary Andrew Comstock devised a phonetic "purfekt alfabet" for his "Filadelfia" New Testament of 1848. But these and similar efforts met with little success.

Only with the production of the American Standard Version in 1901 did publishers begin to enjoy a market for newer versions. But that market remained fairly small until after World War II, when a host of new translations became popular. Among these new versions, some of the most widely used have been the Revised Standard Version (sponsored by the National

401

In a scene that helps explain how religion has functioned powerfully in American public life alongside a formal separation of church and state, President Harry Truman receives the first copy of the Revised Standard Version of the Bible from Dr. Luther Weigle of the National Council of Churches. *National Council of Churches*

Council of Churches), the New English Bible (imported from Britain), the Jerusalem Bible and the New American Bible (under Catholic auspices), the Living Bible (a paraphrase by Kenneth Taylor), the Good News Bible (a common-language version sponsored by the American Bible Society), the New International Version (from the International Bible Society and an evangelical coalition), and TANAKH, a version of the Hebrew Scriptures from the Jewish Publication Society. Burgeoning sales of new translations notwithstanding, it is still usually the case that more copies of the King James Version are distributed than any other single version (although according to some counts the evangelically sponsored New International Version now occasionally registers more sales than the KJV). Accurate publication figures are difficult to come by, since in 1990 there were at least 7,000 different editions of the Bible from hundreds of publishers. But it is safe to say that since World War II, American publishers have printed about two Bibles for every American.

The study and reading of Scripture has now become a nonsectarian

Monsignor Patrick Skehan of the Catholic University of America is shown here in 1970 as he studies galley proofs for the New American Bible, a Roman Catholic contribution to the flood of new biblical translations that appeared after World War II. *Courtesy of the Dapartment of Archives and Manuscripts of the Catholic University of America*

free-for-all in which Catholics are unusually active. Catholics may read editions of the Living Bible and Good News Bible, both produced under strictly Protestant auspices, with the official blessing of the church hierarchy. Catholic scholars sit on the revision committee of the Revised Standard Version, and Protestant purchasers swell the sales of the Catholic Jerusalem Bible. Official delegates were exchanged between the Catholic Biblical Association and the Society of Biblical Literature for the first time only in 1959, yet by 1966 a Catholic had been elected president of the SBL. It was a sign of new times when the Catholic Sacred Heart League placed record orders from the American Bible Society for 775,000 New Testaments in 1979 and 800,000 in 1983.

Since the early history of the United States, Bible societies have aggressively promoted the distribution of Scripture. Although Britain had the first formal Bible society, American groups soon took the lead. After its founding in 1816, the American Bible Society boldly exploited the new technology of stereotype printing and was soon publishing more than 70,000 volumes per year on eight hand-operated presses running nearly around the clock. By 1830, the American Bible Society's annual production had reached over 300,000 volumes per year at a time when the national population was not quite 13,000,000. Since its founding in 1816, the Society has distributed nearly 4,000,000,000 complete Bibles, testaments, portions of Scripture, and selections.

Bible societies received the support of many who held traditional Christian views on the Bible's special character, such as the first president of the United States Congress, Elias Boudinot of New Jersey, who also became first president of the American Bible Society. But they also were patronized by others with unconventional religious ideas such as Thomas Jefferson, who twice prepared editions of the Gospels with the references to supernatural events removed.

A Cultural Force

The many ways in which the Bible is put to use have combined to exert a great influence on how Americans write, talk, think, and perceive themselves. In 1864, for instance, a group of grateful blacks from Baltimore presented President Lincoln — as a token of their respect for his efforts on their behalf — with a pulpit Bible bound in violet-tinged velvet, finished in gold, with a raised design depicting the emancipation of the slaves. In response, Lincoln called the Bible "God's best gift to man." Some years before, the skeptical John Adams wrote to his even more skeptical friend Thomas Jefferson that the Bible "contains more of my little philosophy than all the libraries I have seen." Such views on Scripture have regularly proceeded from public leaders.

America's common people have also reflected a pervasive respect for Scripture. The use of biblical names for children continues into the late twentieth century, and extends a much longer pattern of employing biblical nomenclature. As Americans in the nineteenth century settled new towns and named new features of the terrain, it was instinctive to turn to the Bible for names like Zoar (from Gen. 13:10) in Ohio and Mount Tirzah (Josh. 12:24) in North Carolina, or the forty-seven variations on Bethel to be found across the country, sixty-one on Eden, and ninety-five on Salem.

In American social history the Bible has provided both a conservative and a radical force. As we have seen, it played a large role in the circumstances leading to the Civil War and in the interpretations of that war, as well as in many of the other dramatic events of American history. The potential for Scripture to be used in contradictory ways is also a part of the national history. The Bible, for instance, has provided a vocabulary for traditional deference but also innovative egalitarianism. It has been used to promote both stability in the face of anarchy and freedom in the face of tyranny. The Bible has served as a charter of social liberty for many who have felt constrained by traditional boundaries or dominating cultural fashions. "The Bible only" was the liberating cry of the energetic men and women who formed many of the new denominations established between the Revolution and the Civil War. On the other side of the picture, the Bible has also played a part in reinforcing social conformity. When the Roman Catholic bishop of Philadelphia Francis Patrick Kenrick petitioned city officials in 1842 to allow school children of his faith to hear readings from the Douay version instead of the King James Version, strong Protestant protests followed. Evangelical ministers formed national anti-Catholic organizations and Protestant laymen vented their anger by rioting against Philadelphia's Catholic churches.

The most important instance of the Bible's social liberation in America belongs to the history of African Americans. Slaves made a sharp distinction between the Bible that their owners preached to them, with its emphasis on not stealing and obeying masters, and the Bible they discovered for themselves, with its message of liberation for the captive and redemption for the oppressed. Under slavery, stringent regulations often existed against unsupervised preaching and sometimes even against owning Bibles. But with permission or not, slaves went to great lengths to possess Scripture for themselves. Many made a special effort to hear black preachers preach in circumstances unsupervised by masters. One slave left a striking testimony of the difference: "a yellow [light-complexioned] man preached to us. She [the slave owner] had him preach how we ought to obey our master and missy if we want to go to heaven, but when she wasn't there, he came out with straight preachin' from the Bible."

Blacks sang and preached about Adam and Eve and the Fall, about "wrestlin' Jacob" who "would not let [God] go," about Moses and the exodus from Egypt, about Joshua possessing the Promised Land, about Daniel in the lions' den and Daniel's three friends in the fiery furnace, about Jonah in the belly of the fish, about the birth of Jesus and his death and future return. The narratives of the Old Testament in particular undergirded the powerful social dimension of the Bible among slaves. The figure of Moses assumed a special importance among them as the one whom God had raised up to free his people. To the hope of liberation in this world the slaves added a concentration on the figure of Jesus, who suffered innocently and who ministered particularly to the oppressed, as the source of hope for the future. The slave's profound embrace of Scripture created the climate for the sustained importance of Bible reading and biblical preaching among blacks since the Civil War.

The Bible has also played an important role in efforts to define the character of the United States. Borrowing liberally from Old Testament

If the United States has never been "God's Country" in any legitimate sense, its one universal book has nonetheless been the Bible. Here a Missouri sharecropper reads the Scriptures by the light of a kerosene lantern in 1939. *Library of Congress*

precedents, many early Americans and not a few in more recent days have regarded the United States as God's New Israel, a nation established in this New World Canaan as a land flowing with wealth and freedom. To balance the picture, however, we must also note a different perspective for the role of the United States. Black slaves before the Civil War and not a few Christian radicals in the late twentieth century have reversed the typology: America is Egypt, and *escape* from American institutions is the Exodus. Particularly at moments of crisis, however, the themes of Scripture have easily slid over into the terms of national identity, whether apocalypse during the Revolutionary and Civil Wars, redemption during the Civil War by the one whom some called "Father Abraham," or judgment during national disasters. Late into the twentieth century, these themes can still be heard in the American landscape.

As a parallel and yet a contrast, Canadians have sometimes also applied biblical language to themselves. But as is regularly the case when Canadians consider questions of their own national identity, that application can be stimulated by the intrusion of the United States. In 1880, the Methodist educator Egerton Ryerson published a book on the founding Loyalists who had first settled in Upper Canada (Ontario) after the American Revolution. Looming large in his account are both the transgressions of Americans against Canada and the use of biblical language to describe what had gone on. After writing at some length about the American invasions of Canada during the War of 1812, he drew on biblical images to show how the conflict came out: "the Gideon hordes of loyal Canadians repelled and scattered, for more than two years, the Midian and Amalekite thousands of democratic invaders." By putting such language to use, Ryerson was affirming that he felt God had called out these Canadian Loyalists to do a special work in the world and that they would accomplish it despite the efforts of Americans. Such views of a divinely guided destiny have not been as common in Canada as in the United States, but they do continue. The authors of a volume published in 1981, *God Keep Our Land,* in fact applied some of the same biblical texts to Canada that the New Christian Right was at the same time using to describe the United States.

The Bible has become part and parcel of North American culture because it has been constantly read, discussed, and studied. As great as the quantity of Bibles printed in America is, even greater is the quantity of literature about the Bible. The Library of Congress's catalogues of books on Scripture held in American libraries as of 1956 amounted to four large volumes with 63,000 entries in 700 languages. The *Subject Guide to Books in Print* contains sixty pages of fine print listing biblical materials available at the present. Five thousand academics belong to the Society of Biblical Literature. They are responsible for a substantial portion of the eighty-six columns of Bible-related citations from 1989 in the two major indexes of religious literature. For many years in the 1950s and 1960s, the periodical *Christianity Today* published each spring a review of recent books on Scripture; it regularly ran over more than ten pages. By themselves, three large religious publishers in Grand Rapids, Michigan (Baker, Eerdmans, Zondervan), currently have in print more than thirty commentary series on Scripture. All this is to say that even in the more secular twentieth century, a lot of people are still spending a lot of time pondering the messages of Scripture.

The most prominent role of the Bible in American history has almost certainly been its presence as the source (or at least a reference point) for sermons, homilies, meditations, or harangues in church after church, week after week, throughout the length and breadth of the land.

In many other ways the Bible has played a part in American culture, often shaping that culture by the power of its own message, but also often being shaped by the social, economic, and artistic patterns of life in America. The Bible has informed the spirituals of blacks and Shakers as well as more formal hymnody, provided material for artwork appealing to elites and the masses, served as a textbook in many schools and a decisive influence on the curriculum in many more, been a factor in legal decisions and jurisprudential reasoning, and provided the raw material for historical novels, plays, mass art, country music, humor, broadcasting, children's literature, and much much more. In 1990, a Gallup Poll reported that, as of the mid-1980s, 47 percent of the United States population read the Bible at least once a month (up from 41 percent in 1978), while 20 percent reported reading it at least two or three times a week. The same poll reported that 55 percent of the populace believed that the Bible was the "actual" or "inspired" word of God which, whether interpreted literally or symbolically, made no mistakes. It is ironic that more people hold such views than possess basic knowledge about Scripture. But it is still fairly impressive that, when this same poll was taken, over 40 percent of the population knew that Jesus had preached the Sermon on the Mount and could name the four gospels. In other words, the staying power of the Bible has outlived the period when Protestant denominations dominated public life.

In sum, the Bible has been an ever-present force in North American life. Americans have perhaps been more prone than people elsewhere to bend, twist, and abuse the Bible for their own sometimes very un-Christian purposes, but from its pages they have also drawn insight, strength, and wisdom that accord far better with Scripture's central themes.

A Literature Preoccupied with God

The legacies of "Christian America" include also a constant literary fascination with the themes of faith. Like Puritan-evangelical politics and the continual engagement with Scripture, the centrality of religion in American literature demands nuanced interpretation. Regarding that body of American novels and poems preoccupied with themes of sin and redemption, given over to developing a Christ figure, or devoted to the promotion of traditional Christian morals, it cannot be argued that all have advanced either the faith or literature. But on the other hand, many literary compositions in which nothing overtly Christian appears nonetheless reflect visions of human existence fully compatible with the faith. As in so many other aspects of North American history, Christianity has made an incalculable impact on literature. It has provided the stuff of poems, plays, novels, short stories, and essays without number. It has shaped the aesthetic expectations of writers, reviewers, and readers in every generation since European settlement. In some ways, the Christian presence in literature has become even sharper and more powerful over the course of the twentieth century, at the same time that the general culture has slipped more obviously beyond the control of Christian institutions. Yet having noted the centrality of Christian or more generally religious concerns in North American literature, we would still have to undertake a case-by-case investigation in order to say where preoccupation with religious themes has comported well with the ideals of Christianity and where it has undermined those ideals.

The Christian presence in literature reflects the same characteristics of the general history. Just as the churches in America have been more democratic and more entrepreneurial than their counterparts elsewhere in the world, so too have the religious preoccupations of American literature been more populist and commercial. If sermons in America have tended to be moralistic rather than doctrinal or traditionalist, so too has much American literature with religious themes aimed to shore up morality rather than promote specifically Christian dogmas or defend the claims of a particular church. Christianity in America has been marked by a persistently optimistic tone — whether Puritan reform from the colonial period, nineteenth-century evangelical millennialism, the liberal theological belief in cosmic progress, spiritual uplift from Higher Life and Victorious Living, or Possibility Thinking from the late twentieth century. In such an environment, it is not surprising that literature with religious overtones is often marked by an idealistic Romanticism that in the end boils down to an affirmation of cozy domestic bliss.

The limits of this kind of literature were once noted by the twentieth-century Catholic writer Flannery O'Connor; speaking of fiction by her fellow Catholics, she said, "novels that, by the authors' efforts to be edifying, leave out half or three-fourths of human existence . . . are therefore not true either to the mysteries we know by faith or those we perceive simply by observation." There has been every bit as much of this sort of material written by Protestants as by Catholics.

Remembering that questions of quality are not the same as questions of simply being there, a survey of the many levels at which Christian themes have permeated North American literature still shows how significant the Christian legacy remains in North American culture. This significance holds up even if a discrimination is made between literature with general religious concerns and literature that engages Christian questions more directly. It is safe to say that almost all the most widely studied works of American literature are "religious" in some sense of the term. Ralph Waldo Emerson and Henry David Thoreau, in their different varieties of post-Unitarian Transcendentalism, no less than Walt Whitman and Hart Crane as poets of human possibility, are preoccupied with generally religious matters. The same could be said of novelists Henry James, Ernest Hemingway, F. Scott Fitzgerald, Joyce Carol Oates, Ralph Ellison, and many, many more whose fiction constantly addresses questions of ultimate meaning through the use of religious or even Christian symbols. But to set such writers aside and concentrate only on those who have exploited distinctly Christian themes still leaves legions of authors of almost every kind and quality.

Literature of Christian Moral Purpose

In the eighteenth and early nineteenth century, English-speaking North Americans were often suspicious of novels. Part of that suspicion came from the pragmatic character of New World settlement, and part came from a lingering Puritan distaste for wasting time on made-up, unreal stories. In the early nineteenth century, that suspicion was largely overcome by a corps of earnest novelists whose works showed that a good story could be moral as well as entertaining. Once established as a genre, the religious novel with moral purpose became a mainstay in American publishing.

Early authors of this kind of fiction, such as Catherine Sedgwick, Lydia Child, Sylvester Judd, and William Ware, were likely to express liberal or anti-Calvinist opinions. But the great example of such writing in the nineteenth century was Harriet Beecher Stowe (1811-1896), the daughter of Congregationalist-Presbyterian stalwart Lyman Beecher. Stowe did modify certain aspects of her Calvinist heritage, but in such novels as *Oldtown Folks* (1869) and *The Minister's Wooing* (1859) she wrote fondly of the clerical world in which she had grown up. The general approach that dominated her books was a combination of moral earnestness and modified Calvinist spirituality. She is best known for *Uncle Tom's Cabin* (1852), an extraordinarily effective polemic against slavery. Stowe's hero, who suffers the lash of Simon Legree so that two other slaves, Cassy and Emmeline, might escape, was a Christ figure meant to encourage others in the spiritual struggle against human bondage.

Novels like *Uncle Tom's Cabin* — in which explicit Christian values provide resources for their protagonists — have never lost their appeal for North American readers. They have appeared in great numbers in almost all Christian communities, directed to children and young people as well as adults, and have been written by many kinds of authors. Orestes Brownson, for example, one of the most notable converts to Catholicism in the nineteenth century, wrote several such novels for appreciative Catholic audiences. At the turn of the twentieth century, several novels promoting variations of the Social Gospel became runaway best-sellers. They included books by Harold Bell Wright (1872-1944), a Disciples of Christ minister whose *The Shepherd of the Hills* (1907) showed how a manly, clear-eyed Christianity embodying the rural values of the Midwest could survive in an

Orestes Brownson tried out various forms of Protestantism (e.g., Presbyterianism, Universalism, Unitarianism) and transcendentalism before he became a Roman Catholic in 1844. For the rest of his life he was the chief American spokesman for the proposition that the Catholic faith of old Europe was destined to flourish even more vigorously in harmony with the best of the new American world. *Courtesy of the Department of Archives and Manuscripts of the Catholic University of America*

increasingly urban America. A Presbyterian who spent much of his career in Western Canada, Charles Gordon (1860-1937) was the most popular Canadian author of his day on the strength of such Social Gospel novels as *The Sky Pilot* (1899), which he wrote under the name Ralph Connor. By far the most popular novel of this sort, however, was *In His Steps* (1897) by Charles Sheldon (1857-1946), a Congregationalist minister in Topeka, Kansas. Sheldon, who looked for the realization of God's kingdom through evangelism and reform, hoped that his readers would take with great seriousness the question that structured his story — "What would Jesus do?" Since the time of Wright, Gordon, and Sheldon, the flood of novels promoting reassuring Christian visions of the world has not ceased.

One particular variety of this fiction has been the embellished biblical narrative or story from the biblical times. Academic critics have not responded kindly to such books, but the American people have never been able to get enough of them. Lew Wallace's *Ben Hur* (1880), which climaxed in a breathtaking chariot race, has sold into the millions, and it was also the inspiration for an immensely successful touring drama (complete with surging horses on a treadmill) and two motion pictures. But many other such

411

Charles Gordon, who wrote under the name Ralph Connor, was one of Canada's most popular novelists early in the twentieth century. His optimistic presentations of the Social Gospel are now hard to read, but they were greately appreciated when they first appeared. *National Archives of Canada*

books have also been hugely successful best-sellers, including Henryk Sienkiewicz's *Quo Vadis?* (1896), Lloyd Douglas's *The Robe* (1942), and Marjorie Holmes's *Two from Galilee* (1972). One of the best examples of this kind of fiction, *Pontius Pilate,* appeared in 1968 from Paul Maier, a historian of ancient Rome who is also the son of a long-time preacher on *The Lutheran Hour,* Walter Maier.

Christianity in the Literary Canon

Fiction and poetry that have been accepted as "canonical" by academic scholars show as much preoccupation with Christian themes as the more popular books not usually studied in formal literature classes. In such books, however, the Christian elements are more complicated. Since the beginning of "classic" American writing in the 1830s and 1840s, this literature, as James Barcus has put it, "reflected the loss of faith in creeds, but the best creative minds continued throughout the nineteenth and twentieth centuries to wrestle with religious issues." That judgment is something of an understatement, for many critically acclaimed authors have professed as well as written about Christian faith. But in general it is true that America's best writers have more engaged than advocated Christianity.

An important subgenre of North American fiction persistently occupied with Christian themes is made up of novels on the experience of immigrants or other ghettoized minorities. The very best of these works have regularly dealt fully with the way that the church, Christian convictions, and the struggle for faith define the meaning of life. The novels of Abraham Cahan (1860-1951), Canadian A. M. Klein (1909-1972), Saul Bellow (b. 1915), and Chaim Potok (b. 1929) are books of this sort in which Jewish faith and self-identity are always near the focus of concern.

Many different Christian groups have enjoyed novelists of the same sort, although "enjoyed" is not always the word to describe how the faith communities have reacted to seeing their lives dissected in fiction. It is possible to mention examples of only some of these writers, but their works are constantly being rediscovered and appreciated anew. *Giants in the Earth* (1929) by Ole Rölvaag, an immigrant from Norway, is a profoundly moving account of a Norwegian family's experience on the Dakota prairies in which God (or his absence) features centrally. Mention has already been made of Willa Cather's *Death Comes for the Archbishop* (1927) as a novel drawing on the experiences of the Catholic Southwest; several of her other novels, though not as directly, explore religious dimensions of the distinct society created by settlers in the plains states. *The Blood of the Lamb* (1961) is only one of the novels of Peter De Vries that reflects a similar preoccupation, and ambiguity, about the world of Dutch Reformed immigrants in which he was reared. Shirley Nelson's *The Last Year of the War* (1978) is an unusually successful story about the separatistic fundamentalist world of the 1940s. Rudy Wiebe's *Peace Shall Destroy Many* (1962) subjects a Mennonite subculture in Manitoba to the same kind of painful, but also respectful, scrutiny. In *The Stone Angel* (1964), Margaret Laurence weaves a domestic history set in the Saskatchewan plains in which alienation from a divine covenant is a central theme. Among black writers, a growing number of forceful authors are becoming known for capturing, among many other aspects of experience, the historically central role of the church for African Americans. Like fiction drawing on other closed communities, this work is not simplistic or necessarily uplifting, but it often takes with deep seriousness the crucial role of the church. Prominent examples include Zora Neale Hurston's *Their Eyes Were Watching God* (1937), James Baldwin's *Go Tell It on the Mountain* (1953), and Alice Walker's *The Color Purple* (1982).

A different kind of preoccupation with Christianity appears among authors often placed in the pantheon of American literature. In the select

413

group from which assignments are made in college literature classes, an unusually large proportion deal relentlessly with Christian questions. These include, at a minimum, the works of Nathaniel Hawthorne, Herman Melville, Emily Dickinson, Mark Twain, and William Faulkner. None of these great authors provides unambiguously Christian affirmations, and some explicitly disavow the faith. But a persistent return to spiritual questions, a steady employment of biblical language, and moving accounts of a fall, vicarious passion, and redemption are central features of their work.

Such preoccupations dominated, for example, the works of Nathaniel Hawthorne (1804-1864). Hawthorne was repulsed by what he considered the bigotry of his Puritan ancestors, but he was also transfixed by the realism with which they tested themselves. His novel *The Scarlet Letter* (1850) and many of his stories, such as "Young Goodman Brown" (1835), are intensely empathic accounts of Puritan wrestling with God. Hawthorne's younger friend Herman Melville once commented shrewdly on this theme:

> whether Hawthorne has simply availed himself of this mystical blackness as a means to the wondrous effects he makes it to produce in his lights and shades; or whether there really lurks in him, perhaps unknown to himself, a touch of the Puritanic gloom, — this I cannot altogether tell. Certain it is, however, that this great power of blackness in him derives its force from its appeal to that Calvinistic sense of Innate Depravity and Original Sin, from whose visitations, in some shape or other, no deeply thinking mind is always and wholly free. For, in certain moods, no man can weigh this world, without throwing in something, somehow like Original Sin, to strike the uneven balance.

As it happens, these comments from 1850 reveal something important about the literary vision of Melville (1819-1891) as well as that of Hawthorne. An abiding rumination on themes of good and evil, providence and fate, colors Melville's work even more clearly than Hawthorne's. Melville may have been further estranged from conventional Christianity than was Hawthorne, but his writing remains, among much else, a deeply probing reflection on the ways of God among humanity. His greatest books were haunted by the language and images of Christian tradition. *Moby Dick* (1851) begins with the evocative words, "Call me Ishmael." And almost the last lines of *Billy Budd,* written four decades later, came out of a similar world: "at the same moment it chanced that the vapory fleece hanging low in the East was shot through with a soft glory as of the fleece of the Lamb of God seen in mystical vision, and simultaneously therewith, watched by the wedged mass of upturned faces, Billy ascended; and, ascending, took the full rose of the dawn."

Although Nathaniel Hawthorne was repulsed by certain aspects of his Puritan heritage, he repeatedly draws upon it in his most memorable novels and short stories. *The Bettman Archives*

Similarly preoccupied, but even less affirming, was Emily Dickinson (1830-1886), possibly the greatest American poet. Dickinson, who lived a cloistered life in Amherst, Massachusetts, published only a handful of verses during her lifetime. But the 1,500 meticulously crafted poems discovered posthumously showed that her telling reflections on the human experience had come from the angle of her Puritan forebears. Ultimately the Puritan answers were not enough:

> Of course — I prayed — And did God care?
> He cared as much as on the Air
> A Bird — had stamped her foot — And cried
> "Give Me" — My Reason — Life —
> I had not had — but for Yourself . . .

Dickinson's reaction to faith was not always so stark. Often she seemed ready to believe that God could reveal himself as both powerful and loving. But most of her poems reveal what critic Roger Lundin has called "a piety of homeless devotion." Her poetry did not make a Christian affirmation, but it was defined by questions believers have always asked.

415

Emily Dickinson had little use for conventional religious practice, but wrestling with God is a constant theme in her poems, which are among the best ever written by an American.
The Bettman Archives

Almost the same could be said about the work of Mark Twain (1835-1910). It moved from playful employment of church practices and environments to frank revulsion at the pronouncement of Christian dogma. The former is illustrated by the wonderful scene in *Huckleberry Finn* where Huck describes going to a Presbyterian church with the Grangerfords: "It was pretty ornery preaching — all about brotherly love, and such-like tiresomeness; but everybody said it was a good sermon, and they all talked it over going home, and had such a powerful lot to say about faith and good works and free grace and preforeordestination, and I don't know what all, that it did seem to me to be one of the roughest Sundays I had run across yet." The latter was his response when, as an old man, he read Jonathan Edwards's treatise *On the Freedom of the Will:* "I wallowed and reeled with Jonathan in his insane debauch; rose immediately refreshed and fine at 10 this morning, but with a strange and haunting sense of having been on a three days' tear with a drunken lunatic. . . . All through the book is the glare of a resplendent lunatic gone mad. . . . By God I was ashamed to be in such company." Twain could not be a Christian, but through his last embittered works he wrestled with the faith.

It was otherwise with William Faulkner (1897-1962), whose stories

William Faulkner's novels include many extended and sympathetic portrayals of the intense religious passions of the rural South, black and white. *The Bettman Archives*

about the fictional Yoknapatawpha County, Mississippi, created a gothic world of profound moral seriousness. Titles of such novels as *Absalom, Absalom!* (1936) and *Go Down Moses* (1942) hint at the biblical framework for his art. Even more important are what literary scholar Randall Stewart once called "the basic Christian concepts" that inform the novels. As Stewart put it, "there is everywhere in his writings the basic premise of Original Sin; everywhere the conflict between the flesh and the spirit. . . . Man in Faulkner is a heroic, tragic figure. He may on occasion rise to spiritual greatness. The greatness is measured by the distance between the heights he attains and the depths to which he descends, or, but for the grace of God, might have descended." Faulkner is not a "Christian writer" in any simple sense of the term, but like the great figures in American literature who preceded him, he seems to have shaped his art instinctively with the resources of Christian tradition.

A host of other writers could be cited who, perhaps with slightly less attention, have also wrestled profoundly with Christian themes. Robertson Davies (b. 1913), the contemporary Canadian, is one such figure. Davies's novels and stories are much concerned with the integrity of art, they constitute an ongoing commentary on the provincial character of Canadian intellectual life, and they are molded by Davies's grasp of Jungian psychology. But each of his three major trilogies — Salterton, Deptford, and Cornish — also features instincts, actions, or reflections on Christian matters inspired by Scottish-Canadian Presbyterianism, Anglicanism in Canada and Britain, and observations on Christian expressions as diverse as gypsy Catholicism and storefront rescue missions.

Especially in the twentieth century, North American literature has witnessed something even more remarkable than writers whose imaginations are shaped by Christian faith. Society as a whole may be moving in a more secular direction, and the arts may increasingly be co-opted by ideological propaganda or vulgar commercialism. But at the same time, the prominence of "serious" writers who go beyond wrestling with the resources of Christianity to actually embrace the faith has never been higher. Because these writers take seriously the modern condition and the internal demands of their craft, their works are rarely reassuring, complacent, or even overtly moral. In ways attuned to modern and even postmodern writing, they affirm the ideals of Christian faith at least as clearly as the more conventional and more obviously moral writing that has always been produced so powerfully in North America.

Poet-critics with English connections were pioneers of such affirmation, especially T. S. Eliot (1888-1965), who was raised in St. Louis and educated at Harvard but exerted his literary influence from London, and W. H. Auden (1907-1973), English-born and educated, who wrote some of his most frankly Christian works after becoming an American citizen in 1946. In their train has come a remarkable crop of writers whose work is as literarily diverse as it is religiously varied. The novels of John Updike (b. 1932) can combine detailed sex of the sort never even hinted at in Victorian "Christian fiction" with theological acumen of a sort also rarely found in those works. Frederick Buechner (b. 1926) belies the stereotype of a Presbyterian clergyman (which he is) by being pithy, funny, and frank in his Christ-haunted books. Michael Malone (b. 1942) and John Irwin (b. 1940) are younger novelists whose works move implicitly and sometimes explicitly in Christian directions.

Since World War II, Roman Catholics from the South have produced some of the most riveting literature imbued with faith. It may be because they were alienated losers twice over — as Southerners in a culture dominated by Northern industriousness and as Catholics in an overwhelmingly Protestant South — but Walker Percy (1916-1990) and Flannery O'Connor (1925-1964) have expressed Christian visions more powerful than those of writers from the Protestant North. Percy's grasp of the absurd and the maniacal, in such novels as *Love among the Ruins* and *The Thanatos Syn-*

Though not "Catholic writing" in any simple sense, the novels and essays of Walker Percy still testify powerfully to the shape his Roman Catholic faith gave his entire life. *Religious News Service*

drome, proceeded from a conscience defined by normative Christian virtues. O'Connor, whose life is described in greater detail in Chapter 19, exercised the same ability to startle toward faith.

Still other Catholic writers have added measurably to postwar fiction. The novels and stories of J. F. Powers (b. 1917) featuring Catholic priests are wittily sardonic and yet also suffused with deep reverence for the Catholicism that shapes their milieu. Much the same could be said about the fiction of Ralph McInerny (b. 1929), a philosopher at Notre Dame whose Father Dowling is the most successful cleric-detective since G. K. Chesterton's Father Brown. (The only comparable figure in contemporary detective fiction is Rabbi David Small, who appears in a series of books by Harry Kemelman that exploit the values, quirks, and circumstances of a Jewish community north of Boston just as effectively as McInerny does his fictional world of Catholics in suburban Chicago.)

The Anglo-Oxford authors J. R. R. Tolkien and C. S. Lewis are an inspiration, or at least the appropriate context, for the fantasy of Madeleine L'Engle (b. 1918), one of whose poems is quoted at the start of this chapter. Her fiction is the best example of much work that has been written in imitation of Lewis, Tolkien, and their friends.

The poets who pursue (or are pursued by) Christian themes are as varied as the novelists. Margaret Avison (b. 1918), a Canadian Baptist, and Luci Shaw (b. 1928), born among Plymouth Brethren but conveyed by art into the Episcopal Church, are inspired by clear-eyed visions of the pain, as well as the comfort, of faith. Poets who were preoccupied with Christian themes without promoting them include Robert Lowell (1917-1977), who moved in and out of the Catholic Church during his adult life, and John Berryman (1914-1972), a self-preoccupied and self-destructive friend of the postwar generation's most celebrated poets, who expressed frank Christian affirmations in the poems he wrote shortly before he took his own life.

The list could be extended nearly indefinitely. But what is most significant for a general history of Christianity in North America is to realize how profoundly the culture's literary sensibilities have been touched by Christian themes. These themes appear in almost every imaginable form. They have jolted conventional faith as often as soothed it. In altered form, they continue to be as powerful in the late twentieth century as ever they were in the heyday of "Christian America."

❀   ❀   ❀

The legacies of "Christian America" are not unambiguous. Puritan-evangelical politics promotes self-righteousness as well as public-minded morality. Fascination with Scripture veers into closed-minded anti-intellectualism even as it draws humans to God. Christians who write novels and poems produce mountains of kitsch as well as gems of insight. For historical purposes, the point in recording such legacies is to make sure that those who live at the end of the twentieth century, in a more secular America, remember that they are the heirs of a civilization deeply influenced by Christian institutions, foibles, habits, conventions, eccentricities, and instincts.

Further Reading

Barcus, James E. "Literature, Christianity and." In *The Dictionary of Christianity in America*, pp. 655-58. Downers Grove, IL: InterVarsity Press, 1990.

Frederick, John T. *The Darkened Sky: Nineteenth-Century American Novelists and Religion*. Notre Dame, IN: University of Notre Dame Press, 1969.

Gallup, George, Jr. *Religion in America 1990*. Princeton: Princeton Religion Research Center, 1990.

Hatch, Nathan O., and Mark A. Noll, eds. *The Bible in America: Essays in Cultural History*. New York: Oxford University Press, 1982.

Howe, Daniel Walker. "The Evangelical Movement and Political Culture in the North during the Second Party System." *Journal of American History* 77 (March 1991): 1216-39.

Jeffrey, David L. "The Influence of the Bible upon North American Literature." In *The Oxford Companion to the Bible.* Edited by Bruce M. Metzger. New York: Oxford University Press, 1992.

Marty, Martin E. "America's Iconic Book." In *Humanizing America's Iconic Book.* Edited by G. M. Tucker and D. A. Knight. Chico, CA: Scholars Press, 1982.

Noll, Mark A. "The Bible in America." *Journal of Biblical Literature* 106 (1987): 493-509.

————. *One Nation under God? Christian Faith and Political Action in America.* San Francisco: Harper & Row, 1988.

Nord, David Paul. "The Evangelical Origins of Mass Media in America." *Journalism Monographs* 88 (1984): 1-30.

Reynolds, David S. *Faith in Fiction: The Emergence of Religious Literature in America.* Cambridge: Harvard University Press, 1981.

Siegfried, André. *America Comes of Age: A French Analysis.* New York: Harcourt, Brace, 1927.

Stewart, Randall. *American Literature and Christian Doctrine.* Baton Rouge: Louisiana State University Press, 1958.

Sweet, Leonard I. "Nineteenth-Century Evangelicalism." In *Encyclopedia of the American Religious Experience,* vol. 2, pp. 875-900. New York: Scribner's, 1988.

PART V

WILDERNESS ONCE AGAIN?

FOR THE PERIOD SINCE THE 1920S, IT HAS BECOME EXCEEDINGLY DIFFICULT to relate the history of Christianity in North America as a unified story. For one thing, we are simply so close to the recent past that important patterns of development are hard to separate from more ephemeral circumstances. But the very nature of recent history also contributes to the difficulty. The United States and Canada have become more pluralistic in their religions, and that pluralism extends to varieties of the Christian faith. In a setting where there are now more black Baptists than white Methodists, more Orthodox of Greek, Russian, and other Eastern European stock than either of the colonial period's leading denominations (Episcopalians and Congregationalists), where families of denominations that did not exist in 1900 (e.g., the Pentecostals) are now much larger than a historic American body such as the Presbyterians — the story must indeed be complex.

Diversity also reaches far beyond denominational allegiance. In modern North America the profusion of Christian styles of life stretches as broad as the landmass from sea to sea. Twentieth-century believers apply the faith in hot tubs and picket lines. Their artistic tastes range from Bach to Bill Gaither, from Simone Weil to Marjorie Holmes, from Rembrandt to Charles Schultz. Theologically, there are intense Christian conservatives and radical Christian progressives, as well as countless variations in the middle. Old standoffs, such as those between Protestants and Catholics, still count in some venues, but there are also new ones, such as that between pro-life and pro-choice forces on the question of abortion. No longer will it do, in other words, to talk as if there were simply one main plot for Christianity in North America.

Likewise, fresh sources of information about the churches serve both to help us see the picture more clearly and make it more difficult to say

423

what is going on. Since World War II, systematic surveys of public opinion and practice have added a fresh dimension to analyses of Christian experience. Polls often provide firm information on how many people attended church in the previous week and what sorts of churches they were. They also provide a great deal of information on attitudes, personal religious practices, and connections between religion and other spheres of life. Although the results of these surveys by Gallup and other reputable organizations are not infallible, their general reliability has been well demonstrated. But sometimes adding polling information to the other kinds of records that historians have always used makes it harder to pick out patterns rather than easier. How important are changes and continuities that the pollsters miss? How should national attention to one individual or one crisis be related to broader, underlying trends? What weight should be given the statements of acknowledged leaders over against mass data from the people as a whole? Such questions indicate some of the potential, but also some of the problems, afforded by the new surfeit of information.

But complexity notwithstanding, the kaleidoscopic permutations of modern America do reveal what seem to be observable patterns for the history of Christianity. For one thing, a relative rise in the number of Catholics dating from the mid-nineteenth century has continued throughout the twentieth. For another, a decades-long process of consensus in the United States, which involved Jews as well as Catholics and Protestants, seemed to culminate in the 1950s, only to give way to renewed outbursts of public strife among Christians and between certain groups of Christians and some nonreligious elements. A general pattern is also visible among Protestants in terms of their church adherence: previously marginal groups have become larger and more important, while previously central groups have moved to the margins. In Canada, the postwar years first brought a greater boom for the churches than was experienced in the United States, but then a more precipitate falling away than ever took place in the States. Some patterns of religious belief and practice seem to have changed only slightly, if at all, over the last three quarters of a century. These changes and these continuities are the patterns with which this last section of the book is concerned.

At the same time, the concluding chapters will also focus on questions of interpretation. The major events of the twentieth century — including two global wars, the Great Depression of the 1930s, the North American engagement with the world economy, several revolutions in communications, and the cultural upheavals of the 1960s and 1970s — have restructured patterns of ordinary life to such a degree that they bear little resemblance to life at the time of the Civil War. These social changes raise prominently the question of secularization — that is, whether, and in what ways, the focus of North American life has shifted away from the sacred toward a greater concentration on the circumstances of this world. On closer analysis, however, the notion of secularization itself turns out to be complicated. Part of the problem has to do with facts that seem to move in opposite directions. For example, since the 1920s, the percentage of North Americans claiming to be members of churches has *risen*. But over the same period, the preoccupation of major public media with matters concerning religion has *declined*. Another part of the problem is interpretive. "Secularization" often implies that the power or reality of religion is fading in a society. But from other angles, "secularization" might be a good thing for the churches, as, for example, when the disestablishment of state religions allows many kinds of Christian groups more freedom for their activities.

To raise such questions is to approach what is perhaps the most important question of all for the twentieth-century history of Christianity in North America. The question is sharpest for Protestant descendants of the denominations that were prominent in early periods, but it also affects all Christians who care about the integrity of their faith. The question is whether a North American culture that seems to have less interest in religious matters has become a moral wilderness like the physical wilderness that European settlers first encountered four centuries ago. Put a different way, how should the health of Christianity itself be evaluated in the late twentieth century? Is it better off or worse off as a result of its passage through the recent past? Or maybe it is *both* better off and worse off at the same time. Such interpretive questions are much more difficult than questions about personalities, the growth or decline of denominations, and interactions between the faith and politics or between the faith and intellectual life. But they are questions that must be addressed, if only briefly, before we come to the end of this book.

CHAPTER 16

Turbulent Decades

I'll Overcome Some Day

This world is one great battlefield,
With forces all arrayed;
If in my heart I do not yield
I'll overcome some day.
I'll overcome some day,
I'll overcome some day.

Both seen and unseen powers join
To drive my soul astray,
But with His Word a sword of mine,
I'll overcome some day.
I'll overcome some day,
I'll overcome some day.

*   *   *   *   *

Tho' many a time no signs appear
Of answer when I pray,
My Jesus says I need not fear,
He'll make it plain some day.
I'll be like Him some day,
I'll be like Him some day.

Charles A. Tindley (1851-1933), the pioneering composer of gospel music, published this song in his New Songs of Paradise *(1916). When it was amal-*

gamated with the spiritual "I'll Be All Right" and sung to the tune of the same spiritual, it became the anthem of the civil rights movement of the 1950s and 1960s, "We Shall Overcome."

❧   ❧

IT IS A SLOPPY INTELLECTUAL HABIT TO THINK THAT THE DYNAMICS OF lived human experience can be neatly packaged into discrete decades. Historians are given to the same kind of habit when they think that the reigns of monarchs or the tenures of presidents provide the most important divisions of the past. Shortcomings of this sort notwithstanding, it may still be valuable, as an effort to capture something of the recent development of Christianity in North America, to attempt a rough decade-by-decade account of that history.

This kind of survey must, by its nature, concentrate on public events and controversies. But it is also important to remember that the visible, public "events" of Christian faith rest on the week-by-week gatherings of believers in stately churches, dingy storefronts, rented public schools, and magnificent cathedrals, where attention is paid to Scripture, where the faithful take part in the sacraments or ordinances of their churches, and where Christians share the joys and sorrows of their fellow believers. Newsworthy public events rest on a thick substratum of daily prayer, Bible reading, family worship, and interpersonal support (and sometimes conflict) that rarely receives attention. Some evidence suggests that Christian observances in churches, among families, and by individuals may have declined throughout the course of the twentieth century, but they remain the warp and woof of Christian history in North America and in every other place on the earth. The public events to which we now turn are important in themselves, but a proper understanding will view them as patterns in a carpet densely interwoven with the threads of daily Christian life and weekly Christian assembly.

Legacies of the 1920s

The great crash of the stock market in October 1929 provided a dramatic symbol for the end of an era in the United States as well as Canada. The 1920s had begun in the United States with extraordinary church support for the restoration of national stability after the tumult of World War I.

428

The resurgence of the Ku Klux Klan in the first decades of the twentieth century was fueled, in part, by Protestant fear of other religions. This photo shows a march in Florida early in the century. *California Museum of Photography, Keystone-Mast Collection, University of California, Riverside*

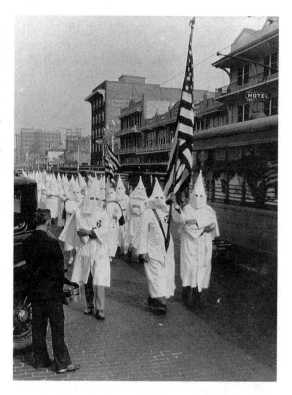

Persistent if vague affirmations of trust in an English-speaking Protestant God featured large in the rhetoric of Presidents Harding and Coolidge. The same affirmations also shaped the small-town midwestern values that sociologists Robert and Helen Lynd described in *Middletown* (1929), a detailed study of life in Muncie, Indiana. In addition, they provided the backdrop for the moral boosterism of merchandiser Russell Conwell (who gave his speech "Acres of Diamonds" on thousands of occasions) and of businessman Bruce Barton, whose 1925 book, *The Man Nobody Knows*, portrayed Jesus as the first great entrepreneur. These uses of the Protestant past came close to trivialization through over-familiarity.

Other uses were more sinister. The assumption that there was a normative national Protestantism helped fuel the Red Scare, the frenzied attack on suspected communists that took place immediately after World War I. It stood behind the growing antagonism to immigrants, especially from Eastern Europe and Asia, that led the United States Congress in 1924 to pass laws restricting immigration. In the lower Midwest and upper South this same hereditary religion was involved in the resurgence of the Ku Klux Klan and its desire to keep American power in white Protestant hands. Uncertain Christian responses to the growing tensions between capital and labor sometimes showed a similar prostitution of the faith to narrowly partisan values. A great general strike in Winnipeg, Manitoba, in 1919 became, for example, an occasion for some Anglican, Methodist, and Baptist ministers to revile and others to baptize the aspirations of working people.

To repeat a previous conclusion, demographics were working against the assumption of a Protestant America. The Catholic Church was growing rapidly. Black Baptist and Methodist churches were as strong as ever in the South, and, because of migration during and after World War I, they were growing in the urban North. Immigration brought in large numbers of Jews to New York, Los Angeles, Chicago, and other Northern cities.

The decline of Protestantism throughout the 1920s owed as much to internal difficulties, however, as to the growth of alternatives. As we have seen, this was the decade of the highly publicized controversy between fundamentalists and modernists in the North. It was the decade of the Scopes Trial, which at least some intellectual arbiters interpreted as traditional Christianity reeling from the blows of modern science. In Canada, where there was no systematic fundamentalist-modernist division, echoes of the American battles still could be heard. The dynamic T. T. Shields of Toronto did not succeed in mounting a full-scale fundamentalist movement across Canada, but he did manage to take nearly eighty churches with him out of the Baptist Confederation of Ontario and Quebec. Even more important than the issues themselves, the fundamentalist-modernist battles discredited the illusion of a dominant cultural Protestantism. Even if the Protestant hegemony forged in the generation of Charles Finney and Francis Asbury had never been as thorough as some Protestant leaders thought it was, it had been a dominant force. But now, in the era of Harry Emerson Fosdick and J. Gresham Machen, that hegemony came to an end. The historian Martin Marty has caught some of the importance of those divisions: "the tearing apart of Protestantism in the twenties . . . is one of the major incidents of American religious history. Its full consequences for culture and society keep revealing themselves differently with each passing decade."

The internal struggles of Protestantism were matched by failed expectations for ecumenical ventures. It was the era when great hopes for the Interchurch World Movement were dashed by the realities of limited funding and widespread lack of interest. In Canada, some leaders of the new United Church felt that after its creation in 1925 it could go on to become a great national church inspiring all Canadians to moral greatness. Although the United Church did survive and continued to exert a considerable influence, it never realized those earlier goals.

430

Al Smith, here at a whistle stop in Montana during the 1928 presidential campaign, was the first Catholic nominee of a major political party for the nation's highest office.
Museum of the City of New York

A straw in the wind for future religious configurations was the nomination by the Democrats in 1928 of a Roman Catholic for president. If Al Smith (the Catholic) did not defeat Herbert Hoover (descended from Quakers) in the election, he nevertheless did receive 60 percent more votes than any Democratic candidate had ever garnered before. And if Protestant opposition to his candidacy was intense, Smith still had shown the increasing political strength of non-Protestants (Catholics, Jews, the unchurched) in several of the nation's major cities. Smith's candidacy pointed to perhaps the most important religious development of the decade — the growing awareness that American life was no longer exclusively dominated by white, Anglo-Saxon, Protestant culture.

Hard Times, 1929-1939

The 1930s proved to be a difficult decade for the older Protestant denominations. With the traumas of the fundamentalist-modernist debate behind them, these groups did display a measure of bureaucratic unity. But they

431

also suffered greatly from the difficulties of the era, especially economic uncertainty. Theological uncertainty was almost as pronounced. The older mainline churches struggled, and often failed, to maintain numbers and contributions on a par with the 1920s. They were the groups who experienced an institutional "religious depression" to match the nation's economic depression.

Yet other, more sectarian Protestant bodies knew better how to redeem the times. The fundamentalists, while vanquished in the old denominations, sustained a thriving variety of evangelistic, educational, and missionary activities. By exploiting the burgeoning fundamentalistic networks, Wheaton College in suburban Chicago became the nation's fastest growing institution of higher learning for several years during the early 1930s. Charles E. Fuller of Pasadena, California, experienced a similar success when in 1937 he took his local radio program to the nation. Within two years "The Old-Fashioned Revival Hour" was reaching a weekly audience of about 10,000,000 over the Columbia Broadcasting System. Some of the traditionally more sectarian denominations also prospered throughout the decade by providing a religious home for ordinary people and by offering a convincing Christian interpretation of daily life. The Southern Baptist Convention, for instance, grew in the decade from fewer than than 4,000,000 members to well over 5,000,000; Seventh-Day Adventists went from about 112,000 to 181,000. Some urban black churches, several holiness denominations, and many newer Pentecostal groups, both black and white, experienced similar growth. What were hard times for the mainline Protestants turned out to be good times for others.

Throughout the decade Protestant theologians struggled to express a convincing Christian faith. Fundamentalists became a self-aware minority largely content with the anti-intellectual label with which they had been identified in the 1920s. Yet by the end of the decade, a few younger fundamentalists were searching for a less combative, more intellectually respectable faith. Some of them, including Edward John Carnell, Carl F. H. Henry, and George Eldon Ladd, were later recruited to staff the first "neo-evangelical" attempt at a full-fledged seminary. Located in Pasadena, California, it was named after Charles Fuller and funded by contributions to his radio broadcast.

More liberal Protestants experienced considerable difficulty in clarifying theological issues. Some were eager to dilute even further the particularities of their Christian faith. In 1932 the Commission of Appraisal of the Layman's Foreign Missions Inquiry issued a report entitled *Rethinking Missions* that called on foreign workers to stress social outreach rather than evangelistic preaching. The principal author of the report, William Hocking of the Harvard philosophy department, felt that the goal of missionary work should be to find points of unity between Christianity and the other religions of the world. From a contrary perspective, other Protestant theologians bent under the pressure of events — especially economic collapse and the rise of the Nazis — and began to propound a theology more attuned to the limits of human nature and more open to the notion of divine transcendence. Such Protestants were also influenced by questions being raised by the neo-orthodox theologies of Europeans Karl Barth and Emil Brunner. A 1935 manifesto expressing this viewpoint, *The Church against the World,* presented the argument that cultural captivity was the great enemy of authentic Christian faith. Its authors — a Southern Presbyterian layman, Francis Miller; an expatriate church historian from Germany, Wilhelm Pauck; and a young professor of theology from Yale, H. Richard Niebuhr — criticized fundamentalists for providing false answers to the crises of the era. But they also joined fundamentalists in criticizing liberal platitudes about the goodness of humanity and the inevitable progress of the human race. Their manifesto echoed many of the themes found in the larger work of Richard Niebuhr and his brother, Reinhold.

In the Catholic Church, which continued its steady rise in numbers and (despite the Depression) economic resources, a different theological climate prevailed. During the decade a neoscholastic synthesis, rooted in the thought of Thomas Aquinas, became the dominant influence. Neo-Thomism, which stressed the Church's authority, the value of disciplined reasoning, and the unifying spirituality of the sacraments, provided ballast for a considerable intellectual exercise in which academics from many disciplines organized societies to explore Thomistic conceptions of their work. Catholic thought of the age was formally similar to fundamentalistic thought. The two groups differed markedly between themselves, but both were practicing the life of the mind on their own, without addressing the larger intellectual community.

In society, Catholic energies received a fresh boost from an Italian import. "Catholic Action" was both a concept and an organization. The concept was that the laity, supported by an active liturgical life and intensive involvement in small groups, could shape economic and social spheres in a distinctly Christian fashion. Through the leadership of such priests as Reynold Hillenbrand of Chicago and a network of laymen, Catholic Action was by the end of the 1930s representing a growing network of organizations dedicated to Christian outreach and renewal. In Quebec, Catholic Action introduced several young Canadians, including the future prime minister Pierre Elliott Trudeau, to larger worlds of social responsibility. Later Canadian history was marked by the irony that not a few veterans of Catholic Action from the 1930s

433

Under the leadership of Dorothy Day, the Catholic Worker movement was one of the most conscientious Christian organizations that attempted to address the physical and psychological traumas of the Depression. This is a breadline outside a New York City Catholic Worker office in 1937. *Marquette University Archives*

and 1940s led Quebec out from under the control of the Catholic Church in the 1960s and 1970s. Catholic Action was not as well known outside of the Church as the Catholic Worker movement of Dorothy Day and Peter Maurin, which is discussed in Chapter 19, but until the changes brought about by the Second Vatican Council in the early 1960s, it was probably the Catholic Church's strongest lay witness in American society.

Social and economic strain no doubt contributed to the sensational, apocalyptic voices that arose in the churches during the 1930s. Premillennialist evangelist Gerald B. Winrod from Kansas saw a plot behind Franklin Roosevelt's "Jewish New Deal" and tried to rally fundamentalists to oppose the president. The most noticeable public religious voice, however, belonged to a Detroit Catholic priest, Father Charles Coughlin. After having supported FDR on his extraordinarily popular radio broadcast for a time, Coughlin turned against him in a vitriolic campaign that soon became an embarrassment to his Catholic superiors. In general, however, political influence from American churches grew quite diffuse during this period. Because so many contending religious groups were trying to push President Roosevelt and the state governments in so many different ways, the pushing led to little significant movement.

Tommy Douglas, who carried the liberal evangelical values of his Baptist upbringing into politics, became the Co-operative Commonwealth Federation premier of Saskatchewan during the 1940s. Here he is shown speaking to strikers at a Hamilton, Ontario, steel mill in 1949. *National Archives of Canada*

In Canada a different situation prevailed. While the main denominations suffered many of the same disabilities as their counterparts in the United States, politics inspired by religion flourished, especially in the western provinces. From one side, former leading proponents of the Social Gospel, such as Methodist James S. Woodsworth and Baptist T. C. "Tommy" Douglas, were leading figures in the creation of the Co-operative Commonwealth Federation. The CCF, which in the 1930s won seats in the national parliament and in 1944 became the ruling party in Saskatchewan, sought a socialist alternative to capitalism, at least in part out of a desire to Christianize the social order. From the other side, a fundamentalist radio preacher, William Aberhart, cut a wide swath politically in Alberta by championing "Social Credit," a scheme of Englishman C. H. Douglas to distribute money to all residents. Under the Social Credit banner, Aberhart won two provincial elections (in 1935 and 1940). As time wore on, the party became more conservative in its social and economic policies, but even after Aberhart's death in 1943 it remained a powerful influence in Alberta and neighboring provinces. The United States also contained religious figures who shared the socialism of the CCF and who came close to the populism of Aberhart. But it is again a commentary on differences between the two societies that these religious connections made a more noticeable impact on the politics of the 1930s in Canada than in the United States.

The Depression era also saw the beginning of more significant involvement by immigrant churches in American and Canadian life. When the United States Congress passed restrictive immigration legislation in the 1920s, it greatly cut back the connections with Old World cultures as well as the numbers of immigrants. Some former enclaves actually began to reach out to the wider society, as, for example, the Lutheran Church–Missouri Synod, which sponsored a successful radio program called "The Lutheran Hour," on which the scholarly Walter Maier preached effectively, and in English. The immigrant churches were not yet part of mainstream American life, but the assimilation process was accelerating. Canada received fresh infusions of European immigrants in the 1920s and, unlike the United States, continued to accept significant numbers of European immigrants after the Second World War. The result was that by 1950 Canada was home to a much wider array of Christian bodies than was the case at the start of the twentieth century.

This period like all others was filled not only with momentous public events but also with private tragedy, growth, reversal, joy, and despair. The 1930s was a time when many in the churches worried that communism would erode traditional religious values. What was harder to see at the time was the way that traditional faith worked as an antidote to Marxist faith for some who had became communists. It was during this decade, for example, that Joy Davidman, who later became the wife of the British apologist C. S. Lewis, and Will Herberg, a Jew who later wrote a classic study of American religious life, began their pilgrimages away from Marx toward faith in God. In other dimensions of life, similarly unnoticed events would come to have as much importance as those covered in the *New York Times* or debated in denominational assemblies. We have already seen that, despite secularizing trends, notable literature with Christian themes has flourished in recent decades. Cause and effect is opaque beyond resolution, but it is striking that four of the notable writers who most seriously engaged the Christian faith in the 1950s and later had, as children or teenagers, lost their fathers in the interwar years: Flannery O'Connor, whose father died of lupus in 1941, and John Berryman, Walker Percy, and Frederick Buechner, each of whose fathers committed suicide. Such domestic tragedies do not fit easily into normal historical accounts, but they may be the developments that in the long run count most.

War and Its Aftermath, 1939-1960

For the decade of the 1940s the dominant influence in North American religion, as in almost everything else, was World War II. After the war a period of readjustment and consolidation took place that lasted through the presidency of Dwight Eisenhower (1953-1961). In Canada a similar drive for stability lasted nearly as long through the Liberal regimes of wartime prime minister William Lyon Mackenzie King and his hand-picked successor, Louis St. Laurent, a stately grandfatherly figure cut from the same comforting cloth as General Eisenhower.

During the war itself, the social changes resulting from all-out mobilization had considerable impact on generally religious matters. The recruitment of troops and industrial expansion on the home front changed traditional gender roles, family structures, geographical living patterns, and occupational demographics. When a grateful United States government provided the G.I. Bill for veterans to attend college, social change was accelerated yet further. The war also brought women and blacks more centrally into the public view. Women, who had managed factories and other traditionally masculine domains, were not always eager to resume traditional roles after the war. Blacks, who served in great numbers to fight for the Allies' freedom, gained firmer notions of what freedom *within* American society might mean.

Both good and evil, from strictly Christian perspectives, occurred during the conflict. Most believers in the United States and Canada maintained a shameful silence when ethnic Japanese, many of them Christian, were interned for much of the war. More positively, the churches through chaplains and social agencies offered consistent ministry to troops at home and abroad. The war was also a harbinger of ecumenical activity as it drew together in common tasks, often for the first time, representatives of most of the nation's denominations. The economic prosperity that unexpectedly followed the war also provided denominations and local churches with resources missing during the long period of Depression and war.

Wartime gave way to an era of booming growth for the two nations, and also for their churches. The vast surge in the population — the postwar Baby Boom — created countless new families for whom attachment to church became as normal as increased personal prosperity and a move to the suburbs. Church membership and the building of new houses of worship both increased dramatically. From 1945 to 1949, Southern Baptists grew by nearly 300,000 members; Catholics baptized something on the order of 1,000,000 infants a year; and Methodists reported growing more rapidly in the four years after the war than in any period since the mid-1920s. By 1950 Protestant and Jewish seminaries were enrolling twice their prewar numbers, and Catholic institutions also experienced substantial increases. The Canadian boom may have been even stronger, with countless new associations such as Sunday Schools and adult study groups drawing tens of thousands into active church participation. In the twenty years after the war, the

The executive committee of the National Association of Evangelicals, which came into existence as an alternative to the Federal Council of Churches, is shown here in an early meeting from 1942. *Archives of the Billy Graham Center*

United Church of Canada by itself constructed 1,500 churches and over 600 manses, and these were figures that most other denominations matched proportionately.

Also on the increase was interdenominational or parachurch cooperation among Christians. Prosperity after the war seemed to make many denominations more confident in their own capacities for outreach, nurture, and social influence. But the strengthening of the individual church bodies was also matched by ecumenical breakthroughs. Theologically conservative Protestants organized the National Association of Evangelicals in 1942, and they continued after the war to form myriads of new organizations for evangelism, missions, publishing, and youth work. For their part, the older Protestant churches took the lead in 1950 to form the National Council of Churches. These same denominations were also in the forefront of church union. The two largest bodies of northern Presbyterians merged in 1958, and in 1959 the Congregationalists and the Evangelical and Reformed Church joined to form the United Church of Christ. North of the border, the Canadian Council of Churches and the Baptist Federation of Canada, both organized in 1944, testified to a similar unitive direction.

Despite the increasingly pluralistic character of North American religion, Protestants who participated in these mergers and new federations sometimes retained the nationalistic aspirations of their predecessors. Leaders

A snowstorm prevented President Truman from appearing at the constituting convention of the National Council of Churches in late November 1950. But the banner emblazoned over the gathering spoke eloquently of the Council's national aspirations.
National Council of Churches

of the new Youth for Christ movement thought that their ability to draw a crowd — for example, the 70,000 who showed up in Chicago's Soldier Field on Memorial Day, 1945 — heralded an impending national revival in which conservative evangelicals would once again define the agenda. In Cleveland on November 28, 1950, when the National Council of Churches was born, a huge banner proclaimed "One Nation under God." And Henry Knox Sherrill, the Council's first president, stated that the Council's formation "marks a new and great determination that the American way will be increasingly the Christian way, for such is our heritage. . . . Together the churches can move forward to the goal — a Christian America in a Christian world."

One facet of this Protestant nationalism was a continued distrust of Roman Catholics. In 1939 President Roosevelt had tried to name a personal representative to the Vatican, a move that sparked fierce Protestant opposition. After the war, fundamentalist spokesmen continued to rail at Catholicism. But the strongest attack came in a book from the Protestant mainstream, Paul Blanshard's *American Freedom and Catholic Power* (1949). Continuing agitation over the rights of Catholics to school funding in Ontario kept alive the same sort of Protestant antagonisms in parts of Canada. These anti-Catholic sentiments loomed large in the immediate postwar period. It is clearer now than it was then, however, that they were remnants of the past rather than guideposts for the future.

The postwar period also brought a notable increase in concern for the psychological dimensions of religion. The national effort to adjust to postwar conditions as well as persistent uncertainty internationally (communism, the atomic bomb) fostered a climate in which religion was enlisted in the search for psychological repose. Beginning with Rabbi Joshua Loth Liebman's *Peace of Mind* in 1946, a series of influential best-sellers showed how religion could lead to a fuller and more settled existence. The most widely distributed of these books came from some of the era's major religious figures — Norman Vincent Peale's *Guide to Confident Living* (1948) and *The Power of Positive Thinking* (1952), Bishop Fulton J. Sheen's *Peace of Soul* (1949), and Billy Graham's *Peace with God* (1953).

Christianity of different sorts also had much to do with reactions to the Cold War. The "fall" of China to Mao Tse-tung seemed especially tragic for many Americans in both liberal and fundamentalist camps, since a wide spectrum of Protestant missionaries had invested decades of evangelizing, teaching, and healing in that corner of the world. At the start of the 1950s, Sen. Joseph McCarthy from Wisconsin grabbed headlines and wrenched hearts with sensational charges about communists in the U.S. state department and elsewhere.

The fact that Senator McCarthy was a Roman Catholic pointed to the increasing visibility of Catholics in the nation's public life. Postwar affluence increased the ability of Catholics to mobilize for the strengthening of their communities. Catholic schools, colleges, service organizations, publishers, and learned societies all came into existence or were strengthened in the postwar period. In 1960, the election of the nation's first Catholic president, John F. Kennedy, signaled how far this influential Christian community had come in moving out from its earlier enclaves.

Theologically, the postwar period was calm at the center but beginning to boil at the periphery. A rising generation of Protestant conservatives was growing increasingly dissatisfied with fundamentalist bromides. Manifestos from this group included a collection of Carl F. H. Henry's lectures published in 1947 under the title *The Uneasy Conscience of Modern Fundamentalism*, in which he appealed for renewed social and intellectual engagement, and Bernard Ramm's *The Christian View of Science and Scripture* (1954), in which he defended the compatibility of modern science and traditional views of the Bible. An even greater jolt to a larger Christian community was administered in 1955 by Monsignor John Tracy Ellis. Ellis's essay "American Catholics and the Intellectual Life," which he expanded the next year into a book, called for Catholics to devote more resources and expend more mental energy in mastering the complicated academic disciplines of the twentieth century. By failing to demonstrate a mature, respected intellect, said Ellis, Catholics were short-changing the character of their faith and crippling the outreach of Catholicism into the larger society. A great and varied literature arose in response to Ellis — a literature that anticipated the vigor, but also the fragmentation, that would soon characterize Catholic thought.

From the perspective of the 1990s, it is difficult to assess the postwar mood objectively. On the one hand, the growth of the churches, the widespread dedication to reach adults and children with the Christian message, and the effort to find useful social values in a general "Judeo-Christian" heritage represented significant accomplishments. What the alienated of that generation came to regard as complacency may have been, in reality, a hard-earned stability. On the other hand, this postwar "era of good feelings" was also self-indulgent, conformist, and unimaginative. Beneath the surface, churchgoers seem to have participated quite eagerly in social trends that thinned out the faith. With almost no serious analysis, Christians welcomed television — and its relentless materialism — as an intimate member of the household. Long before the papal encyclical *Humanae Vitae* reaffirmed the Catholic prohibition of artificial birth control in 1968, the size of Catholic families was shrinking — even in Quebec, North America's most traditional Catholic enclave. Conservative evangelicals such as the leaders of the new Youth for Christ movement translated the gospel into forms of entertainment that looked as much like versions of youthful diversion as alternatives to it. Mainline Protestants, while exerting themselves to build bureaucracies, prepare Sunday School literature, and provide for a larger clergy, were also busy creating a religion of the lowest common denominator with less and less that was distinctly Christian.

It may have been, to borrow a phrase from Charles Dickens, the worst of times as well as the best of times.

Revolutions and Counterrevolutions, 1960-1980

Whatever may have been happening beneath the surface in the postwar era, the upsetting developments of the 1960s and 1970s were right out front for everyone to see. If the postwar years represented wide-ranging growth and

441

diversification for the churches, the 1960s were simply a shock. Prominent images signaled the rapid shift from a settled order in the 1950s to the tumults of the 1960s — from the grandfatherly President Eisenhower in the United States and the beneficent "Uncle Louis" St. Laurent in Canada to the assassination of two Kennedys and Martin Luther King, Jr., and a rising tide of separatist terrorism in Quebec. Such tumults seemed also to have defined the course of Christianity in North America since that time.

During the 1960s — marked by moral revolution — older mainline churches received the greatest public attention as they sought an accommodation with the times. During the next decade — marked by moral reaction — fundamentalists seized the initiative and tried to redirect society in a conservative direction. The legacy of these contentious times was a pervasive division between liberal and conservative approaches to both public issues and the life of faith. This division came to dwarf the significance of the traditional denominations.

The 1960s were tumultuous in many particulars. Black Americans, long frustrated by painfully slow progress in realizing the nation's vaunted freedom, agitated for civil rights in a movement guided by clergymen such as Martin Luther King, Jr. Violence broke in upon the public with unprecedented force with the assassination of John F. Kennedy in 1963 and of both Robert Kennedy and Martin Luther King in 1968. The death of 50,000 less-well-known Americans who perished in Vietnam left an even more permanent scar.

Disorder in public life seemed also to be matched by disorder in private. Whether an actual sexual revolution occurred in the 1960s or there was simply a new frankness about practices already habitual in private, the public became ineluctably aware of shifting values. More and more people talked about a relaxation of sexual standards; less and less restraint hindered public discussion of sexual issues. The feminist movement, the increased participation of women in the job market, the rising divorce rate, the widespread availability of pornography, and the public advocacy of homosexuality were symptoms of upheaval in family and sexual ethics.

In the churches, efforts to respond to the crises of the times led to deep intramural divisions. While the relative importance of the denominations had been declining throughout the century, they were moved further to the sidelines by the controversies of the 1960s and following years. Within most large denominations, caucuses emerged to promote individual causes or clusters of actions. Outside the denominations religious organizations for almost every imaginable purpose — from motorcycle evangelism, support for the divorced, and the distribution of the Bible to organizations for ecological awareness, open housing, and ethical

The march on Washington for Jobs and Freedom, August 28, 1963, enlisted many church groups, as did other civil rights activities of the period. *Religious News Service*

After the assassination of Dr. Martin Luther King, Jr., in the spring of 1968, arson and looting occurred in several American cities. This photo was taken in New York City's Harlem. *Religious News Service*

investment on Wall Street — multiplied beyond counting. The result of these divisions within denominations and the proliferating array of special interest groups was a new pattern for religious organization. What historian John Webster Grant has written about the Canadian churches pertains as well for those in the United States:

> among all the churches there appeared a new line of fissure that bore little relation to traditional denominational and party differences. . . . Demands quickly followed for the more effective representation of groups that felt themselves to be deprived of power in the church — the laity generally, but especially women, youth, and ethnic minorities. Even those who showed no great desire for radical change seemed reluctant to trust decisions to boards or committees on which their peers were not strongly represented. Hierarchical and conciliar churches alike were pressed to institute participatory democracy.

Nor were explicit indictments of the churches lacking. In 1961, Peter Berger took his theme and his title, *The Noise of Solemn Assemblies,* from words in the book of Amos ("I hate, I despise your feasts, and I take no delight in your solemn assemblies"). According to Berger, a German-born sociologist, the churches were sacrificing their essential message of encounter with God for fascination with the machinery of bureaucracy. A few years later the Anglican Church of Canada asked journalist Pierre Berton, who had been raised in a Yukon parish of that denomination, to critique the church from which he had dropped out. The result was Berton's *The Comfortable Pew* (1965), a book that chastised the churches for their complacency, their lack of connection to modern concerns, and their inattention to the struggles of modern individuals. Both books, and several others of the same stripe, became best-sellers and sparked much debate.

Christian voices in sympathy with the revolutionary character of the times were the ones most frequently heard in the 1960s. While many religious figures supported the war in Vietnam, those who opposed it — such as William Sloane Coffin of New York's Riverside Church and the Catholics Philip and Daniel Berrigan — made a larger public impact. The Vietnam conflict also stimulated a questioning of national military policy and fed directly into a pacifistic trend. For the first time since the interwar period, representatives of mainline Protestant churches and some Catholics campaigned against the military, and some joined such traditional pacifists as the Mennonites and Quakers in arguing against warfare of any sort. Socially progressive denominations also took the lead in supporting appeals for resistance to oppression based on gender, race, and class.

In the wake of the Supreme Court's ruling in *Roe v. Wade,* conservatives from across the denominational spectrum joined in protesting the liberalized acceptance of abortion. This photo was taken at the 1978 "March for Life" in Washington, D.C. *Religious News Service*

During the 1970s, there was considerable reaction against the main developments of the 1960s (which had been either "breakthroughs" or "disasters," depending on one's point of view). Most visible was the rise of a political movement known as the "New Religious Right." Three events seemed to have stimulated the renewal of the kind of evangelical political action that was standard in the nineteenth century but that had largely diminished after the 1930s. The first was the ruling of Supreme Court on abortion in 1973. Many religious conservatives viewed the *Roe v. Wade* decision legalizing abortion on demand as an explicit affront to Judeo-Christian reverence for life and an implicit sanction of the morally reprehensible sexual revolution. The second event was the nation's Bicentennial in 1976, an occasion exploited by aggrieved conservatives to appeal for a return to the nation's Christian heritage, which they pictured as once strong but now in grave peril. The third event was the election as president at the end of the decade of Ronald Reagan, a conservative voice who won overwhelming approval from theologically conservative Protestants and who also had unprecedented success, for a Republican, among Roman Catholics. With spokesmen skillful in the use of the media, such as Jerry Falwell of the Moral Majority, conservative Christians rallied to the cause of what they regarded as "traditional values."

The sorts of Protestant conservatives who backed the Moral Majority were also active in education. Since the nineteenth century, Catholics and a few denominations of European confessional background (Lutherans, Christian Reformed) had maintained parochial schools. In the twentieth century they had been joined by Seventh-Day Adventists and Pentecostals, who also sponsored considerable numbers of their own schools. But in the 1960s and following years, hundreds of new "Christian academies" were founded by evangelical and fundamentalist Protestants opposed to the "secular humanism" they believed was taking over public education. In these new schools, politically or socially sensitive topics could be treated in accord with the wishes of the parents and churches who organized, staffed, and funded them. One especially sensitive topic was the teaching of biological evolution, which, in the turbulence of the late twentieth century, functioned much more on the level of a contest between supernatural and materialistic cosmologies than on the level of a scientific debate. In these new schools, assertions that the earth had been created relatively recently and that the earth's geological strata were laid down by Noah's flood became defiant marks of a resurgent conservative confession.

Christian higher education also underwent its traumas in the 1960s and 1970s. As religious vocations for men and women declined among Catholics, a growing number of Catholic colleges and universities began to recruit non-Catholics for their faculties. Catholic boards of trustees were also opened to lay and non-Catholic participation. Contending voices called for these institutions to heed more carefully the wisdom of the modern world or to shun it as a corrosive influence. Among the older Protestant churches, church-related colleges faced increasing problems. Fewer and fewer of what had once been the dominant kind of American colleges were able to tell their constituencies how they differed from secular private colleges. On the other side of the Protestant spectrum, almost all of the period's most visible media entrepreneurs (Jerry Falwell, Oral Roberts, Pat Robertson, Jimmy Swaggart, and John MacArthur, to mention only a few) founded their own colleges as alternatives to the existing institutions of secular higher education.

The Second Vatican Council

Among Catholics, the great event of the 1960s was the Second Vatican Council (1962-1965). However the Council was understood by later popes and their advisors, in the United States it was seen as a liberalizing event. In response to Pope John XXIII's call for opening the windows of the church, the Council appealed for greater collegiality, more scope for the laity, and more interaction with modern scholarship. By the mid-1960s American

One of the major changes in the Roman Catholic Church after the Second Vatican Council was the willingness to bring "church" out into the daily lives of parishioners. Here mass is being celebrated at a private home in the inner city of West Philadelphia.
Religious News Service

Catholics had set aside lingering doubts about full participation in the American democratic process, doubts that had persisted among the hierarchy at least into the 1950s. Since the Council, American Catholics have also found it much more acceptable to "dialogue" with Protestants and members of other faiths. The most notable of these ecumenical dialogues have been discussions with Lutherans, out of which has come a series of path-breaking statements. Although these statements recognize remaining differences between the two historic communions, they also point to a much broader range of agreement — including a near agreement on the historically critical question of justification by faith — than was thought possible as recently as 1960.

The Vatican Council's attitude toward the Bible encouraged a contrasting pair of developments. Catholic biblical scholars began to look more like liberal Protestants as they put to use conventional critical approaches to Scripture. But groups of lay Catholics began to look more like evangelical Protestants as they adopted patterns and habits of small-group Bible study. Among this latter segment, the Catholic charismatics were especially important.

447

A thorny development after the Council was the publication of Pope Paul VI's encyclical *Humanae Vitae* in 1968, which forbade any form of artificial birth control. For perhaps the first time in American history, legions of Catholics chose to ignore a major teaching of the Church and in practice sanctioned the use of artificial forms of family planning.

Because of events in the 1960s, Roman Catholics have become more oriented to lay ministry, more internally pluralistic, more socially conscious, more attuned to the larger academic community, more active politically, and more self-consciously ideological than ever before in American history. It is a fact welcomed by some Catholics and deplored by others that the Catholic Church now seems to contain within itself many of the differences and much of the energy (both creative and fragmenting) that are evident in the many Protestant denominations.

A Quiet Revolution

In Canada, the 1960s and 1970s also witnessed considerable change, agitation, and disruption in the churches. In the early 1970s the Lutherans surpassed the Presbyterians to become Canada's third largest Protestant denomination, and other European-rooted churches also grew substantially in these decades. Ecumenical dialogue increased dramatically, especially after the Second Vatican Council. Controversy continued over the funding of Catholic schools in Ontario, but, beginning in 1965, worship services under joint Catholic-Protestant auspices also took place, a development inconceivable only a few short years before. Catholic, United Church, and Anglican spokespeople led the way in promoting advanced social reform, criticizing the United States' involvement in Vietnam, and warning about cultural imperialism from Canada's aggressive southern neighbor. At the same time, however, evangelicals within the larger denominations and a whole host of smaller conservative bodies (e.g., the Pentecostal Assemblies of Canada, the Christian and Missionary Alliance, the Mennonite Brethren) either increased their numbers or looked outward in new ways and so became more visible in the nation's religious life. Following the National Association of Evangelicals from the United States, an Evangelical Fellowship of Canada was formed in the early 1960s. But only in 1967, when the Evangelical Fellowship sponsored an exhibition at Montreal's world fair in competition with the ecumenical pavilion planned by Catholics, Orthodox, and the Canadian Council of Churches, did the lineaments of a trans-Canadian evangelical network come into view.

The most important Christian story in Canada since World War II was

In April 1957, Pierre Elliott Trudeau, later the prime minister of Canada, was photographed with Gérard Picard, president of the Confederation of Catholic Workers of Canada. Trudeau's political liberalism had earlier been nurtured by his participation in Quebec's reformist Catholic labor movement. *National Archives of Canada*

the revolution of Catholicism in Quebec. For more than a century, Quebec had been the most thoroughly Catholic region in North America and also the region with the highest rate of participation in weekly church activities. Harbingers of a new situation appeared, however, during and after the Second World War. In 1943, the province for the first time made education compulsory for all children, and during the war more and more people moved to the cities. Shortly thereafter, key church leaders supported striking asbestos workers in their push for better working conditions, a move that signaled a sharp break from earlier cooperation between elites in church and industry. In 1960, Quebec's labor unions, which had always been Catholic organizations, broke their ties with the Church. In that same year, the Liberal Party won a decisive provincial election, and the outward-looking cultural style that would be associated with Pierre Elliott Trudeau on the national level secured its hold.

What followed in the 1960s has sometimes been called "the Quiet Revolution," but it *was* a revolution. Many different voices called for greater autonomy for Quebec over against Canada as a whole, but the stress was now on economic or linguistic distinctives rather than on Quebec's Catholic heritage. Charles de Gaulle's 1967 visit from France, during which he appealed publicly for a "free Quebec," brought political agitation to the boiling point. Urban terrorists in the late 1960s and politicians appealing for a separate Quebec propounded Marxist, socialist, capitalist, and several other ideologies, but rarely did they mention the church. In 1964 a provincial Ministry of Education was created, and for the first time in Quebec history the Catholic Church was not in control of the schools. Criticism of Catholic institutions of a sort once rarely heard now became widespread. Attendance at mass plummeted. Vocations to the priesthood and for service in women's religious orders experienced a comparable decline.

Almost overnight, it seemed, a stable synthesis of Catholic, French, rural, conservative, isolationist, and precapitalist values had disappeared. In May 1980 Quebec voters rejected a move toward secession from Canada, but the former Catholic-cultural synthesis was nonetheless gone forever. Earlier weaknesses in the Church's response to modern intellectual and social arrangements as well as the powerful inroads after World War II of market forces help to account for Quebec's rapid change. But fully satisfactory explanations for this extraordinary — and extraordinarily rapid — revolution have yet to be published.

Charismatic Renewal

Within the churches of both Canada and the United States, the most dramatic channel of renewal during the 1960s and 1970s was the charismatic movement. The emphasis on a special filling of the Holy Spirit after conversion had been moving out from the Pentecostal churches since at least the 1940s. After the war, the labors of a new wave of Pentecostal itinerants, led by William Branham and Oral Roberts, broadened the appeal of faith healing beyond traditional Pentecostal denominations. The Full Gospel Business Men's Fellowship International, founded in 1953 by Demos Shakarian, brought an emphasis on the special work of the Spirit to broader circles of Catholics and Protestants. Numerous independent movements, some ephemeral and some affecting thousands, likewise stressed these charismatic themes. Soon after Episcopal clergyman Dennis Bennett experienced baptism in the Holy Spirit with speaking in tongues in 1959, more and more groups in the traditional Protestant churches began to look for this special work of the Spirit. In 1967 a band of Roman Catholics at Pittsburgh's Duquesne University received the baptism of the Spirit. The next year, additional groups of Catholics at the University of Notre Dame and at several locations in Michigan were likewise affected. Simultaneously, several large independent churches or ministries, including those of Kenneth Hagin, Kenneth Copeland, Chuck Smith, Pat Robertson, and John Wimber, were also promoting an emphasis on the extraordinary gifts of the Spirit.

What is now known as the charismatic movement includes at least three centers — Catholic, traditional Protestant, and independent Protestant. Generally speaking, charismatics do not specify the steps of the Spirit's extraordinary work as specifically as Pentecostals, even though the gift of

450

The dramatic spread of the charismatic movement came very early to
include Roman Catholics along with
many kinds of Protestants. This photo
was taken at the 1976 Eastern General
Conference of the Catholic Charismatic Renewal in Atlantic City,
which drew some 28,000 people.
Religious News Service

tongues is usually considered (as among Pentecostals) the most obvious sign
of the Spirit's work. The concerns of charismatics are as broad as American
religion itself, with a proliferation of groups promoting family support,
urban outreach, overseas missions, exorcisms, "deliverances," and a wide
variety of other special works. Charismatics and independent Pentecostals
were early exploiters of radio and then became leaders in the use of television. Oral Roberts, whose career spans a transition from tabernacle itinera-
tion to upbeat television productions, was a leader in exploiting the media.

The charismatic renewal movement is hard to describe, both because
it is so recent and because it is so diverse. Not surprisingly, its rapid spread
has been the source of considerable controversy. Theological liberals often
look askance at charismatic spirituality as an escape from social responsibilities in this world. Large conservative denominations such as the Lutheran
Church–Missouri Synod and the Southern Baptist Convention have rejected
charismatic interpretations of the Bible. After considerable early uneasiness,
the Catholic hierarchy has followed Pope Paul VI and Pope John Paul II in
approving the movement but with the caution that charismatic Catholics
not undermine the Church's authority by their practice of the gifts. Parallel
developments in Africa, South America, and Asia have contributed to
making the charismatic movement one of the most dynamic, if also most
debated, recent movements in the history of the church.

451

State in Church

Since the Depression era, churches in the United States have had to contend with an ever-growing role for government in public life. The growth of government involvement in daily life is one of the reasons for the flourishing of the religious voluntary societies concerned about public policy. In a political system in which institutions as such are not the focus of law, except as they embody the will of individuals, it has become increasingly necessary to organize for special purposes. The end result is that the consequences of government action are heightened and all interchanges in the public square — including religious interchange — are politicized.

A growing sphere of government action can be highly disturbing to religious organizations, since traditions, biblical interpretations, and commonly accepted procedures in the churches do not always conform to the standards of fairness developed in the democratic, market-oriented, and individualistic history of the United States. At the same time, the churches' discontent with government intrusion is sometimes a result of their own culpable inaction. It was Christian individuals, not the churches as a whole, who agitated to gain civil rights for blacks, Native Americans, and other ethnic minorities. The same may be said about earlier efforts to protect children and women from overwork in factories and to insure that laborers received the sort of humane treatment due all human beings: a few religious leaders spoke out against existing injustices, but it was the government that, however clumsily, brought about the needed changes. If government defense of human rights is ham-fisted or goes too far, churches have mostly themselves to blame for not working more effectively toward better solutions.

A series of decisions by the Supreme Court has also brought the government more directly into contact with religious spheres. The most controversial cases were decided in the 1960s, and so contributed to the general tumult of those times. But foundational decisions had come earlier. In a case from 1940 involving the rights of Jehovah's Witnesses, *Cantwell v. Connecticut*, the Court ruled that on the basis of the Civil War–era Fourteenth Amendment, it had a right to apply the standards of the First Amendment to the states. Thus, both the free exercise of religion and the prohibition against establishing religion found in the First Amendment could be applied to local and state circumstances as well as to actions of the national Congress. A further decision in 1947, *Everson v. Board of Education*, in which the use of public school buses to transport children in parochial schools was under consideration, defined "the separation of church and state" in much sharper terms than had been the case before. These decisions in turn served as the basis for some controversial opinions of the 1960s — *Engel v. Vitale* (1962), which prohibited the recitation of prayers in public schools, and *Abington School District v. Schempp* (1963), which made a similar prohibition against the reading of Scripture in a public school's opening exercises. (Later Supreme Court decisions affirmed the propriety of studying the Bible and other religious texts as part of literature or history classes, but not as a religious observance expected of all children.) Unhappiness with these decisions helped fuel the rise of the New Religious Right.

Unlike the United States, Canada has never tried to divide the spheres of religion and government with thorough precision. Yet in the 1980s the role of Canada's government also grew in importance for the churches. An action by the British parliament in 1982 to give Canada complete control over its own constitution was accompanied by new laws and legal procedures in Canada itself. The most important of these was a Charter of Rights and Freedoms that spelled out, along the lines of the United States' Bill of Rights, a specific set of protections for citizens and prohibitions concerning governmental actions. The final implications of the new Charter are not yet clear, but it seems to have encouraged a rights-centered, individualistic approach to many social relationships (families, schools, labor unions, churches) that contradicts the traditional Canadian respect for the privileges of ethnic, religious, and educational groups.

In larger perspective, the growing government has taken over more and more of the functions that churches and their members once performed for themselves. This development is both a testimony to the diversity of contemporary populations and a challenge for the churches. As more and more religious voices compete to be heard in public debates (in the process drowning one another out), the influence of government seems destined to grow only larger. As the Canadian author Robertson Davies recently put the matter, "the parson has lost his control over us but the squire moves on from strength to strength."

The Reagan Era and Beyond

In light of the tumults of the 1960s and 1970s, as well as the growing role of national governments in North American life, it is not surprising that the decade of the 1980s seemed to be dominated by politics. Whether the situation was actually different than in the past or simply appeared to be because of concentrated political coverage in the national media, the impression is strong that church life was also politicized in the eighties.

Connections between religious adherence and political choices became as definite in the 1980s as they had been in the mid-nineteenth century. In

Ronald Reagan's two victorious campaigns for president in 1980 and 1984, for instance, the divisions were very clear-cut. The Jewish vote for Reagan's Democratic challengers was much higher than the national average. But the Democratic advantage among blacks who attended church weekly or more was even higher; Reagan received about only 10 percent of their votes. On the other side of the political spectrum, the vote for Reagan among white Protestants whose denominations were large enough to show up in national surveys was considerably higher than the national average. And among white Protestants who attended church regularly, the Reagan advantage was even greater than with nominal members who did not attend regularly. As just one example of these pluralities, white Baptists not part of the Southern Baptist Convention who regularly attended church gave Reagan 85 percent and 90 percent of their votes in the two elections. After decades of favoring Democratic presidential candidates, Catholics voted for Reagan in numbers that came very close to national averages.

In Canada, where figures for individual elections are not as readily available, similar correlations can still be found between religious and political allegiances. In 1985 Catholics, both in Quebec and in other regions, were more than twice as likely to support the Liberal party than were Anglicans, adherents of the conservative Protestant denominations, or members of the United Church. The latter, in turn, were more than twice as likely as Catholics to identify with the Progressive Conservative Party. Support for the socialist New Democratic Party was more than three times greater among members of the United Church than among Quebec Catholics, and it received even greater favor from those who were not members of any religious group. By 1990, Canada also witnessed several attempts to form political parties with distinct religious values. One of these, the Reform Party, made considerable headway in the Canadian West. In sum, for both Canada and the United States, one of the consequences of a broadened governmental presence was tighter connections between church affiliation (or its absence) and political choice.

Contentions about politics also spilled over into notions about how churches were to relate to public life more generally. During the 1980s there were religious people who sought self-consciously to recapture earlier patterns of Christian influence. There were anti- or nonreligious people who wished to order public life by "enlightened," scientific, or secular goals. There were religious people (sometimes Protestant, but more often Catholic, Jewish, and adherents of other faiths) who wanted morality in public life but not traditional American Protestantism. And, drawn from each of the above groups, there were significant numbers trying to figure out how to act with religious integrity while still respecting the religious, moral, and political pluralism that had become a fact of life.

Put more generally, the religious landscape seemed to be divided between those who favored a "civil religion" of tolerance, expression, and civility on the one hand and those who favored a "civil religion" of tradition, restraint, and moral courage on the other. The spectacular rise in the number of religious voluntary associations continued. Virtually every interest group with even the most elementary organization constructed a platform for promoting its cause. Most of these groups were low-key (e.g., neighborhood Bible studies or local agencies to house the homeless), but some (e.g., gay causes or antiabortion groups) went public with a vengeance. The fact that these special-interest groups usually divided between conservative and liberal proclivities, often in alignment with other voluntary associations drawing on similar constituencies, reinforced the depth of division. A systematic split over the role of government in areas of moral, family, or economic life — with conservatives generally opposed and liberals generally in favor — added to the systematic tension in the 1980s.

A cluster of volatile family and sexual controversies drove a particularly deep wedge between constituencies in North American churches. Spectacular revelations about the sexual indiscretions of television evangelists in the United States and about the involvement of Catholic priests with young boys in several Canadian regions heightened the public awareness of such issues. While some denominations offered formal judgments on abortion or AIDS, many were split down the middle. Most Christian bodies agreed on the undesirability of abortion, but they remained deeply divided on what to do about it. Some — generally the more liberal theologically — considered free access to abortion a lesser evil than the social cost of undesired pregnancies or any restriction of women's right to control reproduction. Others — generally the more conservative theologically — considered abortion on demand an affront to moral law and the fabric of civilization itself. Advocates of the latter view, however, had considerable difficulty agreeing on tactics to halt legal abortions. Constitutional amendments, normal legislation, and a judicial reversal of *Roe v. Wade* were all proposed. Issues that once were shielded in discrete silence were private no more. The resulting clamor both mobilized and divided the churches.

Among Catholics political matters also had an unusual salience throughout the decade. The Vatican's effort to firm up support for the Church's official teachings at Catholic colleges and universities led to widely reported conflicts over the views of individual professors. It has also been the occasion for a great deal of hand-wringing, some fruitful negotiation, and a small amount of sound reasoning on the emotional issue of "academic freedom." For all of its efforts to maintain the spiritual and liturgical life of the Church, the National Conference of Catholic Bishops received greatest attention when it issued pastoral letters on nuclear arms (1983) and the economy (1986). The specific conclusions of the papers were important (verging close to nuclear pacifism in the first and seeking significant curbs on capitalistic excesses in the second), but even more significant was the way the letters promoted highly visible and emotional debate within the Church and without. Similar letters, provoking similar controversy, were also regularly published by Canada's Roman Catholic bishops.

The politicization of the university also affected Christian life in the 1980s. A wave of militant rhetoric proposing to expose the evils of class, gender, ethnic, and sexual oppression stimulated a counterwave of protest defending Western intellectual traditions. In the process, Christianity became both more suspect (as a despised tool of oppression) and more acceptable (as a grounding for academic inquiry no more suspect than any other grounding). Observers such as the sociologist Hans Mol wondered why scholars favoring academic freedom found it any more intellectually "respectable to be obsessed with ecology, feminism or nuclear disarmament than with being saved by Jesus." But the major conclusion should probably be that institutions of higher learning were no more immune to the religious-political enthusiasms of the era than any other domain.

Important books of the 1980s looked back with alarm at trends in modern society while holding out at least some hope that Christian resources might provide an answer. In 1987 Reginald Bibby, of the University of Lethbridge in Alberta, published *Fragmented Gods: The Poverty and Potential of Religion in Canada*. A sociologist who grew up in Nazarene and Baptist churches, Bibby contended that religion has become just another commodity for Canadians fixated on the choices of the market — a prospect that dismayed him: "when religion becomes nothing more than a consumer item, the customer is in charge. The gods, relegated to an a la carte role, have little to say about everyday life. In Canada, the stability of religious affiliation is matched by the poverty of religious significance."

Bibby's book generated unusual attention, but it did not match the debate touched off two years before by the publication of *Habits of the Heart: Individualism and Commitment in American Life*. This volume, authored by Episcopalian Robert Bellah and a team of cooperating sociologists, tracked the increasing tendency of Americans to define themselves and their values as simple expressions of personal choice. Against this evil fruit of modernity, Bellah and his colleagues proposed a recommitment to covenanted forms of life. The authors argue that the commitment of covenant would draw on America's republican tradition as well as on virtues described a century and a half before by Alexis de Tocqueville (who first used the phrase "habits of the heart"). But covenant would also benefit from Judeo-Christian notions of divine transcendence and the sacredness of life under God. Books such as *Fragmented Gods* and *Habits of the Heart* offered encouraging, but also ironic, evidence of how the objective, detached methods of the modern social sciences — which once systematically neglected the spiritual dimensions of existence — could themselves be used to call for spiritual renewal.

A survey of the decades since the 1920s cannot do justice to the complexity of Christian experience in North America over the intervening years. But it might serve to provide an outline map on which to trace both continuations of past circumstances and innovations of the recent past. It might also provide a context for more detailed examination of specific trends, communities, and leaders in the recent history of the churches, while preparing us for the difficult task of asking what all this confusion has meant.

Further Reading

Gleason, Philip. *Keeping the Faith: American Catholicism Past and Present.* Notre Dame, IN: University of Notre Dame Press, 1987.

Grant, John Webster. *The Church in the Canadian Era.* Expanded ed. Burlington, ON: Welch, 1988.

Harrell, David Edwin, Jr. *All Things Are Possible: The Healing and Charismatic Revivals in Modern America.* Bloomington: Indiana University Press, 1975.

Hutchison, William R., ed. *Between the Times: The Travail of the Protestant Establishment in America, 1900-1960.* New York: Cambridge University Press, 1989.

Lotz, David W., ed. *Altered Landscapes: Christianity in America, 1935-1985.* Grand Rapids: Eerdmans, 1989.

Kellstedt, Lyman A., and Mark A. Noll. "Religion, Voting for President, and Party Identification, 1948-1984." In *Religion and American Politics from the Colonial Period to the 1980s.* Edited by Mark A. Noll. New York: Oxford University Press, 1990.

Marsden, George M., ed. *Evangelicalism and Modern America.* Grand Rapids: William B. Eerdmans, 1984.

Marty, Martin E. *Modern American Religion.* Vol. 2, *The Noise of Conflict, 1919-1941.* Chicago: University of Chicago Press, 1991.

Mol, Hans. "The Secularization of Canada." *Research in the Social Scientific Study of Religion* 1 (1989): 197-215.

Rawlyk, George A., ed. *The Canadian Protestant Experience 1760 to 1990*. Burlington, ON: Welch, 1990. In this volume, see especially Robert A. Wright, "The Canadian Protestant Tradition, 1914-1945"; and John G. Stackhouse, Jr., "The Protestant Experience in Canada since 1945."

Wuthnow, Robert. *The Restructuring of American Religion: Society and Faith since World War II*. Princeton: Princeton University Press, 1988.

CHAPTER 17

Trends

As the darkness draweth nigh,
Daylight fadeth from the sky:
Father, unto Thee we call,
Thou Who rulest over all.
Light that cannot know decline,
Come within our souls to shine!

All our hearts to Thee are known;
Come, possess them as Thine own.
Thou alone these hearts can fill,
And their deepest yearning still.
Love that never groweth old,
In Thy love our lives enfold! . . .

Thou Whose eye doth never sleep
O'er our slumber vigil keep,
That our hearts may wakeful be
While we take our rest in Thee,
And the darkness of earth's night
Fade in everlasting light.

Despite the large number of Roman Catholics in the United States since early in the nineteenth century, Catholic hymn-writing did not flourish so long as congregations were bound to the liturgies of Europe. After the Second Vatican Council, however, there has been a dramatic upsurge in the number of hymns being written by Catholics. Among the leaders of that movement are the Do-

minican Nuns of the Monastery of Our Lady of the Rosary in Summit, New Jersey, who published these stanzas of an evening hymn in 1982.

A LONG WITH THE SOCIAL AND ECONOMIC CHANGES OF TWENTIETH-century North American life there have also been major shifts in the relative size of churches. Some of these changes represent major breaks with past experience, others are the last stages of long evolutionary development. One conclusion from examining the relative fates of Christian groups is that the growth of denominations often depends upon an ability to speak the language of the moment but with some sort of distinctive Christian accent. Groups that shape their message completely to current trends, as well as those that present their vision of Christian faith in a completely alien idiom, do not prosper. Another conclusion, however, is that numerical success cannot be simply equated with Christian integrity or the blessing of God. Any number of reasons exist for the rise and decline of denominations, some obviously spiritual, some obviously social or demographic, and some clearly a complex intermingling of factors.

By examining first the relative size of the denominations in the 1920s, we will be in a position to track some of the major shifts in denominational size since that time. These denominational figures, in turn, provide the context for another set of trends as disclosed by the work of pollsters. In this chapter, we will look at sketches of recent developments in several groups with distinctive histories along with associated numerical information. By combining the broad view with narrower descriptions, perhaps we will be able to see both the forest and the trees, as well as the relationships between them.

The Christian Map in the 1920s

For several decades surrounding the beginning of the twentieth century, the United States government took a census of the American churches every ten years. In Canada, every ten-year census since 1871 has asked about citizens' religious preferences. Even with the precision aspired to by the census departments of both countries, these figures are no more than solid estimates. But they do convey something of the big picture with respect to relative denominational size.

The growing diversity of Christian organizations by the 1920s is illustrated by this photo of an African-American Catholic high school in Louisville, Kentucky.
Archives of the University of Notre Dame

The United States census of 1926 provides considerable support for conclusions drawn in the preceding chapters: church life had become pluralistic; the age of simple Protestant domination was over.

In 1926 the largest Christian communion by far was the Roman Catholic Church, with almost 19,000,000 members in nearly 20,000 churches. The largest Protestant bodies were the Methodists and the Baptists, each with slightly more than 8,000,000 members and 60,000 churches. To indicate the relative strength of these three major traditions a different way, about 43 percent of America's 117,000,000 citizens were members of churches in 1926; 37 percent of the church members were Roman Catholic and about 16 percent each were Methodists and Baptists.

The range of Protestant churches in 1926 reflected the divergent history of Christianity in the United States. Among the Methodists the largest denominations were the white bodies that had divided before the Civil War (about 4,000,000 in the North; about 2,500,000 in the South) and the black African Methodist Episcopal and the African Methodist Episcopal Zion churches (each with about 500,000). Approximately 1,290,000 Baptists belonged to the Northern Baptist Convention, while the Southern Baptist Convention and the

461

black Baptist denominations each numbered about 3,500,000. Other Protestant families with over 1,000,000 members were the Lutherans (3,966,000 in 21 different bodies), the Presbyterians (2,625,000 with about three quarters of that number in the largest northern denomination), the Protestant Episcopal Church (1,859,000), and the Disciples of Christ (1,378,000). Many bodies, reflecting broad ethnic and theological diversity, numbered over 100,000 (including Adventists, the German Church of the Brethren, Christian Church, Churches of Christ, Congregationalists, Eastern Orthodox, Evangelical Church, Evangelical Synod of North America, Friends, Latter-Day Saints, Reformed Dutch, and Church of the United Brethren). And literally scores, with even more extensive diversity in origins, beliefs, and practices, had at least 10,000 members (including the Assemblies of God, Plymouth Brethren, Christian and Missionary Alliance, Church of God, Church of God [Anderson, Indiana], Church of the Nazarene, Mennonites-Amish, Moravians, Old Catholics, Pilgrim Holiness, Polish National Catholic Church, Salvation Army, Unitarians, and the Scandinavian Evangelical "Free" churches). What census data in the aggregate show is that the United States had provided a lush soil for the flourishing of many different Christian groups.

The 1921 Canadian census showed less diversity but still a situation in which the number of denominations was appreciably larger than earlier. As in the United States, the different Canadian regions reflected different denominational strengths. Catholics predominated in Quebec, of course, but they were also strong in the Atlantic provinces and Ontario, and they had a large presence in the Canadian West. There were substantial numbers of Anglicans and Methodists in all of English-speaking Canada, with Presbyterians and Baptists strongest in the Atlantic provinces and Ontario. Most of the older Protestant bodies had established a fair number of churches in the prairie provinces and British Columbia, but these western areas were also home to many immigrant groups, such as the Mennonites (German-speakers from Russia), Doukhobors (mystical communalists from Russia), Ukrainian Catholics, Greek Orthodox, and offshoots of several evangelical and fundamentalist groups from the United States.

Well over 3,000,000 of Canada's nearly 9,000,000 citizens identified themselves as Catholics in the census. The largest Protestant bodies — Anglicans, Presbyterians, and Methodists — were named by more than 1,000,000 Canadians each as their preferred church. Over 400,000 identified as Baptists, almost 300,000 as Lutherans, about 170,000 as Greek Orthodox, and another 125,000 as Jewish. There were an additional five denominational families numbering between 10,000 and 100,000: Mennonites, Congregationalists, Salvation Army, Mormons, and the Evangelical Church. In 1925, the creation of the United Church brought together the Methodists,

Table 17.1   Proportions of Church Adherents, 1920s: United States and Canada

United States (1926)*		Canada (1921)†	
Roman Catholics	37%	Roman Catholics	39%
Methodists	16	Anglicans	16
Baptists	16	Presbyterians	16
Lutherans	8	Methodists	13
Presbyterians	5	Baptists	5
Episcopalians	4	Lutherans	3
Disciples of Christ	3	Greek Orthodox	2

*Calculated as a percentage of actual church adherents
†Calculated as a percentage of church preference identified by the total population in a national census

Congregationalists, and about two-thirds of the Presbyterians to create Canada's largest Protestant denomination.

A comparison of proportions of church adherents in the 1920s shows considerable similarities between Canada and the United States (see Table 17.1). Protestants as a whole constituted the largest group, but the Catholics were the largest single communion, and by wide margins. The Anglican Church was much more broadly distributed in Canada than the Episcopal Church in the States, as were Presbyterians. There was a larger number of Baptists in the United States than in Canada, a difference that only increased throughout the course of the twentieth century. In addition, every Protestant family in the United States was divided into more subunits (often many more subunits) than in Canada.

The number of church adherents in the 1920s serves as a useful base for analyzing trends that developed throughout the rest of the century. The Roman Catholics were becoming more numerous. The traditional Protestant churches were in flux. Both the number and the size of new groups were increasing. Regardless of whether any observer in 1926 could have foreseen the changes of the next decades, the figures from the 1920s do provide a pocket-sized map of a dynamic ecclesiastical landscape.

Rises and Declines since World War II

In the United States, the denominations that have grown most rapidly in the twentieth century all either arrived late on the scene or existed earlier at the margins of national influence. For example, the Roman Catholic Church is now beyond question the major Christian presence in a once overwhelmingly Protestant nation. Although fewer men are becoming priests and fewer women nuns since the early 1960s, the size and diversity of the American Catholic Church is still remarkable. Between 1965 and 1984 the number of sisters dropped by over 60,000, and the number of priests by over 35,000. Yet at that later date there were still more priests (57,000) than there was total membership in some Protestant denominations, such as the Moravians or the largest body of Quakers. And there were still more sisters (118,000) than there was total membership in such denominations as the Evangelical Covenant Church or the Evangelical Free Church. Despite financial pressures and painful cutbacks, the Catholic Church in 1984 still ran 239 colleges, 319 seminaries, 731 hospitals, and almost 9,500 primary and secondary schools. Each week, a greater number of Catholic school-children receive instruction in church or parochial schools than the total number of Southern Baptists or Methodists who go to church.

Among Protestants there has been a changing of the guard. The Southern Baptists, once marginalized as inhabitants of a supposedly backward region, have become the largest Protestant denomination in the country. Groups that once seemed but pesky sects — the Mormons, the Adventists, and various Pentecostal and fundamentalist bodies — have grown rapidly in recent decades. On the other hand, most of the denominations that dominated America's religious life in the nineteenth century — Congregationalists, Episcopalians, Presbyterians, and Methodists — are in decline.

Since the 1940s, public polls conducted by the Gallup Organization and other survey institutes have provided a regular accounting of the professed religious allegiance of Americans. The most general results, from 1947 to 1988, as summarized recently by George Gallup, Jr., and Jim Castelli, reveal a considerable growth for Catholics (from 20 to 27 percent of the total population), a corresponding loss for Protestants (from 69 to 56 percent), a serious decline for Jews (from 5 to 2 percent), and considerable enlargement in the categories of "Other" (from 1 to 4 percent) and "None" (from 6 to 8 percent). In addition, because the proportion of young people is much higher among Catholics, present trends suggest that the country will have about the same numbers of Catholics and Protestants sometime early in the twenty-first century. The numbers in Table 17.2 show some of these general trends more clearly.

Mostly White Denominations

Interpreting the changes represented by these numbers is more difficult than noting them. Catholic growth arises in part from continued immigration

464

**Table 17.2   United States Denominational Size, 1940-1988
(All denominational figures given in thousands)**

	1940	1960	1980	1988	% change 1940-88	% change 1980-88
U.S. population (in millions)	132	178	227	246	+86	+8
Roman Catholics and Southern Baptists						
Roman Catholics	21,284	42,105	50,450	54,919	+158	+9
Southern Baptists	4,949	9,732	13,600	14,812	+199	+9
Newer Denominations (Fundamentalist, Pentecostal, "Sectarian")						
Assemblies of God*	199	509	1,064	2,147	+978	+102
Christian and Missionary Alliance*	23	60	190	260	+712	+37
Church of God (TN)	63	170	435	582	+824	+34
Mormons	724	1,487	2,811	4,000	+452	+42
Seventh-Day Adventists	176	318	571	687	+290	+20
Jehovah's Witnesses	n.a.	250	565	805	—	+42
Church of the Nazarene	166	308	484	552	+233	+14
Presbyterian Church in America	—	—	150	217	—	+45
Salvation Army	238	318	417	433	+82	+4
Older "Ethnic" Churches						
Lutheran Church–Missouri Synod	1,277	2,391	2,625	2,604	+104	0
Christian Reformed Church	122	236	212	226	+85	+7
Mennonite Church	51	73	100	93	+82	-7
Evangelical Lutherans†	3,118	5,296	5,276	5,251	+68	0
Wisconsin Evangelical Lutherans	257	348	407	419	+63	+3
Baptist General Conference	n.a.	72	133	135	—	+2
Older "American" Denominations						
Reformed Church in America	255	355	346	334	+31	-3
Episcopal Church	1,996	3,269	2,786	2,455	+23	-12
United Methodist	8,043	10,641	9,519	9,055	+13	-5
Presbyterian Church in the U.S.**	2,691	4,162	3,362	2,930	+9	-13
United Church (Cong.)	1,708	2,241	1,736	1,645	-4	-5
Disciples of Christ	1,659	1,802	1,178	1,073	-35	-9

*Growth rates for the Assemblies of God and the Christian and Missionary Alliance are exaggerated by a change in enumeration that took place in the 1980s, from tallying only duly processed members to counting church constituencies, including children and attending nonmembers (from *Yearbook of American and Canadian Churches: 1990*, ed. C. H. Jacquet, Jr. [Nashville: Abingdon, 1990] and information provided by Robert Patterson, National Association of Evangelicals).

†Evangelical Lutherans = the Evangelical Lutheran Church in America, which was formed by the union of the American Lutheran Church and the Lutheran Church in America.

**Presbyterian Church in the U.S. = northern and southern Presbyterians (most recently, Hispanic) as well as from relatively good success at retaining the allegiance of those who grow up in that Church. Analysts regularly ascribe the growth of Southern Baptists, Mormons, Pentecostal denominations, and other evangelical or fundamentalist groups to a combination of factors. These churches define doctrine firmly and make high demands of commitment and conformity in daily practice (and so counter the culture's general trends toward permissiveness and "value neutrality"). But at the same time, their very numbers communicate an aura of success and sometimes even socioeconomic optimism (and so conform well to American myths of progress and improvement).

Of the denominations included in Table 17.2, the Assemblies of God and the Church of God (Cleveland, Tennessee) are both Pentecostal bodies formed only in this century. The Church of the Nazarene, the Salvation Army, and the Christian and Missionary Alliance are holiness or holiness-influenced denominations established late in the previous century. Seventh-Day Adventists have moved in recent decades closer to evangelical Protestants, but their origins in the wake of William Miller's nineteenth-century Adventism and their practice of worship on Saturday have kept them distinct from main Protestant traditions. The Presbyterian Church in America is a recent breakaway from the larger Presbyterian denominations; it is marked by a self-conscious adherence to the Westminster Confession that passed from fashion sometime hence in the older Presbyterian bodies. The Church of Jesus Christ of Latter-day Saints (Mormons) has likewise become more patriotic, middle class, and nationally prominent, but it too retains the distinctiveness of its earlier teachings and so has never fit a standard Protestant mold. The Jehovah's Witnesses, dating from the work of Charles Taze Russell at the end of the nineteenth century, constitute an intensely apocalyptic, sectarian movement that opposes obeisance to national governments; they have never aspired to mainline status. To be sure, some of these groups are ready and willing to engage society in various ways. But even where they do seek approval from the broader religious or secular culture, they have retained distinctives of faith and practice. They have also attempted to inculcate their members with these distinctives. In addition, most also foster a sense of intimate community which, along with the harder-edged concern for defining faith and practice, may explain their above-average rates of growth.

A footnote on changes over time, as well as a caution concerning the use of numbers, is relevant with respect to the recent history of the Assemblies of God, the largest mostly white Pentecostal denomination in the States. During the 1980s, it changed from counting only adults to counting its entire constituency in determining the total number of adherents, and so

The Pentecostal movement spread rapidly among America's Hispanics, as with this Assemblies of God congregation in Mercedes, Texas, shown with its pastor, Manuelita Gonzáles, on the right. *Assemblies of God Archives*

its index of growth has naturally been increased. In addition, figures released by the denomination early in 1991 show that most of the Assemblies' recent growth has taken place among its Hispanic and Korean ministries. The Assemblies of God have charted a phenomenal story of success over the course of the twentieth century, but that very success may have brought with it some of the same problems of complacency and bureaucratic uncertainty that bedevil the older Protestant churches.

Largely white Protestant churches of ethnic heritage have lagged behind the growth of sectarian groups, but they have fared better than the traditional mainline denominations. The pattern for a wide variety of these ethnic denominations is strikingly similar, as suggested by the growth curves indicated in Table 17.2. Whatever the ethnic origin — German (Wisconsin Evangelical Lutheran Synod and the Mennonite Church), German and Scandinavian (the Lutheran Church–Missouri Synod and the Evangelical Lutheran Church in America that combined the former American Lutheran Church and Lutheran Church in America), Dutch (Christian Reformed Church), or Swedish (the Baptist General Conference) — the general pat-

467

tern is a modest growth since World War II that tailed off in the 1980s. Strictness in defining doctrine or practice does not seem to affect growth rates within this group of churches. Those that could be called conservative — the Wisconsin Evangelical Lutheran Synod, the Lutheran Church–Missouri Synod, and the Mennonite Church (which has worked to maintain its pacifist stand) — fare about the same as those that might be labeled moderately conservative (the Christian Reformed Church and the Baptist General Conference) as well as those that could be characterized as moderate or pluralistic (the Evangelical Lutheran Church in America). A common passage from isolated ethnic communion to assimilated American denomination — with common problems of retaining the rising generations while reaching out to those beyond the ethnic group — may account for the similarities in patterns of growth.

The fate of the older Protestant churches that once constituted the most visible religious institutions in the country has been the source of considerable publicity in recent decades. Given the magnitude of their decline, that publicity is fully justified. To look at the situation with slightly different figures than those in Table 17.2, during the two decades from 1965 to 1985 the United Methodist Church lost 17 percent of its members, the United Church of Christ lost 19 percent of its members, the Episcopal Church lost 20 percent of its members, the two largest Presbyterian bodies lost 28 percent of their members, the American (i.e., northern) Baptists lost 37 percent of their members, and the Disciples of Christ lost 42 percent of their members.

As we have seen, these older Protestant churches were never as dominant as they may have appeared. But it is also true, as historian William Hutchison has written, that they once "served to provide and articulate moral norms for American society." But now, due to internal losses and the transformation of the religious landscape generally, these churches, again in Hutchison's words, have "abdicated that function or lost the power to perform it."

The reasons for that loss probably have more to do with changes in the larger society than with changes in these churches. But their own choices have no doubt played a role. Stung by the encounter with fundamentalists, mainline Protestant churches became exceedingly wary of sharply defined doctrine or carefully circumscribed practice. Disillusioned with infighting over theology, these denominations internalized the pluralism that was growing in American public life. A historian of twentieth-century Presbyterianism, Bradley Longfield, concludes that the choice for internal pluralism "made sense to many wise and devout Presbyterians in the 1920s when there seemed to be little danger that the Presbyterian Church would ever suffer from an unfocused identity." But the generation for whom pluralism amounted to a slight loosening of previous commitments gave way to a generation for whom pluralism was more simply an open forum for new directions. "In the long run," Longfield continues, "this course has contributed to the current identity crisis of the church and helped to undermine the foundation of the church's mission to the world." The difficulties of the older Protestant denominations may also stem from their willingness to embrace ideas and trends as defined by the nation's media and educational elites — elites that are remarkably unrepresentative of the religions espoused by the great mass of the nation's population. From one perspective, the promotion of radical social causes or the acceptance of alternative lifestyles, as defined by these elites, could be seen as a prophetic effort to keep the Christian message relevant to a changing world. From another perspective, it could be seen as simply selling out to that world.

Whatever reasons lie behind the different growth rates of the American churches over the last half-century, the principal result is clear. A major reorientation has taken place in what constitutes the nation's religious center of gravity.

Black Denominations

Categories applicable to the mostly white churches do not fit as well with the black denominations. Most of the large African-American churches combine mainline and sectarian characteristics. They have been the source of moral direction, an arena for personal leadership, and the center of social as well as religious life within black communities. But over against white society, they have been churches of protest or withdrawal. Functioning as both establishment and separatist churches, the black denominations have grown steadily since the 1920s at a rate that matches or even exceeds the growth of the national population. Estimates provided by C. Eric Lincoln and Lawrence H. Mamiya place membership in 1989 at about 11,000,000 in the major Baptist bodies (National Baptist Convention, U.S.A., Inc., 7,500,000; National Baptist Convention of America [unincorporated], 2,400,000; and the Progressive National Baptist Convention, 1,200,000). The three large Methodist denominations total about 4,000,000 (the African Methodist Episcopal Church approximately 2,200,000, the African Methodist Episcopal Zion Church approximately 1,200,000, and the Christian Methodist Episcopal Church approximately 900,000). In addition, the largest black Pentecostal body, the Church of God in Christ, numbers between 3,500,000 and 4,000,000 members. Several other holiness and Pentecostal bodies have substantial memberships as well. And it is estimated that

Dr. L. K. Williams was the long-time pastor of the Olivet Baptist Church in Chicago, one of the many large urban congregations of African-Americans that developed after the first World War. *Courtesy of the Billy Graham Center Museum*

about 1,200,000 blacks are members of mostly white Protestant denominations and that another 2,000,000 are Catholics. The meaning of these figures in light of the tumultuous recent history of African Americans receives more attention in Chapter 18.

Canada

As is evident in Table 17.3, general patterns of denominational growth and decline in the United States have also prevailed in Canada. The proportion of Canadians identifying themselves as Catholics continues to rise, and the numbers associated with the formerly dominant Protestant churches continue to decline. More conservative churches do show increases, but these groups remain much smaller proportionately than in the United States. There is also no Canadian equivalent to the very large evangelical Protestant denominations such as the Southern Baptist Convention or the Assemblies of God.

Canadian census figures are not good indices of active membership, but they do provide a sense of religious loyalties that linger even after active participation ceases. In general, the more conservative Protestant churches, the Anglicans, and the Catholics have more active members among those

Table 17.3 Percentage of Canadians Who Identify with Different Denominations

	Figures from National Censuses			
	1941	1961	1971	1981
Roman Catholic	43.4%	45.8%	46.2%	46.5%
United Church	19.2	20.1	17.5	15.6
Anglican	15.2	13.2	11.0	10.1
Presbyterian	7.2	4.5	4.0	3.4
Baptist	4.2	3.3	3.1	2.9
Lutheran	3.5	3.6	3.3	2.9
Eastern Orthodox and Greek Catholic	n.a.	2.4	2.5	n.a.
Mennonite	1.0	.8	n.a.	.8
Pentecostal	.5	.8	1.0	1.4
Salvation Army	.3	.5	.6	.5
None	n.a.	.4	4.3	7.4
Population in millions	11.5	18.2	21.6	24.3

identifying with the denominations than do the older Protestant bodies. Thus, in 1981 among Protestants, 37 percent of Pentecostals and 36 percent of Anglicans participated regularly in their churches, but only 24 percent of those in the United Church and 20 percent of Presbyterians did so.

One of the important factors distinguishing the situations in the two countries is that Canada has far fewer denominations. Part of the reason for this is simply that Canada's population is barely one-tenth that of the United States. But the difference is also due to the fact that the American democratic ethos has encouraged fragmentation more than consolidation, for both immigrant and home-grown denominations. The *Yearbook of Canadian and American Churches: 1990* lists more denominations in the United States with over 1,000,000 members each (23) than there were in Canada with over 100,000 members each (9). And it counted more American denominations numbering between 100,000 and 1,000,000 (40) than those in Canada numbering between 10,000 and 100,000 (22). Similarities between denominational patterns in Canada and the United States do outweigh the differences, but the differences point to instructive contrasts between Christian life in the two nations, to which we will return.

Regional Strengths

Both the United States and Canada are large countries with diverse populations. It is little wonder, then, that the pattern of denominational distribution is irregular. It is also no surprise that the Catholic Church, as the largest

Christian body in each country, is the most widely dispersed, or that the United Church, as Canada's largest Protestant denomination, is also distributed in many regions. (On the other hand, the Baptists, America's largest Protestant denominational family, show more regional concentration — a point to which we will return.) There is, however, still enough sheer space in both countries that smaller denominations can predominate in individual localities and even, within those limited regions, take on some of the proprietary functions often exercised by the nationally larger bodies.

The Glenmary Research Center in Atlanta periodically prepares color-coded maps that chart the relative strength of denominations county-by-county throughout the United States. On these maps each county is given the color of the denomination that makes up at least fifty percent (a dark color) or at least twenty-five percent (a lighter shade of the same color) of the church members in that county. On these maps the Catholic Church is assigned the color blue, and, looked at from a few feet away, the range of solid or light blue is stunning. The map is almost solidly dark blue in New York and New England, around the shores of Lake Michigan, in much of Alaska and all of Hawaii, in the southeastern United States, and in the southern portions of Texas, Louisiana, and Florida. Examined a little more closely, smaller pockets of blue can be found almost everywhere except in most of the states of the old Southern Confederacy.

Those Southern states, by contrast, are a sea of red, the color of the Baptists. On the 1974 map (reporting data from 1971), Baptists in at least 98 percent of the counties in Alabama, Arkansas, Georgia, and Mississippi made up the largest group of church members. At least 80 percent of the counties in Oklahoma, South Carolina, North Carolina, Tennessee, Florida, Kentucky, and Missouri contained the same preponderance of Baptists, as did at least 50 percent of the counties in Texas, Virginia, and Louisiana, and about 30 percent of the counties in West Virginia and New Mexico. But beyond these states and the southern parts of Indiana and Illinois, Baptists were very much in the minority. In only thirteen other counties in the other thirty-two states did Baptists constitute the largest denomination. The implications of these numbers for the Southern Baptist Convention, the recent history of which is sketched in Chapter 18, is very great. But it is also helpful to remember that although the Southern Baptist Convention is the largest Protestant denomination in the United States, there are more Baptists who are not Southern Baptists than those who are.

Elsewhere, Methodists exhibited special strength in a broad band of states from Delaware (the state with the highest concentration of Methodists in the country) through Nebraska. Their home, as historian Martin Marty puts it, is "the north of the South and the south of the North." The regional

472

strength of the Churches of Christ and the Disciples of Christ roughly paralleled that of the Methodists; each of these denominations, which are descended from the Restorationist movement of the early nineteenth century, enjoyed a plurality in several counties of the upper South and lower Midwest. Lutherans were strong in the upper Midwest. In 1971, they made up at least half of the church members in 109 counties, more than two-thirds of which were in Minnesota and North Dakota, and almost all the rest in Wisconsin, Iowa, South Dakota, Nebraska, and Montana.

The locations where other denominations predominate were random and depend heavily on past patterns of immigration and subsequent settling. Presbyterians were the largest denomination in widely scattered counties from nine states. Because of early missionary work among the Dakota Indians of South Dakota and among Alaskan Inuits, Episcopalians constituted a plurality of church members in isolated regions in those two states. Mormons dominated every county in Utah as well as many in the adjacent states. The holiness Church of God (Anderson, Indiana) was the largest denomination in several counties in northern Kentucky. Dutch migration accounted for the preponderance of the Reformed Church in America and the Christian Reformed Church in western Michigan, northwestern Iowa, and northern Washington. Mennonites are the largest denomination in two Kansas counties and one in Michigan. And for reasons that local historians could no doubt elucidate, the Quakers were the largest denomination in Kobuk County, Alaska, the Church of the Nazarene in Adams County, Idaho, and Skamania County, Washington, and the Plymouth Brethren in Morrow County, Washington. When thinking about the large shifts affecting the country's religious history as a whole, we would do well to remember that a big country has room for many smaller stories that, for specific localities, are every bit as important as what has happened in the nation to Catholics, Southern Baptists, Methodists, and other large denominations.

The same is true in Canada. The Roman Catholic Church is a dominating presence throughout the country — not only in Quebec, where almost 90 percent of the population still identifies itself as Catholics, but also in each of the Atlantic provinces and Ontario, where the Catholic Church is the largest communion. And in each of the four western provinces — Manitoba, Saskatchewan, Alberta, and British Columbia — there are roughly as many Catholics as members of the United Church, the dominant Protestant body in the region. For its part, the United Church is the largest Protestant denomination in each of Canada's provinces except Quebec and Newfoundland, where the Anglican Church is larger, and in New Brunswick, where there are more Baptists. After the United Church, the Anglicans are the Protestant denomination represented most widely throughout Canada.

Change has been the order of the day in Canada since World War II as it has been in the United States. Here we see the last service in the old Cooksville United Church, Mississauga, Ontario, November 1957. *Archives of the United Church of Canada*

But, as in the United States, there are also pockets of regional strength for smaller denominations — Presbyterians in Ontario and Prince Edward Island, Pentecostals and the Salvation Army in Newfoundland, Baptists in Nova Scotia and New Brunswick, Ukrainian Catholics and Mennonites in Manitoba, and Lutherans in the four western provinces. As in the United States, the histories accounting for local concentrations of particular churches are as significant, in miniature, as the national histories of the bigger denominations are at large.

Finally, there is also a distinct regionalism to the absence of Christian faith. Polling since World War II has confirmed a general pattern for both Canada and the United States — the further west, the lower the levels of church affiliation. In the United States, the states in which the largest numbers of people reported having no religious attachment of any kind were, in 1991, Oregon (17 percent), Washington and Wyoming (14 percent each), California (13 percent), and Arizona (12 percent). In Canada, it is the same. While only a handful of Canadians in the Atlantic provinces and Quebec report no religious affiliation, the "nones" in Saskatchewan are almost as numerous as the Lutherans, in Alberta they are more numerous than the Anglicans, and in British Columbia the number reporting no religious connection is higher than the number of Catholics, the United Church, or any other denomination.

General Trends

Public polling opens a window that was not available for previous generations. As carried out by George Gallup, Jr., Andrew Greeley, Reginald Bibby, and other experts, these polls generate data that provide rough accounts of more general patterns of religious belief and practice. Some of the findings are surprising; others merely reinforce common knowledge. This kind of information is not as extensive for Canada as for the United States, but results from Canada show significant differences, as well as some similarities, with larger patterns in the United States.

The most stable elements in twentieth-century religion seem to be those associated with beliefs. Since the beginning of popular polling in the United States, well over 95 percent of the population has persistently affirmed belief in God, and the proportion is almost as high in Canada. Affirmation of belief in such traditional Christian doctrines as the deity of Christ, life after death, and the real existence of heaven and hell also remains very high. By comparison with European countries, only the Republic of Ireland, Northern Ireland, and Poland report levels of belief in traditional Christian doctrines that are close to those in the United States. On these questions of belief, Canadians are not far behind.

For several decades, the Gallup polls have also showed that roughly a third of Americans have reported having had a "religious experience" or "a moment of religious insight or awakening that changed the direction of their lives." Pollsters have also discovered a consistent pattern in how life-cycle changes affect religious behavior. The point at which a striking number of people begin to go back to church is with the birth of children. The least religious group in America, defined demographically, is childless couples. When a marriage ends in divorce, the separated spouses become less likely to participate in religious activities; when it is ended by death, the remaining spouse is more likely to take part.

If religious beliefs and connections with life cycles seem to have been fairly stable in both the United States and Canada, there are major differences between the two countries in church attendance, and there are also important distinctions within the two. Since the 1940s, Gallup has been asking Americans if they attended a church or synagogue within the last seven days, a question also posed to Canadians since 1955. Two important trends seem to have taken place since World War II. First, Canadians were

Mainstream Protestant churches enjoyed a boom after World War II, as illustrated by this throng waiting to enter the New York Avenue Presbyterian Church in Washington, D.C. *Library of Congress*

once much more likely to have been in church than Americans, but since the mid- or late 1970s they have become considerably less likely to attend church regularly. Second, Catholic Church attendance was once much higher than regular participation by Protestants, but since the late 1960s or early 1970s the gap has narrowed considerably.

In the United States, total church attendance has tracked a fairly stable curve from 41 percent in 1937 to 43 percent in 1989, with high points of 49 percent in 1955 and 1958, a low of 37 percent in 1940, and several years at 40 percent since 1970. In Canada, by contrast, pre-Gallup figures show as many as two-thirds in church on a typical Sunday immediately after World War II, and well over 50 percent into the mid-1960s. But then a precipitate decline occurred: in the late 1980s only slightly more than one-fourth of Canadians were likely to be in church on any given Sunday.

In the United States, church attendance by Protestants has risen slightly since the 1940s (from 30 percent in 1940 to about 37 percent in 1989), while it has declined substantially for Catholics (from 65 percent as late as 1965 to about 50 percent by 1989). In Canada, regular attendance has fallen off considerably, by Protestants from a high of 60 percent in 1946 to well under 30 percent in the late 1980s, and by Catholics from above 80 percent in the early 1960s to barely 40 percent in the late 1980s. The Catholic drop-off has

476

been most spectacular in Quebec, where religious practice was once most secure. In 1955, the year of the first Gallup survey of Canadian religion, 93 percent of Quebec Catholics reported being in church the previous week. By the late 1980s, the proportion had fallen to nearly 30 percent.

Affirmation of church membership and stances toward the Bible show the same kind of national differences. In the United States, the proportion of those claiming church membership is down only slightly from 73 percent of the population in 1937 to 69 percent in 1989, while in Canada the percentage has fallen by half in only the last fifteen years (58 percent in 1975, 29 percent in 1990). In the United States, actual knowledge of Scripture remains quite low, but more people in the late 1980s said they read the Bible daily (about 15 percent) than in 1950 (about 10 percent), and a higher percentage can tell who preached the Sermon on the Mount. Canada, on the other hand, has witnessed a precipitate drop in Bible reading, from over 40 percent who reported reading at least once a week in 1960 to less than 10 percent in 1980. Belief that the Bible should be interpreted literally has declined somewhat over the last quarter century, especially among Roman Catholics. But respect remains high for Scripture, with over half of the Americans polled by Gallup in 1988 affirming that Scripture is "God's word" without errors (whether interpreted literally or figuratively).

A few results from the pollsters indicate comparable declines in both the United States and Canada. A question asked regularly since the 1950s is whether religion is important in a respondent's life. Into the 1960s, close to three-fourths in the United States typically replied that it was "very important," a figure that has dropped to a few percentage points over half in the late 1980s. To a different kind of question Canadians show a similar result. When asked whether they had a great deal of confidence in religious leaders, about three-fifths responded affirmatively in 1980, but within a decade that proportion had dropped to only slightly more than one-third.

Finally, pollsters allow a glimpse at what social scientists call variables, or general factors associated with religious belief and practice. One of their clearest results merely confirms the less scientific conclusions of previous generations. Women remain substantially more committed and active in Christian churches than men. In 1989, for example, 48 percent of American women had been in church or synagogue within the previous week, but only 38 percent of the men, while 62 percent of the women said that religion was very important in their lives, but only 47 percent of the men. About the same differences are observed in Canada, where, for example, a 1985 poll found that 70 percent of women but only 60 percent of men believed in life after death, and 62 percent of Canadian women but only 45 percent of Canadian men prayed privately.

Another commonly accepted truth that pollsters confirm is that region makes a difference. In Canada, church attendance and traditional beliefs are both highest for Protestants and Catholics in the Atlantic provinces and lowest in British Columbia. In this regard, the Atlantic provinces are, in effect, Canada's "religious South," for in the American South levels of belief and practice are also higher, on average, than in any other region of the country.

⁂   ⁂   ⁂

The information provided by polls must always be interpreted. But what the polls do provide is an alternative approach to the history of the churches offered by a chronicle of major events. Polls shift attention away from spokespeople to the laity. They highlight long-term trends rather than spectacular occurrences. They do not reveal the health or integrity of belief, but they do indicate something about participation and nominal understanding. For the United States, they reveal a situation since World War II with more overall stability than change. For Canada, they show a substantial falling away in traditional Christian practice. For both countries, survey research demands deeper, more interpretative understanding of major developments over time. To some of these key developments among groups with distinctive twentieth-century histories we now turn.

Further Reading

Bibby, Reginald W. *Fragmented Gods: The Poverty and Potential of Religion in Canada.* Toronto: Irwin, 1987.

Carroll, Jackson W., Douglas W. Johnson, and Martin E. Marty. *Religion in America: 1950 to the Present.* San Francisco: Harper & Row, 1979.

Coalter, Milton J., John M. Mulder, and Louis B. Weeks, eds. *The Mainstream Protestant "Decline": The Presbyterian Pattern.* Louisville: Presbyterian/John Knox, 1990.

Gallup, George, Jr. *Religion in America 1990.* Princeton: Princeton Religion Research Center, 1990.

Gallup, George, Jr., and Jim Castelli. *The People's Religion: American Faith in the 90's.* New York: Macmillan, 1989.

Greeley, Andrew M. *Religious Change in America.* Cambridge: Harvard University Press, 1989.

Hutchison, William R., ed. *Between the Times: The Travail of the Protestant Establishment in America, 1900-1960.* New York: Cambridge University Press, 1989.

Jacquet, C. H., Jr., ed. *Yearbook of American and Canadian Churches: 1990.* Nashville: Abingdon, 1990.

Kelley, Dean M. *Why Conservative Churches Are Growing.* New York: Harper & Row, 1972.

Lincoln, C. Eric, and Lawrence H. Mamiya. *The Black Church in the African American Experience.* Durham, NC: Duke University Press, 1990.

Longfield, Bradley J. *The Presbyterian Controversy: Fundamentalists, Modernists and Moderates.* New York: Oxford University Press, 1991.

Roof, Wade Clark, and William McKinney. *American Mainline Religion: Its Changing Shape and Future.* New Brunswick, NJ: Rutgers University Press, 1987.

CHAPTER 18

Communities

Un día Jesús andaba
predicando en Nazareth.
La gente muy asombrada
decía no puede ser.

ESTRIBILLO:
Es hijo del carpintero.
Profeta no puede ser.
Es uno de nuestro barrio.
Profeta no puede ser. . . .

La virgen miró a Juan Diego
con ojos de mucho amor.
El obispo estaba ciego.
Por eso no le creyó.

ESTRIBRILLO

*As Hispanics came to constitute a larger portion of America's Christian popu-
lation, it was only to be expected that they would also contribute by writing
hymns. These verses, which show a traditional wariness of church hierarchy,
are by the Mexican-American composer Carlos Rosas, from San Antonio, Texas.
They can be translated as follows: "One day Jesus came preaching in Nazareth.
The people, amazed, said this could not be. Refrain: It is the son of the carpenter.
He cannot be a prophet. He is one of us from our village. He cannot be a
prophet. . . . The Virgin looked at Juan Diego [a Christianized Aztec who*

received a vision of the Virgin in 1531] with eyes of great love. The bishop was blind. That's why he did not believe."

CHRISTIANITY IN TWENTIETH-CENTURY NORTH AMERICA WEARS MANY faces. The four general profiles sketched here are not representative of all Christian communities, but the stories of Europeans who have faced the challenge of Americanization, of Southern Baptists who have begun to venture outside of the South, and of Hispanics and African Americans who are expanding their presence in American church life are all important. Moreover, they also show some of the diversity, as well as some of the different ties to the past, that make up the broader Christian picture. Individually, they add color to the general statistical patterns provided by social scientists. Together, they point to the dynamic interaction of religious and social realities that always constitute the journey of faith.

European Ethnic Enclaves

A most important general development of the twentieth century is the public emergence of groups previously segregated by the immigrant experience. The largest examples of this process are found within the Catholic Church and include its Irish, southern European, and now Hispanic subcommunities. But it has also been a process at work among ethnic Protestants.

Dutch Protestants

Dutch immigration, for example, has produced two moderately large denominations that have moved out from earlier preoccupation with ethnic preservation to fuller interaction with public religious life. The older of the two bodies, the Reformed Church in America (RCA), was established in the colonial period by Dutch immigration to New York and the surrounding region. By the early nineteenth century it had assimilated to the point of participating in many of the common evangelical movements of the day. But as it assimilated, it retained a guiding role for its Old World doctrinal standard, the Heidelberg Catechism, and it continued to welcome a continuing flow of immigrants from Holland.

Abraham Kuyper, prime minister of the Netherlands in the early years of the twentieth century, inspired a neo-Calvinist revival that influenced the Dutch Reformed churches of the United States and Canada as thoroughly as the churches in his native Holland. *Calvin College Heritage Hall Collection*

Fresh surges of immigration in the years before the Civil War and then in the 1870s and 1880s added substantially to the RCA but also led to the creation of a new Dutch Reformed denomination eager to maintain Continental distinctives and somewhat uneasy about the RCA's accommodation to what new immigrants often called "Methodism" (by which they meant the revivalistic practices of American Protestants in general). The new denomination eventually became known as the Christian Reformed Church. For several generations it zealously maintained a Dutch Christian ethos. The denomination promoted heartfelt piety but never adopted the behaviors common to American evangelicals (hymn singing and theological discussion, for instance, were often lubricated by lager and pursued through clouds of cigar smoke). It kept strictly to the doctrinal standards of the Dutch Reformation. The CRC also created its own distinctive cultural institutions, especially schools, along lines articulated by Abraham Kuyper (1837-1920), a masterly theologian, editor, and politician who flourished in the Netherlands at the time of resurgent migration to America. During and after World War II, a new wave of Dutch immigrants to Canada eagerly joined the CRC and extended the same distinctly Dutch mix of piety and culture-formation in Ontario and some of the western provinces.

Since World War II the CRC has begun to move out its ethnic enclave, very much as the Reformed Church in America did in the nineteenth century. While still jealous of its distinctives, the CRC has provided academic leadership to a broader range of evangelicals. Its Canadian congregations have promoted distinctly Christian organizations in labor and politics. And a network of publishers centered in Grand Rapids, Michigan, broadened their perspectives to take in a wide variety of evangelical and fundamentalist audiences as well as moderate groups associated with the National and World Council of Churches. In the process, the CRC has endured several internal debates on issues picked up from growing involvement in larger American circles, such as the proper stance toward liberal or conservative politics, the role of women in church, and the interpretation of cosmological passages in the book of Genesis. More than most groups, the CRC has preserved its Old World distinctives, but it could not preserve itself indefinitely from the broader American experience. At the end of the twentieth century a mingled judgment is possible on the process of assimilation undergone by the CRC: it has pushed members of this denomination into positions of leadership in the larger Christian world, but it has also forced the denomination as a whole to act on the often controversial issues of American experience rather than simply to rely on traditions inherited from the past.

Lutherans

Interesting as developments in the relatively small Dutch immigrant community have been, the prime example of ethnic Protestant evolution is provided by the Lutherans. Their story is one of consolidation following on the heels of fragmentation. The waves of German and Scandinavian immigration, which grew especially strong after the 1840s, led to the creation of myriad small Lutheran bodies — as many as sixty-six independent organizations at one time. Not until the twentieth century — not, that is, until two generations had passed from the start of massive Lutheran immigration — did real consolidation take place. World War I, with its intense anti-German antagonism and its forced cooperation in many spheres, set the backdrop for important mergers. In 1917 most of the Norwegian bodies joined to form the Norwegian Lutheran Church. In the next year, the United Lutheran Church came into existence through the merger of several different groups. Also in 1918 the influential Iowa and Ohio synods established fellowship for preaching and communion. In 1930, the Ohio, Iowa, and Buffalo, Texas, synods joined to form the American Lutheran Church, a body that later merged with the larger Evangelical Lutheran Church (the name assumed in

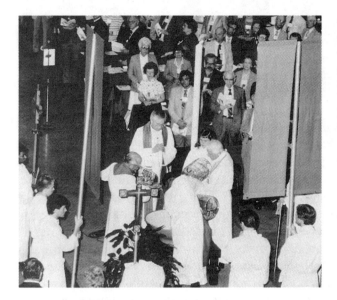

The three bottles of water being poured together here symbolized the three denominations that joined in 1988 to form the Evangelical Lutheran Church in America. *Courtesy of the Evangelical Lutheran Church in America*

1946 by the Norwegian Lutheran Church) to make up The American Lutheran Church. To this merger came also smaller bodies of Danish-American and Norwegian-American Lutherans. The creation of The American Lutheran Church in 1960 was significant as the first major merger of American Lutherans involving both Germans and Scandinavians. Two years later the United Lutheran Church joined the Augustana Lutherans (Swedish), a smaller Danish church, and the largest of the Finnish bodies to form the Lutheran Church in America. From 1967 a Lutheran Council in the United States of America provided a forum for discussion among the ALC, the LCA, and the Lutheran Church–Missouri Synod, a more conservative body that was itself the product of synodical mergers. In 1988 the process of consolidation reached a climax when The American Lutheran Church, the Lutheran Church in America, and the Association of Evangelical Lutheran Churches joined to create the Evangelical Lutheran Church in America. With more than 5,000,000 members, the ELCA has become the third largest predominantly white Protestant denomination in the country. This new Lutheran body looks increasingly like a mainline Protestant church. Whether it will do better than other mainline bodies at preserving its historical distinctives, while taking a larger place in America, only time will tell.

In Canada the number of separate Lutheran branches was never as large as that in the States, but a similar process of consolidation took almost as long to develop. After establishing less formal connections in the 1950s and 1960s, the groups corresponding to the ELCA in the United States joined together in 1986 into the Evangelical Lutheran Church of Canada. And in 1989, the Canadian branch of the Lutheran Church–Missouri Synod became a fully independent denomination.

Meanwhile, the Missouri Synod Lutherans in the United States underwent a traumatic internal division that, in some particulars, resembled the nineteenth-century clash between Samuel Schmucker and his European opponents. Throughout the postwar period, leading academics in the Missouri Synod urged the denomination to take a more open attitude toward modern biblical scholarship. A number of influential leaders were not pleased with this proposal, which in part reflected an effort to bring the denomination into closer fellowship with the main movements in American religious thought. It seemed at once too much a concession to contemporary academic conventions and too obvious a deviation from the traditional positions on Scripture contained in historic Lutheran confessions. The result was a major struggle during the late 1960s and early 1970s in which the majority of the denomination backed the traditionalists. In opposition to the majority decision, a small group (Evangelical Lutherans in Mission) broke from Missouri and eventually (as the Association of Evangelical Lutheran Churches) contributed significantly to the new Evangelical Lutheran Church in America. Weighty differences over the nature and use of Scripture were at the heart of the Missouri Synod's strife, but an additional factor was cultural. The majority, perhaps drawing on the strength of conservative trends in the 1970s, concluded that it simply was not necessary to take their cue from larger developments in American academic life. Whatever the drift in other Lutheran bodies, they were resolved to make the sacrifices required to keep the denomination in line with what its leaders felt was the Old World confessional heritage.

American Lutherans have not yet contributed to American public or religious life in proportion to their numbers. There are, to be sure, Lutheran academics who have become American leaders in the interpretation of Christianity to the broader American public. At the end of the 1980s, for example, the Lutheran Martin Marty of the University of Chicago was the most knowledgeable and most often quoted commentator on America's religious past, and the Lutheran Jaroslav Pelikan of Yale University was widely regarded as the nation's leading historian of Christian doctrine. At the same time, however, no Lutheran has ever been the nominee of a major political party for President, Lutheran efforts in publication are directed mostly to other Lutherans rather than the broader American community, and Lutheran literary voices, though often outstanding, have typically served, like Ole Rölvaag, to chronicle immigrant experience rather than shape American perceptions more generally.

The Southern Baptist Convention

The experience of Southern Baptists since the 1960s resembles both sides of the Lutheran story. Like the groups that went into the Evangelical Lutheran Church in America, Southern Baptists have been moving from isolated, self-contained communities (in their case, regional rather than ethnic) into broader social, political, and academic worlds. Like the Missouri Synod Lutherans, on the other hand, Southern Baptists have also been engaged in a vigorous internal debate concerning the preservation of distinctive denominational (and perhaps also regional) convictions.

Controversy in the SBC came from a growing belief among a few key laypeople and several pastors of large churches that liberal forces were undermining the denomination, especially its central bureaucracy and its seminaries. During the 1960s, conservatives were worried when Bible study materials published by the SBC's Sunday School board made moderate use of modern biblical criticism. Heads of departments funded by the denomination's Cooperative Program (its apparatus for gathering contributions) insisted that unity in traditional Baptist activities was more important than detailed considerations of doctrine, a response not to the liking of the conservatives. Some of them in 1973 organized a Baptist Faith and Mission Fellowship to urge a literal reading of its confessional Statement of Faith and Mission. These conservatives insisted that recent trends were drawing Southern Baptists away from a commitment to the inerrancy of the Bible, a view they felt had been implicitly or explicitly espoused throughout the Convention's history.

Beginning in 1979 and continuing through the 1980s, conservatives successfully organized to elect one of their own as the Convention's president. Since the president appointed the boards that nominated trustees for the six Convention seminaries and directors of the denomination's bureaucracy, it was not long until new faces on seminary boards and in the SBC's Nashville offices were cracking down on what they regarded as dangerous liberalism. A wounded contingent of "moderates" fought back, arguing that there was very little liberalism present in the denomination and that the "fundamentalist" eagerness to enforce biblical inerrancy violated traditional Baptist standards of "soul liberty" and congregational autonomy. "Moderates" raised interesting points for discussion, but the "fundamentalist" organization proved superior, as did their support from the Convention as a whole. Like the situation in the Missouri Synod from the 1970s — but unlike the struggles among northern Presbyterians and Baptists in the 1920s — the conservative forces carried the day.

Describing this Southern Baptist debate is much easier than determin-

At this annual meeting of the Southern Baptist Convention in 1979, theological conservatives elected Adrian Rogers as the denomination's president, setting in motion a chain of events that eventually led these conservatives to almost complete control of the Southern Baptists' institutional life. *Courtesy of the Southern Baptist Convention*

ing what it means. The Southern Baptist Convention, despite its imposing strength when viewed from the outside, has always been defined as much by its region as by its religion. Called into being in 1845 in order to protect slaveholding, "baptized in blood" during the Civil War, deeply enmeshed in anti-Yankee, antimodern regionalism, Southern Baptist life also partook substantially of Southern norms and experiences. Within the Convention, there have always been several identifiable religious traditions — Charleston (Regular and orderly), Sandy Creek (Separate and revivalistic), Georgia (regional), Landmark (primitivistic), evangelical (pragmatic and theologically conservative), and Texas (culture influencing). And within within each of these emphases, there have been numerous conflicting opinions about the correct content of doctrine, the appropriate norms of piety, and the best way to influence the culture. "Southernness," much more than uniformity of belief and practice, kept the denomination united around its goals of evangelism and cultural maintenance.

Given this diversity, it was almost inevitable that, when the SBC began to move out from its Southern heartland, tension would result. Since World War II such movement has been obvious both geographically and culturally.

Increases in education, a rise in mobility, and growth in income affected the Southern Baptists as they did the country at large. As a result of these broader social factors, it became ever harder for the denomination to remain an entirely Southern entity. Many Southern Baptists, moreover, were pleased with their growing national presence because it provided additional opportunities for the evangelism and church planting that have always been Southern Baptist trademarks.

When controversy arose, both sides tried to appropriate the Southern Baptist heritage. "Moderates" claimed to be following the practices of past denominational statesmen such as E. Y. Mullins and Herschel H. Hobbs, one of the great preachers in the era after World War II. As they saw it, they were submerging minor theological differences in order to preserve a widespread coalition of fellowship and so get on with the great task of outreach. "Fundamentalists," by contrast, claimed to be adhering to the intended meaning of earlier doctrinal formulations. They were taking a stand on principle in order to preserve the theological integrity of the denomination and so get on with the great task of outreach. Both sides claimed to be doing the Baptist thing in the Baptist way.

Both sides may have been right. But in a changing America, the residual Southernness was no longer a strong enough glue to keep diverging interpretations of Baptist principles together. Both sides drew on wider national trends for allies and moral support — "fundamentalists" from the conservative political movements that arose in the 1970s, and "moderates" from the standards of the major Northern universities that more and more Southern Baptist educators attended. The specific result of actions in the 1980s was that the SBC aligned itself with nationally conservative sympathies. The more general fact, however, was that the rest of the nation had begun to mean more for the Southern Baptists. The almost inevitable consequence of that development is that Southern Baptists will soon begin to mean more for the nation.

Hispanics

The growing number of Hispanic Americans, mostly from heritages with some church connections, has added a new dimension to the history of Christianity in twentieth-century North America. Generalizations are as suspect for this as for any other large population, especially since the Hispanics include Mexican Americans, Cuban Americans, Puerto Rican Americans, and various descendants of immigrants from Spain, Central America, and South America. Although Mexican Americans predominate (constituting about 60 percent of the total Hispanic population), representatives of other regions have also contributed measurably to the growth of Christian faiths in North America.

Historically, Hispanic Americans have been mostly Catholic, although never in predictable ways. One of the first Catholic leaders in what became the southwestern United States, for example, was Antonio José Martinez, an energetic priest who established Catholic churches in a broad region straddling the present Mexican-American border. He labored during the unsettling times of the Mexican and American civil wars but still succeeded in creating strong churches and leading many families into active church life. However, when New Mexico came under the government of the United States and when the redoubtable Bishop Jean Baptiste Lamy was sent to the Southwest to regularize Catholic authority in the region, there was trouble. Among his exceptions to standard Catholic practice, Padre Martinez had openly married and had been joined by his wife, "Madre Teodorita," in guiding the churches. Bishop Lamy barely tolerated this breach of Catholic norms, and he also alienated Martinez and his flocks by insisting on a process of Americanization. When Bishop Lamy put pressure on Hispanic priests to collect tithes, Father Martinez responded that the Church should be giving money to the poor, not taking it away. Finally, after long years of conflict, Martinez was eased out of his ministry, although several churches remained loyal to him and set up an independent Catholic network in northern New Mexico.

The relationship between Padre Martinez and Bishop Lamy illustrates a long-standing feature of Hispanic Catholic life. While most Hispanics have been Catholic, their faith has existed on two levels. First, the official Church has in many cases been run by bishops (and often even priests) of other nationalities and has worked to assimilate Hispanics into a body dominated by other religious, ethnic, or educational practices. Second, however, a church oriented more to the masses also developed. From the earliest days of Spanish settlement, when stalwarts like Bartolomé de Las Casas spoke out against abuse of New World Indians, this "second" Catholic church has sought ways to inculcate the Christian message through, rather than against, Hispanic culture. As theologian and historian Justo L. González has put it, "from its very beginning Spanish American Roman Catholicism has been torn between a hierarchical church which has generally represented and stood by the powerful, and a more popular church, formed by the masses and led by pastors who have ministered at the very edge of disobedience."

This bipolar division of Catholicism prevailed well into the twentieth century, even after the Hispanic population began to constitute a growing proportion of the Catholic Church. One of the results of this two-track Catholicism was that Hispanic spirituality tended to focus on the home and

Outdoor processions were one of the religious expressions imported to North American from Latin America. This procession took place at a Catholic festival in Chimayo, New Mexico. *Courtesy of the Maryknoll Fathers*

on community festivals more than on the official ecclesiastical activities. A common expression among Hispanics has been "soy católico a mi manera" (I am a Catholic in my own way). Perhaps 90 percent of Hispanic Catholics throughout most of American history have fallen into this category of a religious but only lightly churched people.

Beginning in the 1950s, however, a number of factors transformed the face of Hispanic Catholicism in the United States. The first was a large increase in immigration from Mexico, Cuba, Puerto Rico, and Latin America that has made the Hispanic population a significant proportion of the nation. In 1930, the Mexican-American population in the United States was estimated conservatively at about 1,400,000. But by 1989 the Census Bureau estimated that there were over 20,000,000 people of Hispanic origins in the country. And this total makes little provision for undocumented (and, therefore, uncounted) immigrants. About 80 percent of Hispanics are baptized Roman Catholics.

Even more important than mere numbers, however, was a rise in self-confidence and self-definition prompted by the example of the black civil rights movement and by indigenous cultural developments among Hispanics themselves. These movements stimulated distinctly Hispanic forms of organization, such as the *communidades eclesiales de base* (Christian base communi-

In 1970, Patricio Flores, who once worked as a migrant agricultural laborer, became the first Hispanic bishop in the American Roman Catholic Church. *Courtesy of the Maryknoll Fathers*

ties) that had earlier arisen in Latin America as a form of popular Christian mobilization. Their leaders asked for the same rights to seek ethnic expression of the faith that French, German, Irish, Italian, and Polish Catholics had enjoyed. A third factor transforming Hispanic Catholic life was much greater attention from the hierarchy. In 1945 a Bishops' Committee for the Spanish Speaking was set up; it promoted especially the rights of migrant Hispanic laborers. Through its work, leaders of the Hispanic community as a whole, such as Cesar Chavez, were introduced to labor organizing.

But church promotion of Hispanic concerns did not become a serious concern until the civil rights movement had worked its effects. The National Conference of Catholic Bishops set up a new office for Hispanics in 1969, and the next year Patricio Flores, a former migrant worker, was appointed the auxiliary bishop of San Antonio, the first Hispanic to be named a bishop in the American Church. Since that time, the number of Hispanic leaders has mounted dramatically. By 1990 there were two Hispanic archbishops, nineteen other bishops, about 1,600 priests, and 2,000 nuns. In addition, by that time the archbishop and the hierarchy in Puerto Rico were entirely Puerto Rican. The American Church has also organized three national *en-*

cuentros, or pastoral conferences (in 1972, 1977, and 1985), in which distinctive themes of Hispanic life assumed theological and practical shape. In the report of the third *encuentro,* for example, there is an affirmation that "the Word of God gives us strength to denounce the injustices and abuses that we suffer; the marginalization and scorn, the discrimination and exploitation. It is in the Word of God that we, as pilgrim people, find the motivation for our daily Christian commitment." Similar statements about the church's mission have directed Catholic activity in Hispanic communities since the 1970s. As Jay Dolan, a historian of American Catholicism, put it, "Hispanic Catholics have moved up from the rear of the church."

The American Catholic Church sanctioned distinctly Hispanic aspirations as a response to the growing population and the growing assertiveness of Hispanics in North America. But it was also responding to larger developments in the Spanish-speaking world, especially the assemblies of bishops from throughout Latin America that took place in Medellín, Colombia, in 1968 and Puebla, Mexico, in 1979. At these meetings, the bishops were addressed by Pope Paul VI and Pope John Paul II, respectively, both of whom called upon the Church to act constructively on behalf of the poor. The popes also applied principles from the Second Vatican Council to distance the Church from its traditional alliance with the cultural and economic elites of Latin America. As the flow of people, ideas, and information continues between Hispanics in the United States and Latin America, these themes have exerted increasing force in the American Church.

As large as the Catholic Church has loomed in the consciousness of American Hispanics, there has also been a variety of active Protestant movements almost from the first years of American life. The great liberators of South America in the early nineteenth century — Bernardo O'Higgins, José de San Martín, and Simón Bolívar — welcomed representatives of the British and Foreign Bible Society, for example, since they felt Protestant initiative would aid the liberalizing of South American life. In Latin America, small Protestant communities emerged in the nineteenth century, sometimes led by missionaries from Britain and the United States but even more often by expatriates returning from Protestant areas. These churches were intensely anti-Catholic, both because of Catholic opposition to their existence and because of their own commitment to bourgeois freedoms as well as Protestant theology. Some of these Latin American Protestants eventually settled permanently in the United States and helped establish small but active communities of Presbyterians and Methodists. Vincente Martinez, a son of Padre Antonio Martinez, was one of the early leaders of Hispanic Presbyterians in the Southwest.

In the twentieth century, Hispanic Protestantism has been given a great

Part of the liturgical renewal following the Second Vatican Council was a much greater flexibility in holding masses. This one was held outdoors after a walking pilgrimage to a tiny shrine in Champayo, New Mexico.
Courtesy of the Maryknoll Fathers

boost by the spread of Pentecostalism. As early as 1916, Puerto Ricans who had received the gift of tongues returned to their native island to establish a Pentecostal presence. From there Hispanic Pentecostalism spread rapidly to the Puerto Rican population in New York City and then to other major urban centers in the United States. Unlike the Presbyterians and Methodists, who waffled on the issue of establishing special districts for their Spanish-speaking members, Pentecostal denominations such as the Assemblies of God have followed this practice more consistently, with the result that Hispanic sections flourish in several of the Pentecostal bodies.

Hispanic Protestants are people in the middle. Many of them, like those participating in the churches founded by refugees in the Miami area after Fidel Castro's Cuban revolution, are vigorous promoters of Americanization. But the promotion of Americanization is often regarded by other Hispanics as a sellout to an alien culture. In addition, although Protestant churches often align their worship and service with the family-centered patterns of traditional Hispanic piety, they almost always do so by incorporating large elements of anti-Catholic teaching. But this emphasis can create further alienation from the preponderance of Hispanics who remain Catholics. In the United States, Hispanic Protestants, like Hispanic Catholics, are living in a culture with norms that have been defined by the descendants of Europeans. As American culture becomes more genuinely pluralistic, and as American churches acknowledge more directly the universal implications of the Christian message, contacts between Hispanics and "Anglo" churches should increase. But even if they do, it will probably be some time before Hispanic churches, Catholic and Protestant, are recognized for the important part they have played in defining the Christian history of twentieth-century North America.

African Americans

Throughout the twentieth century, the black churches have reflected the social strains of modern America even as they have continued practices of self-organization dating back for two centuries. The large Baptist and Methodist denominations formed in the nineteenth century still enlist a majority of black Christians, but a wide range of independent churches and several denominations formed in the twentieth century also minister to significant segments of the black population. Among the former are energetic urban ministries, some of which press or exceed the traditional bounds of black Christian teaching. Johnnie Coleman, for example, was an exception on a number of counts. For one thing, it has been rare for a woman to experience her success in building a church. And her theology is clearly unorthodox, making room for reincarnation and a frank pursuit of material riches. But during the 1980s her Christ Universal Temple was Chicago's largest black congregation.

More representative of recent developments is the rapid growth of the Church of God in Christ, America's largest black Pentecostal denomination. Pentecostal and charismatic expressions are widespread in black churches among both independent fellowships and some churches of the more traditional denominations. But the Church of God in Christ has been the leading organization for black Pentecostalism. Its founder, Charles Mason (1866-1961), exercised leadership over the denomination for more than a half-century stretching from his Spirit-baptism at Azusa Street in 1907 to his death during the administration of President John Kennedy. What is even more remarkable for someone of such longevity is that Mason was respected more for his spirituality than for his organizational success. The Church of God in Christ passed through a crisis of leadership after Mason's death, but a governing board of twelve bishops was in place by 1968, and it succeeded in preserving the main emphases of the church's earlier days.

From 1907 until his death in 1961, C. H. Mason was the senior bishop of the Church of God in Christ, the largest and still fastest growing black Pentecostal denomination. *Assemblies of God Archives*

One of the factors propelling the growth of the Church of God in Christ — it may be the fastest growing large denomination of any kind in the United States — has been its exuberant use of black gospel music. "Gospel" and successor forms of music that combine elements of traditional spirituals with hints of white hymnody and a full exploitation of the blues are trademarks of black churches. But they also generate considerable controversy. Just as established black leaders initially opposed the introduction of spirituals in the nineteenth century and the use of C. A. Tindley's and T. A. Dorsey's gospel songs in the first half of this century, so concern has also arisen about the use of drums, electronic instruments, and themes from the world of jazz. In the Church of God in Christ, however, there has been far less resistance to musical innovation. In fact, leaders in the church have embraced dancing and shaking in worship as both justified by Scripture and faithful to black traditions. Musicians such as Andrae Crouch, the Hawkins Singers, and the Clark Sisters, all of whom were raised in the Church of God in Christ, have taken music from this tradition to ever broadening audiences.

Throughout the twentieth century, both the older black denomina-

Andrae Crouch, who grew up in the Church of God in Christ, is one of many African-American singers in the twentieth century who have moved out from the churches to broader popularity. *Religious News Service*

tions and new bodies such as the Church of God in Christ have largely maintained the dual character that makes them so difficult to classify by standards of the white denominations. In the form and content of their spiritual message, most black churches have maintained evangelical or even fundamentalistic convictions. But with respect to life beyond the church walls, they have practiced a form of social engagement more radical than that of almost any of the white churches. The extensive research of C. Eric Lincoln and Lawrence H. Mamiya on black churches in the 1980s points up these tendencies. Of the more than 1,800 ministers surveyed, nearly two-thirds affirmed that their churches exist to proclaim the same message as white churches. One Baptist minister told Lincoln and Mamiya that "the ministry of both black and white preachers is the same: the saving of souls. . . . Skin color is of no great significance in relating the message of Jesus." On the other hand, most of the ministers reported that distinct elements of black experience gave shape to their message. More than 70 percent, for example, taught the children in their churches about distinctive features of black church history. Only about one-third of the black ministers made self-conscious use of theologians promoting a distinctly African-

496

Adam Clayton Powell, pastor of the Abyssinian Baptist Church in New York City, later also served for many years in the United States Congress. *Courtesy of the Billy Graham Center Museum*

American theology. But nearly two-thirds said they drew on the themes of black consciousness or black power that had been stimulated by the civil rights movement. The picture that this extensive research provides is of churches conservative in their view of salvation through Christ but liberal in their conception of how Jesus should be transforming the contemporary social order.

Since the civil rights movement of the 1950s and 1960s, the black churches as a whole have experienced modest growth. They remain "the hub of traditional black life," in the words of James Forbes, one of the most visible black preachers in contemporary America and the successor to Harry Emerson Fosdick and William Sloane Coffin at New York's Riverside Church. The burial societies, insurance agencies, political caucuses, schools, food pantries, housing cooperatives, and other self-help organizations that grew up around the churches in the course of black history still remain. But since blacks won more access to the larger society through the gains of the civil rights movement, the church does not dominate black society as thoroughly as it once did. The change can be seen in a subtle shift in the always close relationship between religious and political leadership. In the 1950s and 1960s, Adam Clayton Powell, minister of Harlem's Abyssinian

Baptist Church, was a black community leader who served simultaneously as a pastor and as a U.S. congressman. More recently, Andrew Young (President Carter's ambassador to the United Nations) and Jesse Jackson (who made a serious run for the democratic presidential nomination in 1988) gave up their careers as active Baptist ministers when they entered full-time into national political life.

One of the most morally poignant episodes of recent American history grows directly out of the triumphs of the civil rights movement. For generations, black churches had sustained a struggling middle class of African Americans that provided leadership, direction, and support for segregated black communities in the rural south as well as in cities throughout the country. Over the last quarter century, many in that class have been able to leave urban ghettos for better housing, education, jobs, and living conditions elsewhere. For at least a few years after the 1960s, newly successful middle-class blacks tended to drift away from their traditional churches into largely white congregations. Over the course of the 1980s, this pattern has reversed, as successful businessmen and women and professionals have returned in considerable numbers to the predominantly black churches. Other changes in the wake of the civil rights movement have proved more problematic for the black churches. For example, with more and more vocations opened to blacks, the ministry is no longer the obvious choice for capable young leaders. As a result, the average age of the black clergy had crept beyond 50 by 1990, and efforts to recruit new ministers were proceeding with difficulty.

The sharpest irony in the wake of the civil rights movement, however, is that blacks left in urban enclaves have been deprived of the support of some of the most capable leaders groomed in black churches precisely at a time when the multiplying traumas of modern urban life — single-parent families, drug abuse, educational stagnation — have become most intense. It is cruel that the exercise of rights won long after they should have been given has, to some extent, undermined the work that churches labored to perform in days of more overt oppression. This sad fact is almost certainly not the last of the sins of the slave-tolerating fathers to be visited upon subsequent generations.

As in the mostly white churches, African-American women are more active in week-to-week activities than men. The black churches have mirrored the more conservative white churches, however, by opening positions of public leadership only slowly to women. Nonetheless, the role of the "church mother," widely venerated matriarchs whose family and spiritual connections bind whole congregations together, remains a distinctive feature of black life. African-American churches also show higher levels of participation by members than comparable white churches. In 1989, for example,

Gallup polls showed that blacks were somewhat more likely than whites to be members of churches and to have attended church within the last week, and much more likely than whites to say that religion remains "very important" in their lives.

In such ways, black churches remain exceptions in the history of Christianity in North America. Although African-American churches share a great deal with both more evangelical and more liberal white churches, the distinctive history to which they have been subjected and the singular institutions that they have developed both continue to set them apart from the standard expectations of white American society.

❀   ❀   ❀

Histories of individual Christian communions or groups of communions provide an alternative reading of recent developments to those found in polling data. The aggregate data point in the direction of a somewhat thinner Christian presence in the United States and a very much thinner presence in Canada. To turn from aggregate data to the histories of individual communities of faith is to discover, however, that the whole is never simply the sum of the parts. Dramatic changes in ethnic communities, as well as evolutionary developments in traditional denominations, make it impossible to reach easy conclusions about the general direction of Christianity in America. The one thing that seems to be clearest is that nothing is clear. The faith seems to be weaker everywhere while nonetheless showing widespread signs of life. Depressing crises in one corner are matched by encouraging developments in another. Since the fate of Christianity in America is no longer tied to the fate of any one group of Christians (if it ever was), the story has grown more complicated (and perhaps more interesting) rather than less. In Chapter 19 we will add another element to the mix as we look at the stories of well-known individuals and how they have fit into the developing tales of recent decades.

Further Reading

Ammerman, Nancy Tatom. *Baptist Battles: Social Change and Religious Conflict in the Southern Baptist Convention.* New Brunswick, NJ: Rutgers University Press, 1990.

Bratt, James D. *Dutch Calvinism in Modern America.* Grand Rapids: William B. Eerdmans, 1984.

Dolan, Jay P. "Religion and Social Shange in the American Catholic Community." In *Altered Landscapes: Christianity in America, 1935-1985*. Edited by David W. Lotz. Grand Rapids: William B. Eerdmans, 1989.

González, Justo L. *The Theological Education of Hispanics*. New York: Fund for Theological Education, 1988.

Leonard, Bill J. *God's Last and Only Hope: The Fragmentation of the Southern Baptist Convention*. Grand Rapids: William B. Eerdmans, 1990.

Lincoln, C. Eric, and Lawrence H. Mamiya. *The Black Church in the African American Experience*. Durham, NC: Duke University Press, 1990.

Nelson, E. Clifford, ed. *The Lutherans in North America*. Philadelphia: Fortress Press, 1975.

Wills, David W. "Beyond Commonality and Plurality: Persistent Racial Polarity in American Religion and Politics." In *Religion and American Politics from the Colonial Period to the 1980s*. Edited by Mark A. Noll. New York: Oxford University Press, 1990.

CHAPTER 19

Personalities, Leaders, Exemplars

Take My Hand, Precious Lord

Precious Lord, take my hand, lead me on, let me stand,
I am tired, I am weak, I am worn.
Thru the storm, thru the night, lead me on to the light,
Take My Hand, Precious Lord, lead me home.

When my way grows drear, Precious Lord, linger near,
When my life is almost gone.
Hear my cry, hear my call, Hold my hand, lest I fall —
Take My Hand, Precious Lord, lead me home.

When the darkness appears and the night draws near
And the day is past and gone,
At the river I stand, Guide my feet, hold my hand,
Take My hand, precious Lord, lead me home.

The composer of this hymn, Thomas A. Dorsey, transformed the world of black religious music — indeed, the world of all American music — by incorporating elements of the blues into gospel hymns like this one, published in 1938. Dorsey, a tireless promoter and publisher, first wrote his hymns for congregations, but then they became the material for choirs, quartets, and such well-known black soloists as Mahalia Jackson, Willie Mae Ford Smith, and Sallie Martin.

501

HISTORICALLY, LEADERSHIP IN AMERICAN CHURCHES HAS INVOLVED A combination of factors. At least since the days of George Whitefield, personal charisma — the native ability to communicate urgency, energy, and truth — has always played a part. So it was with Barton W. Stone, Charles G. Finney, and Dwight L. Moody in the nineteenth century, and so it continues to be with many examples in the twentieth century. In the past the most visible leaders were those with special skills that others could not do without. The skill might be pastoral or administrative, as was the case with Richard Allen, who gathered the African Methodist Episcopal Church, and Bishop John Carroll, who shepherded the Catholic Church in the early United States. It might also be intellectual, as was the case with many nineteenth-century theologians who were widely respected as faithful expounders, defenders, and communicators of the Christian message. In addition, leaders in the churches have traditionally been masters of organization. They have learned how to exploit channels of communication provided by denominations, by institutions of higher learning, by periodicals, and by networks of their own creation. Charles Hodge of Princeton Seminary was a leading nineteenth-century Presbyterian not just because he was a solid theologian but also because a wide circle of readers valued his annual reports on the Presbyterian General Assembly that appeared in the journal from his seminary. Similarly, James Cardinal Gibbons was a leading Catholic at the turn of the twentieth century not just because he wrote persuasively about the compatibility of Catholicism with American values but because he had mastered the internal mechanics of his Church in the United States and its connections with the Vatican.

In the more pluralistic twentieth century, Christian leaders are still marked by these traits. The individuals who become best known in the churches usually have a personal "presence" that demands attention. They possess some skill or capacity that others value. And they are masters of organization. Increasingly, however, the nature of twentieth-century life has altered the balance among these leadership traits. Populations are now more mobile and so less tied to the static institutions of a particular place. People live longer, have fewer children, and divorce more frequently, which means that family patterns are diverse and complicated. The number of religious groups, as well as associations of every other kind, has multiplied, with the result that the group loyalties of individuals now tend to be much more widely distributed than was the case a century ago. As the conditions of modern life change, so also do the churches. Schisms and unions, tense debates and strenuous efforts to avoid controversy, social activism and social conservatism — all can be found in the churches, and all can alienate or attract different constituencies in the general population.

The effect of these conditions on religious leadership is considerable. Mastering such traditional organizations as denominations has become less important than mastering ways of getting along in newer ad hoc, voluntary networks. The skills or capacities that are valued most tend to be less intellectual and more relational, having less to do with formulating doctrine than with guiding faith through experience. Charisma is no less important, but charisma in the modern world has come to be defined more as the ability to communicate through the mass media than through face-to-face speaking.

These changes are in many cases simply extensions of established trends. A leader's ability to draw his or her own crowd has always been essential in North America, where formal establishments were weak or nonexistent. Mastering radio and television, in these terms, is only a logical extension of mastering a preaching circuit. In other ways, however, twentieth-century leadership is categorically different. The organizations that count most tend to be those created by the leader's own efforts; they are less and less likely to be the traditional denominations. Martin Luther King, Jr., for example, is widely recognized as a civil rights leader, and it is also known that he played a leading role in the Southern Christian Leadership Conference, which coordinated the work of churches and ministers in the struggle for equitable treatment of blacks. What is less well known, however, is that King was ordained in the National Baptist Convention, U.S.A., Inc., and was later one of the founding members of the Progressive National Baptist Convention, Inc. Similarly, Billy Graham is widely recognized as an evangelist and the founder of the Billy Graham Evangelistic Association, but his membership in a Southern Baptist Church and his regular worship with Presbyterians is less well known. Leaders called "Cardinal" are easy to identify as Roman Catholics. Yet many of the twentieth-century Catholics who have become known outside their own church came to the attention of the public for nonecclesiastical activities, such as John Ryan's support of New Deal politics and Father James Groppi's civil rights efforts.

The biographical sketches that follow are meant to illustrate some of the qualities that have distinguished Christian leaders in the last two-thirds of this century. We will consider the cases of individuals who became well known through the media, women who have entered more visibly into public leadership, and theologians whose work has been widely recognized. It would have been possible to profile any number of individuals in this way, but the stories of those that were selected should suggest how the conditions of modern life have in some cases redirected the public work of the churches and in other cases simply offered new venues for continuing traditional activities.

Personalities, Leaders

The revolution in communications media has made it possible for radio, television, satellite, and cable services to carry messages from, and stories about, leading figures in all walks of life to unprecedented numbers of private homes. In an age defined by the media, it is almost inevitable that religious leaders too would take on a larger-than-life status, especially those with the savvy to exploit the media for the causes they champion. So it was that in the 1920s and 1930s, radio pioneers such as Fr. Charles Coughlin, the Protestant liberal Harry Emerson Fosdick, and Charles Fuller (host of "The Old-Fashioned Revival Hour") gained national reputations. In that same period, editors of periodicals that crossed denominational lines, such as Charles Clayton Morrison of *The Christian Century* and Charles Trumbull of the *Sunday School Times*, were cultural and theological arbiters, conveyers of news and entertainment, as well as personalities in their own right. The media also helped give a number of local Catholic leaders national influence, such as Cardinals O'Connell and Cushing in Boston, Cardinals Mundelein and Strich in Chicago, and Cardinal Spellman in New York. An occasional Protestant, such as Eugene Carson Blake, who served as stated clerk of the northern Presbyterians and then as general secretary of the World Council of Churches, received the same exposure. In the past several decades, involvement in highly publicized political controversies has also provided a springboard to broader recognition for individuals with religious concerns, as it was for William Sloane Coffin and Philip and Daniel Berrigan as clerical opponents of the Vietnam War and, more recently in the era of Ronald Reagan, for Michael Novak and Richard Neuhaus as proponents of neoconservative social theory.

The age of television has also been the age of the religious "celebrity." Because of their skill or chutzpah on television, a number of religious entrepreneurs — Oral Roberts, Jerry Falwell, James Robison, Jim and Tammy Bakker, Jimmy Swaggart, Kenneth Copeland, Robert Schuller, and Rex Humbard — have become much better known than the elected leaders of the major denominations. Even before their sales reached astronomical heights, popular religious books by such authors as Hal Lindsey, Rabbi Harold Kushner, and Frank Peretti became media events. The same process also transforms an occasional academic book — for instance Will Herberg's *Protestant, Catholic, Jew* (1960) or *Habits of the Heart* (1985), from a team headed by Robert Bellah — into a volume that more people talk about than read. In this regard, the churches reflect some of the same forces at work in the broader world of popular culture.

The mass media's fascination with "the expert," even if such experts are rarely allowed more than a sound bite or two, also means that otherwise retiring academics enjoy a more visible public role than was the case before World War II. Network television, the weekly newsmagazines, and other media have heightened the visibility of expert commentators even as the commentators attempted to explain the inner workings of religious events in forums more suited to analyzing the events of this world than of the next. In the 1980s, Martin Marty of the University of Chicago provided such expertise for the whole gamut of religion in modern America, as did novelist-sociologist Andrew Greeley for Catholics as a whole, Auburn's David Harrell for Pentecostals and charismatics, Duke's George Marsden for evangelicals and fundamentalists, Brigham Young's Leonard Arrington for Mormons, and for Catholic factions from left to right, Charles E. Curran of Southern Methodist, David O'Brien of Holy Cross, and James Hitchcock of St. Louis University.

Religion, like politics, commerce, and other spheres of life, has had its share of charlatans and quacks exploiting the potential of this media revolution. But it has also had a number of exemplary figures who have maintained the integrity of their message even while putting the media to use. Three of those individuals — Martin Luther King, Jr., Bishop Fulton J. Sheen, and William Franklin ("Billy") Graham — have consistently ranked among the most admired Americans since World War II. Brief sketches of their lives show both something of their personal contributions and something of how each became a significant voice for an important segment of the Christian community.

Martin Luther King, Jr.

Martin Luther King, Jr. (1929-1968), was America's most visible civil rights leader from 1955 until his assassination in April 1968. The son of a prominent black Baptist pastor in Atlanta, King studied at Morehouse College, Crozer Theological Seminary, and Boston University (where he received his doctorate) before becoming the pastor of the Dexter Avenue Baptist Church in Montgomery, Alabama. He vaulted into national prominence when in 1955-56 he led a successful bus boycott in Montgomery that brought an end to the racial segregation of the city's public transportation. In 1957 King helped organize the Southern Christian Leadership Conference (SCLC), which rapidly became one of the foremost civil rights groups in the country. Its leaders, including King and his successor, Ralph David Abernathy, were mostly black Baptist ministers.

Dr. King's own personal prestige was at its height in the early and mid-1960s. He keynoted the massive march on Washington in August 1963 with his moving "I Have a Dream" speech. And he helped organize the

In 1965, Martin Luther King, Jr., led 25,000 civil rights marchers from Selma to Montgomery, Alabama. Here, at the end of that journey, he is confronted by a solid wall of state troopers outside the state capitol in Montgomery. *Religious News Service*

well-publicized Selma-to-Montgomery march in the spring of 1965. The first of these events marshaled major support for the Civil Rights Act of 1964, the second for the federal Voter Registration Act of 1965. During the presidencies of John Kennedy and Lyndon Johnson, King was consulted by the White House. He was awarded the Nobel Prize for Peace in 1964.

Yet even as he gained an international reputation, the struggle went on. On Good Friday, 1963, King was arrested in Birmingham, Alabama, and imprisoned for eight days. In jail he read in the *Birmingham News* printed criticism of his work from white ministers. In response, King penned a "Letter from Birmingham Jail — April 16, 1963," one of his most effective brief statements. He first justified coming from his church in Atlanta to Alabama:

I am in Birmingham because injustice is here. Just as the prophets of the eighth century B.C. left their villages and carried their "thus saith the Lord"

506

far beyond the boundaries of their home towns, and just as the Apostle Paul left his village of Tarsus and carried the gospel of Jesus Christ to the far corners of the Greco-Roman world, so am I compelled to carry the gospel of freedom beyond my own home town. Like Paul, I must constantly respond to the Macedonian call for aid.

King then answered charges leveled against his movement by church leaders who feared instability or disorder. He defended his methods, which, "through the influence of the Negro church," had always been "the way of nonviolence." He closed by saying he had never written a letter of such length before, "but what else can one do when he is alone in a narrow jail cell, other than write long letters, think long thoughts and pray long prayers?"

Toward the end of his life, King's influence was contested. Excursions into the North (Chicago, 1966, for example) cost him the support of those who viewed civil rights as a strictly Southern problem. His criticism of the Vietnam War angered other Americans. And he was caught in the ideological crossfire resulting from the the rioting that occurred in American cities during the mid- and late 1960s. Some whites held King responsible for these outbursts because of his promotion of black civil rights. Some blacks felt that King betrayed their cause by continuing to repudiate the use of violence to attain racial justice.

During the 1950s and 1960s King was a living example of black preaching at its best. His speeches and writings drew heavily on the rich reservoirs of black Christian history. His ideology was constructed on an evangelical realism concerning the nature of human evil and a scriptural defense of nonviolence ("love your enemies"). As was customary in African-American Christianity, however, King made little distinction between spiritual and social problems involved in the civil rights struggle. Other influences also shaped his thinking — the pacifism of Gandhi, the civil disobedience of Thoreau, the philosophical idealism that he had studied at Boston University, and the American faith in democratic equality. In the moving rhetoric of Dr. King, it was often hard to tell where, if at all, the Christian substratum of his thought left off and the superstructure of his social theory began. In any case, he was beyond question the most important Christian voice in the most important movement of social protest after World War II.

Bishop Fulton J. Sheen

For millions of Americans in the first decades of electronic mass communication, Fulton J. Sheen (1895-1979) was the embodiment of Christian

Here shown at his most typical, while making a point on television, Bishop Fulton J. Sheen was one of the first — and best — Christian communicators on that medium. *Religious News Service*

proclamation. In 1940 he was the first individual to conduct a televised religious service. Ten years before, he had become the regular speaker on the "Catholic Hour," a Sunday evening radio program broadcast by the National Broadcasting Company that eventually reached four million listeners a week. In 1951 he added a regular appearance on television to his already busy schedule when he began the weekly series "Life Is Worth Living." From these broadcasts Bishop Sheen received a tremendous correspondence, once reaching thirty thousand letters in a single day and averaging forty thousand per week. The Bishop's message went out even further through his newspaper columns in both the Catholic and secular press, through his many speaking engagements in this country and abroad, and through nearly seventy books.

Casual observers of the American scene who equated popular preaching with a lack of formal education and a surplus of mindless emotion could not fathom Bishop Sheen or his popularity. He had been born in El Paso,

Illinois, where he took his turn at chores on the family farm before moving with his parents and three brothers to Peoria. He excelled first in the local Catholic schools and then at St. Viators College (Illinois), St. Paul Seminary (Minnesota), the Catholic University of America, the Sorbonne, the University of Louvain, and the Pollegio Angelico in Rome. He held earned doctorates in philosophy and theology and taught philosophy for a quarter century at the Catholic University of America. He was an influential delegate to the Second Vatican Council, an auxiliary bishop of New York from 1951, Bishop of Rochester from 1966, and titular archbishop of Newport (Wales) from 1969. Honors came to him from around the world and in the United States, including an Emmy for his television work.

On radio and television as well as in person, Bishop Sheen was a compelling speaker. It was his habit to talk without notes after hours of rigorous preparation, a practice that enabled him to communicate informally while still having something to say. Bishop Sheen employed a time-honored missionary strategy by attempting to move his audience from the known to the unknown, from significant circumstances in everyday life to the church's message of hope in God. His tapes still circulate and continue to attract individuals to the Christian faith.

For all his fame, Bishop Sheen never lost the common touch, nor did he slight the inner world. Nearly every day of his adult life he set aside an hour to meditate upon Scripture and the teachings of the Church. On October 2, 1979, in New York's St. Patrick's Cathedral, two months before the bishop's death, Pope John Paul II embraced Fulton Sheen and said, "you have written and spoken well of the Lord Jesus. You are a loyal son of the Church." As a representative of an old Church, Bishop Sheen was still eager to exploit the newest media available. His skill at using the new to communicate the old made him one of the most respected Christian figures of his generation.

Billy Graham

The same judgment can be rendered about the most visible Protestant evangelical of the late twentieth century, Billy Graham (b. 1918). Graham was raised in North Carolina in a conventionally fundamentalist home and then attended Wheaton College in Illinois, at a time when that institution was cautiously shifting its self-designation from an aggressive fundamentalism to a somewhat more open "evangelical" stance. An impressive preacher from a very early age, Graham became in 1944 the first full-time employee of the Youth for Christ movement, one of a number of such

509

By the 1960s, the well-publicized prayer breakfast had become a fixture on the Washington scene. Here Billy Graham joins President John F. Kennedy in one of these events. *Courtesy of the Billy Graham Center Museum*

organizations founded by evangelicals after World War II. Graham traveled extensively on behalf of Youth for Christ, was briefly president of an evangelical Bible college, and conducted periodic tent crusades. In the summer of 1949, Graham and associates planned such a three-week meeting in Los Angeles. Newsworthy conversions of athletes, mobsters, and entertainers toward the close of the third week led to the extension of the campaign. Publisher William Randolph Hearst got wind of the event and instructed his newspapers to promote the young evangelist. The results were spectacular. The meetings extended for another nine weeks, crowds jammed the 6,000-seat "Canvas Cathedral," and a new star rose on the religious horizon.

Graham's message is a modern variation of the message that evangelical itinerants have been preaching since the time of Whitefield. What sets Graham apart from other revivalists is his winning charisma and an unusual freedom from the eccentricities and incivilities with which other American itinerants have so often been marked. Graham has also been unusually eager to cooperate with a wide range of Christian groups. A major campaign in New York City in 1957 marked something of a turning point in his career. When Graham insisted on including representatives of mainline Protestant churches in planning the crusade and on directing some who made decisions for Christ at his meetings to these same churches, separatistic fundamentalists wrote him off as soft on liberalism. In subsequent years, Graham has even won the guarded support of various Catholic bishops. Much earlier he had been a pioneer in integrating blacks and whites in his crusades, even in the South.

Graham's conventional evangelical faith was matched in his early career by a conventional faith in America. In 1950 the first broadcast of his long-running radio program "The Hour of Decision" offered what was then a typical mixture of evangelical and anticommunist fervor. "The Battle Hymn of the Republic" provided the backdrop for an appeal for spiritual repentance, and the evangelist's message was filled with alarm about "the tragic end of America" and the "hour of tragic crisis all across the world." Graham has been invited to the White House by every president since Harry Truman, but for a long time he enjoyed closer relationship with more conservative political leaders, and especially with Richard Nixon. Only a last-minute intervention by Bobby Kennedy kept Graham from publishing an endorsement of then Vice President Nixon on the eve of the 1960 election. The resignation of President Nixon in 1974, and even more the earlier revelations of sordid doings in the Nixon White House, sobered Graham politically. Since then, he has been more circumspect and more determinedly nonpartisan in his political associations. He has also departed significantly from the conventional views of his evangelical constituency to advocate greater controls on nuclear arms and increased efforts to establish world peace. In the 1980s Graham made several well-received visits to China and the Soviet Union. Almost as remarkable as the constancy of Graham's preaching, therefore, is the evolution of his politics, from aggressive cold warrior to widely respected advocate for world peace and religious toleration.

Like Martin Luther King, Jr., and Fulton Sheen, Graham also knew how to exploit the media. He early used radio, television, and motion pictures to promote the gospel. Several of his books have sold over a million copies, and *Decision* magazine, which he supervises, is one of the most widely circulated religious periodicals in the world. The Billy Graham Evangelistic Association has been a leader in office efficiency, to the point that it has been called upon to advise other organizations, religious and secular, on how to maintain connections with a far-flung constituency.

Graham does not speak authoritatively for American Protestant evangelicals any more than King did for blacks or Sheen for Catholics. Nor is Graham any more insulated from criticism than were these other leaders. Efforts that have been made to discredit the work of King because of personal moral lapses and of Sheen because of his fidelity to Thomistic conceptions of Christian faith are paralleled by attacks on Graham's political naïveté. In an age of media exaggeration, it is entirely appropriate to remember that these are fallible human beings. At the same time, the ability of each to proclaim an authentic Christian message with telling effect made them justifiably respected voices. Each has been a model of the qualities by which their larger constituencies would like themselves to be judged in the larger world.

A Public Role for Women

The opening of American society in the era after World War II has also made a great deal of difference for the practice of Christianity by women. By the 1980s women were active at every level of Christian life, including traditionally personal and domestic spheres as well as more public spheres of responsibility historically reserved for men. One thing that has not changed, however, is the fact that women still continue to be more active in churches than men. Public surveys now confirm more broadly what had been the regular report of observers throughout American history. In the late 1980s, for example, women were about ten percent more likely than men to attend worship, pray, or affirm that religion was very important in their lives. In a 1989 Gallup poll, 48 percent of American women reported being in church sometime during the previous week, compared to only 38 percent of the men. Conversely, of Americans who said they had no religion, 61 percent were men.

Increasingly, women have also taken on public positions as ministers, chaplains, parish assistants, and denominational officials. To some extent, this development simply mirrors broader changes in American society, as women stayed in school longer and took on a broadening range of careers. Patterns of education reveal the scope of change. In 1894, less than 20 percent of the bachelor's and master's degrees conferred by American colleges and universities went to women, and far less than 10 percent of the doctoral degrees. By the mid-1980s, women were receiving almost exactly half of the bachelor's and master's degrees, and well over a third of the doctorates. In 1972 the Association of Theological Schools in the United States and Canada reported that barely 10 percent of the students in its member institutions were women, whereas by 1987 that figure had climbed to over 27 percent. Churches were no more insulated from changing expectations about gender roles than any other sphere of North American life.

Among the Protestant denominations, something of a flip-flop has taken place during the twentieth century with respect to women's participation in the church's public life. On the one side, the older, traditional denominations were slow to allow women to participate in positions of leadership. The Methodist Episcopal Church, for example, voted in 1924 to ordain women, but did not grant women ministers equal opportunity for placement until 1956. Other mainline Protestant groups were even later in opening ministerial ranks to women — northern Presbyterians waiting until 1956, Episcopalians until 1976, and Lutherans until 1979. But having once taken such steps, representatives of these established Protestant churches have moved to the forefront in advancing the clerical activity of women. By contrast, Protestant bodies of a more sectarian cast were often pioneers in allowing women to serve as itinerant revivalists, missionaries, and pastors. By the first decades of the twentieth century, women had entered into public activity among most of the Wesleyan and Holiness denominations, some of the independent and Baptist groups of the North, and in almost all branches of the Pentecostal movement. Over the course of the century, however, the public leadership by women in these groups has declined, and since World War II conservative Protestants have revived theological objections to the ordination of women. Among Catholics and the Orthodox bodies, women have never been ordained as priests, although they have been called upon to fill an increasingly broad array of tasks beyond the convents and schools that once were their main centers of activity outside the home.

The careers of exemplary women leaders in the twentieth century do not satisfactorily describe the range and extent of women's activities, but they do provide some sense of the achievements in public venues by Christian women in this century. Five examples of women who worked with very different constituencies suggest something about the diversity of these opportunities.

Aimee Semple McPherson

Aimee Semple McPherson (1890-1944) was one of America's most flamboyant revivalists in the 1920s and 1930s. She married first a man who had been influential in her conversion, Robert Semple, a Pentecostal preacher, with whom she went to China as a missionary in 1908. When Semple died, she returned to the United States with their daughter Roberta. She then married Harold McPherson, from whom she was subsequently divorced. A third marriage and another divorce came later. With her mother as companion, Aimee Semple McPherson began a very successful series of revival tours across the United States after World War I.

"Sister Aimee" was a physically attractive woman who knew how to exploit her good looks and vibrant personality to capture the attention of the

One of the best known in a long line of prominent women evangelists in American history, Aimee Semple McPherson was among the first to understand the potential of radio for spreading her message. *Courtesy of the Billy Graham Center Museum*

media. Always keen for new means to proclaim her message, she very early recognized the potential of radio. As she put it in 1924, it was now possible to "carry on the winged feet of the winds, the story of hope, the words of joy, of comfort, of salvation." At least initially, her teaching was probably not as important as her personality for her considerable success. But in the course of her career she maintained standard fundamentalistic and Pentecostal emphases: entire sanctification, baptism of the Holy Spirit and the gift of tongues, Christ as Savior and Healer (hence faith healing), and the imminent return of Christ. In 1922 she settled in Los Angeles, where thousands came each week to her Angelus Temple, an architectural wonder that cost the very large sum of $1,500,000. In 1927, her ministry led to the founding of the International Church of the Foursquare Gospel in the United States, a denomination led for several decades by her son that has grown to over 200,000 members. Her career illustrates both the impetus to public proclamation provided by the early Pentecostal movement and the success awaiting those, whether male or female, who knew how to capture the imagination of the public.

Dorothy Day

When Dorothy Day (1897-1980) died, the historian David O'Brien called her "the most significant, interesting, and influential person in the history

514

By the end of her life, Dorothy Day had come to be known not only for the considerable influence she wielded in modern America but also for her saintliness. This iconographic portrait was painted by Robert Lentz. *Religious News Service*

of American Catholicism." Of this claim, the editor of her selected writings, Robert Ellsberg, wrote that "such a statement is all the more extraordinary considering that it refers to someone who occupied no established position of authority, and whose views, after all, met with virtually universal rejection throughout most of her career."

For almost fifty years, Dorothy Day found a voice — practically and verbally — through leadership of the Catholic Worker movement, a lay ministry that she and Peter Maurin (1877-1949) founded in 1931. Her commitment to the Catholic Worker's cause came only several years after her conversion to Catholicism. In *From Union Square to Rome* (1938), she told the story of a tempestuous adolescence and early adulthood, which included first an affair and an abortion and then a common-law marriage that broke up when she was converted.

In their work together in the 1930s, Day and Maurin sought a radical expression of the social philosophy of the Catholic Church, which had been the object of considerable attention since the publication of the 1893 encyclical *Rerum Novarum* by Pope Leo XIII. Maurin, who had immigrated to the United States via Canada from France, espoused a form of personalist theology like that being taught in his native country by renovators of the thought of Thomas Aquinas. Together Maurin and Day published their views in the pages of their newspaper the *Catholic Worker,* and they gave them tangible shape in a network of "Houses of Hospitality," in which Christ's acts of mercy — feeding the hungry, clothing the naked, sheltering the homeless — were carried out by his contemporary disciples. To these houses came a motley assortment of seekers, the down-and-out, troubled youths, simple misfits, and the would-be pious. Concerning this mélange, one observer noted that "the Catholic Worker consists of saints and martyrs, and the martyrs are those who have to live with the saints."

Despite practical difficulties, suspicion of her pacifism, opposition to her critique of capitalism, and simple uneasiness at such single-mindedness, Day sustained the movement through the Depression, the Second World War, the Korean and Vietnam conflicts, and the civil rights upheavals of the 1950s and 1960s. Throughout those years, she sought to retain the basic program of the movement, the spiritual sensibility of which she defined as follows: "sacrifice, worship, a sense of reverence." In her writing Day displayed an unusual kind of piety that combined absolute, even simplistic, fidelity to Catholic teaching with a passionate desire to bring the message of the Gospel to bear upon the suffering of the modern world.

Mahalia Jackson

Mahalia Jackson (1911-1972), the "queen" of gospel music, was an inspiration to her fellow blacks and a window for whites into one of the most dynamic aspects of African-American religious experience. Her parents in New Orleans were devout Baptists who made the church the central part of her life. In her own church she learned the hymns of Isaac Watts and the eighteenth-century evangelical revival (e.g., "Amazing Grace"). But among her aunts and uncles were professional entertainers who introduced her to the blues and the influence of Bessie Smith. She also drank in the music she heard in the Sanctified (or Holiness) church next to her home, where, as she later put it, everybody "clapped and stomped their feet and sang with their whole bodies."

Mahalia Jackson left New Orleans for Chicago in 1927. There she soon was singing leads with the Greater Salem Baptist Church choir. And there she soon came under the influence of Thomas A. Dorsey (b. 1899). Following a path blazed by Charles Albert Tindley (1856-1933), a black Methodist minister in Philadelphia, Dorsey became the motivating force in the creation of modern gospel music. Mahalia Jackson traveled widely with Dorsey, who served as composer, arranger, and accompanist. In 1937 she made her first recording (including a new song by Antonio Haskell entitled "God Shall

No one could "bring it" like Mahalia Jackson in her prime. *Religious News Service*

Wipe All Tears Away"). Just as in the nineteenth century some black church leaders, such as Bishop Daniel Payne, had tried to keep black folk music out of the churches, so some black leaders opposed Mahalia Jackson's free-flowing "gospel" music, with its Southern and Sanctified enthusiasm, its rocking beat, and its tendency to invoke infectious hand-clapping. One observer from the 1930s remembered that "she was known for hollering and getting happy and lifting her dress . . . an inch or two." But after years of constant performing and sensationally popular records (including her 1946 rendering of "Move on up a little higher, meet with Paul and Silas, / Move on up a little higher, meet the lily of the valley!"), she became a much-loved symbol of authentic black experience.

In the 1950s and 1960s white audiences "discovered" Jackson. With the help of these groups as well as black churches, she managed to raise money for civil rights causes and to take part in some of the most visible moments of the era. She sang at John Kennedy's inauguration in 1961, for example, and on August 28, 1963, at the request of Martin Luther King, Jr., she sang "I Been 'buked and I Been Scorned" just before King delivered his "I Have a Dream" speech in Washington, D.C. Less than four years later she sang Thomas Dorsey's "Take My Hand, Precious Lord," at King's funeral.

Mahalia Jackson may have been the best-known black woman in

America at the midpoint of the twentieth century. *That* she could sing explained much of her fame. *What* she sang — recapitulating slave experience as well as the urban black faith of more recent times — was part of the reason as well.

Flannery O'Connor

When Flannery O'Connor (1925-1964) was about twenty-five years old, at a time when she was trying to make her way as a writer, friends took her to a high-toned literary party in New York City. Several years later she recorded an exchange from that evening:

> Mrs. Broadwater said when she was a child and received the Host [at communion], she thought of it as the Holy Ghost, He being the "most portable" person of the Trinity. Now she thought of it as a symbol and implied that it was a pretty good one. I then said, in a very shaky voice, "Well, if it's a symbol, to hell with it." That was all the defense I was capable of but I realize now that this is all I will ever be able to say about it . . . except that it is the center of existence for me; all the rest of life is expendable.

Both the striking character of this confession and its deep roots in Roman Catholic Christianity typified the short but telling life of the century's most memorable Christian writer.

Flannery O'Connor was born in Savannah and lived most of her life on the family farm near Milledgeville, Georgia. As a teenager in 1941 she watched her father succumb to disseminated lupus. After training at the University of Iowa Writing Workshop and a brief residence in Connecticut, she returned to the South, which provided the stuff of her stories as well as the arena of her own life. When she was twenty-five she was diagnosed with her father's disease, which she bore with dignity while writing increasingly well-received books and carrying on a large correspondence, often on the themes of the faith. Among her best-known works were the novels *Wise Blood* (1952) and *The Violent Bear It Away* (1960) and two collections of short stories, *A Good Man Is Hard to Find* (1955) and *Everything That Rises Must Converge* (1965).

O'Connor's writing was early acclaimed by Christian and non-Christian readers alike for its eerie truthfulness to experience, its masterly depiction of character, and its challenging moral implications. O'Connor set almost all of her stories in her native South, a region that she claimed was,

Although she was diagnosed with lupus in young adulthood, Flannery O'Connor never lost her unique sense of humor. After the session that produced this publicity photo in 1953, for example, she wrote that the pictures "were all bad. The one I sent looked as if I had just bitten my grandmother and that this was one of my few pleasures, but all the rest were worse."
Ralph Morrissey,
Photographic Archives,
Vanderbilt University

if not Christ-centered, at least "Christ-haunted" in a way that the rest of the nation was not. Her stories often dealt with individuals on the fringe. Some were itinerant laborers, who, though illiterate and inarticulate, acted according to deeply felt reasons of the heart. Others concerned "respectable" people whose time had come and gone and who clung to dead patterns of belief and behavior in a frightening world. Usually these characters were Protestants about whom O'Connor could write more easily than her fellow Catholics because, as she once said in a self-deprecating remark, "they express their belief in diverse kinds of dramatic action which is obvious enough for me to catch. I can't write about anything subtle." Whatever their makeup, Flannery O'Connor's characters had to confront the Truth that consumes before it consoles. Most of her stories contain a moment when a character's expectations or fortunes are shockingly overturned. It is this moment of judgment that also serves as the prelude to the word of grace and forgiveness.

For two decades readers experienced Flannery O'Connor's stories with mystified delight and read her occasional essays with great interest. After she died, the publication of her occasional prose and letters revealed even more clearly the Christian faith motivating her remarkable literary achievement.

519

Noted author Catherine Marshall maintained in her writings the religious proprieties of former generations, but did so by showing their continuing relevance in the era after World War II. *Religious News Service*

Catherine Marshall

Like Mahalia Jackson and Flannery O'Connor, Catherine Marshall (1914-1983) was from the South. But in most other respects, her life followed a very different pattern. Marshall was descended from a long line of white Protestants, she came to public recognition first through the position of her husband, and her published writing championed conventional Protestant virtues. For all that, however, her career also testified to the way in which the traditionally domestic sphere of women's religious concerns became increasingly public throughout the course of the century.

Marshall was born into the home of a Presbyterian minister in Tennessee. The rural upbringing she enjoyed there later became the raw material for her inspirational novel *Christy* (1967). Before this book appeared, however, she had become widely known as the editor of her husband's sermons and the author of his biography. When Catherine Ambrose married Peter Marshall in 1936, she entered immediately into the public eye. Peter Marshall was an eloquent Presbyterian minister and immigrant from Scotland who eventually became the minister of the New York Avenue Presbyterian Church in Washington, D.C., and, in the the last years of his life, chaplain of the U.S. Senate.

Peter Marshall's death in 1949 was a crushing blow to his wife, but it did not undermine her pluck and determination. In that same year she published a collection of Marshall's sermons entitled *Mr. Jones, Meet the Master,* which achieved great popularity. And soon she was at work on the story of his life. The book that resulted, *A Man Called Peter: The Story of Peter Marshall,* was not an "objective" biography, but neither was it a sanitized, predictable memorial. Its sparkling prose and clear-sighted assessment of a preacher's life conveyed persuasively the reasons for her husband's popularity. The book proved successful at a very difficult task: showing that a pious man of God could also be a knowledgeable man of this world.

From this success, Catherine Marshall went on to a varied career. She wrote books of inspiration, became an editor of *Guideposts* magazine, helped establish a publishing firm, and remained active as a speaker at conferences. From conventional beginnings, and through a career that affirmed the best of those conventions, she nonetheless had become publicly visible in ways that were common only in this century.

⁂   ⁂   ⁂

The lives of Aimee Semple McPherson, Dorothy Day, Mahalia Jackson, Flannery O'Connor, and Catherine Marshall cannot be categorized easily. Each was her own person; each spoke most forcefully to a different segment of the Christian population. Yet the fact that each was also recognized outside her original constituency is a significant fact of twentieth-century religion. It has become less and less remarkable for at least some women in the churches to add other dimensions — as activist, writer, preacher, singer — to the domestic religious tasks that women and men together have continued to carry out in this century as in all others.

Personalities of Theology

Formal religious thought has never been of utmost importance in the history of Christianity in North America. Faith has been more active than contemplative, more pragmatic than intellectual. Still, since 1925 a number of capable individuals have articulated convincing theological statements. Given the pluralism of Christianity in North America, it is not surprising that these statements have been extraordinarily varied.

In light of the continuing importance of influences from abroad, it is also not surprising that American theology has reflected the themes of Christian thought elsewhere. Thus, in the 1930s and 1940s the neo-

521

orthodoxy of Karl Barth and Emil Brunner found significant echoes on this side of the Atlantic, as did the neo-Thomist Catholic theologies of Etienne Gilson and Jacques Maritain. The works of the German pastor Dietrich Bonhoeffer, who was put to death by Hitler's agents near the end of World War II, are still read with great interest. Somewhat later comparable direction was offered Catholics by the work of Karl Rahner, Hans Urs von Balthasar, and Hans Küng. From Britain, the process philosopher Alfred North Whitehead influenced academic theology, and the pungent "mere Christianity" of C. S. Lewis, expressed in several literary genres, has had an even broader impact on laity and clergy from many denominations. The works of liberation theologians such as the Catholic Gustavo Gutiérrez from South America and the Reformed Allan Boesak from South Africa brought still other influences to these shores.

A catalogue of names can only hint at the main concerns of twentieth-century theologians. but it can suggest something of the theological diversity that has become commonplace. And it can serve as an introduction to more extended consideration of the work of brothers Reinhold and H. Richard Niebuhr, who were probably the best-known American theologians of the century.

Among Roman Catholics, John Courtney Murray (1904-1967) served an especially important role in providing Catholics with an articulate defense of democratic procedures in state and church. Thomas Merton (1915-1968) showed how much a silent Trappist monk could contribute to theological discussion by drawing on resources of both Oriental thought and the monastic tradition. The Canadian Bernard Lonergan (1904-1984) offered a sophisticated interpretation of Catholic faith based both in the certainties of neo-Thomism and the subtleties of phenomenology. More recently, the biblical scholar Raymond Brown (b. 1928) and such theologians as Avery Dulles (b. 1918), David Tracy (b. 1939), and the Canadian Gregory Baum (b. 1923) have proposed various strategies for defining the faith in a changing world.

Theology in the old-line Protestant churches has been buffeted by the more general changes affecting these bodies. During the 1930s and 1940s, neo-orthodox themes were prominent in the work of Walter Marshall Horton (1895-1966), ethicist John Bennett (b. 1902), historian Joseph Haroutunian (1904-1968), and W. W. Brydon of Knox College, Toronto. In the War years and after, the German émigré Paul Tillich (1886-1965) gained a wide following by describing God as the "being beyond being" who transcends all human efforts at description. In Tillich's wake, such writers as Langdon Gilkey (b. 1919) and Schubert Ogden (b. 1928) have sought ways of preserving elements of historic Christianity in forms suggested by twentieth-century thought. A mixture of modern and traditional themes likewise shapes the work of theological ethicists James Gustafson (b. 1925) and Max Stackhouse (b. 1935). An eccentric deviation from mainstream Protestant theology came in the 1960s when several theologians, including Thomas J. J. Altizer, argued that twentieth-century theological trajectories combined with the dislocations of the time revealed the death of God.

The older Protestant bodies, after considerable initial resistance, have become especially receptive to liberationist themes. Harvey Cox is one of the Protestants who is most attuned to controversies and formulations from Third World contexts. Catholic voices have made even more of liberationist themes. Biblical scholars such as Elisabeth Schüssler Fiorenza (b. 1938) and the historian-ethicist Rosemary Radford Ruether (b. 1936) now draw tight links between justice for women, the poor, and marginalized races.

Black theology has emerged in the twentieth century as a more distinct version of such liberationist themes. In 1938, Benjamin E. Mays suggested in *The Negro's God as Reflected in His Literature* that "a continuous insistence upon the view that God is no respecter of person" set African-American theology apart. In the 1960s, proponents of an even more distinctive black theology such as Albert Cleage (b. 1911) carried Mays's insights further. They have received their fullest expression in the work of James Cone (b. 1938), who argues that the particular character of African-American experience provides a normative setting for understanding Christ's message of freedom. Since the 1960s, more blacks have articulated several versions of Cone's theme, some more separatistic and others less so. A younger voice, Cornel West (b. 1953), has added elements from classical philosophy to his passionate proclamation of black Baptist themes.

During the 1930s and following, leaders moving out of American fundamentalism also struggled to proclaim a less sectarian, more intellectually rigorous theology. Led by E. J. Carnell (1919-1967), biblical scholar George Eldon Ladd (1911-1982), and others at Fuller Seminary in California, these "neo-evangelicals" engaged in dialogue with other theological traditions to make their conservative case. Carl F. H. Henry (b. 1913), an early Fuller professor who later edited the evangelical periodical *Christianity Today,* wrote an ambitious defense of propositional revelation and, through a number of projects, encouraged evangelicals to wrestle meaningfully with the intellectual and social structures of the twentieth century. Significant assistance in renewing evangelical theology has also come from Canada, with notable contributions from the Arminian Clark Pinnock (b. 1937) and the Reformed immigrant from Britain James I. Packer (b. 1926). The Presbyterian Francis Schaeffer (1912-1984), the Nazarene H. Orton Wiley (1877-1961), and the Anabaptist Ronald Sider (b. 1939) are among others who, with quite different emphases, have called wider evangelical circles to more thoughtful Christian reflection on theological concerns.

Some of the most compelling theological labor among Protestants since World War II has come out of a series of efforts to recover significant elements of historic Christian confessions in sophisticated ways appropriate to the late twentieth-century. This kind of work, though different in many particulars, is united by a greater skepticism regarding modern thought than is found among Protestant liberals and a more faithful adherence to historic confessions than is found among Protestant neo-evangelicals. Some of those who pursue what might be called neoconfessional themes circulate among more liberal Protestants, some among evangelicals, and some among both groups as well as Roman Catholics. Elton Trueblood (b. 1900), who has applied Quaker themes along with traditional Protestant elements to questions of family, education, and formal philosophy, exemplifies this approach, but it is found quite widely among others. Notable examples have been the Methodists Paul Ramsey (1913-1988), Albert Outler (1908-1989), and Thomas Oden (b. 1931), the Lutherans Robert Jenson (b. 1930) and Carl Braaten (b. 1929), the Dutch Reformed Nicholas Wolterstorff (b. 1932), the Mennonite John Howard Yoder (b. 1927), the Congregationalist Gabriel Fackre (b. 1926), and an informal group of Lutheran-leaning academics at the Yale Divinity School including Hans Frei (1922-1988), George Lindbeck (b. 1923), and the biblical scholar Brevard Childs (b. 1923). These theologians have not been concerned about the same things, nor have their constructive labors pointed in the same direction, but they do indicate some of the potential remaining in historic formulations of Protestantism, even in the late twentieth century.

The doing of Christian theology since World War II has also been regularly enriched by fruitful interchange with Jewish religious thinkers. Will Herberg, for example, drew helpful attention to questions of religious integrity in his influential book *Protestant, Catholic, Jew* (1960). More explicitly theological stimulation came through interchange with major Jewish thinkers such as Abraham Heschel (1907-1972).

A whole host of sociologists, philosophers, historians, and even political scientists and economists has also enriched the character of Christian reflection in the twentieth century. Three of many such examples indicate the range of such work. The Jesuit literary theorist Walter Ong (b. 1912) pioneered in showing how changes in communication strategies are bound inextricably to changes in religious conceptualization. The Dutch Reformed philosopher Alvin Plantinga (b. 1932) has been a leader in making discussion of "the God question" intellectually compelling among professional philosophers. And the Episcopalian sociologist Robert Bellah (b. 1927) regularly examines the meaning of Christian faith for the social order as well as the reverse. Without denying the secularization of modern university life, the work of academics such as Ong, Plantinga, and Bellah suggests that Christian faith may have as significant an intellectual potential in the late twentieth century as it ever had.

Among the best-known theologians of the twentieth century are two brothers, Reinhold and H. Richard Niebuhr. Their histories are important in narrowly religious terms but also for revealing something about the contribution of immigrant Christian perspectives to the ongoing task of theological reflection. The Niebuhrs were not necessarily the most creative theologians since the 1920s, nor is there any guarantee that their insights will continue to receive concentrated attention. But since their work has had a broad influence, a more extensive consideration of it will provide insights concerning more general developments in twentieth-century theology.

Reinhold Niebuhr

The theology of Reinhold Niebuhr (1892-1971) is often linked to the theology of European neo-orthodoxy, but the perspective of "Christian realism" that he developed did not have the same shape as neo-orthodoxy. Niebuhr's theology is more concerned with ethics than theology proper, it focuses more on the doctrine of man than on the doctrine of God, and it shows more concern for life in society than for life in the church. On the other hand, it does share the conviction of such neo-orthodox theologians as Karl Barth and Emil Brunner that liberalism has placed too much faith in humanity and given too little attention to human self-deception.

Niebuhr was the son of an immigrant pastor in the German Evangelical Church. He attended his denomination's college and seminary (Elmhurst and Eden) before coming into fuller contact with modern Protestant liberalism at Yale Divinity School. In 1915 he accepted the pastorate of Bethel Evangelical Church in Detroit, where he served for thirteen years. Niebuhr came of age theologically in this urban church as his liberalism encountered the harsh realities of industrial America. He was particularly upset with what industrial life did to the laborers. And he wondered what hope there was for American civilization when, as he put it, "naive gentlemen with a genius for mechanics suddenly become the arbiters over the lives and fortunes of hundreds of thousands." While still in Detroit, Niebuhr began to advocate radical solutions to the human crisis as he saw it — socialism and pacifism for life in society, a new "Christian Realism" for theology.

When Niebuhr moved to New York's Union Theological Seminary in

By the end of his life, Reinhold Niebuhr was being feted often for his contributions to public theology. Here he is receiving the Grand Cross of the Order of Merit from the Federal Republic of Germany during a New York ceremony in 1960. *Religious News Service*

1928, he carried with him the commitments formed in Detroit. The coming of World War II led him to abandon his socialism and pacifism, but he remained a dedicated activist, serving on scores of committees in the 1930s and 1940s, helping to form Americans for Democratic Action and New York's Liberal Party, editing the journal *Christianity and Crisis,* and writing prolifically for newspapers and magazines.

His theological ethics were developed more systematically in a long list of major books. Of these the most important are *Moral Man and Immoral Society* (1932) and *The Nature and Destiny of Man* (1941, 1943). In the former he criticizes liberal optimism severely, arguing that social groups are selfish almost by their very definition. He also condemns the notion that human beings are perfectible as individuals and inherently good in groups. In the latter work he provides a more systematic discussion of what he calls mankind's "most vexing problem. How shall he think of himself?" In this work as elsewhere Niebuhr proposes a series of "dialectical" relationships to answer his own question: humanity as sinner and saint, subject to history and social forces but also shaper of history and society, creature of the Creator but potential lord of the creation, egotistical but capable of living for others. In explaining these tensions or paradoxes, Niebuhr draws on the symbols of Scripture. What he calls the biblical "myth" of creation helps show humanity's potential (made in the image of God) for both true good and radical evil. Niebuhr felt Scripture supported his contention that humans sin inevitably but not by moral necessity. In the person of Christ, Niebuhr found a unique example of an individual who used power only for good and not — as all other people — for evil. The cross of Christ was a particularly important theme for Niebuhr since it reveals the great paradox of powerlessness turned into power.

Niebuhr showed little interest in formal Christian doctrines except where they helped develop his ethics. Because of this lack of interest, his theology has been criticized for losing touch with the supernatural, or at least transcendent, dimensions of faith. Significantly, one of those critics was his own brother.

H. Richard Niebuhr

H. Richard Niebuhr (1894-1962) shared his brother's convictions about the weaknesses of theological liberalism, but in his own theology he offered more serious consideration of strictly theological themes and more direct concern for the church, both in itself and in its relationship to society. Like his brother, Richard Niebuhr was ordained in the Evangelical and Reformed Church (a successor to the German Evangelical Church) after attending the denomination's schools. In 1931 he accepted a position at Yale Divinity School, where he remained until his death.

Niebuhr's published work draws on diverse influences. From the older liberalism he took a commitment to the essentially experiential nature of religion. From the same source he took the view that humankind, immersed in history, can never transcend that history to see truth unbiased and whole. From European neo-orthodoxy he took a sharply critical view of liberal optimism concerning humanity and its potential. This new realism was the most notable contribution of the Niebuhrs to American neo-orthodoxy. From the classical orthodoxy of Augustine, the Reformers, and Jonathan Edwards, Niebuhr also gained a high conception of God's sovereignty and a firm belief in the utter dependency of all existence upon God.

These influences combined with Niebuhr's own creativity to produce a stimulating flow of influential books. One group of them deals broadly with the church in society. *The Social Sources of Denominationalism* (1929) shows how securely church structures are bound up with the cultural customs and patterns of Western life. *The Kingdom of God in America* (1937) provides a brilliant portrait of the way in which the idea of God's kingdom has shifted content throughout American history — from God's sovereignty

Photos of H. Richard Niebuhr are much rarer than those of his brother Reinhold. While Reinhold pursued subjects with obvious public importance, Richard worked longer, harder, and perhaps with greater long-lasting effect on background questions concerning the nature of Christianity itself. *Religious News Service*

in the time of Jonathan Edwards, to the kingdom of Christ during the 1800s, and finally to the coming kingdom for twentieth-century liberals. He offers criticisms of each era, but looks most fondly on the earliest period, when some Americans seemed truly to believe in the ultimacy of God. The book also contains the best short critical description of theological liberalism ever written: "A God without wrath brought men without sin into a kingdom without judgment through the ministrations of a Christ without a cross." In *Christ and Culture* (1951) he provides a classic schematization for the different ways in which believers over the centuries have interacted with their surrounding worlds. Its five categories — Christ against culture, the Christ of culture, Christ above culture, Christ and culture in paradox, and Christ the transformer of culture — have become standard ways to describe Christian approaches to political, economic, and social affairs.

Niebuhr's more directly theological works have not been as widely read, but they have exerted a lasting influence on formal religious thought. In *The Meaning of Revelation* (1941) he argues that when God reveals himself to people, all other events and questions become relative. The work has been criticized for making revelation overly subjective, but here as elsewhere

Niebuhr points to the Christian community as a body providing standards (albeit relative standards) for describing and communicating God's revelation. *Radical Monotheism and Western Culture* (1960) was Niebuhr's last full statement of his convictions. In it he looks to God as the source of all being, as Being itself, and he decries all that would detract from his all-sufficiency.

❀   ❀   ❀

The concerns of North American theologians in the twentieth century do not by any means encompass the concerns of all Christians in North America. Nevertheless, they remain important for their efforts at spelling out how an ancient faith can be expressed in a modern environment and for describing the ways in which the conditions of modern culture can shape expression of the ancient faith.

Theologians in the twentieth century have felt as strongly as others the erosion of institutions and the shifting contexts of personal life. That theology of any sort persists as the traditional supports for theology give way is itself remarkable. But that theology has become as much the expression of personal viewpoints as the articulation of a church's position should also not be surprising in this "age of personality."

Further Reading

Boyer, Paul. "Minister's Wife, Widow, Reluctant Feminist: Catherine Marshall in the 1950s." *American Quarterly* 30 (1978): 703-21.

Branch, Taylor. *Parting the Waters: America in the King Years, 1954-1963.* New York: Simon & Schuster, 1988.

Fackre, Gabriel. "Theology: Ephemeral, Conjectural, Perennial." In *Altered Landscapes: Christianity in America, 1935-1985.* Edited by David W. Lotz. Grand Rapids: William B. Eerdmans, 1989.

Ferm, Deane William. *Contemporary American Theologies: A Critical Survey.* New York: Seabury, 1981.

Fox, Richard Wightman. *Reinhold Niebuhr: A Biography.* New York: Pantheon, 1985.

Jackson, Mahalia, with Evan McLeod Wylie, *Movin' on Up.* New York: Hawthorn Books, 1966.

McPherson, Aimee Semple. *This Is That: Personal Experiences, Sermons and Writings.* Los Angeles: Bridal Call Publishing House, 1919.

Martin, William. *A Prophet with Honor: The Billy Graham Story.* New York: William Morrow, 1991.

Miller, William M. *Dorothy Day: A Biography.* San Francisco: Harper & Row, 1982.

O'Connor, Flannery. *The Habit of Being: Letters of Flannery O'Connor.* Edited by Sally Fitzgerald. New York: Farrar, Straus & Giroux, 1978.

Ramsey, Paul, ed. *Faith and Ethics: The Theology of H. Richard Niebuhr.* New York: Harper, 1957.

Sheen, Fulton J. *Treasures in Clay: The Autobiography of Fulton J. Sheen.* Garden City, NY: Doubleday, 1980.

CHAPTER 20

American Christianity, Christianity in America

We come, O Christ, to you, true Son of God and man,
by whom all things consist, in whom all life began.
In you alone we live and move
and have our being in your love.

$$* \qquad * \qquad * \qquad * \qquad *$$

You are the living truth; all wisdom dwells in you,
the source of every skill, the one eternal True!
O great I AM! in you we rest,
sure answer to our every quest.

$$* \qquad * \qquad * \qquad * \qquad *$$

We worship you, Lord Christ, our Savior and our King;
to you our youth and strength adoringly we bring:
so fill our hearts that all may view
your life in us and turn to you.

In its music, the postwar evangelical movement is associated mostly with Scripture songs and "gospel rock." It has, however, also inspired more traditional hymns, including these verses by a Canadian, Margaret Clarkson (b. 1915), which were written in 1946 at the request of the director of Canada's Inter-Varsity Christian Fellowship.

THE BLOWS RAINED ON NORTH AMERICAN SOCIETY IN THE TWENTIETH century have included two world wars, a great economic depression followed by unprecedented (if unevenly distributed) affluence, and a major cultural upheaval at the time of the Vietnam War. Shocks only slightly less powerful — such as the Red Scare after World War I, the Korean and Gulf Wars, the continuing problem of Quebec's relationship with the rest of Canada, and violent business cycles in widely scattered regions on the continent — have rolled by almost without number. As part of society, the Christian churches have felt the effects of those shocks as fully as any institutions.

At the same time, however, powerful forces have also been at work to remind North Americans Christians that they are part of a worldwide movement. One of these is involvement in missionary work. The great contribution of North Americans to overseas service has had a measurable impact on world Christianity, but it has also shaped the sending churches of Canada and the United States. Other events drawing attention away from local developments to the world have been the remarkable ecumenical breakthroughs between Catholics and Protestants since the 1960s. The fact that controversies begun long ago and far away have been at least partially resolved in late-twentieth-century North America reinforces a sense of participation by those churches in world Christian experience. It is, therefore, appropriate in the concluding chapter of a history of Christianity in North America to examine both the missionary movement and the recent steps that have been taken toward Catholic-Protestant reconciliation.

The book ends, however, not with more information but by asking what, in Christian terms, the record of the past means. To gain the perspective necessary to consider such a question, we must look at the differences between white and black experiences of the faith, between rates of secularization in different regions of North American, and between the Christian experience in Canada and in the United States. In a concluding section we will seek to define a Christian way of assessing the recent history of Christianity in North America.

Twentieth-Century Missions

One of the most striking developments in the history of Christianity has occurred in the twentieth century. It is the shift in the centers of world

This band of China Inland Mission workers, with a typical proportion of women outnumbering men, was photographed in Vancouver shortly before sailing for the Far East. *Courtesy of the Billy Graham Center Museum*

Christianity from the West to the non-Western world. In 1900 something like 85 percent of Christians lived in the West. By the year 2000 it has been predicted that nearly 60 percent will live in the Third World. The story of Christian missions from America since World War I has played a part in that redistribution. It is a story illuminating important changes in domestic religion as well.

The major twentieth-century shifts in American denominational strength have been reflected in the size of missionary populations. For their part, Catholics in America have become the main financial supporters of the worldwide missionary efforts of their Church. Although the recruitment of Catholic personnel lagged somewhat behind the raising of funds, by the mid-twentieth century Americans, led by the Catholic Foreign Mission Society (Maryknoll) and by the Jesuits, contributed several thousand missionaries, about a third of the worldwide Catholic total. (The numbers of American Roman Catholics serving overseas rose to nearly 10,000 by 1968, but by the end of the 1980s had declined to slightly over 6,000.)

Among Protestants the high point of missionary activity among the older ecumenical denominations came in the 1920s. At the time of the famous Edinburgh Conference of 1910, missionaries from the United States and Canada made up about one-third of the 21,000 Protestant missionaries worldwide. By 1925, half of the world's 29,000 missionaries were Americans or Canadians. In that year there were more than 3,300 American mission-

The China Inland Mission, like many other missionary agencies from the United States and Canada, worked especially hard at constructing schools and academies in the lands to which they went. The 1921 graduating class of China's Hunan Bible Institute, sponsored by the CIM, respresented one of the fruits of that effort. *Courtesy of the Billy Graham Center Museum*

aries in China alone. Canada's great interest in Asian missionary activity is suggested by the immense popularity of Toyohiko Kagawa during the early 1930s. Kagawa, a Japanese Presbyterian who pioneered Christian work among the urban poor of his own country, preached throughout Canada to great crowds in the years just before Japanese military expansion cut contacts between Asia and North America. By the mid-1950s, the proportion of Christian missionaries from the United States and Canada had reached two-thirds of the world total. It has subsequently declined, because of the rise in missionary activity among Third World Protestants, but the contribution of North America to Protestant missions remains very great.

By the 1950s, however, a significant change was taking place in the source of these Protestant missionaries. Whereas mainline denominations had taken the lead in the period between the Edinburgh Conference and the Second World War, independent evangelical agencies grew more rapidly thereafter. As late as 1953, about half of the nearly 19,000 Protestant missionaries from North America were affiliated with the National or Canadian Councils of Churches. By 1985 only slightly more than 10 percent of the nearly 40,000 American career missionaries were so affiliated. Instead, most were members of independent mission boards, some of which had been established around the turn of the century (e.g., the Africa Inland Mission, the China Inland Mission, the Sudan Interior Mission). Others were part of the postwar surge of evangelical voluntary agencies (e.g., Missionary Aviation Fellowship, Far Eastern Gospel Crusade, Greater European Mission). In 1985, over 3,000 were at work translating the Scriptures with Wycliffe Bible Translators. In addition, substantial numbers of missionaries were being sponsored by the Southern Baptists (over 3,000 in 1984), the Assemblies of God (over 1,500 in 1986), and other conservative denominations such as the Christian and Missionary Alliance and the Seventh-Day Adventists.

The situation in Canada mirrored that in the States. In 1966 there were about 5,100 Canadians ministering overseas. Catholics accounted for 1,700 of this number, missionaries associated with the Canadian Council of Churches another 700, and conservative Protestants the remaining 2,700. By 1985 several of Canada's small evangelical denominations such as the Christian and Missionary Alliance and the Associated Gospel Churches were each sponsoring more missionaries than the Presbyterians, the Anglicans, and the United Church all together.

This surge of mission effort reflected in part the general growth of fundamentalists and evangelicals in American church life. But it also came about as a result of significant institutional developments. Since 1946, the Inter-Varsity Christian Fellowship has held a missionary conference for students every three years with upwards of 20,000 young people receiving a missionary challenge. The first of these gatherings was held in Toronto, with subsequent meetings at the University of Illinois in Urbana. In 1974 American evangelicals were leaders in calling an International Congress on World Evangelization at Lausanne, Switzerland, a meeting that has led to an active continuing committee engaged especially in bringing Third World evangelists to the fore as leaders of such pan-evangelical gatherings. At meetings in the wake of Lausanne, cosponsored by the World Evangelical Fellowship, Third World evangelicals have pressed their American counterparts to modify the notion of evangelism so that it might fit local circumstances in all regions of the world.

Concerns for social justice and religious tolerance have advanced much further in the ecumenical denominations that once were leaders in world evangelization. Since World War II, general theological uncertainty in the mainline churches has been matched by an increasing uncertainty about the idea of evangelization itself. Voices can still be heard in such bodies defending the need to proclaim the gospel as the sole hope of the world. More typical, however, are two other stances. One is the growing conviction that although Christianity enjoys a unique status as God's fullest revelation, other world religions share part of that truth. The other is the belief that Christianity is an important expression of human religion but that it need not necessarily be promulgated as a replacement for the religions practiced by the other peoples of the world. In the estimation of ecumenical spokesman W. Richey Hogg, this "shift marks a move away from a Western Christian evangelistic crusade to the world and toward an engagement with the world

Many Americans and Canadians participated in the 1974 Lausanne Congress on World Evangelization, but that meeting also marked the emergence of Third World evangelical movements out from under the shadow of their North American counterparts. *Religious News Service*

in what is regarded as a total evangelistic response to the world's needs and the religious beliefs of the people."

For their part, American Catholic efforts have always nurtured a two-pronged approach, seeking to draw non-Christians into the church while also working extensively at social efforts including education, medicine, and the care of orphans. Since the Second Vatican Council published views that showed a greater acceptance of non-Christian faiths, Catholics have had some of the same debates as their Protestant ecumenical associates concerning traditional assertions about the uniqueness of the Christian gospel.

The engagement of American Christians with the rest of the world through missions is nearly two centuries old. But much has changed in that time. Previous certainties now appear less secure — for instance, the belief that the civilization of the United States is distinctly Christian and as such is to be linked with the proclamation of the gospel. In addition, the rapid spread in the West of secular opinions and secular habits of life has created a situation in which efforts toward conversion are as urgently needed in Western countries as in regions of the Third World. When more Koreans practice the faith than citizens of most European countries, and when Roman Catholicism is expanding much more rapidly in Africa than in North America, the missionary picture is bound to change. Still, it would be wrong to deemphasize the great importance of North American mission efforts in the twentieth century. They have brought American visions of the Christian faith to millions around the world. They have also instructed both mission-aries and believers in North America about the ability of the missionary message to take on a life of its own once it has been integrated into cultures with conventions different from those in the West.

Ecumenism

Since World War II the most visible ecumenical activities in the United States and Canada have been carried out by agencies aiming directly at increased interdenominational cooperation. Of these groups, the National Council of Churches of Christ has played an especially prominent part. With its record of support for causes that others have deemed radical, it is also the most controversial. Not surprisingly, given the relative decline of the older Prot-estant denominations, the National Council in which those groups have been prominent also suffered through difficult times in the 1970s and 1980s. A combination of decreased funding and continuing opposition from theo-logical and social conservatives made for ongoing strain within the organi-zation. At the same time, however, a wide range of other ecumenical groups has taken on the same kind of cooperative tasks that the National Council exists to promote. The National Association of Evangelicals (founded in 1942), the Christian Holiness Association (a successor to the National Campmeeting Association for the Promotion of Christian Holiness), the Pentecostal Fellowship of North America (established in 1948), and the Baptist Joint Committee on Public Affairs are examples of lower-keyed organizations that have each carved out a niche for themselves. These agen-cies promote cooperation among sister denominations, lobby governments on issues of special concern to constituencies, and provide national meetings for fellowship and encouragement.

But the most significant ecumenical breakthrough of recent decades has been the calming of previous antagonism between Roman Catholics and Protestants. No one group alone is responsible for this improved state of affairs, but it is certainly one of the most intriguing stories of the century.

As late as the post–World War II era, feelings between Catholics and Protestants were still very sensitive. In 1945, for example, a fundamentalist radio preacher, Carl McIntire, argued publicly that the Catholic Church posed a greater threat to America than even the Communist menace. "If one had to choose between the two [Communism or Catholicism]," he wrote, "one would be much better off in a communistic society than in a Roman Catholic Fascist set-up." When President Truman later proposed assigning a formal representative to the Vatican, it was the Protestant estab-

Ecclesiastical dignitaries from around the world assembled at Chicago's Soldier Field for a Festival of Faith during the second assembly of the World Council of Churches, which met August 15-31, 1954, in Evanston, Illinois. *Religious News Service*

lishment, led by G. Bromley Oxnam, president of the Federal Council of Churches, that led the opposition. Such a move, Oxnam said, would encourage an "un-American policy of a union of church and state" of the sort supposedly favored by Catholics. But suspicion did not turn up on one side only. When the second General Assembly of the World Council of Churches met at Evanston, Illinois, in 1954, Chicago's influential Cardinal Samuel Strich forbade Catholic priests to attend its sessions. A year earlier, Catholics protested the release of a motion picture depicting the life of Martin Luther on the grounds that it constituted a scurrilous attack on their faith. Quebec's bishops banned the movie in their province.

But then the situation changed with lightning speed. The most visible public signal of a shift in the United States was the election of a Catholic president in 1960. John F. Kennedy's victory was itself a milestone. To be sure, his candidacy did split voters to an unprecedented degree along religious lines. Catholics had given Democratic presidential candidate Adlai

Stevenson 51 percent and 45 percent of their vote in 1952 and 1956, respectively. In 1960, 82 percent of Catholics voted for Kennedy, the Democrat. White Protestants who regularly attended church had given Dwight Eisenhower, the Republican, about two-thirds of their votes in in 1952 and 1956. In 1960 they gave the Republican, Richard Nixon, three-quarters. Even black Protestants, who since World War II had usually voted strongly for the Democratic candidate, gave almost half their votes to Nixon. But Kennedy proved adept at allaying Protestant fears. During the campaign, in a widely publicized speech to Protestant ministers in Houston, he pledged strict fidelity to American traditions of separation between church and state. When he became president, Kennedy scrupulously held to his word, even to the point of opposing any sort of governmental aid to parochial schools. Because of these actions, controversy over Catholics in national office was calmed almost to the vanishing point. (Some Catholics, it may be added, were disappointed that Kennedy's faith seemed to mean so little for his policies or style of government.)

Even more important for improved Catholic-Protestant relations were events coming from Rome and the Second Vatican Council convened by Pope John XXIII in 1962. In the wake of the Council's Decree on Ecumenism, which "commends this work to the bishops everywhere in the world for their diligent and prudent guidance," the Conference of American Bishops in November 1964 set up its own Ecumenical Commission. One year later, joint Protestant-Catholic worship services were taking place even in Quebec. In both the United States and Canada, Roman Catholics were soon deep in discussion with Eastern Orthodox churches as well as with several of the major Protestant bodies. Catholic-Protestant dialogue now occurs at almost every imaginable level. Of these discussions, the one between Catholics and Lutherans has borne the most fruit. Representatives of these long-time antagonists could even agree in the early 1980s that their convictions on justification by faith were now very close to each other.

The improvement in Catholic-Protestant relations has also been accelerated by other modern circumstances. Alliances on social or political issues have broken down barriers between those Catholics and Protestants who, for example, together favor greater government assistance to the poor or who together oppose abortion on demand. Even more important, though also more difficult to document, are a wealth of new Catholic-Protestant connections in neighborhood Bible studies, local agencies for housing the homeless, attendance at concerts featuring "Christian rock," and a host of other activities.

To be sure, all is not rosy on the ecumenical front. Protestant fear of Catholicism is not entirely dead; it continues to appear at the extremes of

Angelo Giuseppe Roncalli became Pope John XXIII in 1958 and served only five years as the head of the Roman Catholic Church. But his policy of "opening windows," most evident in the Second Vatican Council, deeply affected Catholic churches around the world, and perhaps nowhere more dramatically than in the United States and Canada. *Religious News Service*

the Protestant spectrum, among arch-conservatives still characterizing the pope as the Whore of Babylon and among arch-liberals whose sensitivities are offended by Catholic efforts to guide the faithful on social and moral questions. In addition, other religious antagonisms have arisen to replace traditional differences. North American Christians still differ sharply on political questions (budget for defense versus budget for social programs), on social issues (support for traditional families and traditional marriages versus support for alternative life-styles), and on general approaches to ethical behavior itself (grounded in timeless truths versus adjustable according to the circumstances of the times). It is always possible that these differences might flare into religious warfare, at least of the verbal sort. But even as such differences continue to divide churches, and to divide membership within churches, it is still true that modern breakthroughs in charity among churches, especially between Catholics and Protestants, distinguished the postwar years as one of the most remarkable ecumenical eras in the recent history of Christianity.

Making Sense of the Story

As reference to missionary activity makes clear, Christianity is a worldwide movement. As discussion of historic divisions between Catholics and Protestants indicates, Christianity existed long before the European settlement of North America. These larger, worldwide realities help put our story into perspective. Although the Christian faith has played an important role in the development of North America, never has a majority of the world's Christians lived in Canada and the United States, never have worldwide habits of Christian worship and devotion been entirely dominated by North Americans, and never have the most prominent patterns of Christian thought uniformly followed North American examples.

At the same time, American versions of the ancient faith have been unusually influential in the modern world. Pentecostalism, which began humbly on Los Angeles's Azusa Street, is the world's most dynamic, most rapidly growing form of Christianity. American Catholics contributed substantially to the discussions of the Second Vatican Council when that ancient Church adjusted its age-old traditions to modern conditions. The United States may be the place where Eastern Orthodoxy breaks through the barriers of historic ethnic divisions. The older Protestant bodies in the United States and Canada have been key supporters of the World Council of Churches. Canadian Anglicans were in the vanguard that established the Lambeth Conferences (periodic gatherings of Anglicans and Episcopalians from around the globe). More recently, North Americans have taken the lead in promoting greater fellowship among Protestant evangelicals throughout the world. All of this shows that North Americans have made a difference in world Christianity. Although their influence has never been absolute, it has been great, especially in the past century. It is, therefore, all the more important to ask what has been American and what Christian in the history of the ancient faith in North America.

To answer such a question is, however, immensely difficult. It may be easy to label some expressions of the faith as mere "culture Christianity," simply a veneer of traditional Christian language on indigenous social patterns. We might point to scriptural defenses of the slave system as an example of this sort of thing, or the Christianized resistance to immigration, or the hyper-Christian patriotism that cropped up during many of the nation's wars. But the question is really much more complicated. Christian abolitionism, Christianized one-worldism, and Christian antipatriotism could, in fact, be just as culturally conditioned as the religious movements they opposed. Religion and culture do not coexist like pieces of bread in a sandwich; they are, rather, interwoven deeply one into the other.

One way to consider the fate of Christianity in North American history is to approach the topic by way of comparisons. Those that follow are only some of the important ones that could be made, but they serve as a starting point for viewing the course of the faith from contrasting perspectives. This

541

way of looking at the faith does not serve to extract it from culture, but it does help to bring the meaning of its cultural connections into clearer focus.

Black and White

The history of Christianity among African Americans is basic to the history of Christianity in America. From a religious viewpoint, the great scandal of American history is the support that white believers found in Scripture and Christian traditions for slavery and even longer-lasting convictions about black racial inferiority. From the same viewpoint, the triumph of African-American history is the flourishing of the gospel in black communities. To African Americans, Christianity has brought comfort, consolation, and even power, to the surprise of representatives of the dominant society, who more often expected it to bring passivity, complacency, and servility.

Such a history is not, however, any less complex than other aspects of our story. Some blacks did find in Christianity merely a compensatory religion with little meaning for life on earth. Some whites did realize that the Christian message they communicated to blacks had the potential to revolutionize conditions in this life as well as in the life to come. As organizations, black congregations and denominations have been no less free of the infighting and power-mongering that have infected white churches. Christian practice can become a vacant form among blacks almost as easily as it can for staid Presbyterians, theatrical Episcopalians, or conventional Catholics. But having made all necessary qualifications, it still is true that among the most remarkable reversals in the history of American Christianity were the conversion of blacks, the growth of strong African-American denominations, and the continuing reservoir of hope provided by the churches to black communities.

The character of African-American Christianity shines through most obviously in the sermon. Since the days of George Whitefield and before, North America has been home to many powerful preachers in almost all of the denominations. But the sermon has played an especially powerful role in the African-American experience. Some of these sermons are well known, such as the messages of Martin Luther King, Jr., but most have never been appreciated beyond the congregations that hear them and heed them.

The potential of black sermons arises from both form and substance. In form, the preacher's call with the congregation's response draws all who are present deep into the gospel story, as in this transcript (from about 1970) recorded by Eleanor Dickinson and Barbara Benzinger of a revival sermon by J. M. Kimball at First Calvary Baptist Church, Knoxville, Tennessee.

I have a feeling that somebody ought to join the church tonight. Somebody that's not attached ought to join.
Yes. Amen.

Somebody that never has been a member of a church ought to join.
Yes, yes.

Or somebody ought to deem it necessary to choose First Calvary as his church home. Is there anybody —
Yes.

That has ever been in trouble? Is there anybody here
Yes.

That has a burden on your shoulders?
Yes.

Is there anybody here
Yes.

That has been mistreated?
Yes.

Is there anybody here
Yes, yes.

That has ever been out at night
Yes, yes.

In the cold alone?
Yes, yes.

I don't have any weapons, but I can open a door for you.
Yes.

He can open a door for you.
Yes, yes.

Is there anybody here
Yes, yes.

That's ever gotten lonesome?
Yes, yes.

I want to search them out tonight.
Yes.

If you're out of the church
Yes.

You ought to come home.
Yes.

While the wind
Yes

Is still blowing,
Yes.

You ought to come home.
Yes.

While the sun is still shining on everything,
Yes.

You ought to come home.
Yes.

While God is still on his throne, you ought to come home.

Beyond the form, as in J. M. Kimball's appeal, the secret of power in black sermons is the substance. As Garry Wills has written, "hope welling up from the darkest places remains the miracle of African-American Christianity." So it was with a sermon by James Bevel, one of many preached at the funeral of Martin Luther King, Jr., as recorded by Wills:

> There's a false rumor around that our leader's dead. *Our* leader is not dead. Martin Luther King is not our leader. [Some hesitation here, on the *"Talk it!"* cries.] Our leader is the man who led Moses out of Israel. [*"Thass the man!"*] Our leader is the man who went with Daniel into the lions' den. [*"Same man!"*] Our leader is the man who walked out of the grave on Easter morning. Our leader never sleeps nor slumbers. He cannot be put in jail. He has never lost a war yet. *Our* leader is still on the case. Our leader is not dead. One of his prophets died. We will not stop because of that.

In such a sermon, the biblical story of alienation, death, and redemption parallels, defines, and expresses the lived realities of a particular people's story.

Christianity is a religion in which believers can draw upon the Scriptures in their efforts to stabilize society, to work to construct institutions, and to realize the potentials of the self. But even more profoundly it is a religion in which God is praised, in the words of the Authorized Version that was the first Bible preached to and by blacks, for choosing "the foolish things of the world to confound the wise . . . the weak things of the world to confound the things which are mighty; and base things of the world, and things which are despised, hath God chosen, yea, and things which are not, to bring to nought things that are: that no flesh should glory in his presence." The historian Donald Mathews phrases it similarly when he describes how evangelical Protestantism in the antebellum South needed the faith of blacks to enjoy a full understanding of the faith itself: "Southern Evangelicalism could never really constitute a balanced Christian ideology apart from the values and beliefs of blacks because without them there was no successful identification of believers with a Christ at once crucified and victorious. Because of their place in society, white Evangelicals were too conscious of their own respectability and too crippled by their ethnocentricism or racism to sense the agony and alienation of the cross and therefore to understand the Gospel as a truly liberating force." In these terms, the history of African-American Christian faith may be for North America *the* fundamental story.

The United States and Canada

The value of comparing Christian history in the United States and Canada is different than the value of comparing the experiences of whites and blacks. But for providing other unexpected insights, as well as fresh ways to conceive the relation of North American Christianity to world Christianity, the Canadian-American comparison is almost as valuable.

Canada is both too similar to the United States and too different to make for easy comparisons. On the one hand, there are the same European-based forms of Christianity facing many of the same perils and opportunities in an open New World; the same heritage of British political ideals; the same participation in revivalistic, intellectual, and social movements. On the other hand, the differences are not slight. Where the United States' most critical social tension has been between blacks and whites, Canada's has been between those who speak French and those who speak English. Where the Catholic Church was a late force in the development of American Christianity, it was there from the start in Canada. Where Americans laud the ideals of their Revolutionary heritage, Canadians celebrate the virtues of Loyalism. Moreover, these differences are played out on two very different demographic landscapes. Canada remains, by the standards of Asia, Europe, or even the United States, a scarcely inhabited land. (Canada's second most populous province, Quebec, is bigger than Alaska but has considerably fewer people than New Jersey. There are more people living in California than in all of Canada.)

Despite such differences, and perhaps even despite such similarities, conclusions about the history of Christianity in Canada turn out to reveal much about the parallel story in the States.

One such conclusion has to do with the remarkable degree of Canada's Christianization in the nineteenth century. A generation ago, historian W. L. Morton wrote that "religion — not wealth, and not politics — was the chief concern, the main ideal occupation of Canadians, both British and French [in the Victorian Era]. The Age is indeed to be comprehended only in terms of the idea of Providence, that God and His Church were very present actors in the World. The fact indeed even transcended the differences between French and English." The perception of Canada as a "Christian nation" was, however, always blurred. Part of the blurring concerned "Christianity," since Protestants and Catholics found it difficult to recognize one another as truly of the same faith. But a larger part of the blurring involved the Canadian national identity. Canada has always lacked the sort of compelling myths that fuel American ideology. South of the border there is "Give me liberty or give me death," "We hold these truths to be self-evident," "We the people of the United States of America," "now we are engaged in a great civil war," and "with malice toward none, with charity toward all." These moving slogans, moreover, were all spoken in the belief that God was singularly concerned about the great national experiment to which they referred.

North of the border, by contrast, there have been no civil wars worthy of the name and certainly no revolution (the local skirmishes of 1837-1838 are sometimes called "rebellions," but their long-term impact was mostly to show Canadians why nothing similar should ever happen again). The establishment of modern Canada in 1867 involved little that could be turned into legend, with railroad magnates and hard-drinking politicians meeting behind closed doors in the wake of the American Civil War to propose a hasty piece of legislation for the British Parliament in order to keep their defenseless provinces from falling into the grasp of the rising American empire. Although it is true, as we have seen, that some Canadians did feel that God had singled out their nation for special concern, that belief almost always remained in the background.

Yet despite a national history without the ideology of special divine blessing, Canada has an even better objective argument for being considered a "Christian nation" than does the United States. The list of comparisons with the United States is striking: Canada did not tolerate slavery, it has not thrown its weight around in foreign adventures, it has not done quite so poorly with its Native Americans, it has not puffed itself up with messianic pride, it has tolerated much less social violence, until very recently its rates of church attendance were considerably higher, its believers have promoted missionary outreach at home and abroad at least as vigorously, its churches have had much more (Quebec) or considerably more (Ontario, Maritimes) impact on local public life, it has cared more humanely for the poor and weak members of its society, and its educational structures make some provision for teaching religion. In other words, if believers want to find a more convincing history of "Christian America," they should look to Canada.

To draw this conclusion is not to deny the significant Christian influences on life in the United States. Nor is it to pretend that Canada's Christian heritage is flawless. It is, rather, to suggest that if we want historical standards against which to judge the nature of the Christian presence in the United States, we will make better judgments if we include comparisons with the northern neighbor that chose not the way of revolution and independence but of Loyalism and peaceful change.

In the decades after World War II, the Canadian situation has changed dramatically. Emphasis on personal rights has become just as vigorous as in the States. As fewer Canadians attend church regularly, the immense Catholic and Protestant contributions to Canadian history are fading from sight, and so also from memory. But the prominence of Christianity in both English- and French-speaking regions constitutes a remarkable historical legacy. The virtues and vices of Christians in Canada have been similar to those of believers in the States. Yet where things were different, it remains instructive to ask why.

To consider Canada's more recent history is to approach the question of secularization directly. How are present realities connected to history? How do we explain the fact that Christian observance in the States seems to be holding to about the same levels as it has for decades, while in Canada it has been in a steep decline for the better part of thirty years? And is it enough regarding the situation in the States to note that pollsters find substantial numbers at church each Sunday if other aspects of national life seem increasingly anti-Christian? Such questions demand brief treatment on their own.

The Varying Pace (and Diverse Meanings) of Secularization

At least two issues are involved in any consideration of secularization. The first explains why rates of Christian observance and adherence change at different rates in different regions. The second defines the connections between rates of adherence and observance on the one hand and the health of a people's faith on the other.

With respect to the first question, the British sociologist David Martin has proposed a plausible theory to explain different patterns and rates of secularization. Martin notes that "at certain critical periods in their history societies acquire a particular frame and . . . subsequent events persistently move within the limits of that frame." When applied to North America, this concept helps explain some of the dramatic contrasts of recent decades — why, for example, the rates of church attendance in Canada, which were considerably higher than those in the States for probably the entire century before 1960, have subsequently fallen considerably below those in the States; why rates of church adherence in Canada have fallen fastest and furthest in Quebec, where once they were highest; and how the United States has managed to develop the most "modern" society in the West without experiencing the dramatic fall in church adherence that has taken place in other "modern" Western societies. ("Modern" in discussions of secularization usually connotes such factors as economic and educational expansion, increased geographic and social mobility, and heightened affluence.)

In simplest terms, secularization has developed differently in the United States and Canada because the societies have developed differently. Until recently, Canada was consistently more conservative, group oriented, and traditional than the United States, and Quebec more so than the rest of Canada. Significantly, the largest communions in Canada — the Catholics, Anglicans, and Presbyterians — all enjoyed some measure of governmental establishment in the Old World or the New or, as in the case of the United Church, aspired to a quasiofficial role as the nation's church. In the United States, by contrast, church and state were constitutionally separated early in the nation's history. Even if several varieties of Christians have tried to re-create informal establishments, the influence of dissenters who welcome disestablishment has usually been stronger. In the United States even Catholics became "dissenters" who made their way by their own wits without the assistance of the state.

Since World War II, the changes that have most significantly shaped North American culture have stressed technology instead of morality, personal enrichment instead of altruistic service, and the potential for individual development instead of the force of historical traditions. These secularizing forces have had a variety of effects. In Canada, they seem to have moved the entire society away from traditional religious practices. Quebec, the society that was most tightly bound to a religious-social union, moved the fastest. In the United States, the same trends have come to coexist with traditional religious practices. Both countries have experienced what sociologist David Martin calls "erosion of religious ethos" in public life, and yet in both (as pollsters have shown) vast majorities retain many traditional religious beliefs. The difference has come, again in Martin's terms, with "institutional erosion" of the churches in Canada contrasted to "institutional expansion" of the churches in the States. The forces of modernity, in other words, have worked *through* the communal, top-down structures of traditional Canadian religion, while they have worked *alongside* the more fragmented, populist structures of American churches. The vast freedoms of the United States may have thinned out the content of Christianity, but those freedoms also resulted in more room for the faith in a modernizing world. Canada, a society more cohesive and deferential to authority, has experienced rapid losses in church adherence as its political, economic, cultural, and educational leaders turned from traditional faith. The United States, a sprawling, diffuse society in which leadership remains largely a function of democratic appeal, has absorbed secularizing changes with fewer obvious changes in patterns of church attendance or adherence.

But if this analysis helps make sense of differences in recent history between the United States and Canada, it does not provide an interpretation of the changes. The question can be put in two ways: Was Christianity healthier in Canada when its rates of church attendance were higher than in the United States? Is Christianity now more vigorous in the States because rates of church adherence are higher? Even to ask these questions is to suggest that the situation is more complicated, that formal rates of attendance or adherence do not necessarily tell the full story. Certain aspects of Canadian Christian life may indeed have once been healthier, and certain aspects in the United States may actually now be more vigorous. But simply to equate rates of adherence with resistance or capitulation to secularization is too simple. Historian George Marsden has posed this issue well: "If we use 'secularity' in a normative context to refer to the decline or retreat of *true* religion, then it should be evident that secularity can increase even as religious (or even 'Christian') profession and practice increases. For instance, if Christians simply baptize worldly practice (e.g., pure self-interest or materialism), the resultant increase in the popularity of Christianity will not retard the growth of true secularity."

It would be hard to deny that a fixation on material concerns, narrow self-interest, and hedonistic life-styles has affected citizens of the United States as strongly, or nearly so, as their counterparts in Canada. To be sure, over the past 125 years vigorous forms of ultramontane Catholicism and evangelical Protestantism have moved from shaping Canadian life to competing within it, and then to being shaped by it. But, even with higher rates of church attendance today, the same could perhaps be said about the United States.

If these things are so — if there is a form of secularization in the States that advances within the churches, and if there is another form in Canada that advances by taking people away from the churches — we are in a position to address the question with which this last section of the book began: Has Christianity in North America at the end of the twentieth century once more entered into a wilderness? With religious pluralism the norm in the States and with Christian adherence declining rapidly in Canada, but also with many signs in the two societies of faithful Christian witness, how should believers judge the situation of recent decades?

Wilderness Once Again?

Evaluation of the immediate past can be viewed as a balance between gains and losses. On the debit side, it is clear that standards of Christian culture have lost considerable power in the course of the twentieth century. In French-speaking Canada, the Catholic Church's intrinsic authority is only a shadow of what it once was. In the rest of Canada and in the United States, the Protestant mainstream that once dictated cultural values, provided standards for private and public morality, assumed primary responsibility for education, and powerfully shaped the media — that Protestantism is fragmented and culturally feeble. In short, institutions and values constructed with great sacrifice have been weakened and are now threatened with collapse.

Yet on the credit side, it is clear that some varieties of the Christian faith, such as Pentecostalism, advance with vigor. Others, such as Roman Catholicism, may be experiencing numerous difficulties but are nonetheless finding new respect and broadening their influence. Selected voluntary agencies (e.g., Bible societies) continue to expand. New sensitivity to the Christian contributions of African Americans and Native Americans has brought Christian traditions that were once neglected further into the light. Overt Christian participation in politics is always a risky thing, but, despite questionable actions, the New Christian Right did succeed in reintroducing questions of traditional morality into spheres that needed ethical renewal. In Canada, where twentieth-century traditions of religious-political involvement are more discrete, leaders from several denominations and coalitions have made at least some positive contributions to resolving the constitutional crises of the late 1980s.

From a completely different angle, however, it may be that toting up a balance sheet of gains and losses is more a North American way of analyzing the contemporary situation than a distinctly Christian way. A common feature of North American church history — whether written by the heirs of the Puritans, by Catholics, by representatives of sectarian bodies, or by mainline and evangelical Protestants — is a tendency to concentrate on the churches in their relationship to the broader society. Matters of greatest interest (as also in this book) have been visible relationships: Who gained influence? Who gained respectability? Did a reforming crusade work? Did an "outsider" pay too high a price to move to the "inside"? Or, in words once applied to Catholic Americans, "Has the immigrant kept the faith?"

Yet there are other ways to present the history of Christianity, ways that shift the focus back toward internal questions concerning the nature of the faith itself. For this kind of analysis, the internal character of the gospel provides the interpretive standard more than external measures of success in North America. From the central fact of the Christian story, the Incarnation of Jesus Christ, believers know that the most important things in life are likely to be the least conspicuous and that circumstances of severest defeat lead to the clearest apprehension of God. From the angle of the Incarnation, in other words, the main goal in life is not to gain power but to undertake a journey guided by the ideals of the gospel.

In these terms, the history of *Christianity* in North America, as opposed to the history of *North American* Christianity, might not be so much about the gain or loss of cultural influence but stories about "signs of contradiction," moments when the faith offered something unexpected to a person, a problem, a situation, or a region. Such "signs of contradiction" existed, for example, when slave owners — perhaps against their better judgment — gave Bibles to their slaves. They were illustrated during the 1930s by the conversion of a few social radicals, such as Dorothy Day, from left-wing utopias to Christian faith. They are evident in documents such as Abraham Lincoln's Second Inaugural Address, in which he meditates on the secrets of divine providence rather than on the depths of Southern evil. They are illustrated supremely by the black acceptance of Christianity, offered as it was with a whip.

Whatever we conclude about the public fate of Christianity since World War II, we are able to see many "signs of contradiction" during this period. Among Roman Catholics, Hispanics were once largely neglected, yet from their midst came the Cursillo movement as a lively stimulus to renewal in communities far removed from Hispanic cultures. The relaxing of sexual standards has been a most visible feature of public life since the 1960s, but the same period has also witnessed the dramatic growth of family-strengthening movements such as Marriage Encounter among both Protestants and Catholics. The list could go on. It is an age of cynicism in politics and business but also of dramatic conversions of men and women who had risen to the top. It is an age of unbridled literary license and proliferating literary nonsense but an age in which more excellent writing of a distinctly Christian cast is being published than ever before in North American history. It is a day of death and devastation in inner cities but also a day in which committed churches, ministers, and philanthropists are organizing heroic efforts to hold back the urban night. These "signs of contradiction" do not by themselves constitute a history, but they do suggest that the analysis of Christian history may just as fruitfully follow the form of Christian faith as the norms of a particular host culture.

A Christian effort to tease out the meanings of church history might also look for realities that mirror mysteries of the faith itself. For instance, we might try to describe individual events in what look like contradictory terms, just as it was possible for Israel to place itself in peril by prospering and for Jesus to share the profoundest truths with children. As an example from recent history, the pioneering fundamentalistic and Pentecostal use of the radio may have brought genuine Christian encouragement to many people at the same time it encouraged a pursuit of standards, influence, power, and wealth deeply alien to the Christian faith.

Another theme at the heart of Christianity is the "theology of the cross" — the belief that God displayed his greatest power and most illuminating revelation when Christ suffered most abjectly and most forlornly for his people. Following this principle, we will not be surprised to discover some of the purest expressions of Christian faith in, say, the activities of Japanese-American Christians in the internment camps of World War II or among the ill-paid teachers, Catholic and Protestant, who toil away in the largely thankless task of educating young people in the faith.

Following the theme of the cross still further could lead us to view the passing of "Christian America" or "Christian Canada" as a blessing as well as a tragedy. So long as Protestants in the States and in English Canada or Catholics in Quebec thought that the land belonged to them, the temptation to view themselves as gods — to live by sight instead of faith — was nearly irresistible. But now, with these Christian establishments mostly a memory, there are blessings to count as well as vanishing monuments to mourn. Now Catholic, Orthodox, and the full spectrum of Protestants might learn from each other as fellow-believers instead of fearing each other as antagonists with turf to protect. Freed from the burden of American messianism, churches may find it possible to concentrate more on the Source of Life than on the American Way of Life. Perhaps if Christians evaluate the history of recent decades honestly, they might find it easier to concede their need for the Great Physician.

Has North America became a religious wilderness once again? In considerable measure, the historical record suggests that it has. The glories that have been lost were splendid, if never perfect. The world is indeed a poorer place without the vision of the Puritans, the energies of George Whitefield, Phoebe Palmer, and Cardinal Gibbons, the songs of Mahalia Jackson, the discipline of John Strachan, the faithfulness of Egerton Ryerson, and the conscientious persuasion of Bishop Sheen. Who would not regret leaving such glories behind for the wilderness? Perhaps only those who have been told to listen in the wilderness for a voice to cry and to look in the wilderness for a highway, constructed by God himself, to appear.

Further Reading

Anderson, Gerald H. "American Protestants in Pursuit of Mission: 1886-1986." *International Bulletin of Missionary Research* 12 (July 1988): 98-118.

Barrett, David B., ed. *World Christian Encyclopedia.* New York: Oxford University Press, 1982.

Carpenter, Joel A., and Wilbert R. Shenk, eds. *Earthen Vessels: American Evangelicals and Foreign Missions, 1880-1980.* Grand Rapids: William B. Eerdmans, 1990.

Dickinson, Eleanor, and Barbara Benziger. *Revival!* New York: Harper & Row, 1974.

Hutchison, William R. *Errand to the World: American Protestant Thought and Foreign Missions.* Chicago: University of Chicago Press, 1987.

Marsden, George M. "Are Secularists the Threat? Is Religion the Solution?" In *Unsecular America.* Edited by Richard John Neuhaus. Grand Rapids: William B. Eerdmans, 1986.

Martin, David. *A General Theory of Secularization.* New York: Harper & Row, 1978.

Mathews, Donald G. *Religion in the Old South.* Chicago: University of Chicago Press, 1977.

Morton, W. L., ed. *The Shield of Achilles: Aspects of Canada in the Victorian Age.* Toronto: McClelland & Stewart, 1968.

Noll, Mark A. "The Eclipse of Old Hostilities between and the Potential for New Strife among Catholics and Protestants since Vatican II." In *Uncivil Religion: Interreligious Hostility in America.* Edited by Robert N. Bellah and Frederick E. Greenspahn. New York: Crossroad, 1987.

Wacker, Grant. "A Plural World: The Protestant Awakening to World Religions." In *Between the Times: The Travail of the Protestant Establishment in America, 1900-1960.* Edited by William R. Hutchison. New York: Cambridge University Press, 1989.

Wills, Garry. *Under God: Religion and American Politics.* New York: Simon & Schuster, 1990.

Bibliography of General Works

BESIDES THE SPECIFICALLY FOCUSED WORKS FOR FURTHER READING PRO-vided with each chapter, the following sources offer more general material on the history of Christianity in America.

Reference Works

The most useful general aids are now the *Dictionary of Christianity in America*, which provides a wide range of shorter articles, and the *Encyclopedia of the American Religious Experience*, which offers extensive essays on approximately one hundred subjects. Each of the other works is also exceedingly helpful for its specific subject.

Dictionary of Canadian Biography. Toronto: University of Toronto Press, 1966ff.

Dictionary of Christianity in America. Edited by Daniel G. Reid, Robert D. Linder, Bruce L. Shelley, and Harry S. Stout. Downers Grove, IL: InterVarsity Press, 1990.

Dictionary of Pentecostal and Charismatic Movements. Edited by Stanley M. Burgess and Gary M. McGee. Grand Rapids: Regency, 1988.

Encyclopedia of the American Religious Experience: Studies of Traditions and Movements. 3 vols. Edited by Charles H. Lippy and Peter W. Williams. New York: Scribner's, 1988.

Encyclopedia of Religion in the South. Edited by Samuel S. Hill. Macon, GA: Mercer University Press, 1984.

Gallup, George, Jr. *Religion in America: Fifty Years, 1935-1985.* Princeton, NJ: The Gallup Report, 1985. See also related reports by Gallup.

Gaustad, Edwin S. *Historical Atlas of Religion in America.* Rev. ed. New York: Harper & Row, 1976.

Harvard Encyclopedia of American Ethnic Groups. Edited by Stephan Thernstrom. Cambridge: Harvard University Press, 1980.

New Catholic Encyclopedia. New York: McGraw-Hill, 1967ff.

Wilson, John F., ed. *Church and State in America: A Bibliographical Guide.* 2
vols. New York: Greenwood, 1986-1987.

Documents

The following are helpful collections of documents, many of which contain
illuminating introductions by their editors.

American Hymns Old and New. Vol. 1: *Hymns.* Edited by Albert Christ-Janer,
Charles W. Hughes, Carleton Sprague Smith. Vol. 2: *Notes.* Edited by
Charles W. Hughes. New York: Columbia University Press, 1980.

Carey, Patrick W., ed. *American Catholic Religious Thought.* New York: Paulist,
1987.

Ellis, John Tracy, ed. *Documents of American Catholic History.* Milwaukee: Bruce,
1962.

Farina, John, series ed. *Sources of American Spirituality.* Mahwah, NJ: Paulist. A
series of almost twenty volumes presenting primary sources from American religious life.

Gaustad, Edwin S., ed. *A Documentary History of Religion in America.* 2 vols.
Grand Rapids: William B. Eerdmans, 1982-1983.

Lundin, Roger, and Mark A. Noll, eds. *Voices from the Heart: Four Centuries of
American Piety.* Grand Rapids: William B. Eerdmans, 1987.

Ruether, Rosemary Radford, and Rosemary Skinner Keller, eds. *Women and
Religion in America.* 3 vols. San Francisco: Harper & Row, 1981-1986.

Sernett, Milton C., ed. *Afro-American Religious History: A Documentary Witness.*
Durham, NC: Duke University Press, 1985.

Smith, Hilrie S., Robert T. Handy, and Lefferts Loetscher, eds. *American Christianity: An Historical Interpretation with Representative Documents.* 2 vols.
New York: Scribner's, 1960.

Wilson, John F., and Donald L. Drakeman, eds. *Church and State in American
History.* 2d ed. Boston: Beacon, 1987.

Texts and General Studies

The following are among the best works or texts on the history of Christianity in North America. All of them offer further insight into the matters
discussed in this book and much else besides.

Ahlstrom, Sydney E. *A Religious History of the American People.* New Haven: Yale University Press, 1972.

Dolan, Jay P. *The American Catholic Experience.* Garden City, NY: Doubleday, 1985.

Eerdmans' Handbook to Christianity in America. Edited by David F. Wells, Mark A. Noll, George M. Marsden, Nathan O. Hatch, and John D. Woodbridge. Grand Rapids: William B. Eerdmans, 1983.

Handy, Robert T. *A Christian America: Protestant Hopes and Historical Realities.* 2d ed. New York: Oxford University Press, 1984.

————. *A History of the Churches in the United States and Canada.* New York: Oxford University Press, 1977.

Hennesey, James, S.J. *American Catholics: A History of the Roman Catholic Community in the United States.* New York: Oxford University Press, 1981.

Grant, John Webster. *The Church in the Canadian Era.* Rev. ed. Burlington, OT: Welch, 1988.

Holifield, E. Brooks. *A History of Pastoral Care in America: From Salvation to Self-Realization.* Nashville: Abingdon, 1983.

Hudson, Winthrop S. *American Protestantism.* Chicago: University of Chicago Press, 1961.

————. *Religion in America.* 4th ed. New York: Macmillan, 1987.

Lincoln, C. Eric, and Lawrence H. Mamiya. *The Black Church in the African-American Experience.* Durham, NC: Duke University Press, 1990.

Marsden, George M. *Religion and American Culture.* San Diego: Harcourt Brace Jovanovich, 1990.

Marty, Martin E. *Pilgrims in Their Own Land: Five Hundred Years of Religion in America.* Boston: Little, Brown, 1984.

————. *Protestantism in the United States: Righteous Empire.* 2d ed. New York: Scribner's, 1986.

Mead, Sidney E. *The Lively Experiment: The Shaping of Christianity in America.* New York: Harper & Row, 1963.

Moir, John S. *The Church in the British Era.* Toronto: McGraw-Hill Ryerson, 1972.

Pierard, Richard V., and Robert D. Linder. *Civil Religion and the Presidency.* Grand Rapids: Zondervan, 1988.

Rawlyk, George A., ed. *The Canadian Protestant Experience, 1760 to 1990.* Burlington, OT: Welch, 1990.

Sweet, Leonard I., ed. *The Evangelical Tradition in America.* Macon, GA: Mercer University Press, 1984.

Synan, Vinson. *The Holiness-Pentecostal Movement in the United States.* Grand Rapids: William B. Eerdmans, 1971.

Walsh, H. H. *The Church in the French Era.* Toronto: Ryerson, 1966.

Wells, Ronald A., ed. *The Wars of America: Christian Views.* Grand Rapids: William B. Eerdmans, 1981.

Index

Hume, David, 154
Hundley, Daniel, 318
Hunt, Robert, 36
Hunter, Jane, 310
Hunter, John E., 278
Hunter, William, 318
Huron Indians, 9, 19-21
Hurston, Zora Neale, 413
Hutcheson, Francis, 154-55
Hutchinson, Anne, 60-62
Hutchison, William R., 388, 457, 468, 478, 553
Hutterites, 328
Huxley, Thomas, 367

Illinois Indians, 19
Illinois, University of, 535
Inglis, Charles, 129, 262
Inglis, John, 262
Innocent (Saint), 346
Inskip, John S., 378
Institut Canadien, 253-54
Interchurch World Movement of North America, 309, 430
International Bible Society, 402
International Church of the Foursquare Gospel in the United States, 514. *See also* McPherson, Aimee Semple
International Congress on World Evangelization, 535-36
Inter-Varsity Christian Fellowship, 535
Ireland, John, 356-57, 359
Ireland, emigration of: Catholics, 206, 212, 349; Presbyterians, 7, 68, 73, 90, 160; other Protestants, 206, 257
Iroquois Indians, 19-21, 75
Irving, Edward, 266
Irwin, John, 418
Isaac, Rhys, 113
Italy, emigration of Catholics, 350

Jackson, Andrew, 176, 188-89, 242, 392
Jackson, Jesse, 498
Jackson, Mahalia, 501, 516-18, 529, 553
Jackson, Sheldon, 326
Jacob, Henry, 56
Jacobs, B. F., 229-30
Jacobs, George, 49
Jacquet, C. H., Jr., 479
James I (of England), 26, 32, 35, 38
James II (of England), 48
James, Henry, 409
Jamestown settlement, 13-14
Japanese internment, 437, 552
Jarvis Street Baptist Church (Toronto), 283. *See also* Shields, T. T.

Jay, John, 133, 139-40
Jefferson, Thomas, 118, 134, 155, 233, 404
Jeffrey, David L., 421
Jehovah's Witnesses, 308, 452, 465-66
Jenson, Robert, 524
Jerusalem Bible, 402-3
Jewish Publication Society, 402
Jews, 73, 145, 220, 311, 328, 348, 361, 424, 430, 431, 454, 464
John XXIII (Pope), 446, 539, 540
John Paul II (Pope), 451, 492-93, 509
Johns Hopkins University, 365
Johnson, Douglas W., 478
Johnson, James Weldon, 336
Johnson, Lyndon, 506
Johnson, Thomas H., 53
Jolliet, Louis, 18-19
Jones, Absalom, 202
Jones, C. P., 338
Jones, Charles Colcok, 204
Jones, Evan, 189
Jones, John B., 189
Judd, Sylvester, 410
Judson, Adoniram, 186-87
Judson, Ann Hasseltine, 187

Kagawa, Toyohiko, 534
Kaplan, Sidney, 142
Keane, John Joseph, 358, 362
Keith, George, 89
Kelley, Dean M., 479
Kellstedt, Lyman A., 457
Kemelman, Harry, 419
Kennedy, John F., 261, 440, 442, 506, 510, 517, 538-39
Kennedy, Robert, 442, 511
Kenrick, Francis Patrick, 208
Keswick Higher Life movement. *See* Holiness movement
Ketcham, Ralph, 135
Kimball, J. M., 542-44
King, Martin Luther, Jr., 442-43, 503, 505-7, 511, 517, 542, 544
King, Starr, 326
King, William Lyon Mackenzie, 437
King James Version of the Bible, 219, 401, 405
King Philip's War, 74
King's Business, The, 382
Klein, A. M., 413
Knights of Labor, 352
Know-Nothing Party. *See* American Party
Know Nothings, 209-10
Korean War, 516, 532
Krauth, Charles Porterfield, 216

Moody Bible Institute, 290
Moore, James R., 389
Moore, R. Laurence, 218
Moorhead, James H., 334
Moral Majority, 445
Moral Reform, 295
Moravians, 71, 75-77, 187, 464; as pacifists, 131
Morgan, Edmund S., 53
Mormons, 192, 195-97, 216-17, 326, 354, 397, 464-66, 473; in Canada, 266. *See also* Reorganized Church of Jesus Christ of Latter-day Saints
Morris Brown College, 339. *See also* African Methodist Episcopal Church
Morrison, Charles Clayton, 504
Morton, W. L., 285, 546, 553
Mott, John R., 291, 308
Mott, Lucretia Coffin, 184-85
Moule, H. C. G., 381
Mountain, Jacob, 251, 269
Muhlenberg, Henry Melchior, 71, 214
Mulder, John M., 310, 478
Mullins, Edgar Young, 372, 381, 488
Mulroney, Brian, 261
Mundelein, Cardinal, 504
Munger, Theodore, 374
Murray, Iain, 113
Murray, John (Universalist), 150
Murray, John Courtney (Jesuit), 398, 522
Murray, Robert, 256-57
Murton, John, 56

Napoleon, Prince, 211
Natchez Indians, 136
National Association for the Advancement of Colored People (NAACP), 336
National Association of Evangelicals, 438, 448, 537
National Baptist Convention, 337, 340. *See also* National Baptist Convention of the U.S.A., Inc.
National Baptist Convention of America, 469
National Baptist Convention of the U.S.A., Inc., 337-38, 469, 503
National Campmeeting Association for the Promotion of Christian Holiness. *See* Christian Holiness Association
National Catholic War Council, 309. *See also* National Catholic Welfare Conference
National Catholic Welfare Conference, 360
National Conference of Catholic Bishops, 360, 455-56, 491

National Council of Churches of Christ, 534, 537
National Council of the Churches of Christ, 13, 401-2, 438-39. *See also* World Council of Churches
Native Americans, and early colonies, 12-13, 25, 58-59, 67, 73-77, 101, 105-6; missionary work among, 7, 11-20, 105; removal of, 187-89
Nazarenes, 379-80
Nelson, E. Clifford, 500
Nelson, Shirley, 413
Neo-evangelicals, 432, 523-24
Neo-orthodoxy, 433, 522
Neuhaus, Richard John, 504
Nevin, John William, 176, 239
New American Bible, 402-3
New Brunswick, 246, 256
New Democratic Party (Canada), 454
New England, effect of Great Awakening in, 91, 97; Puritan disunity in after Great Awakening, 98; and Second Great Awakening, 168-69; secularization of Protestantism in, 223; and support of War for Independence, 119-20; and tightening of church organization, 88-89
New England, home of: Baptists, 56-62, 100, 150-51, 179; Catholics, 207, 472; Congregationalists, 89; Presbyterians, 68; Puritans, 7, 38-41; Quakers, 60, 65; Universalists, 150
New English Bible, 402
Newfoundland, 22, 250
New Hampshire Baptist confession, 178
New Haven Theology, 233
New International Version of the Bible, 402
New Jersey, College of, 100, 107, 120, 134, 156-57, 159, 235, 260. *See also* Princeton University
"New Lights," 98
"New measures," 175-76
"New School" Presbyterians, 232, 240, 243, 316
Newton, Sir Isaac, 97, 156
New York, home of: Catholics, 207, 472; Church of England, 63, 65; Presbyterians, 7, 68; Reformed, 7; Shakers, 150
New York Avenue Presbyterian Church (Washington, D.C.), 322, 476, 520
Nez Percé Indians, 327
Nicea, Second Council of, 344
Niebuhr, H. Richard, 397, 433, 522, 527-29

574